Assembly Language
Fundamentals
360/370
OS/VS DOS/VS

RINA YARMISH   Kingsborough Community College
JOSHUA YARMISH   Pace University

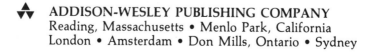
ADDISON-WESLEY PUBLISHING COMPANY
Reading, Massachusetts • Menlo Park, California
London • Amsterdam • Don Mills, Ontario • Sydney

To our children
GABRIEL, MICHAEL, DANIEL, BETH, AND GAIL

Reproduced by Addison-Wesley from camera-ready copy prepared by the authors.

ISBN 0-201-08798-7
GHIJ-MA-8987654

Preface

Assembler language, particularly assembler language for the IBM Sys/360 and 370 computers, has not traditionally been the "first" language of exposure for students of Data Processing, Computer Technology, or Business. Assembler language is "closer" to machine language than are higher-level languages such as FORTRAN or COBOL, and writing programs in assembler language therefore requires a deeper understanding of the computer and of programming technique. When coding in assembler language, the programmer must do much of the "work" which, when coding in other languages, would be performed by the compiler.

The authors' experience has shown that individuals who study assembler language become better programmers in higher-level languages such as COBOL, FORTRAN, PL/1, and BASIC. Assembler language thus has an important function in that it serves as a base for the study of future languages. It also provides deeper understanding of the workings of the computer and of programming languages in general, for those already involved in applications programming in higher-level languages.

This text is designed to prepare the reader to write a variety of simple assembler language programs quickly and "painlessly". Moreover, the text will allow the student to actively participate, almost immediately, in the programming experience. The first complete program is developed as early as chapter 2.

There are no prerequisites to the use of this text. However, a basic understand-

ing of what a computer is and what is involved in programming will be helpful. In our experience, most students of assembler language have had some
exposure to at least one higher-level language.

The text is intended for use by students of Data Processing or Business, or by
professionals whose educational objectives include acquiring the facility to
program in assembler language for the solution of typical business problems. It
should also afford an excellent supplement for self-study to students of Computer Science who require a knowledge of the machine best gained through
the study of assembler language. It may be used in a course which parallels
Course B2, Computers and Programming in the curriculum presented by the
ACM Curriculum Committee on Computer Science in *Communications of the
ACM*, March 1968, pp. 151–197.

It has been our experience that formal explanation reinforced by well-done
graphical description leads to longer-lasting retention. Many explanations in
the book are therefore highlighted by pictorial and/or graphical descriptions.

From time to time, sections marked "Towards Deeper Understanding" or
"Programming Tip" have been incorporated. These sections will include
"extra" information: knowledge of technique which distinguishes the novice
from the pro, and deeper explanations of how the computer performs certain
tasks. The instructor may avoid presentation of this material, if that is desired.

Each assembler language instruction presented is summarized for easy reference. Each summary includes the instruction name, mnemonic, instruction
type (machine, assembler, macro), machine format (if any), symbolic format,
and a brief list of rules governing the use of the instruction. Summaries are
boxed to distinguish them visually from the main body of the text. The introduction of new instructions and techniques is effected during the solution of
particular programming problems described in the text, so that they are seen
at the time of presentation to have practical application. Each new instruction
and technique is followed by appropriate example(s) illustrating its use.

Assembler language for IBM 360/370 under both OS and DOS control has
been presented. Both OS and DOS have been treated equally. However, to
avoid unnecessary duplication, computer programs have been run on an
IBM/370 under OS control. Comments have been included when appropriate,
indicating what changes would need be incorporated, had the program been
run on a system operating under DOS control.

Moreover, portions of the text relating strictly to DOS (including comments on
the program listings) have been shaded to visually distinguish them from the
main body of the text.

Each chapter is followed by a brief summary of the information presented and
a list of the important terms discussed and considered in the chapter. This list

of words should provide a checklist for the reader to test his grasp of the material presented in the chapter. In addition, a glossary is provided which lists and defines important programming terms used in the text.

Questions on new material presented follow each chapter; these questions are of various levels of difficulty. Answers to odd-numbered questions are given in Appendix D. When appropriate, chapter questions are followed by suggested programming project(s) which may be assigned to students. Such projects give input layout descriptions, desired output formats, and a statement of what the required program is to accomplish.

Design of the text is modular. Briefly, the text may be considered to be comprised of the following units:

Unit 1 Introduction to Assembler Language
    This comprises chapters 1, 2, and 3.
    Chapter 1   provides a discussion of what a computer is and of the components of a computer system. A description of machine language, of basic machine formats in the 360 and 370, and of the meaning and structure of assembler language are also included. Parts of this chapter will be review for students who have taken a previous programming course.
    Chapter 2   presents a complete assembler language program, along with explanations of the instructions introduced and examples of their use.
    Chapter 3   describes a systematic approach to computer problem solution, along with explanations of constant definition (the DC instruction), storage definition (the DS instruction), and the use of literals in assembler language.

The material in Unit I provides a basis upon which the remaining chapters will be built, and should be studied first.

Unit 2 The Decimal Instruction Set
    This comprises chapters 4, 5, and 6.
    Chapter 4   discusses arithmetic operations with decimal (packed) integer values.
    Chapter 5   describes a method for simple editing of zoned fields, including the use of the decimal compare.
    Chapter 6   presents techniques for arithmetic operations with non-integer decimal (packed) values, including techniques for truncation and rounding to a desired accuracy.

Unit 3 Binary and Hexadecimal Numbers, and the Standard Instruction Set
    This comprises chapters 7, 8, and 9.
    Chapter 7   discusses positional representation, including the binary and

hexadecimal number systems, two's complement representation, and conversion of numbers from one number system to another.

Chapter 8   introduces binary arithmetic with integer values, including the binary conversion instructions and the instructions which load numbers into registers and store numbers in main storage locations.

Chapter 9   describes instructions and techniques for performing binary arithmetic with non-integer values.

Unit 4 Editing, and More Advanced Branching and Looping
   This comprises chapters 10 and 11.

Chapter 10   discusses editing,. including the insertion of floating characters into edited fields. Forms control using the CNTRL and PRTOV macros is considered, along with a discussion of spooled systems, and the use of ANS control characters to control printer spacing. The chapter also considers the retrieval of the date and time from the supervisor for programmer use.

Chapter 11   describes techniques for branching and loop control. A variety of techniques are used for incrementing and/or decrementing counter values, and for testing for exit from the loop.

Unit 5 Operating Systems Concepts
   This comprises chapters 12, 13, and 14.

Chapter 12   describes subroutines and subroutine linkage, using the standard linkage conventions. Both internal and external subroutine linkage are considered. Topics covered include entry to and return from subroutines, passage of data between calling and called routines, saving and restoring register contents, and the SAVE, RETURN, and CALL macros.

Chapter 13   is an introduction to virtual storage systems and other operating systems concepts. Topics considered include storage allocation, static and dynamic relocation, segmentation and paging, the PSW, and the interrupt system. The IBM 3033 processor is introduced.

Chapter 14   presents a systematic approach to the debugging of assembly language programs, including desk-checking, correction of program diagnostics, and testing the program output. Students are shown how to locate specific fields in a dump through use of the base register and the displacement.

The order of presentation of material after Unit 1 may be varied to some extent. Students of Business may find the decimal instruction set useful, and the production of attractive report output a major goal. In such a case, a recommended chapter sequence would be chapters 1, 2, 3 (introduction), 4, 5, 6 (the decimal set), 10 (editing and forms control), 14 (debugging), and chapters 12 and 13 as additional topics.

Students of Computer Science would find the standard instruction set more useful. A recommended chapter sequence would thus be chapters 1, 2, 3 (introduction), 7, 8, 9 (the standard set), 11 (branching and looping), 14 (debugging), followed by chapters 12 and/or 13 in any order.

Actually, chapters 12, 13, and 14 are rather independent and may be included at any point within the chapter sequence (after Unit 1) that the instructor feels is appropriate. Chapter 14 may be especially useful to introduce earlier, perhaps about the time that the first class programming project is assigned.

We should like, at this point, to note several usages which have been employed in the text program listings, whose availability may vary among installations. In particular, the CNTRL and PRTOV macros (sections 10.3.2 and 10.3.3) are used in our program listings to control vertical printer spacing. These macros may not work on spooled systems, since on such systems the programmer cannot communicate directly with the printer's carriage control tape. For this reason, the use of ANS control characters has been presented in section 10.3.4 as an alternate method for effecting such spacing, and the counting of output lines is illustrated in the first program example of chapter 12.

Note too that register conventions (saving and restoring register contents) at the start and end of each program have not been employed in the earlier program examples. We have instead chosen to explain these conventions at that point in the text discussion at which the reader is adequately prepared to fully understand the workings of and rationale for such usage (section 12.3). If register conventions are required usage at the reader's installation, they may simply be indicated by the instructor as a convention which must be followed until full explanation is provided in chapter 12.

We wish to express our sincere thanks and appreciation to all those who have helped in the completion of this text. In particular, we wish to thank Adena Rosin, for her masterful typing of the manuscript; Esther Kobre, for her imaginative art work; the reviewers, whose comments were most helpful; the Kingsborough Community College computer center and Mr. Louis Lampert for providing computer time and programming support for the development of the program examples presented in the text. Finally, we wish to acknowledge the generosity of IBM Corporation for granting us permission to use some materials from their publications.

We hope that you enjoy reading this text. If you do, and feel that you have gained in knowledge and in expertise through its use, the authors are well rewarded.

New York, N. Y. R. Y.
May, 1979 J. Y.

Contents

Unit 2   The Decimal Instruction Set

Unit 3   Binary and Hexadecimal Numbers, and the Standard Instruction Set

Unit 4   Editing, and More Advanced Branching and Looping

Unit 5   Operating System Concepts

Unit

1

Introduction to Assembly Language

Chapter 1

Meet the Computer

MEET THE COMPUTER

In this chapter, we will be introduced to the computer: its capabilities, its organization, and methods for communicating with it. Some basic terminology required for effective understanding of this book will also be discussed.

The information in this chapter is a condensed review of some of that which is normally taught in many one semester introductory data processing courses. Although the information presented is sufficient for an understanding of this text, those who wish to delve more deeply into some particular area might refer to one of the many fine introductory texts which are available. There is a substantial amount of detail presented here, which is intended to serve as reference throughout your reading.

1.1   WHAT IS A COMPUTER?

"The Computer" is spoken of and used almost everywhere, in almost every phase of life. In banks, tellers deposit and withdraw your money by communicating with a computer; in laboratories, computers are used to interpret experimental results; the military uses computers to guide "smart" bombs to their targets; computers control many factory operations, and even the timing of traffic lights. And these are a very few of the many applications of today's computers.

But what *is* a computer? In a nutshell, it is a "data manipulator" of a special kind. It is an electronic machine which transforms incoming data (**input**) into outgoing information (**output**), by following a set of instructions (a stored program) given to it ahead of time.

When something is totally electronic, it has no moving parts. This implies that any movement and manipulation of data, from the time it enters the computer (input) until it leaves (output), is done by electronic signals within the computer which move at tremendous speeds, much as electricity is transmitted at great speeds through wires. The absence of moving parts also means that the machine will require little maintenance.

What really makes the computer so powerful, however, is its ability to follow sets of instructions (**programs**). We can change the program, and the computer will change what it is doing. The computer can thus perform an unlimited number of jobs, since there is no limit to the number of programs that can be written. The computer cannot instruct itself; the "thinking" must be done by a human being. The computer has no "intelligence", no ability to think; its greatness lies in that it is an accurate, fast, highly reliable general-purpose tool whose operations are controlled.

As you read this book, you will be learning how to instruct the computer through writing programs.

1.2   A COMPUTER SYSTEM

A typical computer system has six basic components. The first three (figure 1.1), which may or may not be housed in the same physical unit, are the

- **Storage unit** (sometimes referred to as main storage, internal storage or primary storage)
- **Arithmetic and logical unit** often referred to as the **ALU**
- **Control unit**

These three units are often collectively called the **CPU**, or **Central Processing Unit**. (An alternate definition, proposed by the American National Standards Institute (ANSI), considers the CPU to contain only the ALU and the control unit, although the storage unit must certainly be present as well, as a separate unit.) The actual manipulation of data takes place in the CPU. Throughout this book, the terms "CPU" and "computer" will be interchangeable.

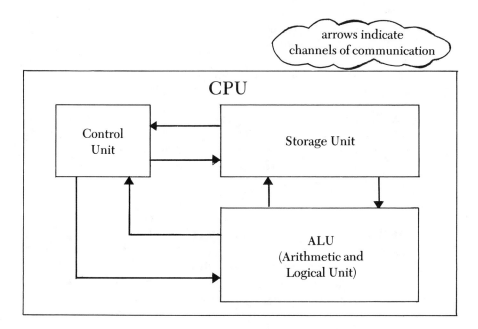

Figure 1.1

The other three components are:

- **Input** ⎫
- **Output** ⎬ ———————————→ | I/O is used to mean: input and/or output |
- **Auxiliary storage** ⎭

The six components above comprise what is known as a **computer system**. Let us briefly examine each of these components in turn.

1.2.1   Storage Unit

Just as a human must have information stored in his memory before he can act upon it, so the computer must have data in its own memory bank, along with instructions which tell it what to do. These instructions comprise a **stored program**. Physically, some computer memories are composed of tiny rings called **cores**, which are arranged in rows strung on wires. It is for this reason that the computer memory itself is sometimes referred to as **core**. Electrical currents passing through these wires may selectively magnetize individual cores in one of *two* ways, clockwise or counter-clockwise.

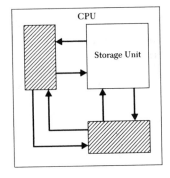

Actually, recent trends in computer technology have resulted in memories composed of faster, solid state circuitry, and monolithic circuits. Laser technology has likewise been incorporated into the design and construction of many modern-day computers. However the term core storage persists, as applying to main memory.

Binary Numbers

A light switch may be on (connected) or off (disconnected); electrical circuits may be open or closed; a plug may be connected or disconnected. In each situation described, there are two possibilities: technically we may refer to each **state** as "yes" or "no" or, more commonly, as "1" or "0". When data is stored in the computer memory it is represented as a sequence of cores, each one pointing in one of two directions: that is, as a sequence of the digits 0 and 1. It is for this reason that a core will henceforth be referred to as a bit (binary digit). Just as in the Morse Code, where each symbol is represented as a unique sequence of dots and dashes, so computer symbols are represented as unique sequences of bits. In the Morse Code, not every symbol has the same length; however, computer memory is divided into segments of equal size called **bytes**; each byte may house one symbol (like the letters, digits, special symbols such as an "&" sign, and the like). On IBM computers, each byte is 8 bits long.

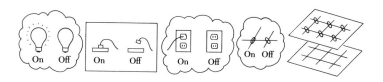

Computers use the **binary number system** to represent numbers, by placing appropriate combinations of the digits 0 and 1 in columns whose values are powers of 2:

binary column
values: $\ldots$ $2^3=8$ $2^2=4$ $2^1=2$ $2^0=1$ $2^{-1}=\frac{1}{2}$ $2^{-2}=\frac{1}{4}$ $2^{-3}=\frac{1}{8}$ $\ldots$

A "1" digit in a binary column is "worth" the amount of the column value itself. A "0" digit does not contribute to the value of the number, and serves only as a placeholder.

For example, the binary number 1101 is equivalent to 13 since

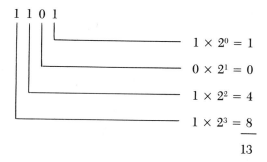

$$1 \times 2^0 = 1$$
$$0 \times 2^1 = 0$$
$$1 \times 2^2 = 4$$
$$1 \times 2^3 = 8$$
$$13$$

Likewise, the binary number 110.11 is equivalent to 6¾, since

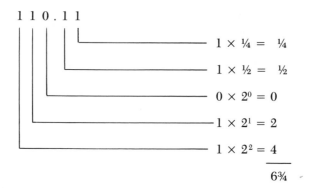

$$1 \times \tfrac{1}{4} = \tfrac{1}{4}$$
$$1 \times \tfrac{1}{2} = \tfrac{1}{2}$$
$$0 \times 2^0 = 0$$
$$1 \times 2^1 = 2$$
$$1 \times 2^2 = 4$$

$$6¾$$

Hexadecimal Representation

One major disadvantage of working with binary numbers is that the numbers tend to be rather long and difficult to read. For this reason, we often use a representation called **hexadecimal representation** as a compact way of representing strings of 0's and 1's.

Hexadecimal representation substitutes an appropriate hexadecimal digit for each group of 4 binary digits, as follows:

Hexadecimal digit	Binary digits
0	0000
1	0001
2	0010
3	0011
4	0100
5	0101
6	0110
7	0111
8	1000
9	1001
A	1010
B	1011
C	1100
D	1101
E	1110
F	1111

Thus the following conversion

binary: 1101 0101 1010 1111

hexadecimal: B   5   A   F

Binary and hexadecimal representations are discussed at length in chapter 7.

Note that the largest binary number using 4 bits is 1111 or 15 ($2^4 - 1$), and the largest binary number using 8 bits is 11111111 or 255 ($2^8 - 1$). In general, the largest binary number using n bits is $2^n - 1$. Thus the number of binary numbers that can be represented using n bits is one more (to take zero into account) than the largest binary number which uses n bits, that is, $(2^n - 1) + 1$ or 2^n.

EBCDIC Code

It is possible to represent 256 unique combinations of 0's and 1's in 8 bits ($2^8 = 256$). Computer manufacturers have associated symbols with certain of these combinations. The particular combinations which we will be using throughout this book are known as **EBCDIC** (**E**xtended **B**inary **C**oded **D**ecimal **I**nterchange **C**ode) **Code**. It is convenient to divide the byte into two parts and to number the bits from left to right starting from 0 and ending with 7:

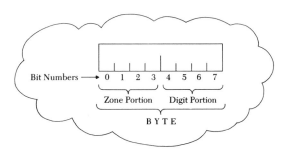

The EBCDIC code for the digits and capital letters is given in figure 1.2.

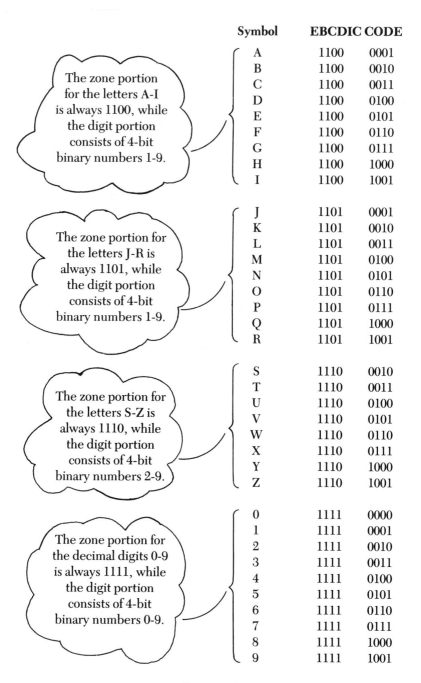

Symbol	EBCDIC CODE	
A	1100	0001
B	1100	0010
C	1100	0011
D	1100	0100
E	1100	0101
F	1100	0110
G	1100	0111
H	1100	1000
I	1100	1001
J	1101	0001
K	1101	0010
L	1101	0011
M	1101	0100
N	1101	0101
O	1101	0110
P	1101	0111
Q	1101	1000
R	1101	1001
S	1110	0010
T	1110	0011
U	1110	0100
V	1110	0101
W	1110	0110
X	1110	0111
Y	1110	1000
Z	1110	1001
0	1111	0000
1	1111	0001
2	1111	0010
3	1111	0011
4	1111	0100
5	1111	0101
6	1111	0110
7	1111	0111
8	1111	1000
9	1111	1001

The zone portion for the letters A-I is always 1100, while the digit portion consists of 4-bit binary numbers 1-9.

The zone portion for the letters J-R is always 1101, while the digit portion consists of 4-bit binary numbers 1-9.

The zone portion for the letters S-Z is always 1110, while the digit portion consists of 4-bit binary numbers 2-9.

The zone portion for the decimal digits 0-9 is always 1111, while the digit portion consists of 4-bit binary numbers 0-9.

Figure 1.2
EBCDIC Representation for Letters and Digits

For example, the word "RAIN" would require 4 consecutive bytes for its EBCDIC storage representation, as follows:

1101 1001	1100 0001	1100 1001	1101 0101
R	A	I	N

A typical computer memory has enough room to store many thousands of EBCDIC characters.

Addressing Memory

Mailboxes in a post office are uniquely and consecutively numbered. Likewise the computer manufacturer associates each byte of main storage with a unique number which is used by the programmer to identify that particular byte or storage location. This number is called an **address**.

We may thus conceptualize the computer memory as a box which is subdivided into a number of smaller numbered boxes, each of which is one byte in size.

000	001	002	003	004	005	006	007	008	009
		R	A	I	N				

010	011	012	013

010
.
.
.

020	021	022	023

In the above diagram, the word "rain" is stored *beginning* with location 002 and extending 4 locations in *length*.

It is an IBM convention to rate storage size in units of **K**, each K being 1024 bytes ($1024 = 2^{10}$). A typical computer can have, say, 128K units of storage.

(K stands for the metric measure "kilo" and means "roughly 1000".) Additional storage, as needed, may be purchased from vendors. Core is usually sold in units of 4K.

1.2.2   The Arithmetic and Logical Unit (ALU)

The arithmetic and logical unit consists of electronic circuits whose function is to perform operations such as addition. Subtraction, multiplication, and division are seen by the computer as extensions of addition. The ALU can also compare two values to determine whether one value is greater than, equal to, or smaller than another, and it can determine whether stated expressions are true or false.

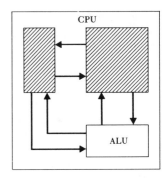

The manipulations are facilitated by the availability of several 32-bit units of storage technically known as **registers**. These registers are used for temporary storage of small units of information during processing, such as intermediate results of series of calculations.

1.2.3   The Control Unit

The control unit acts as a "general manager", controlling the various operations of the computer. For example, it controls the input and output to the computer and the communication between the 6 computer components (input, output, control unit, ALU, storage unit, and auxiliary storage). The control unit interprets program instructions, initiates input/output devices, commences execution of computer programs, and ensures that everything is done at the proper time and in the right sequence. It is similar in this respect to a policeman directing traffic at a busy intersection.

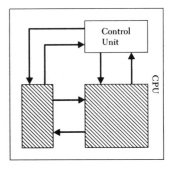

1.2.4   Input

Input and Output

There are many means of getting information into the computer (input) and of transferring information out of the computer (output). They differ in the medium used, and hence in speed, cost, convenience, and types of applications for which they are suited.

In this book, we will be using punched cards and the card reader as the input medium and device respectively. For output, we will use the printer as the device; its medium is continuous form paper. These devices were chosen since they are among the most commonly used and are particularly suited for the novice.

The Punched Card

The punched card described in figure 1.3 was first introduced by Herman Hollerith in the late 1880's. Since then it has been known as the **Hollerith card** or in more recent times as the IBM card. We will refer to it simply as the punched card.

The following discussion is a quick guide through the world of the punched card. We first note that the punched card may be sliced in two ways: horizontally or vertically.

If we look at the horizontal division, we note from the diagram that there are 12 horizontal sections, called **rows**. Starting from the top, the first 3 rows are called the 12-row, the 11-row (or X-row) and the 0-row respectively; these three rows are collectively known as the **zone rows** and any punch (hole) in these rows is known as a zone punch. Proceeding downward, the 0-row is followed by the 1-row, the 2-row, and so on, through the 9-row. The 0-row through the 9-row inclusive are known as the **numeric rows**, and any punch in these rows is known as a numeric punch. Note that the zero row is both a zone row and a numeric row.

Now let us examine the card vertically. Notice the very bottom printed line on the card in our diagram, which is labeled "column number". (This line is repeated below the zero row.) The numbering on this line extends from 1 to 80; each number identifies one **column**; when we wish to refer to a specific column, we use the identifying number.

You may notice from the diagram that each symbol has a unique number of punches which identifies it, However, each symbol occupies exactly one column, just as on a typewriter, a typed symbol occupies one print position.

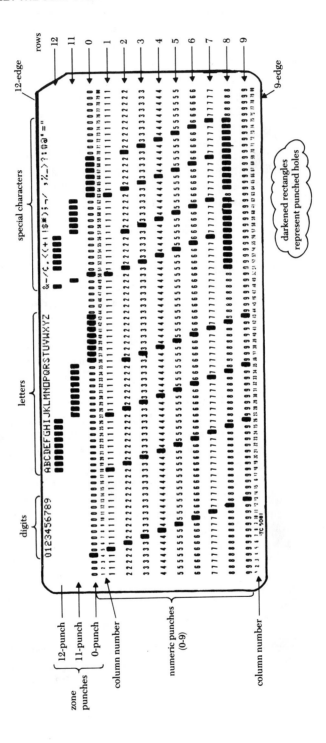

Figure 1.3
The Hollerith Card

Note that for representation of the digits 0-9, a numeric punch in the respective numeric row designates that digit. For example, a 4-punch in column 8 of our card means that the digit 4 is represented. Only one hole is necessary.

The alphabetic symbols are each represented by 2 punches in a column, one zone punch and one numeric punch. The letters A-I use a 12-punch together with numeric punches 1 through 9, respectively; the letters J-R use an 11-punch together with numeric punches 1 through 9, respectively; the letters S-Z use a 0-punch together with numeric punches 2 through 9, respectively. Note that this code is different from the EBCDIC code used for character representation in memory.

The printed numbers on the punched card identifying rows and columns, or any other printed information, as well as the color of the card, are totally irrelevant to that which is stored (punched) on the card. It is the positioning of the holes or punches in the card which determines what information is represented.

The Card Reader

The contents of a punched card are transferred into the storage unit by a machine called the **card reader** (figure 1.4). A typical card reader "reads" (transfers information) at the rate of 600 cards/minute, although machines are available which read at rates varying from 100 to 2000 cards/minute.

Courtesy of IBM Corporation

Figure 1.4
IBM 3505 Card Reader

The cards are placed by an operator into a compartment of the reader, called the read hopper. When the computer desires to read data, an electronic signal is sent to the card reader directing it to read a card. The card moves into the machine, where it passes over a series of 80 brushes or photoelectric cells which sense the presence or absence of holes in each particular column of the card. Each specific configuration generates its own particular electronic impulse(s) which store the respective EBCDIC character in the main memory of the computer as the proper sequence of 0's and 1's.

1.2.5 Output

The Printer

The **printer** (figure 1.5) is one of the most popular output devices, since it provides information in a readable form. The medium generally used is continuous paper (each sheet is attached to the next along perforated lines).

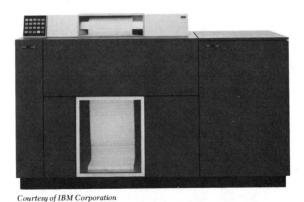

Courtesy of IBM Corporation

Figure 1.5
IBM 3211 Printer

The number of characters which may be printed on a line varies between models. The most typical is the line capacity used in this book: 132 or 133 **print positions** per line. A typical printer is capable of producing 1200 lines/minute. Fifty lines per page at 1200 lines/minute will produce 24 pages each minute.

1.2.6 Auxiliary Storage

Typical examples of auxiliary storage (or secondary storage) media are magnetic tape and disk, illustrated in figures 1.6 and 1.7.

Courtesy of IBM Corporation

Figure 1.6
IBM 3420 Magnetic Tape Unit

Courtesy of IBM Corporation

Figure 1.7
IBM 3350 Disk Storage

The computer must have the program data, along with the program instructions, in storage at the time of program execution. However data and/or instructions which are not being used immediately may be stored on auxiliary devices such as tape or disk, where they may be retrieved quickly. The widespread use of auxiliary devices may be partly credited to the fact that they are considerably less expensive than main memory units, and yet serve a similar function for many purposes.

Tying It All Together

Input device(s), output device(s), and the CPU must each be present for any meaningful data processing to take place. The CPU together with one or more input and output units constitute a **computer system**.

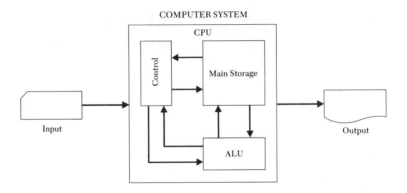

Figure 1.8
A Schematic Diagram of a Computer System

Typically, data is processed by a computer system as follows: A program is read by an input device which stores the instructions in the computer memory. If arithmetic or logical operations are requested by the program, the control unit will direct the transfer of information needed for processing to the ALU, where these operations will take place. The results are then placed back into main storage. If the program requires output, the finished product is transmitted to an output device.

Courtesy of IBM Corporation

Figure 1.9
A Typical Computer System
IBM 3033 Processor for System/370

1.3   DATA ORGANIZATION: FIELD, RECORD, FILE

Data is organized in businesses to provide for its more efficient handling. **Data** is defined as facts about something. For example, "blue eyes, 5 foot 8 inches" are facts which describe the physical characteristics of some person. Data may be numeric, alphabetic, or a mixture of the two.

Every organization collects facts necessary for its own operations. For example, a retail business might have facts on its salesmen: names, addresses, salesman number, sales performance, territory, salary and the like. This data is organized to provide for its more efficient handling. For example, a file cabinet may be set aside, containing many alphabetically arranged sheets of paper. Each sheet of paper contains all the relevant data about an individual salesman. The handling of data may be done manually, by humans, who can select the data needed for processing wherever it is placed on the paper. When machines were first used for data processing, the placement of data on storage media was standardized.

Data is organized into units called fields, records, and files. On a punched card, data is represented as a group of columns which belong together as a logical unit of information. Such a collection of columns is called a **field**.

```
JOHNSON MANUF CO        07216820000
  I       I  I I
II I II I    I     I
         NAME         DATE   AMT
0000 00000 0 0000000 0 00000 0 0000 00000000000000000000000000000000000000000000
1 2 3 4 5 6 7 8 9 10 11 12 13 14 15 16 17 18 19 20 21 22 23 24 25 26 27 28 29 30 31 32 33 34 35 36 37 38 39 40 41 42 43 44 45 46 47 48 49 50 51 52 53 54 55 56 57 58 59 60 61 62 63 64 65 66 67 68 69 70 71 72 73 74 75 76 77 78 79 80
1111111 I 11111111 111 I 1 1111111111111111111111111111111111111111111111111111111
2222 2222222222222222 22 222 2222 2222222222222222222222222222222222222222222222222
3333333333333333 33333 333333 333333333333333333333333333333333333333333333333333333
4444444 44 4444444444 444444 44444 4444444444444444444444444444444444444444444444444
555 55 555 555555555 5555555 55555 5555555555555555555555555555555555555555555555555
6 666 666666 66 6666 6666 6 66666 666666666666666666666666666666666666666666666666666
7777777777777777777 7 7777 777777 7777777777777777777777777777777777777777777777777
88 8888888888888888 88888 88888 8888888888888888888888888888888888888888888888888888
99999999999999999999 99999 99999 9999999999999999999999999999999999999999999999999999
1 2 3 4 5 6 7 8 9 10 11 12 13 14 15 16 17 18 19 20 21 22 23 24 25 26 27 28 29 30 31 32 33 34 35 36 37 38 39 40 41 42 43 44 45 46 47 48 49 50 51 52 53 54 55 56 57 58 59 60 61 62 63 64 65 66 67 68 69 70 71 72 73 74 75 76 77 78 79 80
JTC 5081
```

Figure 1.10
Fields on a Punched Card

The punched card of figure 1.10 contains 3 fields, each of which tells us something. The term *field* refers to the smallest meaningful collection of characters.

A **record** is an organized collection of related fields. (The emphasis here is on "organized" and "related".) The punched card of figure 1.10 is an example of a record, since the fields each refer to the same company (the Johnson Manufacturing Company).

A **file** is an organized collection of related records; one possible example is illustrated in figure 1.11.

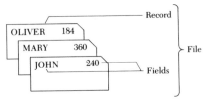

Figure 1.11
Fields, Records and File

In a typical business there are many different types of files: Accounts Receivable file, Accounts Payable file, Name and Address file and the like.

The terms field, record, and file are independent of the medium used. That is, one may have files stored on tape, disk, paper, or any other desirable medium.

1.4   COMMUNICATING WITH THE COMPUTER

1.4.1   Computer "Languages"

Any human language contains a collection of symbols which are grouped into units called words according to the grammar rules of the particular language. Words may be combined into sentences by following certain language rules.

A computer language also has rules, as well as symbols which are used to form allowable words, which are in turn combined to form statements or commands. However, a computer language has a much smaller available vocabulary: typically about 100 words, which may be combined with other elements to form commands which are meaningful to the computer.

For example, if we want the computer to read a card in COBOL (a commercially used computer language) we might say READ CARD; in assembler language (the language we will study) you might say GET CARD. As is the case with human languages, each computer language has its own style and its own rules.

Computer languages are classified into several categories: machine language, assembler language, and higher-level language.

1.4.2   Machine Language

A SNEAK PREVIEW: REGISTERS, ADDRESSING, RELATIVE ADDRESSING

In this section, we will discuss several important topics whose relevance will become apparent later in this chapter and throughout the book.

A.   REGISTERS

Registers are discrete storage units of fixed length which are conceptually similar to, but are physically separate from, main storage. In the IBM System/360 and System/370 computers, there are three types of registers: control registers, floating point registers, and general purpose registers (GPR's). They are capable of receiving, holding, and transferring data, but are typically used to hold data temporarily, such as, for example, intermediate results in a series of calculations.

The **storage** (placement into) and **retrieval** (removal from) of a letter from a mailbox takes a certain amount of time; likewise, it takes time to store and retrieve information from main storage. The exact amount of time required varies from computer to computer. The possession of those higher speed (approximately 2 to 4 times faster) memory units called registers greatly improves machine efficiency in terms of **execution time** (the amount of time it takes a computer to perform the operations specified in the instructions).

Control Registers

When a computer malfunctions, the repairman utilizes the control registers to locate the cause of the trouble. They are not of use to the programmer and will therefore not be discussed in this text.

Floating Point Registers

The floating point registers are not available in every model, and are primarily used for scientific applications. We will not discuss the instructions which utilize these registers; however, upon completion of this text, you will be prepared to study this aspect of 360 and 370 programming without difficulty.

General Purpose Registers (GPR's)

There are 16 general purpose registers, each 32 bits (4 bytes) in length. The registers are numbered from 0 through 15 (in hexadecimal, 0 through F). Note that the first register is labeled 0, the second is labeled 1, the third is labeled 2, and so on.

The data in these registers is stored in straight binary format. The numbers will consist of two parts: a sign portion which occupies the leftmost bit (0 means positive, 1 means negative) and the numeric portion which occupies the remainder. Binary numbers will be explained in detail in chapter 7.

In a 32-bit register, the number + 58 is represented as illustrated in figure 1.12.

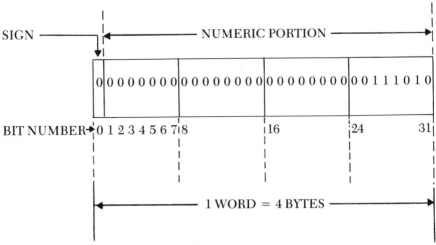

Figure 1.12
The Number + 58 in Binary

Note: 1. To facilitate referencing particular bits within a register, it is the practice to number them from left to right starting from 0 (which is the **high-order** bit) through 31 (which is the **low-order** bit). In figure 1.12, bit number 30 contains a 1, and bit number 31 contains a 0.

2. It is often convenient to group bytes into units. A unit of 2 bytes is called a **halfword**; a unit of 4 bytes (2 halfwords) is called a **fullword** or **word**; a unit of 8 bytes (2 words) is called a **doubleword** (see figure 1.13).

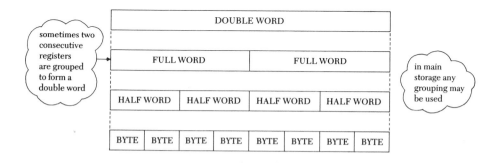

Figure 1.13
Byte, Halfword, Fullword, Doubleword

The 16 general purpose registers may be referenced both by the computer system and by the programmer. When the system needs registers, it selects among registers 0, 1, 13, 14, and 15; the machine's choice among these five will depend upon the particular application to which the registers are being put. In order to avoid conflict, it is the general practice for the programmer to use only registers 2 through 12 inclusive. (Although the machine language itself permits using any general purpose register.)

B.   ADDRESSING

At this point we will discuss techniques for referencing locations in main storage. Recall (section 1.2.1) that in an instruction, the programmer refers to particular locations in main storage by specifying numbers called addresses assigned by the manufacturer to those locations.

There are several methods of addressing. One is **absolute addressing**, which means specifying the location number itself. In order to provide for efficient management of storage, this method is not used in IBM 360 and 370 computers. The IBM 360 and 370 computer systems include a variety of models, with memory sizes varying to a maximum of 16,777,216 bytes of computer memory. These bytes are numbered consecutively: the first location is numbered 0, the second is 1, and so on, through 16,777,215. It is in this memory that the data which a computer manipulates is placed.

We tell the computer what to do with the data by using computer instructions. In general, the instructions contain the address in which the data to be acted upon is stored, so that for an instruction to reference all possible locations using straight binary, 24 bits will be necessary for each address. (The number $16,777,215 = 2^{24}$ is 111111111111111111111111 in binary, necessitating 24 bits.) If 2 values are to be acted upon, 48 bits would be necessary each time the data is referenced! Since computer storage is very expensive and therefore limited in size, a technique was developed for addressing locations using only 16 bits, thus saving one byte (8 bits) of memory every time a location is referenced. This technique is known as **relative addressing**.

C. RELATIVE ADDRESSING

Relative addressing is a technique for addressing locations. The technique uses some fixed addresses as a reference point. The IBM 360 and 370 computers use two methods for computing relative addresses: The base-displacement and index-base-displacement methods.

Base-Displacement Method

In short, the method follows: a programmer chooses an address called a **base address** which he places in a general purpose register. When used for this purpose, the register is called a **base register**. The programmer has in this way provided a reference point called a **base**, and this is the starting point which will be used by the computer to calculate actual addresses (sometimes called **effective addresses**) in his program. Thus:

effective address = contents of base register + displacement

where the displacement represents the number of storage locations which the address is displaced from (removed from) the number in the base register. The programmer also chooses the general purpose register to be so used, and notifies the computer of his choice.

For example, if the base register contains the number 1027, and we wish to reference address 4127, we would say that 4127 may be expressed as 3100 storage locations *displaced from* the location numbered 1027 (contents of base register, see figure 1.14).

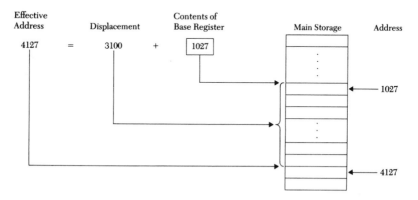

Figure 1.14
Illustrating the Base-Displacement Method

Index-Base-Displacement Method

In this method, the programmer chooses two general purpose registers: one is the base register as described above, and the other is called the **index register**. The index register will contain another number which is utilized in calculating the effective address (see figure 1.15).

$$\text{effective address } = \text{ contents of base register}$$
$$+ \text{ contents of index register}$$
$$+ \text{ displacement}$$

The base register, once **loaded** (that is, once a number has been placed into it), may not be modified during program execution. The index register, however, may be modified. This fact sometimes proves very useful in programming, as we will see. The question of which method of addressing is preferable will depend upon the type of instruction being used, as will be explained later in the text.

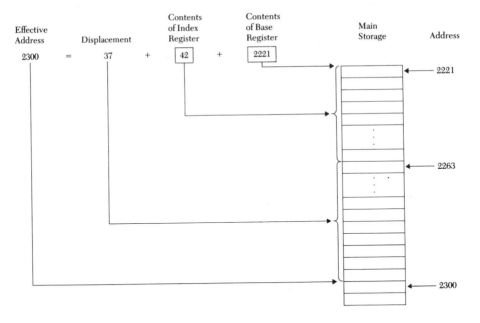

Figure 1.15
Illustrating the Index-Base-Displacement Method

Instructions which use the base-displacement or index-base-displacement method allocate 12 bits for the displacement. A displacement specifies a number of bytes which a location is displaced from the base address (the number in the base register), and is thus always a positive value. For this reason, the 12 bit displacement is an unsigned positive binary number; its maximum value, $2^{12} - 1$, is 111111111111 or 4095_{10}. As a result, if register 5 is used as a base register and is loaded with the value 100_{10}, then the program may reference addresses thus:

Base displacement	Effective address
contents of register 5 + 0 = 100 + 0 =	100
contents of register 5 + 1 = 100 + 1 =	101
.	
.	
.	
contents of register 5 + 4095 = 100 + 4095 =	4195

Note that the smallest displacement value is 0, hence 4096 bytes of memory may be referenced using base register 5.

The Displacement Concept

Figure 1.16

If our program required referencing higher numbered locations in memory, we might choose a second base register, for example register 8. We would place the next address to be referenced into register 8; in this example, the number 4196 would be loaded into register 8. Then

Base displacement	Effective address
contents of register 8 + 0 = 4196 + 0 =	4196
contents of register 8 + 1 = 4196 + 1 =	4197
.	
.	
.	
contents of register 8 + 4095 = 4196 + 4095 =	8291

We see that specifying an additional base register enables one to reference an additional 4096 memory locations.

In an instruction, 4 bits are allocated for describing a register number. The registers are numbered from 0 to 15, and 4 bits can describe any of these; that is, 0000_2 (the binary number 0) through 1111_2 (the binary number 15). The displacement (12 bits) and the register number (4 bits) together will specify any location number using 16 bits (up to a maximum of $2^{31} - 1 + 4096$, for $2^{31} - 1$ is the largest possible number that may be represented in a register, and 4096 is the largest possible 12-bit displacement value).

Another benefit of relative addressing is that it provides for **program relocation**. Each time a program is run, the computer may place it in different memory locations. The computer is not required to modify the addresses of instructions and data in the relocated program. The only modification is the value of the base address. The relative distances of other program addresses from the base will of course remain constant, since the displacement is the same. This would not be the case were absolute addressing to be used, for then the use of the location numbers themselves would require that those exact memory locations be used.

D.   THE MACHINE LANGUAGE INSTRUCTION FORMATS

The unit of control of a digital computer is an instruction. That is, all operations of a computer are directed by sequences of instructions. Such a sequence is called a **program** and one who writes programs is called a **programmer**. The activity of writing programs is known as **programming** or **coding**.

Every computer is manufactured with the facility to understand one language, called its **machine language**. Machine languages differ from one computer to another, so that a machine language program written for one computer cannot be understood by another. However, different machine languages do have common characteristics, so that knowledge of one does facilitate the learning and understanding of others.

As you know, instructions to a computer must be stored in the main memory; it thus follows that they are represented as sequences of 0's and 1's. For example:

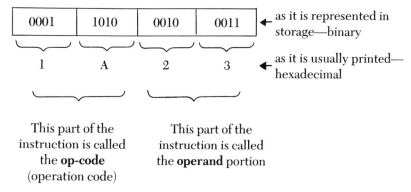

The **op-code** is the part of the instruction which specifies what action the computer should take. Every computer instruction has an op-code. In this example, hexadecimal 1A means "add the contents of two registers as specified in the operand portion".

An **operand** is a part of the instruction which contains the information to be acted upon or which contains the address of information to be acted upon. The concept of an operand will be clarified as we introduce the instructions themselves. In the operand portion of the instruction above, the first 4 bits specify register 2, and the second 4 bits specify register 3. Thus, the computer would, upon execution of this instruction: add the contents of register 3 to the contents of register 2, placing the sum into register 2.

Machine instructions in some computers are of fixed length; that is, they occupy the same number of storage positions. However, the IBM 360 and 370 have instructions which may occupy either 2 bytes, 4 bytes, or 6 bytes of storage. Regardless of instruction length, the first byte of each instruction is occupied by the op-code—the part of the instruction which determines what operation is to take place: addition, subtraction, reading, writing, and the like. The remaining parts of the instructions will depend on the **instruction format**. There are six different machine language instruction formats. However we shall discuss only five. All instructions of the sixth type, called the S format, are concerned with advanced functions, and are beyond the scope of this text.

The instruction formats outlined below serve to describe the general appearance of the instructions classified into each group. If you are told that a particular instruction (even one with which you are unfamiliar) falls into a particular category, you will have a basic idea of how the instruction is organized and of the types of locations with which it deals.

In the text, therefore, as each new instruction is introduced, we will include its associated format along with the instruction; the following five format descriptions will be useful as reference throughout the reading of the text.

1.   RR (Register to Register) Instruction Format

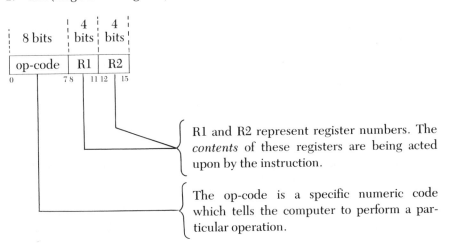

R1 and R2 represent register numbers. The *contents* of these registers are being acted upon by the instruction.

The op-code is a specific numeric code which tells the computer to perform a particular operation.

In RR instructions, the data being acted upon resides in two registers, which are mentioned in the instruction. In the above diagam, R1 refers to the first register and R2 refers to the second register.

When the RR format is used, operands contain binary data. In the RR instruction format, R1 is the first operand, and R2 is the second operand.

2.   RX (Register and Indexed Storage) Instruction Format

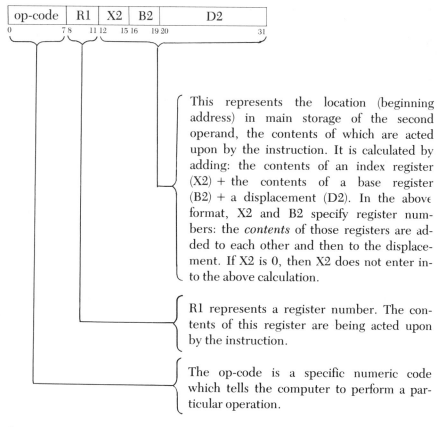

op-code	R1	X2	B2	D2
0	7 8 11 12	15 16	19 20	31

This represents the location (beginning address) in main storage of the second operand, the contents of which are acted upon by the instruction. It is calculated by adding: the contents of an index register (X2) + the contents of a base register (B2) + a displacement (D2). In the above format, X2 and B2 specify register numbers: the *contents* of those registers are added to each other and then to the displacement. If X2 is 0, then X2 does not enter into the above calculation.

R1 represents a register number. The contents of this register are being acted upon by the instruction.

The op-code is a specific numeric code which tells the computer to perform a particular operation.

The RX instruction format is used for operations on binary values in which one operand is located in a register and the other is located in main storage.

Example:

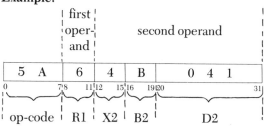

5 A	6	4	B	0 4 1
0	7 8 11 12	15 16	19 20	31

first oper-and   second operand

op-code   R1   X2   B2   D2

(5A means "add")

This instruction tells the computer to add the contents of the second operand to the contents of register 6 (R1). The result replaces the previous contents of register 6. The second operand is calculated by adding the contents of X2 (register 4) to the contents of B2 (register 11, since B is 11 in hexadecimal) and adding that sum to the displacement value 41_{16} (hex), equivalent to 65_{10} (decimal).

As you see from figure 1.17, the sum was placed into register 2 (first operand), replacing (erasing) the number which was previously there. Most instructions in this machine language format operate from right to left (that is, results of the operation replace the previous contents of the first operand).

3. RS (Register and Storage) Instruction Format

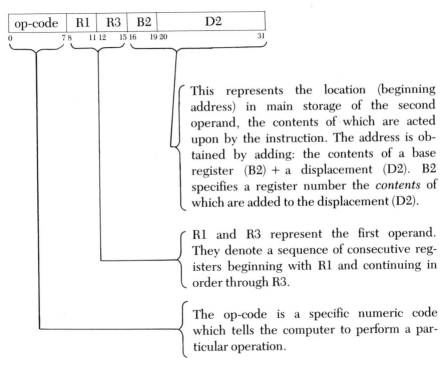

This represents the location (beginning address) in main storage of the second operand, the contents of which are acted upon by the instruction. The address is obtained by adding: the contents of a base register (B2) + a displacement (D2). B2 specifies a register number the *contents* of which are added to the displacement (D2).

R1 and R3 represent the first operand. They denote a sequence of consecutive registers beginning with R1 and continuing in order through R3.

The op-code is a specific numeric code which tells the computer to perform a particular operation.

The RS instruction format is used for operations on binary values in which the first part (what we call the first operand) is located in registers and the other is located in main storage.

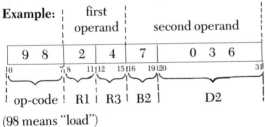

Example:

first operand | second operand

| 9 8 | 2 | 4 | 7 | 0 3 6 |

op-code | R1 | R3 | B2 | D2

(98 means "load")

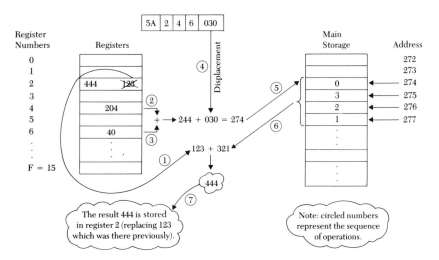

Figure 1.17
Executing a Machine Language Instruction in RX Format

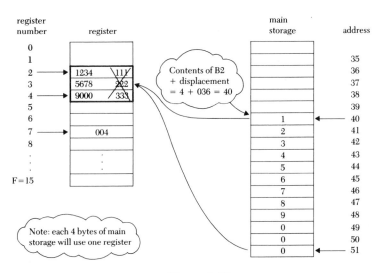

Figure 1.18
Executing a Machine Language Instruction in RS Format

This instruction tells the computer to "load" (copy) the contents of storage, beginning with the second operand location, into registers 2 through 4 (that is, registers 2, 3, and 4). The number of bytes moved is determined by the number of bytes in R1 through R3. As usual, the previous contents of registers 2 through 4 are destroyed and replaced by the new value(s) coming in (see figure 1.18).

Notice from figure 1.18 that the number of bytes "loaded" is determined by the length of the first operand. Since three registers occupy 12 bytes, 12 bytes of storage beginning with the second operand location (that is, locations 40 through 51) replace the previous contents of registers 3, 4, and 5.

4.   SI (Storage and Immediate Operand) Instruction Format

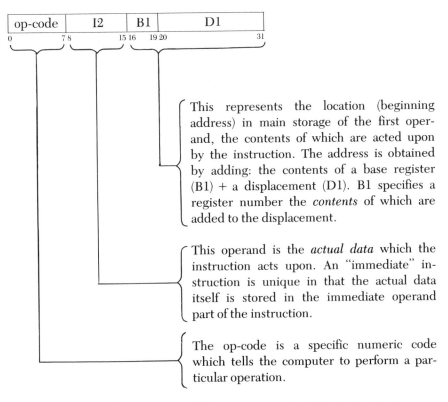

This represents the location (beginning address) in main storage of the first operand, the contents of which are acted upon by the instruction. The address is obtained by adding: the contents of a base register (B1) + a displacement (D1). B1 specifies a register number the *contents* of which are added to the displacement.

This operand is the *actual data* which the instruction acts upon. An "immediate" instruction is unique in that the actual data itself is stored in the immediate operand part of the instruction.

The op-code is a specific numeric code which tells the computer to perform a particular operation.

Instructions in SI format are used for operations in which it is advantageous for data to be included in the instruction itself.

Example:

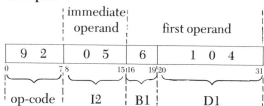

(92 means "move immediate")

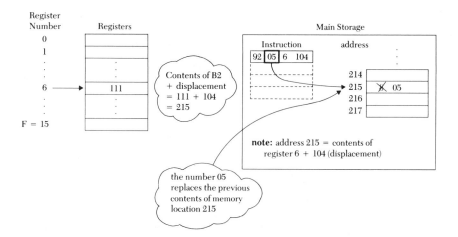

Figure 1.19
Executing a Machine Language Instruction in SI Format

5.   SS (Storage to Storage) Instruction Format

The SS instruction format is used for operations in which both operands are located in the main storage.

Version 1:

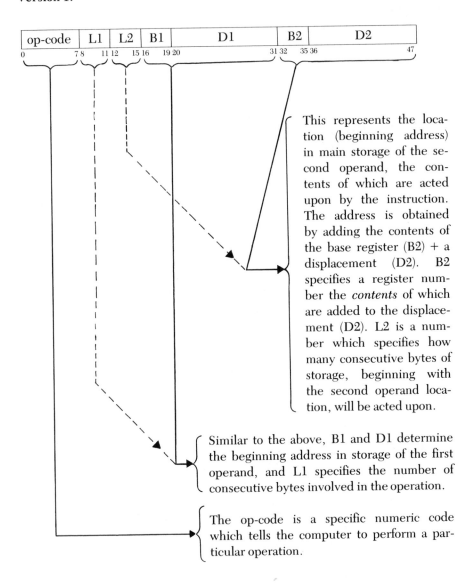

This represents the location (beginning address) in main storage of the second operand, the contents of which are acted upon by the instruction. The address is obtained by adding the contents of the base register (B2) + a displacement (D2). B2 specifies a register number the *contents* of which are added to the displacement (D2). L2 is a number which specifies how many consecutive bytes of storage, beginning with the second operand location, will be acted upon.

Similar to the above, B1 and D1 determine the beginning address in storage of the first operand, and L1 specifies the number of consecutive bytes involved in the operation.

The op-code is a specific numeric code which tells the computer to perform a particular operation.

Example:

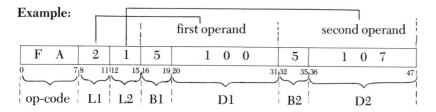

(FA means "add")

This instruction tells the computer to add the contents of the second operand, which is 2 bytes long (the length used is one byte more than $L2 : L2 + 1 = 1 + 1 = 2$), to the contents of the first operand, which is 3 bytes long (the length used is one byte more than $L1 : L1 + 1 = 2 + 1 = 3$). Of course, the previous contents of the first operand are destroyed by the sum (see figure 1.20).

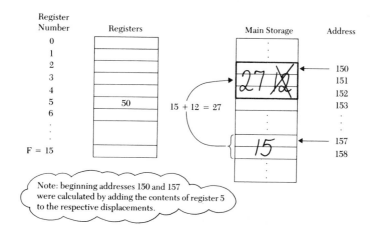

Figure 1.20
Executing a Machine Language Instruction in SS Format, Version 1

Version 2:

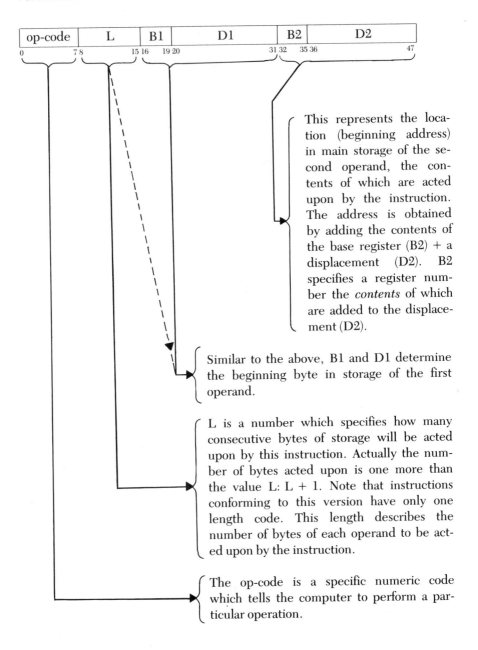

This represents the location (beginning address) in main storage of the second operand, the contents of which are acted upon by the instruction. The address is obtained by adding the contents of the base register (B2) + a displacement (D2). B2 specifies a register number the *contents* of which are added to the displacement (D2).

Similar to the above, B1 and D1 determine the beginning byte in storage of the first operand.

L is a number which specifies how many consecutive bytes of storage will be acted upon by this instruction. Actually the number of bytes acted upon is one more than the value L: L + 1. Note that instructions conforming to this version have only one length code. This length describes the number of bytes of each operand to be acted upon by the instruction.

The op-code is a specific numeric code which tells the computer to perform a particular operation.

Example:

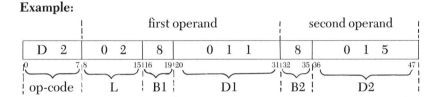

(D2 means "move")

This instruction tells the computer to move (copy) the information in the second operand into the first operand location. The operand length is three bytes (the length used is one byte more than $L : L + 1 = 2 + 1 = 3$). We see (from figure 1.21) that the direction of the operation is from left to right, with the previous contents of the first operand replaced by the contents of the second operand.

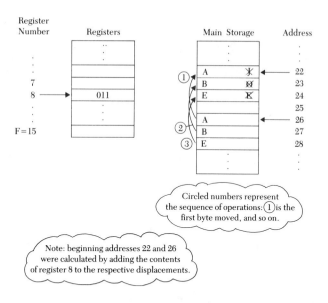

Figure 1.21
Executing a Machine Language Instruction in SS Format, Version 2

1.4.3 Assembler Language

At one time, all computer programming was performed in machine language, with the instructions coded as sequences of 0's and 1's.

However the activity of writing programs was very costly, time-consuming, error-prone, and inefficient. The programmer found himself spending a disproportionate amount of time in clerical activity: calculating addresses, keeping track of thousands of storage positions, remembering large numbers of codes, and the like. Since computer instructions are stored sequentially in memory, the addition or deletion of an instruction required an adjustment of addresses in all subsequent instructions. Recall too, that machine language instructions were prepared by the programmer as long sequences of 0's and 1's, which made it tedious and difficult to locate errors and to correct them.

It was obvious that harnessing the computer to do this clerical work would lead to greater efficiency and speed, and would make programming much more pleasurable. The programmer would be freed of much of the tedious work, and would be able to more fully concentrate on method rather than on detail.

This led to the development of what is known as **assembler language**. In this language, each op-code, instead of being written in binary, was replaced by a symbolic name, often called a **mnemonic**. For example, 5A (hex) or 01011010 (binary) was replaced by "A" which means "add"; 5C (hex) or 01011100 (binary) was replaced by "M" which means "multiply"; and so on. The operands which previously used numbers (which pointed to the addresses of data) were replaced by symbolic names. Thus displacements and base registers no longer occupied the programmer's attention. He was allowed, within certain limitations, to select names such as PRICE, ITEM, ACCOUNT, and the like.

For example, the machine language instruction (written in hexadecimal for convenience):

D 2	0 3	8 0 1 1	8 0 1 5
op-code	length	operand 1	operand 2

could be written in assembler language as:

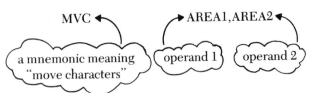

The instruction, when executed, will move (copy) the contents of the location called AREA2 into the location called AREA1.

As you see, instructions written in assembler language are much easier to write and to understand than are machine language instructions. But in order for us to use assembler language, the computer must be able to understand it! (The computer understands only sequences of 0's and 1's.) To accomplish this goal, computer manufacturers supply programs whose purpose is the translation of symbolic or assembler language into machine language. The assembler language program is henceforth referred to as the **source program**; if punched on cards, as the **source deck**; and when printed, as the **source listing**. The translated machine language version is henceforth referred to as the **object program**; if punched on cards, as the **object deck**; and when printed, as the **object listing**. The translating program is called the **assembler program** or the **assembler** and the process of translation is called **assembly**. Although there are quite a few new terms here, their frequent use throughout the text will make them easy to remember.

In our concern with the translating activities of the assembler, we neglected to mention all the other clerical work which it performs. The assembler associates a particular address in main storage with each symbolic name assigned by the programmer; in the event that modifications of the program are necessary, the assembler will make all the necessary clerical adjustments. A modern assembler also performs numerous other chores which will be explained throughout the text.

1.4.4   Why Assembler Language?

As we have seen, assembler language was developed as an alternative to machine language. It is not, however, the only alternative. "Higher-level" languages such as COBOL, FORTRAN, PL/1, BASIC, and the like were introduced in the late 1950's and during the 1960's. (These names are acronyms: COBOL means **CO**mmon **B**usiness **O**riented **L**anguage, FORTRAN means **FOR**mula **TRAN**slation, PL/1 means **P**rogramming **L**anguage **1**, BASIC means **B**eginners **A**ll-purpose **S**ymbolic **I**nstruction **C**ode.)

A characteristic of higher-level languages is that one source statement, after translation (for these languages, we call the translation process **compilation** and the translator a **compiler**), will usually generate many machine language instructions. By contrast, an assembler language instruction, after being assembled (translated), typically generates one machine language instruction. Thus assembler language has an important advantage over the higher level languages in that it is "closer" to machine language and therefore utilizes the power of the machine in a more efficient manner. No unnecessary instructions are generated, resulting in economical use of storage and of machine time during program execution.

A Computer Needs a Translator

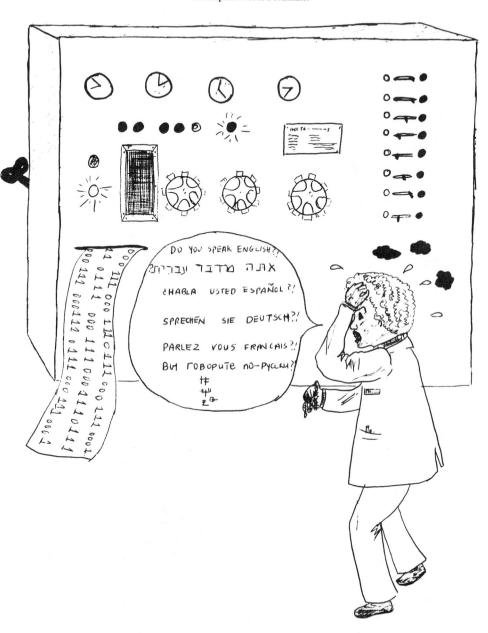

Figure 1.22

There are many situations in which the use of assembler language becomes imperative as opposed to higher level languages because of restrictions on storage and time available.

Assembler language is thus a necessary tool for the serious programmer. Even when programs are written in higher-level languages, a true understanding and most efficient use of those languages necessitates a certain knowledge of assembler. Some such understanding can also help when **debugging** (correcting) and analyzing malfunctioning programs written in higher-level languages.

Summary

In this chapter, we have been introduced to the computer. In particular, we have become acquainted with
- what a computer is
- the basic components of a computer
- the punched card
- Hollerith code
- EBCDIC code
- a computer system
- data organization: fields, records, files
- machine language
- the instruction formats
- registers
- addressing and relative addressing
- assembler language: what it is and why we use it

The information in this chapter is foundation material upon which the remaining chapters of the text will build.

Important Terms Discussed in Chapter 1

absolute addressing	base register
address	bit
arithmetic and logical unit (ALU)	byte
assembler	
assembler language	card reader
assembler program	central processing unit (CPU)
auxiliary storage	coding

compiler
compilation
computer
computer language
computer system
control register
control unit
core

data
debugging
disk
displacement
doubleword

EBCDIC
effective address
execution time

field
file
floating point
floating point register
fullword (word)

general purpose register

halfword
high-order bit
Hollerith card

index register
input
instruction format
I/O

loading
low-order bit

machine language
magnetic tape

numeric punch

object deck
object listing
object program
output

printer
program
programmer
programming
program relocation
punched card

record
relative addressing
register
retrieval

secondary storage
source deck
source listing
source program
storage
stored program
storage unit

zone portion
zone punch

Questions

1-1. At a recent meeting of stockholders of a company called Bank-rupt, a discussion arose when one stockholder suggested investing in a computer which would be used to handle the company's paperwork (data processing). A number of other stockholders voiced strong objections, claiming that a computer was no more than an overpriced adding machine. Is this true? Explain.

1-2. What is a computer program?

1-3. List the six basic components of a computer system.

1-4. What do the letters CPU stand for? What does the term refer to?

1-5. What is the basic building block of main storage?

1-6. What is a byte? How is the byte divided?

1-7. In the following table, fill in the missing entries.

Phrase	Phrase as it appears in storage			
TOV	_____			
HIY	_____			
_____	1111	0111	1111	0110

1-8. Does the following statement completely describe the functions of the ALU? "The ALU performs logical operations, and determines the relationship in size between two numbers."

1-9. Which computer component oversees the communication between the other five components and between each of these and itself?

1-10.

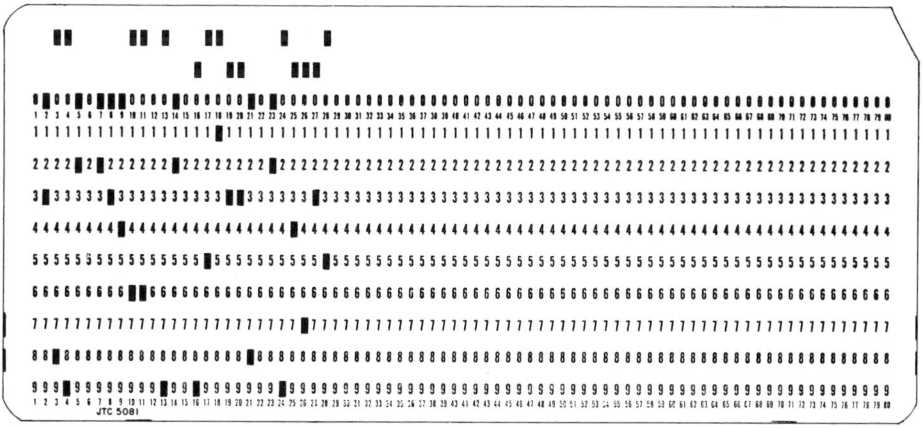

Figure 1.23

Looking at the punched card of figure 1.23 above, determine what information is punched on it.

1-11. What is the maximum number of symbols that may be punched on a Hollerith card?

1-12. In what way do punched alphabetic representations differ from punched numeric representations?

1-13. If you wished to have the contents of a Hollerith card stored in computer memory, what device would you use?

1-14. How many symbols may be output on a line produced by a typical printer?

1-15. Is the card reader an input or output device? What about the printer?

1-16. What is auxiliary storage used for? Name some devices used for this purpose.

1-17. Explain in your own words what is meant by the terms field, record, and file.

1-18.

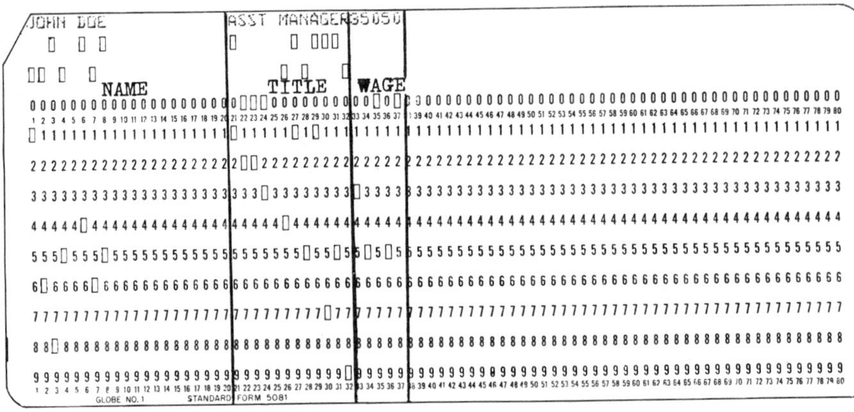

Figure 1.24

How many fields are on the above card? What are thay called?

1-19. What types of files would one find in a typical business organization?

1-20. In what way are computer languages similar to human languages?

1-21. What is a register?

1-22. In what respect do registers differ from units of main storage?

1-23. What types of registers are available in the IBM 360 and 370 computers? Identify the types by name.

1-24. How does a programmer reference a general purpose register?

1-25. Can alphabetic information be placed in a general purpose register?

1-26. What is the length of a general purpose register in bits? in bytes? Are there any other terms which may be used to describe the length of a register?

1-27. A programmer trainee has written a computer program in assembler language in which several registers were used, among them register 0. The program produced satisfactory output several times; however, one day it started to produce strange results, to everyone's surprise. What do you think might have happened?

1-28. What are the two methods of addressing? Which one is used by the IBM 360 and 370 computers?

1-29. Assume that registers 5, 6, 8, 9, and 11 contain hexadecimal information as outlined below:

Register address	Register content (in hex)
5	0 0 0 0 2 3 7 1
6	0 0 0 0 0 2 C 2
8	0 0 0 0 0 6 5 4
9	0 0 0 0 0 0 8 A
11	0 0 0 0 3 A B 1

Complete the missing entries in the table below.

Base Register	Displacement (in hex)	Effective Address
5	6 2 A	_____
8	2 4 F	_____
9	_____	F F F
11	_____	4 0 0 0

1-30. Assuming the same register contents as in question 1-29 above, complete the missing entries in the following table:

Base Register	Index Register	Displacement	Effective Address
8	9	111	——
5	Not used	237	——
6	8	——	ABC
11	9	——	4F2C

1-31. Mr. I.M. Confused has just finished writing a very important assembly language program and discovered that it requires 5000 consecutive storage locations. Can all those location numbers be expressed using one base register? Explain.

1-32. Mr. I.M. Confused could not solve problem 31 on his own, so he consulted with Dr. Moor Register, who found a solution. What do you think it was?

1-33. Name the two main parts of a typical machine language instruction.

1-34. The IBM 360 and 370 computers have machine language instructions in three lengths. Express these lengths in terms of bits, bytes, and halfwords.

1-35. Identify the machine language formats by name.

1-36. How many bits do the op-code, register, base register, index register, immediate operand, and displacement occupy, if present, in a machine language instruction?

1-37. How many bits are required in a machine language instruction to reference a location in main storage?

1-38. List three disadvantages of machine language.

1-39. How is a main storage address specified in assembler language?

1-40. How is an op-code specified in assembler language?

1-41. What enables the computer to understand assembler language?

1-42. Distinguish between the terms source program and object program.

Chapter 2

Our First Program

OUR FIRST PROGRAM

2.1 OUR FIRST PROBLEM—DESCRIBED

The Mickey Mousetrap Company, a subsidiary of United Meatpackers Incorporated, had a great deal of trouble handling its inventory, payroll, accounts receivable, and accounts payable. Its executives therefore decided to purchase an IBM 370 model 135 computer, which the manufacturer claimed could efficiently handle their operation. The computer arrived amidst great excitement. In order to show that the computer was functioning properly, Mr. I.M. Sharp, the IBM custom engineer, demonstrated a series of programs to the management. The first program involved reading a deck of cards which was processed by the computer to produce a picture; some of the employees were so excited that they asked for an explanation of how the computer was able to manage such a feat.

The systems engineer said, "This program makes use of three pieces of equipment in this room: the card reader, the printer, and the CPU.

"Do you you see the deck of cards which I am holding? Actually we may consider it to be composed of two parts: the program, that is, the assembler language instructions which tell the computer what to do, and the data: the information being acted upon. Each data card contains one line of the picture, and when printed consecutively, the lines will look like that which you now see" (figure 2.1).

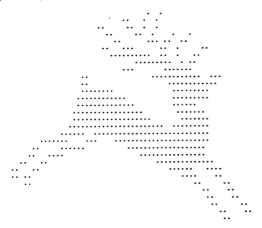

Figure 2.1
Mr. Sharp's Program Output

"The steps which the computer follows," the engineer continued, "are as follows:

- "The information in the first part of the deck, that is, the punched instructions, are read by the card reader and directed by the control unit into predetermined consecutive storage locations. After this is done,
- "The computer starts **executing** the program; that is, doing what the instructions tell it to do. The first instruction in this program tells the computer to read a data card and to store its contents in a fixed location, which we call the **input area**, similar to the "receiving area" your company has for raw materials arriving to be processed.
- "The information is then **processed**, that is, **moved** (or copied) into different storage locations which the programmer set aside for output, similar to the "shipping area" into which your finished products are placed when ready to be shipped. We call this part of storage the **output area**.
- "Finally, an instruction tells the computer to have the printer print the contents of the output area, that is, to in effect print out the contents of the original data card. This is analagous to placing finished goods on a truck for transfer to their final destination.
- "This process, that is, input ⟶ processing ⟶ output, is repeated for every card. The second card is handled in the same manner as the first, resulting in a second line printed beneath the first. This process is repeated until all the cards have been read; the final result is the picture you see (figure 2.1).

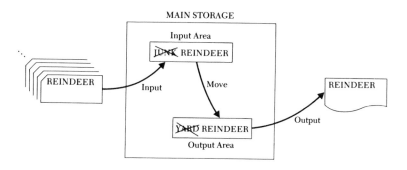

Figure 2.2
Input, Move, Output

- "In your company, once materials have left the receiving area, incoming materials are placed in the evacuated space. Likewise the computer places information from subsequent cards into the *same* input area as was used for previous cards. However in the case of computer storage, we

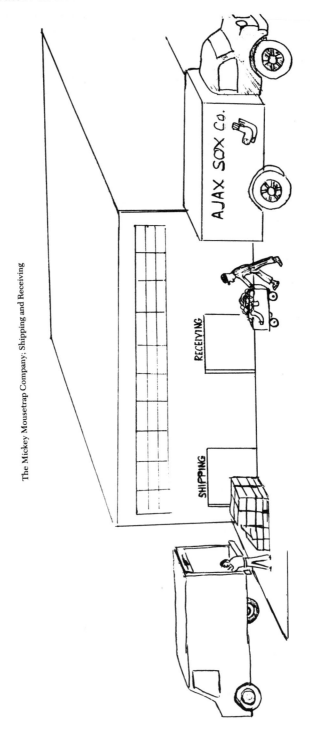

The Mickey Mousetrap Company; Shipping and Receiving

must be careful to observe that incoming information replaces (destroys) any previous data stored there. In this respect, the process is similar to recording music on a used tape, thereby destroying that which was previously recorded. This implies that stored information remains in its location indefinitely, unless it is replaced by incoming information.

- "The 'destruction' of information in memory is effected *only* by new information coming in; 'moving' information from one storage area to another actually only destroys the previous contents of the receiving area, while the contents of the sending area remains the same. We thus think of the 'move' as a 'copy'. You may understand this process more fully if you compare this to the recording of music from one tape onto another, resulting in two copies of the same music.

"Computer output may be thought of as a 'playback' of the copied music; the music can be played for an indefinite number of times without affecting its storage on the tape; computer information may be output many times without affecting its storage if the programmer so instructs.

"In conclusion, we may thus say that the 'input' and 'move' operations are destructive, while the 'output' is non-destructive."

- "The above implies one other thing. As you have seen, the information from our first card was printed, and was therefore no longer needed when the second card was read. It is the practice, therefore, to use the same input area and output area for every data card read and printed. This has the advantage of limiting the amount of storage needed by the program, and furthermore implies that the amount of storage needed for input and/or output is independent of the number of data cards used."

"What you said sounds all right," one employee said, "but of what use is a savings of storage, if the instructions have to be repeated for every card read and processed?"

The engineer smiled and remarked that programmers have considered this problem, and the answer is a simple one: since the instructions are independent of the data used, and depend only upon the input/ouput equipment used and the locations being acted upon, then use of the same memory locations implies that the instructions themselves can be reused for every data card processed. This idea has great application potential, for it implies that writing programs should involve a limited number of instructions executed in sequence and repeated for every record until the required problem has been solved.

The employees thanked the engineer for his very lucid explanation, and for copies of the computer program, the workings of which he had explained.

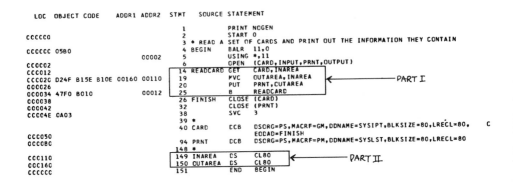

```
  LOC   OBJECT CODE   ADDR1 ADDR2  STMT    SOURCE STATEMENT
                                      1            PRINT NOGEN
CCCCC0                                2            START 0
                                      3  * READ A SET OF CARDS AND PRINT OUT THE INFORMATION THEY CONTAIN
CCCCCC  05B0                          4  BEGIN     BALR  11,0
                             00002    5            USING *,11
CCC0C02                               6            OPEN  (CARD,INPUT,PRNT,OUTPUT)
CCC012                               14  READCARD  GET   CARD,INAREA
CCC02C  D24F B15E B10E 00160 00110   19            MVC   OUTAREA,INAREA          ◄──────── PART I
C00026                               20            PUT   PRNT,OUTAREA
0C0034  47F0 B010              00012 25            B     READCARD
CCC038                               26  FINISH    CLOSE (CARD)
C00042                               32            CLOSE (PRNT)
CCCC4E  0A03                         38            SVC   3
                                     39  *
                                     40  CARD      DCB   DSORG=PS,MACRF=GM,DDNAME=SYSIPT,BLKSIZE=80,LRECL=80,  C
CCC050                                             EODAD=FINISH
0CCCBC                               94  PRNT      DCB   DSORG=PS,MACRF=PM,DDNAME=SYSLST,BLKSIZE=80,LRECL=80
                                    148  *
CCC110                              149  INAREA    DS    CL80                    ◄──────── PART II
C0C160                              150  OUTAREA   DS    CL80
CCCCCC                              151            END   BEGIN
```

Figure 2.3
Mr. Sharp's Program—OS Version

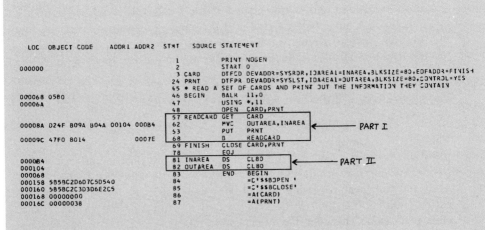

```
  LOC   OBJECT CODE   ADDR1 ADDR2  STMT    SOURCE STATEMENT
                                      1            PRINT NOGEN
000000                                2            START 0
                                      3  CARD      DTFCD DEVADDR=SYSRDR,IOAREA1=INAREA,BLKSIZE=80,EOFADDR=FINISH
                                     24  PRNT      DTFPR DEVADDR=SYSLST,IOAREA1=OUTAREA,BLKSIZE=80,CONTROL=YES
                                     45  * READ A SET OF CARDS AND PRINT OUT THE INFORMATION THEY CONTAIN
000068  05B0                         46  BEGIN     BALR  11,0
00006A                               47            USING *,11
                                     48            OPEN  CARD,PRNT
                                     57  READCARD  GET   CARD
00008A  D24F B09A B04A 00104 000B4   62            MVC   OUTAREA,INAREA          ◄──────── PART I
                                     53            PUT   PRNT
00009C  47F0 B014              0007E 68            B     READCARD
                                     69  FINISH    CLOSE CARD,PRNT
                                     78            EOJ
0000B4                               81  INAREA    DS    CL80                    ◄──────── PART II
000104                               82  OUTAREA   DS    CL80
000068                               83            END   BEGIN
000158  5B5BC2D6D7C5D540             84            =C'$$BOPEN '
000160  5B5BC2C3D3D6E2C5             85            =C'$$BCLOSE'
000168  00000000                     86            =A(CARD)
00016C  00000038                     87            =A(PRNT)
```

Figure 2.4
Mr. Sharp's Program—DOS Version

Before departing, they were invited to call upon him should any difficulty arise.

Here are copies of two different versions of the program as they were presented. Figure 2.3 shows the program as it would be written for a computer directed by a collection of control programs known as OS (Operating System). Figure 2.4 shows the program as it would be written by a computer directed by a collection of control programs known as DOS (Disk Operating System). The concept of operating systems and what they do will be considered in chapter 13. Let it suffice for now to say that certain assembly language instructions will vary from one operating system to another. We will consider both OS and DOS versions in this text. Shaded areas of the text and of the programs describe assembly language for DOS systems only.

Mr. I.M. Sharp was thoughtful in that he enclosed those program instructions which he touched upon in his explanation. The copies of the programs shown in figures 2.3 and 2.4 were produced by the assembler (that is, the manufacturer-supplied program which translates the source program into an object program). Henceforth, such a copy will be called a **listing**. In the listing, the rightmost portion, under the heading "source statement", is a copy of the original program. The source statements (instructions) are numbered for convenience by the assembler program under the printed heading STMT (standing for "statement"). The leftmost portion represents the object program, that is, the machine language version of the program which the computer understands. The programmer codes (writes) the source program, which is then translated by the assembler into the object program, which is then executed.

Let us examine the boxed sections in the listing to see if we can relate the commands to what we know the program is doing.

In part II, the first statement will reserve (technically DS = **D**efine **S**torage) 80 consecutive storage locations which will serve as the input area for our program. The programmer named this area INAREA. The second statement will reserve 80 consecutive storage locations which will serve as the output area for our program. The programmer named this area OUTAREA.

In part I, the first instruction will read (in assembler language we say GET) a card from the file which the programmer called CARD (the name CARD was assigned by the programmer) and will place its contents into INAREA. The second instruction will move (in assembler language, MVC = **M**o**V**e **C**haracters) the information from INAREA into OUTAREA. The third instruction will print (in assembler language we say PUT) the contents of OUTAREA. Finally, the computer is instructed to go back to the first instruction labeled READCARD to repeat the process for the second card and for subsequent cards. In assembler language, B stands for **B**ranch and means that the next instruction to be executed is that which is located at (labeled) READCARD.

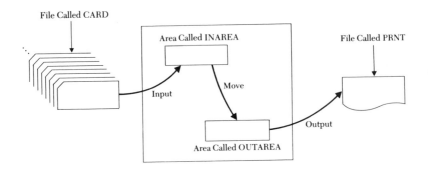

Figure 2.5
Mr. Sharp's Program Logic Illustrated

2.2   THE PROGRAM INSTRUCTIONS

Assembly language instructions may be grouped into three categories:
- **Assembler instructions**—needed to provide the translator (assembler) with directions for proper translation
- **Machine instructions**—instructions written by the programmer in a symbolic language and subsequently translated by the assembler into machine language instructions
- **Macro instructions**—instructions each of which will be replaced by the assembler with more than one machine language instruction.

Each of these three instruction categories contains a fixed repertoire of instructions. The programmer selects the proper instructions to suit his purpose and pieces them together so that they will provide a logical solution to his problem. This is similar to the choosing of proper English vocabulary in writing. The art of programming involves choosing the proper instructions, using them according to their correct rules, and placing them into an appropriate sequence to yield a correct and efficient solution to the problem. There may be many correct ways to code a problem solution; programs vary in style just as does writing in any human language. In the chapters which follow, we will examine and illustrate many assembly language instructions.

Note that both the terms "machine instruction" and "machine language instruction" are used here. Do not confuse them. Recall that

- machine language instructions are instructions in machine language: the language which the computer understands. All other instructions must be first translated into machine language before the computer can do that which they instruct the computer to do (chapter 1, section 1.4.2).
- machine instructions are instructions in assembly language which are translated by the assembler on a one-to-one basis into machine language instructions.

Similarly, be sure that you understand the difference between the terms "assembly language instruction" and "assembler instruction" before proceeding. Recall that

- assembly (or assembler) language instructions are instructions written in mnemonic code (chapter 1, section 1.4.3).
- assembler instructions are a category of assembler language instructions which you will use whenever you want to provide direction to the assembler.

2.2.1 Assembly Language Instructions: Assembler Instructions, Machine Instructions, and Macros

- **Assembler instructions** are written by the programmer to communicate wth the assembler program, in order to provide direction and assistance during the translation process.

To fully understand what is meant by the term "assembler instruction" consider the following analogy. A book is to be translated from English to Chinese by a professional translator. Often it is imperative to provide the translator with special instructions which do not relate directly to the subject of the text and yet are necessary for proper translation.For example, we might tell him to translate only certain portions of the text, or indicate that he is free to provide certain additions or deletions. Likewise, assembler instructions give special instructions to the assembler program, detailing procedures to be followed in translation. In this program, the PRINT NOGEN, START, USING, DS, and END instructions are assembler instructions.

Assembler instructions have fulfilled their mission during the translation process and are therefore not translated into machine language. We thus consider them non-executable instructions. It follows that the instruction formats discussed in chapter 1, section 1.4.2, do not apply to assembler instructions.

- **Machine instructions** are those instructions which are coded by the programmer and are subsequently translated by the assembler into machine language for execution. Each statement written by the programmer (**source statement**) is translated into *one* machine language instruction (**object statement**). For example, the MVC and BALR instructions in our program are machine instructions.

- **Macro instructions** are written by programmers to represent a set sequence of instructions which may be repeated several times in the same program or in different programs.

In order to afford a savings of cost, time, and programming effort, the manufacturer supplies sequences of prewritten generalized instructions (in machine language) which may be readily incorporated into any assembly language program, and which may be customized to fit the needs of independent users. Many such instruction sequences are provided, and are stored in a "library" called a **macro library**. The programmer may retrieve those sequences from the library, when needed, and may have them incorporated into the appropriate part of his program. The method for accomplishing this is the writing of a **macro instruction**.

In a macro instruction (henceforth referred to as a **macro**), the name portion is optional. The operation code is a mnemonic which identifies the appropriate instruction sequence in the library so that it may be retrieved; the operation code is required. The third part may consist of operands whose purpose is to tailor the generalized routine to fit the user's program, just as a customer buying a suit has the suit tailored to fit him properly.

The retrieval of the appropriate sequence of instructions occurs during the assembly process. The assembler locates the appropriate program segments corresponding to the specific macro, and copies those sequences into the object program which it produces; such retrieval leaves the original copy in the library for future use. Since the macro is simply a means of retrieving machine language instructions, the instruction formats discussed in chapter 1, section 1.4.2, do not apply.

It is possible for the programmer to create his own macros and store them in the system library under an appropriate name for future use. However we shall use the manufacturer-supplied macros in this text. Examples of macros in the DOS version of our program are the OPEN, GET, PUT, CLOSE, EOJ, DTFCD, and DTFPR instructions. Examples of macros in the OS version of our program are the OPEN, GET, PUT, CLOSE, and DCB instructions. Note that the DOS and OS programs are similar, with the following exceptions: the operand portions of the OPEN and CLOSE macros differ; the DOS macro EOJ corresponds to the OS machine instruction SVC 3; the DOS macros DTFCD and DTFPR correspond to the two DCB macros in the OS version of our program.

2.2.2   Instructions—Common Features

Every assembly language instruction is composed of four parts, some of which may be optional. One of these parts (the operation portion) is always dictated by the assembler language, while the others are in most cases programmer-supplied. The four parts are:

- The **name** portion
- The **operation** portion
- The **operand** portion
- The **comment** portion

In writing the instructions, you must take extreme care to separate these parts by at least one space. A space is a signal to the assembler program that the part of the instruction being identified is terminated. To ensure that the programmer strictly adhere to this rule, the computer manufacturers supply special **coding forms**, which we will discuss in section 2.2.3.

Beware that the instruction portions follow in the above order. The instruction below is correct:

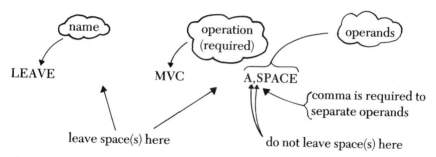

The instruction

MVC   LEAVE   A,SPACE

is incorrect, since the operand portion and the name portion of this instruction are not in the proper order.

The Name Portion

We know from our discussion thus far that instructions and data must be stored in memory before the computer can use them. Frequently during program execution, the computer finds it necessary to reference a particular instruction or a specific piece of data. This means that the computer must know exactly where in memory the data and/or instructions are stored; that is, he must have an address (number) for reference purposes.

Since the computer depends for its guidance on the programmer, it is the programmer's responsibility to provide addresses for its use. Numeric addresses are difficult to remember and to keep track of; assembly language therefore allows one to reference storage locations by using names. For example, we may refer to the instruction

LEAVE   MVC   A,SPACE

as the instruction stored in the location called LEAVE. By the time execution occurs, the system assures that a specific numeric address is associated with the programmer-assigned name.

The name itself has two meanings: it stands for a location number (that is, the beginning location number: to be discussed in chapter 3) in main storage, and it also refers to the *contents* of the location associated with it (just as when we say "the president" we may mean the office, or the man who occupies the office). Thus whenever a name is mentioned in a program, either meaning or both may be implied.

The purpose of a name is to identify a location. It follows that it is *necessary* to assign a name only when a location is to be referenced; however you may always assign a name if you feel that is desirable.

When you choose to name a location, the following rules must be observed:

- The name may consist of from one to eight characters inclusive.
- The first character must be alphabetic (A-Z). Remaining characters may be alphabetic, numeric (0-9), @, #, or $.
- Spaces are separators and therefore may not be embedded between any two other characters.

A programmer in the Mickey Mousetrap Company has written the following names for inclusion in his first assembly language program. Which of these will be accepted by the assembler? Which will be rejected, and why?

A.   THIS
B.   3S
C.   AGREATTEXT
D.   RIGHT?
E.   IT IS

"A" is correct, while the others are not, since they violate the rules for assigning names. "B" has a digit as its first character; "C" exceeds eight characters in length; in "D" the symbol "?" is not allowed; "E" contains an embedded blank.

You must also observe that when assigning names, each name must be unique. Otherwise the assembler will politely remind you that an error has been made.

Names need not be English words, or even words at all, although meaning-ful names do considerably improve the readability of a program. Whenever a particular name is repeated, be sure to spell it in exactly the same way as its original form. The assembler will always notify you if any discrepancies are found.

The Operation Portion

The operation is the part of the instruction that tells the computer what to do; consequently it must always be present in every instruction. The form and spelling of the operation portion is determined by the manufacturer.

Each instruction has a unique operation code. For example, A means "add", MVC means "move character(s)" and so on.

In addition, the operation code tells the assembler program what format the instruction is to conform to, as discussed in chapter 1, section 1.4.2.

The operation portion must be preceded by at least one blank.

For convenience, you may wish to refer to the IBM/360 Reference Data Card (GX20–1703) or to the IBM/370 Reference Summary (GX20–1850), each of which contains a list of all the machine instructions in the appropri-ate assembler language, along with other important reference information which will be explained in this text. The IBM/370 Reference Summary is reproduced in Appendix A for your use.

The Operand Portion

The operand portion identifies and/or describes the data to be acted upon by an instruction. Operands may be optional, however when required, their number is determined by language specifications which we will discuss for each instruction in turn.

If present, the first operand of an instruction must be preceded by at least one blank. If several operands are required, they must be separated by commas, with no embedded blanks permitted, and no blanks either preceding or following the comma.

The Comment Portion

Comments are short explanatory remarks which the programmer may add in order to explain the workings of his program. The comment itself does not affect program execution in any way, since it is not stored in main storage along with the instruction. It is merely printed along with the instruction on the program listing.

Comments must be preceded by at least one blank and may contain anything the programmer might desire.

2.2.3   The Coding Form

In the beginning of this chapter, you observed that Mr. I.M. Sharp used the punched card as a means of entering his instructions into the computer. The practice of using the punched card format as a means of entering instructions is traditionally followed throughout the computer industry.

To ensure that the person who punches the cards strictly adheres to the rules for separating the different instruction parts, a special form called an **assembler coding form** (henceforth referred to simply as a coding form) was developed by the computer manufacturer, and is available through vendors. The following discussion will explain the coding form and its use.

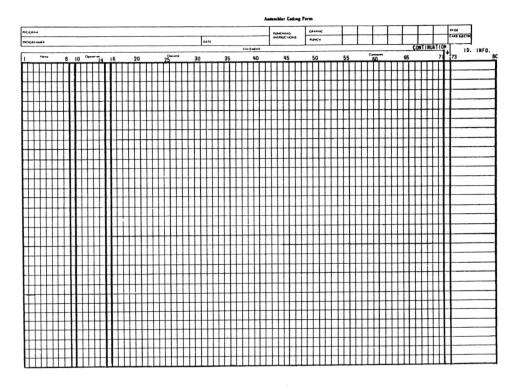

Figure 2.6
The Assembler Coding Form

The coding form of figure 2.6 consists of two parts. The upper part is used for identification and special instructions, and the lower part is used for coding instructions.

The upper part of the coding form contains preprinted sections labeled for specific purposes. The information entered here includes the program name (a name assigned by the programmer for identification purposes); the name of the programmer; the date the program was written. The area labeled "punching instructions" is used to provide information to the keypunch operator. This becomes necessary since some characters, when handwritten, can be interpreted in more than one way. For example, the letter "O" may be confused with the digit "0", the letter "I" with the digit "1", and the letter "Z" with the digit "2".

When using the coding sheet in this text, the following conventions will be used (you can make up your own conventions):
the letter "O" will be slashed, that is, Ø
the letter "Z" will be crossed, that is, Ƶ
the letter "I" will be written I
the digit "7" will be crossed, that is, 7̵

Whenever several coding sheets are necessary, it is helpful to consecutively number the pages in the space provided for this purpose on the coding sheet (the upper right hand corner). The information in this upper section of the coding sheet is not punched.

The remainder of the coding sheet consists of horizontal rows. Each row will contain information which will be punched on one card (unless a time-sharing system is being used, a discussion of which is beyond the scope of this book).

Recall (section 2.2.2) that each instruction has four parts: the name part, the operation part, the operand part, and the comment part, each of which is designated on the coding sheet. The coding form is helpful in that it is pre-lined to delineate separate areas for each instruction part.

Under the heading "name" (columns 1 through 8), one enters the symbolic name, beginning with column 1 and continuing in sequence without extending beyond column 8. The programmer enters the operation code under the heading "operation", starting in column 10. Starting in column 16, one or more operands are entered, if required. Comments will follow the operand(s), provided that at least one blank character separates the operand(s) from the comment. Operands and/or comments may not extend beyond column 71. If an operand requires space beyond column 71, it may be continued onto a second line only (for DOS programs), or onto a second and then onto a third line (for OS programs). When an operand is to be continued onto a succeeding line, we place any nonblank character in column 72, and continue writing the statement starting in column 16 of the succeeding line, leaving columns one through fifteen blank. The **continuation character** is not part of the instruction; it merely indicates (to the assembler) that the following line is a continuation of the instruction on the present line.

Note that columns 9 and 15 are always left blank.

Comments are usually short explanatory remarks which explain the program. Whenever longer comments are desired, one may place an asterisk (*) in column 1 of the line to notify the assembler that the entire line is not part of the program (not translated). The comment will appear on the program listing produced by the assembler. As many comments as are desired may be used, as long as column 1 of each comment card has an asterisk.

The use of columns 73–80 is optional. They are used for identification and sequencing, if desired. For example, one might place one's initials in columns 73 and 74 of each statement, the coding sheet page number in columns 75 through 77 and line numbers in columns 78 through 80. This part of the instruction is for documentation purpose only, and is not translated by the assembler. Typical entries are illustrated in figure 2.7.

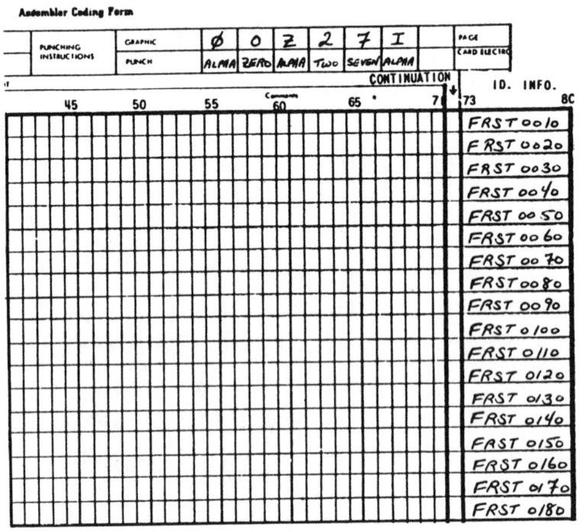

Figure 2.7
Identification and Sequencing on a Coding Form

It is convenient to sequence the statements in a manner which will allow for insertion of additional instructions into the program, as is often necessary. The above numbering allows for additions of nine cards between every two cards. If a deck of cards should be accidentally dropped, the sequencing will prove very helpful in quickly restoring the original order.

If you are a nonconformist, or if for any reason you would prefer not to use a coding form, you may do without it. The instruction parts must be written in the following order: the name portion must begin in column 1; the operation code must be preceded by at least one blank; the operand and comment portions, if present, must be separated from the operation code and from each other by at least one blank; and your coding may not extend beyond column 71. Technically we call these latter guidelines **free-form coding.** Figures 2.8 and 2.9 show examples of instructions correctly entered on coding forms.

2.3   MAKING THE COMPUTER TICK: TRANSLATING AND EXECUTING A PROGRAM

The IBM 360 and 370 computers have been designed with the facility to perform certain basic operations. These basic operations involve manipulation of data. The manufacturer supplies unique 8-bit binary codes varying in value from 0_{10} to 255_{10}, each of which identifies a particular operation; we call these **operation codes.** In assembly language, these codes appear as mnemonics.

To invoke a computer operation, we must use an instruction which, in general, consists of two parts: the operation code, and operand(s). An operand supplies the computer with information regarding the data upon which the computer is to operate; the operand may be in binary form, or in a more convenient form, as we will demonstrate. A programmer will write a sequence of such instructions, which in turn will invoke a sequence of operations which the computer is to perform.

As we know, instructions may be written in various ways. If written in machine language, the instruction components must be written as specified in chapter 1, section 1.4.2. If you prefer to code in assembly language, as is done in this text, the instruction components must follow a prescribed format which we will describe as we present each instruction.

You have seen your first assembly language program. Now, you may be surprised to find that this program must go through a number of stages before the computer can follow the operations which we have specified, that is, before the execution of the program.

The first stage is the translation of the program into machine language. This is accomplished by a translating program called an **assembler**, and we call this stage the **assembly phase** or **assembly time**. The assembler will at this time replace the mnemonic op-codes with 8-bit machine language codes, and will replace all symbolic references to locations with references in base-displacement form. Of course you will be notified of any syntax errors which may have been present in your original source program. The end product of the assembly phase is referred to as the **object module**.

The second stage is the transformation of the object module into a revised form called the **load module** by the **linkage editor** program. (The activities of the linkage editor will be discussed in chapter 12.)

The third stage involves the **execution** of the load module. We also refer to this stage as the **execution phase** or as **execution time**. It is at this time that the computer will fulfill your instructions and will therefore produce (hopefully) the desired results.

2.4   EXPLAINING MR. SHARP'S PROGRAM INSTRUCTIONS

In this section, we will discuss the individual instructions in the two versions (DOS and OS) of the program described in section 2.1. For convenience, we present the programs as they would appear on the assembler coding forms. We have numbered the instructions to the right of the coding forms for reference in this chapter. These numbers are not part of the coding forms (see figures 2.8 and 2.9).

Henceforth, in describing symbolic formats of assembler instructions, straight brackets will surround each entry whose use is optional for a particular instruction. Curly brackets designate a choice of operand entries. Capitalized portions must appear as indicated, and lowercase portions are to be provided by the programmer.

Some of the instructions discussed below are macro instructions. The macros are used either to define files (declarative macros) or to effect actions against files (imperative macros). It is common to refer to "files" when DOS macros are used, and to "data sets" when OS macros are used. We shall adhere to this practice in our discussion.

The first instruction of Mr. Sharp's program is

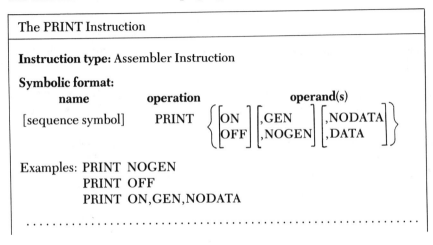

The PRINT Instruction

Instruction type: Assembler Instruction

Symbolic format:

name	operation	operand(s)
[sequence symbol]	PRINT	$\left\{ \begin{bmatrix} \text{ON} \\ \text{OFF} \end{bmatrix} \begin{bmatrix} ,\text{GEN} \\ ,\text{NOGEN} \end{bmatrix} \begin{bmatrix} ,\text{NODATA} \\ ,\text{DATA} \end{bmatrix} \right\}$

Examples: PRINT NOGEN
              PRINT OFF
              PRINT ON,GEN,NODATA

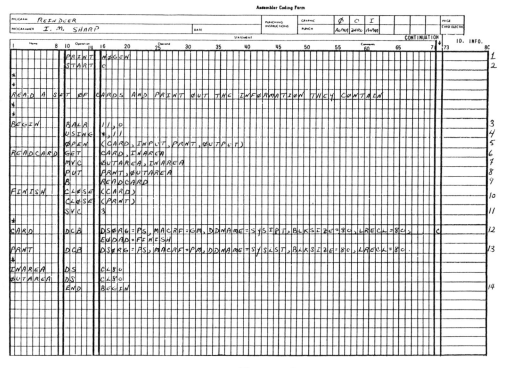

Assembler Coding Form

```
        PRINT   NOGEN                                                    1
        START   O                                                       2
*
*
READ A SET OF CARDS AND PRINT OUT THE INFORMATION THEY CONTAIN
*
*
BEGIN   BALR    11,0                                                     3
        USING   *,11                                                    4
        OPEN    (CARD,INPUT,PRNT,OUTPUT)                               5
READCARD GET     CARD,INAREA                                            6
        MVC     OUTAREA,INAREA                                         7
        PUT     PRNT,OUTAREA                                           8
        B       READCARD                                                9
FINISH  CLOSE   (CARD)                                                 10
        CLOSE   (PRNT)
        SVC     3                                                      11
*
CARD    DCB     DSORG=PS,MACRF=GM,DDNAME=SYSIPT,BLKSIZE=80,LRECL=80, C 12
                EODAD=FINISH
PRNT    DCB     DSORG=PS,MACRF=PM,DDNAME=SYSLST,BLKSIZE=80,LRECL=80.   13
*
INAREA  DS      CL80
OUTAREA DS      CL80
        END     BEGIN                                                  14
```

Figure 2.8
Mr. Sharp's Program Coded—OS Version

Assembler Coding Form

```
        PRINT   NOGEN                                                    1
        START   O                                                       2
CARD    DTFCD   DEVADDR=SYSRDR,IOAREA1=INAREA,BLKSIZE=80,EOFADDR=FINISH 12
PRNT    DTFPR   DEVADDR=SYSLST,IOAREA1=OUTAREA,BLKSIZE=80,CONTROL=YES   13
*
*
*  READ A SET OF CARDS AND PRINT OUT THE INFORMATION THEY CONTAIN
*
*
BEGIN   BALR    11,0                                                     3
        USING   *,11                                                    4
        OPEN    CARD,PRNT                                                5
READCARD GET     CARD                                                    6
        MVC     OUTAREA,INAREA                                          7
        PUT     PRNT                                                     8
        B       READCARD                                                9
FINISH  CLOSE   CARD,PRNT                                               10
        EOJ                                                             11
INAREA  DS      CL80
OUTAREA DS      CL80
        END     BEGIN                                                  14
```

Rules:
- The name portion, if present, contains a sequence symbol. A sequence symbol has the following form:

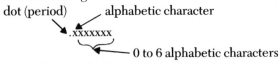

- At least one operand must be specified
- At most one option from each of the 3 operand groups may be specified
- The options specified are in force until the assembler encounters a contradictory option in another PRINT instruction
- The options specified take place *after* the PRINT instruction. For example if PRINT OFF is specified (meaning that a listing is not to be produced), the PRINT OFF instruction will itself be printed, but the statements after it will not.
- The options which are inherent in the assembler program are ON, GEN, and NODATA. Thus the PRINT instruction need be used only if we wish to override those standard options
- The operands may be specified in any order

The PRINT instruction controls the amount of detail printed in our program listings. The three possible operands and their respective meanings are presented below:

Hierarchy	Description	PRINT options
1	A listing is printed	ON
	A listing is not printed	OFF
2	All statements generated by processing macro instructions are printed	GEN
	Statements generated by processing macro instructions are not printed	NOGEN
3	Constants are printed in their entirety on the listing	DATA
	Only the first (leftmost) 8 bytes of constants are printed on the listing	NODATA

The hierarchy may be understood as follows: if OFF is specified, then GEN and DATA do not apply; if NOGEN is specified, then DATA — the printing of generated constants in full — does not apply. (The meaning of program constants will be considered in detail in chapter 3).

The instruction PRINT NOGEN in Mr. Sharp's program implies that a listing will be produced (since the first operand option ON is inherent in the assembler program). The statements generated by macro instructions will not appear, although the macros themselves will. The third operand does not apply.

Instruction number 2 of the program is

The START Instruction

Instruction type: Assembler Instruction
Symbolic format:

name	operation	operand
[symbolic name]	START	[unsigned integer]

Examples: BEGIN START 0
  START 8192
  START

. . . .

Rules:
- The START instruction should be present in every assembly language program. If omitted, START 0 is assumed.
- The START instruction must precede all machine and/or macro instructions
- If the operand is present, the integer must be divisible by 8.
- If the operand is not present, the assembler assumes a 0 value.

The START instruction is an assembler instruction. It alerts the assembler to the fact that an assembly language program will follow.

In the operand portion (if used), we may request that the assembler reserve the stated location number for storage of the first machine language instruction of the program beginning in that location. In our program, START 0 will result in the first machine language instruction being stored starting in location number 0. This is accomplished by the assembler.

Program instructions are stored in consecutive storage locations. The assembler keeps track of what location to use for storage of each instruction by using a counter, technically known as the **location counter**. The function of the START instruction is to initialize the location counter to the value specified in the operand portion. The instruction START 8192 initializes the counter to the decimal value 8192 (hexadecimal 2000). As instructions are translated, the counter is incremented by the assembler by the amounts 2, 4, or 6, depending upon the format and hence the length in bytes of the last machine language instruction stored. Thus the current setting of the location counter indicates to the assembler the location number or address beginning at which the next instruction should be placed.

The name portion of the START instruction, if used, will assign a symbolic name to the program.

Instruction number 3 of our program is

The BALR Instruction (**B**ranch **A**nd **L**ink **R**egisters)

Instruction type: Machine Instruction

Machine format: RR Instruction (Register to Register Instruction)

05	R1	R2
0	7 8 11 12	15

Symbolic format:

name	operation	operands
[symbolic name]	BALR	R1,R2

where R1 and R2 specify general register numbers. Registers are specified using decimal numbers.

Examples: BEGIN   BALR   11,0
           HELLO   BALR   2,3
                   BALR   3,4

The BALR instruction takes the address of the next machine language instruction (the instruction which follows the BALR) in the program and places it into that register which is designated as the first operand of the instruction.

After this is done, the program branches to the instruction which is stored in that location specified in the second operand register. If 0 is specified for the second operand, however, no branching occurs; instead, the next instruction in sequence will be executed.

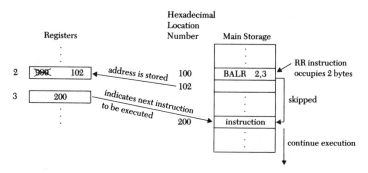

Figure 2.10
Executing the Instruction BALR 2,3

Instruction number 4 of our program is

The USING Instruction

Instruction type: Assembler Instruction

Symbolic format:

name	operation	operands
[symbolic name]	USING	v,r1,r2,...,r16

where v indicates a numeric variable
      r1,r2,...r16 are register numbers

Examples: USING *,11
                    USING B,2

The USING is an assembler instruction which provides the assembler with information necessary for calculating addresses.

You will recall from chapter 1 that the IBM 360 and 370 computers use a special method for calculating addresses called the base-displacement method. A location of data and/or instructions is calculated by adding 2 numbers:

        contents of base register + displacement

The assembly language programmer is not responsible for performing these calculations. This job is delegated to the assembler program at assembly time. In order to enable the assembler to function properly, however, it is the programmer's responsibility to provide it with two pieces of information:

1. Which register(s) are used as base register(s)
2. The contents of the base register(s) at execution time

These facts will provide the assembler with a reference point (the contents of the base register(s)), and the assembler will now express addresses in terms of their relative distance or displacement in bytes from this reference point.

By the instruction USING *,11 we are committing register 11 to be used by the assembler as the base register. We are also telling the assembler that we plan to place the current setting of the location counter into this register at execution time. An asterisk (*) in the operand portion of an assembly language instruction is a variable representing the number which is the "current setting of the location counter". Thus we ensure that the current setting of the location counter, which will be the contents of register 11, will be used as a reference point for address calculation by the assembler.

You have learned in chapter 1 that the displacement cannot exceed 4095 bytes. Thus, if your program is to exceed 4096 bytes in length, you may consider using additional base registers. Your USING statement should reflect this choice. For example, if your program requires 20,000 storage locations, you will need 5 base registers, since each register services a maximum of 4096 bytes. You may therefore write

    USING   *,2,3,4,5,6

Base register 2, it is assumed, will contain the current contents of the location counter; register 3 will contain the current contents + 4096; register 4 will contain the current contents + (2 × 4096); and so on.

The instruction USING B,2 designates register 2 to be used as the base register for the program, and informs the assembler that the register will, at execution time, be loaded with the number which is in some location called B. Of course, the placement of the contents of B into register 2 is the programmer's responsibility, and should be done immediately prior to this USING instruction.

A Marriage: The USING and the BALR

It is common practice to use both the USING and the BALR instructions to ensure effective addressing.

Examine the following pair of instructions:

    BALR   11,0
    USING   *,11

In this example, the USING instruction (an assembler instruction, it is not translated and therefore does not occupy storage) makes a commitment to the assembler: that it may expect the current setting of the location counter (*) to be in register 11 at execution time, so that register 11 may be used as a base register for addressing purposes during assembly time. This commitment is fulfilled during the execution of the program. It is then that the BALR instruction will place an actual value in register 11: namely, the value of the location counter *after* the execution of the BALR instruction. The USING directly follows the BALR instruction on the coding form; you may therefore note that the value of the location counter used by the USING is the same value which is ultimately placed into register 11 by the BALR instruction. It follows that the order of these instructions is critical for the proper fulfillment of the commitment made by the USING instruction to the assembler. The USING must follow the BALR if both instructions are used.

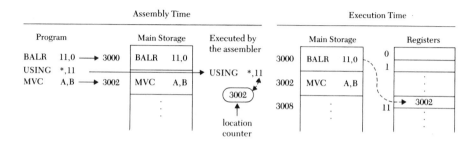

Figure 2.11
Executing the USING and BALR Instructions

Instruction number 5 of our OS program is

The OPEN Instruction

Instruction type: Macro Instruction

Symbolic format:

name	operation	operand(s)
[symbolic name]	OPEN	(dcbname−1,[(option−1[,option−2])] [,dcbname−2,[(option−1[,option−2])] ...)

Examples: OPEN   (INFILE,INPUT)   INPUT is option−1
OPEN   (INFILE,INPUT,OUTFILE,OUTPUT)

. . . .

Rules:
- Dcbnames used must have been previously defined by DCB statements. They must appear and be spelled in the same manner as in the name portions of the DCB's for those data sets.
- Option−1 must be one of the words INPUT, OUTPUT, INOUT, OUTIN, RDBACK(for magnetic tape which we wish to read backwards) or UPDAT (for direct access data sets). We shall use either INPUT or OUTPUT in our programs to open respective input or output data sets. Use of the other option − 1 choices is beyond the scope of this text.
- The default option for option−1 is INPUT. That is, if option−1 is not specified for a dcbname, it is assumed to be INPUT.
- Option−2 must be one of the words DISP, REREAD, or LEAVE. It controls the positioning of the data sets. However if we wish to start reading or writing the data set from the beginning, option−2 may be omitted. We shall omit option−2 in our programs, for such use is beyond the scope of this text.
- If option−2 is omitted, we need not enclose option−1 within parentheses. However the entire operand list must always be enclosed within parentheses.

Instruction number 5 of our DOS program is

The OPEN Instruction

Instruction type: Macro Instruction

Symbolic format:

name	operation	operand(s)
[symbolic name]	OPEN	filename−1[,filename−2,...

Examples:	OPEN	CARD
	OPEN	CARD,PRNT

Rules:
- A maximum of 16 files may be opened by one OPEN statement
- Filenames used must have been previously defined by DTF statements. They must appear and be spelled in the same manner as in the name portions of the DTF macros for those files.

Assembly language requires that every file be OPENed before it is used—that is, before reading records from input files or writing records onto output files. In practice, files are usually opened at the beginning of the program.

For card and printer files, the instruction transforms the file(s) from inactive to active status. For other files, such as magnetic tape and disk files (which we will not discuss), the OPEN performs certain other operations, such as checking that the correct file was mounted, whether it is expired, and so on.

Instruction number 6 of our OS program is

The GET Instruction

Instruction type: Macro Instruction

Symbolic format:

name	operation	operands
[symbolic name]	GET	dcbname [,area address]

Example: GET   CRD,INAREA

. . . .

Rules:
- The dcbname must appear and be spelled in the same manner as in the name portion of the DCB for that data set
- The data set must be opened before this statement is used

For OS programs, the GET statement retrieves one record from the input device associated with the dcbname by the DCB for that data set. If the MACRF operand of the DCB macro specifies "move mode" (MACRF=GM meaning **MACR**o **F**orm is the **GET** macro in **M**ove mode), then the record retrieved will be placed by the supervisor into main storage beginning at the area address specified in the second operand of the GET statement. The OS operating system provides for buffering (along with various other functions), and the programmer need not describe buffer areas, as is necessary for DOS systems. Records may also be retrieved using what is known as "substitute mode"; however we will not use substitute mode in this text.

Instruction number 6 of our DOS program is

The GET Instruction

Instruction type: Macro Instruction

Symbolic format:

name	operation	operands
[symbolic name]	GET	filename [,area address]

Examples: GET   CARD
             GET   CARD,WORKAREA

· ·

Rules:
- The filename must appear and be spelled in the same manner as in the name portion of the DTF for that file
- The file must be opened before this statement is used

For DOS programs, the GET statement retrieves one record from the input device associated with the filename by the DTF macro for that file. If the WORKA=YES operand is not specified in the DTF, the GET macro will store the record in the area designated by the DTF as the IOAREA1 or

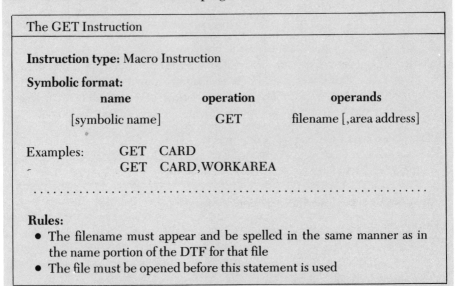

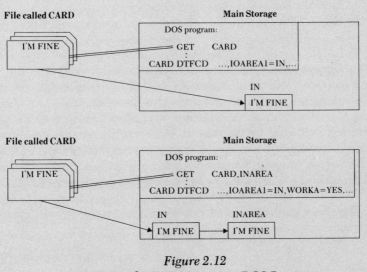

Figure 2.12
Executing the GET Macro in a DOS Program

IOAREA2 for the file; in such case, the second operand of the GET statement should be omitted. However if the WORKA=YES operand is specified in the DTF for the file, the GET macro will store the record first in the IOAREA1 or IOAREA2 for that file (now used as buffer—or intermediate—areas for holding contents of input records); the record will then be moved to the "work area"—the area named in the second operand of the GET macro (see figure 2.12).

Instruction number 7 of our program is

The MVC Instruction (MoVe Characters)

Instruction type: Machine Instruction

Machine format: SS Instruction (Storage to Storage Instruction)

D2	L	B1	D1	B2	D2
0	7 8	15 16 19 20	31 32	35 36	47

Symbolic format:

name	operation	operands
[symbolic name]	MVC	name1,name2
or [symbolic name]	MVC	D1(L,B1),D2(B2)

where D1 and B1 are the displacement and base register respectively used to calculate the first operand address.

D2 and B2 are the displacement and base register respectively used to calculate the second operand address.

L is a length factor which applies to both operands, where L = 0 means that 1 byte will be acted upon, L = 1 means that 2 bytes will be acted upon, and so on.

The operand portion of a symbolic SS (storage to storage) instruction may be specified using two different forms, as outlined above. The first form (which is discussed in this chapter) uses symbolic operands as demonstrated in our examples, and is the form most commonly used by assembly language programmers. The second form allows the programmer to specify the base registers and displacements himself. The second form will be used in program examples presented in chapters 11 and 12.

. . . .

Rules:
- Data is moved from the second operand location (**sending field**) to the first operand location (**receiving field**). The content of the sending field is not altered by this instruction.
- The instruction moves the data one byte at a time.
- The number of bytes moved from the second operand is determined by the length of the first operand.
- The MVC instruction processes data from left to right. The leftmost byte of the sending field is moved first, into the leftmost byte of the receiving field. The second byte from the left of the sending field is then moved in a similar manner, followed by the third byte, and so on, until the receiving field has been filled.
- The storage areas represented by the first and second operands may overlap in memory.
- A maximum of 256 bytes may be moved by one MVC instruction.

Note to the curious:

A maximum of 256 bytes may be moved by one MVC instruction for the following reason. The length factor L in the machine language format of the MVC instruction is 8 bits long. The smallest non-negative binary number which may be represented in 8 bits is 0; the largest binary number which may be represented in 8 bits is $(2^8 - 1)$ or 255_{10}. A length factor of 0 means that 1 byte will be moved; a length factor of 1 means that 2 bytes will be moved, and so on. Therefore a length factor of 255 (the largest possible length factor) means that 256 bytes will actually be moved. Note that

$$\text{length factor} + 1 = \text{number of bytes moved}$$

The MVC instruction will copy the contents of one area (the second operand) into another area (the first operand). Consequently, after the MVC has been executed, the previous contents of the second operand will remain unchanged, while the previous contents of the first operand will be destroyed and replaced with some or all of the data from the second operand. The amount of data copied will depend upon the amount of room available in the first operand.

Note:

The examples below utilize the DS (Define Storage) instruction, which will be fully explained in chapters 3 and 7. The DS is an assembler instruction. As used in these examples, it instructs the assembler to set aside storage locations in memory and to associate a name and a length with them. Its basic form for our purpose in this chapter is

[symbolic name]   DS   CLn

where CL means "character length", and n is a positive integer specifying the number of storage locations (bytes) to be set aside by the assembler. The symbolic name, when used in other instructions, refers to the beginning address of the area reserved, as will be demonstrated through examples.

It is important to note here that the use of the DS instruction is to reserve the main storage locations, and not to place information into those locations. If placement of information into storage locations is necessary, the programmer will use other means, such as the MVC instruction, or other instructions which will be discussed in later chapters.

Example 1:
The number of bytes in the first and second operands is equal:

```
TRAP        DS      CL5
ANIMAL1     DS      CL5
            MVC     TRAP,ANIMAL1
```

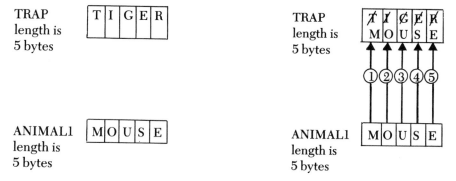

Before execution of the MVC

TRAP
length is
5 bytes

| T | I | G | E | R |

After execution of the MVC

TRAP
length is
5 bytes

ANIMAL1
length is
5 bytes

| M | O | U | S | E |

ANIMAL1
length is
5 bytes

| M | O | U | S | E |

Circled numbers represent the sequence of movement: ① is the first byte moved, ② is the second byte moved, and so on.

Example 2:
The first operand has a smaller length than the second operand:

```
TRAP        DS      CL5
ANIMAL2     DS      CL8
            MVC     TRAP,ANIMAL2
```

Before execution of the MVC   **After execution of the MVC**

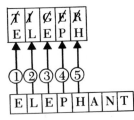

TRAP
length is
5 bytes

| T | I | G | E | R |

TRAP
length is
5 bytes

ANIMAL2 | E | L | E | P | H | A | N | T |
length is
8 bytes

ANIMAL2 | E | L | E | P | H | A | N | T |
length is
8 bytes

Circled numbers represent the sequence of movement: ① is the first byte moved, ② is the second byte moved, and so on.

Note that the receiving field has 5 bytes; therefore, 5 bytes were moved. (The size of the receiving field determines the length of the move.)

Example 3:
The first operand has a larger length than the second operand:

```
TRAP       DS    CL5
ANIMAL3    DS    CL3
           MVC   TRAP,ANIMAL3
```

Before execution of the MVC   **After execution of the MVC**

TRAP
length is
5 bytes

| T | I | G | E | R |

TRAP
length is
5 bytes

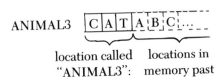

ANIMAL3 | C | A | T | A | B | C | ...

location called   locations in
"ANIMAL3":   memory past
3 bytes long   ANIMAL3

ANIMAL3 | C | A | T | A | B | C | ...

location called   locations in
"ANIMAL3":   memory past
3 bytes long   ANIMAL3

Circled numbers represent the sequence of movement: ① is the first byte moved, ② is the second byte moved, and so on.

Note that the first operand is 5 bytes in length; therefore, 5 bytes will be moved. The MVC begins moving from the leftmost byte of the second operand location and continues rightward until 5 bytes have been moved (even though this might mean going beyond the defined 3-byte length of the location called "ANIMAL3").

The size of the first operand in an MVC instruction can be controlled in two ways:

Implicit Length

In the three examples above, which demonstrated the use of the MVC instruction, the first operand was the name of a location. This location was assigned a length in a DS instruction; when the assembler translates the MVC into machine language, it takes the length (in bytes) of the first operand, as defined in the DS, to be the number of bytes to be moved. Whenever the assembler determines the length in this way, we call this **implicit length**.

Explicit Length

If you are a do-it-yourselfer, you may override the length implied by the assembler, by using the technique demonstrated in the following example. We call this **explicit length**.

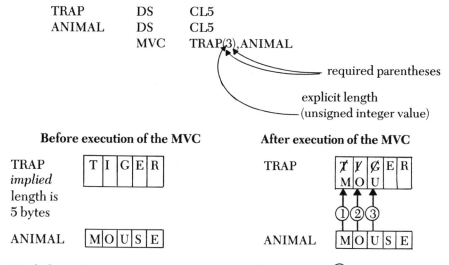

```
TRAP        DS        CL5
ANIMAL      DS        CL5
            MVC       TRAP(3),ANIMAL
```

required parentheses

explicit length
(unsigned integer value)

Before execution of the MVC   **After execution of the MVC**

Circled numbers represent the sequence of movement: ① is the first byte moved, ② is the second byte moved, and so on. In this example, 3 bytes were explicitly indicated to be the length of the first operand; therefore 3 bytes were moved. Remember this technique if you wish to become a pro. It eliminates assembler control and lets *you* control the workings of the instruction.

Address Adjustment

Another very useful technique allows you to adjust the beginning location of a field. This is demonstrated in the following example:

```
TRAP        DS      CL5
ANIMAL      DS      CL5
            MVC     TRAP+2(2),ANIMAL
```

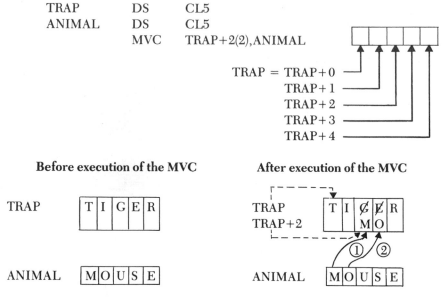

TRAP = TRAP+0
TRAP+1
TRAP+2
TRAP+3
TRAP+4

Before execution of the MVC   **After execution of the MVC**

TRAP | T | I | G | E | R |

TRAP | T | I | G̸ | E̸ | R |
TRAP+2 | M | O |

① ②

ANIMAL | M | O | U | S | E |

ANIMAL | M | O | U | S | E |

Circled numbers represent the sequence of movement: ① is the first byte moved; ② is the second byte moved.

In this example, the computer copies the contents of memory, beginning with the leftmost byte of ANIMAL, into the leftmost byte of TRAP+2(2). TRAP+2(2) is the area which starts 2 bytes past the beginning of TRAP (which is what is meant by "plus 2"), and continues for a length of 2 bytes (which is meant by "(2)").

This method of address adjustment may be used for one or more operands in any instruction which references main storage (as opposed to registers). When the adjustment is made, the length assumed by the assembler no longer applies, so that the length must be explicitly provided by the programmer.

In the MVC instruction, the length is relevant only in the first operand, and must be provided there. The second operand length is optional, and will be rejected by the assembler even if supplied. The instruction

MVC   TRAP+2(2),ANIMAL(5)

will therefore be rejected, although it appears to request the same function as the instruction

MVC   TRAP+2(2),ANIMAL

The MVC Instruction With Overlapping Operands

Consider the following instructions:

```
LOVE          DS     CL4
              MVC    LOVE,LOVE-1
```

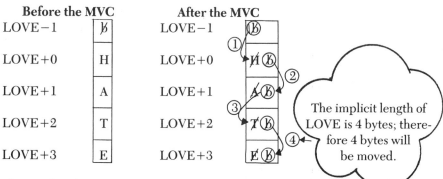

Before the MVC

LOVE−1	ƀ
LOVE+0	H
LOVE+1	A
LOVE+2	T
LOVE+3	E

After the MVC

LOVE−1	ƀ
LOVE+0	ƀ
LOVE+1	ƀ
LOVE+2	ƀ
LOVE+3	ƀ

The implicit length of LOVE is 4 bytes; therefore 4 bytes will be moved.

This is what the computer does:

Step 1: LOVE−1 contains a blank, and this blank is moved (copied) into the storage location LOVE+0. Now LOVE+0 also contains a blank.

Step 2: The second byte of LOVE−1 (LOVE+0 or LOVE) contains a blank (from step 1). This blank is moved into the second byte of LOVE (LOVE+1).

Step 3: The third byte of LOVE−1 (LOVE+1), which contains a blank (from step 2), is moved into the third byte of LOVE (LOVE+2).

Step 4: The fourth byte of LOVE−1 (LOVE+2), which contains a blank (from step 3), is moved into the fourth byte of LOVE.
...and now HATE (the original contents of LOVE) has been wiped out.

We may summarize thus:

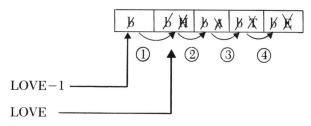

This technique may be used to propagate any character throughout a field; you will find it useful on many occasions, particularly in "clearing" memory locations, that is, filling them with blanks.

Instruction number 8 of our OS program is

The PUT Instruction

Instruction type: Macro Instruction

Symbolic format:

name	operation	operands
[symbolic name]	PUT	dcbname [,area address]

Examples: PUT   PRNT
           PUT   PRNT,OUTAREA

. . . .

Rules:
- The dcbname must appear and be·spelled in the same manner as in the name portion of the DCB for that data set
- The data set must be opened before this statement is used

For OS programs, the PUT statement outputs one record onto the output device associated with the dcbname by the DCB for that data set. If the MACRF operand of the DCB macro specifies "move mode" (MACRF=PM meaning **MACR**o **F**orm is the **PUT** macro in **M**ove mode), then the record output will be retrieved by the supervisor from main storage beginning at the area address specified in the second operand of the PUT statement. The OS operating system provides for buffering (along with various other functions), and the programmer need not describe buffer areas, as is necessary for DOS systems. Records may also be output using what is known as "substitute mode"; however we will not use substitute mode in this text.

Instruction number 8 of our DOS program is

The PUT Instruction

Instruction type: Macro Instruction

Symbolic format:

name	operation	operands
[symbolic name]	PUT	file [,area address]

Examples: PUT   PRNTFL
            PUT   PRNTFL,OUTAREA

. . . .

Rules:
- The filename must appear and be spelled in the same manner as in the name portion of the DTF for that file
- The file must be opened before this statement is used

For DOS programs, the PUT statement outputs one record onto the output device associated with the filename by the DTF macro for that file. If the WORKA=YES operand is not specified in the DTF, the PUT macro will retrieve the record from the area designated by the DTF as the IOAREA1 or IOAREA2 for that file; in such case, the second operand of the PUT statement should be omitted. However if the WORKA=YES parameter is specified in the DTF for the file, the PUT macro will retrieve the record from the "work area": the area named in the second operand of the PUT macro. The record will then be transferred to the area designated as the IOAREA1 or IOAREA2 for that file (now used as buffer—or intermediate— areas for holding contents of output records), from which the data is output.

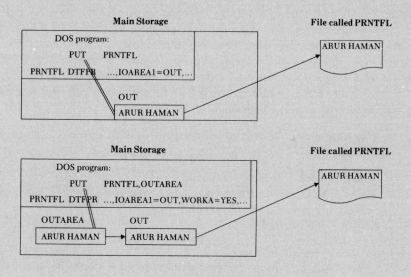

Figure 2.13
Executing the PUT Macro in a DOS Program

Instruction number 9 of our program is

The B Instruction (**B**ranch)

Instruction type: Machine Instruction (Extended Mnemonic)

Machine format: RX Instruction (Register and IndeXed Storage Instruction)

47	R	X2	B2	D2

0   7 8   11 12   15 16   19 20   31

Symbolic format:

	name	operation	operand
	[symbolic name]	B	symbolic name
or	[symbolic name]	B	D2(X2,B2)

where D2 and B2 are the displacement and base register respectively used to calculate the second operand address. X2 is the register used as an index register in this instruction.

Note: The B instruction belongs to a special group of instructions called **extended mnemonics**. For the convenience of the programmer, the manufacturer supplies extended mnemonics as alternate forms of some machine instructions. They are simpler in their symbolic form than the original machine instructions, since the symbolic op-code of an extended mnemonic instruction incorporates both the operation and the first operand information of the original.

In our program, the original instruction would have been

BC   15,READCARD

which means "branch on condition 15" to the instruction called READCARD. This original machine instruction, the BC instruction, will be fully discussed in chapter 11.

The extended version is

B   READCARD

Before instruction execution, the load module is stored with the instructions arranged in sequence; the computer is a simple-minded machine, and executes the instructions one after another unless instructed otherwise. If we want the computer to alter the order of execution, we use a branch instruction, of which only one variation is presented here: the unconditional branch. The operand portion of the unconditional branch provides the computer with the address of the next instruction to be executed. Thus the computer will alter its normal order of execution and branch directly to the address specified in the operand portion; it will then continue execution in sequential order, continuing from that location.

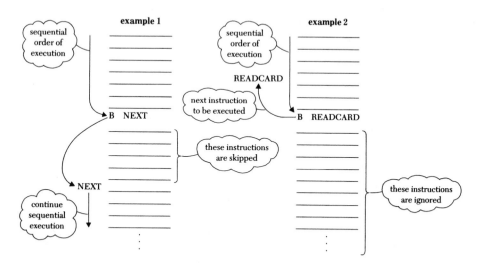

Figure 2.14
Executing the B (Branch) Instruction

Instruction number 10 of our OS program is

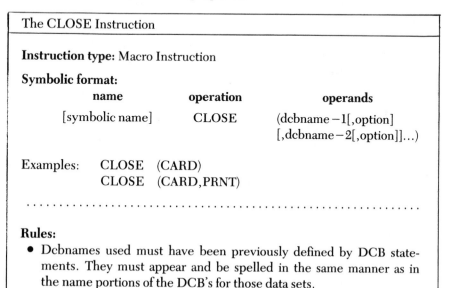

The CLOSE Instruction

Instruction type: Macro Instruction

Symbolic format:

name	operation	operands
[symbolic name]	CLOSE	(dcbname −1[,option] [,dcbname −2[,option]]...)

Examples: CLOSE (CARD)
             CLOSE (CARD,PRNT)

. . . .

Rules:
- Dcbnames used must have been previously defined by DCB statements. They must appear and be spelled in the same manner as in the name portions of the DCB's for those data sets.

- The option may be one of the words DISP, REREAD or LEAVE, and it refers to the positioning of the data set after it is closed. DISP lets the DISP parameter of the DD statement (see section 2.5) decide what shall be done. REREAD will position the data set for rereading, LEAVE leaves it at the end. This text will not use any of the option choices.
- The operand list must always be enclosed within parentheses.

Instruction number 10 of our DOS program is

The CLOSE Instruction

Instruction type: Macro Instruction

Symbolic format:

name	operation	operand(s)
[symbolic name]	CLOSE	filename−1[,filename−2...

Examples: CLOSE   CARD
             CLOSE   CARD,PRNT

. . . .

Rules:
- A maximum of 16 files may be closed by one CLOSE statement
- Filenames used must have been previously defined by a DTF statement. They must appear and be spelled in the same manner as in the name portions of the DTF macros for those files.

Assembler language requires that all files that were OPENed be CLOSEd. For card and printer files, the CLOSE statement deactivates the file so that it is no longer available for processing. For other media, such as magnetic tape and disk, it performs such functions as rewinding tapes, writing labels, and the like.

Instruction number 11 of our OS program is

The SVC Instruction (SuperVisor Call)

Instruction type: Machine Instruction

Machine format: RR Instruction (Register to Register Instruction)

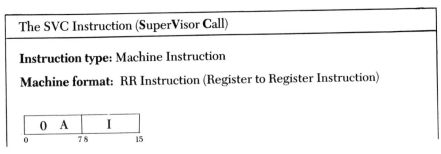

Symbolic format:

name	operation	operand	
[symbolic name]	SVC	I ←	a numeric code

Example: SVC   3

....

Rule:
- The SVC instruction is an RR instruction, but does not reference registers. Bits 8-15 are a byte of "immediate" data: a code which requests a certain action on the part of the supervisor.

The SVC   3 instruction is a request to terminate execution of the program. (The second byte of the SVC instruction may be used to request other actions on the part of the supervisor, in which case different operand codes will be used.)

Instruction number 11 of our DOS program is

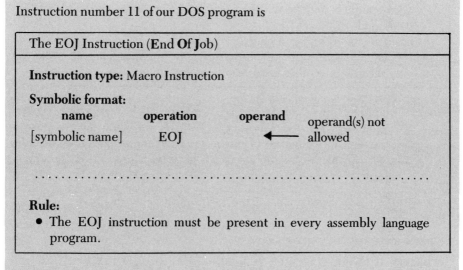

The EOJ Instruction (**End Of Job**)

Instruction type: Macro Instruction

Symbolic format:

name	operation	operand	
[symbolic name]	EOJ	←	operand(s) not allowed

....

Rule:
- The EOJ instruction must be present in every assembly language program.

The EOJ instruction informs the computer to terminate execution of the program.

The instructions numbered 12 and 13 of our OS program are

DCB Macros (**D**ata **C**ontrol **B**lock)

Instruction type: Macro Instruction

Symbolic format:

name	operation	operands
dcbname	DCB	a,b,c,d,...

where a,b,c,d,... are operands which characterize elements associated
with the data set

. . . .

Rules:
- The operands of the DCB macro are keyword operands of the form
  keyword=value
  where "keyword" is the operand name, and "value" is the quantity
  or meaning to be assigned to the keyword by the assembler. Keyword operands may be written in any order (as opposed to positional operands).
- The dcbname is a programmer-supplied name.
- The DCB macro must be present in order for the dcbname to be
  referenced by any other instruction in the program.

Note: A complete discussion of the DCB macro will be very confusing for
the beginner. The exact form of a DCB will vary with the equipment
used and with a number of other factors. Here we will present only
those forms of the instruction which have been used in our program;
a complete list of DCB operands may be found in Appendix B.

We will use DCB instructions of the following form in this text:
For input card files,

name	operation	operands
dcbname	DCB	DSORG=code,MACRF=code,DDNAME=SYSIPT, BLKSIZE=unsigned integer,RECFM=code, LRECL=unsigned integer,EODAD=symbolic name

For output printer files,

name	operation	operands
dcbname	DCB	DSORG=code,MACRF=code,DDNAME=SYSLST, BLKSIZE=unsigned integer,RECFM=code, LRECL=unsigned integer

A Data Control Block may be thought of as a table of constants which describe the data set and specify how we wish this data set to be processed. The "dcbname" supplied by the DCB instruction is a name assigned to the Data Control Block, and the operands specify details concerning our processing of the data set.

Each data set used by the program must be described by a DCB instruction.

In our program, the following DCB statements have been used:

```
CARD   DCB    DSORG=PS,MACRF=GM,DDNAME=SYSIPT,
              BLKSIZE=80,LRECL=80,EODAD=FINISH

PRNT   DCB    DSORG=PS,MACRF=PM,DDNAME=SYSLST,
              BLKSIZE=80,LRECL=80
```

DSORG (**D**ata **S**et **ORG**anization) This operand is required. It chooses one of four data set organizations provided by the OS operating system. We will use DSORG=PS (**P**hysical **S**equential organization) for both our input card files and our output printer files. This means that our data sets will be processed sequentially: in the order in which they are stored on the input or output medium. (Other possibilities are DSORG=IS (**I**ndexed **S**equential organization); DSORG=PO (**P**artial **O**rganization); DSORG=DA (**D**irect **A**ccess organization); however their use is beyond the scope of this text.)

MACRF (**MACR**o **F**orm) This operand is required. It indicates which macro instruction will be used for data set input or output, as well as certain processing options which will be employed.

- MACRF=GM will describe our input card data set. This means that the **MACR**o **F**orm for input is the **GET** macro in **M**ove mode. That is, the GET macro will be used to read input records, and the records will be moved to a work area (specified in the GET instruction) after being first read into a buffer (intermediate) area in main storage.
- MACRF=PM will describe our output printer data set. This means that the **MACR**o **F**orm for output is the **PUT** macro in **M**ove mode. That is, the PUT macro will be used to print output records, and the records will be moved from a work area (specified in the PUT instruction) to a buffer (intermediate) area in main storage, from which they will be output.
- Other options may be chosen for use with the MACRF operand; however we shall not consider them here.

DDNAME (**D**ata **D**efinition **NAME**) This operand is required. It specifies which data set is to be used and associated with the data set characteristics supplied by the other DCB operands. The value of the DDNAME operand must be the same as the name of another statement called a DD statement, which is supplied to the computer before our actual assembly language instructions. The DD is a statement in a special language called JCL (for OS systems), and will be presented in section 2.5.

In this text, we shall use DDNAME=SYSIPT (**SYS**tem **InPuT**) for input card files and DDNAME=SYSLST (**SYS**tem **LiST**) for output printer files.

The three DCB operands described above — DSORG, MACRF, and DDNAME— are required. The operands described below supplement those three with descriptions of yet other processing options.

BLKSIZE (**BL**oc**K SIZE**) and LRECL (**L**ogical **REC**ord Length) describe the respective lengths in bytes of units of information called blocks and records. Card and printer data sets are "unblocked", that is, the block size is the same as the record length. In this book, punched card data sets will be associated with 80-byte records and printer data sets with records which are 132 bytes or less in size.

RECFM (**REC**ord **F**or**M**at) describes the format of the records in the data set: whether they are of **F**ixed length and unblocked (value F); of **F**ixed length and **B**locked (value FB); of **V**ariable length (value V); of **V**ariable length and **B**locked (value VB); or of so-far **U**ndefined format (value U).

LRECL (**L**ogical **REC**ord Length) This operand describes the record size (in bytes) associated with the data set described by the DCB macro. In our book, a punched card file will always be associated with 80-character records, and a printer file with records which are 132 characters or less in size.

EODAD (**E**nd **O**f **D**ata **AD**dress) is used only for input files. The symbolic name entered here designates the location of another instruction in the program to which the computer will transfer control when an **end of data condition** is detected; that is, when the input device attempts to read a record and there are no more to be found (for a card data set, the end of data condition is determined by the reading of a card with the characters "/*" in columns 1 and 2).

Thus the DCB statements in our program define data control blocks to describe the following data sets:
- A data set called CARD is associated with the card reader (SYSIPT). Its organization is physical sequential and its records will be accessed by the GET macro in move mode. Records are unblocked and 80 characters long. When, during the reading of such records, the end of data condi-

tion is detected ("/*" card is read), program control will be transferred to an instruction called FINISH.

- A data set called PRNT is associated with the printer (SYSLST). Its organization is physical sequential, and its records will be output by the PUT macro in move mode. Records are unblocked and 80 characters long.

The instructions numbered 12 and 13 of our DOS program are

DTF Macros (Define The File)

Instruction type: Macro Instruction

Symbolic format:

name	operation	operands
filename	DTFxx	a,b,c,d,...

where xx is a code representing the input/output equipment associated with the file

a,b,c,d,... are operands which characterize elements associated with the file

. . . .

Rules:
- Filename is a programmer-supplied name which follows the rules for symbolic names discussed in section 2.2.2, with the exception that no more than 7 characters may be used.
- The DTF macro must be present in order for the filename to be referenced by any other instruction in the program.

Note: A complete discussion of the DTF macro will be confusing for the beginner. The exact form of a DTF will vary with the equipment used and with a number of other factors. Here we will present only those forms of the instruction which have been used in our program; a complete list of DTF operands may be found in Appendix B.

We will use DTF instructions of the following form in this text:

name	operation	operands
filename	DTFCD	DEVADDR=SYSRDR,IOAREA1=symbolic name, BLKSIZE=80,EOFADDR=symbolic name
filename	DTFPR	DEVADDR=SYSLST,IOAREA1=symbolic name, BLKSIZE=unsigned integer,CONTROL=YES

where DTFCD defines a file associated with a card reader

DTFPR defines a file associated with a printer

As you know, a macro represents a program segment located in the system library, which whenever used in your program, will be incorporated into the object program by the system. All DTF instructions are general purpose macros which the programmer must tailor to fit his own purposes. This means that he must make some choices which will determine the operand entries to be used. A limited number of possible choices will be provided here. If, however, you experience any difficulty in running a program using these operands, you should consult with your computer center management to determine just which entries its system may require. A reference to the appropriate manufacturer's manual will also prove very helpful. The manual should be available at your computer center.

The purpose of the DTF is to provide certain necessary information required by the system for proper handling of the file. In this program, the following DTF statements have been used:

CARD   DTFCD DEVADDR=SYSRDR,IOAREA1=INAREA,
BLKSIZE=80,EOFADDR=FINISH

PRNT   DTFPR DEVADDR=SYSLST,IOAREA1=OUTAREA,
BLKSIZE=80,CONTROL=YES

DEVADDR (**DEV**ice **ADDR**ess) provides a symbolic name associated with the device used. For the card reader, you will use SYSRDR (**SYS**tem **ReaDeR**); for the printer, you will use SYSLST (**SYS**tem **LiST**).

IOAREA1 (**I**nput and/or **O**utput **AREA 1**) associates a symbolic name with the file. The symbolic name represents the "receiving" area (input area) for input files, or the "shipping" area (output area) for output files. The amount of storage to be reserved for the input and output areas must be specified later in the program, using the same name specified here and the same area size (called blocksize) specified in the BLKSIZE operand. The symbolic name is supplied by the programmer by following the rules   specified in section 2.2.2.

BLKSIZE (**BL**oc**K SIZE**) is used to specify the record size associated with the file used. In our book, a punched card file will always be associated with 80-character records, and a printer file with records which are 132 characters or less in size .

EOFADDR (**E**nd **O**f **F**ile **ADDR**ess) is used only for input files. The symbolic name entered here designates the location of another instruction in the program which the computer will execute when the card reader attempts to read a record and there are no more to be found; technically, the situation is called an **end of file condition**.

CONTROL=YES is an operand whose use in the DTF instruction permits the programmer to issue a CNTRL macro instruction to the file at some later point in the program. The CNTRL macro is used to specify spacing and skipping for printer files; and the selection of cards into particular stackers of the card punch (the device which issues punched card output) for card files, a process known as **pocket selection** or **stacker selection**. The CNTRL macro will be explained in chapter 10.

Thus, the DTF macros in our program define files as described below:
- The DTFCD statement defines a file called CARD which is associated with the card reader; the symbolic name SYSRDR is provided for the reader. An input area called INAREA is associated with the file, and the record size (which is also the size in bytes of INAREA) is specified to be 80 characters. When the card reader attempts to read a record and no more are available, the computer is directed to immediately execute the instruction called FINISH and to continue further execution from that point.
- The DTFPR statement defines a file called PRNT which is associated with the printer; the symbolic name SYSLST is provided for the printer. An output area called OUTAREA is associated with the file, and the record size (which is also the size in bytes of OUTAREA) is specified to be 80 characters.

Instruction number 14 of our program is

The END Instruction

Instruction type: Assembler Instruction

Symbolic format:

name	operation	operand
	END	[symbolic name]

. . . .

Rules:
- The END instruction must be the last statement of the source program (the assembly language program)

This instruction notifies the assembler that the assembly phase is terminated, and that the computer may proceed to the link-edit phase and execution phase, upon successful assembly.

The operand portion, if present, is a symbolic name which designates, to the assembler, that location number to which the computer will pass control after the object program is loaded into main storage. Therefore, the operand portion of the instruction will usually contain the symbolic name of the first executable instruction of the program.

The operand portion may be omitted, in which case control will be passed to the first byte of the program, after the object program is loaded into memory. This is not always desirable, since the first byte of the program might not necessarily be an executable instruction, as in the following example:

```
            START
AREA1       DS      CL80
FIRST       BALR    11,0
            USING   *,11
              .
              .
              .
            END
```

A better choice for the last instruction would have been   END   FIRST , so that control would be passed to the BALR instruction at execution time, in order for proper execution to begin.

2.5 MEET JCL: JOB CONTROL LANGUAGE

Now that you have studied our first program's instructions, you might be tempted to write your own program. However, there is one additional thing you must know; namely, how to guide your program through the assembly, link-edit, and execution phases. This guidance is provided by instructions in a special language called **Job Control Language** or **JCL**. These instructions are not part of the assembly language; their exact form will vary from one computer installation to another, and may even vary in the same installation from time to time. Therefore, it is advisable that before you actually attempt to run your program, you verify the instructions used with an authority at the relevant computer installation.

Here we will present those JCL instructions which we used in running the programs presented in this chapter and which will be used in most of our subsequent programs. They are presented as they would appear on punched cards.

The JCL statements immediately below were used with our OS program:

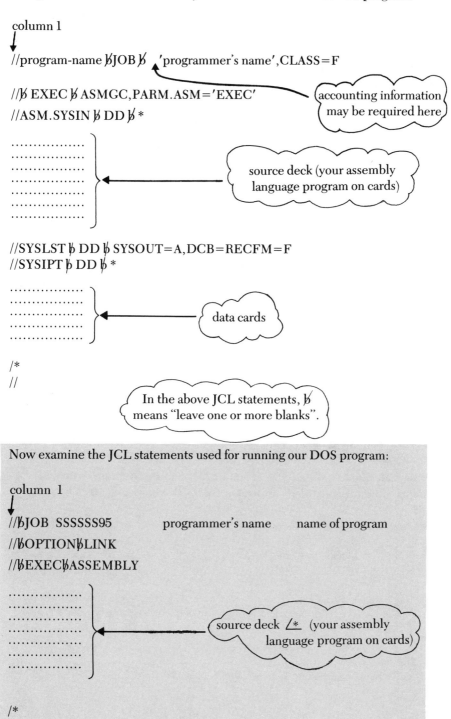

column 1

//program-name ⱕJOB ⱕ 'programmer's name',CLASS=F

//ⱕ EXEC ⱕ ASMGC,PARM.ASM='EXEC'
//ASM.SYSIN ⱕ DD ⱕ *

accounting information may be required here

source deck (your assembly language program on cards)

//SYSLST ⱕ DD ⱕ SYSOUT=A,DCB=RECFM=F
//SYSIPT ⱕ DD ⱕ *

data cards

/*
//

In the above JCL statements, ⱕ means "leave one or more blanks".

Now examine the JCL statements used for running our DOS program:

column 1

//ⱕJOB SSSSSS95   programmer's name   name of program
//ⱕOPTIONⱕLINK
//ⱕEXECⱕASSEMBLY

source deck ⁄* (your assembly language program on cards)

/*

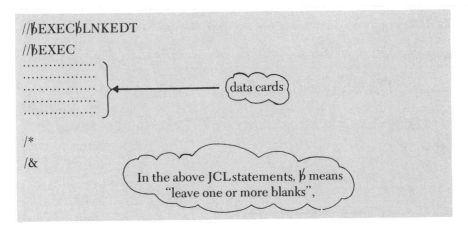

The JCL instructions, whether for DOS or OS systems, must be entered in the exact order specified. A slash (/) must always be in column 1, for it identifies a JCL card to the computer. The entries must be spelled exactly as they appear.

Full explanations of these JCL statements and of their relationship to the operating system will be confusing to the novice and are beyond the scope of this book. The formats of the JCL statements, along with operand choices available, are summarized in Appendix C.

2.6   THE PROGRAM IN ITS ENTIRETY

This section will summarize how Mr. Sharp's program was written, submitted, and brought through execution.

2.6.1   On Coding Sheets

Figure 2.15 illustrates the OS version of Mr. Sharp's program, with JCL, on a coding sheet. Figure 2.16 illustrates the DOS version of Mr. Sharp's program.

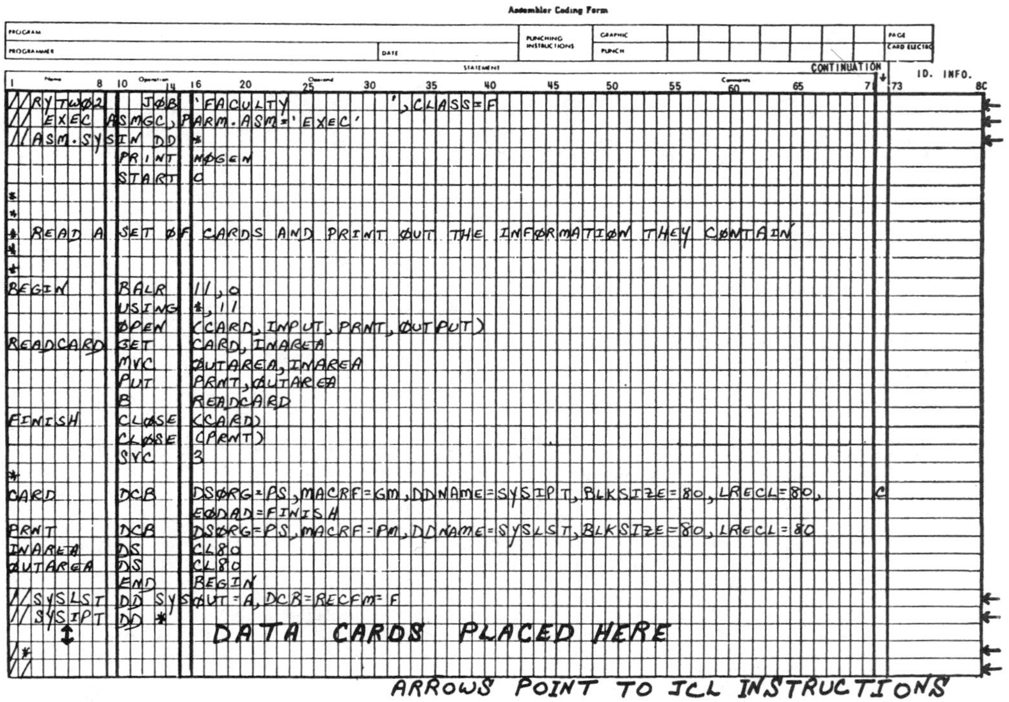

Assembler Coding Form

```
//RYIW02  JOB  'FACULTY'
//    EXEC ASMGCL,PARM.ASM='EXEC'                    ,CLASS=F
//ASM.SYSIN DD *
        PRINT NOGEN
        START 0
*
*  READ A SET OF CARDS AND PRINT OUT THE INFORMATION THEY CONTAIN
*
*
BEGIN    BALR  11,0
         USING *,11
         OPEN  (CARD,INPUT,PRNT,OUTPUT)
READCARD GET   CARD,INAREA
         MVC   OUTAREA,INAREA
         PUT   PRNT,OUTAREA
         B     READCARD
FINISH   CLOSE (CARD)
         CLOSE (PRNT)
         SVC   3
*
CARD     DCB   DSORG=PS,MACRF=GM,DDNAME=SYSIPT,BLKSIZE=80,LRECL=80,
               EODAD=FINISH
PRNT     DCB   DSORG=PS,MACRF=PM,DDNAME=SYSLST,BLKSIZE=80,LRECL=80
INAREA   DS    CL80
OUTAREA  DS    CL80
         END   BEGIN
//SYSLST DD SYSOUT=A,DCB=RECFM=F
//SYSIPT DD *
*
```

DATA CARDS PLACED HERE

ARROWS POINT TO JCL INSTRUCTIONS

Figure 2.15

Mr. Sharp's Program with JCL—OS Version

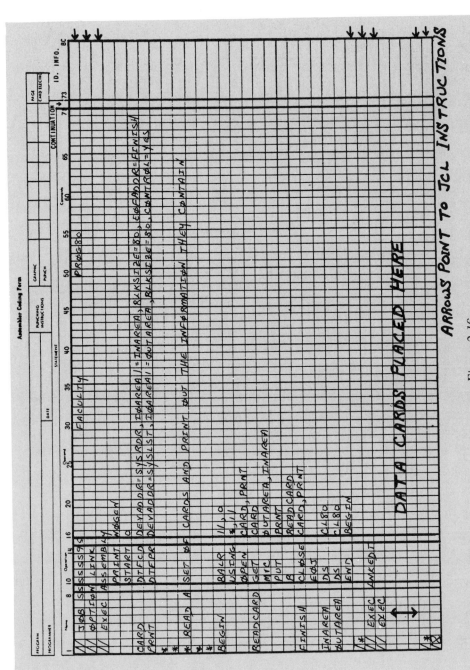

Figure 2.16

Mr. Sharp's Program with JCL—DOS Version

The entries on the coding sheets are then keypunched, one card per line.

2.6.2   The Program Keypunched

Figures 2.17 and 2.18 illustrate the cards to be submitted to the computer for assembly, link-editing, and execution. They are arranged in the sequence in which they are to be submitted.

Figure 2.17 illustrates the OS version of our program; figure 2.18 illustrates the DOS version.

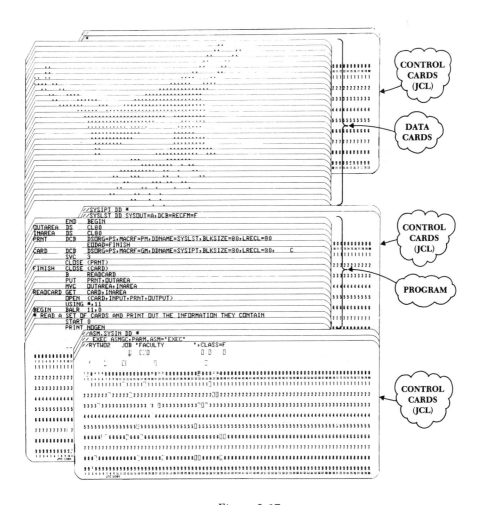

Figure 2.17
Mr. Sharp's Program on Cards — OS Version

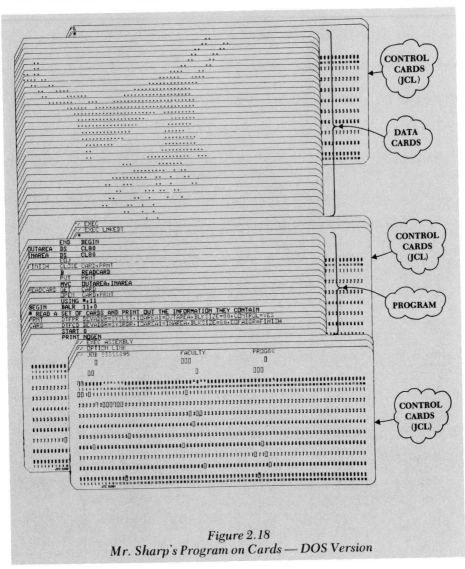

Figure 2.18
Mr. Sharp's Program on Cards — DOS Version

2.6.3   Output of Assembler, Linkage Editor, and Program Execution

Figures 2.19 and 2.20 illustrate the complete program output of OS and DOS programs, obtained each time the respective assembly language program is assembled, link-edited, and executed. The computer output will comprise several pages; each section (sections are separated by wavy lines) originally appeared as one or more full pages of computer output.

The output of the OS assembler is in figure 2.19, sections ③, ④, ⑤, ⑥, ⑦, ⑧, and ⑨; section ⑤ is the program listing and is so labeled. Section ⑩ is the result of program execution.

The output of the DOS assembler is in figure 2.20, sections ②, ③, ④, and ⑤; section ③ is the program listing and is so labeled. Sections ⑥, ⑦, and ⑧ relate to the linkage editor, while section ⑨ is the result of program execution.

The meanings of those parts of the program output which are of most relevance to the assembly language programmer will be considered in chapters 12 and 14.

```
ISV4C JOB ORIGIN FROM GRCUP=KBCO1   , CSP=CR , DEVICE=K8001RC1, 037
//RYTW02   JOB 'FACULTY          ',CLASS=F
// EXEC ASMGC,PARM.ASM='EXEC'
//ASM.SYSIN DD *
//SYSLST DD SYSOUT=A,DCB=RECFM=F
//SYSIPT DD *
/*
//
```
①

```
1C1CC4 M2 R= IEF403I RYTWC2   STARTEC
101119 M2 R= IEF45CI RYTWC2  .ASM      .       ABEND S706      TIME=10.11.27
1C1122 M2 R= IEF4C4I RYTWC2   ENDED


//RYTWC2   JOB 'FACULTY          ',CLASS=F
// EXEC ASMGC,PARM.ASM='EXEC'
XXASM       PROC MACLIB='SYS1.MACDUM',BLKSIZE=3200,SCBJ=30,SUT1=150,    XCCCCC1CO
XX              TYPE=G                                                   CCCCC2CO
XXASM          EXEC PGM=ASMGTYPE                                        CCCCC3CC
IEF653I SUBSTITUTION JCL - PGM=ASMG
XXSYSLIB      DD DSN=GMACLIB,DISP=SHR                                   CCCCC4CO
IEF653I SUBSTITUTION JCL - DSN=SYS1.MACDUM,CISP=SHR
XX            DD DSN=SYS1.MACLIB,DISP=SHR                               CCCCC5CO
XX            DD DSN=SYS1.CLMACS,DISP=SHR                               CCCCC6CO
XXSYSLIN      DD UNIT=SYSDA,CISP=(MCO,PASS,DELETE),CCB=BLKSIZE=GBLKSIZE, XCCCCC7CO
IEF653I SUBSTITUTION JCL - UNIT=SYSDA,DISP=(MCO,PASS,DELETE),CCB=BLKSIZE=3200,
XX            SPACE=(64CO,GSCBJ),DSN=GGLCADSET                          CCCCC8CO
IEF653I SUBSTITUTION JCL - SPACE=(6400,30),DSN=GLCADSET
XXSYSPRINT    DD SYSOUT=A,CCB=BLKSIZE=1936                              CCOCC9CO
XXSYSPUNCH    DD SYSOUT=B                                               CC001CCO
XXSYSTERM     DD SYSOUT=A                                               CC0011CO
XXSYSUT1      DD UNIT=SYSDA,SPACE=(6440,GSUT1)                          CC0012CO
IEF653I SUBSTITUTION JCL - UNIT=SYSDA,SPACE=(6440,150)
XXSYSLT2      DD UNIT=SYSDA,SPACE=(6440,GSUT1)                          CCCC13CO
IEF653I SUBSTITUTION JCL - UNIT=SYSDA,SPACE=(6440,150)
XXSYSLT3      DD UNIT=SYSDA,SPACE=(6440,GSUT1)                          CCCC14CO
IEF653I SUBSTITUTION JCL - UNIT=SYSDA,SPACE=(6440,150)
//ASM.SYSIN DD UNIT=(CTC,,CEFER),DSN=GGASPIO001,VCL=SFR=012503,     *
// CISP=(OLD,DELETE),DCB=(LRECL=80,BLKSIZE=80,RECFM=F)
//SYSLST DD SYSOUT=A,DCB=RECFM=F
//SYSIPT DD UNIT=(CTC,,DEFER),DSN=GGASPIO002,VCL=SER=022503,     *
// CISP=(OLD,DELETE),DCB=(LRECL=80,BLKSIZE=80,RECFM=F)
//
IEF236I ALLOC. FOR RYTWO2   ASM
IEF237I 751    ALLOCATED TC SYSLIB
IEF237I 751    ALLOCATED TO
IEF237I 751    ALLOCATED TC
IEF237I 1D8    ALLOCATED TC SYSLIN
IEF237I C78    ALLOCATED TC SYSPRINT
IEF237I C7F    ALLOCATED TO SYSPUNCH
IEF237I C81    ALLOCATED TO SYSTERM
IEF237I 1D8    ALLOCATED TO SYSUT1
IEF237I 769    ALLOCATED TO SYSUT2
IEF237I 768    ALLOCATED TO SYSUT3
IEF237I C86    ALLOCATED TC SYSIN
IEF237I C85    ALLOCATED TO SYSLST
IEF237I C87    ALLOCATED TC SYSIPT
IEA7C3I 706    RYTWO2   ASM     MODULE ACCESSED CG,-G-P
COMPLETION CODE - SYSTEM=706  USER=CCOO
```
②

Figure 2.19 (Part 1)
Mr. Sharp's Complete Program Output—OS Version

```
IEF285I   SYS1.MACDUM                                   KEPT
IEF285I   VOL SER NOS= SYS002.
IEF285I   SYS1.MACLIB                                   KEPT
IEF285I   VOL SER NOS= SYS002.
IEF285I   SYS1.CUMACS                                   KEPT
IEF285I   VOL SER NOS= SYSC02.
IEF285I   SYS78321.T100233.RV001.RYTWO2.LOADSET        PASSED
IEF285I   VOL SER NOS= DRM002.
IEF285I   SYS78321.T100233.RV001.RYTWO2.ASPCA001       DELETED
IEF285I   VOL SER NOS= ASPC78.
IEF285I   SYS78321.T100233.RV001.RYTWO2.R0001899       DELETED
IEF285I   VOL SER NOS= DRM002.
IEF285I   SYS78321.T100233.RV001.RYTWO2.R0001900       DELETED
IEF285I   VOL SER NOS= SCR002.
IEF285I   SYS78321.T100233.RV001.RYTWO2.R0001901       DELETED
IEF285I   VOL SER NOS= SCR001.
IEF285I   SYS78321.T100233.RV001.RYTWO2.ASPI0001       DELETED
IEF285I   VOL SER NOS= 012503.
IEF285I   SYS78321.T100233.RV001.RYTWO2.ASPOA004       DELETED
IEF285I   VOL SER NOS= ASPC85.
IEF285I   SYS78321.T100233.RV001.RYTWO2.ASPI0002       DELETED
IEF285I   VOL SER NOS= 022503.
```

```
** START - STEP=ASM        JOB=RYTWO2      DATE=11/17/78   CLOCK=10.10.12   PGM=ASMG
** END -                                   DATE=11/17/78   CLOCK=10.11.29   CPU=    2.32 SEC   CC= S706  **
** EXCPS - DISK=  250,    CTC=   105,   TAPE=    0,   TOTAL=    355   REGION USED=  126K OF  130K **

    DDNAME      EXCP COUNT    PCI CCUNT
    LINK/SVC        26            22
    SYSLIB         108
                     0
                     0
    SYSLIN           4
    SYSPRINT         6
    SYSPUNCH         0
    SYSTERM          0
    SYSUT1          99
    SYSUT2           7
    SYSUT3           6
    SYSIN           24
    SYSLST          38
    SYSIPT          37
```

```
IEF285I   SYS78321.T100233.RV001.RYTWO2.LOADSET        DELETED
IEF285I   VOL SER NOS= DRM002.
```

```
** START - JOB=RYTWO2      DATE=11/17/78   CLOCK=10.10.12
** END -                   DATE=11/17/78   CLOCK=10.11.30   ACCOUNTING TIME=    2.32 SECONDS    MAX REGION USED=  126K **
```

```
                              OS/360 ASSEMBLER

LEVEL=G    RELEASE=21MAR76    SYSTEM=MVT 21.7   MODEL=168   TIME=10 10 25   DAY=FRIDAY    DATE=17 NOV 78

OVERRIDING PARM=EXEC

ASSEMBLER OPTIONS=ALGN,BATCH,CALIGN=0,COLUMN=3,NODECK,ESD,EXECUTE,EXTEN,EXTIME=5,INSTSET=1,LINECNT=55,
          LIST,LCAD,LREF,LSETC=8,NUM,OS,PRINTER,NORENT,RLC,SEQUENCE,SPACE=MAX-4K,STMT,SYSPARM=,
          NOTERM,NOTEST,UMAP,UPCOND=12,NOUPDATE,UPLIST,UTBUFF=3,FULLXREF,YFLAG.
```

(3)

```
          $JOB
```

```
                              EXTERNAL SYMBOL DICTIONARY                    PAGE   1

                                                                           17 NOV 78
SYMBOL   TYPE ID  ADDR  LENGTH LD ID
    PC   01 COC000 OOC1B0
```

(4)

Figure 2.19 (Part 2)
Mr. Sharp's Complete Program Output—OS Version

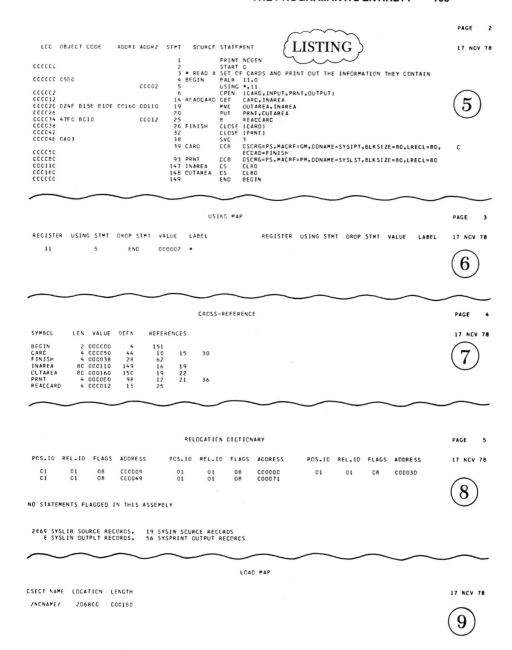

```
LCC   OBJECT CODE   ADDR1 ADDR2  STMT   SOURCE STATEMENT         LISTING          17 NOV 78
                                  1            PRINT NOGEN
CCCCCC                            2            START 0
                                  3     * READ A SET OF CARDS AND PRINT OUT THE INFORMATION THEY CONTAIN
CCCCCC C5BC                       4 BEGIN      BALR 11,0
                        CCC02     5            USING *,11
CCCCC2                            6            OPEN (CARD,INPUT,PRNT,OUTPUT)
CCCC12                           14 READCARD   GET  CARD,INAREA
CCCC2C D24F B15E B10E C0160 C0110 19           MVC  OUTAREA,INAREA
CCCC26                           20            PUT  PRNT,OUTAREA
CCCC34 47FC BC10        CCC012    25            B    READCARD
CCCC38                           26 FINISH     CLOSE (CARD)
CCCC42                           32            CLOSE (PRNT)
CCCC4E 0A03                      38            SVC  3
                                 39 CARD       CCB  DSORG=PS,MACRF=GM,DDNAME=SYSIPT,BLKSIZE=80,LRECL=80,   C
CCCC5C                                              EODAD=FINISH
CCCCBC                           93 PRNT       CCB  DSORG=PS,MACRF=PM,DDNAME=SYSLST,BLKSIZE=80,LRECL=80
CCC11C                          147 INAREA     DS   CL80
CCC16C                          148 OUTAREA    DS   CL80
CCCCCC                          149            END  BEGIN
```

                                    USING MAP   PAGE   3

```
REGISTER  USING STMT  DROP STMT  VALUE  LABEL        REGISTER  USING STMT  DROP STMT  VALUE  LABEL   17 NOV 78
   11         5          END    000002   *
```

                                  CROSS-REFERENCE   PAGE   4

```
SYMBOL    LEN   VALUE   DEFN   REFERENCES                                          17 NOV 78

BEGIN      2  000000    4     151
CARD       4  CCCC50   44      10    15    30
FINISH     4  00C038   28      62
INAREA    8C  000110  149      16    19
CUTAREA   8C  000160  150      19    22
PRNT       4  0000C0   98      12    21    36
READCARD   4  CCC012   15      25
```

                               RELOCATION DICTIONARY   PAGE   5

```
POS.ID  REL.ID  FLAGS  ADDRESS     POS.ID  REL.ID  FLAGS  ADDRESS     POS.ID  REL.ID  FLAGS  ADDRESS   17 NOV 78

  C1      01     08   CCCC09        01      01     08   CC0000        01      01     08   C00030
  C1      01     08   CC0049        01      01     08   C00071
```

NO STATEMENTS FLAGGED IN THIS ASSEMBLY

```
2E65 SYSLIB SOURCE RECORDS,    19 SYSIN SOURCE RECORDS
   E SYSLIN OUTPUT RECORDS,    56 SYSPRINT OUTPUT RECORDS
```

                                    LOAD MAP

```
CSECT NAME  LOCATION  LENGTH                                                       17 NOV 78
/NONAME/    2068CO    C001BC
```

Figure 2.19 (Part 3)
Mr. Sharp's Complete Program Output—OS Version

Figure 2.19 (Part 4)
Mr. Sharp's Complete Program Output—OS Version

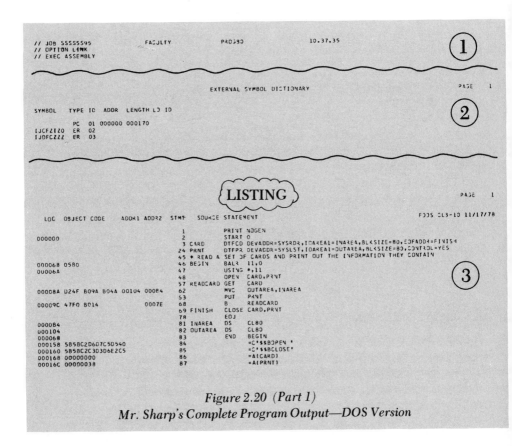

Figure 2.20 (Part 1)
Mr. Sharp's Complete Program Output—DOS Version

```
                                    RELOCATION DICTIONARY                              PAGE   1

  POS.ID   REL.ID   FLAGS    ADDRESS                                                   11/17/78

    01       01       0C     000008
    01       02       18     000011
    01       01       0C     000018
    01       01       0C     00001C
    01       01       08     000021
    01       01       0C     000040
    01       03       18     000049
    01       01       0C     000050
    01       01       08     000061
    01       01       0C     000074
    01       01       0C     000078
    01       01       0C     0000A8
    01       01       0C     0000AC
    01       01       0C     000168
    01       01       0C     00016C
```
④

```
NO STATEMENTS FLAGGED IN THIS ASSEMBLY
```
⑤

```
// EXEC LNKEDT
```
⑥

```
JOB  SSSSSS95  11/17/78   DISK LINKAGE EDITOR DIAGNOSTIC OF INPUT

ACTION TAKEN  MAP
LIST    AUTOLINK    IJCFZIZO
LIST    AUTOLINK    IJDFCZZZ
LIST    ENTRY
```
⑦

```
11/17/78  PHASE  XFR-AD  LOCORE  HICORE  DSK-AD   ESD TYPE  LABEL      LOADED  REL-FR

          PHASE***  005068  005000  005227  24 00 1  CSECT                005000  005000

                                                     CSECT     IJCFZIZO   005170  005170

                                                     CSECT     IJDFCZZZ   0051D8  0051D8
                                                   * ENTRY     IJDFZZZZ   0051D8
```
⑧

```
// EXEC
```
⑨

```
EOJ SSSSSS95                                    10.40.05,DURATION 00.02.27
```
⑩

Figure 2.20 (Part 2)
Mr. Sharp's Complete Program Output—DOS Version

2.6.4   Recap: What Has the Program Done

In the following summary, the statement numbers referred to are those appearing on the DOS listing. The instructions are numbered in sequential order. The explanation for instructions on the OS listing is similar, however the statement numbers are, of course, different.

The first instruction, statement number 1, is an assembler instruction. Its purpose is to suppress the printing of the machine language equivalent of macro instructions (see chapter 4 for more detail). Statement number 2 marks the beginning of the program and initializes the location counter. Statement number 3 is a macro defining the card file. As you can see, this macro produced 21 machine language instructions, since the next instruction has statement number 24. Statement number 24 is a macro defining the printer file; it also generated 21 machine language instructions. Statement numbers 41, 42, 43, 44, and 45 are comments, some of which provide spacing. Statement number 46, the BALR, places the beginning location number of statement number 48 (the next executable instruction) into register 11. Statement 47 is an assembler instruction which notifies the assembler that register 11 is to be used as a base register for this program, and tells the assembler to assume the contents of register 11 to be that value which the BALR placed into register 11.

The OPEN instruction, statement number 48, is a macro. It makes the card and printer files available for processing. This macro generated 9 machine language instructions. The GET instruction, statement number 57, is a macro instruction which reads a card and stores its contents in the area called INAREA (which the DTFCD associated with the file called CARD). Statement 62 moves the contents of INAREA to OUTAREA. Statement 63 prints the contents of OUTAREA (the area associated by the DTFPR with the file called PRNT); it generated 5 machine language instructions. Statement number 68 tells the computer to go back to statement number 57, that is, to the instruction located at the address known as READCARD. The computer will then read another card into main storage, and continue sequential execution from that point through statement number 68, which will again direct the computer to branch back to the instruction called READCARD. This process is repeated until the computer, upon attempting to execute the GET instruction, finds that no more records (cards) are available. At this point, control will pass to that location designated in the definition of the file called CARD (that is, in the DTFCD instruction) as the EOFADDR: that is, control will pass to the statement called FINISH (statement number 69). The files are then deactivated by the CLOSE instruction, and program execution is terminated by statement number 78, the EOJ instruction.

Summary

In this chapter, we were introduced to a complete assembly language program. The program was first shown in its entirety, after which the individual
instructions were discussed in detail. Finally, the chapter considered how
the program is translated into machine language and how one requests the
computer to produce the desired results.

In particular, the chapter has acquainted us with
- assembler instructions
- machine instructions
- macro instructions
- the general form of an assembler language instruction
- the use of the assembler coding form
- the use of, and the associated rules for, the following assembler language
  instructions:
  > PRINT, START, BALR, USING, OPEN, GET, MVC, PUT, B,
  > CLOSE, SVC, EOJ, DCB, DTFCD, DTFPR, END
- the formats of some statements in a language called JCL.

Important Terms Discussed in Chapter 2

assembler instruction
assembly phase
assembly time

coding form
comment
continuation character

end-of-file condition
execution
execution phase
execution time
explicit length
extended mnemonic

free form coding

implied length
input area

Job Control Language (JCL)

linkage editor
load module
location counter

machine instruction
macro instruction
macro library

object module
object statement
operand
operation (code)
output area

pocket selection
processing

receiving area

sending field
source statement
stacker selection

Questions

2-1. Name the three categories of assembly language instructions.

2-2. The terms "machine instruction" and "machine language instruction" sound almost the same. Do they mean the same thing? Explain.

2-3. Distinguish between the terms "assembly language instruction" and "assembler instruction".

2-4. Explain the purpose of an assembler instruction.

2-5. Which of the three categories of assembly language instructions is translated into machine language?

2-6. Which category of assembly language instruction may be termed nonexecutable? Explain.

2-7. A macro represents a sequence of two or more machine language instructions. Where may they be found?

2-8. Why would a programmer find it convenient to use macros?

2-9. If the assembler retrieves a sequence of instructions from the macro library, can this sequence be reused?

2-10. Name the four parts of which assembly language instructions may be composed.

2-11. Is the order of instruction components (see question 2-10) important?

2-12. What is the purpose of a name portion?

2-13. What is the maximum number of characters which may comprise a name?

2-14. Must every instruction have an operation code? Explain.

2-15. What is the function of an operand?

2-16. Why is it helpful to write instructions on a coding sheet?

2-17. If you choose not to use a coding sheet, what rules should you observe?

2-18. What instruction informs the assembler that an assembly language program will follow?

2-19. Write a START instruction which will initialize the location counter to the decimal value 4096.

2-20. Must a START instruction have an operand portion?

2-21. How does the assembler determine the location of the next instruction?

2-22. What is the main purpose of a DCB (or DTF) instruction?

2-23. What instruction(s) identify(ies) to the computer an area in storage to be used as an input area or as an output area?

2-24. Write a DCB (or DTF) instruction which defines a card data set (file) called JDL, associated with a card reader and with an input area called RECEIVE. When the end of file condition is encountered, we wish the computer to branch to an instruction stored in a location called NOMORE.

2-25. Given the following instruction
     BALR   5,0
explain what it will do.

2-26. Write an instruction which notifies the assembler that registers 2 through 6 will be used as base registers, with the current contents of the location counter being placed into register 2.

2-27. Write instructions which will activate and deactivate the data sets (files) called FBIFILE (an input data set) and CIAFILE (an output data set).

2-28. Correct the errors, if any, in the following nonsense DOS program segment:

```
MITLA    DTFCD    DEVADDR=SYSRDR,IOAREA1=IN,BLKSIZE=80,
                  EOFADDR=FINAL
PASS     DTFPR    DEVADDR=SYSLST,IOAREA1=OUT,BLKSIZE=132,
                  CONTROL=YES
         OPEN     IN
         GET      OUT
         PUT      OOT
         CLOSE    MITLA,PAS
         EOJ
```

2-29. In the following instruction:
     MVC   BOTTLE,WATER
which is the receiving field and which is the sending field?

2-30. Given the fields WATCH and OUT containing information as indicated below, what will be the contents of these fields after the execution of each of the following statements?

WATCH | S | T | R | E | E | T |

OUT | A | V | E | N | U | E |

(a) MVC   WATCH(3),OUT
(b) MVC   WATCH+2(4),OUT
(c) MVC   WATCH+2(4),OUT+1

2-31. Given the information below, what will the fields CHANGE and ME contain after execution of the instruction

MVC   CHANGE,ME

	before		after	
(a) CHANGE	B O D Y	CHANGE	☐☐☐☐	
ME	S O M E	ME	☐☐☐☐	
(b) CHANGE	B O	CHANGE	☐☐	
ME	S O M E	ME	☐☐☐☐	

2-32. Which operand of a MVC instruction determines the number of bytes moved, and what is the maximum number of bytes which may be moved?

2-33. Explain the meaning of the term "extended mnemonic".

2-34. What will result when the following instruction is executed?

DOOMSDAY B   DOOMSDAY

2-35. What is the function of the SVC 3 and EOJ instructions?

2-36. Is it possible to have instructions following the END instruction? Explain.

2-37. The program of figure 2.21 has one or more errors. Can you find them? (For reference we have numbered the instructions starting from 1 through 15.)

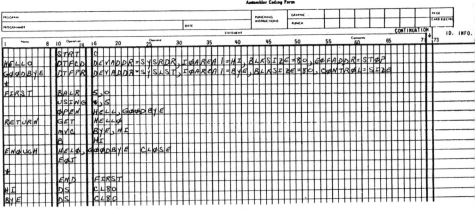

Figure 2.21

2-38. Which of the following instructions has an instruction format? START, DTFCD, DTFPR, BALR, USING, OPEN, GET, MVC, PUT, B, CLOSE, EOJ, END.

Chapter 3

Defining Storage and Defining Constants

DEFINING STORAGE AND DEFINING CONSTANTS

The program presented in chapter 2 used an instruction called the DS (Define Storage) instruction to reserve areas of storage which held the program input and the program output.

In this chapter we shall discuss the DS instruction in more detail, along with an instruction—the DC (Define Constant) instruction—which not only reserves storage area, but also places constant data into computer memory. We shall then demonstrate the use of these instructions through a programming example.

3.1   HOW AND WHY IS DATA PLACED INTO STORAGE?

In chapters 1 and 2, you have seen and used several assembly language instructions. Many of these instructions used names in their operand portions to refer to storage locations in memory. The names used were assigned by the programmer for convenience. It is easier to call a friend by name than by social security number; likewise names are more easily remembered than numbers for reference to computer storage.

How will the computer know which particular memory locations are being referred to when specific names are used? It is one of the functions of the assembler to associate names with storage locations. The programmer uses the DS and DC assembler instructions to tell the assembler which names should be assigned to main storage areas. The instructions also request the assembler to reserve those areas for use by the program, and to designate the exact area length in bytes.

The DC instruction has an additional function: placing constant data into main storage. A **constant** is a symbol or group of consecutive symbols stored in computer memory by the assembler program for use during program execution. For example, the heading to be printed on top of a report, messages to the computer operator, tax tables, or any similar information which is fixed in value and useful to the program during execution is considered constant.

From the programmer's point of view, the DC and DS instructions are very similar. Our discussion of the DC will precede that of the DS, for many of the options specified by the DC will apply to the DS as well. Therefore if you thoroughly understand the DC, the explanation of the DS should follow easily.

3.2 THE DC INSTRUCTION—CONSTANT DEFINITION

The DC instruction serves to direct the assembler to perform the following:
- Define and reserve one or more areas in storage
- Specify the size of the area being reserved
- Associate a name with the area (optional). This name may be used to refer either to the address of the area or to the contents of the area.
- Place constant data into the reserved location.

For example, consider the instruction

        FORTY   DC   CL2'40'

This instruction sets aside an area in memory to contain Character data (data coded in EBCDIC form); the area is of "Length 2", that is, 2 bytes in length. The constant value "40" will be placed into this area by the assembler. The name "FORTY" is associated with the address of the defined area, so that whenever reference to the contents of this area (the number 40) is required, the programmer will refer to FORTY and the computer will act upon "the contents of FORTY", that is, "40".

The Anatomy of the DC Instruction

The DC instruction, like other assembler instructions, is composed of three portions: the name portion, the operation portion, and the operand portion.

1. The name portion:
   As you already know, the assembler associates a beginning address with a name that the programmer has chosen. The name is a means by which the programmer refers to the beginning location of the constant. If the programmer does not wish to refer to the constant, then no name is required. For rules concerning the composition of names, refer to chapter 2, section 2.2.2.

2. The operation portion:
   The mnemonic DC comprises the operation portion of this instruction. This is the part of the instruction which directs the assembler to establish some storage (or none at all, as will be explained shortly) and place a constant into that storage area, as specified in the operand portion.

3. The operand portion:
   This is the part of the instruction which details the form and value of the constant to be stored and provides other information required by the assembler such as the length of the reserved area. The operand portion consists of four subfields:
   a) Duplication factor

b) Type
c) Modifiers
d) Constants

The first three describe the constant, and the fourth provides the constant itself. Modifiers describe the length in bytes used for storage of the constant.

Our discussion of the DC instruction will deal with different designations of the type subfield separately. Different type designations within the DC instruction will cause data to be stored in the computer in different forms. We know that the same numeric value may be represented in Roman numerals or Arabic numerals. However Arabic numerals are more convenient for arithmetic purposes. Similarly, computers allow a choice of methods through which a programmer may choose to represent numbers. For example,

- Alphabetic and alphameric data in the 360 and 370 may be stored in EBCDIC code (the "C" type designation)
- Numeric data may be stored in
  EBCDIC form (the "C" type designation)
  packed form (the "P" type designation)
  zoned form (the "Z" type designation)
  binary form (the "H", "F" type designations)
  and other forms as are available for the computer you use.

Each data form has its own advantages and disadvantages, and is best suited for specific purposes. As you read this text and the manufacturer's manuals, and as you gain programming experience, you will develop a proficiency for determining the data form to most efficiently serve your specific purpose.

It is useful at this point to note that many assembly language instructions (other than the DC and DS) are grouped according to the form of the data upon which they act. We shall therefore discuss particular type subfields as they become relevant. The chapters immediately following this one (chapters 4, 5, and 6) will use numeric values in EBCDIC, packed, and zoned forms. We will also discuss the "X" type (hexadecimal) and "B" type (binary) storage specifications by the DC; the "X" type is used in chapter 6. Similarly, we will consider the storage of binary constants immediately before we introduce the instructions which act upon binary numbers (in chapter 7), and the storage of address constants when we study applications which use those constants (in chapter 12).

3.2.1 EBCDIC Constants

If we wish to store letters or special symbols (such as ?, !, =, and so on) in computer memory, we would specify EBCDIC representation. Numbers which are not to be used in arithmetic operations may also be stored in

EBCDIC. If you are not certain that you recall the EBCDIC representation, refer back to chapter 1, section 1.2.1.

For convenience, we use what is known as "hexadecimal code" or "hexadecimal notation", as a shorthand form for representing combinations of bits (0's and 1's). In particular, one of the **hexadecimal digits** 0,1,2,...,9,A,B,C, D,E,F replaces a group of four bits. The hexadecimal digit—bit correspondence is given in figure 3.1.

hexadecimal digit	bits	hexadecimal digit	bits
0	0000	8	1000
1	0001	9	1001
2	0010	A	1010
3	0011	B	1011
4	0100	C	1100
5	0101	D	1101
6	0110	E	1110
7	0111	F	1111

Figure 3.1
Hexadecimal Digit—Bit Correspondence

The hexadecimal notation derives from the digits of the **hexadecimal number system**, which is discussed in chapter 7, section 7.2.2.

In figure 3.2, we reproduce the EBCDIC representations of alphabetic, numeric, and some of the more frequently used special characters, along with the corresponding hexadecimal codes. Representations of other special characters may be looked up in the System/370 Reference Summary (Appendix A).

Symbol	EBCDIC CODE (bits)	EBCDIC CODE (hexadecimal)
A	1100 0001	C1
B	1100 0010	C2
C	1100 0011	C3
D	1100 0100	C4
E	1100 0101	C5
F	1100 0110	C6
G	1100 0111	C7
H	1100 1000	C8
I	1100 1001	C9
J	1101 0001	D1
K	1101 0010	D2

Symbol	EBCDIC CODE (bits)	EBCDIC CODE (hexadecimal)
L	1101 0011	D3
M	1101 0100	D4
N	1101 0101	D5
O	1101 0110	D6
P	1101 0111	D7
Q	1101 1000	D8
R	1101 1001	D9
S	1110 0010	E2
T	1110 0011	E3
U	1110 0100	E4
V	1110 0101	E5
W	1110 0110	E6
X	1110 0111	E7
Y	1110 1000	E8
Z	1110 1001	E9
0	1111 0000	F0
1	1111 0001	F1
2	1111 0010	F2
3	1111 0011	F3
4	1111 0100	F4
5	1111 0101	F5
6	1111 0110	F6
7	1111 0111	F7
8	1111 1000	F8
9	1111 1001	F9
Ƀ(blank)	0100 0000	40
,	0110 1011	6B
.	0100 1011	4B
'	0111 1101	7D
+	0100 1110	4E
−	0110 0000	60
&	0101 0000	50

Figure 3.2
EBCDIC Character Representation

To define and store EBCDIC constants, we use the following form:

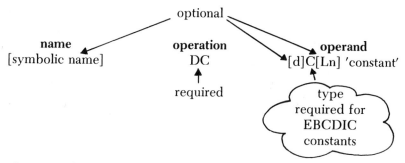

The discussion below will demonstrate several variations in the manner in which EBCDIC constants may be specified.

Explicit vs. Implicit Lengths

Suppose we wished to store the constant: I LIKE ASSEMBLER, which would be referred to at some point in our program as "FRSTLOVE". We would code

      FRSTLOVE   DC   C'I LIKE ASSEMBLER'

or

      FRSTLOVE   DC   CL16'I LIKE ASSEMBLER'

Did you recognize the difference? If you did not, don't feel badly. These instructions really do the same thing. They result in identical constants being stored, as we will now explain.

In the first instruction, the length is *implied*. Since we do not specify the length of the constant, the number of storage positions required to store the constant is determined by the assembler by counting the number of characters specified within the quotes (including blanks).

In the second instruction, we have *explicitly* specified the length, by writing "L16". That is, the assembler is no longer required to count the number of storage positions necessary to store the constant; we have already done it for the assembler. In EBCDIC code each character requires one byte of storage; consequently, sixteen consecutive bytes of storage are set aside.

What If Explicit and Implicit Lengths Disagree?

What do you think the assembler would do with the following?

    (1)   FRSTLOVE   DC   CL11'I LIKE ASSEMBLER'
    (2)   FRSTLOVE   DC   CL20'I LIKE ASSEMBLER'

Don't panic. The answer is forthcoming.

In these examples, explicit and implicit lengths disagree. Whenever this is the case, the rule is: explicit length supercedes.

In instruction (1), the explicit length factor is 11 ("L11") while the implicit length is 16. Instruction (1) will therefore store the leftmost 11 positions of the specified constants (including blanks); that is IƀLIKEƀASSE will be stored. Instruction (2) will use 20 consecutive storage locations; that is, IƀLIKEƀASSEMBLERƀƀƀƀ. As you may note, instruction (1) **truncates** (eliminates) the rightmost symbols of the constant which do not "fit into" the allocated length. In instruction (2) the explicit length exceeds the implicit length. In such a case the assembler **pads** (adds onto) the defined constant with blanks on the rightmost end.

In summary, when a length is specified, the assembler will allocate just that amount of storage. If the constant fits in exactly, there is no problem. If the constant is too large, it is truncated on the right. If the constant is too small, it is placed in the area beginning at the low-order byte (left justified), and any unused bytes at the high-order portion of the area are padded with blanks.

Trick of the trade:
Suppose a programmer is asked to clear (fill with blanks) an area of 132 storage locations. He could code this as

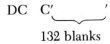

$$\text{DC} \quad \text{C}' \underbrace{\hspace{3cm}}' $$

132 blanks

but a much slicker method is to code   DC   CL132' '. There are many other opportunities to use this technique, as you will discover yourself.

Note: In designating the storage of an ampersand (&) or an apostrophe ('), we must indicate these characters twice. For example, the statement 'PROGRAMMING'S FINE' (including the apostrophes) is stored by

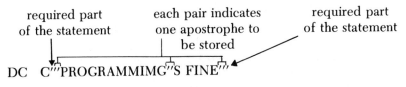

required part of the statement	each pair indicates one apostrophe to be stored	required part of the statement

DC   C'''PROGRAMMIMG''S FINE'''

Likewise, the statement BOB & TED is stored by

DC   C'BOB && TED'

Let us show you what the assembler will do with the following DC instructions:

Instructions written by us			Values generated in storage by assembler (shown in hexadecimal code)
NIGHT	DC	C'MOON'	D4D6D6D5
COMMA	DC	C'A,B'	C16BC2
PAD	DC	CL5'123'	F1F2F34040
TRUNCATE	DC	CL2'123'	F1F2

During the assembly process, the assembler will ask the following questions:
- What type of constant is it? In the above examples, "C" (EBCDIC type) is indicated.
- How many bytes are required to store the constant? If a length is explicitly stated, the modifier length will apply; otherwise the amount of storage required will be determined by the constant.

The assembler will then represent the characters in consecutive memory locations, each by its equivalent 8-bit EBCDIC code.

Summary

In its translating activity, the assembler will be cognizant of the following rules for the storage of EBCDIC constants:
1. left justify
2. right truncation
3. padding with blanks to the right
4. assemble the constant in EBCDIC form
5. maximum constant length is 256 bytes

Let us pretend to be the assembler. What EBCDIC constants will we generate when given the instructions below?

(i)	THIS	DC	C'CHEER'
(ii)	IS	DC	CL1'UP'
(iii)	VERY	DC	CL10'IT''S NOT'
(iv)	EASY	DC	C'HARD,ANYMORE'

The assembler will generate the following constants:
- (i) C3C8C5C5D9
- (ii) E4
- (iii) C9E37DE240D5D6E34040
- (iv) C8C1D9C46BC1D5E8D4D6D9C5

3.2.2   Packed Constants

A packed number is a signed number stored in memory in a special form suitable for use in some arithmetic operations.

In a packed constant, digits are "packed" two per byte with the exception of the low-order byte (the rightmost byte). The second half (digit portion) of the low-order byte contains the sign. A positive constant will have a hexadecimal C (or binary 1100) in the sign position; a negative constant will have a hexadecimal D (or binary 1101) in the sign position.

Below is a schematic diagram of packed representation:

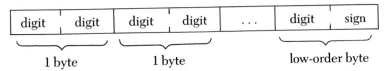

The digital representations are binary forms of the individual digits; that is, each digit will be represented in 4 bits.

Examples:

As specified in the DC	Internal representation	Equivalent in hexadecimal
+5	0101 1100	5 C
−7	0111 1101	7 D
+874	1000 0111 0100 1100	8 7 4 C
+56	0000 0101 0110 1100	0 5 6 C

To define and store packed constants, we use the following form:

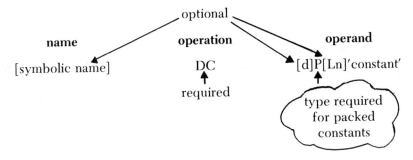

Whenever packed numbers are placed into a storage area of predetermined length, the number is placed with its low-order portion into the low-order part of the area, and extending to the left. If the area is of exactly the right length to accommodate the constant, there is no problem. If the area is too small, the leftmost digits of the constant are truncated. If the area is too large, the constant is padded with high-order packed zeros, two hexadecimal zeros per byte. We know, of course, that appending high-order zeros does not alter the value of a number.

We may specify the length, that is, the number of bytes desired for a packed constant, either explicitly or implicitly, as we have seen for EBCDIC constants.

Explicit vs Implicit Lengths

Instruction		**Internal Representation**	**Comments**
DC	PL2'345'	3 4 5 C	Explicit and implicit factors agree
DC	PL2'6789'	7 8 9 C ↗ truncation	Implicit length exceeds explicit length
DC	PL2'6'	0 0 6 C ↳ padding	Explicit length exceeds implicit length

Note: The length factor in a DC instruction refers to the number of bytes in storage to be filled by the stored constant and not necessarily to the number of digits in the constant.

For example:

Constant	Necessary number of bytes in storage
+52	2
1234	3
5	1
768	2

Let us consider the following examples:

1.	DC	PL3'1234'
2.	DC	PL3'+1234'
3.	DC	PL3'−1234'

The respective constants which will be stored (using hexadecimal notation) are:

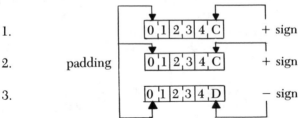

1.   0 1 2 3 4 C   + sign

2.   padding   0 1 2 3 4 C   + sign

3.   0 1 2 3 4 D   − sign

Instructions 1 and 2 generated the same internal representations. An unsigned number and a positive signed number both generate a plus sign (hexadecimal C) in the digit portion of the low-order byte. However, in example 3, a minus sign generated a hexadecimal D.

Did you notice too that padding (an extra hexadecimal zero) occurred in the leftmost portion of the high-order byte? This will occur whenever we have an even number of packed digits.

Note that although 4 digits (actually 5 with the padding digit) are being stored, only 3 bytes of storage were necessary. This results from the fact that packed digits are stored two per byte with the exception of the rightmost byte, which contains only one digit.

Here is a formula to find the number of bytes required to store a packed number:

$$\text{\# of bytes} = \text{integer part of } (\text{\# digits}/2) + 1$$

Examples:

Packed constant to be stored	Number of bytes	
1. 245	2	# of bytes = (integer part of 3/2)+1=1+1 = 2
2. 1078	3	# of bytes = (integer part of 4/2)+1=2+1 = 3
3. −5	1	# of bytes = (integer part of 1/2)+1=0+1 = 1

Implicit Length Factor

Now consider the same examples with an implicit length factor:

Instruction	Stored representation
1. DC P'1234'	

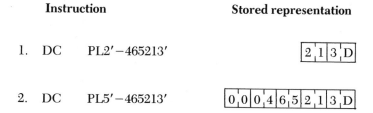

2. DC P'+1234'	
3. DC P'−1234'	

When explicit and implicit lengths disagree, the assembler will make appropriate adjustments, similar to that which is done for EBCDIC constants.

For example:

Instruction	Stored representation
1. DC PL2'−465213'	|2|1|3|D|
2. DC PL5'−465213'	|0|0|0|4|6|5|2|1|3|D|

In example 1, truncation occurred in the high-order portion of the number. In example 2, padding occurred. The padding characters are packed zeros appended to the high-order portion of the number.

Decimal Points

Decimal points within a number are handled by the assembly language programmer rather than by the computer itself. Therefore, although the assembler permits mentioning a decimal point within the DC instruction defining a packed number, the decimal point will not occur in storage.

Example:

Instruction	Stored representation
DC P'+1.5'	|0|1|5|C|

Note that the decimal point is not stored.

In this chapter we restrict ourselves to whole numbers. Later in the text we will consider the question of how to perform arithmetic operations with numbers containing decimal points.

Multiple Constants

One further convenience allowed when specifying packed constants with the DC instruction is the definition of several constants with one instruction. We call such constants **multiple constants**.

The technique involved is simply the separation of the requested constants by commas. The commas themselves are not stored, since they are not numeric characters.

Example:

$$DC \qquad P'+4,-5.2,+63'$$

is equivalent to

$$DC \qquad P'+4'$$
$$DC \qquad P'-5.2'$$
$$DC \qquad P'+63'$$

The constants are stored in consecutive locations as follows:

4	C	0	5	2	D	0	6	3	C

When a length factor is specified with multiple constants, it applies to each individual constant.

A useful tip:

When the constants are not equal in size, one should generally avoid specifying a length factor. This will eliminate unnecessary padding and truncation.

Example:

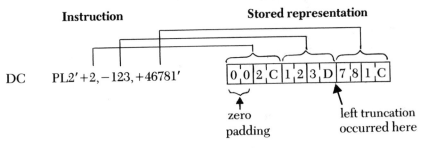

| | Instruction | | | Stored representation |
| DC | PL2'+2,−123,+46781' |

zero padding

left truncation occurred here

Note: The maximum number of stored bytes for packed constants is 16 (that is, 31 decimal digits; the sign occupies ½ byte).

Summary

In its translating activity, the assembler will be cognizant of the following rules for the storage of packed constants:
1. right justify
2. left truncation
3. padding with packed zeros to the left
4. assemble the constant in packed form
5. maximum constant length is 16 bytes

Let us again pretend to be the assembler and indicate those constants to be generated by the DC instructions:

(i)	THIS	DC	PL4'68'
(ii)	IS	DC	P'+3,71,−4'
(iii)	TRICKY	DC	C'+3,71,−4'
(iv)		DC	PL1'+46'

The following will be generated:
(i)	0000068C
(ii)	3C071C4D
(iii)	4EF36BF7F16B60F4
(iv)	6C

3.2.3   Zoned Constants

A zoned number is a signed number in which each digit occupies one byte and consists of two parts: the zone portion and the digit portion. Each byte, with the exception of the low-order (rightmost) byte, must have the bit configuration "1111" or hexadecimal F in the zone portion, and a 4-bit representation of the decimal value of the digit in the digit portion. The low-order byte will contain the sign of the number in the zone portion (binary 1100 or hexadecimal C for plus, binary 1101 or hexadecimal D for minus), with a 4-bit representation of the low-order digit value in the digit portion.

Below is a schematic diagram of zoned representation:

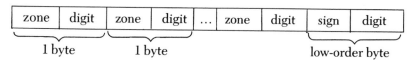

Examples: (The same decimal values are used here as were used in the discussion of packed representation.)

As specified in the DC	Internal representation	Equivalent in hexadecimal
+5	1100 0101	C 5
−7	1101 0111	D 7
+874	1111 1000 | 1111 0111 | 1100 0100	F 8 | F 7 | C 4
+56	1111 0101 | 1100 0110	F 5 | C 6

To define and store zoned constants we use the following form:

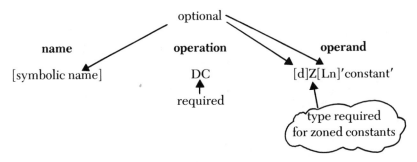

optional

name	operation	operand
[symbolic name]	DC	[d]Z[Ln]′constant′

required

type required for zoned constants

The rules which apply to assembler storage of zoned numbers are the same as those applying to assembler storage of packed numbers. The handling of
- explicit vs implicit length factors
- decimal points specified within the constant
- multiple constants
- maximum length allowed a constant (16 bytes)

is identical to the treatment accorded packed representation. However, the number itself is represented in zoned form and therefore any padding which may take place will be in the form of zoned zeros (F0 for each zero).

Consider the following examples:

Instruction	Internal representation	Comments
DC ZL2′6789′	F 8 | C 9 ← truncation	Implicit length exceeds explicit length: left truncation
DC ZL2′6′	F 0 | C 6 padding	Explicit length exceeds implicit length: zero padding

DC	ZL1'1'	$\boxed{\text{C} \mid 1}$	Implicit and explicit lengths agree: positive constant
DC	ZL1'+1'	$\boxed{\text{C} \mid 1}$	Implicit and explicit lengths agree: positive constant
DC	ZL1'−1'	$\boxed{\text{D} \mid 1}$	Implicit and explicit lengths agree: negative constant
DC	Z'+2.7'	$\boxed{\text{F} \mid 2 \mid \text{C} \mid 7}$	Decimal points mentioned within an instruction do not occur in storage
DC	Z'+4,−5,+63'	$\boxed{\text{C} \mid 4 \mid \text{D} \mid 5 \mid \text{F} \mid 6 \mid \text{C} \mid 3}$	Multiple constants are stored in consecutive storage locations

Summary

In its translating activity, the assembler will be cognizant of the following rules for the storage of zoned constants:

1. right justify
2. left truncation
3. padding with zoned zeros to the left
4. assemble the constant in zoned form
5. maximum constant length is 16 bytes

3.2.4   Hexadecimal Constants

A hexadecimal constant is one in which a group of one or more hexadecimal digits (0 through F) is indicated in the operand portion of the DC instruction. Those hexadecimal digits will be translated into appropriate combinations of 0's and 1's and stored in the computer memory. Each hexadecimal digit translates into a group of exactly 4 bits, so that a pair of such digits will occupy one byte (8 bits). If an even number of hexadecimal digits is specified, one byte will be occupied per pair of digits. If an odd number of digits is specified, the assembler will pad the leftmost byte of the constant with a high-order hexadecimal zero.

To define and store hexadecimal constants, we use the following form:

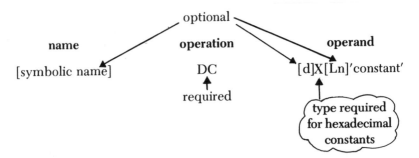

If the implicit length of the constant (the number of hexadecimal digit pairs) exceeds the explicit length, truncation of high-order digits will occur to conform to the explicit length. If the implicit length is smaller than the explicit length, the constant is padded with high-order hexadecimal zeros.

Consider the following instruction examples:

Instruction	Internal representation	Comments
DC X'FF13'	F F 1 3	Explicit length not specified
DC XL1'FF13'	1 3	Implicit length exceeds explicit length: left truncation
DC XL3'FF13'	0 0 F F 1 3	Explicit length exceeds implicit length: zero padding on left
DC X'ABC'	0 A B C	Odd number of hexadecimal digits: high-order zero padding
DC XL2'456FE'	5 6 F E	Implicit length (odd number) exceeds explicit length: left truncation

Only one hexadecimal constant may be specified per operand: multiple constants are not permitted.

Note a major difference between the EBCDIC, packed, and zoned constants and the hexadecimal constants. In the former case, decimal values specified in the operand portion were first translated by the assembler from the decimal into the type of format requested by the DC instruction. In the case of hexadecimal constants, the *hexadecimal digits themselves* (not the decimal equivalent!) are specified by the instruction.

Hexadecimal constants are used to specify *configurations of bits* desired, as opposed to specifying data to be stored in a particular format. For this reason we do not include a sign or specify multiple constants or decimal points. Hexadecimal constants will be used in chapter 6.

Summary

In its translating activity, the assembler will be cognizant of the following rules for the storage of hexadecimal constants:
1. two hexadecimal digits per byte; right justify
2. left truncation
3. padding with hexadecimal zeros to the left
4. maximum constant length is 256 bytes (512 hexadecimal digits)

3.2.5 Binary Constants

A binary constant is specified by a group of bits (0's and 1's) in the operand portion of a DC instruction. The bits will be stored exactly as written in the DC instruction, with appropriate truncation and padding. The implicit length is the number of bytes occupied by the constant itself with any necessary high-order zeros so that entire bytes will be filled (for example, if a combination of 12 bits is specified, requiring one and a half bytes, then 4 high-order zeros will be appended, to require 16 bits or 2 bytes).

As we have seen for other constant types, when explicit and implicit lengths disagree, the explicit length is adhered to by the assembler in assigning storage. Appropriate padding (with 0 bits) or truncation occurs on the left. As in the case of hexadecimal constants, the "B" type operand is used when we are interested in storing specific bit configurations, as opposed to storing specific numeric values.

To define and store binary constants, we use the following form:

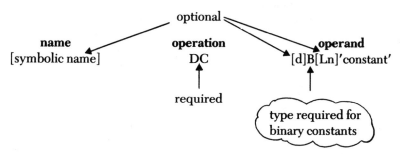

Consider the following examples:

Instruction	Internal representation (bits)	Internal representation (hex)
DC B'11110000'	11110000	F 0
DC B'11101'	00011101	1 D
	padding	
DC BL2'11101'	0000000000011101	0 0 1 D
	padding: explicit length exceeds implicit length	
DC BL1'111100001001'	00001001	0 9
	↑ left truncation	

Summary

In its translating activity, the assembler will be cognizant of the following rules for the storage of binary constants:
1. eight bits per byte; right justify
2. left truncation
3. padding with 0-bits to the left
4. maximum constant length is 256 bytes

DUPLICATION FACTOR

One moment! We almost forgot something very important: the duplication factor.

The function of the duplication factor is to allow repetition of a constant a number of times in consecutive storage locations. For packed and zoned numbers, repetition may be specified as many times as needed up until but not exceeding the allowed 16 bytes; however, for EBCDIC, hexadecimal and binary constants, a total of 256 bytes are allowed.

Examples:

    1.   DC   4CL8'MOSQUITO'
    is equivalent to
        DC   CL8'MOSQUITO'
        DC   CL8'MOSQUITO'
        DC   CL8'MOSQUITO'
        DC   CL8'MOSQUITO'

2. DC   3PL2'123'
    is equivalent to
        DC   PL2'123'
        DC   PL2'123'
        DC   PL2'123'

3. DC   2Z'23,42,6'
    is equivalent to
        DC   Z'23,42,6'
        DC   Z'23,42,6'
    and to
        DC   Z'23'
        DC   Z'42'
        DC   Z'6'
        DC   Z'23'
        DC   Z'42'
        DC   Z'6'

A constant will be repeated in storage only after the appropriate length (implicit or explicit) has been assigned. That is, the instruction

A	DC	2XL2'F0'	will generate	00 F0 00 F0;
B	DC	2XL2'F0D0C0'	will generate	D0 C0 D0 C0;
C	DC	4XL1'F0D0C0'	will generate	C0 C0 C0 C0.

Another important point with regard to duplication is that the name assigned by the DC instruction will refer *only* to the leftmost field stored by the instruction. Thus, for the storage contents generated above, we have

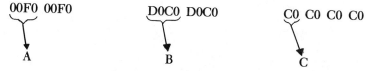

In order to refer to duplications (repetitions) of the named fields, the programmer would resort to relative addressing. Thus the duplication of A would be referred to as

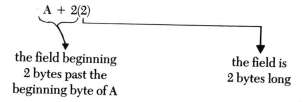

The respective duplications of B and C would likewise be referred to as:

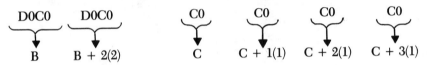

$$\underbrace{\text{D0C0}}_{B} \quad \underbrace{\text{D0C0}}_{B + 2(2)} \qquad \underbrace{\text{C0}}_{C} \quad \underbrace{\text{C0}}_{C + 1(1)} \quad \underbrace{\text{C0}}_{C + 2(1)} \quad \underbrace{\text{C0}}_{C + 3(1)}$$

The DC Instruction (**D**efine **C**onstant)

Instruction type: Assembler Instruction

Symbolic format:

name	operation	operand
[symbolic name]	DC	[d]t[Ln]'constant'

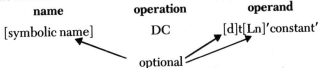

optional

where d is an unsigned integer (it may also be zero) which is a duplication factor. It tells the assembler how many identical areas are
desired. When one area is required, the duplication factor may
be omitted.

t is the type of constant to be represented. These types include:

Type	Remarks	Max Length in Bytes	Adjust-ment	Padding and Truncation	Padding Character
C	character (EBCDIC) constant	256	left	on the right	blank
X	hexadecimal constant	256	right	on the left	hex 0
B	binary constant	256	right	on the left	binary 0
P	packed constant	16	right	on the left	packed 0
Z	zoned constant	16	right	on the left	zoned 0
H	halfword	8	right	on the left	binary 0 or 1, depending upon sign
F	fullword	8	right	on the left	

(fixed point binary constants)

Types also include "address constants" (to be explained in chapter 12). Yet other constant types, which are not used in this book, are described in the manufacturer's manual.

Ln is the length of the storage area in bytes, explicitly specified.

L stands for length.

n is an unsigned integer representing the number of bytes to be allocated.

'constant' designates the actual symbols we want to store. The single quotation marks must enclose the constant.

. . . .

Rules:
- The entries specified for the operand portion of the instruction, if used, must appear in the order specified.
- Other format rules were summarized for each type subfield separately, along with our discussion of those subfields.

3.3 LITERALS

A literal is a specification of data to be used in a program. It is written in exactly the same way as the operand of a DC instruction (with a few differences, which we shall list) but is preceded by an equality sign (=). For example,

$$= \text{C'HOW ARE YOU'}$$
$$= 2\text{P'23'}$$
$$= \text{Z'}-4'$$
$$= \text{X'F0'}$$

are literals. The main advantage of literals is that they may be used in the operand portions of instructions, so that the programmer avoids having to write a DC assembler instruction to store the data. (The DC would be written in order to use the name assigned by the DC in the instruction operand.) That is

```
          MVC     BOX,=C'APPLE'
BOX       DC      CL5'PEARS'
```

performs the same function as:

```
          MVC     BOX,FRUIT
BOX       DC      CL5'PEARS'
FRUIT     DC      C'APPLE'
```

When a literal is specified in an instruction, the assembler program will:

1. Assemble the specified data—that is, represent the data in the format requested by the literal
2. Store the assembled data in a special place called the **literal pool**, which is usually at the end of the program
3. Place the address of the data (the location number within the literal pool at which the data is stored) into the operand portion of the instruction which specifies the literal

Thus we see that the machine language version of an instruction which specifies a literal references the *contents of an address* in which the desired constant is stored (this address will be in the literal pool), and *not* the constant itself! This way of interpreting instruction operands—as contents of locations—is of course typical of assembly language instructions. (There is a category of machine instructions—the SI or Storage Immediate instructions—in which *data itself*, rather than the address of data, is assembled into the instruction. Do *not* confuse literals with this category. Literals are assembled into instructions as addresses—we merely save the work of defining the constant separately.)

The programmer must adhere to several rules when using literals:

- A literal may only appear in one operand of an instruction.
- A literal may not be used in the receiving field of an instruction. Literals introduce *data* to a program, but names are not assigned to the addresses of literals. A literal is not to be altered by the programmer. It is used when we wish to introduce constant data to the program *without* reserving storage area which need be referenced.
- Literals may not be used as part of assembler instructions.
- The duplication factor of a literal may not be 0. (In other words, storage must be assigned.)
- The duplication factor and length modifiers, when used, must be unsigned decimal numbers.

Duplicate Literals

If identical literals, which cause identical constants to be stored, are designated to be placed within the same literal pool, the assembler will only store one.

For example,

$$
\left.\begin{array}{l} = X'01' \\ = B'00000001' \end{array}\right\}
\quad
\begin{array}{l} \text{both literals will be stored,} \\ \text{although both result in the} \\ \text{same combination of stored bits} \end{array}
$$

$$
\left.\begin{array}{l} = X'F2' \\ = C'2' \end{array}\right\}
\quad
\begin{array}{l} \text{both are stored, although the} \\ \text{assembled constants are identical} \end{array}
$$

$$= C'2' \quad \left.\begin{array}{l} \\ \\ \end{array}\right\} \quad \text{only one is stored}$$
$$= C'2'$$

$$= P'4' \quad \left.\begin{array}{l} \\ \\ \end{array}\right\} \quad \text{both are stored; the assembled}$$
$$= Z'4' \quad \quad\quad\quad \text{constants are different}$$

Program examples throughout this text will use literals when it is convenient to do so. Remember, however, that their use is limited, for the locations in which literals are stored may not be referenced by name, nor may literals be used in the receiving fields of machine instructions.

3.4   THE DS INSTRUCTION: STORAGE DEFINITION

The DS instruction directs the assembler to perform the same functions as the DC, with one exception: the DS does not place constant data into computer storage. It thus directs the assembler to:
- Define and reserve one or more storage areas
- Specify the size of the area being reserved
- Associate a name with the area (optional)

For example, the instruction

        AREA   DS   PL4

directs the assembler to set aside an area in memory called AREA to contain data in packed form (type P). The area will be 4 bytes long (L4). The instruction does *not*, however, cause any constant data to be placed into AREA, nor is AREA set to zeros. In other words, the programmer may not make any assumption as to the contents of AREA.

The DS Instruction (**Define Storage**)

Instruction type: Assembler Instruction

Symbolic format:

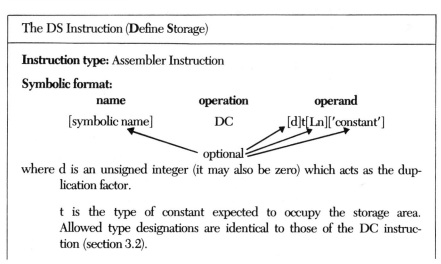

where d is an unsigned integer (it may also be zero) which acts as the duplication factor.

t is the type of constant expected to occupy the storage area. Allowed type designations are identical to those of the DC instruction (section 3.2).

Ln is the length of the storage area in bytes, explicitly specified.

L stands for length.

n is an unsigned integer representing the number of bytes to be allocated.

'constant' is an *optional* subfield in the DS instruction. It is some constant value which is meant only to indicate the general form of the data which the programmer expects to be placed into the storage area during execution. The DS instruction will *not* actually place the constant data into this area, nor will it place the data anywhere else.

. . . .

Rules:
- The entries specified for the operand portion of the instruction, if used, must appear in the order specified.
- All other format rules for the DS operand are identical to those of the DC operand, as explained for the C (character), P (packed), Z (zoned), X (hexadecimal), and B (binary) type subfields in section 3.2 above, with two differences:
    - (i) The 'constant' subfield is optional in a DS operand. However if it is specified, it must be valid (it must conform to the specified type designation for that operand. For example, if the type designation is P, the constant must be numeric and must conform to all rules for the P type designation).
    - (ii) The maximum constant length for field types C (character) and X (hexadecimal) is 65,535 bytes. (In the DC instruction, the maximum length was 256 bytes for field types C and X).

Examples:

DS Instructions			Field(s) defined
FLD1	DS	CL60	One 60-byte character field named FLD1.
FLD2	DS	60CL1	Sixty 1-byte character fields. The leftmost field is named FLD2.
FLD3	DS	XL3	One 3-byte hexadecimal field called FLD3.

FLD4	DS	X'FF'	One 1-byte hexadecimal field called FLD4. The constant 'FF' is *not assembled or stored*. It serves merely to indicate that one byte (the implicit length) is to be reserved.
FLD5	DS	X'FFD'	One 2-byte hexadecimal field called FLD5. (The constant is *not* stored).
FLD6	DS	XL2'FD'	One 2-byte hexadecimal field (Explicit length supercedes implicit length).

Subdividing a Storage Area

A DS assembler instruction with a duplication factor of zero may be used to assign a name to a storage area without actually reserving that area. Subsequent combinations of DS and/or DC instructions may then be used to actually reserve the area.

For example, we may wish to define an input area to hold data being read into memory. Let us assume that we have an 80-character input record with a "name" field in positions 1-20, a "salary" field in positions 21-25, and a "commission" field in positions 27-30. We define the input area as follows:

```
INAREA    DS    0CL80
NAME      DS    CL20
SALARY    DS    CL5
          DS    CL1
COMMIS    DS    CL4
          DS    CL50
```

The first DS instruction above assigns the name INAREA to an 80-character main storage area (CL80). However the duplication factor of 0 designates that the area not yet be reserved. The name INAREA will thus refer to the 80 main storage locations which are defined next. The subsequent 80 bytes will thus be *part of INAREA*, and will describe the appropriate field layout within INAREA. The NAME field constitutes the first 20 characters followed by a 5-character SALARY field. One unused character separates the SALARY field from the 4-byte COMMIS field. Fifty unused character positions complete the description of INAREA.

Notice that the area subdivision demonstrated above enables us to assign a name (INAREA) to the entire input area while assigning other names to individual fields within the area. This technique is particularly useful for describing input and output data layouts, but will be helpful for other situations as well. For example, if an "employee number" assigned by a business firm identifies the division and the department of the firm in which the employee works, the field which represents the employee number may be subdivided so that those values may be separately identified and referenced:

```
EMPNO      DS      0CL8
DIVISION   DS      CL3
DEPT       DS      CL3
NUMB       DS      CL2
```

Moreover, the employee number may be subdivided even if it is itself part of a larger subdivision:

```
INAREA     DS      0CL80
EMPNO      DS      0CL8      ⎫ employee
DIVISION   DS      CL3       ⎬ number:
DEPT       DS      CL3       ⎪ 8 bytes
NUMB       DS      CL2       ⎭
NAME       DS      CL20
SALARY     DS      CL5
           DS      CL1
COMMIS     DS      CL4
           DS      CL42
```

⎫ input area: 80 bytes

It is also possible for the subdivision to be effected by combining DS and DC instructions. For example, let us describe an output line in which output fields are to be separated by blanks, as follows:

We present the definition of an appropriate output area below:

```
OUTAREA    DS      0CL132
           DC      CL1' '
DIVISION   DS      CL3
           DC      CL1' '
DEPT       DS      CL3
           DC      CL1' '
NUMB       DS      CL2
           DC      CL6' '
NAME       DS      CL20
           DC      CL6' '
SALARY     DS      CL5
           DC      CL6' '
COMMIS     DS      CL4
           DC      CL74' '
```

The use of DC instructions for placing blanks in locations which separate output fields eliminates the need for placing blanks into those locations during program execution. (Remember that the DC and the DS are assembler instructions and are effected during the assembly phase which precedes program execution.)

3.5   OUR SECOND PROGRAM

Let us now consider a programming problem which will make use of the DC and DS instructions. In chapter 2 we have seen how the employees of the Mickey Mousetrap Company were introduced to programming through an application which read input data from cards and produced printed output. In that program, each ordered input record contained a line of a picture. When the input records were output in printed form, the printed output was a picture of a reindeer.

The basic logical step of the reindeer problem was to read input records and print exact copies of those records. Suppose that in an effort to expand that basic step, the company attempted to change the input data in some way before printing. That is, rather than simply "copying" our input records, we wish to produce output in which the input fields are separated by blanks on the output line.

A simple application of this type of logic is the development of an employee telephone directory. Each input record will have information about a particular employee: the name, title, division and department, telephone number and extension. Output will consist of a printed directory listing the input information, appropriately spaced on output lines. For simplicity, we will assume that the input data is in alphabetical order, so that the printed directory will be easy and practical to use. (It is of course possible for the computer to alphabetize the names as well. However the instructions necessary for "comparing" data will first be introduced in chapter 5.)

Before embarking on writing the computer instructions for our telephone directory problem, it will be very useful for us to examine the various steps through which problem solution should be approached. Having a clearly defined way of approaching a problem will make it simpler for us to solve more difficult problems in the future. The following discussion is applicable to computer solution in general.

3.6   THE ROAD TO PROBLEM SOLUTION

The road to the solution of a problem by the computer consists of several steps. They are outlined below and will be explained in this chapter and in chapter 14. When you are assigned a computer program in this book, the first step will usually be provided by us; however in industry this job will usually be performed by a systems analyst in consultation with a programmer; the programmer will do the rest.

The steps for problem solution are:

1. Understanding the problem
      A. Defining the input
      B. Defining the output
      C. Describing the steps required to produce the desired output (flowcharting)

2. Coding—Writing instructions for computer solution.

3. Recording—The instructions and the data are transcribed onto a medium for transfer to computer memory.

4. Assembly, link-editing, and execution—These were briefly described in chapter 2 and will again be considered in chapter 12.

5. Testing and debugging—Just as a car manufacturer will check the workings of his product before it is sold, so will a programmer check his programs to ensure that they function properly. If errors are found, the programmer will correct them. A program error is called a **bug**, and the process of detecting and correcting bugs is called **debugging**. Chapter 14 will describe various techniques and aids which may be used by the programmer for debugging. An ordered, step by step approach to debugging will be used.

6. Documentation—After the job has been completed and debugged and is functioning as intended, the programmer organizes the documents (layout forms, flowcharts, listings and the like) generated in each step, with detailed explanations of each. He includes directives for future users of the program. This package (the set of documents together with explanations and directives to users) created is his program **documentation**.

3.6.1   Understanding the Problem

A.   Defining the input

The process of describing the input to a problem involves several decisions on the part of the programmer.

First he must decide what data is to be included. For the employee telephone directory problem described in section 3.5, we will need the following fields (items): employee name, title, division and department, telephone number and extension. The programmer must then choose the medium on which these fields will be recorded for computer processing; in our text the input medium will be the punched card, so that the data will be transferred into storage by a card reader. In many real life applications, it may be most convenient to choose tape or disk.

Furthermore, the "layout" of input data on the punched card must be determined. This means that you will have to examine each data item (field), and decide on the length to be allocated. This decision will naturally be influenced by your estimate of the maximum lengths of the fields to be used for the particular application. For example, it may suffice in your judgement to allocate the following lengths: the name is to occupy 20 columns, the title 15 columns, the division 2 columns (each division is assigned a unique 2 digit number), the department 3 columns (each is assigned a unique 3 digit number), the telephone number 10 columns (a 3 digit area code followed by a 7 digit telephone number), the extension 3 columns. In addition to determining field length, you must decide where and in what order each field is to be placed on the medium. On-job experience will teach you how to do this most efficiently. Many firms will require (and most programmers will find it convenient) that the layout be specified in pictorial form; a special form is used for this purpose, called a **card layout form** (figure 3.3).

If you examine figure 3.3, you will notice that fields were planned to appear adjoining each other with no spaces separating them. This arrangement minimizes keypunching time, and leaves more room for additional fields if they should be needed. It is obvious that human readability is compromised here, since the intent of the punched card is for machine consumption.

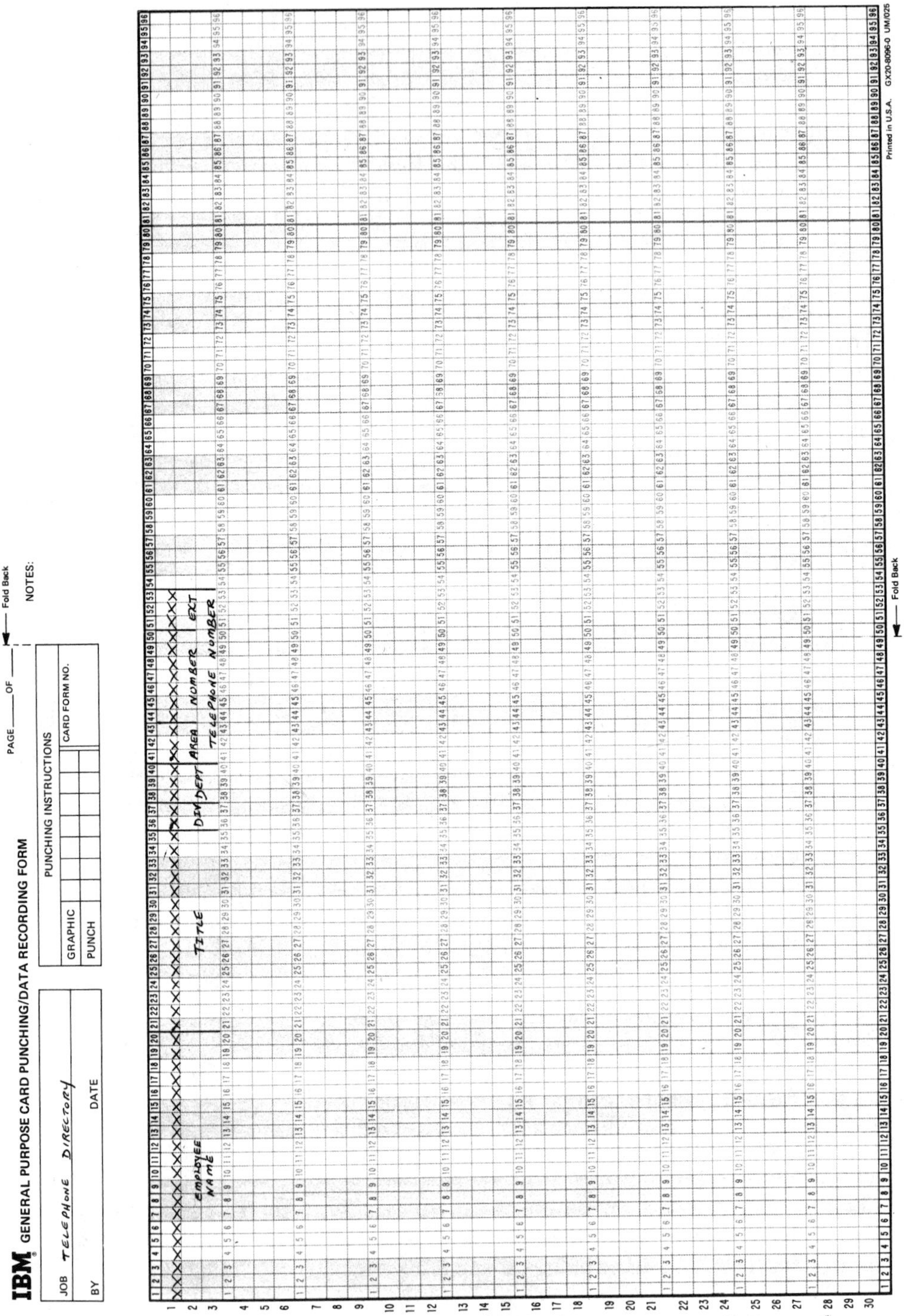

Figure 3.3
Card Layout Form for Telephone Directory Problem

The fields first defined are related to each other and are organized in a specific manner; they thus constitute a **record**, as we explained in chapter 1.

B.   Defining the Output

The user provides the programmer and/or the systems analyst with information as to the desired output medium and the form of the information the computer is to produce. In our example, the output medium will be continuous form paper to be produced by a machine called the printer. On this paper, each line constitutes an output record with a maximum size of 132 characters (the size of printer records may vary, but 132 characters is typical). Computer manufacturers provide a special form called a **printer layout form** (figure 3.4) to assist the programmer in planning the arrangement of program output.

For our telephone directory problem, we have 2 types of output lines: a **heading line** which is composed of constant information determined by the user and implemented by the programmer and **detail lines** which contain information which varies from record to record.

The programmer uses the printer layout form to plan the appearance and arrangement of the data on the output record. The programmer also uses this form to communicate layout information to the user as part of the program documentation.

C.   Flowcharting

In order to produce output from input, the computer must be supplied with a well organized sequence of detailed instructions. When writing a program, the programmer is concerned with selecting the proper instructions and arranging them in a correct and logical sequence so that the specified output will be produced. The detail of writing the instructions themselves is at times overwhelming enough to cause the programmer to lose perception of the overall logic of the problem. This loss of perception might cause him to commit errors of several types, among them missing instructions or the arrangement of instructions in incorrect order.

A tool called a **flowchart template** was developed to aid the programmer in developing a pictorial description or **flowchart** of his problem logic. Thus the programmer need not memorize the details of program logic, and may concentrate fully on coding the individual instructions, using the flowchart as a guide. The template pictured in figure 3.5 has many shapes outlined. Most of them, however, are used by systems analysts in systems design.

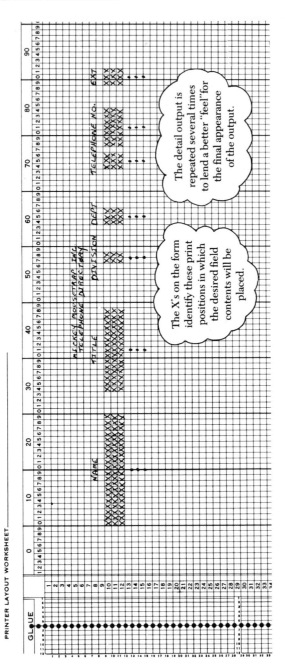

Figure 3.4

Printer Layout Form for Telephone Directory Problem

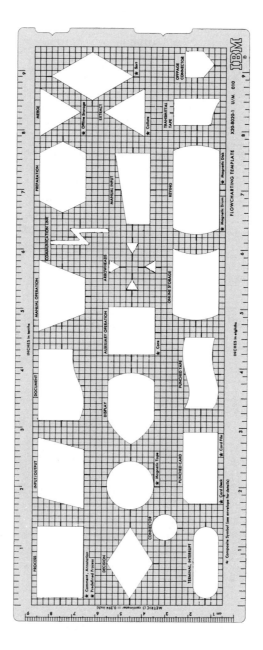

Figure 3.5
Flowchart Template

The computer programmer is primarily concerned with the following symbols:

The **terminal symbol**: used to depict the beginning and the end of a program.

The **decision symbol**: used to indicate alternate paths which may be chosen by the computer in the course of processing. The choice of path will depend upon the presence or absence of some condition.

The **input/output symbol**: used to describe input and output operations.

The **process symbol**: used for any other processing operation aside from those mentioned above.

The **connector symbol**: used to indicate entry to or exit from another part of the program flowchart.

It is the authors' feeling that flowcharting is a technique for which time, effort, and considerable practice is required before true proficiency is developed. In this text, we will generally provide flowcharts along with our problem descriptions; if you study the flowcharts presented, you should develop the confidence to flowchart on your own.

Before attempting to flowchart a problem, you must first have a clear understanding of the logic (sequence of steps) necessary for the computer to solve the problem. Let us now describe the logic necessary to solve the employee telephone directory problem.

The employee telephone directory problem will begin with **housekeeping** (preparatory) operations: opening the files (the OPEN macros), and setting up the base register (BALR and USING instructions). These steps are followed by printing the heading information.

The programmer's main concern from this point on is to instruct the computer to read one card at a time; to place the data into the input area; to rearrange the fields in the output or buffer area so that they will be positioned relative to each other in the same manner that the programmer indicated in his plan on the printer layout form. This will require movement of individual fields from the input area to the output area. Finally we will tell

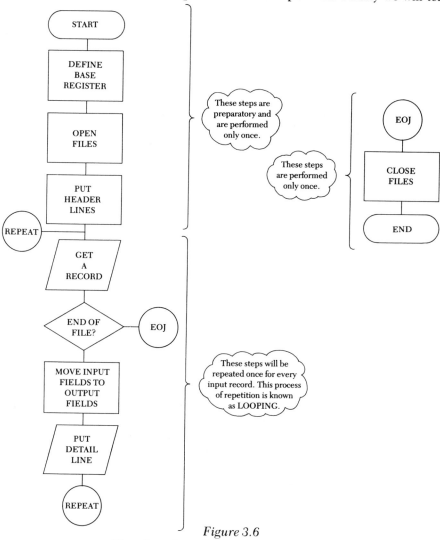

Figure 3.6
Flowchart for Telephone Directory Problem

the computer to print the newly arranged output record. This process will be repeated for every input record. These steps constitute the program **mainline**: the main body of program logic.

When all records have been exhausted, we will instruct the computer to close the program files and stop execution.

Our verbal description may be formalized in flowchart form as in figure 3.6.

Note that:
- A flowchart is developed and read from top to bottom and from left to right.
- The flowchart symbols may be hand drawn, or drawn with a template.
- Ordinary paper may be used to draw a flowchart, or you may use special forms designed for this purpose (see figure 3.7).
- The choice of wording used for description within flowchart symbols (shapes) is relatively arbitrary. A flowchart should clearly and efficiently communicate the steps to be followed in writing the program; the only requirement is for clarity and conciseness. You might find it useful to use wording which is similar to the instructions in your program.
- A flowchart symbol may describe one or more steps. It is the programmer who decides how many steps to include in each flowchart symbol.
- The amount of detail presented in a flowchart is variable. As a consequence, the size of the flowchart for a particular program may vary from programmer to programmer.

3.6.2   Coding the Solution

After describing the problem logic in a flowchart, we use a coding form to write the computer instructions; the flowchart serves as a guide.

Below you will find the coded solution, in assembly language, to the employee telephone directory problem, along with the flowchart solution presented above. As you read the program, you will notice that all the instructions, up until the area definitions, were fully discussed in chapter 2. The part of the program in which the main storage areas are reserved and constants are defined makes use of the DC and DS instructions explained in sections 3.2 and 3.4 above.

Read the assembly language code of figure 3.8 carefully, paying special attention to the use of DC and DS instructions. Note that the input and output areas are defined using a zero duplication factor. We also have a subdivision within a subdivision (IPHONE, which is comprised of IAREA, INUM, and IEXT, is itself part of INAREA). If you have a question with regard to the use of a particular instruction, refer back to the appropriate section of the text.

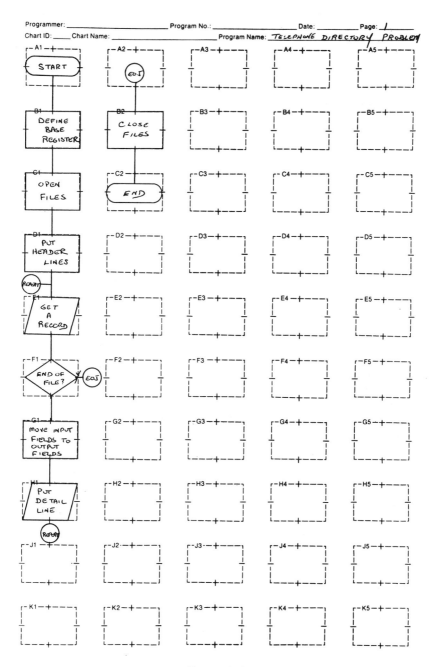

Figure 3.7
Program Flowchart on Flowchart Form

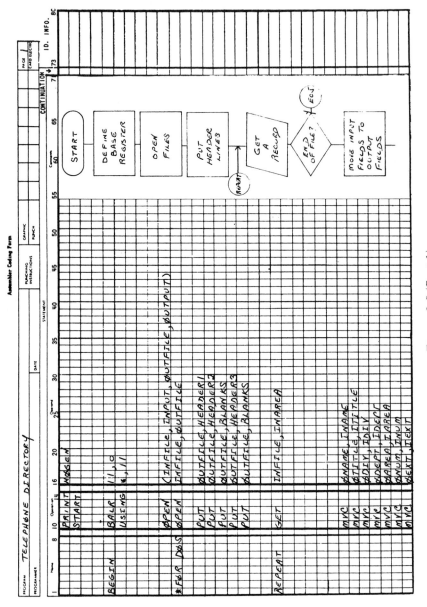

Figure 3.8 (Part 1)
Code for Telephone Directory Problem

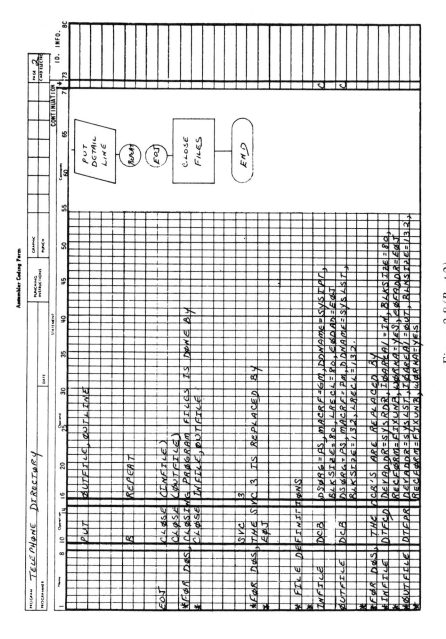

Figure 3.8 (Part 2)
Code for Telephone Directory Problem

Assembler Coding Form

PROGRAM TELEPHONE DIRECTORY   PAGE 3

Name	Operation	Operand	Comments
IN	DS	CL80	IN IS NAME OF INPUT BUFFER AREA FOR DES
OUT	DS	CL132	OUT IS NAME OF OUTPUT BUFFER AREA FOR DES
*			
* AREA DEFINITIONS			
*			
* INPUT AREA			
INAREA	DS	0CL80	
INNAME	DS	CL20	
ITITLE	DS	CL15	
IDIV	DS	CL2	
IDEPT	DS	CL3	
ITPHONE	DS	0CL13	
IAREA	DS	CL3	
INUM	DS	CL7	
TEXT	DS	CL3	
	DS	CL27	
* HEADER LINES			
HEADER1	DC	CL132'ETRAP INC.'	MILKEY MOUSE
HEADER2	DC	CL132'DIRECTORY'	TELEPHONE C
HEADER3	DC	CL132'DIVISION DEPT NAME TELEPHONE NO. TITLE'	TITLE C
BLANKS	DC	CL132' EXIT'	
* OUTPUT LINE			
OUTLINE	DS	0CL132	
	DC	CL9' '	
ONAME	DS	CL20	

Figure 3.8 (Part 3)
Code for Telephone Directory Problem

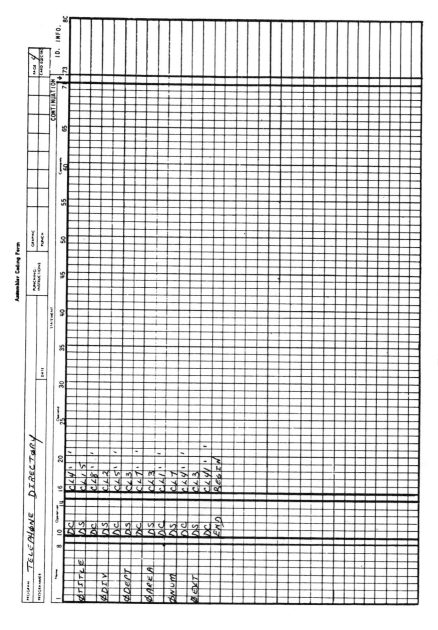

Figure 3.8 (Part 4)
Code for Telephone Directory Problem

After writing the program solution on a coding form, we must record the instructions and data on an appropriate input medium, in this case punched cards, for input to the computer. Assembly, link-editing, and execution then take place, to be followed by testing and debugging to ensure that the program works. The programmer then documents the entire package. These steps were listed at the beginning of section 3.6.

The program listing and output are presented in figure 3.9.

```
  LOC  OBJECT CODE    ADDR1 ADDR2  STMT   SOURCE STATEMENT

                                     1  *
                                     2            PRINT  NOGEN
  CCCCCC                             3            START
                                     4  *
  CCCCCC  C580                       5  BEGIN    BALR   11,0
                             CCCU2   6            USING  *,11
                                     7  *
  CCCCC2                             9            OPEN   (INFILE,INPUT,OUTFILE,OUTPUT)
                                    16  *
                                    17  *FOR DOS,OPEN  INFILE,OUTFILE
                                    18  *
  CCCC12                            19            PUT    OUTFILE,HEADER1
  CCCC2C                            24            PUT    OUTFILE,HEADER2
  CCCC2E                            29            PUT    OUTFILE,BLANKS
  CCCC3C                            34            PUT    OUTFILE,HEADER3
  CCCC4A                            39            PUT    OUTFILE,BLANKS
                                    44  *
  CCCC58                            45  REPEAT   GET    INFILE,INAREA
                                    50  *
  CCCC66  D213 B3E3 B17A  CC3F5 CO17C  51        MVC    CNAME,INAME
  CCCC6C  D2CE B3FB B1BE  CC3FD CC190  52        MVC    CTITLE,ITITLE
  CCCC72  C201 B412 B19D  CU414 CO19F  53        MVC    CCIV,ICIV
  CCCC78  D202 B419 B19F  CC41B CO1A1  54        MVC    CCEPT,ICEPT
  CCCC7E  D202 B423 B1A2  CO425 CO1A4  55        MVC    CAREA,IAREA
  CCCC84  D2C6 B427 B1A5  CO429 CO1A7  56        MVC    ONUM,INUM
  CCCC8A  D2C2 B432 B1AC  CC434 CC1AE  57        MVC    CEXT,IEXT
                                    58  *
  CCCC9C                            59            PUT    OUTFILE,OUTLINE
                                    64  *
  CCCC9E  47F0 BC56        CCC58    65            B      REPEAT
                                    66  *
  CCCCA2                            67  EOJ      CLOSE  (INFILE)
  CCCCAE                            73            CLOSE  (OUTFILE)
                                    79  *FOR DOS,CLOSING PROGRAM FILES IS DONE BY
                                    80  *            CLOSE  INFILE,OUTFILE
                                    81  *
  CCCCBA  CAC3                      82            SVC    3
                                    83  *FOR DOS,THE SVC 3 IS REPLACED BY
                                    84  *            EOJ
                                    85  *
                                    86  * FILE DEFINITIONS
                                    87  *
                                    88  INFILE   DCB    DSCRG=PS,MACRF=GM,DDNAME=SYSIPT,   C
  CCCCBC                                                BLKSIZE=80,LRECL=80,EODAD=EOJ
  CCCC11C                          142  OUTFILE  DCB    DSCRG=PS,MACRF=PM,DDNAME=SYSLST,   C
                                                        BLKSIZE=132,LRECL=132
                                   196  *
                                   197  *FOR DOS, THE DCB'S ARE REPLACED BY
                                   198  *INFILE  DTFCD DEVADCR=SYSRDR,IOAREA1=IN,BLKSIZE=80,
                                   199  *            RECFORM=FIXUNB,WORKA=YES,EOFADDR=EOJ
                                   200  *OUTFILE DTFPR DEVADDR=SYSLST,IOAREA1=OUT,BLKSIZE=132,
                                   201  *            RECFORM=FIXUNB,WORKA=YES
                                   202  *IN       DS    CL80   IN IS NAME OF INPUT BUFFER AREA FOR DOS
                                   203  *OUT      DS    CL132  OUT IS NAME OF OUTPUT BUFFER AREA FOR DOS
                                   204  *
```

Figure 3.9 (Part 1)
Telephone Directory Program: Listing

```
LOC    OBJECT CODE      ADDR1 ADDR2  STMT    SOURCE STATEMENT
                                     205 * AREA DEFINITIONS
                                     206 *
                                     207 * INPUT AREA
CCC17C                               208 INAREA   DS    OCL80
CCC17C                               209 INAME    DS    CL20
CCC15C                               210 ITITLE   DS    CL15
CCC19F                               211 IDIV     DS    CL2
CCC1A1                               212 IDEPT    DS    CL3
CCC1A4                               213 IPHCNE   DS    OCL13
CCC1A4                               214 IAREA    DS    CL3
CCC1A7                               215 INUM     DS    CL7
CCC1AE                               216 IEXT     DS    CL3
CCC1B1                               217          DS    CL27
                                     218 *
                                     219 * HEADER LINES
                                     220 *
CCC1CC 4C404C404C4C4040              221 HEADER1  DC    CL132'                MICKEY MOUSC
                                                        ETRAP INC.'
CCC25C 404040404C4C4040              222 HEADER2  DC    CL132'                   TELEPHONE C
                                                        DIRECTORY'
C0C2D4 4C4C4C4C4C4C4C4C              223 HEADER3  DC    CL132'          NAME            TITLE         C
                                                        DIVISION  DEPT   TELEPHONE NO.   EXT'
CCC358 4C4040404C4C4C4C              224 BLANKS   DC    CL132' '
                                     225 *
                                     226 * CUTPUT LINE
                                     227 *
CCC3CC                               228 CUTLINE  DS    OCL132
CCC3CC 4C40404C4C4C4040              229          DC    CL9' '
CCC3E5                               230 CNAME    DS    CL20
CCC3F9 40404C4C                      231          DC    CL4' '
CCC3FD                               232 CTITLE   DS    CL15
CCC4CC 404040404C4C4040              233          DC    CL8' '
CCC414                               234 ODIV     DS    CL2
CCC416 4C40404C4C                    235          DC    CL5' '
CCC41E                               236 CDEPT    DS    CL3
CCC41E 404040404C4C4040              237          DC    CL7' '
CCC425                               238 OAREA    DS    CL3
CCC428 40                            239          DC    CL1' '
CCC429                               240 CNUM     DS    CL7
CCC43C 40404040                      241          DC    CL4' '
CCC434                               242 OEXT     DS    CL3
CCC437 4C4C4C4C4C404040              243          DC    CL41' '
CCCCCC                               244          END   BEGIN
```

Figure 3.9 (Part 2)
Telephone Directory Program: Listing

```
                        MICKEY MOUSETRAP INC.
                        TELEPHCNE CIRECTCRY

         NAME              TITLE          DIVISION  DEPT    TELEPHONE NO.   EXT

    CAMPBELL ANNE      ASST MANAGER          01      001    214 2445324     444
    FARR HAROLD        MANAGER               12      345    670 2345557     772
    GEORGE WINNIE      ASST MANAGER          02      100    456 789C123     221
    JEANS BLUE         BUYER                 03      032    456 789C123     544
    JOHNSON CALVIN     SALESMAN              04      022    456 789C123     521
    MEIR GOLDA         PRIME MINISTER        05      044    788 2134502     024
    SMITH JOHN         MANAGER               10      034    456 789C123     655
```

Figure 3.9 (Part 3)
Telephone Directory Program: Output

Summary

In this chapter, two techniques for placing constant data into main storage were discussed. These involved use of the DC (Define Constant) instruction and the use of literals in the operand portion of machine instructions. In addition, the DS (Define Storage) instruction for defining main storage areas was presented.

We described the sequence of steps which a programmer should follow in analyzing and solving a programming problem. This process of planning the program logic, describing it in flowchart form, and coding the solution, is carried out for a program which produces a printed telephone directory.

Important Terms Discussed in Chapter 3

binary constant
bug

card layout form
connector symbol
constant

debugging
decision symbol
detail line
documentation
duplication factor

explicit length

flowchart
flowchart template

heading line
hexadecimal constant
housekeeping

implicit length
input/output symbol

left justify
length factor
literal
literal pool

mainline
modifier
multiple constant

packed constant
pad (padding character)
printer layout form
process symbol

right justify

terminal symbol
truncation

zoned constant

Questions

3-1. Name the 5 steps involved in solving a problem through use of the computer.

3-2. What is the purpose of a *card layout form*? Of a *printer layout form*?

3-3. What is the purpose of a flowchart? May there be more than one correct flow-chart for a particular problem? Explain.

3-4. What will be the contents of computer memory generated by each of the DC instructions below? Use hexadecimal notation.

(a)	ONE	DC	C'THIS IS EASY'
(b)	TWO	DC	CL4'ARE YOU SURE?'
(c)	THREE	DC	CL10'YES'
(d)	FOUR	DC	C'''LET'S GO'''
(e)	FIVE	DC	C'''''''
(f)	SIX	DC	CL12'1122&&''44AA'
(g)	SEVEN	DC	CL8'1,234,567'
(h)	EIGHT	DC	CL8'1234567'

3-5. Represent each of the numbers below in both packed and zoned formats.

(a)   75
(b)   − 42
(c)   − 800
(d)   0

3-6. What will be the contents of computer memory generated by each of the DC instructions below? Use hexadecimal notation.

(a)	D	DC	P'12'
(b)	E	DC	PL2'143444'
(c)	C	DC	PL5'0'
(d)	I	DC	2PL1'1.2'
(e)	M	DC	P'76,−44,8.95'
(f)	A	DC	2PL2'−1,+22,−33.3,+9444,−50'
(g)	L	DC	ZL2'482'
(h)		DC	2Z'+891'
(i)	N	DC	3ZL1'500'
(j)	O	DC	ZL6'−7'
(k)	S	DC	2ZL2'−6.68,−1,+99'
(l)		DC	Z'7.777'

3-7. Write three *different* DC instructions to store *each* of the following hexadecimal values.

    (a) C1D8E4
    (b) F1F3F8
    (c) F4F9D2
    (d) C8

3-8. What will be the contents of computer memory generated by each of the DC instructions below? Use hexadecimal notation.

(a)		DC	2X'F0C0'
(b)		DC	XL2'C4'
(c)		DC	XL4'00'
(d)		DC	X'FED'
(e)	B	DC	B'111'
(f)	I	DC	2BL2'11'
(g)	T	DC	3BL1'0101010110101010'
(h)	S	DC	2B'11110000'

3-9. What is the maximum constant length for EBCDIC constants? packed constants? zoned constants? hexadecimal constants? binary constants?

3-10. What are "multiple constants"?

3-11. What is the function of the duplication factor?

3-12. Answer the following questions as they apply to
        EBCDIC constants
        packed constants
        zoned constants
        hexadecimal constants
        binary constants

    (i) Does justification occur to the right or to the left?
    (ii) Does truncation, when necessary, occur on the right or on the left?
    (iii) What characters, if any, are used for padding?

3-13. What is the main advantage to using literals in an assembly language program?

3-14. May a literal be used in the receiving field of an instruction? Explain.

3-15. What is a *literal pool?*

3-16. Suppose that program instructions designate five different identical literals. How many such literals will be stored?

3-17. Distinguish between the functions of the DC and DS instructions.

3-18. Assume that we are coding an assembly language program which is to accept input records on punched cards, with the following input layout:

field	card columns
A	1-3
B	4-5
C	7-10
D	12

Write the assembler instructions to describe an appropriate input area for these records. Call the input area IN.

3-19. The program which accepts the input records discussed above (question 18) is to produce printed output as described below, with blanks separating the output fields.

field	print positions
A	4-6
B	13-14
C	21-24
D	31

Write the assembler instructions to describe an appropriate output area. Call the output area OUT.

3-20. Write an assembly language program which accepts the card input described in question 18 above and produces printed output along with heading lines, as described in figure 3.10 below:

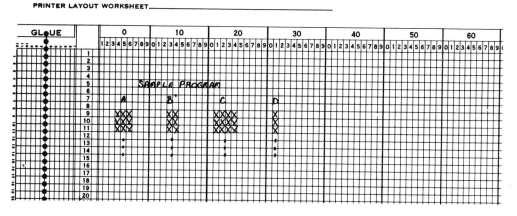

Figure 3.10

Unit

2

The Decimal Instruction Set

Chapter 4

Decimal Arithmetic— Operations with Packed Integer Values

DECIMAL ARITHMETIC—
OPERATIONS WITH PACKED INTEGER VALUES

Now that we are familiar with EBCDIC, packed, and zoned data formats, it is time that we apply our knowledge to solve a problem. We will see how important it is to keep track of the form in which data is stored, as well as where in memory such data is located. We will also see how to perform calculations (addition, subtraction, multiplication, and division) with integers that are in packed form in main storage.

4.1   A PAYROLL PROBLEM

4.1.1   The Problem Described

Let us consider a problem which is rather typical in today's business world—producing a payroll. As you know, before we can attempt to "solve" a problem, we must first be sure that we understand it completely and know exactly what input information will be supplied and what output is desired. We will consider input in the form of employee records on punched cards. Each card will contain three fields, as described in figure 4.1.

That is, one card will be supplied for each employee. An employee number (a unique identifying number assigned by the employer, sometimes the individual's social security number) will be recorded in columns 2 through 7; the number of hours the employee has worked during the week will be recorded in columns 8 and 9; and his hourly rate of pay will be recorded in columns 10 and 11. Every such employee card will have the same "layout": that is, the same items of information will be punched in the same card columns for each such card.

The purpose of our program will be to instruct the computer to consider the input data and to produce output in the form of a printed report. The report will contain a "heading" to make the report more easily understandable to the person who reads it. The main body of the report consists of "detail information", or "detail lines". There will be one detail line per employee (that is, per input card) containing his employee number, number of hours worked, and hourly rate as determined by the input information, along with his gross pay for that week, the weekly tax he will pay, and his net pay (gross pay less tax). The "total" output will then give the total weekly amount of all employees' gross pay and net pay. The program output is described on the printer layout worksheet of figure 4.2.

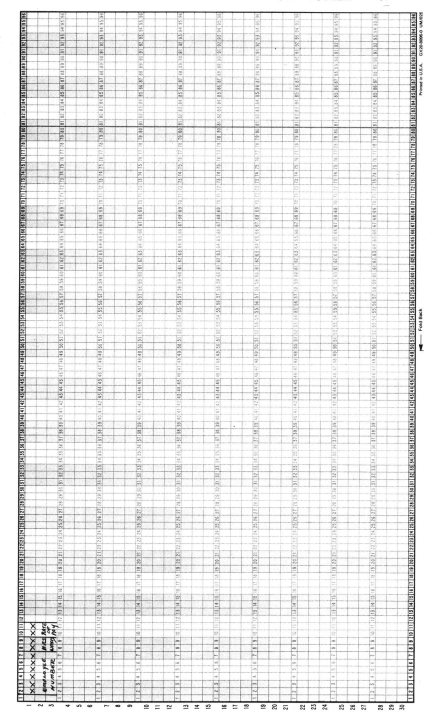

Figure 4.1
Input Layout for Payroll—1

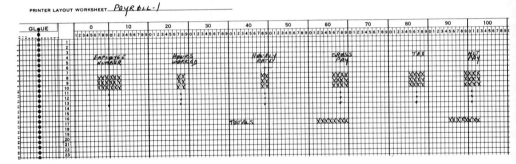

Figure 4.2
Output Layout for Payroll—1

As you have probably noticed, the output detail records all have the same layout: similar fields will occupy the same print positions for each record. We have seen that the same concept applies to input layout. This way of organizing records is very important to the design of the program which will act upon them. It means that instructions which will accept data from certain card columns or produce output in definite print positions may be used over and over again for each record of similar layout.

4.1.2 Zoned vs Packed Forms

At first, it might seem that the program logic involves only reading a card, performing computation, and printing the output line for each record. However arithmetic operations in assembly language require us to consider an additional factor: the format of the numbers being acted upon. You will recall that it is possible to cause data to be stored in computer memory in various forms; in chapter 3 we have seen how the DC instruction may store numbers in various forms such as EBCDIC, packed, zoned, hexadecimal, and binary forms.

When data is read into main storage by the card reader, the information is stored in memory in accordance with set codes, called the   System/360-370 eight-bit alphameric character set (see chapter 1, section 1.2.1 and Appendix A). Decimal numbers which have just been read appear in memory in EBCDIC format (with "F" or "C" or "D" as sign, similar to zoned format), which may be thought of as a subset of the eight-bit character set.

The EBCDIC format, however, is not used in arithmetic operations. Instead, the computer performs arithmetic on packed numbers (in chapters 7, 8, and 9, we will see yet other ways of performing arithmetic). Assembly language provides special instructions for "packing" numbers (converting numeric data from EBCDIC or zoned form into packed form) and for "unpacking" numbers (converting numeric data from packed form into signed EBCDIC or zoned form). In this way, **decimal arithmetic** may be performed on data in packed format, and communication with an I/O device afterwards for the purpose of output would be with numbers which have been converted back into signed EBCDIC or zoned form. If you are not certain that you remember the EBCDIC, zoned and packed representations, refer back to chapter 3.

Let us recap the above. Numeric values are generally input to the computer memory in EBCDIC form. In order to use these values in arithmetic computation, they must first be "packed"; arithmetic is then performed with numbers in packed format, and the results are in packed format. Results (to be readable) should be transformed to zoned format before they are output.

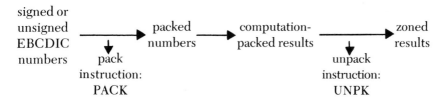

Conversion of data from one form to another is thus a very important part of any assembly language program in which arithmetic computation takes place.

4.1.3 Payroll Program Logic

Keeping the purpose of our payroll program in mind (that is, computing the weekly gross pay, tax, and net pay for a file of employees, and producing the report of section 4.1.1), we may now consider the program logic that will yield our desired output.

The flowchart of figure 4.3 describes one possible way of solving our problem. Let us examine it carefully.

You have probably noticed, upon examining the flowchart, that the special form upon which it is written does more than simply arrange our steps neatly in columns and rows. Every flowchart symbol is contained within a labeled box; thus, if we wish to refer, in our discussion, to a specific flowchart step, we may refer to the appropriate box label.

The first step undertaken by our flowchart is opening our files, both the input file (the card file) and the output file (the printer file). Opening files is

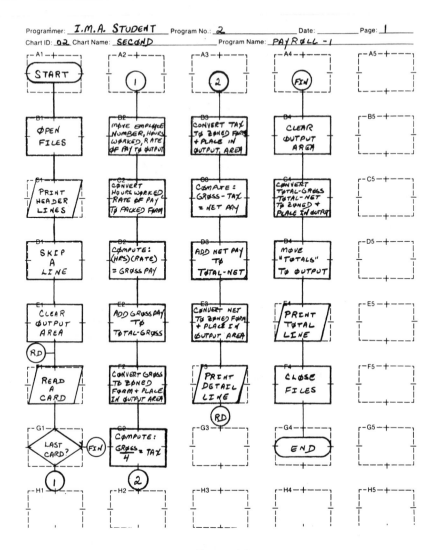

Figure 4.3
Flowchart for Payroll—1

one of the first things done in many programs, since data which is part of a file may not be input or output in Assembly Language until the file has been opened.

Symbol C1 specifies that the next step to be performed is the printing of header lines, which are to be the first lines of our printed output. We then skip a line (symbol D1), as specified on the printer layout worksheet for our problem: notice that the line following the header lines is blank on our layout form (figure 4.2). We next "clear" the output area. You will recall from chapter 2 that "clearing" an output area means replacing its contents at a particular time with blanks. Why do you suppose that is necessary here? If you do not see a reason immediately, you might want to examine the printer layout worksheet a bit more carefully, keeping in mind the fact that all output lines produced by our program will actually be copies of our 132-position output area in main storage. Thus any line which will be printed must first be arranged in the output area exactly the way we wish it to be printed, usually by "moving" information into the appropriate positions. Since at this point of our program the last line to be printed was the second header line (line 5 on the layout form), the word "NUMBER" is still in positions 7-12 of the output area, the word "WORKED" in positions 26-31, the word "RATE" in positions 47-50, the word "PAY" in positions 67-69 and 100-102 of the output area. Let us suppose, now, that we wish to arrange our first detail line (line 8 on the worksheet) by moving numeric data into their appropriate positions. If we move the amount of "hours worked" into output positions 27 and 28, as required, the letter "W" from the header will remain in position 26, and the letters "KED" will remain in 29-31. If the individual worked 38 hours, attempting to print an output line in this way will give us "W38KED" in the "hours worked" field! In order to avoid situations in which data from one output arrangement inteferes with a second arrangement, the output area is "cleared" (that is, filled with blanks) between routines that produce header output and those that produce detail output, and again between routines that produce detail output and those that produce total output. The area is cleared between any routines which produce output lines that differ in the arrangement of their fields.

Flowchart symbols C1, D1, and E1 comprise the program's "header routine"—the part of the program that produces the header lines.

Labeled boxes in the first 3 columns of our flowchart, starting with symbol F1 and ending with symbol F3, comprise the "detail routine"—the computation and output of detail lines, the main part of our program's output. The first step of the detail routine (step F1) is the reading of an input record (a card), for an individual's payroll results cannot possibly be computed unless we first know who the person is, how many hours he has worked, and his hourly wage. Step G1 asks whether the card just read is the last card, that is, whether it is the "/*" card which appears at the end of every data deck. This step is included in our problem flowchart, even though the source program itself will not ask the question at this point.

You may recall that, for DOS programs, the "EOFADDR=" parameter of the DTFCD macro instruction requests the computer to check every card for "/*" as it is read. When it finds the "/*", a branch is immediately effected to the designated location. EOFADDR=HERE will thus cause a branch to the instruction called HERE as soon as the "/*" card (the last card of the data deck) is read. Likewise, for OS programs, the "EODAD=" parameter of the DCB macro instruction which describes the input card data set requests the computer to check every card for "/*" as it is read. When it finds the "/*", a branch is immediately effected to the designated location. EODAD=THERE will thus cause a branch to the instruction called THERE as soon as the "/*" card (the last card of the data deck) is read. In this program, an automatic branch to FIN (symbol A4) will be taken as soon as the "/*" card is read.

Let us assume for the moment, however, that we have just read our first detail record, containing the employee number, hours worked, and rate of pay for a particular employee. The contents of those fields are part of the output description for detail lines; therefore they may just as well be "moved" (copied) into their appropriate output positions right away (symbol B2).

The next field required for output will contain the gross pay, that is the product of the individual's hourly rate and hours worked. The original numeric values were read into computer memory in EBCDIC form, therefore we must first "pack" them (symbol C2) before computing the gross pay (symbol D2). The gross pay is added into a location which will serve as an accumulator (symbol E2). Every time the gross pay is computed, it will be added into this location, so that at the program's end we will have the total of all the employees' gross pay computed. The gross pay is then converted back to zoned form as it is placed into the output area (symbol F2).

The next field requested by the output description contains the employee's tax, which will be considered in this program to be one fourth his salary. Tax is thus the next value to be computed (symbol G2) and converted to zoned form (symbol B3) as it is placed into the output area. You may have noticed that it was not necessary to convert the gross pay into packed form before computing the tax; the original calculation of gross pay in symbol D2 involved packed numbers, and thus yielded gross pay already in packed form.

In symbol C3, the tax is subtracted from the gross pay (both packed numbers) and the result is the net pay in packed form. The net pay is added to an accumulator (symbol D3)—a location which will, at the program's end, contain the total of all the employees' net pay. The net pay is then converted to zoned form (symbol E3) for placement in the output area.

At this point, we have finished processing this employee's record: his gross pay, tax, and net pay have been determined. All fields are in zoned form in their proper output positions, as designated on the printer layout worksheet. We must now print a line (symbol F3), that is, cause the computer to copy the contents of the output area as arranged, onto the printer's continuous form paper.

The first record has been processed. In order to process succeeding records, the flowchart directs us to return to RD (symbol F1) and repeat the processing with the next sequential record. You have probably noticed that the same instructions are used for the processing of each card. Therefore, the same locations will be used over and over again for every succeeding record. The second employee's input data will destroy that of the first employee as it enters the input area, the third employee's data will destroy that of the second employee, and so on. This fact should not disturb us, however, once we realize that the first record has already been fully processed by the time the branch is taken to RD for the second's processing. It is true that information is being destroyed; however when the destruction takes place, the data which is being destroyed is no longer needed.

Our program has now entered a **loop**. After each input record is processed, the program directs the computer to return to RD to process the succeeding record. This looping will continue until the card read is the "/*" card. At this point, all records have been processed and the program branches to FIN (symbol A4). Here our output area is filled with blanks in preparation for the total line. The total of employees' gross pay and net pay, which have been computed during the loop processing (symbols E2 and D3), are converted to zoned form and moved to the output area along with the word "TOTALS" as required. The total line is then printed (symbol E4), files are closed, and the program ends.

Do you now feel that you have a good understanding of the logic involved in the programming of this payroll problem? If so, you might like to reread the flowchart alone. If not, reread this section. It is very important for a programmer to be able to "read" flowcharts, since flowcharts are often the principle means of communicating program logic to other people. Program flowcharts should be as clear and as concise as possible, yet they should demonstrate the entire scope of the program's logic—all steps which must be followed in order for the computer to process the application.

4.1.4   The Payroll Program—Coded

Now that we understand the logic of the payroll program, it is time to write the appropriate assembly language instructions on coding sheets. All the entries on the coding sheets will then be keypunched, one card per line.

Figure 4.4 shows the payroll program coded.

Assembler Coding Form

PROGRAM: PAYROLL-1
PROGRAMMER: I.M.A. STUDENT

```
          PRINT  NOGEN
          START
*  SET UP BASE REGISTER
BEGIN     BALR   5,0
          USING  *,5
*  PROCEDURES
*  THIS PROGRAM WILL ACCEPT ONE CARD PER EMPLOYEE CONTAINING THE NUMBER
*  OF HOURS WORKED THIS WEEK AND THE RATE OF PAY PER HOUR. IT WILL
*  1.  MULTIPLY THE NO. OF HOURS BY THE RATE OF PAY TO OBTAIN THE
*      GROSS PAY FOR EACH EMPLOYEE
*  2.  1/4 OF THE GROSS PAY WILL THEN BE DEDUCTED (TAX) TO GIVE THE
*      NET PAY FOR EACH EMPLOYEE
*  3.  TOTALS OF BOTH GROSS PAY AND NET PAY ARE ALSO COMPUTED
*  OPEN FILES
          OPEN   (IN,INPUT,OUT,OUTPUT)
*  FOR DOS OPEN PROGRAMS, FILES ARE OPENED BY THE INSTRUCTION
          OPEN   IN,OUT
*  PRODUCE HEADER LINES
          PUT    OUT,BLANKS
          MVC    OUTAREA,HEADER1
          PUT    OUT,OUTAREA
          MVC    OUTAREA,HEADER2
          PUT    OUT,OUTAREA
          PUT    OUT,BLANKS
          PUT    OUT,BLANKS
*  CLEAR OUTPUT AREA
          MVC    OUTAREA,OUTAREA-1
*  PROCESSING OF DATA RECORDS.
READCARD  GET    IN,INAREA
```

Figure 4.4
Payroll—1 Coded (Part 1)

Assembler Coding Form

PROGRAM PAYRØLL-1 — PROGRAMMER I.M.A. STUDENT — PAGE 2

```
         MVC   ØEMPNØ,EMPNØ
         MVC   ØHRS,HRS
         MVC   ØRATE,RATE
         PACK  PHRS,HRS
         PACK  PRATE,RATE
* CØMPUTE GRØSS PAY AND PLACE IN ØUTPUT AREA       ALTERNATE METHØD
         ZAP   PGRØSS,PRATE                              PACK  PGRØSS,RATE
         MP    PGRØSS,PHRS                               MP    PGRØSS,PHRS
         AP    PTGRØSS,PGRØSS
         UNPK  GRØSS,PGRØSS
* CØMPUTE TAX AND PLACE IN ØUTPUT AREA
         ZAP   PTAX,PGRØSS
         DP    PTAX,P4
         UNPK  TAX,QUØT
* CØMPUTE NET PAY AND PLACE IN ØUTPUT AREA          ALTERNATE METHØD
         SP    PGRØSS,QUØT                               ZAP   PNET,QUØT
         AP    PTNET,PGRØSS                              AP    PTNET,PNET
         UNPK  NET,PGRØSS                                UNPK  NET,PNET
*                                            PNET        DS    PL3
*
* PRINT DETAIL LINE
         PUT   ØUT,ØUTAREA
* PRØCEED TØ NEXT RECØRD
         B     READCARD
* EØF/[illegible] - TØTAL RØUTINE
FINISH   MVC   ØUTAREA,ØUTAREA-1
         MVC   TØTAL,CTØTAL
         UNPK  TGRØSS,PTGRØSS
         UNPK  TNET,PTNET
         PUT   ØUT,BLANKS
         PUT   ØUT,BLANKS
         PUT   ØUT,ØUTAREA
```

Figure 4.4
Payroll—1 Coded (Part 2)

Assembler Coding Form

PROGRAM: PAYROLL-1
PROGRAMMER: I.M.A. STUDENT

```
*    CLOSE FILES
     CLOSE (IN)
     CLOSE (OUT)
*    FOR DOS PROGRAMS, THE FILES ARE CLOSED BY
     CLOSE IN,OUT
     SRC   3
*
*    FOR DOS PROGRAMS, EXECUTION IS HALTED BY
     EOJ
*
*    FILE DEFINITIONS
IN   DCB   DSORG=PS,MACRF=GM,DDNAME=SYSIPT,BLKSIZE=80,          C
           LRECL=80,EODAD=FINISH
OUT  DCB   DSORG=PS,MACRF=PM,DDNAME=SYSLST,BLKSIZE=132,LRECL=132
*    FOR DOS PROGRAMS, FILE DEFINITIONS ARE PERFORMED BY THE DTF MACROS
*    AND BUFFER DEFINITIONS
IN   DTFCD DEVADDR=SYSRDR,IOAREA1=INA,EOFADDR=FINISH,WORKA=YES
OUT  DTFPR DEVADDR=SYSLST,IOAREA1=OUTA,BLKSIZE=132,CONTROL=YES,
           WORKA=YES
*
INA      DS   CL80         BUFFER FOR INPUT FILE
OUTA     DS   CL132        BUFFER FOR OUTPUT FILE
*    AREA DEFINITIONS
INAREA   DS   2CL80
EMPNO    DS   CL6
HRS      DS   CL2
RATE     DS   CL69
*
OUTAREA  DC   C' '
         DS   OCL132
         DS   CL6
```

Figure 4.4
Payroll—1 Coded (Part 3)

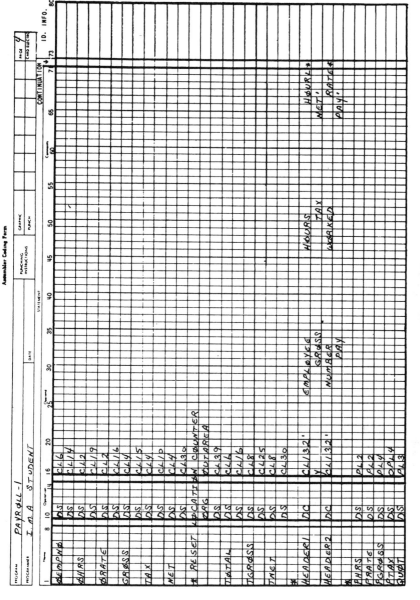

Figure 4.4

Payroll—1 Coded (Part 4)

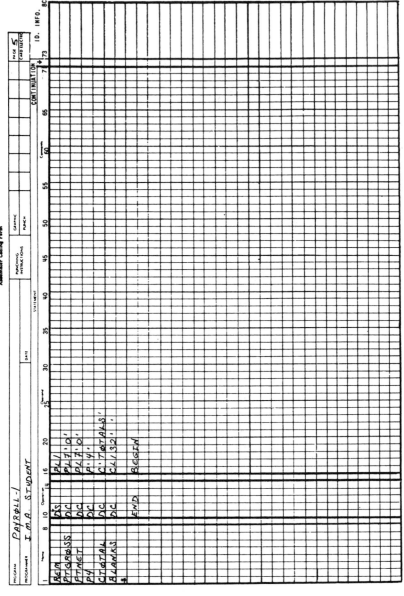

Figure 4.4
Payroll—1 Coded (Part 5)

4.1.5   The Payroll Program—Output

In figures 4.5 and 4.6, we present the results that will be obtained upon assembling and executing the payroll program of section 4.1.4. Figure 4.5 is the program **listing**, and figure 4.6 is the program **output**.

```
LOC   OBJECT CODE    ADDR1 ADDR2   STMT    SOURCE STATEMENT

                                    1               PRINT NOGEN
CCCCCO                              2               START
                                    3  *
                                    4  * SET UP BASE   REGISTER
CCCCCO 0550                         5  BEGIN    BALR  5,0
                          00002     6               USING *,5
                                    7  * PROCEDURES
                                    8  *
                                    9  * THIS PROGRAM WILL ACCEPT ONE CARD PER EMPLOYEE CONTAINING THE NUMBER
                                   10  * OF HOURS WORKED THIS WEEK AND THE RATE OF PAY PER HOUR. IT WILL
                                   11  *   1.    MULTIPLY THE NO. OF HOURS BY THE RATE OF PAY TO OBTAIN THE
                                   12  *         GROSS PAY FCR EACH EMPLOYEE
                                   13  *   2.    1/4 OF THE GROSS PAY WILL THEN BE DEDUCTED (TAX) TO GIVE THE
                                   14  *         NET PAY FOR EACH EMPLOYEE
                                   15  *   3.    TCTALS OF BCTH GROSS PAY AND NET PAY ARE ALSO COMPUTED
                                   16  *
                                   17  * OPEN FILES
CUCCC2                             18               OPEN   (IN,INPUT,OUT,OUTPUT)
                                   26  * FOR DOS PROGRAMS, FILES ARE OPENED BY THE INSTRUCTION
                                   27  *         OPEN  IN,OUT
                                   28  * PRODUCE HEADER LINES
                                   29  *
CCC012 D283 523F 52C3 00241 C02C5  30               MVC    OUTAREA,HEADER1
CCCC18                             31               PUT    OUT,OUTAREA
CCC026 D2B3 523F 5347 00241 00349  36               MVC    CUTAREA,HEADER2
CCCC2C                             37               PUT    OUT,OUTAREA
CCCC3A                             42               PUT    OUT,BLANKS
CCCC48                             47               PUT    OUT,BLANKS
                                   52  * CLEAR CUTPUT AREA
CCCC56 D283 523F 523E C0241 00240  53               MVC    OUTAREA,OUTAREA-1
CCCC5C                             54  * PROCESSING OF DATA RECORDS
CCCC6A D205 5245 51EF 00247 001F1  55  READCARD GET   IN,INAREA
CCCC7C D201 5259 51F5 CC25B 001F7  60               MVC    CEMPNO,EMPNO
CCCC76 D201 526E 51F7 00270 C01F9  61               MVC    OHRS,HRS
CCCC7C F211 53CB 51F5 003CD C01F7  62               MVC    ORATE,RATE
CCCCE2 F211 53CD 51F7 003CF 001F9  63               PACK   PHRS,HRS
                                   64               PACK   PRATE,RATE
                                   65  * COMPUTE GROSS PAY AND PLACE IN OUTPUT AREA     ALTERNATE METHOD
CCCCE9 F831 53CF 53CD 003D1 C03CF  66               ZAP    PGRCSS,PRATE                    PACK  PGROSS,RATE
CCCC8E FC31 53CF 53CB 003D1 C03CD  67               MP     PGROSS,PHRS                     MP    PGROSS,PHRS
CCCC94 FA63 53D7 53CF 003D9 C03D1  68               AP     PTGROSS,PGROSS
CCCC9A F333 5280 53CF 00282 003D1  69               UNPK   GRCSS,PGROSS
                                   70  * CCMPUTE TAX AND PLACE IN OUTPUT AREA
CCCCAC F833 53D3 53CF 003D5 003D1  71               ZAP    PTAX,PGROSS
CCCCA6 FD30 53D3 53E5 003D5 C03E7  72               DP     PTAX,P4
CCCCAC F332 5293 53D3 00295 003D5  73               UNPK   TAX,QUOT
                                   74  * COMPUTE NET PAY AND PLACE IN OUTPUT AREA       ALTERNATE METHOD
CCCCB2 FB32 53CF 53D3 C03D1 003D5  75               SP     PGROSS,QUOT                     ZAP   PNET,QUOT
OCCCB8 FA63 53DE 53CF 003E0 C03D1  76               AP     PTNET,PGROSS                    AP    PTNET,PNET
CCCCBE F333 52A1 53CF 002A3 003D1  77               UNPK   NET,PGROSS                      UNPK  NET,PNET
                                   78  *                                          PNET   DS    PL3
                                   79  *
                                   80  * PRINT CETAIL LINE
CCCCC4                             81               PUT    OUT,OUTAREA
                                   86  * PROCEED TO NEXT RECORD
```

Figure 4.5
Payroll—1 (Part 1)

Note that the values output in the gross pay, tax, net pay, and total fields, end with a non-numeric character. This is the way that zoned numbers are sometimes output. The reasons for this, and a way in which to improve the appearance of this output, are discussed in chapter 5. (A more sophisticated improvement is discussed in chapter 10.)

```
  LOC   OBJECT CODE     ADDR1 ADDR2   STMT    SOURCE STATEMENT

C0C0C2 47F0 505A              CC05C    87        B        READCARD
                                       88  * EOFADDR - TOTAL ROUTINE
CCCCD6 D283 523F 523E   00241 CC240    89 FINISH MVC      OUTAREA,OUTAREA-1
CCCCCC D205 5266 53E6   00268 C03E8    90        MVC      TOTAL,CTOTAL
CCCCE2 F376 527C 53D7   0027E C03D9    91        UNPK     TGROSS,PTGROSS
CCCCE8 F376 529D 53DE   0029F C03E0    92        UNPK     TNET,PTNET
CCCCEE                                 93        PUT      OUT,BLANKS
CCCCFC                                 98        PUT      OUT,BLANKS
CCC1CA                                103        PUT      OUT,OUTAREA
                                      108  * CLOSE FILES
CCC118                                109        CLOSE    (IN)
CCC122                                115        CLOSE    (OUT)
                                      121  * FOR DOS PROGRAMS, THE FILES ARE CLOSED BY
                                      122  *        CLOSE IN,OUT
CCC12E CA03                           123        SVC      3
                                      124  * FOR DOS PROGRAMS, EXECUTION IS HALTED BY
                                      125  *        EOJ
                                      126  *
                                      127  * FILE DEFINITIONS
                                      128 IN     CCB      DSORG=PS,MACRF=GM,DDNAME=SYSIPT,BLKSIZE=80,
CCC13C                                          LRECL=80,EODAD=FINISH
CCC19C                                182 OUT    CCB      DSORG=PS,MACRF=PM,DDNAME=SYSLST,BLKSIZE=132,LRECL=132
                                      236  * FOR DOS PROGRAMS, FILE DEFINITIONS ARE PERFORMED BY THE DTF MACROS
                                      237  * AND BUFFER DEFINITIONS
                                      238 *IN     DTFCD DEVADDR=SYSRDR,IOAREA1=INA,EOFADDR=FINISH,WORKA=YES
                                      239 *OUT    DTFPR DEVADDR=SYSLST,IOAREA1=OUTA,BLKSIZE=132,CONTROL=YES,
                                      240  *             WORKA=YES
                                      241 *INA    DS    CL80               BUFFER FOR INPUT FILE
                                      242 *OUTA   DS    CL132              BUFFER FOR OUTPUT FILE
                                      243  * AREA DEFINITIONS
                                      244  *
CCC1FC                                245 INAREA DS      OCL80
CCC1FC                                246        CS      CL1
CCC1F1                                247 EMPNO  CS      CL6
CCC1F7                                248 HRS    DS      CL2
CCC1F9                                249 RATE   DS      CL2
CCC1FB                                250        CS      CL69
                                      251  *
C0C24C 40                             252        CC      C' '
CCC241                                253 OUTAREA DS     OCL132
00C241                                254        CS      CL6
CCC247                                255 OEMPNO DS      CL6
C0C24D                                256        DS      CL14
CCC25B                                257 OHRS   DS      CL2
C0C25D                                258        CS      CL19
CCC27C                                259 ORATE  DS      CL2
C0C272                                260        DS      CL16
C0C282                                261 GROSS  CS      CL4
00C286                                262        CS      CL15
CCC295                                263 TAX    DS      CL4
CCC259                                264        DS      CL10
CCC2A3                                265 NET    DS      CL4
CCC2A7                                266        DS      CL30
                                      267  * RESET LOCATION COUNTER
C0C2C5                        00241   268        ORG      OUTAREA
```

Figure 4.5
Payroll—1 (Part 2)

```
LOC    OBJECT CODE      ADDR1 ADDR2  STMT    SOURCE STATEMENT

C0C241                               269            DS    CL39
CC02E8                               270 TOTAL      DS    CL6
CC026E                               271            DS    CLI6
00027E                               272 TGROSS     DS    CL8
C0C286                               273            DS    CL25
00C29F                               274 TNET       DS    CL8
C0C2A7                               275            DS    CL30
                                     276 *
                                     277 HEADER1    DC    CL132'    EMPLOYEE          HOURS                    HOURL*
C0C2C5 4040404040C5D4D7                                              Y              GROSS            TAX        NET*
                                     278 HEADER2    DC    CL132'    NUMBER           TAX           WORKED        RATE*
C0C349 40404C404040D5E4                                              PAY                                        PAY'
                                     279 *
C0C3CD                               280 PHRS       DS    PL2
C0C3CF                               281 PRATE      DS    PL2
C0C3D1                               282 PGROSS     DS    PL4
CCC3D5                               283 PTAX       DS    OPL4
CCC3D5                               284 QUOT       DS    PL3
C0C3C8                               285 REM        DS    PL1
C0C3D9 0000CC00C0000C                286 PTGROSS    DC    PL7'0'
C0C3EC 0000C00000000C                287 PTNET      DC    PL7'0'
C0C3E7 4C                            288 P4         DC    P'4'
C0C3E8 E3D6E3C1D3E2                  289 CTOTAL     DC    C'TOTALS'
C0C3EE 4040404040404040              290 BLANKS     DC    CL132' '
                                     291 *
CCCCC0                               292            END   BEGIN
```

Figure 4.5
Payroll—1 (Part 3)

EMPLOYEE NUMBER	HOURS WORKED	HOURLY RATE	GROSS PAY	TAX	NET PAY
CC0001	40	03	012	CC3	009
C00002	37	06	022B	005E	016G
CC0003	38	10	038	009E	028E
C00004	40	06	024	006	018
CC0005	43	03	012I	003B	009G
CC0006	40	04	016	004	012
CC0007	42	C4	016H	004B	012F
CC0008	35	09	031E	007H	023G
CC0009	30	05	015	003G	011C
CC0010	50	02	010	002E	007E
CC0011	4C	03	012	003	009
C00012	40	05	020	C05	015
C00013	40	03	012	003	009
C00014	42	06	025B	C06C	018I
C00015	38	05	019	004G	014C
CC0016	41	04	C16D	C04A	012C
CC0017	40	08	032	008	024
C00018	43	06	025H	006D	019D
CC0019	38	03	011D	002H	008F
C00020	42	03	012F	003A	009E
		TOTALS	0000384H		0000289

Figure 4.6
Payroll—1 Output

4.1.6   What Do the Instructions Accomplish?

We shall discuss the data set (file) definitions and area definitions for this program first, for many of the other instructions refer to the dcbnames and location names in their operand portions.

The statements numbered 128 and 182 are macro instructions which define the input and output data sets, and associate those data sets with appropriate I/O devices. The input and output data sets have been named IN and OUT, respectively. If you do not remember how the DCB macro works, you should refer back to chapter 2, section 2.4, where it was explained in greater detail.

The comments numbered 238 and 239 on the program listing indicate how the respective input and output files would be defined for a DOS program. Of note in these statements is that the files are named IN and OUT, and that they have been assigned buffer areas INA and OUTA. The buffer areas would be defined as indicated in the comments numbered 241 and 246. The DTF macros were discussed in greater detail in chapter 2, section 2.4.

Let us now discuss the storage area definitions for our program. The first storage area defined is called INAREA and is 80 characters in length. The program will use INAREA as the input area (the area into which card input records are read). INAREA is therefore subdivided in accordance with the input description of figure 4.1 with names EMPNO, HRS, and RATE, assigned to the employee number, hours worked, and rate of pay fields respectively. Likewise, the 132-character storage area called OUTAREA will serve as the area from which printer records will be output; it is subdivided according to the format described on the printer layout worksheet of figure 4.2. Field names OEMPNO, OHRS, ORATE, GROSS, TAX, and NET refer to employee number, hours worked, rate of pay, gross pay, tax, and net pay fields respectively. The ORG OUTAREA   instruction resets the location counter to the value it held at the start of OUTAREA, so that the 132-character definition which follows describes the desired total line output. Note that the total line description is a redefinition of OUTAREA and does not occupy any additional space in the computer's main storage. The header lines are defined next. HEADER1 places the 132-character first header line into storage, while HEADER2 places the 132-character second header line into storage. The area definitions which follow describe storage areas to hold packed numbers that will be created by the program: PHRS, PRATE, PGROSS, PTAX, PTGROSS, and PTNET will hold packed versions of hours worked, rate of pay, gross pay, tax, total gross pay, and total net pay fields respectively. Note that the PTAX field is subdivided; the reason will be explained a bit later on. The P4, CTOTAL, and BLANKS fields store constants: a packed 4, the word "TOTALS", and 132 blanks, respectively. These constants will be of use during program execution.

We shall now summarize the meanings of the program instructions. The statement numbers referred to are those appearing on the program listing.

The first instruction, statement number 1, is an assembler instruction which suppresses the printing of the machine language equivalent of macro instructions on the listing (see chapter 2). Statement number 2 initializes the assembler's location counter. Statement 5 places the beginning location number of statement 6 into register 5. Statement 6, the USING instruction, notifies the assembler that register 5 is to be used as a base register for this program. It also tells the assembler to assume that register 5 contains that number which the BALR will actually place into it during execution (the present contents of the location counter). If you feel that a review of the PRINT, START, BALR, or USING instruction would be beneficial for you at this point, refer back to chapter 2, section 2.4.

You may have noticed that the operations described so far were not mentioned at all on the program flowchart. The reason for this apparent omission is that the flowchart is meant to describe program logic only. Since the START instruction, setting up base registers, and defining data sets are parts of virtually all assembly language programs of this nature, it is unnecessary to describe them for every program — that is, their presence is "understood", hence mentioning them would be superfluous. If we wish, we may imply their presence by indicating on the flowchart that "housekeeping" operations will precede the actual problem solution:

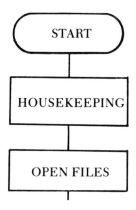

Statements 3, 4, and 7 through 17 are comments. You will notice that many comments appear on the program listing for spacing or discussion purposes.

Statement 18 OPENs the data sets called IN and OUT so that they may be used in program processing.

Statements 28 through 47 comprise the header routine. The first header line is moved to the output area and printed (statements 30 and 31), after which the same is done for the second header line (statements 36 and 37). The identical instructions PUT   OUT,BLANKS cause the computer to "space" two lines by printing two blank lines, that is, to cause output lines to be skipped at this point of program execution. Statement 53 moves blanks into the output area; OUTAREA–1 contains a blank (note the constant definition DC C'𝒃' immediately before OUTAREA) which is propagated throughout the entire OUTAREA field.

Now we are ready to process our data records. Statement 55 reads a record from the data set called IN, into INAREA. In particular, the employee number, hours worked, and rate of pay are placed into the EMPNO, HRS, and RATE fields respectively, subdivisions of INAREA. Statements 60, 61, and 62 move the contents of those fields into OEMPNO, OHRS, and ORATE, the respective output area positions for those values.

The program has now reached the point at which computation is to be performed. Statement 63 considers the contents of the second operand, the value of HRS (a zoned number, since it has just been read into computor memory). The instruction PACKs the number and places the packed version into the memory location called PHRS (the first operand), while the second zoned number, in HRS (the second operand), remains unchanged. Likewise, statement 64 PACKs the zoned number in RATE, placing the packed version into PRATE and leaving RATE unchanged.

The program must now compute the product of those numbers in PHRS and PRATE. Before using the MP (**M**ultiply **P**acked) instruction to accomplish this goal, we first place the contents of PRATE (a 2–byte location) into PGROSS (a 4–byte location). The ZAP (**Z**ero and **A**dd **P**acked) instruction first fills PGROSS with zeros, then adds the contents of PRATE, a packed number, to PGROSS. Since the sum of any number and zero is the number itself, the result of the addition will be a longer, right justified version of PRATE in the PGROSS field. The ZAP instruction thus accomplished very little on its own. Its purpose was, however, to prepare for the MP instruction which follows. The MP (**M**ultiply **P**acked) computes the product of those numbers in PGROSS and PHRS, and replaces PGROSS (the first operand location) by the product. PGROSS now contains the individual's gross pay. Do you see why the ZAP instruction was necessary? Had we attempted to multiply PRATE by PHRS directly, the first operand of the MP would have been at most a 2–byte field and would thus very likely be too short to contain the product of a 3-byte and a 2-byte field. (Note the alternate method described to the right of these instructions. RATE might have been PACKed directly into the larger field, eliminating the need for the ZAP).

Statement number 68 adds the individual's gross pay to the accumulator, a location called PTGROSS, with the sum replacing the previous contents of PTGROSS. PGROSS is then converted to zoned form (i.e., UNPKed) and placed into GROSS, the part of the output area designated for the gross pay.

The next value to be computed is the individual's tax, one fourth of his gross pay. We again use the ZAP instruction to place PGROSS into a larger location, called PTAX. The DP (Divide Packed) instruction divides the number 4 (the contents of P4, the second operand) into PTAX, which at this point contains the employee's gross pay. The results of the division replace PTAX, the first operand. There is one additional factor to take into account in using the DP instruction: both the quotient and the remainder occupy the result field; that is why PTAX has been subdivided, the quotient occupying the first 3 positions, called QUOT, and the remainder occupying the last position, called REM (see statements 283, 284, and 285). The DP instruction will be fully explained in section 4.2.5. The contents of QUOT are then UNPKed, and placed into TAX, the output field designated for that purpose.

The SP (Subtract Packed) instruction subtracts the contents of QUOT (his tax) from the contents of PGROSS (his gross pay). The difference, his net pay, will replace the first operand of the SP instruction. The contents of PGROSS (now his net pay) are then added into an accumulator field (PTNET), to contain the sum of the net pay for all employees. PGROSS is then UNPKed and placed into NET, the appropriate output position for net pay.

Now that the output area contains the employee number, hours worked, hourly rate, gross pay, tax, and net pay, it is time to write a line for that employee (statement 81). We then branch back to read the next record, and execute the same processing steps for that second record. The program has entered a loop, and will continue processing input records in sequence until the GET instruction causes the "/*" card to be read. When that happens, the EODAD=FINISH operand of the DCB macro for the input data set (for DOS programs, the EOFADDR=FINISH operand of the DTFCD macro) will effect an immediate transfer of control to FINISH.

The program will now execute its total routine (statements numbered 89 through 103). The output area is cleared, the word "TOTALS" is moved into positions 40-45 of the output area, the accumulated gross pay and net pay totals are UNPKed into the output area, two lines are skipped (blank lines are printed), and the total line is printed.

The files are then closed, the program terminated.

4.2   EXPLAINING OUR PROGRAM INSTRUCTIONS

In this section, we will discuss those instructions used by our program that we have not encountered in prior chapters. In particular, we will explain the decimal instructions AP, SP, ZAP, MP, DP, PACK, and UNPK.

All these instructions are in SS (Storage to Storage) format; that is, they operate upon values in main storage. You will notice, too, that operand fields are of variable length, and may differ in length within the same instruction. All decimal arithmetic instructions assume packed operands and packed results, with the exception of the PACK instruction (which has a zoned operand) and the UNPK instruction (which has a zoned result).

4.2.1   The AP Instruction

The AP Instruction (**A**dd **P**acked or "add decimal")

Instruction type: Machine Instruction

Machine format: SS Instruction (Storage to Storage Instruction)

FA	L1	L2	B1	D1	B2	D2
0	7 8 11 12	15 16 19 20		31 32	35 36	47

Symbolic format:

	name	operation	operands
	[symbolic name]	AP	name1,name2
or	[symbolic name]	AP	D1(L1,B1),D2(L2,B2)

where D1 and B1 are the displacement and base register respectively used to calculate the first operand address, and L1 is the first operand length. D2 and B2 are the displacement and base register respectively used to calculate the second operand address, and L2 is the second operand length.

. . . .

Rules:
• The first and second operands must both contain packed numbers.

- The first and second operands may overlap in storage; however if they do, their low-order bytes must coincide (it is thus possible to add a number to itself).
- The maximum length of either operand is 16 bytes.

Before execution of the AP instruction, the computer checks all signs and digits to verify that they correspond to the requirement for packed notation. If the value to be acted upon is lacking in length, high-order zeros are supplied. The AP instruction then adds the contents of the second operand location to the contents of the first operand location. The sum is placed into the first operand location (destroying its original contents). The second operand remains unchanged. The sign of the sum is determined algebraically.

Condition Code:

0 if the sum = zero
1 if the sum < zero
2 if the sum > zero
3 if overflow results

Overflow occurs when the result field is not large enough to properly represent the sign and digit portions of the result.

Example:

```
          AP    TOO,SMALL
TOO       DC    P'999'
SMALL     DC    P'88'
```

Before execution of the AP   **After execution of the AP**

TOO $\boxed{9\,9\,9\,C}$ TOO $\boxed{1\,0\,8\,7\,C}$ (overflow)

SMALL $\boxed{0\,8\,8\,C}$ SMALL $\boxed{0\,8\,8\,C}$

Note that TOO was not large enough to contain the sum. Overflow has occurred. The condition code will thus be set to 3, and a program interruption will occur (see chapter 13).

Example:

```
          AP    STEW,SALT
STEW      DC    P'123'
SALT      DC    P'12'
```

Before execution of the AP	After execution of the AP
STEW [1 2 3 C]	STEW [1 3 5 C]
SALT [0 1 2 C]	SALT [0 1 2 C]

Example:

```
              AP       STEW,STEW
STEW          DC       P'–123'
```

Before execution of the AP	After execution of the AP
STEW [1 2 3 D]	STEW [2 4 6 D]

4.2.2   The SP Instruction

The SP Instruction (**S**ubtract **P**acked or "subtract decimal")

Instruction type: Machine Instruction

Machine format: SS Instruction (Storage to Storage Instruction)

FB	L1	L2	B1	D1	B2	D2
0	7 8	11 12	15 16	19 20 31 32	35 36	47

Symbolic format:

name	operation	operands
[symbolic name]	SP	name1,name2
or [symbolic name]	SP	D1(L1,B1),D2(L2,B2)

where D1 and B1 are the displacement and base register respectively used to calculate the first operand address, and L1 is the first operand length. D2 and B2 are the displacement and base register respectively used to calculate the second operand address, and L2 is the second operand length.

. . . .

Rules:
- The first and second operands must both contain packed numbers.
- The first and second operands may overlap, in which case their low-order bytes must coincide (it is thus possible to subtract a number from itself).
- The maximum length of either operand is 16 bytes.

Before execution of the SP instruction, the computer checks all signs and digits to verify that these correspond to the requirement for packed notation. The contents of the second operand location are then subtracted from the contents of the first operand location, and the difference is placed into the first operand location. The contents of the second operand remain unchanged.

The actual method of subtraction used involves 2 steps:

(i)   The sign of the second operand is (temporarily) changed (either + to −, or − to +).

(ii) The contents of the second operand are then *added* to the contents of the first operand.

Thus if we instruct:

	SP	TWO,ONE
TWO	DC	P'2'
ONE	DC	P'1'

then (i)   "1" becomes a "−1"

    (ii) computation: 2 + (−1) = 1

Condition Code:

0 if the difference = 0
1 if the difference < 0
2 if the difference > 0
3 if overflow results

Example:

	SP	NOT,ENOUGH
NOT	DC	P'9'
ENOUGH	DC	P'−9'

Before execution of the SP   **After execution of the SP**

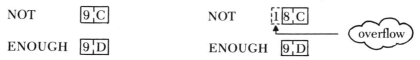

Note that NOT is too small to hold the result of the subtraction. Overflow has occurred. The condition code will be set to 3, and a program interruption will occur (see chapter 13).

Example:

	SP	PEN,INK
PEN	DC	P'42'
INK	DC	P'−4'

Before execution of the SP   **After execution of the SP**

PEN $\boxed{0\,4\,2\,C}$ PEN $\boxed{0\,4\,6\,C}$

INK $\boxed{4\,D}$ INK $\boxed{4\,D}$

Note here that the subtraction of a negative number is equivalent to the addition of its absolute value ("−4" became a "4" after which it was added to
"42").

4.2.3 The ZAP Instruction

The ZAP Instruction (**Z**ero and **A**dd **P**acked)

Instruction type: Machine Instruction

Machine format: SS Instruction (Storage to Storage Instruction)

F8	L1	L2	B1	D1	B2	D2

0   7 8   11 12   15 16   19 20   31 32   35 36   47

Symbolic format:

	name	operation	operands
	[symbolic name]	ZAP	name1,name2
or	[symbolic name]	ZAP	D1(L1,B1),D2(L2,B2)

where D1 and B1 are the displacement and base register respectively
used to calculate the first operand address, and L1 is the first
operand length. D2 and B2 are the displacement and base register respectively used to calculate the second operand address,
and L2 is the second operand length.

. . . .

Rules:
- The second operand must contain a packed number prior to execution.
- The first and second operand locations may overlap; however if they do, the rightmost byte of the first operand must either coincide with, or be to the right of, the rightmost byte of the second operand.
- The maximum length of either operand is 16 bytes.

Before execution of the ZAP instruction, the computer checks the second operand sign and digit codes in order to verify that they correspond to the requirement for packed notation. If necessary, high-order zeros are supplied.

The second operand is then placed in the first operand location, with high-order zeros added in the event of a greater first operand length. The contents of the second operand remain unchanged.

Condition Code:

0 if the result = 0
1 if the result < 0
2 if the result > 0
3 if overflow results

Example:

	ZAP	SMALL,BIG
SMALL	DC	PL1'9'
BIG	DC	PL2'888'

Before execution of the ZAP   **After execution of the ZAP**

SMALL   `9 C`   SMALL `8 8 8 C` (overflow)

BIG   `8 8 8 C`   BIG   `8 8 8 C`

As you can see, an overflow condition results when the first operand is too small to contain the second operand contents.

Example:

```
               ZAP      BIGGER,SMALLER
BIGGER         DS       PL4
SMALLER        DC       PL2'−24'
```

Before execution of the ZAP   **After execution of the ZAP**

BIGGER | u n k n o w n | BIGGER | 0 | 0 | 0 | 0 | 0 | 2 | 4 | D |

SMALLER | 0 | 2 | 4 | D | SMALLER | 0 | 2 | 4 | D |

You have probably guessed by now that the main use of this instruction is for the extension of packed numbers with high-order zeros, that is, to create a longer version of a given number in computer storage.

The ZAP instruction is often an important prerequisite to certain arithmetic operations. In particular, it is used for those in which the operand to be replaced by the result is itself too short to contain the anticipated result.

Consider, for example, the numbers "8" and "9" each in 1-byte storage locations:

			Value in storage
C8	DC	P'8'	8 C
C9	DC	P'9'	9 C

Adding the contents of C8 and C9 would require a 2-byte field to hold the result: 01 7C. The ZAP instruction may be used to provide this extra length. Consider the instruction sequence below:

			Contents of LONGER after execution
C8	DC	P'8'	
C9	DC	P'9'	
LONGER	DS	PL2	
		.	
		.	
		.	
	ZAP	LONGER,C8	0 0 8 C
	AP	LONGER,C9	0 1 7 C

The instruction ZAP LONGER,C8 "extended" the packed 8 in length, converting it from a 1-byte to a 2-byte number. Had we attempted to add *without* first extending the first operand length, an overflow condition would have resulted.

4.2.4   The MP Instruction

The MP Instruction (**M**ultiply **P**acked or "multiply decimal")

Instruction type: Machine Instruction

Machine format: SS Instruction (Storage to Storage Instruction)

FC	L1	L2	B1	D1	B2	D2
0	7 8	11 12	15 16 19 20	31 32	35 36	47

Symbolic format:

	name	operation	operands
	[symbolic name]	MP	name1,name2
or	[symbolic name]	MP	D1(L1,B1),D2(L2,B2)

where D1 and B1 are the displacement and base register respectively
used to calculate the first operand address, and L1 is the first
operand length. D2 and B2 are the displacement and base register respectively used to calculate the second operand address,
and L2 is the second operand length.

. . . .

Rules:
- The first operand (the multiplicand) and the second operand (the
  multiplier) must both contain packed numbers.
- The multiplier and the multiplicand may overlap, if their low-order
  bytes coincide.
- The multiplier (second operand) may not exceed 8 bytes in length
  (15 digits and sign).
- The multiplier (second operand) must be less than the multiplicand
  (first operand) in size.
- The multiplicand must have high-order zeros to make up at least
  the field size of the multiplier. If the extension of the first operand
  with zeros is less than the multiplier in length, a data exception
  occurs and the program is interrupted (see chapter 13).
- The product field (first operand field) may not exceed 16 bytes in
  length (31 digits and sign).

The MP instruction computes the product of the multiplier (the second operand) and the multiplicand (the first operand). The product then replaces

the multiplicand. The sign of the product is determined by algebraic rules, even if operand(s) are zero.

Because the multiplicand field has high-order zeros equivalent at least to the size of the multiplier, overflow will never occur: algebraically,

Maximum number of product digits = number of multiplier digits
+ number of multiplicand digits

Condition Code: The condition code remains unchanged

Example:

	MP	FASTER,FAST
FASTER	DC	PL3'100'
FAST	DC	PL2'132'

Note that the original contents of FASTER, the number 100, required only 2 bytes. However, the product of 132 and 100 is a 5-digit number; hence FASTER needed 3 bytes to be long enough to hold the result:

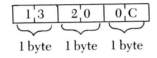

1 byte 1 byte 1 byte

Before execution of the MP   **After execution of the MP**

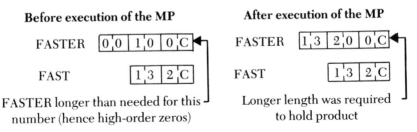

FASTER longer than needed for this
number (hence high-order zeros)

Longer length was required
to hold product

Example: An alternate method to ensure enough room for the product is demonstrated by the following example:

	ZAP	FASTEST,FASTER
	MP	FASTEST,FAST
FASTER	DC	PL2'100'
FAST	DC	PL2'132'
FASTEST	DS	PL3

Here, the original values need occupy only their required lengths, and the multiplicand is ZAPed into a larger field (right justified with leading zeros) to provide enough room for the product.

4.2.5 The DP Instruction

The DP Instruction (**D**ivide **P**acked or "divide decimal")

Instruction type: Machine Instruction

Machine format: SS Instruction (Storage to Storage Instruction)

FD	L1	L2	B1	D1	B2	D2
0	7 8	11 12	15 16 19 20	31 32	35 36	47

Symbolic format:

	name	operation	operands
	[symbolic name]	DP	name1,name2
or	[symbolic name]	DP	D1(L1,B1),D2(L2,B2)

where D1 and B1 are the displacement and base register respectively used to calculate the first operand address, and L1 is the first operand length. D2 and B2 are the displacement and base register respectively used to calculate the second operand address, and L2 is the second operand length.

. . . .

Rules:
- Before execution, the first operand will contain the dividend, and the second operand will contain the divisor.
- After execution, the first operand (the dividend location) will contain the quotient and remainder. The remainder will be rightmost in the operand field, and equal in size to the divisor; the quotient will occupy the rest of the field.
- The maximum size of the dividend is 16 bytes (31 digits and sign).
- The maximum size of the divisor is 8 bytes (15 digits and sign).
- The maximum size of the quotient is 15 bytes (29 digits and sign). (Obtained by considering the dividend of maximum length (16 bytes) replaced by the smallest possible remainder (1 byte) and the quotient (15 bytes left)).
- The dividend must contain at least one leading zero.
- The divisor and dividend may overlap in core, provided their low-order (rightmost) bytes coincide. (Thus it is possible to divide a number by itself.)
- Division by zero is not allowed.
- The first operand location (after the remainder has been stored) must be large enough to hold the quotient.

The. sign of the quotient will be determined according to the rules of algebra. The sign of the remainder will be the same as the sign of the dividend.

Condition Code: The condition code remains unchanged.

Aligning Dividend and Divisor Fields

It is possible to "test" fields to be used as dividend and divisor in a DP instruction, to determine whether or not enough room has been allowed for both the quotient and the remainder. The size of the field(s) may then be adjusted to ensure that sufficient room will be available.

In order to do this, we align the leftmost digit position of the divisor with the second digit position from the left of the dividend. The division is invalid if the divisor, so aligned, is less than or equal to the dividend in value.

Let us consider some examples to clarify this method. Example 1 shows an invalid division. Let us examine it carefully.

Example 1:

```
DVDND       DC      PL3'72460'
DVSR        DC      PL2'2'
            DP      DVDND,DVSR
```

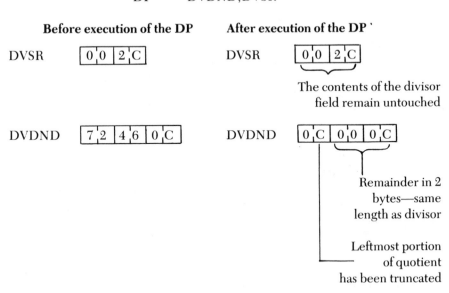

Before execution of the DP   **After execution of the DP**

DVSR   `0 0 | 2 C`   DVSR   `0 0 | 2 C`

                                        The contents of the divisor
                                        field remain untouched

DVDND   `7 2 | 4 6 | 0 C`   DVDND   `0 C | 0 0 | 0 C`

                                        Remainder in 2
                                        bytes—same
                                        length as divisor

                                        Leftmost portion
                                        of quotient
                                        has been truncated

After the DP instruction is executed, the dividend field will contain both the quotient and the remainder, Although the remainder in this problem (zero)

may certainly be represented in 1 byte (as 0C), the amount of actual computer memory assigned will *always* be equal in size to that of the divisor.
Thus, since the divisor in this problem is 2 bytes in length, 2 bytes have
been allocated to the remainder. (Note too that the remainder is the sign of
the dividend [+].) This leaves 1 byte remaining in the dividend field. This is
not enough to contain the quotient. The correct quotient value will be
36230 — 3 6   2 3   0 C   in packed form—which requires 3 bytes. As you
can see, the rightmost byte was stored and the 2 high-order bytes were
truncated.

We could have foreseen these unfortunate results by using the rule stated
above.

Let us align the leftmost digit position of the divisor with the second digit
position from the left of the dividend.

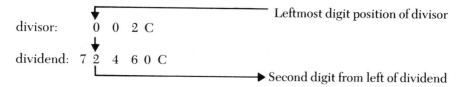

divisor: 0   0   2 C   —————— Leftmost digit position of divisor

dividend: 7 2   4   6 0 C

                                    ——→ Second digit from left of dividend

So aligned, the divisor is smaller in value than the dividend. As we have
already seen from example 1, the division is invalid.

The question which remains is, of course: how can we arrange our data to be
sure that enough room is available for the entire quotient?

The answer is implied by our rule. We adjust the lengths of divisor and dividend fields so that, when they are aligned as described, the divisor will be
larger than the dividend.

Using the values in example 1, we may try shortening the divisor to one
byte in length

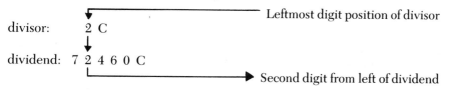

divisor: 2 C   —————— Leftmost digit position of divisor

dividend: 7 2   4 6 0 C

                                    ——→ Second digit from left of dividend

The divisor is still smaller in value than the dividend, although the difference is not as great as it was. This remains unacceptable, however.

Let us try lengthening the dividend by one byte.

divisor: 2 C ⟶ Leftmost digit position of divisor

dividend: 0 0 7 2 4 6 0 C ⟶ Second digit from left of dividend

Now the divisor, so aligned, appears larger than the dividend. These field descriptions will therefore yield correct quotient results.

Example 2 demonstrates the corrected program segment:

Example 2:

DVDND	DC	PL4'72460'	dividend length extended to 4 bytes
DVSR	DC	PL1'2'	divisor length shortened to 1 byte
	DP	DVDND,DVSR	

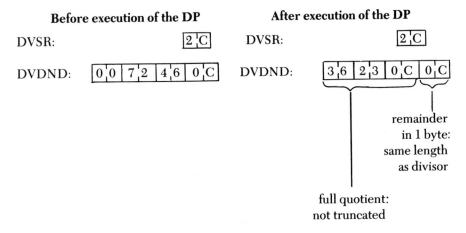

Before execution of the DP

DVSR: [2 C]

DVDND: [0 0 | 7 2 | 4 6 | 0 C]

After execution of the DP

DVSR: [2 C]

DVDND: [3 6 | 2 3 | 0 C | 0 C]

remainder in 1 byte: same length as divisor

full quotient: not truncated

Aligning Dividend and Divisor Fields when Exact Contents are Unknown

You may now be thinking that the above technique is fine when we know the exact values to be divided, but this is not the usual case! More often than not, the same DP instruction will be used over and over again to divide many different values! In our program, for example, the DP instruction will divide new values for every record which is processed.

The technique of aligning fields may be employed even if exact field values are unknown. Only the field lengths need be known—and they always are, for fields must be defined in assembly language.

Let us consider an example to demonstrate the use of our technique in this situation. Assume that we wish to divide the contents of a 3-byte field into the contents of a 4-byte field. Aligning the fields according to our rule and using an "x" to represent each packed digit and an "S" to represent the sign of each field, we see

divisor: x x x x x S

dividend: x x x x x x x S

The divisor, so aligned, may be smaller than the dividend. This is not desirable. (We do *not* know the exact digits, therefore it is possible for the first several dividend digits to be 0's while the divisor digits are not, in which case the divisor would be larger. However we cannot assume this to be the case; the divisor *may* be smaller, and so adjustments are necessary.)

If we extend the dividend on the left with a byte containing zeros, the alignment will be as follows:

divisor: x x x x x S

dividend: 0 0 x x x x x x x S

At first glance, you might say that the divisor is certainly larger here! However consider the following possible divisor and dividend values:

$$0\ 0\quad 0\ 0\quad 1\ C$$

$$0\ 09\quad 99\quad 99\quad 99\ C$$

Remember that the digits are unknown. They may be such that the divisor is still smaller!

In order to be absolutely certain that the division will be valid, *the dividend location must be extended on the left with zeros for as many bytes as are given by the length of the divisor.* Thus if the divisor is 3 bytes long, we extend the dividend on the left with 3 bytes of zeros.

divisor: x x x x x S

dividend: 0 0 0 0 0 0 x x x x x x x S

The divisor cannot have a zero value (division by zero is not permitted). Therefore, the divisor so aligned will be larger in value than the dividend.

4.2.6 The PACK Instruction

The PACK Instruction

Instruction type: Machine Instruction

Machine format: SS Instruction (Storage to Storage Instruction)

F2	L1	L2	B1	D1	B2	D2
0	7 8 11 12	15 16	19 20	31 32	35 36	47

Symbolic format:

name	operation	operands
[symbolic name]	PACK	name1,name2
or [symbolic name]	PACK	D1(L1,B1),D2(L2,B2)

where D1 and B1 are the displacement and base register respectively used to calculate the first operand address, and L1 is the first operand length. D2 and B2 are the displacement and base register respectively used to calculate the second operand address, and L2 is the second operand length.

. . . .

Rules:
- The second operand is assumed to contain a zoned number (the contents are not checked by the computer to see if the second operand indeed contains a zoned number, so exercise caution).
- Overlapping fields are permitted.
- The maximum length of either operand is 16 bytes.

The PACK instruction changes the format of the number in the second operand from zoned to packed. The packed number is placed in the first operand location. The contents of the second operand remain unchanged.

The method used is described below:
(i) The low-order byte is processed first:
- The sign portion (the leftmost 4 bits) of the low-order byte of the se-

cond operand is placed in the rightmost 4 bit positions of the low-order byte of the first operand.

• The digit portion (the rightmost 4 bits) of the low-order byte of the second operand is placed in the leftmost 4 bit positions of the low-order byte of the first operand.

In other words, the sign and digit portions of the rightmost byte are interchanged.

(ii) All other second operand zones are ignored. The digits are moved adjacent to each other in the remainder of the first operand field, proceeding leftward.

(iii) If necessary, the packed result may be extended with high-order zeros.

(iv) If there are more significant digits in the zoned number than can be represented in the first operand length, any extra high-order digits are ignored.

Condition Code: The condition code remains unchanged.

Example 1:

```
            PACK    CASE,BOOKS
CASE        DS      PL2
BOOKS       DC      ZL3'987'
```

Before execution of the PACK	**After execution of the PACK**

CASE
contents
unknown:
2 bytes long

| x | x | x | x |

CASE

| 9 | 8 | 7 | C |

BOOKS

| F 9 | F 8 | C 7 |

BOOKS

| F 9 | F 8 | C 7 |

Example 2:

```
            PACK    BOXES,ROSES
BOXES       DC      CL4'ABCD'
ROSES       DC      ZL4'-1234'
```

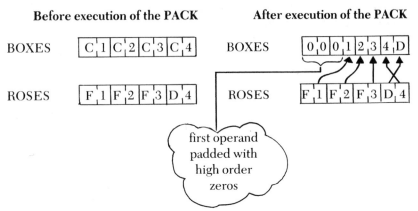

Note 1:

The PACK instruction removes the zone portions of all field bytes, with the exception of the rightmost byte.

If we wish to remove *all* zones (including the rightmost), we simply extend the two operands with dummy (extra) bytes on the right. The zone portions of all the original bytes will be removed, and the programmer will ignore the dummy byte of the result field.

Example 3:

```
          PACK    BOX(3),ROSE(3)
BOX       DC      CL2'AB'
PAD1      DS      CL1
ROSE      DC      ZL2'−12'
PAD2      DC      X'89'
```

Before execution of the PACK   **After execution of the PACK**

BOX | C 1 | C 2 | PAD1 | x x | BOX | 0 0 | 1 2 | PAD1 | 9 8 |

contents unknown

ROSE | F 1 | D 2 | PAD2 | 8 9 | ROSE | F 1 | D 2 | PAD2 | 8 9 |

first operand padded with high-order zeros

Note 2:

By specifying the same address—with a length of one byte—for both operands, the PACK instruction may be used to interchange the zone and digit portions of any byte.

Example 4:

$$\text{PACK} \quad \text{D,D}$$
$$\text{D} \qquad \text{DC} \qquad \text{Z}'+3'$$

Before execution of the PACK   **After execution of the PACK**

note that the zone
and digit portions of
D have been interchanged

4.2.7   The UNPK Instruction

The UNPK Instruction (**UNPacK**)

Instruction type: Machine Instruction

Machine format: SS Instruction (Storage to Storage Instruction)

F3	L1	L2	B1	D1	B2	D2
0	7 8 11	12 15	16 19	20 31	32 35	36 47

Symbolic format:

	name	operation	operands
	[symbolic name]	AP	name1,name2
or	[symbolic name]	AP	D1(L1,B1),D2(L2,B2)

where D1 and B1 are the displacement and base register respectively used to calculate the first operand address, and L1 is the first operand length. D2 and B2 are the displacement and base register respectively used to calculate the second operand address, and L2 is the second operand length.

. . . .

Rules:
- The second operand is assumed to contain a packed number (the sign and digits are not checked to verify that they correspond to the requirements for packed notation, so exercise caution).
- Overlapping fields are permitted. However the low-order position of the first operand must then be to the right of the low-order position of the second operand by the number of bytes in the second operand minus two. If only one or two bytes are to be unpacked, low-order bytes may coincide.
- The maximum length of either operand is 16 bytes.

The UNPK instruction changes the format of the number in the second operand from packed to zoned (unpacked form). The zoned number is placed in the first operand location. The contents of the second operand remain unchanged.

The conversion method uses the following guidelines:
(i) The low-order byte is processed first. The order of the sign and digit portions is interchanged for placement in the first operand location.
(ii) Processing from right to left, zones are then supplied for each second operand byte (zone portions of zoned ("unpacked") digits are coded 1111 for computers using EBCD1C representation) for placement in the first operand.
(iii) If necessary, the second operand will be extended with high-order zeros before unpacking. Zones will then be supplied for those zeros, as for other (original) second operand digits.
(iv) If there are more significant digits in the packed number than can be represented in zone form in the first operand, any extra high-order digits are ignored.

Condition Code: The condition code remains unchanged.

Example:

```
              UNPK   SIT,DOWN
SIT           DS     ZL3
DOWN          DC     PL2'24'
```

Before execution of the UNPK   **After execution of the UNPK**

SIT | x | x | x | x | x | x | SIT | F 0 | F 2 | C 4 |
contents
unknown—
3 bytes long

DOWN | 0 2 | 4 C | DOWN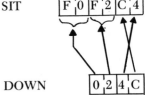

Example:

```
        UNPK    STAND,UP
STAND   DC      ZL5'+12345'
UP      DC      PL2'9'
```

Before execution of the UNPK   **After execution of the UNPK**

STAND | F'1 | F'2 | F'3 | F'4 | C'5 | STAND | F'0 | F'0 | F'0 | F'0 | C'9 |

UP | 0'0 | 9'C | UP | 0'0 | 0'0 | 9'C |

> Second operand has been extended with high-order zeros before unpacking in order that the 1st operand will be filled

Now that all the new instructions have been explained in detail, go back and reread our program to be sure that you understand the whole program as well as the individual statements. Remember that before you can actually code by yourself, you must be able to read and understand an already coded program. You learn to read before you are able to write.

Summary

In this chapter, we have demonstrated the basic decimal arithmetic operations on integers. We have learned to convert numbers to packed form in preparation for arithmetic. The add, subtract, multiply, and divide decimal instructions have been presented and developed. Numbers were then unpacked in preparation for output.

We have also flowcharted and coded the solution to a basic payroll problem, using the instructions introduced in this chapter: the AP (add decimal), SP (subtract decimal), ZAP (zero and add decimal), MP (multiply decimal), DP (divide decimal), PACK, and UNPK (unpack) instructions.

Important Terms Discussed in Chapter 4

decimal arithmetic

overflow

Questions

4-1. After execution of the following sequence of instructions, what will be the contents of the location called ONE? Of the location called TWO?

	AP	ONE,TWO
ONE	DC	P'3'
TWO	DC	PL5'2'

4-2. After execution of the following sequence of instructions, what will be the contents of the location called LNG?

	SP	H,I
	AP	H,J
	ZAP	LNG,H
H	DC	PL2'2'
I	DC	P'50'
J	DC	PL2'100'
LNG	DS	PL3

4-3. After execution of the following sequence of instructions, what will be the contents of the location called HERE?

	PACK	PKX,X
	PACK	PKY,Y
	ZAP	HERE,PKY
	MP	HERE,PKX
X	DC	Z'40'
Y	DC	Z'50'
PKX	DS	PL2
PKY	DS	PL2
HERE	DS	PL4

4-4. After execution of the following sequence of instructions, what will be the contents of the location called AREA1? Of the location called AREA2?

	ZAP	PNUM,NUM	
	MP	PNUM,NUM	
	DP	PNUM,FOUR	
	UNPK	AREA1,PNUM(3)	
	UNPK	AREA2,PNUM+3(1)	
NUM	DC	P'100'	100C
FOUR	DC	P'4'	4C
PNUM	DS	PL4	
AREA1	DS	CL4	
AREA2	DS	CL1	

4-5. Given the following constant definitions:

NUM1	DC	P'100'
NUM2	DC	P'20'
NUM3	DC	P'300'

Write the appropriate assembly language instructions to:
(a) Compute NUM3 + NUM2 − NUM1, and place the packed result into a location called LOC.
(b) Compute $(NUM2)^2$ and place the result into a location called AREA in *unpacked* form.
(c) Compute (NUM3)/(NUM1). Place the quotient into an area called QUOT and place the remainder into an area called REM.
(d) Convert each of the three numbers into zoned form.

4-6. Given A   DS   PL3 containing an unknown packed value, write one assembly language instruction to place a packed zero into A. Then perform the same task using two other methods.

4-7. Write an assembly language program which defines the numbers 10 through 15 in packed form, and which computes their arithmetic average. That is, the program is to find the sum of the numbers 10 through 15 and to divide that sum by the number 6. Convert the arithmetic average into zoned form and place it into a main storage location called RESULT.

4-8. Why is it more often necessary to use the ZAP instruction before decimal multiplication and division, than before decimal addition and subtraction?

4-9. The contents of 5 locations in main storage are given below, along with assembly language instructions which act upon those contents. Examine the instructions and indicate (using hexadecimal notation) what the contents of the first operand will be after each instruction execution.

			Contents
A	DC	P'142'	142C
B	DC	P'15'	015C
C	DC	P'3'	3C
D	DC	P'1'	1C
E	DC	C'100'	F1F0F0

1.	PACK	B,E
2.	AP	A,B
3.	SP	A,C
4.	ZAP	B,C
5.	MP	B,C
6.	ZAP	E,B
7.	DP	E,D

4-10. In the payroll program of this chapter, why is the output area "cleared" after the header lines were printed and at the start of the total routine?

4-11. Why weren't the jobs of the PRINT, BALR, or USING instructions mentioned on the program flowchart of figure 4.3?

4-12. In the program of figure 4.5, what is the purpose of the ZAP instruction of statement 75? Of the PUT instructions of statements 102 and 107?

4-13. What is the machine format of the AP, SP, MP, DP, PACK, and UNPK instructions?

4-14. Which of the decimal instructions AP, SP, MP, DP, PACK, and UNPK, cause the condition code to be set? What do the various condition code settings indicate about the results of the operations?

4-15. Given the area definitions below:

PLACE1	DC	P'100'
PLACE2	DC	P'999'
PLACE3	DC	P'0'
PLACE4	DC	C'20'
LOC	DS	PL3

Indicate whether each of the following instructions is correct or incorrect. If incorrect, tell what is wrong.

```
(a)  AP      PLACE2,PLACE3
(b)  AP      PLACE2,PLACE4
(c)  AP      PLACE1,PLACE2+1(1)
(d)  AP      PLACE1,PLACE2+1
(e)  DP      PLACE2,PLACE1
(f)  DP      PLACE2,PLACE3
(g)  ZAP     LOC,PLACE2
     DP      LOC,PLACE1
(h)  PACK    PLACE4,PLACE4
     AP      PLACE4,PLACE4
(i)  PACK    PLACE4,PLACE4
     MP      PLACE1,PLACE4
(j)  ZAP     LOC,PLACE1
     SP      LOC,PLACE2
```

4-16. Which rule pertaining to the MP instruction assures that overflow will not occur? Explain.

4-17. What are the maximum sizes of operand fields for the AP instruction? SP instruction? ZAP instruction? MP instruction? For the DP instruction, what are the maximum sizes of the dividend and divisor fields? of the resulting quotient?

4-18. Can a zoned number always be PACKed into itself? Explain.

4-19. Why is a ZAP instruction used, as opposed to a MVC instruction, to place packed numbers into longer fields in preparation for arithmetic operations?

4-20. What would happen upon execution of the program segment below? Explain.

```
ADD          AP      A,A
             AP      SUM,A
             B       ADD
A            DC      PL3'10'        00 01 0C
SUM          DS      PL4
```

Program Exercises

4-1. Write an assembly language program which accepts the following input fields:

field	card colums
I	1 - 4
J	5 - 6
K	7 - 9

For each input record, compute
   (i) $X = I + J$
   (ii) $Y = 2I - K$

The program is to print one detail line per input record as follows:

field	print positions
I	2 - 5
J	14 - 15
K	24 - 26
X	35 - 39
Y	48 - 54

4-2. Write an assembly language program which accepts the following input fields:

field	card columns
PRINC (principal amount)	1 - 5
INT (interest rate)	6 - 7

For each input record, compute

PYMNT = (PRINC)(INT)	The yearly payment
MPYMNT = PYMNT/12	The monthly payment

Print one detail line per input record as follows:

field	print positions
PRINC	2 - 6
INT	15 - 16
PYMNT	25 - 31
MPYMNT	40 - 46

Then print a total line with the:
total yearly payment in print positions 23 - 31
total monthly payment in print positions 38 - 46.

Chapter 5

Simple Comparison and Simple Editing

SIMPLE COMPARISON AND SIMPLE EDITING

5.1   INTERPRETING PROGRAM OUTPUT

Chapter 4 has demonstrated how the computer may produce payroll information output. However upon examining the program output, we note that the appearance of signed numeric fields is not exactly as one might have expected. In particular, the contents of gross pay, tax, and net pay fields as well as total fields have been printed with a non-numeric character in the last field position. Let us understand why this happened, and how we interpret these results.

Recall that program output is accomplished by the computer via the PUT instruction, which "copies" the contents of the output area onto the particular output media. That is, every byte in memory is printed out as one EBCDIC character, according to the representation given on the System/370 Reference Summary (see chapter 1 section 1.2.1, and Appendix A).

The representations for letters and digits are given below for ease of reference in this chapter. These particular representations will be encountered so often, however, that committing them to memory will be of great help and will save considerable time in your interpretation of many different types of program output in the future.

EBCDIC character	hex notation SYS/360-370 8-bit code	EBCDIC character	hex notation SYS/360-370 8-bit code
A	C1	S	E2
B	C2	T	E3
C	C3	U	E4
D	C4	V	E5
E	C5	W	E6
F	C6	X	E7
G	C7	Y	E8
H	C8	Z	E9
I	C9	0	F0
J	D1	1	F1
K	D2	2	F2
L	D3	3	F3
M	D4	4	F4
N	D5	5	F5
O	D6	6	F6
P	D7	7	F7
Q	D8	8	F8
R	D9	9	F9

Numbers which are printed as output by the computer can arise in each of the following two situations:

1. Printing numbers which have been converted to zoned form (UNPKed) for output

   Let us assume that a program computed 3 numbers which were converted to zoned form and placed into the output area, as follow: F1F2C3; F7F9D4; D2. From our knowledge of zoned representation, we may interpret these results to have values +123, −794, and −2 respectively. However, the computer will print these numbers EBCDIC character by EBCDIC character, as follows:

internal code:	F1 F2 C3	F7 F9 D4	D2
appearance on output:	1 2 C	7 9 M	K

Thus we see that signed zoned numbers will print with a non-numeric character at the end; the character represents the sign of the number, and its last digit. All zoned numbers which are converted to zoned form by the UNPK instruction will be signed.

2. Printing numbers whose forms have not been altered by the program

   Looking once again at the payroll program output, we see that the contents of the employee number, hours worked, and hourly rate fields do not print with a last non-numeric character. Yet we have insisted throughout that digits to be output must be in zoned form, which we have seen to contain the sign in the last byte! How do we resolve this apparent discrepancy? The answer is really quite simple. The contents of the employee number, hours worked, and hourly rate fields were keypunched as unsigned numbers, and input to the computer via the card reader, where they were stored, character by character, in the computer memory. Thus a punched card with

card columns	1111111111222222222233333333333
	1234567890123456789012345678990123456789...
	ℬℬℬℬℬ87712ℬℬℬℬℬℬℬℬℬℬℬℬℬℬℬℬ40ℬℬℬℬℬℬℬℬℬℬ...

will print as:

   40...40F8F7F7F1F240...40F4F040...40...

Note that hexadecimal 40 is the internal representation for the character ℬ (blank). A complete list of internal character representations is found in Appendix A.

Storage is character by character, and the characters which were punched unsigned are stored unsigned. Therefore the character by character output will also be unsigned. That is, only representations F0 through F9 are in main storage, so that only EBCDIC characters 0 through 9 will be printed.

It is actually possible to keypunch and to read signed numbers, as well as unsigned numbers, into the computer memory. One simply punches the sign ("+" and "−" will appear as a "12-punch" and an "11-punch" respectively) right over the last digit of the number—in the same column! We then observe a very interesting result, namely that this will cause the number to be stored in signed (as opposed to unsigned) zoned form.

For example, imagine that we keypunch the following three numbers:

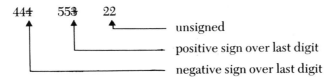

The punched card codes and resultant internal code are demonstrated below:

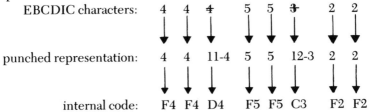

If the internal code were printed, it would appear as 44M, 55C, and 22 respectively. (Note that 11-4, the punched representation for "negative 4", is also the punched representation for "M"; 12-3, the punched representation for "positive 3", is also the punched representation for "C".)

Numbers may thus be input to the computer either in unsigned form or in signed form, as demonstrated above. When converted to zoned form via the UNPK instruction, however, numbers will be signed.

The appearance of numeric output will invariably reflect the signed or unsigned nature of its form in main storage. Signed numeric values will be printed with a non-numeric last character; unsigned numeric values will not.

5.2 IMPROVING THE APPEARANCE OF PROGRAM OUTPUT

Once we understand the meaning of a non-numeric character at the end of a field, it is important that we see how to eliminate it in order that our output be more legible. Improving the appearance of program output is called **editing**. In this chapter we will discuss a very simple form of editing. A more sophisticated approach will be considered in chapter 10.

Consider, for example, the instructions

	UNPK	GROSS,PGROSS	
PGROSS	DC	PL2'12'	PGROSS contains 01 2C
GROSS	DS	CL4	

GROSS before execution   **GROSS after execution**

    unknown | F 0 | F 0 | F 1 | C 2 |

If we were to print the contents of GROSS after execution of the UNPK, they would be printed as follows:

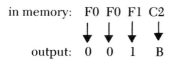

in memory: F0 F0 F1 C2

output: 0   0   1   B

We would prefer it to be printed out as 0012! In order to effect this, however, we must replace the "C" in the zone portion of the last byte with an "F" in that position. Doing this involves moving half a byte—in particular, moving the zone portion of one of the first 3 bytes ("F") to the zone portion of the last byte.

We have a special instruction to accomplish this: the **MoVe Zones** or MVZ instruction. It is a storage to storage (SS) instruction which moves the *zone portion(s) only* of those byte(s) contained in the second operand location to the zone portion(s) of those byte(s) contained in the first operand location.

In the example above, we may issue the following statement:

       MVZ   GROSS+3(1),GROSS+2

This will move the zone portion of GROSS+2 (2 bytes past the beginning byte of GROSS: in other words, the third byte) to the zone portion of GROSS+3 (3 bytes after the byte called GROSS: the fourth byte).

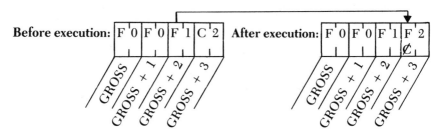

Note that, as in the MVC instruction, the length of the first operand determines how many byte(s) are to be affected by this instruction. If necessary, you may refer back to chapter 2, section 2.4—the MVC instruction—for a discussion of relative addressing as used here.

5.2.1 The MVZ Instruction

The MVZ Instruction (**MoVe Zones**)

Instruction type: Machine Instruction

Machine format: SS Instruction (Storage to Storage Instruction)

D3	L	B1	D1	B2	D2
0	7 8	15 16 19 20	31 32	35 36	47

Symbolic format:

	name	operation	operands
	[symbolic name]	MVZ	name1,name2
or	[symbolic name]	MVZ	D1(L,B1),D2(B2)

where D1 and B1 are the displacement and base register respectively used to calculate the first operand address, and D2 and B2 are the displacement and base register respectively used to calculate the second operand address. L is the operand length.

. . . .

Rules:
- The zone portion (high-order 4 bits) of each byte in the second operand field is placed into the zone portion of the corresponding byte of the first operand field.
- The instruction moves the data through each field one byte at a time.
- The number of zones moved from the second operand is determined by the length of the first operand.
- The MVZ instruction processes data from left to right. The zone portion of the leftmost byte of the sending field is moved first, into the zone portion of the leftmost byte of the receiving field. The zone portion of the second byte from the left of the sending field is then moved in a similar manner, followed by the third byte, and so on, until the receiving field has been filled.
- The storage areas represented by the first and second operands may overlap in memory in any way.

- The numeric portion of each byte (the low-order 4 bits) remains unchanged in both operand fields.
- The second operand remains unchanged upon execution of the MVZ.
- A maximum of 256 zones may be moved by one MVZ instruction.

Condition code: The condition code remains unchanged

Example 1:

```
          MVZ     THERE,HERE
HERE      DC      P'4'
THERE     DC      P'+5'
```

Before execution of the MVZ   **After execution of the MVZ**

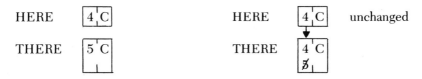

HERE   4 C   HERE   4 C   unchanged

THERE   5 C   THERE   4 C / 5

Example 2:

```
          MVZ     B,A
A         DC      C'AJKL'
B         DC      C'STUVW'
```

Before execution of the MVZ   **After execution of the MVZ**

A | C 1 | D 1 | D 2 | D 3 | A | C 1 | D 1 | D 2 | D 3 | C 2 |

B | E 2 | E 3 | E 4 | E 5 | E 6 | B | C 2 | D 3 | D 4 | D 5 | C 6 |
                                           E / E / E / E / E /

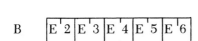

5th byte of A is same as 1st byte of B

Note that the length of the first operand determines the length of the move. B is 5 characters long, hence 5 zones are moved. Note too that the

5th byte of A, the zone portion of which has been moved, is the first character of B, *after* the zone has been changed by the first step of this instruction.

This is an example of overlapping fields in storage. Before execution we had:

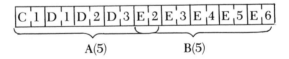

The fifth byte of A is the first byte of B.

After execution we have:

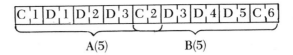

Circled numbers in the instruction diagram represent the sequence of movement: ① is the first zone moved, ② is the second zone moved, and so on.

Example 3:

	MVZ	B+2(2),A+1
A	DC	C'ABCD'
B	DC	C'STUVW'

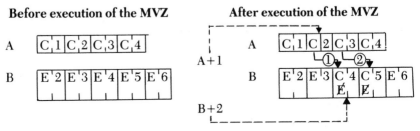

In this example, an explicit length factor of 2 in the first operand field determined that 2 bytes were to be moved. Circled numbers represent the sequence of movement: ① is the first zone moved. ② is the second zone moved.

One very important question has probably entered your mind at this point: It is fine to replace the sign by an "F" in the zone portion of the last byte, as long as the number being dealt with is a positive number, for an unsigned number is always assumed to be positive! But what should be done if the sign of the field is unknown—that is, if it may be either positive or negative? In this event, it will be necessary for the computer to determine, for each value encountered at execution time, whether it is positive or negative. For positive numbers, the sign will be replaced by an "F" in the zone position; the same procedure will be followed for negative numbers, but the numbers should in addition be preceded by a minus sign. Thus the numbers positive twenty-two and negative twenty-two will print as 22 and −22 respectively, instead of 2B (from F2C2) and 2K (from F2D2) as would ordinarily have been the case.

Notice that the method which we have just described involves asking the computer to distinguish between two cases—to determine whether certain values are positive or negative—and to make a decision as to which course of action to follow, depending upon the sign of the particular number. Requesting the computer to distinguish between 2 or more cases is generally the job of certain types of instructions called **compare** instructions, while decision-making would be the work of **branch** instructions. Comparing and branching are of such vital concern to the programmer for almost any but the most trivial computer applications that they certainly merit extensive discussion.

5.3 COMPARISON AND TRANSFER OF CONTROL

Compare instructions in assembly language have the following common purpose: to determine the relationship between the contents of two locations. In particular, compare instructions determine whether the value of one location's contents is equal to, less than, or greater than the value of a second location's contents.

When an instruction compares the contents of two fields, it does not change those contents in any way; instead, it records its findings in a special control field in the CPU called the **condition code**. The condition code is two bits long, so that the only possible configurations that it may contain are: 00, 01, 10, and 11—in other words, the binary representations for 0, 1, 2, and 3 respectively. A compare instruction compares the contents of the first operand field to the contents of the second operand field. If the contents of the first are equal in value to the contents of the second, a 0 (binary 00) will be set in the condition code. If the contents of the first are less in value than the contents of the second, a 1 (binary 01) will be set in the condition code. If the contents of the first are greater in value than the contents of the second, a 2 (binary 10) will be set in the condition code. Since for any two given values, the first must be equal to, less than, or greater than the second—there are no other possibilities—one of either 0, 1, or 2 will be set in the condition code as the result of a compare instruction.

With compare instructions, as with all instructions, cretain procedures must be followed: for example, packed numbers must be compared to other packed numbers, zoned numbers compared to other zoned numbers, and so on. Assembly language provides several compare instructions, and the instruction to use in any particular case will depend upon the formats of the values to be compared, their lengths, and their locations (whether they are in registers or in main storage).

In this chapter, we will discuss the instruction which compares packed numbers, and those which compare logical values (including EBCDIC values) which are located in main storage. In chapter 9 we will discuss those instructions which compare binary numbers.

5.3.1 Comparing Packed Numbers: The CP Instruction

Let us first consider the instruction which compares the values of two numbers known to be in packed form. We will then see how to use this instruction to detemine whether a number is negative, hence whether to precede it by a negative sign for output.

The CP Instruction (**C**ompare **P**acked or "compare decimal")

Instruction type: Machine Instruction

Machine format: SS Instruction (Storage to Storage Instruction)

F9	L1	L2	B1	D1	B2	D2
0	7 8	11 12	15 16	19 20	31 32	35 36	47

Symbolic format:

	name	operation	operands
	[symbolic name]	CP	name1,name2
or	[symbolic name]	CP	D1(L1,B1),D2(L2,B2)

where D1 and B1 are the displacement and base register respectively used to calculate the first operand address, and L1 is the first operand length. D2 and B2 are the displacement and base register respectively used to calculate the second operand address, and L2 is the second operand length.

. . . .

Rules:
- The first and second operands must both contain packed numbers.
- Operands may overlap if their low-order bytes coincide; a number may thus be compared to itself.
- Positive zero is considered equal in value to negative zero.
- Overflow cannot occur, for field values remain unchanged as a result of instruction execution.

The CP instruction compares the first operand with the second; the comparison result is recorded in the condition code. The processing takes place from right to left. Signs (rightmost in packed fields) are checked to see that they conform to the requirements for packed format. Valid plus or minus signs are interpreted as equal to other valid plus or minus signs, respectively. The digits are compared next, proceeding leftward. If the operands are unequal in length, the shorter is extended with high-order zeros for the purpose of comparison.

Condition code:

        0 if operands are equal
        1 if first operand < second operand
        2 if first operand > second operand
        3 cannot result from this instruction

Example 1:

```
          CP      NUM1,NUM2
NUM1      DC      P'4'
NUM2      DC      P'2'
```

Since the contents of NUM1 (a packed "4") are greater in value than the contents of NUM2 (a packed "2"), the CP instruction will set the value "2" in the condition code.

Example 2:

```
          CP      HIGH,LOW
HIGH      DC      P'-3'
LOW       DC      P'+3'
```

The contents of HIGH are lower in value than the contents of LOW; a "1" will therefore be placed in the condition code.

Now let us see how the CP instruction may be used to aid in producing numeric output with a minus sign preceding negative amounts. Let us examine the following program segment, which eliminates the sign from the last character of a zoned number and places a minus sign before negative numbers only. Note also the new instructions BNL and MVI. These will be explained subsequently.

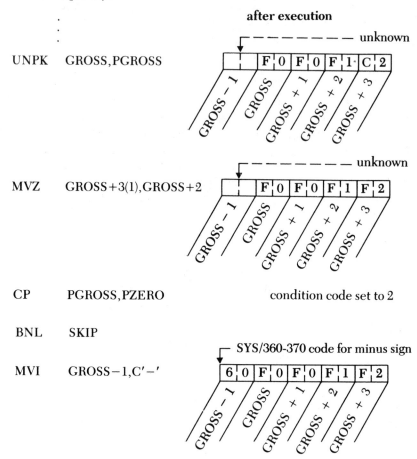

UNPK	GROSS,PGROSS	
MVZ	GROSS+3(1),GROSS+2	
CP	PGROSS,PZERO	condition code set to 2
BNL	SKIP	
MVI	GROSS−1,C′−′	

SKIP

*   AREA DEFINITIONS

PGROSS	DC	PL3′12′	contains 00 01 2C
	DS	CL1	this is GROSS−1
GROSS	DS	CL4	
PZERO	DC	P′0′	contains 0C

The first statement considers the packed number 12 in "PGROSS", converts it into zoned format, and places the zoned result into GROSS. The MVZ instruction eliminates the sign from the last byte of the zoned field; this is desired regardless of whether the field is positive or negative. The CP instruction then compares the packed 12 in PGROSS to the packed 0 in PZERO. Since 12 >0, this execution will place a "2" in the condition code. Had PGROSS contained a negative number or a zero, "1" or "0" would have been indicated in the condition code, respectively. Note that no action which affects these program fields has yet been taken as a result of the comparison. The BNL (**B**ranch **N**ot **L**ow) instruction instructs the computer to examine the condition code, and to **B**ranch to the instruction called SKIP if the condition code has a setting which is anything other than a "1"—any setting which is **N**ot **L**ow (does not reflect a "less than" condition). In this case, the condition code contains a 2: 2 is not low, therefore the computer will continue with SKIP as the next instruction to be executed. Had the condition code contained a "1" (that is, had PGROSS been negative), the branch would not have taken place. The MVI (**Mo**Ve **I**mmediate) instruction would have followed, moving the character "−" (minus) into GROSS−1 (the location preceding GROSS) before continuing to SKIP.

As you can see, the CP instruction distinguished the positive and negative cases, and the BNL instruction actually made the decision as to the course of action to be followed as a result. The BNL is one of many "branch" instructions whose purpose is to test the condition code and to decide whether or not to branch to a specified instruction, depending upon what it finds. The MVI and branch instructions are discussed in a bit more detail below.

The MVI Instruction

The MVI Instruction (**Mo**Ve **I**mmediate)

Instruction type: Machine Instruction

Machine format: SI Instruction (Storage immediate Instruction)

92	I2	B1	D1
0 7 8	15 16	19 20	31

Symbolic format:

	name	operation	operands
	[symbolic name]	MVI	name1,constant
or	[symbolic name]	MVI	D1(B1),I2

where D1 and B1 are the displacement and base register respectively used to calculate the first operand address, and I2 is the immediate operand: a 1-byte constant.

. . . .

Rules:
- The second operand introduces *1 byte* of data from the instruction itself to be copied into one byte of storage (the first operand location).

Condition code: The condition code remains unchanged

Example 1:

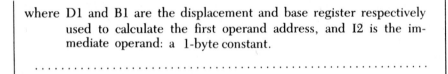

                    MVI   PLACE,C'B'
        PLACE   DC   C'J'

Before execution   **After execution**

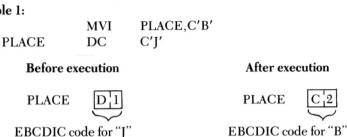

        PLACE |D|1| PLACE |C|2|

    EBCDIC code for "J"   EBCDIC code for "B"

Example 2:

The MVI instruction below accomplishes the same function as that of example 1. We are here explicitly stating the hexadecimal representation for B (in X'C2', X means hexadecimal) instead of implying it (by saying C'B', meaning the character 'B').

                    MVI   PLACE,X'C2'

Note that while the immediate operand is restricted in length to one byte, the description of the value to be moved may be made in a variety of ways. For a review of the methods for describing data format, refer back to chapter 3—the DC instruction—which describes these methods.

5.3.2   Branching with Extended Mnemonics

Branch instructions as a group are those which provide for a departure from normal sequential instruction execution. An extensive discussion of the many ways in which branching can occur and of how the actual transfer of control is effected will be found in chapter 11.

Here we will introduce the very simplest type of **conditional branch** . A conditional branch instruction will cause the computer either to branch (transfer control to another instruction) or not to branch (continue sequential execution) depending upon the setting of the condition code at the time of execution. The condition code, as we have seen, is set by compare instructions or by other instructions to reflect the results of their operations. For example, we have seen that the AP (Add Decimal) and SP (Subtract Decimal) arithmetic instructions will set values in the condition code to reflect negative, zero, positive outputs, or overflow.

The **extended mnemonic** instructions are a set of branch instructions, each of which will test for a specific condition code setting as a condition for branching. We call them "extended mnemonics" because they are actually an "extension" of the BC—Branch on Condition—instruction, which may be used to test for any of those possible conditions. The extended mnemonics, each testing for only one possible condition, are much simpler to use and to remember. (The Branch on Condition instruction is discussed in chapter 11.) Some extended mnemonics for use after comparison and arithmetic instructions are presented below.

	Extended code	Meaning	Condition code setting to cause transfer of control
	B	Unconditional branch	any
	NOP	No operation	none
after comparison: A:B ↓ compared	BH	Branch on A High	2
	BL	Branch on A Low	1
	BE	Branch on A = B	0
	BNH	Branch on A Not High	not 2
	BNL	Branch on A Not Low	not 1
	BNE	Branch on A ≠ B	not 0
after arithmetic operations	BO	Branch on Overflow	3
	BP	Branch on Plus	2
	BM	Branch on Minus	1
	BNP	Branch on Not Plus	not 2
	BNM	Branch on Not Minus	not 1
	BNZ	Branch on Not Zero	not 0
	BZ	Branch on Zero	0

These instructions have one operand, namely the name of the instruction to which control will be transferred should the branch be "successful." For example, we might say

```
            BH      HERE
            AP      A,B
                    .
                    .
                    .
HERE        SP      C,D
```

If the condition code setting is "2" at the time that the BH instruction is executed, the AP instruction will be skipped and control will pass to the instruction called HERE (the SP instruction); otherwise execution will continue sequentially with the AP instruction.

5.3.3   The Payroll Program—Testing for Overtime

We may now use the facility for comparison and branching to expand our payroll program of chapter 4 so that it may provide for computation of overtime pay. Instead of multiplying the number of hours worked by the rate of pay for a particular employee, we shall:

1. Examine the hours worked field and determine whether or not its contents exceed 40; that is, whether or not the individual worked overtime.
   (a) If the employee's hours worked field does not exceed 40, his overtime will be set to 0 (that is, he did not work overtime, hence he receives no overtime pay), and his regular pay (pay for non-overtime hours) will be the product of his rate of pay and hours worked fields.
   (b) If the employee's hours worked field exceeds 40, two computations are required. His overtime pay will be the product of his overtime hours (the number of working hours which *exceed* 40) and his overtime rate of pay (say twice his regular rate). His regular pay will be the product of his regular hours (since he worked more than 40 hours altogether, his regular hours number exactly 40) and his regular rate of pay.
2. Whether or not the individual worked overtime (case (a) or (b)), his gross pay will be the sum of his overtime pay and his regular pay.

We describe this logic in flowchart form in figure 5.1. Note the indication of points 1(a), 1(b), and 2 above on the flowchart itself. The dotted lines denote steps on the original program flowchart (chapter 4) so that we may see exactly where the "overtime" logic belongs.

Do you feel able to code this new portion of the payroll program on your own? It might be beneficial (and fun!) to try before examining the coded solution below. Note that we have extended the output description to allow for separate regular pay and overtime pay fields in addition to the original gross pay field. We have also taken care to remove the sign portion of any field which has been "UNPK"ed—in this case, the gross pay, tax, and net pay fields. The reason that we have not checked these fields for negative amounts is that no individual will

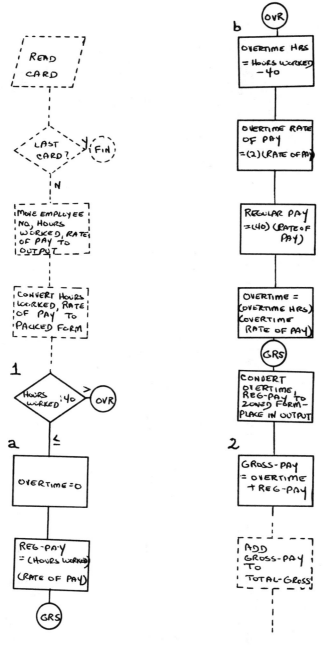

Figure 5.1
Computation of Regular Pay and Overtime Pay

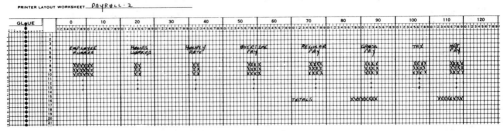

Figure 5.2
Output Layout for Payroll—2

```
LOC   OBJECT CODE    ADDR1 ADDR2  STMT   SOURCE STATEMENT
                                    1  * PAYROLL PROGRAM WITH OVERTIME
                                    2          PRINT  NOGEN
CCCCCC                              3          START
                                    4  * SET UP BASE REGISTER
CCCCCC 0550                         5  BEGIN   BALR  5,0
                           00002    6          USING *,5
                                    7  *
                                    8  * PROCEDURES
                                    9  *
                                   10  * THIS PROGRAM WILL ACCEPT ONE CARD PER EMPLOYEE WITH HIS EMPLOYEE
                                   11  * NUMBER, NUMBER CF HOURS WORKED THAT WEEK, AND HOURLY RATE OF PAY.
                                   12  * IT WILL PRINT ONE LINE PER EMPLOYEE WITH HIS EMPLOYEE NUMBER, HOURS
                                   13  * WORKED, AND RATE CF PAY FROM THE INPUT, ALONG WITH HIS REGULAR PAY,
                                   14  * CVERTIME PAY, GROSS PAY, TAX, AND NET PAY. TOTALS OF GROSS AND NET
                                   15  * PAY FIELDS WILL ALSO BE OUTPUT.
                                   16  *
                                   17  * CPEN FILES
CCCCC2                             18          OPEN   (IN,INPUT,OUT,OUTPUT)
                                   26  * FOR DOS PROGRAMS, FILES ARE OPENED BY THE INSTRUCTION
                                   27  *         OPEN  IN,OUT
                                   28  * PRODUCE HEADER LINES
CCCC12                             29          PUT    OUT,BLANKS
CCCC2C D283 52BB 533F 002BD 00341  34          MVC    OUTAREA,HEADER1
CCCC26                             35          PUT    OUT,OUTAREA
CCCC034 D283 52BB 53C3 002BD C03C5 40          MVC    OUTAREA,HEADER2
CCCC3A                             41          PUT    OUT,OUTAREA
CCCC48                             46          PUT    OUT,BLANKS
CCCC56                             51          PUT    OUT,BLANKS
                                   56  * PROCESSING OF DATA RECORDS
CCCC64                             57  READCARD GET   IN,INAREA
                                   62  * CLEAR OUTPUT AREA
CCCC72 D283 52BB 52BA CC2BD 002BC  63          MVC    OUTAREA,OUTAREA-1
CCCC78 D205 52C0 526B 002C2 026D   64          MVC    CEMPNC,EMPNO
CCCC7E D201 52D2 5271 002D4 00273  65          MVC    CHRS,HRS
CCCC84 D201 52E3 5273 002E5 00275  66          MVC    CRATE,RATE
CCCC8A F211 5447 5271 CC449 00273  67          PACK   PHRS,HRS
CCCC9C F211 5449 5273 0044B C0275  68          PACK   PRATE,RATE
                                   69  * CCMPARE HOURS WORKED TO 40 - SET CONDITION CODE
CCCC96 F911 5447 5465 00449 C0467  70          CP     PHRS,PFORTY
                                   71  * IF PHRS 40, GC TO OVERTIME ROUTINE
CCCC9C 4720 50B4           C00B6   72          BH     CVER
                                   73  * CTHERWISE (PHRS 40 OR PHRS=40) CONTINUE AS FOLLOWS
CCCCA0 F830 544B 5467 0044D 00469  74          ZAP    POVER,PZERO      SET OVERTIME=0
CCCCA6 F831 544F 5449 00451 0044B  75          ZAP    PREG,PRATE
CCCCAC FC31 5447 5447 00451 00449  76          MP     PREG,PHRS        REGULAR PAY
CCCCB2 47F0 50D8           C00DA   77          B      GRS              NOW GO TO GRS
CCCCB6 FB11 5447 5465 00449 00467  78  OVER    SP     PHRS,PFORTY      COMPUTE OVERTIME HRS
CCCCBC F831 544B 5449 0044D 0044B  79          ZAP    POVER,PRATE
CCCCC2 FC30 544B 5468 0044D 00468  80          MP     POVER,P2         COMPUTE OVERTIME RATE OF PAY
CCCCC8 FC31 544B 5447 0044D 00449  81          MP     POVER,PHRS       COMPUTE OVERTIME PAY
CCCCCE F831 544F 5465 C0451 00467  82          ZAP    PREG,PFORTY
CCCCD4 FC31 544F 5449 00451 0044B  83          MP     PREG,PRATE       COMPUTE REGULAR PAY
                                   84  * NOW CONVERT OVERTIME PAY AND REGULAR PAY TO ZONED FORM, ELIMINATE
                                   85  * SIGN, AND PLACE IN OUTPUT AREA.
CCCCDA F333 52F3 544B 002F5 C044D  86  GRS     UNPK   CVERPAY,POVER    UNPACK INTO OUTPUT
```

Figure 5.3
Payroll—2 (Part 1)

receive a negative gross or net pay, or pay taxes in an amount less than zero! Hence we may assume here that field contents are non-negative.

The printer layout worksheet of figure 5.2 describes the desired program output. Note that the output field positions have been somewhat altered from those of the payroll program of chapter 4, in order to allow for the addition of the overtime pay and regular pay fields to the output form.

Now let us examine the listing of our expanded payroll problem (figure 5.3). The portions which have been blocked off represent additions to the original version of chapter 4. Reread the code, paying special attention to the new portions, which we shall discuss.

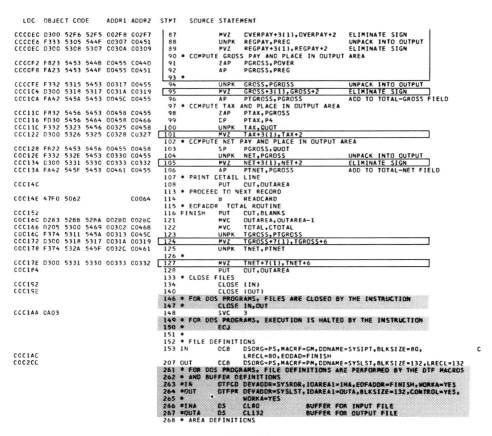

Figure 5.3
Payroll—2 (Part 2)

```
LOC    OBJECT CODE      ADDR1 ADDR2  STMT   SOURCE STATEMENT

                                     269 *
CCC26C                               270 INAREA    CS     OCL80
CCC26C                               271           DS     CL1
CCC26D                               272 EMPNO     DS     CL6
CCC273                               273 HRS       CS     CL2
CCC275                               274 RATE      DS     CL2
CCC277                               275           CS     CL69
                                     276 *
COC2BC  40                           277           DC     C' '
CCC2BD                               278 OUTAREA   DS     OCL132
CCC2BD                               279           CS     CL5
CCC2C2                               280 OEMPNO    DS     CL6
COC2C8                               281           CS     CL12
CCC2C4                               282 OHRS      DS     CL2
CCC2D6                               283           DS     CL15
CCC2E5                               284 ORATE     CS     CL2
CCC2E7                               285           CS     CL14
CCC2F5                               286 OVERPAY   DS     CL4
CCC2F9                               287           DS     CL14
CCC3C7                               288 REGPAY    DS     CL4
CCC3CB                               289           CS     CL12
CCC317                               290 GROSS     DS     CL4
CCC31B                               291           DS     CL10
CCC325                               292 TAX       CS     CL4
CCC329                               293           DS     CL7
CCC330                               294 NET       DS     CL4
CCC334                               295           DS     CL13
                                     296 *
CCC341              CO2BD            297           ORG    OUTAREA
CCC2BD                               298           DS     CL69
CCC3C2                               299 TOTAL     DS     CL6
CCC3C8                               300           CS     CL11
CCC313                               301 TGROSS    DS     CL8
CCC31B                               302           DS     CL17
CCC32C                               303 TNET      DS     CL8
CCC334                               304           CS     CL13
                                     305 *
                                     306 HEADER1   DC     CL132'    EMPLOYEE        HOURS          HOURLY       C
                                                                OVERTIME    REGULAR      GROSS       TAC
CCC341  40404040C5D4D7D3
                                     307 HEADER2   CC     CL132'    NUMBER       WORKED        RATE        C
                                                                PAY         PAY          PAY         C
CCC3C5  4040404040D5E4D4
                                     308 *
CCC449                               309 PHRS      DS     PL2
CCC44B                               310 PRATE     DS     PL2
CCC44D                               311 POVER     DS     PL4
COC451                               312 PREG      CS     PL4
CCC455                               313 PGROSS    CS     PL3
CCC458                               314 PTAX      DS     OPL4
CCC458                               315 QUOT      DS     PL3
COC45B                               316 REM       CS     PL1
CCC45C  0000CCC00C                   317 PTGROSS   DC     PL5'0'
CCC461  C00CC0C00C                   318 PTNET     CC     PL5'0'
CC046E  4C                           319 P4        DC     P'4'
```

Figure 5.3
Payroll—2 (Part 3)

```
LOC   OBJECT CODE      ADDR1 ADDR2  STMT   SOURCE STATEMENT

CCC4E7  040C                         320 PFORTY    DC     P'40'
CCC469  0C                           321 PZERO     DC     P'0'
CCC46A  2C                           322 P2        CC     P'2'
CCC46B  E3D6E3C1D3E2                 323 CTCTAL    CC     C'TOTALS'
COO471  4040404040404040             324 BLANKS    DC     CL132' '
CCCCCC                               325           END    BEGIN
```

Figure 5.3
Payroll—2 (Part 4)

Upon examining the program of figure 5.3, we note that in the latter section —area definitions—few changes have neen made. The description of the input area (INAREA) is unchanged. The description of the output area has been expanded to include fields for the employee overtime pay (OVERPAY) and regular pay (REGPAY), while spacing between the output fields has been adjusted to conform to the revised output description on the printed layout form. In addition, fields POVER and PREG have been added to hold the packed versions of overtime and regular pay computations respectively. The constants 40 (PFORTY), zero (PZERO), and two (P2), have also been stored for use in the overtime routine.

Let us now examine the procedure section of our program. The first portion is unchanged; files are opened, the header lines are output, a record is read, and employee number (EMPNO), hours worked (HRS), and rate of pay (RATE) fields are moved to the output area. The hours worked and rate of pay fields are packed in preparation for further computation.

At this point it is necessary to determine whether the individual whose record is being processed has or has not worked overtime. The number of hours worked (contents of PHRS—a packed number) is compared to 40 using the CP instruction. The CP instruction will set a packed 0, 1, or 2 in the condition code, depending on whether HRS is equal to, less than, or greater than 40, respectively. The BH (Branch on High) instruction, an extended mnemonic, then tests the condition code to see if it contains a 2. The branch instruction will thus result in one of two possible paths, depending upon the condition code setting.

Path 1 – The condition code contains a 2. That means that the individual has worked overtime; a transfer of control will be effected to the instruction called OVER. The number of overtime hours (the number of hours which exceed 40) is then determined by subtracting 40 from the number of hours worked, using the SP instruction. The individual's rate of pay is then "ZAP"ed into POVER (a larger location) after which it is multiplied by two to yield his overtime rate of pay. We then multiply the number of overtime hours by the overtime rate of pay, giving the amount of overtime pay for that employee. The employee's regular pay (pay for the first 40 hours worked) will be determined as usual—by multiplying the regular rate of pay by 40, the number of non-overtime hours for this case. The program then continues to the next sequential instruction (the UNPK instruction at GRS).

Path 2 – The condition code is found by the Branch on High instruction *not* to contain 2. In this case, the determination has been made that the individual has *not* worked overtime. Thus a transfer of control will *not* take place; the computer will continue with sequential execution. A packed zero is "ZAP"ed into

POVER, the packed overtime field, to show that the employee's overtime pay will be zero. The regular pay is computed by multiplying the regular rate of pay by the number of hours worked.

Note that for any particular record, either path 1 or path 2 will be followed, since the cases of having worked overtime and not having worked overtime are the only possibilities. Following the overtime computation, however, the paths once again merge. The overtime pay and regular pay are converted into zoned form, placed in the proper position of the output area, and the signs are eliminated. The contents of overtime pay and regular pay fields are added to yield the gross pay, which is in turn unpacked into the output area, and the sign is eliminated.

The remainder of our program follows the model of the payroll program in chapter 4 for the computation of tax and net pay, the output of detail lines, and the computation and output of "total" fields. The only modification is the addition of those MVZ instructions which eliminate the sign from "UNPK"ed fields; those instructions have been boxed for emphasis in the program listing of figure 5.3.

The program of figure 5.3 was executed on an IBM SYS/370 computer. Output results are shown in figure 5.4. Note the absence of non-numeric characters in the rightmost field positions. If you compare these results with the output of the program in chapter 4, you will most certainly agree that eliminating the sign from output fields is well worth the effort required.

EMPLOYEE NUMBER	HOURS WORKED	HOURLY RATE'	OVERTIME PAY	REGULAR PAY	GROSS PAY	TAX	NET PAY
CCC001	40	03	0000	0120	0120	C030	0090
CC0002	37	06	0000	0222	0222	0055	0167
CCC003	38	10	C000	0380	0380	0095	0285
CCC004	40	06	0000	0240	0240	0060	0180
CCC005	43	03	0018	0120	0138	0034	0104
CC0006	40	04	0000	0160	0160	0040	0120
CCC007	42	04	0016	016C	0176	0044	0132
CCC008	35	09	0000	0315	0315	0078	0237
CC0C09	30	05	0000	0150	0150	0037	0113
CC0010	50	02	0040	0080	0120	0030	0090
CC0011	40	03	0C00	0120	0120	0030	C090
CC0C12	40	05	0000	0200	02C0	0050	0150
CC0013	4C	03	0000	0120	0120	0030	0090
CC0014	42	06	0024	0240	0264	0066	0198
CC0015	38	05	0000	019C	0190	0047	0143
CC0016	41	04	0008	0160	0168	0042	0126
CCC017	40	08	0000	0320	0320	0080	0240
CCC018	43	06	0036	0240	0276	0069	0207
CC0019	38	03	0000	0114	0114	0028	0086
CC0020	42	03	0012	0120	0132	0033	0099

TOTALS   00003925   00002947

Figure 5.4
Payroll—2 Output

5.3.4   The Logical Compare in Main Storage

Our discussion of comparison has so far been limited to the comparison of packed numbers by the CP instruction. It is also possible to compare values in other forms, although care must be taken to ensure that the two numbers being compared share a common format at the time of comparison.

Assembly language actually contains many more compare instructions. The instruction to use in a particular case will depend upon such factors as the formats of the values to be compared, their location (in registers or main storage), and their length.

Operations with packed numbers and EBCDIC values generally take place in main storage; hence we will at this point examine two compare instructions which operate on values in main storage. Their approach is quite different from that of the CP. They belong to a group of compare instructions which perform **logical** comparison. They are the CLC (**Compare Logical Characters**) and the CLI (**Compare Logical Immediate**) instructions.

All Compare Logical instructions treat their operands as though they were unsigned binary values. Thus they may actually be used to compare any code based on ascending or descending binary values. For example, the EBCDIC representation for letters would yield $A = (11000001) < B = (11000010) < \ldots < I = (11001001) < J = (11010001) < \ldots < R = (11011001) < S = (11100010) < \ldots < Z = (11101001)$. The logical compare may thus be used for such purposes as alphabetizing. In a similar manner, the logical compare may be used to compare two numbers both of which are unsigned packed numbers, unsigned zoned numbers, or positive zoned numbers.

The CLC Instruction

The CLC Instruction (**Compare Logical Characters**)

Instruction type: Machine Instruction

Machine format: SS Instruction (Storage to Storage Instruction)

D5	L	B1	D1	B2	D2
0	7 8	15 16 19 20	31 32	35 36	47

Symbolic format:

	name	operation	operands
	[symbolic name]	CLC	name1,name2
or	[symbolic name]	CLC	D1(L,B1),D2(B2)

where D1 and B1 are the displacement and base register respectively used to calculate the first operand address and D2 and B2 are the displacement and base register respectively used to calculate the second operand address. L is the operand length.

. . . .

Rules:
- All operand codes are valid, since comparison is binary and operands are assumed to be unsigned.
- Comparison is left to right.
- Maximum field length is 256 bytes.

Condition code:

0 if operands are equal
1 if first operand < second operand
2 if first operand > second operand
3 cannot result from this instruction

Example 1:

	CLC	ALPHA,BETIZE	
ALPHA	DC	C'LETS'	D3 C5 E3 E2 in storage
BETIZE	DC	C'LOOK'	D3 D6 D6 D2 in storage

Considering the internal representations of the fields being compared as unsigned binary quantities, clearly

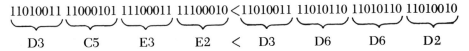

so that this CLC instruction would set the value "1" in the condition code. The value "LETS" has been determined to be "less than" the value "LOOK". We may interpret this to mean that "LETS" would come before "LOOK" in the order of its EBCDIC representation. This technique may be generalized to the extent that field contents may be alphabetized in this way.

Example 2:

	CLC	NOW,NUMBERS	
NOW	DC	C'34'	F3 F4 in storage
NUMBERS	DC	C'43'	F4 F3 in storage

Here   11110011 11110100 $<$ 11110100 11110011

                F3   F4   F4   F3

so that the CLC instruction will place a "1" in the condition code.

Warning:

Caution must be exercised in using the CLC instruction. Should we attempt to compare any values other than those of a form whose collating sequence is based upon ascending or descending binary values, results are unpredictable.

For example, consider the comparison below:

	CLC	TWO,MTWO	
TWO	DC	Z'+2'	C2 or 11000010 in storage
MTWO	DC	Z'−2'	D2 or 11010010 in storage

Here $11000010 < 11010010$ when the representations are treated as unsigned binary values, although obviously $+2$ is not less than -2!

Likewise positive and negative zero will not be considered equal by the CLC, while comparison of two packed or zoned negative numbers will cause the larger to be considered as though it were smaller.

The CLI Instruction

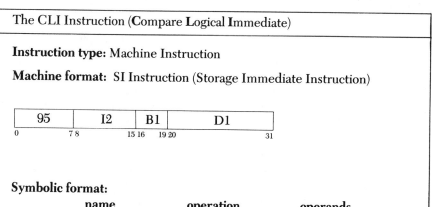

The CLI Instruction (Compare Logical Immediate)

Instruction type: Machine Instruction

Machine format: SI Instruction (Storage Immediate Instruction)

95	I2	B1	D1
0	7 8 15 16	19 20	31

Symbolic format:

	name	operation	operands
	[symbolic name]	CLI	name1,constant
or	[symbolic name]	CLI	D1(B1),I2

where D1 and B1 are the displacement and base register respectively used to calculate the first operand address, and I2 is the immediate operand: a one byte constant.

. . . .

Rules:
- All operand codes are valid, since comparison is binary and operands are assumed to be unsigned.
- Operands are one byte each in length.

Condition code:

    0 if operands are equal
    1 if first operand < second operand
    2 if first operand > second operand
    3 cannot result from this instruction

Example 1:

	CLI	LOC,X'C1'	
LOC	DC	C'A'	C1 in storage

This CLI instruction will set a "0" in the condition code, for LOC contains a hexadecimal C1, which is compared to the hexadecimal constant C1.

Example 2:

	CLI	FLDA,C'2'	
FLDA	DC	P'2'	2C in storage

The CLI instruction will determine that

$$\underbrace{00101100}_{\text{contents of FLDA}} \quad < \quad \underbrace{11110010}_{\text{immediate operand}}$$

and will set a "1" in the condition code. As you can see, had the programmer wished to compare the number "2" to itself, this comparison would not have yielded the proper result. It is incorrect, therefore, to compare numbers in different formats, for results may be highly misleading.

The operation of a compare logical instruction proceeds from left to right. It ends when either an inequality is determined or the end of the fields is reached, whichever occurs sooner. In the case of the CLC instruction, the length of the first operand determines how many bytes will participate in the comparison. For the CLI instruction, each operand must be one byte long.

The CLC instruction might have been used in the payroll program to compare EBCDIC fields, to determine whether or not employees have worked overtime. Do you see how?

The CP instruction in our program compared two packed numbers as follows:

```
            PACK    PHRS,HRS
              .
              .
              .
            CP      PHRS,PFORTY   PHRS contains
              .                   a packed number
              .
              .
PFORTY      DC      P'40'
```

Had we wished to use a logical compare, we might have written

```
            CLC     HRS,CFORTY    HRS contains EBCDIC
              .                   characters
              .
CFORTY      DC      C'40'
```

Perhaps you are wondering why we have not used the CLI instruction here. The reason is quite simple. The CLI instruction can only compare one byte from the instruction itself with one byte in storage; one byte is not enough to accommodate the data for this comparison.

Thus we see that the choice of the proper compare instruction, as indeed the choice of other assembly language instructions for a particular use, should be made with care. But don't worry, for the choice will become much easier as you gain programming experience.

Summary

In this chapter we introduced a method for improving the appearance of program output by eliminating the sign from the low-order portion of output fields.

Comparison and transfer of control (branching) are explained, and are used to expand the basic payroll problem of chapter 4. Employee records are tested for overtime, and regular and overtime pay fields are computed.

Several new instructions were introduced: the MVZ (move zones), the MVI (move immediate), the CP (compare decimal), the CLC (compare logical characters), and the CLI (compare logical immediate) instructions.

Important Terms Discussed in Chapter 5

comparison
condition code
conditional branch

editing
extended mnemonics

immediate (instructions or operands)

logical comparison

Questions

5-1. For each internal code configuration noted below, indicate the appearance of resultant printed output.
    (a) C7D6D6C440C4C1E8
    (b) F1F9F8F4
    (c) F1F9F8C4
    (d) C3C1E3C3C840F2F2

5-2. Suppose that the following character configurations were printed as 3-digit numeric program output. What are their signed numeric values?
    (a) 24M
    (b) 10D
    (c) 10E
    (d) 10J
    (e) 10β
    (f) 99K

5-3. (a) How is numeric punched card data read into the computer in signed form?
     (b) Must all data which is input to the computer be signed? Explain.

5-4. For each of the following stored numeric values in PLACE, tell whether or not
it is necessary or possible to eliminate the sign with an MVZ instruction before
printing the contents of PLACE. When it is necessary, write the appropriate
MVZ instruction.

    (a)   PLACE   DC   C'−40'

    (b)   PLACE   DC   C'40'

    (c)   UNPK   PLACE,NUM
           NUM   DC   P'+496'
           PLACE   DS   CL3

(d)

	UNPK	PLACE,NUM2
NUM2	DC	P'0'
PLACE	DS	CL2

(e)

	UNPK	PLACE,NUM3
NUM3	DC	P'0'
PLACE	DS	CL1

5-5. Given the following defined locations:

UP	DC	C'HIGH'
DOWN	DC	C'LOW'
EXTRA	DC	C'2'

Tell what will be in UP after execution of each of the following MVZ instructions:

(a)	MVZ	UP(3),DOWN
(b)	MVZ	UP+2(2),DOWN+1
(c)	MVZ	UP+1(1),DOWN+2
(d)	MVZ	UP,DOWN

5-6. For the following program segments, tell what value will be set in the condition code as a result of executing each CP instruction. Assume that A, B, and C are defined as:

A	DC	P'− 2'
B	DC	P'+ 2'
C	DS	PL2

(a)	AP	A,A
	CP	A,B
(b)	AP	A,A
	CP	B,A
	AP	A,A
	CP	A,B
(c)	SP	A,A
	SP	B,B
	CP	A,B
(d)	ZAP	C,A
	MP	C,B
	DP	C,=P'−1'
	CP	C(1),=P'4'
	CP	C+1(1),=P'1'
(e)	CP	A,B
	CP	B,A
	CP	A,A
	CP	B,B

5-7. Given:

PNUM	DS	PL2
	DS	CL1
NUM	DS	CL3

where PNUM contains a packed number of unknown quantity, write all instructions necessary to convert the value in PNUM into zoned form in NUM, eliminate the sign from the last character of the zoned number, and place a minus sign before the number in the event that it is negative.

5-8. Follow the instructions of question 5-7, given

PNUM2	DS	PL2
NUM2	DS	CL4

where PNUM2 contains a packed number of unknown quantity. The first byte of NUM2 is to contain either a blank or a minus sign to reflect respective positive or negative values, with the remaining bytes containing the zoned form of the number.

5-9. For each of the following extended mnemonic codes, tell
　　(i)　the meaning of the mnemonic
　　(ii)　the condition code setting(s) upon which the instruction will cause transfer of control.

(a)　B　　　　　　　　　　　　(e)　BP
(b)　NOP　　　　　　　　　　　(f)　BNM
(c)　BL　　　　　　　　　　　　(g)　BZ
(d)　BNE

5-10. In the program of figure 5.3, statements 70 and 72 play a vital role. What is that role?

5-11. What is the function of the MVZ instructions in statements 95, 101, 105, 124, and 127 of figure 5.3? Why were the affected fields not tested to determine the signs of their contents?

5-12. Explain what is meant by logical comparison. How does the operation of the logical compare differ from that of the CP?

5-13. Indicate the condition code setting which will result from the execution of each compare instruction below.

(a)　　　　　　　　CLI　　　PLACE,C'4'
　　　PLACE　　　　DC　　　X'C4'

(b)　　　　　　　　CLI　　　PLACE2,C'4'
　　　PLACE2　　　DC　　　X'F4'

(c)　　　　　　　　CLI　　　PLACE3,C'4'
　　　PLACE3　　　DC　　　P'4'

(d)		CLC	X,Y
	X	DC	C'+2'
	Y	DC	C'−2'
(e)		CLC	X2,Y2
	X2	DC	C'ABC'
	Y2	DC	C'BCD'

5-14. Which of the four valid condition code settings will never result from the execution of a compare instruction? Explain.

5-15. Can the CLC instruction be used to compare packed numbers? zoned numbers? Explain.

Program Exercises

5-1. Write an assembly language program which accepts the following input fields for each record:

field	card columns
FLDA	1-2
FLDB	3-4
FLDC	5-7

For each input record, determine whether FLDA is greater than, equal to, or less than FLDB in value.

(i) If FLDA > FLDB, compute ANS = FLDA − FLDB
(ii) If FLDA = FLDB, let ANS = 100 × FLDC
(iii) If FLDA < FLDB, compute ANS = (FLDA × FLDB)/2

The program is to print one detail line per input record as follows:

field	print positions
FLDA	3-4
FLDB	11-12
FLDC	19-21
ANS	28-32

Arrange a heading line so that field names are centered over field amounts. Skip one line between heading and detail outputs.

Be sure to eliminate the signs from the low-order bytes of zoned fields, and to precede output fields with negative signs, when appropriate.

5-2. Write an assembly language program which accepts the following input fields for each record:

field	card columns
SALENO (salesman number)	2-5
SALARY (base salary)	6-8
AMT (amount sold)	9-11

The program is to determine, for each salesman, whether he sold goods in an amount less than $1000, between $1000 and $5000, or over $5000.

(i) If AMT $\geq$ $5000, add $200 to SALARY
(ii) If $1000 $\leq$ AMT < $5000, add $100 to SALARY
(iii) If AMT < $1000, leave SALARY alone.

Print one detail line per input record as follows, making sure to eliminate signs from low-order field bytes.

field	print positions
SALENO	5-8
SALARY	14-17
AMT SOLD	23-25
BONUS	30-32

BONUS contains: value "YES" for case (i) or (ii) above
value "NO" for case (iii) above

Arrange a double header, with column headings SALESMAN NUMBER, SALARY, AMOUNT SOLD, and BONUS centered over the appropriate field contents. Skip one line between second heading line and first detail output line.

Chapter 6

Decimal Arithmetic with Non-integer Values

DECIMAL ARITHMETIC WITH NON-INTEGER VALUES

Chapters 4 and 5 demonstrated for us how arithmetic may be performed by the computer on packed *integer* values. As you may well imagine, however, virtually all business applications will deal with non-integer fields. For example, money amounts (dollars and cents) or the number of hours worked (what about 1.5 hours?) will involve working with non-integer values. This chapter will discuss some of the more common difficulties in working with packed numbers, as well as some techniques for producing desired results.

6.1   PAYROLL PROBLEM—VERSION 3

Let us reconsider the payroll problem of chapter 5. This time we will use non-integer input values to describe employees' rates of pay and number of hours worked during the week. The employee number will, of course, remain integer.

Input data will be in the form of employee records on punched cards. Each card will contain 3 fields, as described on the input layout of figure 6.1.

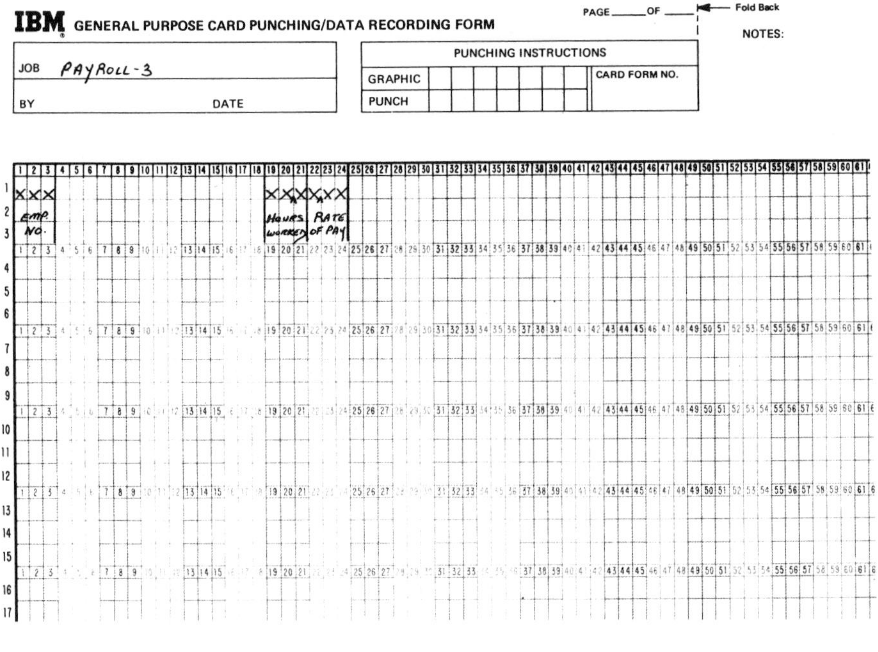

Figure 6.1
Input Layout for Payroll—3

Note that we use the symbol " ∧ "—called a **carat**—to denote an **implied decimal point** here. That is, the decimal point will not be punched on the data card; its presence for the moment is only in the programmer's mind. Don't be concerned about this just yet; we will take care of the decimal point in due time.

The desired output for version 3 of our payroll program is described on the printer layout worksheet of figure 6.2. You will notice that the output description also indicates *implied* decimal points in the output fields; the decimal point will not be printed as part of our output just yet (note that no print positions are alloted on the output form for decimal points). In order to have *real* decimal points (".") printed, assembly language provides special instructions called ED (EDit) and EDMK (EDit and MarK) instructions, which will be discussed in chapter 10. For the moment, we will simply have our numeric digits printed without decimal points, always keeping in mind where the decimal point is supposed to be.

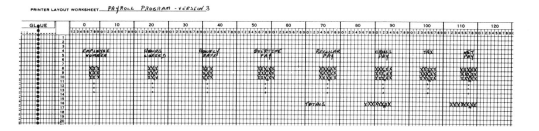

Figure 6.2
Output Layout for Payroll—3

The purpose of version 3 of our payroll program will be essentially the same as that of version 2 of chapter 5. The computer will be instructed to consider the input data (employee records each containing a particular employee's name, hours worked, rate of pay), and to produce the output shown in figure 6.2: header lines; one detail line per employee with the indicated fields; a total line giving the totals for gross pay and net pay fields. Fields involving dollar amounts will be rounded to the nearest two decimal places (that is, to the nearest cent).

Before we attempt to code the solution to this payroll problem, it would be well for us to discuss some of the difficulties which we may encounter. In fact, it is always a good idea to stop and think—to ponder a little—before rushing ahead to solve a programming problem. In this way, we will attempt to find the most straightforward solution to any question which may arise.

Payroll Program—Version 3 will involve several new concepts. We will discuss each of them in turn before applying them to the actual program:

- Alignment of decimal fields for addition and subtraction
- Decimal multiplication with rounding
- Decimal division with shifting

6.2   TECHNIQUES FOR NON-INTEGER DECIMAL ARITHMETIC

6.2.1   Adding and Subtracting Non-integer Fields

DECIMAL ALIGNMENT: WHY?

Let us say that we were asked to compute the sum of the following numbers: 94.43, 72.3, 8. We would almost automatically arrange these values for computation in this way:

$$94.43$$
$$72.3$$
$$\underline{8.}$$

Do you realize what we have done? We have **aligned** the decimal points in these numbers so that they appear one directly above the other. This very conveniently arranges the digits "9" and "7" of the first and second numbers respectively, in the "10's column" (since the digit 9 really represents 9 x 10 or 90 while the digit 7 represents 7 x 10 or 70). The digits 4, 2, and 8 of the second column are in what we call the "1's column" (the digit 4 has the value 4 x 1 or 4, the digit 2 represents 2 x 1 or 2, and the digit 8 has the value 8 x 1 or 8). The third column, the "tenths column", contains digits 4 (meaning 4 x 1/10 or 4/10) and 3 (meaning 3 x 1/10 or 3/10); the fourth column is the "hundreths column" (the digit 3 in this column has the value 3 x 1/100 or 3/100). You are already familiar with the meaning of column positioning in decimal numbers from elementary arithmetic. The column values are based upon the powers of 10, as we indicate below:

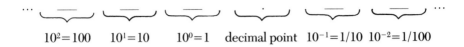

$$10^2=100 \qquad 10^1=10 \qquad 10^0=1 \qquad \text{decimal point} \qquad 10^{-1}=1/10 \qquad 10^{-2}=1/100$$

It is very important for the assembly language programmer to be aware of decimal point positioning and the necessity for proper alignment, for it will be he who will be responsible for its being done. Recall that decimal points within numeric fields in the computer do not exist in any real sense; they are not punched on input cards, nor are they stored as part of the numeric field in computer memory. Thus if the values $94_\wedge 43$, $72_\wedge 3$, $8_\wedge$ (decimal points *implied*) were read and we instructed the computer to add them, the addition would take place thus:

$$94 _\wedge 43$$
$$72 _\wedge 3$$
$$\underline{\qquad 8_\wedge \qquad}$$

with the computer aligning the rightmost (low-order) digits of the fields. As you can see, it will be necessary for the programmer to provide for proper alignment!

TECHNIQUES FOR DECIMAL ALIGNMENT

The computer, upon being instructed to add or to subtract, will automatically align the low-order positions of the operand fields. Considering the numbers above, let us append the digit 0 to the right of the second field and two 0's to the right of the third field. Then aligning the rightmost digits will yield:

$$94 _\wedge 43$$
$$72 _\wedge 30$$
$$\underline{\quad 8 _\wedge 00 \quad}$$

which is fine! It is not even necessary to know the exact constants to be added, as long as we know their lengths and the placement of their decimal points. For example, if we are to subtract a 3-digit number with two decimal places from a 3-digit number with one decimal place, then aligning the decimal points will show us that one 0 need be appended to the minuend in order for the subtraction to be performed:

$$XX _\wedge X0$$
$$\underline{\quad X _\wedge XX \quad}$$

You may find it helpful at the beginning to draw diagrams like the one above to aid in determining how many 0's will be needed and which operand(s) will require them.

There are two approaches which may be taken in order to "pad" a field with zeros on the right. The first approach is arithmetic, while the second involves "shifting" the field to the left. We will consider each in turn.

1. The Arithmetic Approach

The arithmetic approach is quite simple. We know from basic arithmetic that multiplying an integer value by a power of 10 will have the effect of extending the number by as many zeros as are given by the power value itself. That is, multiplying by 10^1 will extend the number with 1 low-order zero, multiplying by 10^2 will extend the number with 2 low-order zeros, and so on. In general, we say that multiplication by 10^n with $n > 0$ will extend the number with n low-order zeros. This technique for extending with low-order zeros can be employed in order to arrange for propei alignment prior to adding or subtracting packed numbers. We have spoken of extending *integer* values with zeros since *all* the numbers we deal with are integer to the computer's mind, regardless of how we wish to interpret them.

Suppose that we wished to find the sum of the following two numbers, with implied decimal points as indicated in the comments to the right of the constant definitions.

NUM1	DC	P'42'	$_\wedge$42,to be interpreted as .42
NUM2	DC	P'+21'	+2 $_\wedge$1,to be interpreted as +2.1

It might be convenient, at this point, to align these numbers as we feel they should be aligned in order to achieve correct results upon addition. Then it will be obvious what modifications, if any, need be made. Remember that the computer aligns rightmost digits for addition and subtraction.

$$\begin{array}{c} _\wedge 42 \\ +2 \,_\wedge 1\ddot{0} \end{array} \quad \longrightarrow \quad \begin{array}{c} _\wedge 42 \\ +2 \,_\wedge 10 \end{array}$$

We see that multiplying the contents of NUM2 by 10 prior to addition will provide the alignment which we seek. The following instructions will find the desired sum:

			Contents of RESULT **after execution**
	ZAP	RESULT,NUM2	02 1C
	MP	RESULT,P10	21 0C
	AP	RESULT,NUM1	25 2C
	.		
	.		
	.		
RESULT	DS	PL2	
NUM1	DC	P'42'	contains 04 2C
NUM2	DC	P'+21'	contains 02 1C
P10	DC	P'10'	

Perhaps you would like to try the following exercise on your own before consulting our solution.

Find the sum of the numbers in the fields A and B:

			Packed form
A	DS	PL1	XS
B	DS	PL2	X$_\wedge$X XS

where "X" symbolizes a packed digit and "S" symbolizes the sign of the appropriate number. The diagram which describes what need be done follows:

$$
\begin{array}{ll}
\text{A:} & \text{X} \wedge \text{00S} \\
\text{B:} & \underline{\text{X} \wedge \text{XXS}}
\end{array}
$$

Thus the contents of A should be extended with 2 low-order zeros before addition.

The coded solution:

			Contents of LOC after execution
	ZAP	LOC,A	00 00 XS
	MP	LOC,P100	00 X0 0S
	AP	LOC,B	0X XX XS: the sum
	.		
	.		
	.		
LOC	DS	PL3	
A	DS	PL1	
B	DS	PL2	
P100	DC	P'100'	

Note that we have defined LOC, the sum location, to be 3 bytes long. This ensures the programmer against the occurrence of overflow, since it is certainly possible for the sum of a 1-byte number and a 2-byte number to require 3 bytes, yet the sum will never exceed 3 bytes.

2. Shifting to the Left

Conceptually, shifting means "pushing" field digits in a particular direction: to the left or to the right. Shifting of decimal fields is accomplished by a combination of instructions (Sys/370 provides a single instruction for this purpose which we will discuss at the end of this chapter). Special attention must be paid to the matter of maintaining the sign in the numeric portion of the last byte of the field. Care must also be taken not to destroy important data when shifting involves the movement of overlapping fields.

Shifting to the Left an Even Number of Places

Consider the following packed field:

FLDA	DC	PL2'−123'	12 3D

We wish to shift this field to the left 2 places; that is, to push it 2 places to the left (adding 2 zeros to the right), maintaining the sign at the end of the field so that the resultant number will be valid for use in packed arithmetic operations. Thus 12 3D will become 12 30 0D. This will certainly require the use of a 3-byte location to hold the finished product.

Examine the following sequence of instructions. The comment portions signify the contents of the respective locations after instruction execution.

		FLDA	**RESULT**
		12 3D	FF FF FF
MVC	RESULT(2),FLDA	12 3D	12 3D FF
MVC	RESULT+2(1),ZERO	12 3D	12 3D 00
MVN	RESULT+2(1),RESULT+1	12 3D	12 3D 0D
MVN	RESULT+1(1),ZERO	12 3D	12 30 0D

FLDA	DC	PL2′−123′
RESULT	DC	XL3′FFFFFF′
ZERO	DC	X′00′

The first MVC instruction simply moves the contents of FLDA into a longer location. Do you see why we have used the Move Characters, instead of the ZAP instruction, for this purpose? The ZAP instruction would have right-justified the contents of FLDA in RESULT (that is, the number would have appeared in the rightmost portion of RESULT). The MVC begins by moving the leftmost byte of te sending field into the leftmost byte of the receiving field, and proceeds rightward until the first operand has been filled. We therefore restricted the length of the first operand with an explicit length: RESULT(2), for we wished that only 2 bytes be moved. The second MVC instruction puts zeros into the last byte of RESULT. (The instruction MVI RESULT+2,X′00′ may also have been used here.)

The third instruction is a MVN—MoVe Numeric—instruction, to be presented in greater detail in section 6.4. It is a machine instruction in storage to storage format. It moves the numeric (low-order) portions of each byte of the second operand into the numeric portions of corresponding bytes of the first operand. Movement occurs from left to right (the numeric portion of the leftmost byte is moved first), and the length of the first operand determines the number of bytes to be affected.

In our example, the instruction MVN RESULT+2(1),RESULT+1 moves the numeric portion of RESULT+1 (which contains the sign of the number) to the numeric portion of RESULT+2 (the last byte of the field). Only one byte is moved, for the first operand has an explicit length of 1. The instruction MVN RESULT+1,ZERO then moves a 0 into the numeric portion of RESULT+1, eliminating the extraneous sign.

Another way of moving and clearing the sign makes use of AND instructions. The AND instructions use 2 operands. The result field will have 1's in those bit positions in which the corresponding bits of both operands were

1's; zeros will be set everywhere else. For example, 1100 AND 0101 yields 0100; the second bit positions of both operands were the only corresponding positions containing 1's.

From a slightly different point of view, 0 AND 0, or 0 AND 1 will always yield 0 in the result; 1 AND 0, or 1 AND 1 will yield the same 0 or 1 respectively in the result. Thus the AND instructions may be used to set bit(s) to zero: simply arrange the bits of the operand to be ANDed so that 1's will correspond to those bits that we wish left alone, and 0's will correspond to those bits that we wish set to zero. This type of process is called **masking**, and the field which performs the process is called the **mask**.

Let us attempt to shift FLDA (from the example above) two places to the left, utilizing the AND instructions:

			FLDA	**RESULT**
			12 3D	88 88 88
	MVC	RESULT(2),FLDA	12 3D	12 3D 88
	MVI	RESULT+2,X'0F'	12 3D	12 3D 0F
	NC	RESULT+2(1),RESULT+1	12 3D	12 3D 0D
	NI	RESULT+1,X'F0'	12 3D	12 30 0D

FLDA	DC	PL2'−123'
RESULT	DC	XL3'888888'

The first instruction, the MVC, moves the contents of FLDA, left-justified, into RESULT. The MVI instruction then places hexadecimal 0F into the rightmost byte of RESULT. The NC—aNd Characters—instruction is a machine instruction in storage to storage format, which ANDs the contents of the two operands and replaces the previous contents of the first operand with the result. In this case the first operand, containing 0F, acts as the mask; 0000 1111 (0F) AND 0011 1101 (3D) yields 0000 1101 in RESULT+2, the last byte of RESULT. As you can see, this NC instruction has in effect transmitted the sign to the rightmost half of the low-order byte. The only thing left to do now is to replace the low-order portion of RESULT+1 with zeros, leaving the high-order portion alone. This can be accomplished by ANDing RESULT+1 with a mask of 1111 0000 binary or F0 hexadecimal. The NI—aNd Immediate—instruction contains the mask itself in the second operand, with the result replacing the first operand in storage. Thus the instruction NI RESULT+1,X'F0' replaces the low-order half of RESULT+1 with zeros.

Incidentally, the examples above moved FLDA to a longer location in order to extend it. That step could be avoided by "padding" FLDA on the right using an extra DS or DC instruction. The revised code for this particular example might look like this:

		FLDA	PAD
		12 3D	?
MVC	PAD,ZERO	12 3D	00
MVN	PAD,FLDA+1	12 3D	0D
MVN	FLDA+1(1),ZERO	12 30	0D

FLDA	DC	PL2′−123′
PAD	DS	CL1
ZERO	DC	X′00′

or like this:

		FLDA	PAD
		12 3D	?
MVI	PAD,X′0F′	12 3D	0F
NC	PAD,FLDA+1	12 3D	0D
NI	FLDA+1,X′F0′	12 30	0D

FLDA	DC	PL2′−123′
PAD	DS	CL1

Note one possible disadvantage of the above instruction sequences: they do not preserve the original number in FLDA.

Shifting to the Left an Odd Number of Places

The techniques just described may be used to shift packed numbers to the left an even number of places. Shifting an odd number of places will require the use of a special instruction, the MVO—MoVe with Offset—instruction, to be presented in greater detail in section 6.4.

The Move with Offset instruction is a machine instruction in storage to storage format with two length factors. It moves the entire contents of the second operand, starting with the *rightmost* byte, into the first operand, starting with the *zone portion of the low-order byte*, and proceeding leftward until the entire second operand has been moved. Any high-order first operand positions which have not been used are then filled with zeros.

For example, consider:

	MVO	FIRST,SECOND	
FIRST	DC	PL4′−9999999′	99 99 99 9D
SECOND	DC	PL3′12345′	12 34 5C

After execution

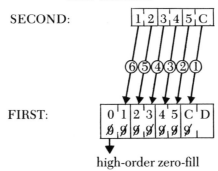

high-order zero-fill

Let us now execute the following statement:

MVN   FIRST+2(1),SECOND+2

After execution

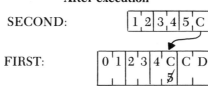

FIRST(3), that is, the first three bytes of FIRST, contains the original contents of SECOND with the last digit truncated.

Note that although the actual truncation was accomplished by the move numeric instruction, it was the MVO instruction which made the truncation possible, for it arranged the number so that the portion to be truncated was in fact in the numeric part of a byte!

Let us now consider the example of the previous section and demonstrate how the MVO will help us accomplish a left shift of an odd number of places. We will assume that the contents of FLDA are to be shifted left three places:

			FLDA	**PAD**
			12 3D	? ?
	MVC	PAD,ZERO	12 3D	00 00
	MVN	PAD+1(1),FLDA+1	12 3D	00 0D
	NI	FLDA+1,X'F0'	12 30	00 0D
	MVO	FLDA(4),FLDA(3)	01 23	00 0D
FLDA	DC	PL2'−123'		
PAD	DS	CL2		
ZERO	DC	X'0000'		

The instruction sequence begins with three instructions (the MVC, MVN, and NI instructions) that accomplish a left shift of four places. The MVO instruction then pushes the field one place to the right with the net result being a left shift of three places. Note that we have used overlapping operands in the MVO, as shown below:

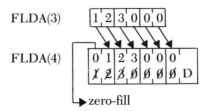

The final result will now be referred to in the program as FLDA(4)

As you can see, this technique can certainly be generalized. In order to accomplish a left shift of an odd number of places, simply shift left one more place than necessary (this will be an even shift) then use the MVO instruction to move rightwards one position.

SOME ADDITIONAL CONSIDERATIONS

Interpreting Our Results

Once decimal alignment has been accomplished and our decimal addition and/or subtraction has been performed, it is important for the programmer to remember where the decimal point belongs.

For example, after proper alignment, adding $95 \wedge 30$ to $8 \wedge 24$ will yield a result with two digits to the right of the decimal point. We must remember where the decimal point belongs. (Recall that as far as the computer is concerned, the point doesn't exist. If the programmer doesn't keep it in mind, no one else will.) If it is deemed desirable, we may insert the point within an output field so that it will appear on our printed output. This procedure makes use of a special instruction, the **ED**it, which is discussed in chapter 10. The number of decimal positions in the result will be the same as the number of such positions in each of the aligned operands.

Avoiding Overflow

Needless to say, it will be important for the addition and subtraction of decimal fieds that our result field be large enough to accommodate the largest possible sum or difference. The result field may require one digit position more in length than does the longer of the two numbers being acted upon.

Thus, the following points may be used for guidance:

1. If the longer of the original numbers contains an even number of significant digits, its location may be used as the result field.
2. If the longer of the original numbers contains an odd number of significant digits, the result field should be one byte longer than that value.

Of course, the programmer's knowledge of his data may serve to modify the determination of the result size. The above rules will allow for the maximum size possible.

6.2.2 Multiplying Non-integer Decimal fields

Preparing the length of the product for multiplication of non-integer fields is really not different from preparing to multiply integer fields. The same rule regardng the length of the product will apply, that is:

The number of bytes in the result = the number of bytes in the multiplier (2nd operand) + the number of bytes in the multiplicand (1st operand).

One additional factor will need consideration, however: the position of the decimal point in the result field. Suppose, for example, that we multiplied two packed numbers of the forms: XXX $\wedge$ XX and XX $\wedge$ X. The length of the result will be, at maximum, eight digits; we will assume three of those digits to be to the right of the decimal point. Thus our product will be of the form: XXXXX $\wedge$ XXX.

Note:

The number of decimal positions in the product = the number of decimal positions in the multiplier + the number of decimal positions in the multiplicand.

Excluding the case of multiplication by an integer, the fact that the product will contain more decimal positions than the original numbers has certain definite implications to the programmer. Suppose we wished to multiply an employee's number of weekly hours worked (format XX $\wedge$ X) by his hourly rate of pay (format X $\wedge$ XX, expressed in dollars and cents). The product, his gross pay, would be at most a six digit number with three decimal positions: XXX $\wedge$ XXX. The employer would hardly issue a check for any amount such as $100.696! Obviously, we have a situation here in which one of two possible alternatives is in order:

- Right truncation—cutting off rightmost digit(s) without regard to their value. (Here, truncating the rightmost digit would yield a salary amount of $100.69.)

- Rounding—Finding the result to a certain accuracy. (Here, rounding to the nearest hundredth would yield $100.70.)

We will consider each of these alternatives in turn.

- *RIGHT TRUNCATION*

Right Truncation may be thought of as a decimal right shift, for it involves "pushing " the number over to the right so that the desired number of digits "fall off". The process is complicated by the special status of the sign, which must remain in the last half-byte in order to preserve the numeric nature of the field.

1. Shifting to the Right

Shifting to the right an even number of places

Let us consider the following problem: John has deposited $30.50 in the bank. He will receive 5% annual interest on his investment. Let us compute the amount of interest that he will receive and truncate the result to yield an amount in dollars and cents.

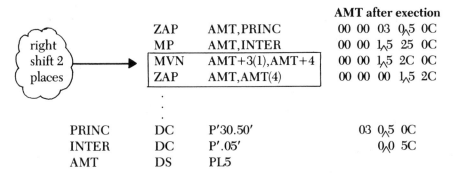

			AMT after exection
	ZAP	AMT,PRINC	00 00 03 0ᴧ5 0C
right	MP	AMT,INTER	00 00 1ᴧ5 25 0C
shift 2	MVN	AMT+3(1),AMT+4	00 00 1ᴧ5 2C 0C
places	ZAP	AMT,AMT(4)	00 00 00 1ᴧ5 2C
		.	
		.	
		.	
PRINC	DC	P'30.50'	03 0ᴧ5 0C
INTER	DC	P'.05'	0ᴧ0 5C
AMT	DS	PL5	

The MVN and ZAP instructions (boxed off above) accomplish a right shift of two places. Let us explain. The first ZAP instruction placed the contents of PRINC (having two implied decimal places), right-justified, into a longer location called AMT. The MP instruction then multiplied the contents of INTER, (INTER also has two implied decimal places) by the contents of AMT. The product will therefore have four implied decimal places; we must truncate two of them in order to achieve a result expressed in dollars and cents.

AMT now contains 00 00 1ᴧ5 25 0C. We wish to truncate the digits 5 and 0 which are rightmost in the field. The MVN instruction will move the numeric portion of the 5th byte of AMT (AMT+4)—the sign—into the numeric portion of AMT+3. This yields 00 00 1ᴧ5 2C 0C in AMT. Note that the truncation has been essentially accomplished. We may now refer to our result as AMT(4) (the first 4 bytes of AMT) if we so wish. In this example, the ZAP instruction right justifies AMT(4) (its second operand) in the AMT field so that the name AMT will now refer to the shifted (truncated) result.

Note that the MVN and ZAP instructions above do not preserve the original (non-shifted) product. If we wished to keep the original product for further reference (perhaps for use in another program computation) the following instructions would accomplish the shift:

MP   AMT,INTER   AMT has 00 00 1ˏ5 25 0C

TRUNC after execution

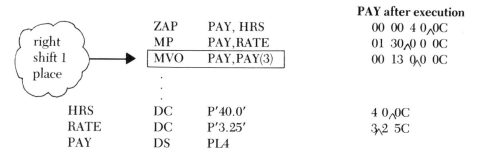

right shift 2 places	MVC TRUNC+1(4),AMT	? 00 00 1ˏ5 25
	MVN TRUNC+4(1),AMT+4	? 00 00 1ˏ5 2C
	MVC TRUNC(1),ZEROS	00 00 00 1ˏ5 2C

```
TRUNC    DS    PL5
ZEROS    DC    X'00'
INTER    DC    P'.05'
AMT      DS    PL5
```

The MVC instruction, by moving only the 4 leftmost bytes of AMT, eliminates the last digit and the sign of AMT from the result field TRUNC. The MVN replaces the digit 5 with the sign, yielding a properly truncated number. The next MVC instruction places zeros in the first byte of TRUNC so that the whole field may be said to contain the shifted result.

Shifting to the right an odd number of places

Suppose that we were to multiply an employee's number of hours worked by his rate of pay and truncate a single last digit, as discussed at the beginning of this section. The instruction sequence below demonstrates how this may be done:

PAY after execution

	ZAP PAY, HRS	00 00 4 0ˏ0C
right shift 1 place	MP PAY,RATE	01 30ˏ0 0 0C
	MVO PAY,PAY(3)	00 13 0ˏ0 0C

```
HRS      DC    P'40.0'          4 0ˏ0C
RATE     DC    P'3.25'          3ˏ2 5C
PAY      DS    PL4
```

The Move with Offset (MVO) instruction has no effect on the sign of the first operand (PAY). It moves the first 3 bytes of pay (these are exactly the digits we want, after truncation) into PAY, beginning immediately to the left of the sign and proceeding to the right with any extra high-order positions filled with zeros. This yields the shifted result in PAY.

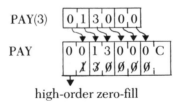

high-order zero-fill

The fact that data movement proceeds from right to left and that movement occurs to the right of the original field contents ensures that problems do not arise with overlapping fields. In general, one must be very careful when overlapping fields, to ensure meaningful results.

Note that in the above example the use of overlapping fields does not preserve the original (non-shifted) product. To preserve that product, it is possible to shift into a different field:

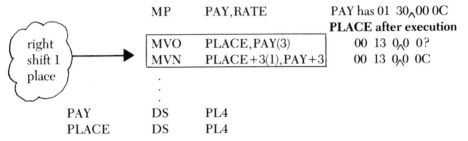

	MP	PAY,RATE	PAY has 01 30∧00 0C
			PLACE after execution
right shift 1 place	MVO	PLACE,PAY(3)	00 13 0∧0 0?
	MVN	PLACE+3(1),PAY+3	00 13 0∧0 0C
	.		
	.		
	.		
PAY	DS	PL4	
PLACE	DS	PL4	

Notice the need for an additional instruction here (the MVN) to move the sign into place.

2. An Arithmetic Approach

Dividing a number by a positive power of 10 has the effect of "moving" the decimal point to the left as many positions as are indicated by that power. This has the same effect as shifting the number to the right that many positions.

Consider, for example, the number 583. Dividing by 10^1 (10 raised to the power 1) and ignoring the remainder yields the quotient 58—equivalent to a 1-position right shift. Dividing by 10^2 and ignoring the remainder yields the quotient 5—equivalent to a 2-position right shift. This technique has the advantage of being applicable to shifting either an even or an odd number of positions.

• *ROUNDING*

Rounding is determining the value of a number to a certain accuracy; for decimal numbers, it would mean determining a value to the nearest tens, whole number, tenth, hundredth, or the like.

For the problem which computes the product of PRINC and INTER, the AMT field contains 00 00 1$_\wedge$5 25 0C after multiplication. Rounding this amount to the nearest cent means incrementing the digit assumed to be in the hundredths column, if the digit to its right is 5 or greater; we do not increment the hundredths position if the thousandths place contains a digit smaller than 5. The job of deciding whether or not to increment can be most easily done by adding a "5" to the digit position immediately to the right of the last digit which we want to keep. In the case of a negative number, of course, we would add "−5" to the same digit position. In our example, this implies the following operation:

$$
\begin{array}{r}
00 \ \ 00 \ \ 1_\wedge5 \ \ 25 \ \ 0C \\
+ \qquad\qquad 05 \ \ 0C \\
\end{array}
$$

Proper field alignment will require that we in fact add a packed 50 to the contents of AMT:

$$
\begin{array}{r}
00 \ \ 00 \ \ 1_\wedge5 \ \ 25 \ \ 0C \\
+ \qquad\qquad 05 \ \ 0C \\
\hline
00 \ \ 00 \ \ 1_\wedge5 \ \ 30 \ \ 0C \\
\end{array}
$$

Note that this resulted in an increment of the hundredths position, as is proper in this case. The instructions below demonstrate how the rounding process may be coded for this example:

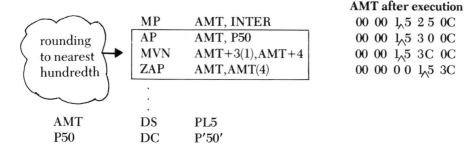

			AMT after execution
	MP	AMT, INTER	00 00 1$_\wedge$5 2 5 0C
rounding	AP	AMT, P50	00 00 1$_\wedge$5 3 0 0C
to nearest	MVN	AMT+3(1),AMT+4	00 00 1$_\wedge$5 3C 0C
hundredth	ZAP	AMT,AMT(4)	00 00 0 0 1$_\wedge$5 3C

AMT	DS	PL5
P50	DC	P'50'

Note that adding 5 to the proper digit position of the number will increment if necessary, and will not increment if not necessary. Truncation of unwanted digits must still be performed in order to complete the rounding process.

Let us pause for a moment to test our understanding. Suppose that we had three fields to be rounded as indicated below. Determine what values need be added to them in order to properly increment before truncation.

(i) $XXX_\wedge XX$ to the nearest tenth
(ii) $XX_\wedge XXX$ to the nearest whole number
(iii) $XXX_\wedge X$ to the nearest hundred (*not* hundredth!)

(i)   requires an addition of 5 (-5 for a negative field value)
(ii) requires an addition of 500 (-500 for a negative field value)
(iii) requires an addition of 500 (-500 for a negative field value)

In section 6.3 of this chapter, we shall see rounding performed as part of the computation of the gross pay and tax in our payroll program.

6.2.3   Dividing Non-integer Decimal Fields

Let us consider a typical division problem with non-integer values. We have a field called EMPSAL (5 bytes long) which contains the sum of employees' salaries for a particular firm, and a field called DIVIS (2 bytes long) which contains the number of divisions in the firm. The average salary per division will be given by the quotient: EMPSAL ÷ DIVIS. We wish our answer expressed to the nearest cent (hundredth).

The division of a 5-byte field by a 2-byte field will look like this:

dd dd dd d$_\wedge$d ds ÷ dd ds

("d" represents a packed digit, "s" represents the sign). If the division is performed in this way, the quotient will be a number with 2 decimal places. To get a result to the *nearest* hundredth, we must carry the division one place further in order to allow for rounding. This implies that we must shift the dividend field 1 place to the left: 0d dd dd dd$_\wedge$dd 0s. Note the implied decimal point in the shifted field. We do not wish to change the value of the field; we wish only to extend it for the purpose of rounding. The high-order zero will be a natural result of our left shift; a field may not occupy 5½ bytes, therefore we require 6 bytes.

One more consideration: will the 6-byte field be long enough to hold both the remainder and the quotient. We know that the remainder will occupy as much space in memory as did the the divisor. In this case, the remainder will occupy 2 bytes, leaving 4 bytes for the quotient. We may check for the possibility of an error occuring when we divide (a divide exception), using the technique described in section 4.2. Arranging dividend and divisor thus,

dividend: 0d dd dd dd dd 0s
divisor: d dd s

we see that it is possible for the divisor to exceed the dividend in size, implying that a divide exception might occur. Assuming that we know the firm to have more than 10 divisions (the programmer must often use his knowledge of the data to help him), we may extend the dividend on the left by one byte, eliminating the possibility of an exception, as we see from the alignment below:

dividend: 00 0d dd dd dd dd 0s
divisor: d dd s

The dividend will thus require 7 bytes. The remainder will occupy 2 bytes, and the remaining 5 bytes will be sufficient to contain the quotient.

Examine the following program segment:

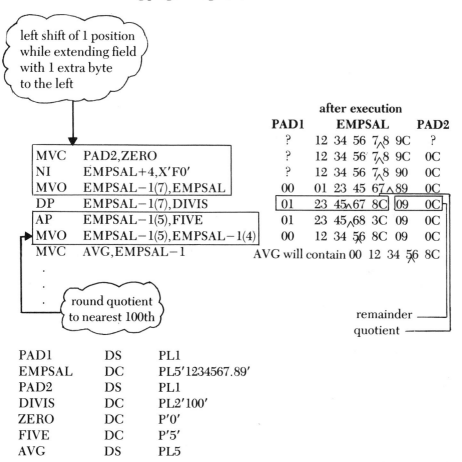

PAD1	DS	PL1
EMPSAL	DC	PL5'1234567.89'
PAD2	DS	PL1
DIVIS	DC	PL2'100'
ZERO	DC	P'0'
FIVE	DC	P'5'
AVG	DS	PL5

Notice that we have extended the dividend field (EMPSAL) by defining PAD1 and PAD2 to its left and right sides respectively. The first three instructions arrange EMPSAL in a field that is in effect 7 bytes long as determined by the discussion above. The DP instruction then divides the contents of DIVIS into the extended EMPSAL field, the field which begins one byte before EMPSAL (that is, at EMPSAL−1) and extends 7 bytes in length (through PAD2). The extended field will contain two numbers as a result of the division: the remainder will occupy the rightmost 2 bytes, and the quotient will occupy the rest.

The AP and MVO instructions round the result to the nearest hundredth using a technique demonstrated above: namely addition of 5 to the digit position immediately to the right of the last digit which we want to keep, and truncation of the now superfluous rightmost digit.

Finally, the MVC instruction places our rounded quotient into a main storage location called AVG.

Most realistic problems involving division of non-integer decimal fields will require the type of logic demonstrated by the example above. We will see another example of this type of division when we compute the tax as part of the new version of our payroll program in section 6.3.

6.3   SOLVING THE PAYROLL PROBLEM WITH NON-INTEGER VALUES

Let us now turn to the flowchart and coded solution to the payroll problem with non-integer values.

The main logic of the problem, described in the flowchart of figure 6.3, is very much the same as the logic of the program in chapter 5. The only difference is the addition of steps G2 and E3: rounding 2 products to the nearest cent, and steps E4 and G4: preparing a field for more accurate division by extending it with a low-order zero, and rounding the quotient to the nearest cent. If you do not remember the program logic, it would be beneficial for you to review this program flowchart carefully.

Now examine the program listing. The blocked-off portions represent additions to the program of chapter 5. In addition, there have been changes in the lengths of certain fields, mostly to accommodate the increased length needed to compute a value to a greater accuracy before rounding and truncation. Study the program of figure 6.4 carefully before reading the discussion which follows .

Upon reading the program, we note very few changes in the sections containing area definitions. The description of the input area (INAREA) is slightly changed, to correspond to our revised program input specification (section 6.1). Likewise, the output area (OUTAREA) description contains output fields with revised lengths, corresponding to the updated input fields (for employee number, hours worked, and rate of pay), and output fields with two decimal places each (overtime pay, regular pay, gross pay, tax and net pay). The POVER and PREG fields (to hold packed overtime pay and packed regular pay respectively) have been extended in length by one byte each, for now they each need accommodate an extra digit, as a result of multiplication. The extra digit will be truncated. The field named PFORTY contains a number which is stored in memory as 40 0C (the number 400) but will be used as a 40 with an implied decimal position. The field P40 contains a packed 40, stored as 04 0C. In addition, the fields P5 and P10, holding the packed numbers 5 and 10 respectively, will be used for rounding and **scaling** (aligning the fields properly in preparation for division) purposes respectively.

We may now examine the procedure section of our program. The beginning is unchanged: files are opened, header lines are printed, and a record is read with employee number (EMPNO), hours worked (HRS) and rate of pay (RATE) moved to the appropriate output area fields. The HRS and RATE fields are packed.

At this point, the CP instruction compares the contents of PHRS (the number of hours worked) to the contents of PFORTY, just identified as the number 400 (40 0C)! Do you understand why the comparison was made to a packed 400 rather than to a packed 40? Recall that the hours worked field on our input was of the form XX$_\wedge$X (with an implied decimal position). This means that a 40-hour work week would be keypunched as 40$_\wedge$0; when read in, it would represented as F4F0C0; and when converted to packed form, it would become 40 0C, the packed number 400! Thus the comparison, to be correct, required the second operand value 400.

The BH instruction then transfers program control to the routine for the non-overtime case or to the routine for the overtime case, depending upon the result of the comparison.

The non-overtime routine places a zero into the overtime field; no computation has been performed, therefore no rounding is required. The computation of the regular pay in the non-overtime case is quite a different matter: the multiplication of hours (format XX$_\wedge$X) by rate (format X$_\wedge$XX) yields a largest possible result of the form XXX$_\wedge$XXX. This is rounded by an addition

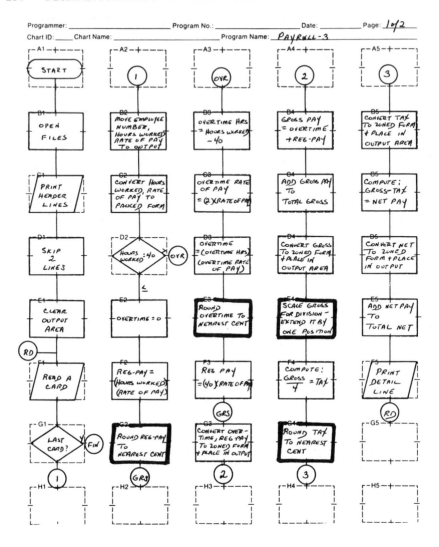

Figure 6.3
Flowchart for Payroll—3 (Part 1)

of 5, and the low-order digit is truncated with the use of the MVO (MoVe with Offset) instruction.

The overtime routine computes the overtime pay by multiplying the number of overtime hours (format $XX_\wedge X$) by the overtime rate of pay (format $X_\wedge XX$),

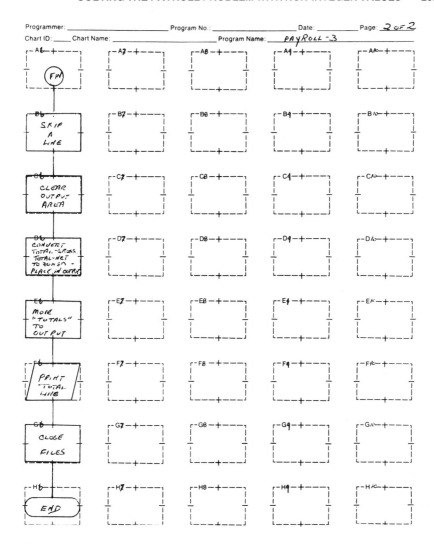

Figure 6.3
Flowchart for Payroll—3 (Part 2)

yielding a largest possible product of the form XXX$_\wedge$XXX. This product is
rounded by adding 5 to the low-order digit and truncating with the use of
the MVO instruction. Note that the Subtract Packed (SP) instruction, which
computes overtime hours, subtracts what is actually the number 400 from

```
LOC     OBJECT CODE        ADDR1  ADDR2   STMT  SOURCE STATEMENT

                                            1  * PAYROLL PROGRAM WITH NON-INTEGER VALUES AND OVERTIME
                                            2          PRINT NOGEN
·CCCCC                                      3          START
                                            4  * SET UP BASE REGISTER
·CCCCC  0550                                5  BEGIN   BALR  9,0
                                     00002  6          USING *,9
                                            7  *
                                            8  * PROCEDURES
                                            9  *
                                           10  * THIS PROGRAM WILL ACCEPT ONE CARD PER EMPLOYEE WITH EMPLOYEE NUMBER,
                                           11  * AND NON-INTEGER HOURS WORKED AND HOURLY RATE OF PAY. IT WILL PRINT
                                           12  * ONE LINE PER EMPLOYEE AS SPECIFIED, WITH FIELDS CONTAINING MONEY
                                           13  * AMOUNTS ROUNDED TO THE NEAREST CENT.
                                           14  *
                                           15  * OPEN FILES
                                           16          OPEN  (IN,INPUT,OUT,OUTPUT)
OCCC2                                      24  * FOR DOS PROGRAMS, FILES ARE OPENED BY THE INSTRUCTION
                                           25  *       OPEN IN,OUT
                                           26  * PRODUCE HEADER LINES
CCC12                                      27          PUT   OUT,BLANKS
00CC20  D283 52E3 5367    002E5  00369    32          MVC   OUTAREA,HEADER1
CCC26                                      33          PUT   OUT,OUTAREA
CC034   D283 52E3 53EB    002E5  003ED    38          MVC   OUTAREA,HEADER2
CCC3A                                      39          PUT   OUT,OUTAREA
CCC048                                     44          PUT   OUT,BLANKS
CCC56                                      49          PUT   OUT,BLANKS
                                           54  *
                                           55  * PROCESSING OF DATA RECORDS
                                           56  *
CCCC4                                      57  READCARD GET  IN,INAREA
                                           62  * CLEAR OUTPUT AREA
CC072   D283 52E3 52E2    002E5  002E4    63          MVC   OUTAREA,OUTAREA-1
                                           64  *
00CC78  D202 52E9 52EB    002EB  00294    65          MVC   CEMPNO,EMPNO
00C07E  D202 52FA 52A4    002FC  002A6    66          MVC   OHRS,HRS
00CC84  D202 530A 52A7    0030C  002A9    67          MVC   CRATE,RATE
00CC8A  F212 52A4 54F3    002A6  004F5    68          PACK  PHRS,HRS
00CC9C  F212 54F5 52A7    004F7  002A9    69          PACK  PRATE,RATE
                                           70  * COMPARE HOURS WORKED TO 40 - SET CONDITION CODE
00CC96  F911 54F3 5513    004F5  00515    71          CP    PHRS,PFORTY
                                           72  * IF PHRS 40 GO TO OVERTIME ROUTINE
00CC9C  4720 50C0                500C2    73          BH    OVER
                                           74  * OTHERWISE (PHRS 40 OR PHRS=40) CONTINUE AS FOLLOWS
                                           75  * ROUTINE FOR NON-OVERTIME CASE              SET OVERTIME=0
00CCAA  F840 54F7 551A    004F9  0051C    76          ZAP   PCVER,PZERO
00CCA6  F831 54FC 54F5    004FE  004F7    77          ZAP   PREG,PRATE
00CCAC  FC31 54FC 54F3    004FE  004F5    78          MP    PREG,PHRS      REGULAR PAY 0XXX,XXXS
00CCB2  FA30 54FC 5517    004FE  00519    79          AP    PREG,P5        ROUND
00CCB8  F132 54FC 54FC    004FE  004FE    80          MVO   PREG,PREG(3)   AND TRUNCATE 00XXX,XXS
00CCBE  47F0 50F0                000F2    81  * ROUTINE FOR OVERTIME CASE
                                           82  *
00CCC2  F811 54F3 5513    004F5  00515    83  OVER    SP    PHRS,PFORTY    OVERTIME HRS  XX,X - 40,0
00CCC8  F841 54F7 551B    004F9  0051D    84          ZAP   PCVER,PRATE
00CCCE  FC40 54F7 54F5    004F9  004F7    85          MP    POVER,P2       OVERTIME RATE 00 00 00 X,X XS
00CCD4  FC41 54F7 54F3    004F9  004F5    86          MP    PCVER,PHRS     OVERTIME PAY  00 0X XX,XX XS
```

Figure 6.4
Payroll—3 (Part 1)

LCC	OBJECT CODE	ADDR1	ADDR2	STMT	SOURCE STATEMENT	
0CC0CA	FA40 54F7 5517	004F9	00519	87	AP PCVER,P5	ROUND
0CCCE0	F143 54F7 C4F9	004F9	004FE	88	MVO POVER,POVER(4)	AND TRUNCATE 00 0X XX XX XS
0CCCE6	F831 54FC 5515	004FE	C0517	89	ZAP PREG,P40	
0CCCEC	FC31 54FC 54F5	004FE	C04F7	90	MP PREG,PRATE	REGULAR PAY 00 0X X,X XS
				91	* NCW CONVERT CVERTIME PAY AND REGULAR PAY TO ZONED FORM, ELIMINATE	
				92	* SIGN, AND PLACE IN OUTPUT AREA	
0CCCF2	F364 531A 54F7	0C31C	004F9	93	GRS UNPK OVERPAY,POVER	UNPACK INTO OUTPUT
0CCCF8	D300 531E 031D	0320	0031F	94	MVZ OVERPAY+4(1),OVERPAY+3	ELIMINATE SIGN
0CCCFE	F343 532C 54FC	0032E	C04FE	95	UNPK REGPAY,PREG	UNPACK INTO OUTPUT
0CC1C4	D300 5330 532F	0332	C0331	96	MVZ REGPAY+4(1),REGPAY+3	ELIMINATE SIGN
				97	* CCMPUTE GRCSS PAY, PLACE IN OUTPUT AREA	
0CC1CA	F824 54F7 5500	00502	004F9	98	ZAP PGROSS,POVER	
0CC1C...	F423 5500 54FC	00502	004FE	99	AP PGROSS,PREG	
0CC116	F342 533C 5500	0033E	00502	100	UNPK GRCSS,PGROSS	UNPACK INTO OUTPUT
0CC11C	D300 5340 533F	00342	00341	101	MVZ GROSS+4(1),GROSS+3	ELIMINATE SIGN
0CC122	FA42 5508 55C0	050A	C0502	102	AP PTGROSS,PGROSS	ADD TO TOTAL-GROSS
				103	* CCMPUTE TAX, PLACE IN OUTPUT AREA	
0CC128	F842 5503 5500	0505	00502	104	ZAP PTAX,PGROSS	PTAX 00 00 XX XX,X XS
0CC12E	FC41 5503 5518	0505	0051A	105	MP PTAX,P10	SCALE FOR DIVISION
				106	*	
0CC134	FD30 5503 5512	0505	00514	107	DP PTAX,P4	PTAX 00 0X X,X XX 0S
0CC13A	FA30 5503 5517	0505	00519	108	AP QUOT,P5	ROUND
0CC140	F132 5503 5503	0505	C0505	109	MVO QUCT,QUOT(3)	AND TRUNCATE 00 XX X,X XS
0CC146	F343 5349 5503	034B	00505	110	UNPK TAX,QUOT	UNPACK INTO OUTPUT
0CC14C	D300 534D 534C	034F	C034E	111	MVZ TAX+4(1),TAX+3	ELIMINATE SIGN
				112	* CCMPUTE NET PAY, PLACE IN OUTPUT AREA	
0CC152	FB23 5500 5503	05C2	00505	113	SP PGROSS,QUOT	
0CC158	F342 5355 5500	0357	0502	114	UNPK NET,PGROSS	UNPACK INTO OUTPUT
0CC15E	D300 5359 5358	035B	C035A	115	MVZ NET+4(1),NET+3	ELIMINATE SIGN
0CC164	FA42 5508 550D	050F	00502	116	AP PTNET,PGROSS	ADD TO TOTAL-NET
				117	* PRINT DETAIL LINE	
0CC16A				118	PUT OUT,OUTAREA	
				123	* PROCEED TO NEXT RECORD	
0CC178	47F0 5062		00064	124	B READCARD	
				125	* ECFADDR B TOTAL ROUTINE	
0CC17C				126	FINISH PUT OUT,BLANKS	
0CC18A	D283 52E3 52E2	02E5	C02E4	131	MVC OUTAREA,OUTAREA-1	
0CC19C	D205 5328 551C	032A	C051E	132	MVC TOTAL,CTOTAL	
0CC19E	F374 5339 5508	033B	0050A	133	UNPK TGROSS,PTGROSS	
0CC19C	D300 5340 537F	0342	00341	134	MVZ TGROSS+7(1),TGROSS+6	
0CC1A2	F374 5352 550D	0354	0050F	135	UNPK TNET,PTNET	
0CC1A8	D300 5359 5358	035B	C035A	136	MVZ TNET+7(1),TNET+6	
0CC1AE				137	PUT OUT,OUTAREA	
				142	* CLOSE FILES	
0CC1BC				143	CLOSE (IN)	
0CC1C6				149	CLOSE (OUT)	
				155	* FGR DDS PROGRAMS, FILES ARE CLOSED BY THE INSTRUCTION	
				156	* CLOSE IN,OUT	
0CC1D2	0A03			157	SVC 3	
				158	* FGR DDS PROGRAMS, PROGRAM EXECUTION IS HALTED BY THE INSTRUCTION	
				159	* EOJ	
				160	*	
				161	* FILE DEFINITIONS	
0CC1C4				162	IN CCB DSORG=PS,MACRF=GM,DDNAME=SYSIPT,BLKSIZE=80,	C
					LRECL=80,EODAD=FINISH	

Figure 6.4
Payroll—3 (Part 2)

```
LOC      OBJECT CODE          ADDR1 ADDR2   STMT  SOURCE STATEMENT

CCC234                                      216  OUT      DCB   DSORG=PS,MACRF=PM,DDNAME=SYSLST,BLKSIZE=132,LRECL=132
                                            270  * FOR DOS PROGRAMS, FILE DEFINITIONS ARE PERFORMED BY THE DTF MACROS
                                            271  * AND BUFFER DEFINITIONS
                                            272  *IN       DTFCD  DEVADDR=SYSRDR,IDAREA1=INA,EOFADDR=FINISH,WORKA=YES
                                            273  *OUT      DTFPR  DEVADDR=SYSLST,IOAREA1=OUTA,BLKSIZE=132,CONTROL=YES,
                                            274  *                WORKA=YES
                                            275  *INA      DS    CL80          BUFFER FOR INPUT FILE
                                            276  *OUTA     DS    CL132         BUFFER FOR OUTPUT FILE
                                            277  * AREA DEFINITIONS
                                            278  *
CCC294                                      279  INAREA   DS    0CL80
CCC294                                      280  EMPNO    DS    CL3
CCC297                                      281           DS    CL15
CCC2A6                                      282  HRS      DS    CL3
CCC2A9                                      283  RATE     DS    CL3
CCC2AC                                      284           DS    CL56
                                            285  *
CCC2E4  40                                  286  CUTAREA  DC    C' '
CCC2E5                                      287  OUTAREA  DS    0CL132
CCC2E5                                      288  OEMPNO   DS    CL6
CCC2EB                                      289           DS    CL3
CCC2EE                                      290  OHRS     DS    CL14
CCC2FC                                      291           DS    CL13
CCC3CC                                      292  ORATE    DS    CL13
CCC3CF                                      293           DS    CL13
CCC31C                                      294  OVERPAY  DS    CL5
CCC321                                      295           DS    CL5
CCC32E                                      296  REGPAY   DS    CL5
CCC333                                      297           DS    CL11
CCC33E                                      298  GROSS    DS    CL5
CCC343                                      299           DS    CL8
CCC34B                                      300  TAX      DS    CL5
CCC350                                      301           DS    CL7
CCC357                                      302  NET      DS    CL5
CCC35C                                      303           DS    CL13
                                            304  *
CCC369               C02E5                  305  *
CCC369                                      306           CRG   OUTAREA
CCC32A                                      307           DS    CL69
CCC33C                                      308  TOTAL    DS    CL6
CCC33B                                      309           DS    CL11
CCC354                                      310  TGROSS   DS    CL8
CCC35C                                      311           DS    CL17
                                            312  TNET     DS    CL8
                                            313           DS    CL13
                                            314  *
CCC369  4040404040C5D4D7D3                  315  HEADER1  DC    CL132'       EMPLOYEE      REGULAR HOURS   OVERTIME   GROSS HOURLY   NET   TAX C'
CCC3ED  4040404040D5E4D4E4                  316  HEADER2  DC    CL132'       NUMBER        PAY     WORKED   PAY        PAY   RATE    PAY       C'
CCC471  404040404040404040                  317  BLANKS   DC    CL132' '
                                            318  *
CCC4F5                                      319  PHRS     DS    PL2
```

Figure 6.4

Payroll—3 (Part 3)

PAGE 5

17 NOV 78

LOC	OBJECT CODE	ADDR1	ADDR2	STMT	SOURCE STATEMENT	
CCC4F7				320	PRATF	DS	PL2
CCC4F9				321	PCVER	DS	PL5
CCC4FE				322	PREG	DS	PL4
CCC5C2				323	PGROSS	DS	PL3
CCC5C5				324	PTAX	DS	OPL5
00C5C5				325	QUCT	DS	PL4
CCC5C9				326	REM	DS	PL1
CCC5CA	C000C0C00C			327	PTGROSS	DC	PL5'0'
00C50F	C000000000C			328	PTNET	DC	PL5'0'
CCC514	4C			329	P4	DC	P'4'
C0C515	400C			330	PFORTY	DC	P'40.0'
C0C517	040C			331	P40	DC	P'40'
00C519	5C			332	P5	DC	P'5'
CCC51A	010C			333	P10	DC	P'10'
CCC51C	0C			334	PZERO	DC	P'0'
CCC51D	2C			335	P2	DC	P'2'
C0051E	E3D6E3C1D3E2			336	CTOTAL	DC	C'TOTALS'
				337	*		
CCCCC0				338		END	BEGIN

Figure 6.4
Payroll—3 (Part 4)

the HRS field. This is necessary for proper alignment, since PHRS is of the form XX$_\wedge$X! The computation of regular pay in the overtime case requires no rounding, for the multiplication of a whole number (P40 contains a packed 40) by a 2-decimal place number (PRATE is of the form X$_\wedge$XX) yields a product with 2 decimal positions. Had PFORTY been used here instead of P40, rounding would have been required!

The program continues, converting overtime and regular pay fields to zoned form and placing them in the output area. Gross pay is computed, unpacked, and placed in the output area. Note that the instructions

$$\text{ZAP} \qquad \text{PGROSS,POVER}$$
$$\text{AP} \qquad \text{PGROSS,PREG}$$

each have a receiving field (first operand) which is shorter in length than the sending field (second operand)! This situation is generally not desirable, however it may sometimes be valid. POVER and PREG at this point each have a minimum of two leading zeros, for they contained longer numbers which have since been truncated. Thus POVER and PREG are only apparently—not actually—longer operands than PGROSS. In addition, the programmer may always use knowledge of his data as a basis for decision making. PGROSS is 3 bytes long hence may contain packed numbers of the form XX X$_\wedge$X XS; we need only be sure that our employees do not earn a weekly gross amount exceeding \$999.99, in order to ensure that PGROSS is large enough.

The computation of TAX follows. Note that the gross pay is extended with one low-order zero in order that the quotient may be first computed to greater accuracy, then rounded after division.

The remainder of the program is essentially unchanged from that of chapter 5, for the computation of net pay, the output of detail lines and the computation and output of "total" fields.

The program was executed on an IBM Sys/370 computer. Sample output records are presented in figure 6.5.

You will note that although we have assumed all our field values (with the exception of the employee number field) to contain decimal positions, decimal points have not apeared as part of our output. We assume that they are implied (imagined). Producing printed output with actual decimal points (as well as possible commas, slashes, question marks, or any other non-numeric characters) within numeric fields will require the use of special instructions called "editing" instructions. A detailed discussion of "editing" can be found in chapter 10.

EMPLOYEE NUMBER	HOURS WORKED	HOURLY RATE	OVERTIME PAY	REGULAR PAY	GROSS PAY	TAX	NET PAY
CC1	400	250	CCOOO	100CC	10000	025C0	07500
CC2	400	283	00000	1132C	11320	02830	08490
C03	400	328	00000	13120	13120	03280	09840
C04	400	210	00000	08400	08400	02100	06300
C05	400	529	CCC00	21160	21160	05290	15870
C06	400	432	C0000	17280	17280	04320	12960
C07	400	324	00000	12960	12960	03240	09720
C08	400	222	00000	08880	08880	02220	06660
C09	400	421	00000	16840	16840	04210	12630
C10	400	460	00000	18400	18400	04600	13800
C11	400	200	00000	08000	08000	02000	06000
C12	400	258	C0000	10320	10320	02580	07740
C13	0C0	583	00000	00000	00000	00000	00000
C14	350	276	00000	09660	09660	02415	07245
C15	400	500	00000	20000	20000	05000	15000
C16	6C0	452	18080	18080	36160	09040	27120
C17	285	299	00000	08522	08522	02131	06391
018	450	486	04860	19440	24300	06075	18225
C19	470	384	05376	15360	20736	05184	15552
C20	580	236	08496	09440	17936	04484	13452
C21	540.	599	16772	23960	40732	10183	30549
C22	2C0	356	00000	0712C	07120	01780	05340
C23	160	421	C0000	0673€	06736	01684	05052
C24	430	521	03126	2084C	23966	05992	07974
C25	400	200	00000	08000	08000	02000	06000
				TOTALS	00380548		00285410

Figure 6.5
Payroll—3 Output

6.4   INSTRUCTIONS FOR SHIFTING DECIMAL FIELDS

The MVN Instruction

The MVN Instruction (**MoVe** Numeric)

Instruction type: Machine Instruction

Machine format: SS Instruction (Storage to Storage Instruction)

D1	L	B1	D1	B2	D2
0	7 8	15 16	19 20	31 32	35 36	47

Symbolic format:

name	operation	operands
[symbolic name]	MVN	name1,name2
or [symbolic name]	MVN	D1(L,B1),D2(B2)

where D1 and B1 are the displacement and base register respectively used to calculate the first operand address, and D2 and B2 are the displacement and base register respectively used to calculate the second operand address. L is the operand length.

. . . .

Rules:

- The numeric portion (low-order 4-bits) of each byte in the second operand field is placed in the numeric portion of the corresponding byte of the first operand field.
- The instruction moves the data through each field one byte at a time.
- The number of numerics moved from the second operand is determined by the length of the first operand.
- The MVN instruction processes data from left to right. The numeric portion of the leftmost byte of the sending field is moved first, into the numeric portion of the leftmost byte of the receiving field. The numeric portion of the second byte from the left of the sending field is then moved in a similar manner, followed by the numeric portion of the third byte, and so on, until the receiving field has been filled.
- The storage areas represented by operand 1 and operand 2 may overlap in memory in any way.
- The zone portion of each byte (the high-order 4 bits) remains unchanged in both operand fields.
- The second operand remains unchanged upon execution of the MVN.
- A maximum of 256 numerics may be moved by one MVN instruction.

Condition Code: The condition code remains unchanged.

Example:

```
        MVN    X,Y
X       DC     P'8'
Y       DC     P'-2'
```

Before execution of the MVN	After execution of the MVN
Y 2|D	Y 2|D
X 8|C	X 8|D

Example:

```
        MVN    HARD+2(2),EASY
HARD    DC     PL4'1234'
EASY    DC     C'ABC'
```

Before execution of the MVN   **After execution of the MVN**

EASY | C 1 | C 2 | C 3 | EASY | C 1 | C 2 | C 3 |

HARD | 0 0 0 | 1 2 3 4 C | HARD | 0 0 0 | 1 2 1 4 2 |

Note that the first operand length determines how many numerics are moved. The first operand has an explicit length factor of 2, therefore 2 numerics are moved. Circled numbers represent the sequence of movement. ① is the first numeric moved, ② is the second.

The MVO Instruction

The MVO Instruction (**MoVe** with **Offset**)

Instruction type: Machine Instruction

Machine format: SS Instruction (Storage to Storage Instruction)

F1	L1	L2	B1	D1	B2	D2
0	7 8 11 12	15 16	19 20	31 32	35 36	47

Symbolic format:

	name	operation	operands
	[symbolic name]	MVO	name1,name2
or	[symbolic name]	MVO	D1(L1,B1),D2(L2,B2)

where D1 and B1 are the displacement and base register respectively used to calculate the first operand address, and L1 is the first operand length. D2 and B2 are the displacement and base register respectively used to calculate the second operand address, and L2 is the second operand length.

. . . .

Rules:

- The second operand is moved into the first operand location, starting with the zone portion of the low-order byte of the first operand, and continuing leftward.
- The numeric portion of the first operand's low-order byte will remain untouched.
- If the first operand field is longer than is needed to contain the second operand, it will be filled with high-order zeros.
- If the first operand field is too short to contain the second operand, left truncation will occur.
- Fields are not checked to verify that they correspond to the requirements for packed notation.
- Overlapping fields are permitted.

Condition Code: The condition code remains unchanged.

Example:

```
              MVO      TRUNC,NUMB(1)
NUMB          DC       P'732'
TRUNC         DC       P'-99999'
```

Before execution   **After execution**

NUMB | 7 | 3 | 2 | C | NUMB | 7 | 3 | 2 | C |

                                                              (2)(1)

TRUNC | 9 | 9 | 9 | 9 | 9 | D | TRUNC | 0 | 0 | 0 | 7 | 3 | D |

                                            high-order
                                            zero-fill

                                                          remains
                                                          unchanged

Example:

```
              MVO      A,A(3)
A             DC       P'123456789'
```

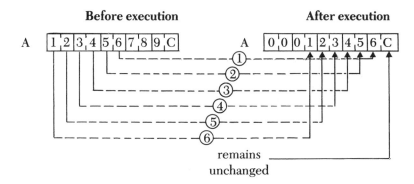

In the examples above, circled numbers represent the sequence of movement: ① is the first digit moved, ② is the second, and so on.

AND Instructions (The NC and NI instructions)

The AND instructions find the **logical product** of the bits of the first and second operands. The result is placed in the first operand location. The result will have 1's in those positions where the corresponding bits of both operands were 1's, while zeros will be set everywhere else. Processing occurs bit by bit from left to right.

The NC Instruction (aNd Character)

Instruction type: Machine Instruction

Machine format: SS Instruction (Storage to Storage Instruction)

D4	L	B1	D1	B2	D2
0	7 8	15 16	19 20	31 32	35 36	47

Symbolic format:

name	operation	operands
[symbolic name]	NC	name1,name2
or [symbolic name]	NC	D1(L,B1),D2(B2)

where D1 and B1 are the displacement and base register respectively used to calculate the first operand address, and D2 and B2 are the displacement and base register respectively used to calculate the second operand address. L is the operand length.

. . . .

Rules:
- All operands (packed, binary, hexadecimal, and so on) are permitted.
- The maximum operand length is 256 bytes.

Condition Code: 0   if the result is 0
1   if the result is not 0
2   cannot result from this instruction
3   cannot result from this instruction

Example:

	NC	NUMB,ZERO	
NUMB	DC	P'999'	99 9C
ZERO	DC	X'0000'	00 00

The operation to be performed may be expressed as 999C AND 0000 (in hexadecimal) or 1001 1001 1001 1100 AND 0000 0000 0000 0000 (in bits). ANDing 0 with either 1 or 0 yields a zero result. Thus NUMB will contain all zeros after execution of the NC instruction.

Example:

	NC	NUMB+1(1),LOC	
NUMB	DC	P'999'	99 9C
LOC	DC	X'0F'	0F

This operation is 9C AND 0F (in hexadecimal) or 1001 1100 AND 0000 1111 (in bits). The first 4 bits of the first operand will be ANDed with zeros, hence they will be replaced by zeros. The second 4 bits of the first operand will be ANDed with ones, hence they will remain the same. After execution, therefore, NUMB+1(1) will contain 0C and the field NUMB will contain 99 0C.

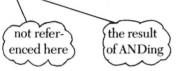

not referenced here the result of ANDing

The NI Instruction (aNd Immediate)

Instruction type: Machine Instruction

Machine format: SI Instruction (Storage Immediate Instruction)

94	I2	B1	D1
0	7 8	15 16 19 20	31

Symbolic format:

	name	operation	operands
	[symbolic name]	NI	name1,constant
or	[symbolic name]	NI	D1(B1),I2

where D1 and B1 are the displacement and base register respectively used to calculate the first operand address, and I2 is the immediate operand: a one-byte constant.

. . . .

Rules:
- All operands (that is, all combinations of zeros and ones) are permitted.
- Operands are each one byte in length.

Condition Code: 0   if the result is 0
1   if the result is not 0
2   cannot result from this instruction
3   cannot result from this instruction

Example:

	NI	A,X'0F'	
A	DC	P'4'	4C

The operation is 4C AND 0F (in hexadecimal) or 0100 1100 AND 0000 1111 (in bits). The result will be 0C (hexadecimal) in A after execution.

Example:

	NI	X,X'F0'
X	DC	B'11110000'

The operation is F0 AND F0 (in hexadecimal) or 1111 0000   AND   1111 0000   (in bits). The result will be F0 (hexadecimal) in X after execution.

6.5   SHIFTING AND ROUNDING DECIMAL FIELDS WITH SYSTEM/370

System/370 users may make use of a special instruction not to be found in the 360 computers: the Shift and Round Packed (SRP) instruction. This instruction can shift a packed number to the right (up to 32 digit positions) or left (up to 31 digit positions) as specified by the programmer. In addition, it may round the shifted result down (truncation), up, or to a nearest accuracy (to the nearest integer, tenth, hundredth, or the like).

The SRP Instruction (**S**hift and **R**ound **P**acked or Shift and Round Decimal)

Instruction type: Machine Instruction

Machine format: SS Instruction (Storage to Storage Instruction)

F0	L1	I3	B1	D1	B2	D2
0	7 8 11 12	15 16	19 20	31 32	35 36	47

Symbolic format:

	name	operation	operands
	[symbolic name]	SRP	name1,D2(B2),I3
or	[symbolic name]	SRP	D1(L1,B1),D2(B2),I3

where (i) D1 and B1 are the displacement and base register respectively used to calculate the first operand address, and L1 is the first operand length.

(ii) D2 + (B2) i.e., the number D2 + the contents of register B2, are calculated. The sum is represented as a 32-bit 2's complement number, the last 6 bits of which (bits 26-31 of that address) determine the number of decimal positions the first operand is to be shifted.

(iii) I3 is the rounding factor, an integer value.

. . . .

Rules:

- The first operand address must contain a number in packed format.
- The second operand address (the number D2 + the contents of register B2) must contain a signed binary number in its low-order 6 bits. This number specifies a left shift if positive and a right shift if negative.
- The third operand (I3) is an integer value specifying the rounding factor to be implemented in the case of a right shift.
- The maximum shift amount is 31 digit positions for a left shift, 32 digit positions for a right shift. (This is enough to completely clear any decimal field.)
- If B2 is zero, the number of positions to be shifted is equal to the value of the low-order 6 bits of D2 alone.
- The computer checks the first operand, even when no shift is specified, to ensure that its digit and sign positions conform to the specifications for packed numbers.
- The computer checks the rounding factor, even when no addition for rounding is to take place, to ensure that its digit code is integer.
- Decimal overflow occurs when significant high-order digit(s) are shifted out during a left shift.
- Overflow cannot occur during a right shift or no shift at all.
- The sign of the result is the original sign, with the exception that a zero result (barring overflow) will be positive.

Condition Code: 0   if shifted result $= 0$
1   if shifted result < 0.
2   if shifted result > 0
3   if overflow occurs

The SRP instruction considers the first operand field and shifts its contents as specified by the low-order 6 bits of the second operand—the shift value. The absolute value of the shift value is the number of digit positions to be shifted, and the sign specifies the direction of the shift. A positive shift value implies a left shift, while a negative shift value implies a right shift. Vacated positions are filled with zeros. Only the digit positions are shifted; the sign position is not.

The third operand—the rounding factor—is added to the first operand by aligning the low-order digit of the rounding factor with the leftmost digit to be shifted out, and propagating the carry, if any, into the first operand field. The addition is performed as though both fields were positive. Thus the programmer need not concern himself with the sign of the first operand field when determining the rounding factor to use. Rounding is *not* performed in the case of a left shift.

In the following examples, we will use a new instruction—the LH or Load Halfword instruction. This instruction will be fully explained in chapter 8.

Example 1:
Let us consider a field called NUM1 which contains the packed number 738∧395, with three implied decimal positions. We wish to round this number to the nearest hundredth.

```
        LH      8,M1
        SRP     NUM1,0(8),5
          .
          .
          .
M1      DC      H'-1'
NUM1    DC      P'738.395'          07 38∧39 5C
```

In order to truncate the rightmost decimal digit, we wish a right shift of one decimal position. Therefore the shift value (the value of the second operand, D2 + (B2)), must be − 1. The LH (**Load Halfword**) instruction copies the binary number − 1 from memory location M1 into register 8. Thus the shift value

$$0(8) = 0 + \text{ contents of register } 8 = 0 + (-1) = -1$$

The rounding factor, the number 5, is added to the leftmost digit to be shifted out (in this case there is only one digit). We have

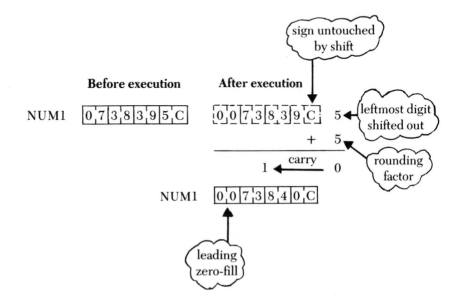

Example 2:

Now examine the field NUM2 containing the packed number $-483_\wedge 4492$. We wish to round this number *up* to the next higher integer.

```
          LH      6,M4
          SRP     NUM2,0(6),10
            .
            .
            .
M4        DC      H'-4'
NUM2      DC      P'-483.4492'     48 34 49 2D
```

In this case we require a right shift of 4 places, thus a shift value of -4. The Load Halfword instruction copies the contents of a halfword location which contains the value -4 into register 6. The SRP instruction interprets the second operand as follows:

$$0(6) = 0 + \text{contents of register } 6 = 0 + (-4) = -4$$

The low-order digit of the rounding factor, 10, is added to the leftmost digit to be truncated. Note here that the rounding factor and the first operand (NUM2) are added *as though they were both positive*, although in this case they are not.

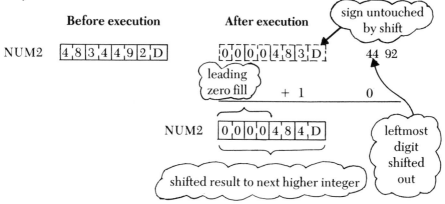

Example 3:

Suppose now that we have a field called NUM3 which we wish shifted to the left two places (that is, multiplied by 100).

```
          LH      4,P2
          SRP     NUM3,0(4),0
            .
            .
            .
P2        DC      H'2'
NUM3      DC      PL3'472'
```

Before execution   **After execution**

NUM3 $\boxed{0\,|\,0\,|\,4\,|\,7\,|\,2\,|\,C}$ NUM3 $\boxed{4\,|\,7\,|\,2\,|\,0\,|\,0\,|\,C}$

                                                       ⌣
                                           trailing zero fill

Note that rounding is not performed in the case of a left shift. Although we specified the rounding factor here to be zero, we might have specified anything. The rounding would not take place in any case.

Note too that had we wished NUM3 to be shifted 4 positions to the left, overflow would have resulted, with significant high-order digits shifted out. This possible condition may be avoided by use of the ZAP.

		LONGER after execution
ZAP	LONGER,NUM3	00 00 47 2C
LH	4,P4	
SRP	LONGER,0(4),0	47 20 00 0C
	.	
	.	
	.	
P4	DC	H′4′
NUM3	DC	PL3′472′
LONGER	DS	PL4

In the examples above, we have used the contents of base register B2 to specify the shift value.

If we wish, we may use the displacement D2 instead, to specify the shift value, or we may use a combination of the two: D2 + (B2). The displacement must be a valid decimal integer. Let us rewrite the SRP instructions for the three examples above, using D2 for the shift value.

Before execution	**Shift instruction**	**After execution**
NUM1 $\boxed{0\,|\,7\,|\,3\,|\,8\,|\,3\,|\,9\,|\,5\,|\,C}$	SRP NUM1,63,5	$\boxed{0\,|\,0\,|\,7\,|\,3\,|\,8\,|\,4\,|\,0\,|\,C}$
NUM2 $\boxed{4\,|\,8\,|\,3\,|\,4\,|\,4\,|\,9\,|\,2\,|\,D}$	SRP NUM2,60,10	$\boxed{0\,|\,0\,|\,0\,|\,0\,|\,4\,|\,8\,|\,4\,|\,D}$
NUM3 $\boxed{0\,|\,0\,|\,4\,|\,7\,|\,2\,|\,C}$	SRP NUM2,2,0	$\boxed{4\,|\,7\,|\,2\,|\,0\,|\,0\,|\,C}$

For NUM1 and NUM2, negative shift values (− 1 and − 4 respectively) were desired. To obtain the binary value for − 1 (in 2's complement form, − 1 is represented as 111111) in the low-order 6 bit positions of the second operand, we use the number 63, whose 6 low-order bit positions comprise − 1 in 2's complement form. The same procedure was followed for NUM2.

NUM3 required a left shift, therefore a positive shift value is represented above in the form of a positive decimal number.

Towards Deeper Understanding

In order to equate the representation of a negative binary number with the representation of a positive decimal number, one may utilize the following rule:

$$\text{2's complement of N} = 2^n - N$$

where n is the number of bits used to represent the value

N is the value to be complemented

Thus for a 6-bit representation:

$$-1 = \text{2's complement of } 1 = 2^6 - 1 = 64 - 1 = 63$$
$$-4 = \text{2's complement of } 4 = 2^6 - 4 = 64 - 4 = 60$$

Summary

In this chapter we examined techniques for performing arithmetic with non-integer decimal values. We discussed the alignment of fields for addition and subtraction. Methods for truncating and rounding the results of decimal multiplication were examined. We have also seen various ways of scaling decimal fields in preparation for division, and truncating and rounding quotient fields.

Several new instructions were introduced: the MVN (move numerics), the MVO (move with offset), the NC (and character), the NI (and immediate), and the SRP (shift and round decimal) instructions.

Important Terms Discussed in Chapter 6

alignment

carat

logical product

mask

rounding

shifting

truncation

Questions

6-1. Distinguish between implied decimal points and real decimal points.

6-2. Given the following fields, with implied decimal points as indicated:

FLDA	DC	P'4.45'
FLDB	DC	P'+50'
FLDC	DC	P'1.1'
FLDD	DC	P'1.222'

Write the appropriate assembly language instructions to:
(a) Compute   FLDA + FLDB
(b) Compute   FLDB − FLDC − FLDD
(c) Compute   FLDD − FLDA
Use the arithmetic approach to align decimal positions.

6-3. Given
      FIELD   DC   PL3'+ 9876'
Write the instructions necessary to shift this field 2 places to the left. Use *three* different approaches to perform the same task.

6-4. Given
      PLACE   DC   PL4'999'
Write instructions necessary to:
(a) Shift the contents of PLACE one place to the left, with the shifted result in a location called PLACE2, and with the contents of PLACE left unchanged.
(b) Shift the contents of PLACE one place to the left, with the shifted result remaining in PLACE.
(c) Shift the contents of PLACE three places to the left, with the shifted result remaining in PLACE.

6-5. Indicate the form of the product after performing each of the multiplications indicated below. (X represents a digit, and $\wedge$ represents an assumed or implied decimal point.) In each case, tell what field size will be necessary to hold the product.
(a) $(XX) (XX_\wedge XX) =$
(b) $(XX_\wedge XXX) (XXX_\wedge XX) (X) =$
(c) $(X_\wedge X) (X_\wedge X) (X_\wedge X) (X_\wedge X) =$
(d) $(XX) (XXX) =$

6-6. Distinguish between the guidelines used for determining the size of the result field after addition or subtraction, and the size of the result field after multiplication.

6-7. Assume that we have fields in the formats shown below, to be rounded as indicated. Tell what integer values need be added to these field contents in order to increment properly, before truncation.
(a) $XX_\wedge XX$ to the nearest whole number
(b) $XX_\wedge XX$ to the nearest tenth

(c) XX∧XX to the nearest ten
(d) XXXXX∧ to the nearest thousand
(e) XXX∧XXXX to the nearest hundredth
(f) XXX∧XXX to the nearest hundred
(g) XX∧XXXX to the nearest thousandth
(h) X∧XXX to the nearest whole number

6-8. Given fields, with formats indicated below:

X	DS	PL3	XX X∧X XC
Y	DS	PL3	XX ∧XX XC
Z	DS	PL2	XX∧ XC

Write the instructions necessary to compute
(a) X + Y   rounded to the nearest hundredth
(b) X × Y   rounded to the nearest hundredth
(c) X × Y × Z   rounded to the nearest whole number
(d) Y − Z   *truncated* to the nearest tenth
Use the arithmetic approach to accomplish all necessary truncation.

6-9. Perform the operations of example 6-8 above, this time using decimal shifting to accomplish all necessary truncation.

6-10. Distinguish between the meanings of the terms *truncation* and *rounding*.

6-11. Consider the following fields:

TOTAL	DC	PL4'98765.43'
NUMB	DC	PL3'67.1'

Write the instructions necessary to compute TOTAL ÷ NUMB, with the quotient determined to the nearest thousandth. Place the quotient into a location called RESULT.

6-12. In the payroll program of figure 6.4, what was the purpose of the MVO instruction in statement 80? Could some other shifting technique have been used which would avoid the use of MVO? Explain.

6-13. Explain the need for statement 105 in the payroll program of figure 6.4.

6-14. What condition code settings (if any) will result from the execution of the MVN instruction? The MVO instruction? The NC instruction? The NI instruction?

6-15. Use the SRP instruction to round the fields shown below to the accuracies requested.
(a) CONS1 DC P'682.444' to the nearest hundredth
(b) CONS2 DC P'−76.89'   to the next higher integer (rounding up)
(c) CONS3 DC P'98.69' to the nearest tenth
(d) CONS4 DC P'66.666' to the next higher tenth (rounding up)

6-16. Use the SRP instruction to shift each field indicated below, 2 places to the left.
(a) FLD1   DC   P'875'
(b) FLD2   DC   P'68.11'

Program Exercises

6-1. Write an assembly language program which accepts input records of the following form:

field	card columns	field format
FLDA	4-9	$XXX_\wedge XXX$
FLDB	10-13	$X_\wedge XXX$
FLDC	14-18	$XXX_\wedge XX$
FLDD	19-21	$XX_\wedge X$
CODE	22	X

For each input record, determine whether CODE contains the value 1, 2, 3, or some other character. Then

(i)   If the contents of CODE = 1, compute

$RES1 = (FLDB) (FLDD) + 8 = (X_\wedge XXX) (XX_\wedge X) + 8$

(ii) If the contents of CODE = 2, compute

$RES2 = (FLDA) \div (FLDC) = (XXX_\wedge XXX) \div (XXX_\wedge XX)$

(iii) If the contents of CODE = 3, compute

$RES3 = (FLDD) (FLDB) \div 4 = (XX_\wedge X) (X_\wedge XXX) \div 4$

(iv) If the contents of CODE are not equal to 1, 2, or 3, then do not perform any computation.

Output will consist of a header line, followed by one detail line per input record. The detail line will consist of fields FLDA, FLDB, FLDC, and FLDD from the input record, along with *either* RES1, RES2, or RES3, depending upon whether the record resulted in case (i), (ii), or (iii) above. If the record resulted in case (iv), then neither RES1 nor RES2, nor RES3 should be printed. Instead the message "CODE DID NOT CONTAIN 1,2, or 3" should appear on the detail line.

The format of the detail line follows:

field	print positions	field format
FLDA	3-8	$XXX_\wedge XXX$
FLDB	18-21	$X_\wedge XXX$
FLDC	31-35	$XXX_\wedge XX$
FLDD	45-47	$XX_\wedge X$
RES1	57-63	$XXXXX_\wedge XX$
RES2	74-79	$XXXX_\wedge XX$
RES3	90-94	$XXX_\wedge XX$

Note: 1. Heading lines should be arranged so that field names are centered over field contents.

2. Skip one line between heading and detail outputs.

3. RES1, RES2, and RES3 should be *rounded to the nearest hundredth* before being printed.

4. Each detail line should contain *either* RES1 *or* RES2 *or* RES3, *or* the printed message; no two of these items should appear on the same line.

6-2. Write an assembly language program which accepts input records of the following form:

field	card columns	field format
ACCT NUMBER	1-6	XXXXXX
PRINCIPAL	7-13	XXXXX$_\wedge$XX
INTEREST RATE	14-17	$_\wedge$XXXX

For each input record, the program should calculate

(i)   MONTHLY INTEREST = (PRINCIPAL) (INTEREST RATE) ÷ 12

(ii) NEW PRINCIPAL = PRINCIPAL + MONTHLY INTEREST

Both monthly interest and new principal amounts should be rounded to the nearest cent (hundredth).

Program output will consist of header lines as indicated below, with one detail line per input record in the field formats indicated. Two lines should be skipped between headings and detail output.

	ACCOUNT	PRINCIPAL	MONTHLY	NEW
	NUMBER		INTEREST	PRINCIPAL
	XXXXXX	XXXXX$_\wedge$XX	XX$_\wedge$XX	XXXXX$_\wedge$XX
print positions:	6-11	20-26	37-40	51-57

Unit 3

Binary and Hexadecimal Numbers and The Standard Instruction Set

Chapter 7

Working With Binary Numbers

7.1   THE STANDARD INSTRUCTION SET

The IBM S/360 and S/370 computers work with what is known as fixed length organization. That is, numeric values are represented in binary form (a way of representing numbers in a number system of base 2), and are allowed only certain lengths. Moreover, along with the fixed length requirement there is a restriction on which of the numbered memory locations the value is permitted to occupy. The IBM S/360 and S/370 also have a set of machine language instructions to deal with those numbers. We call those instructions the **standard instruction set** for the 360 and the 370, since it is "standard" — that is, always supplied with the machine. (The **decimal instruction set** described in chapters 4, 5 and 6 is not standard, although it is very widely used, especially for programming business applications.)

In particular, we shall see that binary numbers in the 360 and 370 are permitted three lengths: 16 bits (halfword), 32 bits (fullword) and 64 bits (doubleword). Binary addresses will occupy 24 bits. The address in main storage which a binary number may occupy is also restricted, and will depend upon its length. Binary numbers may also occupy the general registers.

Why Binary?

There are many reasons why a programmer might choose the standard instructions over the decimal instruction set. Arithmetic computation is generally less time consuming with binary numbers. In most cases, storage of binary numbers is more compact than storage of the equivalent value in packed decimal form. Recall that in packed form, each group of four bits will represent one decimal digit, hence may take on 10 different bit combinations ranging from 0000 to 1001. We then have an additional four bits for the sign. In binary form, each group of four bits may take on 16 different bit combinations, ranging from 0000 to 1111, with only one bit allocated for the sign.

In addition, the IBM S/360 and S/370 series represent address values in binary form, and perform address arithmetic in binary. It is, therefore, quite important for programmers to be able to understand and manipulate binary numbers, even if most of the computation performed by their programs will not use the standard instruction set. Even the proper understanding of much of the output of the assembler program and the linkage editor (location numbers and object code on the listing, External Symbol Dictionary and Relocation Dictionary, and program dumps which are important for debugging) requires a familiarity with binary representation.

7.2   POSITIONAL REPRESENTATION: BINARY AND HEXADECIMAL NUMBERS

By **positional representation**, we mean a representation of numbers in which numeric digits may assume different values depending upon the position, or column, of the number that they occupy.

For example, the decimal number system (the way in which we are generally accustomed to writing numbers) is a positional representation in which values assigned to the columns of the decimal number are "based" upon powers of 10. We may interpret the decimal number 2 as 2×10^0 (or 2×1, for any non-zero number raised to the zero power has the value 1), the decimal number 20 as 2×10^1, the decimal number 200 as 2×10^2, the decimal number 2000 as 2×10^3, and so on. The 0 digits in the decimal numbers above have no value in themselves. They serve merely as "place holders", to ensure that the digit 2 occupies the proper position, or column, of the number. Notice that the positional value assumed by the digit 2 in each of the decimal numbers above is obtained by multiplying its "digit" value (2 units) by the appropriate "column" value (some power of 10).

The interpretation of any decimal number may be performed by following the same procedure to determine the positional value of every decimal digit, and then finding the sum of those values:

$$
\begin{aligned}
482 \quad &= \quad 4 \times 10^2 \quad + \quad 8 \times 10^1 \quad + \quad 2 \times 10^0 \\
&= \quad 4 \times 100 \quad + \quad 8 \times 10 \quad + \quad 2 \times 1 \\
&= \quad 400 \quad + \quad 80 \quad + \quad 2
\end{aligned}
$$

$$
\begin{aligned}
6190 \quad &= \quad 6 \times 10^3 \quad + \quad 1 \times 10^2 \quad + \quad 9 \times 10^1 \quad + \quad 0 \times 10^0 \\
&= \quad 6 \times 1000 \quad + \quad 1 \times 100 \quad + \quad 9 \times 10 \quad + \quad 0 \times 1 \\
&= \quad 6000 \quad + \quad 100 \quad + \quad 90 \quad + \quad 0
\end{aligned}
$$

$$
\begin{aligned}
7.23 \quad &= \quad 7 \times 10^0 \quad + \quad 2 \times 10^{-1} \quad + \quad 3 \times 10^{-2} \\
&= \quad 7 \times 1 \quad + \quad 2 \times 1/10 \quad + \quad 3 \times 1/10^2 \\
&= \quad 7 \quad + \quad 2/10 \quad + \quad 3/100
\end{aligned}
$$

The decimal number system is thus a way of writing numbers by combining any of the digits 0, 1, 2, 3, ..., 9 in appropriate columns. Any of the columns which have been "skipped" after assigning all necessary digits to other columns should be "filled in" with zeros. The decimal column values are:

$$\ldots \quad \overline{} \ \overline{} \ \overline{} \ \overline{} \ \overline{} \ \overline{} \ \underset{\downarrow}{} \ \overline{} \ \overline{} \ \overline{} \ \ldots \quad \text{decimal}$$
$$\quad\quad 10^5 \ \ 10^4 \ \ 10^3 \ \ 10^2 \ \ 10^1 \ \ 10^0 \qquad 10^{-1} \ 10^{-2} \ 10^{-3} \qquad \text{point}$$

We say that the decimal number system is a system of **base** 10 or **radix** 10 ("deci" means "10").

These facts are of course familiar to us from our studies in the primary grades. However, the refresher is important, for we shall see that two other forms of numeric representation used by the S/360 and S/370 computers, binary and hexadecimal forms, follow the same representational guidelines.

7.2.1. The Binary Number System

The binary number system is a positional representation with base 2 (or radix 2). Numbers are represented by placing appropriate combinations of the digits 0 and 1 in columns whose values are powers of 2:

$$\ldots \quad \overline{2^3=8} \ \ \overline{2^2=4} \ \ \overline{2^1=2} \ \ \overline{2^0=1} \quad \cdot \quad \overline{2^{-1}=\tfrac{1}{2}} \quad \overline{2^{-2}=\tfrac{1}{4}} \quad \overline{2^{-3}=\tfrac{1}{8}} \quad \ldots$$

binary point

The "fractional" column values (those to the right of the binary point) are relatively unimportant when considering computer usage of binary numbers. We shall see that more often than not, when fractional values are desired, an integer value will in fact be stored, with the point simply assumed by the programmer to be there. The main reason for choosing the latter technique is that many decimal fractional values cannot be accurately represented in binary form. (Consider, for example, the value .3 decimal. Binary .1 ($=\tfrac{1}{2}$) is too large, .01 ($=\tfrac{1}{4}$) is too small, .011 ($=\tfrac{1}{4} + \tfrac{1}{8}$) is again too large. This difficulty will occur when representing fractional values in any two different number systems.) However, any integer value may be accurately converted from one positional representation to another. Our discussion of binary representation and binary arithmetic will consider integer examples only.

Unsigned Binary Numbers

Unsigned binary numbers are assumed to be positive. The numbers have 1's in positions whose column values total the value of the number being represented, and 0's in all other column positions:

decimal   **binary** (using an 8 bit length)

$$
\begin{aligned}
14 \quad 00001110 \quad &= \quad 0 \times 2^7 \;+ 0 \times 2^6 \;\;+ 0 \times 2^5 \;\;+ 0 \times 2^4 \\
&\quad +1 \times 2^3 + 1 \times 2^2 \;\;+ 1 \times 2^1 \;\;+ 0 \times 2^0 \\
&= \quad 0 \quad + \quad 0 \quad + \quad 0 \quad + \quad 0 \\
&\quad + \quad 8 \quad + \quad 4 \quad + \quad 2 \quad + \quad 0 \\
&= 14
\end{aligned}
$$

$$
\begin{aligned}
56 \quad 00111000 \quad &= \quad 0 \times 2^7 \;+ 0 \times 2^6 \;\;+ 1 \times 2^5 \;\;+ 1 \times 2^4 \\
&\quad +1 \times 2^3 + 0 \times 2^2 \;\;+ 0 \times 2^1 \;\;+ 0 \times 2^0 \\
&= \quad 0 \quad + \quad 0 \quad + \quad 32 \quad + \quad 16 \\
&\quad + \quad 8 \quad + \quad 0 \quad + \quad 0 \quad + \quad 0 \\
&= 56
\end{aligned}
$$

$$
\begin{aligned}
21 \quad 00010101 \quad &= \quad 0 \times 2^7 \;+ 0 \times 2^6 \;\;+ 0 \times 2^5 \;\;+ 1 \times 2^4 \\
&\quad +0 \times 2^3 + 1 \times 2^2 \;\;+ 0 \times 2^1 \;\;+ 1 \times 2^0 \\
&= \quad 0 \quad + \quad 0 \quad + \quad 0 \quad + \quad 16 \\
&\quad + \quad 0 \quad + \quad 4 \quad + \quad 0 \quad + \quad 1 \\
&= 21
\end{aligned}
$$

It is particularly useful for the programmer to be able to recognize the binary numbers 0 through 15 by sight.

Decimal	Binary
0	0000
1	0001
2	0010
3	0011
4	0100
5	0101
6	0110
7	0111
8	1000
9	1001
10	1010
11	1011
12	1100
13	1101
14	1110
15	1111

NOTE: To prevent confusion when using number systems of different bases, we may enclose a number in parentheses and follow it with a subscript denoting the base of the system being used. Thus we may say $(14)_{10} = (1110)_2$ and $(15)_{10} = (1111)_2$.

BINARY ARITHMETIC

Arithmetic with binary numbers follows the same rules and guidelines as arithmetic with decimal numbers, or with numbers in any other number system. We need simply recall the rules for decimal arithmetic, and arithmetic in binary will present no difficulty.

From the programmer's point of view, arithmetic procedures with binary numbers may often be avoided by converting the numbers into decimal form, performing decimal arithmetic, and then reconverting the results into binary form. There are times, however, when an understanding of binary arithmetic, particularly addition and subtraction, will be very useful. For example, the programmer should be able to understand the causes of overflow conditions (a situation in which the results are too large for the available space) and to determine how various forms of binary output were obtained.

BINARY ADDITION

Addition is a procedure in which the sum of any two multiple digit numbers may be computed by memorizing the sums of various combinations of digits. If the sum of the digits in a column cannot be represented in one column, then we carry part of that sum into a column to the left. We are familiar with this concept from decimal arithmetic:

$$
\begin{array}{r}
\text{(no carry)} \quad \begin{array}{r} 7 \\ + 2 \\ \hline 9 \end{array}
\qquad
\text{carry of value "10" as a "1" in the 10's column} \quad \begin{array}{r} 1 \\ 9 \\ +4 \\ \hline 13 \end{array}
\end{array}
$$

In binary, the rules of addition may be briefly summarized as:

$0 + 0 = 0$
$0 + 1 = 1$
$1 + 0 = 1$
$1 + 1 = 0$ and a carry of 1 (may be thought of as $1 + 1 = 10$)

Example:

$$
\begin{array}{r}
\text{carry} \quad \begin{array}{r} 1 \\ (0\,0\,0\,1\,0\,1\,0\,1)_2 \\ + (0\,0\,1\,0\,0\,1\,1\,0)_2 \\ \hline (0\,0\,1\,1\,1\,0\,1\,1)_2 \end{array}
\quad
\begin{array}{c} = \\ = \\ = \end{array}
\quad
\begin{array}{r} (21)_{10} \\ +(38)_{10} \\ \hline (59)_{10} \end{array}
\end{array}
$$

Example:

$$
\begin{array}{rcl}
& 1\,1\,1\,1\,1 & \\
(0\,0\,1\,0\,0\,1\,1\,1)_2 & = & (39)_{10} \\
+\,(0\,0\,0\,1\,1\,1\,1\,0)_2 & = & +(30)_{10} \\
\hline
(0\,1\,0\,0\,0\,1\,0\,1)_2 & = & (69)_{10}
\end{array}
$$

Note that the carry generated by the second column from the right in this example resulted in three 1's in the third column. There, $1 + 1 + 1 = 1$ and a carry of 1 into the next column to the left (think of this as an extension of the rules above: $1 + (1 + 1) = 1 + (0$ and a carry of $1) = (1 + 0)$ and a carry of $1 = 1$ and a carry of 1).

BINARY SUBTRACTION

Binary subtraction may be approached in two different ways (later in this section we will demonstrate yet a third approach: subtraction as the addition of a negative).

The first method is the one which we are accustomed to using for decimal subtraction. When the minuend (the value from which we are subtracting) digit is smaller than the subtrahend (the value being subtracted from the minuend) digit in a particular column (we are attempting to subtract a larger digit value from a smaller digit value), then we "borrow" from the nearest column to the left to enable us to complete the subtraction. We summarize the binary rules of subtraction as follows:

$0 - 0 = 0$

$1 - 1 = 0$

$1 - 0 = 1$

$0 - 1 = 1$ after borrowing 1 (may be thought of as $10 - 1 = 1$)

Example:

$$
\begin{array}{rcl}
\overbrace{0\ 10} & & \\
(0\,1\,\cancel{1}\,\cancel{0}\,1\,1\,1\,0)_2 & = & (110)_{10} \\
-\,(0\,0\,0\,1\,0\,1\,0\,0)_2 & = & -\,(20)_{10} \\
\hline
(0\,1\,0\,1\,1\,0\,1\,0)_2 & = & (90)_{10}
\end{array}
$$

(move "1" over to borrow)

Example:

$$
\begin{array}{rcl}
\cancel{1}\ \cancel{1}\ 10 & & \\
0\,1\,1\,\cancel{0}\,10 & & \\
(0\,\cancel{1}\,\cancel{0}\,\cancel{0}\,\cancel{1}\,\cancel{0}\,1\,0)_2 & = & (74)_{10} \\
-\,(0\,0\,1\,1\,1\,1\,0\,0)_2 & = & -(60)_{10} \\
\hline
(0\,0\,0\,0\,1\,1\,1\,0)_2 & = & (14)_{10}
\end{array}
$$

In the latter example, the subtraction performed in the third column from the right required "borrowing" the 1 from the fourth column from the right, leaving a 0 in the fourth column of the minuend. The subtraction in the fourth column thus became 0 − 1, which required borrowing a digit. However, the fifth column had no digit to borrow! We then proceeded to the closest available "1" bit (the seventh column), replacing it with two 1's in the sixth column. One of those 1's was replaced by two 1's in the fifth column. One of the fifth column 1's was then borrowed for subtraction in the fourth column. (Note that the nature of binary column values made the above procedure possible: each column is "worth" twice the column to its right. Therefore, a 1 bit in each column is equivalent in value to two 1 bits in the column to its right.)

A second method for binary subtraction is the "payback" method. When the subtraction requires us to borrow a digit, we add the digit to the subtrahend of the column being borrowed from, rather than deducting it from the minuend. The examples below use the same values as the subtraction examples above, for comparison purposes.

Example:

$$
\begin{array}{r}
10 \\
(0\,1\,1\,\not{0}\,1\,1\,1\,0)_2 \\
-\,(0\,0\,0\,1\,0\,1\,0\,0)_2 \\
1 \\
\hline
(0\,1\,0\,1\,1\,0\,1\,0)_2
\end{array}
$$

Example:

$$
\begin{array}{r}
10101110 \\
(0\,1\,\not{0}\,\not{0}\,\not{1}\,\not{0}\,1\,0)_2 \\
-\,(0\,0\,1\,1\,1\,1\,0\,0)_2 \\
1\,1\,1\,1 \\
\hline
(0\,0\,0\,0\,1\,1\,1\,0)_2
\end{array}
$$

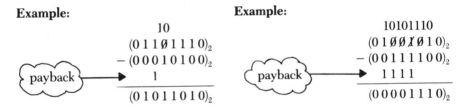

The procedure followed in the second example may be summarized as follows, beginning with the low-order column: 0 − 0 = 0; 1 − 0 =1; 10 (after borrowing) − 1 = 1 and a payback to the subtrahend of the fourth column from the right; 11 (after borrowing) − (1 + 1 = 10) = 1 and a payback to the subtrahend of the fifth column from the right; 10 (after borrowing) − (1 + 1 = 10) = 0 and a payback to the subtrahend of the sixth column from the right; 10 (after borrowing) − (1 + 1 = 10) = 0 and a payback to the subtrahend of the seventh column from the right; 1 -- (0 + 1 = 1) = 0; 0 − 0 = 0.

Signed Binary Numbers

The computer represents addresses (location numbers) in unsigned binary form as described above. For example, when the assembler increments the location counter in order to assign machine language instructions to consecutive storage locations, the computation performed is binary addition. However, when data for a user program is represented in binary form, the numbers are signed (signs are not necessary for address values, since they are always non-negative!), and we call them fixed-point numbers.

In general,

- Positive fixed-point numbers have a **sign bit** (the leftmost bit represents the sign of the number) of 0. The remainder of the number is in true binary form, with 1's in those columns whose values total the value of the number being represented. All other column positions are filled with 0's.

- Negative fixed-point numbers have a sign bit (leftmost bit) of 1. The remainder of the number is in **two's complement form**. Two's complement notation has 0's in those columns whose values total 1 less than the absolute value of the negative number being represented. All other column positions are filled with 1's.

In order for us to fully understand complement representation, we shall begin our discussion with an example of decimal arithmetic using the "ten's complement". This will clarify what complement representation actually means, and the reasons for choosing complement arithmetic as the technique used by the computer.

TEN'S COMPLEMENT

Consider the following decimal subtraction example, with the difference obtained using conventional methods of subtraction.

$$23456 - 14827 = 8629$$

The same result could have been obtained from the following (restated) version of the example:

$$
\begin{aligned}
& 23456 && + && (100000 - 14827) && - && 100000 && \text{ten's} \\
= {} & 23456 && + && 85173 && - && 100000 && \text{complement} \\
= {} & 108629 && && && - && 100000 && \\
= {} & 8629 && && && &&
\end{aligned}
$$

In this example, we call the quantity $(100000 - 14827)$ the **ten's complement** of the number 14827. Subtraction was performed by adding the ten's complement of the subtrahend to the minuend and then subtracting the quantity 100000. However, if we examine the last step in the example above $(108629 - 100000 = 8629)$, we see that the subtraction is actually equivalent to "dropping" the high-order 1 of the minuend. In a computer which performs fixed-point arithmetic, the sum of the two numbers will be allotted the same length as the lengths of the numbers being added. Assuming a fixed-point length of five digits, the addition of the ten's complement of the subtrahend to the minuend in this example would yield

$$\begin{array}{r} 23456 \\ +85173 \\ \hline \cancel{1}08629 \end{array}$$

The high-order 1 would exceed the allotted length and would "drop" off. The last step (subtraction of 100000) is now unnecessary. Thus subtraction using fixed length storage allocation may be performed by *adding the ten's complement of the subtrahend to the minuend*.

In general, the ten's complement of a number N is formed by subtracting it from 10^n where n is the number of digits in N. In the example above, N = 14827, and n = 5, (N is five digits long) so that the ten's complement of $14827 = 10^5 - 14827 = 100000 - 14827$.

> *ten's complement of N = $10^n - N$*
> *where n is the number of digits in N*

In view of the above definition of the ten's complement, we may now note that

$$\begin{array}{lll} & \text{ten's complement of N} & + \quad \text{N} \\ = & 10^n - N & + \quad \text{N} \\ = & 10^n \end{array}$$

If this addition were performed by a computer with fixed length arithmetic, the sum 10^n would be a number of the form 1000...., with n zeros following the digit "1". However, only n positions would be allowed for the sum (both the ten's complement of N and N are n digits long), so that the high-order "1" would drop off. The sum of the number N and the ten's complement of N, using fixed point addition, is 0!

You may recall the definition of a negative number: "−2" is that number which, when added to "+2", yields 0. In general, "−N" is that number which, when added to "+N", yields 0. Note that when fixed-point addition is used, the ten's complement of N conforms to the definition of "−N". Ten's complement numbers may be used in fixed-point arithmetic procedures as valid representations of negative numbers. The procedure for subtraction by adding the complement of the subtrahend to the minuend may be thought of as adding the negative of the subtrahend to the minuend. The expression 17 − (+14) has the same value as the expression 17 + (−14).

One additional note is in order before we leave the discussion of ten's complement notation. The example presented above was the subtraction of a positive number from a larger positive number, yielding a positive difference. What would be the result in a case in which we subtract a larger positive number from a smaller number? The result would be negative and would thus be expressed in complement form! Consider the problem 14827 − 23456 restated as

14827	original minuend
+ 76544	complement of 23456
91371	complement of 8629; therefore the correct result is −8629

In order to properly express the result, it must be recomplemented and a negative sign must then be affixed to it. A situation requiring recomplementing — a negative result — can be recognized by the absence of a high-order 1 "dropping off" after the addition has taken place.

TWO'S COMPLEMENT

Two's complement representation in the binary system is analagous to ten's complement representation in the decimal system.

$$\text{two's complement of } N = 2^n - N$$
$$\text{where } n \text{ is the number of digits in } N$$

Thus if our number $N = 01111$, then $n = 5$ (N has five digits), and the two's complement of $N = 2^5 - 01111 = 100000 - 01111 = 10001$.

In the same manner, if $N = 00101001$ then $n = 8$, and the two's complement of $N = 2^8 - N = 100000000 - 00101001 = 11010111$.

You will notice, from inspecting the examples above or similar examples, that the two's complement of a binary number may be found by:
  (i) inverting the number: changing all 0's to 1's and all 1's to 0's. The result of this step is called the **one's complement**.
  (ii) adding a low-order 1 to the result of step (i).

Thus, for $N = 01111$, we have

(i)	10000
(ii)	+ 1
	10001 two's complement of
	01111

Yet another approach to representing two's complement numbers makes use of the fact that such complement numbers, once formed, have zeros in columns whose values total *one less than the absolute value of the negative number being represented.* Thus the negative number 10001 $(=(-15)_{10})$ has zeros in columns whose values are 2, 4, and 8 ($2 + 4 + 8 = 14$ which is one less than 15, the number's absolute value).

Earlier in this section, we mentioned that the computer represents the sign of a positive binary number with a leftmost bit of 0, while the remainder of the number is in true binary form. Negative binary numbers have a leftmost bit of 1 for the sign, and the rest of the number is in complement form. It is interesting to note at this point that the 0 sign bit will revert to 1 during the complementation process. Likewise, recomplementing a negative number will yield the positive equivalent. (For example, the two's complement of 0001 is 1111; the two's complement of 1111 is 0001.) Moreover, just as positive numbers may be lengthened by expanding leftward with high-order 0's, negative numbers may be expanded on the left with high-order 1's, leaving the numerical value unchanged. (Note that 0101 complemented is 1011; 00101 complemented is 11011; 000101 complemented is 111011; and so on.)

Let us consider some examples which illustrate fixed-point addition as performed in the computer upon signed binary numbers:

Example:

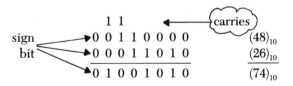

The addition of two positive numbers (sign bit = 0) yields a positive sum.

Example:

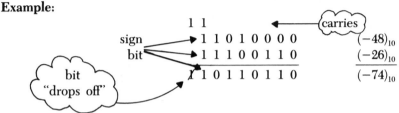

The addition of two negative numbers (sign bit = 1) yields a negative sum.

Example:

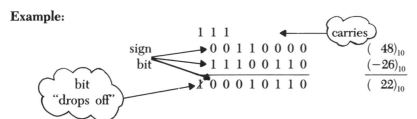

The addition of numbers of unlike sign (one positive, one negative) yields a sum whose absolute value is the difference between the absolute values of the original numbers, and whose sign is equivalent to the sign of the original number with the larger absolute value. $|+48| > |-26|$, therefore the sum is positive.

Example:

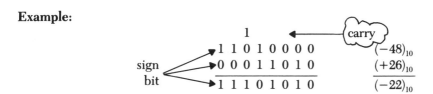

The addition of a negative number with a larger absolute value to a positive number of smaller absolute value yields a negative sum.

Note that negative sums are left in two's complement form. Recomplementation is not necessary, for in the computer, two's complement form is the negative representation. It should also be noted that when the sum is too large to fit into the allotted fixed length, we say that an **overflow condition** has occurred. We shall discuss overflow in chapter 8, when we present the computer instructions to perform binary arithmetic.

Subtraction of signed binary numbers is performed by adding the minuend, the one's complement of the subtrahend, and a low-order one.

Examples:

1.

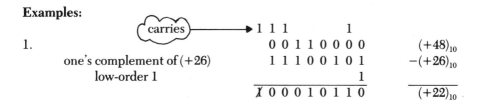

2.

```
        ( carries )  ───────▶    1 1        1
                               0 0 1 1 0 0 0 0        (+48)₁₀
one's complement of (−26)      0 0 0 1 1 0 0 1       −(−26)₁₀
    low-order 1                              1
                              ─────────────────      ──────────
                               0 1 0 0 1 0 1 0        (+74)₁₀
```

3.

```
        ( carries )  ──────▶ 1 1        1
                             1 1 0 1 0 0 0 0        (−48)₁₀
one's complement of (+26)    1 1 1 0 0 1 0 1       −(+26)₁₀
    low-order 1                            1
                            ─────────────────      ──────────
                             1̸ 1 0 1 1 0 1 1 0      (−74)₁₀
```

4.

```
        ( carries )  ───────▶    1        1
                               1 1 0 1 0 0 0 0        (−48)₁₀
one's complement of (−26)      0 0 0 1 1 0 0 1       −(−26)₁₀
    low-order 1                              1
                              ─────────────────      ──────────
                               1 1 1 0 1 0 1 0        (−22)₁₀
```

MAXIMUM BINARY NUMBERS AND THE BINARY ZERO

A maximum positive binary number is represented with a sign bit of zero, and all 1's in the numeric portion of the number. Thus, the largest positive halfword (16-bit number) consists of a zero sign bit and 15 one bits, and has the decimal value 32,767. In the same manner, the largest positive fullword (32-bit number) consists of a zero sign bit and 31 one bits, and has the decimal value 2,147,483,647:

$$01111111 \ 11111111 = 2^{15}-1 = 32,767$$
$$01111111 \ 11111111 \ 11111111 \ 11111111 = 2^{31}-1 = 2,147,483,647$$

A negative binary number of largest absolute value has a sign bit of one, and all 0's in the numeric portion of the number. Thus, the largest negative halfword has a sign bit of 1 and 15 zero bits, and has the decimal value −32,768. The largest negative fullword has a sign bit of 1 and 31 zero bits, with a decimal value of −2,147,483,648:

$$10000000 \ 00000000 = -2^{15} = -32,768$$
$$10000000 \ 00000000 \ 00000000 \ 00000000 = -2^{31} = -2,147,483,648$$

The binary value 0 in two's complement notation is always positive, with a zero sign bit and all zero numeric bits. A halfword zero is thus represented as

00000000 00000000.

sign bit

Towards Deeper Understanding

Binary addition and subtraction (with both signed and unsigned numbers) are important procedures for the assembly language programmer to understand. Binary multiplication and division are less crucial. In terms of understanding the computer's computational procedures, we shall see that multiplication and division are carried out by appropriately combining the operations of addition, complementation and shifting. It is interesting, however, to observe how the multiplication and division take place.

The following discussion of binary multiplication and division in the computer should not be construed in any way to be a comprehensive description of these operations. It is meant merely to give the reader a "feeling" for computer handling of these binary procedures. The discussion is included primarily to improve the reader's understanding of the fixed-point multiplication and division instructions presented in chapter 8.

Binary multiplication on paper is carried out by copying the multiplicand and shifting each time we have a 1-bit in the multiplier, and moving one extra position leftward (equivalent to copying 0's) each time we have a 0-bit in the multiplier:

    0111 multiplicand
    0101 multiplier
    0111 copy multiplicand (mult. by rightmost multiplier digit)
    0000 0's (need not be written)
    0111 shift leftward and copy multiplicand (mult. by third
                multiplier digit from the right)
    0000 0's (need not be written)
carries ⟶111
    0100011

In the computer, the instruction to multiply two fixed-point numbers has the multiplier in an odd-numbered register. The computer then fills the even-numbered register preceding it with 0's so that we have an expanded multiplier in two registers, an "even-odd pair" (say register 4 contains 0's and register 5 contains the original multiplier so that registers 4-5 considered together have the expanded multiplier). The multiplier is the first operand of the instruction. The computer then places the multiplicand (the second operand) into a special register which is nonaddressable (the programmer cannot reference it). The computer then performs the following two steps 32 times, once for each multiplier bit.

1. The low-order multiplier bit is examined. If the bit is 1, the multiplicand is added to the even multiplier register (the high-order register, originally filled with 0's). This is equivalent to copying the multiplicand when we have a 1-bit in the multiplier, for multiplication on paper. Otherwise, addition does not take place; this is equivalent to copying zeros as part of the multiplication on paper.

2. The even-odd multiplier registers are "shifted" to the right one bit position. The low-order bit of the pair (an original multiplier bit) is lost. All other bits are moved to the right one bit position, and the high-order bit position of the pair is filled in with a 0.

Note that after steps 1 and 2 are performed 32 times, all the original multiplier bits will have been shifted out completely and the product will be left in the even-odd register pair.

The diagram below illustrates the multiplication procedure, assuming an even-odd multiplier pair. For brevity we assume 4-bit register lengths, and therefore four repetitions of the two procedural steps listed above. We have chosen positive quantities for our illustration. However, the same procedure is followed for negative values, with complementation of operands and recomplementation of results when appropriate.

multiplicand	multiplier		
	even register	odd register	
0 1 1 1	0 0 0 0	0 1 0 1	even register filled with zeros
0 1 1 1	0 1 1 1	0 1 0 1	multiplicand added to even register
	0 0 1 1	1 0 1 0	right shift
0 1 1 1	0 0 0 1	1 1 0 1	right shift
0 1 1 1	1 0 0 0	1 1 0 1	multiplicand added to even register
	0 1 0 0	0 1 1 0	right shift
0 1 1 1	0 0 1 0	0 0 1 1	right shift

The result in the even-odd register pair is 0 0 1 0 0 0 1 1. We have found that $(7)_{10} \times (5)_{10} = (35)_{10}$.

Binary division on paper is performed as a series of repeated subtractions. When we determine a quotient, we are actually determining how many times we may repeatedly subtract the divisor value from the dividend until we exhaust the dividend value. We may eventually reach a point at which we are left with some dividend quantity which is smaller than the divisor, so that further subtraction is not possible. At such time the series of subtractions will cease, and the quantity left is called the division **remainder**. The number of subtractions which took place is the **quotient**:

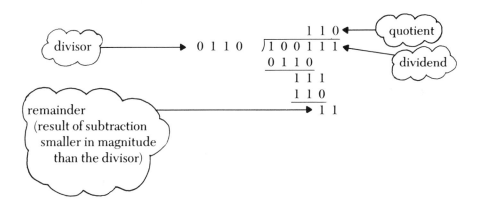

In the computer, the instructions which divide one fixed-point number into another have a dividend which is two fullwords long in an even-odd register pair. The divisor is one fullword long. The computer then performs the following steps 32 times, once for each register bit.

1. The content of the even-odd register pair (the dividend) is shifted leftward one bit position. Then the divisor is subtracted from the contents of the even (high-order) dividend register.

2. If the divisor exceeds the contents of the even-numbered register in magnitude, the divisor is added back, nullifying the subtraction. Otherwise, the low-order dividend bit is changed to 1.

The diagram below illustrates the division procedure, assuming an even-odd dividend pair. As above, we use positive quantities and 4-bit register lengths, with repetitions of the two procedural steps for division.

divisor	dividend		
	even register	odd register	
0 1 1 0	0 0 1 0	0 1 1 1	
0 1 1 0	0 1 0 0	1 1 1 0	dividend shifted left
	1 1 1 0	1 1 1 0	subtracting indicates that divisor exceeds contents of even register
0 1 1 0	0 1 0 0	1 1 1 0	therefore divisor is added back
0 1 1 0	1 0 0 1	1 1 0 0	left shift
0 1 1 0	0 0 1 1	1 1 0 1	subtracting indicates divisor does not exceed contents of even register. low order bit ─▶1
0 1 1 0	0 1 1 1	1 0 1 0	left shift
0 1 1 0	0 0 0 1	1 0 1 1	subtracting indicates divisor does not exceed contents of even register. low order bit─▶1
0 1 1 0	0 0 1 1	0 1 1 0	left shift
	1 1 0 1	0 1 1 0	subtracting indicates divisor does not exceed contents of even register
0 1 1 0	0 0 1 1	0 1 1 0	therefore divisor is added back

After the division process, the remainder is left in the even register, the quotient in the odd register (compare these results with those of the long division above for verification).

7.2.2   The Hexadecimal Number System

The hexadecimal number system is a positional representation with base or radix 16. It is used in the System/360 — 370 as a convenient, compact way of representing strings of 0's and 1's.

The hexadecimal number system has 16 digits: 0,1,2,3,4,5,6,7,8,9,A,B,C,D, E,F, are equivalent in value to the decimal numbers 0 — 15 respectively. Column values are powers of 16:

$$\ldots \quad \overline{16^2=256} \quad \overline{16^1=16} \quad \overline{16^0=1} \quad \cdot \quad \overline{16^{-1}=1/16} \quad \overline{16^{-2}=1/256} \quad \ldots$$

The chart below illustrates the first 33 hexadecimal numbers along with the equivalent values in decimal and binary forms:

Decimal	Hexadecimal	Binary
0	0	0 0 0 0
1	1	0 0 0 1
2	2	0 0 1 0
3	3	0 0 1 1
4	4	0 1 0 0
5	5	0 1 0 1
6	6	0 1 1 0
7	7	0 1 1 1
8	8	1 0 0 0
9	9	1 0 0 1
10	A	1 0 1 0
11	B	1 0 1 1
12	C	1 1 0 0
13	D	1 1 0 1
14	E	1 1 1 0
15	F	1 1 1 1
16	10	0 0 0 1 0 0 0 0
17	11	0 0 0 1 0 0 0 1
18	12	0 0 0 1 0 0 1 0
19	13	0 0 0 1 0 0 1 1
20	14	0 0 0 1 0 1 0 0
21	15	0 0 0 1 0 1 0 1
22	16	0 0 0 1 0 1 1 0
23	17	0 0 0 1 0 1 1 1
24	18	0 0 0 1 1 0 0 0
25	19	0 0 0 1 1 0 0 1

Decimal	Hexadecimal	Binary
26	1A	0 0 0 1 1 0 1 0
27	1B	0 0 0 1 1 0 1 1
28	1C	0 0 0 1 1 1 0 0
29	1D	0 0 0 1 1 1 0 1
30	1E	0 0 0 1 1 1 1 0
31	1F	0 0 0 1 1 1 1 1
32	20	0 0 1 0 0 0 0 0

Notice the correspondence between hexadecimal numbers and their binary equivalents in the chart above. Each hexadecimal digit, considered separately, corresponds to a group of 4 bits in the binary equivalent. Thus, while hexadecimal representation is a number system in itself, one of its main functions from the programmer's point of view is to serve as a "shorthand" notation for long strings of 0's and 1's. We have already seen "hexadecimal notation" used as a compact way of representing packed and zoned representations (chapter 3). We did not then consider the strings of hexadecimal characters as having column values or as having meaning as legitimate numbers in themselves; they served merely as a "notation". Our point here is that when used as a shorthand for *binary* numbers, hexadecimal acquires a new dimension. The groups of hexadecimal digits may be interpreted as numbers in themselves.

Your ability to easily interpret hexadecimal numbers will improve as you gain experience in working with them. Consider the following expansions of hexadecimal numbers:

Decimal   Hexadecimal

420   1A4 $1 \times 16^2 \quad + 10 \times 16^1 \quad + 4 \times 16^0$

$= 256 \quad\quad + 160 \quad\quad + 4$

$= 420$

$172^{33/256}$ AC.21 $10 \times 16^1 \quad + 12 \times 16^0 \quad + 2 \times 16^{-1} \quad + 1 \times 16^{-2}$

$= 160 \quad\quad + 12 \quad\quad + 2/16 \quad\quad + 1/256$

$= 172^{33/256}$

4369   1111 $1 \times 16^3 \quad + 1 \times 16^2 \quad + 1 \times 16^1 \quad + 1 \times 16^0$

$= 4096 \quad\quad + 256 \quad\quad + 16 \quad\quad + 1$

$= 4369$

Some other methods for interpreting and representing hexadecimal values will be presented in section 7.2.3.

Hexadecimal Arithmetic

Hexadecimal arithmetic follows the same rules as does arithmetic in other number systems. We must, of course, accustom ourselves to using the hexadecimal digits 0 through F, and to interpreting numbers which look very much like decimal numbers, according to their hexadecimal meanings. For example, the hexadecimal number 23 is equivalent in value to decimal 35; hexadecimal 46 is equivalent to decimal 70, and so on.

Addition and subtraction of hexadecimal numbers are useful skills for the programmer, especially so when address calculation is required or for interpreting program dumps (chapter 14, section 14.4.3).

HEXADECIMAL ADDITION

Hexadecimal addition is performed by-considering the sums of digits in successive columns, beginning with the rightmost (low-order) column and proceeding leftward. When the sum of two digits exceeds the value of the largest hexadecimal digit $(F = (15)_{10})$, the sum cannot be represented in a single

+	1	2	3	4	5	6	7	8	9	A	B	C	D	E	F	10
1	02	03	04	05	06	07	08	09	0A	0B	0C	0D	0E	0F	10	11
2	03	04	05	06	07	08	09	0A	0B	0C	0D	0E	0F	10	11	12
3	04	05	06	07	08	09	0A	0B	0C	0D	0E	0F	10	11	12	13
4	05	06	07	08	09	0A	0B	0C	0D	0E	0F	10	11	12	13	14
5	06	07	08	09	0A	0B	0C	0D	0E	0F	10	11	12	13	14	15
6	07	08	09	0A	0B	0C	0D	0E	0F	10	11	12 ˙13	14	15	16
7	08	09	0A	0B	0C	0D	0E	0F	10	11	12	13	14	15	16	17
8	09	0A	0B	0C	0D	0E	0F	10	11	12	13	14	15	16	17	18
9	0A	0B	0C	0D	0E	0F	10	11	12	13	14	15	16	17	18	19
A	0B	0C	0D	0E	0F	10	11	12	13	14	15	16	17	18	19	1A
B	0C	0D	0E	0F	10	11	12	13	14	15	16	17	18	19	1A	1B
C	0D	0E	0F	10	11	12	13	14	15	16	17	18	19	1A	1B	1C
D	0E	0F	10	11	12	13	14	15	16	17	18	19	1A	1B	1C	1D
E	0F	10	11	12	13	14	15	16	17	18	19	1A	1B	1C	1D	1E
F	10	11	12	13	14	15	16	17	18	19	1A	1B	1C	1D	1E	1F
10	11	12	13	14	15	16	17	18	19	1A	1B	1C	1D	1E	1F	20

Table 7.1
Hexadecimal Addition

column. A carry of 1 will then be generated to the next high-order column. This carry means that 16 "column units" in some digit position are being replaced by one "column unit" in the next high-order digit position. This interpretation of the carry is valid for any column for which the "carry" procedure takes place. It is the nature of hexadecimal column values that each column's worth is 16 times that of the column to its right. For example, $(D)_{16} + (3)_{16} = (10)_{16}$; $(F)_{16} + (E)_{16} = (1D)_{16}$; $(9)_{16} + (8)_{16} = (11)_{16}$. The sums of all possible combinations of 2 hexadecimal digits are summarized in table 7.1. (Certainly the table should not be necessary, however it is convenient.)

To use the table, we simply find the digits we wish to add, one in the leftmost column and the other in the top or bottom row. The intersection of the appropriate column and row will give the sum. If a carry into a particular column means that the sum of three digits need be computed for that column, then the chart may either be used twice, or the addition of the 1 to one of the digits may be performed mentally, with the next addition performed with the aid of the chart. Alternately, the use of the chart may be avoided altogether, with all computation performed mentally.

The sums obtained in the examples below were verified by conversion of the hexadecimal numbers into decimal form.

Example:

$$
\begin{array}{rcr}
(1\,4\,1\,2)_{16} & = & (5\,1\,3\,8)_{10} \\
+(A\,0\,0\,D)_{16} & = & +(4\,0\,9\,7\,3)_{10} \\
\hline
(B\,4\,1\,F)_{16} & = & (4\,6\,1\,1\,1)_{10}
\end{array}
$$

Example:

carry → 1

$$
\begin{array}{rcr}
(5\,6\,4\,0)_{16} & = & (2\,2\,0\,8\,0)_{10} \\
+ (0\,6\,F\,F)_{16} & = & + (1\,7\,9\,1)_{10} \\
\hline
(5\,D\,3\,F)_{16} & = & (2\,3\,8\,7\,1)_{10}
\end{array}
$$

Example:

carries → $1\,1$

$$
\begin{array}{rcr}
(1\,1\,A\,B)_{16} & = & (4\,5\,2\,3)_{10} \\
(1\,0\,F\,F)_{16} & = & (4\,3\,5\,1)_{10} \\
\hline
(2\,2\,A\,A)_{16} & = & (8\,8\,7\,4)_{10}
\end{array}
$$

HEXADECIMAL SUBTRACTION

Hexadecimal subtraction may be performed using either the "borrowing" method or the "payback" method, similar to the methods used for binary subtraction (section 7.2.1). As we have seen in the case of hexadecimal addition, carrying or borrowing 1 in hexadecimal is carrying or borrowing a quantity equivalent to decimal 16.

The difference obtained from all possible combinations of two hexadecimal digits may be obtained from table 7.1 above. We simply find the subtrahend digit in the topmost row of the table, then follow the column headed by this digit downward until the minuend digit is encountered. Follow the minuend's row across to the leftmost digit. The digit which heads the row is the difference between the minuend and subtrahend values. If the subtrahend is greater in value than the minuend (we are subtracting a larger digit from a smaller digit—a case in which "borrowing" is appropriate) then we simply append a borrow of 1 to the minuend digit before searching for the difference value in the table (in effect we are adding 16 to the minuend digit). Of course, use of the table for hexadecimal subtraction is entirely optional. The table should in any case be considered a convenience only, and the programmer should be able to perform hexadecimal subtraction without it.

Example:

$$
\begin{array}{rcl}
(C\ 4\ A)_{16} &=& (3\ 1\ 4\ 6)_{10} \\
(B\ 1\ 2)_{16} &=& (2\ 8\ 3\ 4)_{10} \\
\hline
(1\ 3\ 8\ )_{16} &=& (\ \ 3\ 1\ 2)_{10}
\end{array}
$$

Example:

$$
\begin{array}{rcl}
\phantom{(A\ 2\ 3)_{16}}\ \ 11 & & \\
\phantom{(A\ 2\ 3)_{16}}\ 9\ \cancel{1}\ 13 & & \\
(\cancel{A}\ \cancel{2}\ \cancel{3})_{16} &=& (2\ 5\ 9\ 5)_{10} \\
(3\ B\ A)_{16} &=& (\ \ \ 9\ 5\ 4)_{10} \\
\hline
(6\ 6\ 9)_{16} &=& (1\ 6\ 4\ 1)_{10}
\end{array}
$$

The latter example utilizes the "borrowing" method. We begin with the low-order column. The digit A (decimal 10) cannot be subtracted from 3, therefore, we borrow 1 from the second column from the right. The borrowed 1 is worth 16 1's in the rightmost column. Therefore, we are now subtracting A from 13 (decimal 19), giving 9. Subtracting B (decimal 11) from 1 (left in the second minuend column after the borrowing took place) is likewise impossible, requiring us to borrow from the third column (the third minuend digit from the right becomes 9). The subtraction in the second column from the right may now be expressed as the subtraction of B (decimal 11) from 11 (decimal

17), yielding the difference value 6. The third column from the right is easily handled: $9 - 3 = 6$.

Example:

$$
\begin{array}{rcl}
(A^1\ 2^1\ 3)_{16} & = & (2\ 5\ 9\ 5)_{10} \\
(3\quad B\ A)_{16} & = & (\ \ 9\ 5\ 4)_{10} \\
\end{array}
$$

$$
\begin{array}{rcl}
\text{carries} \longrightarrow 1\quad 1 & & \\
\hline
(6\quad 6\quad 9)_{16} & = & (1\ 6\ 4\ 1)_{10}
\end{array}
$$

This example is equivalent to the example described above; here we use the "payback" method. Note that each time a digit was borrowed, rather than deducting 1 from the minuend of the column being borrowed from, we add 1 to the subtrahend.

Example: (borrowing method)

$$
\begin{array}{r}
\text{borrows} \longrightarrow \quad 12 \\
1\ \not{2}\ 14 \\
\not{2}\ \not{3}\ \not{4} \\
-\ 1\ A\ E \\
\hline
0\ 8\ 6
\end{array}
$$

Example: (payback method)

$$
\begin{array}{r}
2^1 3^1 4 \\
-\ 1\ A\ E \\
\text{paybacks} \longrightarrow 1\ 1 \\
\hline
0\ 8\ 6
\end{array}
$$

7.2.3 Integer Conversions: Binary, Hexadecimal and Decimal Numbers

It is sometimes necessary for the programmer to convert numbers from one representational system to another. For example, checking binary program output may be more conveniently done if the numbers were first expressed in decimal form. In this section, we shall examine selected methods for converting integer values from one positional representation into another. Conversions between binary, hexadecimal and decimal representations will be considered.

Binary ⟶ Hexadecimal Conversion

To convert a binary number into hexadecimal form, we subdivide the number into groups of 4 bits beginning with the binary point. (For an integer, of course, the binary point occurs immediately to the right of the low-order digit.) Each group of 4 bits is then replaced by a single hexadecimal digit equivalent in value to the 4-bit group considered alone (disregarding the actual place values of those bits within the binary number).

Example:

binary: 0 1 1 0, 1 0 1 0, 1 1 0 1, 1 1 1 1,
hexadecimal: 6 A D F

Example:

binary: 1 0 1 0, 1 0 1 1, 1 1 0 0, 0 0 0 1,
hexadecimal: A B C 1

One question which may be anticipated in the above procedure is what to do if the binary number is of a length which does not divide evenly into groups of 4 bits. The answer would be to simply expand the number with extra high-order bits (for signed numbers, the expansion would be with zeros if positive, with ones if negative) until a length divisible by 4 is obtained. In practice, however, this difficulty will not be encountered. In the S/360 and 370, addresses expressed in binary form will occupy 24 bits, while fixed-point binary numbers are restricted to lengths of 16 bits, 32 bits or 64 bits. All allowed lengths are thus multiples of 4.

Hexadecimal ⟶ Binary Conversion

Conversion of hexadecimal numbers into binary form is the reverse of the above process. We replace each hexadecimal digit with a group of 4 bits equivalent to the digit value.

Example:

hexadecimal: 1 2 A 6
binary: 0 0 0 1 0 0 1 0 1 0 1 0 0 1 1 0

Example:

hexadecimal: 2 3 8 4
binary: 0 0 1 0 0 0 1 1 1 0 0 0 0 1 0 0

It is important here that each hexadecimal digit be replaced by exactly *4* bits, regardless of how many bits might actually be required to represent its value. Note in the first example above, that the hexadecimal digits 1, 2 and 6 were replaced by bit groups 0001, 0010 and 0110 respectively. The high-order zeros in these 4-bit groups were crucial for a correct binary result (omitting them would obviously yield a result with a very different value).

Decimal ⟶ Binary Conversion

One technique for converting a decimal number into binary form involves a series of repeated divisions. We divide the decimal number by 2, noting the remainder (which may be either 0 or 1) near the quotient. We then divide the successive resulting quotients by 2 and note the remainders in a separate column. This process continues until a quotient of 0 is reached. The binary equivalent of the original decimal number is composed of the remainder digits, beginning with the last remainder obtained, which becomes the high-order bit, and continuing through to the first remainder obtained, which becomes the low-order bit.

Example:

Convert $(76)_{10}$ into binary form.

quotients	remainders
2/76	
2/38	0
2/19	0
2/9	1
2/4	1
2/2	0
2/1	0
0	1

Thus $(76)_{10} = (1001100)_2$

Note that the division is so simple, that it may be done mentally.

Example: Convert $(642)_{10}$ into binary form.

quotients	remainders
321	0
160	1
80	0
40	0
20	0
10	0
5	0
2	1
1	0
0	1

Thus $(642)_{10} = (1010000010)_2$

Another approach to this conversion involves successively "fitting" appropriate binary column values "into" the decimal number, until the entire value has been represented. Consider the number $(56)_{10}$. We first determine which binary column value is the largest such value that will "fit into" (is smaller in magnitude than) decimal 56. The value is, of course, 32 (the next larger column value is 64, and that is too large). We place a 1 in that column to denote the high-order bit of our result. We have now represented 32 out of a total 56 units, so that 24 units have yet to be represented. Continuing towards the low-order bit positions, 16 "fits into" 24, leaving 8 more units to represent. The next low-order column has the value 8, so that a 1 in this column completes our representation. Columns valued 4, 2 and 1 are filled with zeros as place holders.

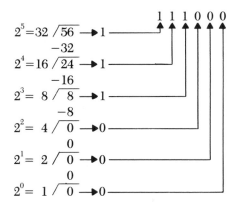

Example:

Convert $(210)_{10}$ into binary form.

Binary ——▶Decimal Conversion

The most direct approach to converting a binary number into decimal form, is to expand it in powers of 2, equivalent to computing the sum of column values which contain a "1" bit. This technique was used earlier (section 7.2.1) when we first introduced binary numbers:

$$(0\ 1\ 0\ 1\ 0\ 1)_2 = 0 \times 2^5 + 1 \times 2^4 + 0 \times 2^3 + 1 \times 2^2 + 0 \times 2^1 + 1 \times 2^0$$
$$= \quad 0 \quad + \quad 16 \quad + \quad 0 \quad + \quad 4 \quad + \quad 0 \quad + \quad 1$$
$$= (21)_{10}$$

Another approach consists of a series of repeated multiplications by 2 and additions. We begin with the high-order bit, double its value, and add the result to the next rightmost bit. Double the sum, then add the result to the next rightmost bit, double, then add, double, then add and so on. Continue in this way until the last bit value has been added. The last step in this process must be an addition. This method is sometimes calle the "double-dabble" method ("double" meaning multiply by 2 when the bit is 0, "dabble" meaning multiply by 2 and add 1 when the bit is 1).

Example:

Convert $(110101)_2$ into decimal form.

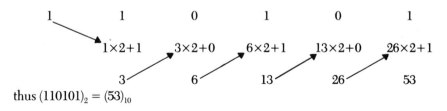

thus $(110101)_2 = (53)_{10}$

Example:

Convert $(10110)_2$ into decimal form.

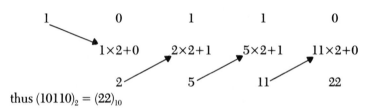

thus $(10110)_2 = (22)_{10}$

Hexadecimal ──▶ Decimal Conversion

A convenient method for converting hexadecimal numbers into decimal form is to expand the number in powers of 16 (just as we expanded binary numbers in powers of 2 to find their decimal equivalents). We multiply each hexadecimal digit value by the value of the column in which it is found, and then sum the results. This technique was used earlier (section 7.2.2).

$$
\begin{aligned}
(5 \ A \ 8)_{16} = \ & 5 \times 16^2 \quad + 10 \times 16^1 \quad + 8 \times 16^0 \\
= \ & 1280 \quad\quad\ + 160 \quad\quad\ + 8 \\
= \ & (1448)_{10}
\end{aligned}
$$

This method will be much simplified by the use of a hand calculator, especially for larger hexadecimal values. You might also like to make use of a chart on the System/370 Reference Summary side ⑯ (see Appendix A) giving the powers of 16 (the hexadecimal column values).

Another approach to this conversion makes use of the hexadecimal-decimal conversion table from the System/370 Reference Summary (Appendix A), reproduced below.

HEXADECIMAL COLUMNS					
6	**5**	**4**	**3**	**2**	**1**
HEX = DEC	HEX = DEC	HEX = DEC	HEX = DEC	HEX = DEC	HEX = DEC
0　　　　0	0　　　　0	0　　　0	0　　　0	0　　0	0　　0
1　1,048,576	1　　65,536	1　4,096	1　　256	1　16	1　1
2　2,097,152	2　131,072	2　8,192	2　　512	2　32	2　2
3　3,145,728	3　196,608	3　12,288	3　768	3　48	3　3
4　4,194,304	4　262,144	4　16,384	4　1,024	4　64	4　4
5　5,242,880	5　327,680	5　20,480	5　1,280	5　80	5　5
6　6,291,456	6　393,216	6　24,576	6　1,536	6　96	6　6
7　7,340,032	7　458,752	7　28,672	7　1,792	7　112	7　7
8　8,388,608	8　524,288	8　32,768	8　2,048	8　128	8　8
9　9,437,184	9　589,824	9　36,864	9　2,304	9　144	9　9
A　10,485,760	A　655,360	A　40,960	A　2,560	A　160	A　10
B　11,534,336	B　720,896	B　45,056	B　2,816	B　176	B　11
C　12,582,912	C　786,432	C　49,152	C　3,072	C　192	C　12
D　13,631,488	D　851,968	D　53,248	D　3,328	D　208	D　13
E　14,680,064	E　917,504	E　57,344	E　3,584	E　224	E　14
F　15,728,640	F　983,040	F　61,440	F　3,840	F　240	F　15
0 1 2 3	4 5 6 7	0 1 2 3	4 5 6 7	0 1 2 3	4 5 6 7
BYTE		BYTE		BYTE	

Table 7.2
Hexadecimal and Decimal Conversion

This chart will help find the decimal equivalent of hexadecimal integers having a maximum length of 6 hexadecimal digits. We consider each digit of the hexadecimal number separately, finding its true value according to its column position. We then sum the positional values obtained.

Example:

Convert $(A\ B\ 6\ 4\ 2)_{16}$ into decimal, using the hexadecimal-decimal conversion table.

	A	B	6	4	2
column	5	4	3	2	1
positional values (from table)	655360 +	45056 +	1536 +	64 +	2 = 702,018

Thus $(AB642)_{16} = (702,018)_{10}$

Yet another approach to the conversion from hexadecimal to decimal form parallels the "double-dabble" approach used to convert binary numbers into decimal format. To convert from hexadecimal, we multiply the high-order hexadecimal digit by 16, add the decimal equivalent of the next digit to the right, multiply the sum by 16, add the value of the next digit to the right, multiply by 16, and so on. The last step is the addition of the low-order digit value.

Example:

Convert $(7\ A\ B)_{16}$ into decimal form.

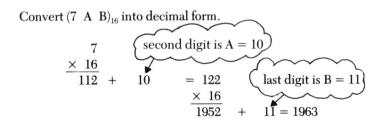

$$
\begin{array}{r}
7 \\
\times\ 16 \\
\hline
112
\end{array}
+\ 10 = 122
\quad
\begin{array}{r}
\times\ 16 \\
\hline
1952
\end{array}
+\ 11 = 1963
$$

second digit is A = 10

last digit is B = 11

Thus $(7AB)_{16} = (1963)_{10}$

Decimal → Hexadecimal Conversion

Conversion from decimal to hexadecimal form may be performed by dividing the decimal number and the successive resulting quotients by 16, noting the remainders in a separate column. Each remainder should be noted as a single hexadecimal digit (remainder values will range from 0 through F). The process is continued until a quotient of zero is obtained. The hexadecimal equivalent of the original decimal number is composed of the remainder digits, beginning with the last remainder obtained (this becomes the high-order digit) and continuing through the first remainder obtained (this becomes the low-order digit).

Example:

Convert $(483)_{10}$ into hexadecimal form.

quotients	remainders
16 /483	
16 /30	3
16 /1	14 = E
0	1

Thus $(483)_{10} = (1E3)_{16}$

Example:

Convert $(1963)_{10}$ into hexadecimal form.

quotients	remainders
16 /1963	
16 / 122	11 = B
16/ 7	10 = A
0	7

Thus $(1963)_{10} = (7AB)_{16}$

An alternate approach to this conversion makes use of the hexadecimal-decimal conversion table above (table 7.2). To convert a decimal number into hexadecimal form, we first search the table to find the largest available entry which "fits into" the decimal value. The table will indicate the hexadecimal digit and column which represent that value. We then continue to search the table to find appropriate entries, the sum of which will be equivalent in magnitude to the value of the decimal number that we wish to convert.

Example:

Convert $(650,478)_{10}$ into hexadecimal, using the hexadecimal-decimal conversion table.

1. Search the table to find the largest entry smaller than 650,478. We find 589,824, represented by the digit 9 in column 5. This leaves 60654 units to represent (650,478 − 589,824 = 60654).
2. Search the table to find the largest entry smaller than 60654. We see 57344, represented by the digit E in column 4. This leaves 3310 units to represent (60654 − 57344 = 3310).

3. Search the table to find the largest entry smaller than 3310. We see 3072, the digit C in column 3. This leaves 238 units (3310 − 3072 = 238).
4. The next digit to use will be the digit E in column 2, valued at 224. This leaves 14 to represent.
5. As we know, 14 is represented by the digit E in column 1.

$$\text{Thus} \quad (650{,}478)_{10} \quad = \quad (9 \quad E \quad C \quad E \quad E)_{16}$$
$$\text{columns} \; 5 \quad 4 \quad 3 \quad 2 \quad 1$$

As you can see, the table is a great convenience when working with numbers of large magnitude.

In this section, we have presented a variety of techniques for converting numbers from one representational system into another. The methods will yield equally accurate results, so that the choice of method for a particular case will depend upon the size of the numbers being converted (some methods will more easily handle large values) and the availability of such aids as hand calculators and tables.

7.3 BINARY NUMBERS WITHIN THE PROGRAM

In this section, we shall discuss some important guidelines which govern the use of binary numbers in an assembly language program. When writing an assembly language program, it is very important to ensure that our numeric values are in the proper format for the job that we wish to perform (zoned, packed or binary format) and that they are in the appropriate place, whether they be in main storage or in registers. We shall also learn how to store binary constants in the computer memory.

7.3.1 The Need for Conversion

When numeric data on punched cards is "read" into the computer memory, the data is stored in zoned form. Zoned numbers cannot, however, be used by the computer in computation. Numbers must be converted either into packed form (see chapter 4) or into binary form, before the computation may take place. When arithmetic is performed upon binary numbers, the results are also in binary form. Results must then be reconverted into zoned form for output.

We shall see that assembly language provides instructions to convert numbers from zoned format into packed format, and from packed format into binary format. Likewise, instructions exist to convert binary numbers into packed format, and packed numbers into zoned format. Instructions are not provided for direct conversion between zoned and binary formats. Performing binary arithmetic upon input data therefore requires the type of instruction sequence described below:

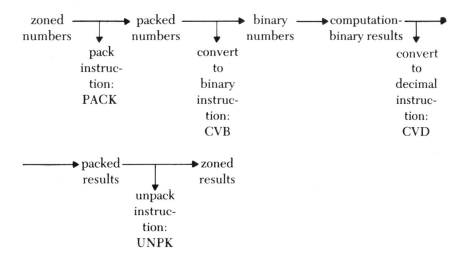

Any assembly language program which performs computation must include appropriate instructions for conversion of data from one format into another.

Zoned and packed representations have been explained in chapter 3. At this point, you may wish to review these concepts in sections 3.2.2 and 3.2.3.

7.3.2 Binary Numbers: Where?

Binary numbers may be found either in the computer's main storage or in the general registers (unlike zoned or packed numbers which may be found only in main storage).

- Binary numbers may occupy the 16 general registers. The registers are numbered 0,1, ..., 14,15 and are each a fullword (32 bits) long. However, registers 0,1,13,14 and 15 are designated for special uses under certain programming conventions. Therefore, in using the general registers for binary arithmetic, we shall assume that only general registers 2 through 12 are available for programmer use. (Special uses for registers 0,1,13,14 and 15 for subroutine linkage are discussed in chapter 12.) Usually we will find that a single binary number occupies an entire register (32 bits, that is 31 bits plus a sign bit). However, there may be instances in which more than one binary number occupies a register, or in which a binary number occupies two adjacent registers (64 bits, that is 63 bits plus a sign bit).

- Binary numbers may also occupy locations in the computer's main storage. Although binary number values may conceivably assume any length (indeed, any combination of 0's and 1's may be interpreted as a binary number), the assembly language instructions which work with binary numbers impose certain requirements upon those numbers.

In general, in order to be valid for use by instructions in the binary instruction set (those instructions which act upon binary numbers), binary numbers must satisfy an **integral boundary** requirement. A number is said to be on an integral boundary if its address (its starting or leftmost location) is a multiple of its length in bytes. To be located on an appropriate integral boundary, the address of a halfword binary number may be 0,2,4,6,8,.... (a multiple of 2, since a halfword is 2 bytes long); the address of a fullword binary number may be 0,4,8,12,.... (a multiple of 4, since a fullword is 4 bytes long); the address of a doubleword binary number may be 0,8,16,24,32,... (a multiple of 8, since a doubleword is 8 bytes long). The binary arithmetic, data movement and comparison instructions operate upon halfword, fullword and doubleword binary values only.

The integral boundary requirements may appear burdensome at first. However, once we learn how to store binary fixed-point constants in main storage and how the binary instructions work, you will see that a great deal of the "work" involved in adhering to those requirements is shouldered by the assembler program.

Note:
Some computer systems may have a special **byte-oriented operand** feature. This allows operands of binary instructions to begin at any address, not necessarily at the appropriate halfword, fullword, or doubleword boundary. However, use of the byte-oriented operand feature does slow execution time. Therefore, we do not recommend use of this feature even in systems in which it is installed. The programs in this chapter and throughout the text do not assume the byte-oriented operand feature.

It is interesting, at this point, to note that *instruction* addresses (besides addresses of data) must also be aligned on halfword (even-byte) integral boundaries; this is true even when the byte-oriented operand feature is installed. An attempt on the part of a branch instruction to transfer control to an odd address results in an error condition.

7.3.3   Fixed Point Constants, Storage Definitions, and Literals

Fixed Point Constants

A fixed point constant is a binary number placed by the assembler into main storage, and **aligned** on a proper integral boundary. The assembler instruction that defines the constant is the DC (**D**efine **C**onstant) instruction of the form

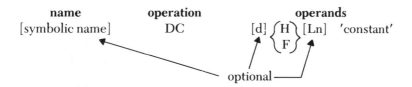

name	operation	operands
[symbolic name]	DC	[d] ⎰H⎱ [Ln] 'constant'

optional

where d is an unsigned integer (it may also be zero) which is a duplication factor. It tells the assembler how many identical areas are desired. When one area is required, the duplication factor may be omitted.

H or F specifies that a halfword or fullword binary fixed point constant is expected to occupy the storage area.

Ln is the length of the storage area in bytes, explicitly specified.

L stands for length.

n is an unsigned integer representing the number of bytes to be allocated.

'constant' is the value of the binary number to be stored, written as a decimal number and enclosed within single quotations. The constant may include a sign and/or decimal point.

When using the DC instruction to store a fixed point constant in main storage,
- The H-type (halfword) constant has an implied length of 2 bytes, and the value will be stored on a halfword integral boundary. The F-type (fullword) constant has an implied length of 4 bytes, and the value will be stored on a fullword integral boundary.
- Lengths of from one to eight bytes may be designated by the optional length specification Ln.
- If the optional length designation is used, the implied 2-byte and 4-byte lengths for the respective H or F constants are overruled. However, in this case, no (halfword or fullword) boundary alignment will be performed.

- Constants are right justified in the fields.
- Truncation, when necessary, occurs on the left.
- Padding, when necessary, occurs on the left with binary zeros (for positive numbers) or binary ones (for negative numbers).
- The decimal number may be followed by the symbol En where n is a signed or unsigned decimal integer. The constant is raised to the nth power of 10. The integer part of the result is then stored in binary form.

Examples:

Instructions	Values Generated in Storage by Assembler		
	hex notation	bits	boundary alignment
DC F'2'	00 00 00 02	00....010 (30 0's)	fullword
DC H'−7'	FF F9	1.....1001 (13 1's)	halfword
DC FL1'−3'	FD	1111 1101	none
DC HL2'+4'	00 04	0.....0100 (13 0's)	none
DC H'16,−16'	00 10 FF F0	0....010000 (11 0's) 1....110000 (11 1's)	halfword
multiple constants stored	↑	↑	
DC HL1'4097'	01	00000001	none
left truncated	↑	↑	
DC FL2'2.145E2'	00D6	0....011010110 (8 0's)	none

value 214, the integer part
of $(2.145 \times 10^{2} = 214.5)$, is
stored

Fullword and Halfword Storage Definitions

The DS (**Define Storage**) instruction is used to:

- reserve areas of main storage which are **aligned** on appropriate fullword or halfword integral boundaries
- specify the size of the area being reserved
- associate a name with the area (optional)

The entries specified for the operand portion of the DS instruction, with H or F type designation, are identical to those of the DC instruction, except that the 'constant' subfield is optional and is meant only to indicate the general form of the data which the programmer expects to be placed into the area. The DS instruction will *not* place the constant data into this area, nor will it place the data anywhere else.

Examples:

DS Instructions			**Field(s) defined**
THIS	DS	F	One aligned fullword (4 bytes long) named THIS.
IS	DS	4F	Four aligned fullwords (four fields, each 4 bytes long). The leftmost field is named IS.
NOT	DS	H'26'	One aligned halfword (2 bytes long) named NOT. The constant is not stored.
DIFFICLT	DS	FL2	One 2-byte field called DIFFICLT (not aligned).

Recall (from chapter 3, section 3.4) that the DS instruction causes storage area to be reserved, but does not cause any value to be stored. The programmer may not make any assumption as to the contents of the reserved areas.

Forcing Alignment

The DS instruction may be used to force the assembler's location counter to an appropriate integral boundary by using a duplication factor of zero with an appropriate field type. For example

```
        DS    0F
LOC     DS    CL13
```

will cause the location counter to advance to the next fullword boundary, and will then reserve a 13-byte storage area called LOC, the leftmost byte of which will be on the fullword boundary.

Fullword and Halfword Literals

Literals are data specifications used in the operand portions of machine instructions. They are written in much the same way as the operands of DC instructions, but are preceded by an "=" sign. The rules governing the use of literals in assembly language have already been discussed in chapter 3, section 3.3. The rules presented in chapter 3 apply to the use of literals with F and H data specifications, as well as with other data types. We shall add a few remarks at this point with regard to the alignment of literal data on integral boundaries.

Recall that the assembler program stores assembled data in a special place called the **literal pool**, which is usually at the end of the program. A literal pool always begins at a doubleword integral boundary, and contains four segments. The first segment contains all literals whose length in bytes is a multiple of 8; the second segment contains all remaining literals with lengths that are multiples of 4; the third segment has all remaining literals with lengths that are multiples of 2. The fourth segment will have any left over literals; these will have odd lengths, since only odd numbers are not multiples of 2.

Note that all literals which are 8 bytes long will be placed in segment one of the literal pool, and must of necessity be doubleword aligned, since these literals are stored consecutively, and the beginning of segment one is on a doubleword integral boundary. Likewise, literals in segment two are fullword aligned, and literals in segment three are halfword aligned. It thus follows that literals need *not* be designated as F or H types to be respectively fullword or halfword aligned. It is sufficient that they be designated to have 4-byte or 2-byte lengths, respectively. In chapter 8, we shall see that the instructions which manipulate binary numbers require alignment of certain operands. Literals may thus be used by those instructions by specifying proper lengths without F or H designations. The following literals will be stored in the literal pool as indicated.

Literal	Literal pool segment	Alignment
=F'2'	2	fullword
=2H'2'	2	fullword
=H'2'	3	halfword
=CL1'1'	4	none

=CL2'1'	3	halfword
=2F'1'	1	doubleword
=BL4'1'	2	fullword
=BL8'1'	1	doubleword

7.3.4   A Program Example Using Binary Values

Program 7.1 considers three zoned constants, converts them into binary format for computational purposes, and performs a simple addition and subtraction. The result is then reconverted into zoned format. The constants are called OLD, representing the amount of certain items stocked by a retail store; RECPT represents the number of such items recently added to stock; ISSUE represents the number of such items depleted from stock. The calculation OLD + RECPT − ISSUE yields NEW, the updated inventory amount.

Note that the zoned numbers were first converted into packed form via the PACK instruction, and then into binary format via the CVB (Convert to Binary) instruction. Binary results were first reconverted into packed form via the CVD (Convert to Decimal) instruction and then into zoned form via the UNPK instruction. The PACK and UNPK instructions were explained in chapter 4, sections 4.2.6 and 4.2.7. The CVB and CVD instructions are explained in section 7.3.5. We defer a full explanation of the binary add and subtract instructions (AR and SR) to chapter 8.

```
                                                                          PAGE    2

  LOC   OBJECT CODE     ADDR1 ADDR2   STMT    SOURCE STATEMENT                    17 NOV 78

000000                                  1          START
CCCCC0 05B0                             2 A        BALR   11,0
                              0C002     3          USING *,11
                                        4 *
CCCCC2 F273 B03E B02E  00040 00030      5          PACK   DBL,OLD    CONVERT OLD INTO PACKED FORM, AND
                                        6 *                         PLACE INTO DBL
CCCCC8 4F40 B03E             00040      7          CVB    4,DBL      BINARY OLD INTO REG 4
CCCCCC F271 B03E BC32  00040 C0034      8          PACK   DBL,RECPT  CONVERT RECPT INTO PACKED FORM, AND
                                        9 *                         PLACE INTO DBL
CCCC12 4F50 B03E             00040     10          CVB    5,DBL      BINARY RECPT INTO REG 5
CCCC16 F271 B03E B034  00040 C0036     11          PACK   DBL,ISSUE  CONVERT ISSUE INTO PACKED FORM, AND
                                       12 *                         PLACE INTO DBL
0CCC1C 4F60 B03E             00040     13          CVB    6,DBL      BINARY ISSUE INTO REG 6
0CCC20 1A45                            14          AR     4,5        ADD    OLD + RECPT INTO REG 4
CCCC22 1B46                            15          SR     4,6        SUBTRACT   (OLD + RECPT)-ISSUE INTO REG 4
0CC024 4E40 B03E             00040     16          CVD    4,DBL      CONVERT BINARY RESULT INTO PACKED FCRM,
                                       17 *                         PLACE INTO DBL
0CC028 F327 B036 B03E  00038 00040     18          UNPK   NEW,DBL    CONVERT PACKED RESULT INTO ZONED FORM,AND
                                       19 *                         PLACE INTO NEW
C0CC2E 0A03                            20          SVC    3          STOP EXECUTION
                                       21 *                         IN DOS, THIS INSTRUCTION IS EOJ
                                       22 *
CCCC30 F1F0F0C0                        23 OLD       CC    Z'1000'
CCCC34 F5C0                            24 RECPT     CC    Z'50'
CCCC36 F7C2                            25 ISSUE     CC    Z'72'
CCCC38                                 26 NEW       DS    CL3
CCCC4C                                 27 DBL       DS    D
CCCCC0                                 28           END   A
```

Program 7.1
A Program Example Using Binary Values

This program performs the most basic inventory calculation. Chapters 8 and 9 will expand upon this application to develop a more realistic approach to the basic inventory problem and to include more extensive use of instructions which work with binary numbers.

7.3.5 Binary Conversion Instructions: CVB, CVD

The CVB Instruction

The CVB Instruction (**Con**Vert to **B**inary)

Instruction type: Machine Instruction
Machine format: RX Instruction (Register and IndeXed Storage Instruction)

4F	R1	X2	B2	D2
0	7 8	11 12 15 16	19 20	31

Symbolic format:

	name	operation	operands
	[symbolic name]	CVB	R1,name2
or	[symbolic name]	CVB	R1,D2(X2,B2)

where R1 is a general register number. D2,X2, and B2 are the displacement, index register and base register respectively used to calculate the second operand address.

. . . .

Rules:
- The second operand must contain a valid packed decimal number.
- The second operand must be a doubleword. IBM S/360 requires that it reside on a doubleword integral boundary.
- The binary equivalent of the packed number replaces the previous contents of R1. (The size of the number is limited to $2^{31}-1$ if positive, -2^{31} if negative: the maximum possible register contents.)

Condition Code: The condition code remains unchanged.

Example:

```
          CVB    4,DBL1
          DS     0D
DBL1      DC     PL8'6'            contains 00 00 00 00
                                            00 00 00 6C
```

Before execution of the CVB	**After execution of the CVB**	
	Binary (hex notation)	**Decimal**
Reg 4: irrelevant	Reg 4: 00 00 00 06	6

The CVB instruction places the binary equivalent of the packed number in DBL1 into register 4.

Note that the second operand DBL1 is a doubleword (8 bytes long). We must also, however, align it on a doubleword integral boundary to conform to the S/360 requirement. That alignment is accomplished by the DS statement, DS   0D, preceding the definition of DBL1. Let us explain.

The type designation D is usually used to store a special category of numbers, called double-precision floating point numbers, in main storage. We do not present the floating point instruction set in this text; however, this particular type designation is useful for us here. The type designation D sets aside an 8-byte area aligned on a *doubleword integral boundary*, required for double-precision floating point numbers. Here, we do not want floating point numbers, only the integral boundary. Therefore, we precede the "D" with a duplication factor of 0: 0D. The "0" tells the computer *not* to reserve any space in memory (recall that a duplication factor tells "how many" of a certain type of area should be defined — "0" means "none"). However, the "D" will still cause the doubleword alignment to be effected. Once the alignment has been performed, we then proceed to define our actual value with the operand PL8 — an 8-byte packed number.

Example:

```
          PACK    PMTWO,ZMTWO
          CVB     5,PMTWO
PMTWO     DS      D
ZMTWO     DC      Z'-2'            contains D2
```

Before execution of the CVB	**After execution of the CVB**	
	Binary (hex notation)	**Decimal**
Reg 5: irrelevant	Reg 5: FF FF FF FE	−2

Here the PACK instruction places a packed negative 2 into the doubleword location PMTWO, as 00 00 00 00 00 00 00 2D. Then the CVB instruction converts the negative 2 into binary form and places it into register 5. Note that the doubleword integral boundary requirement has been satisfied.

The CVD Instruction

The CVD Instruction (**Con**Vert to **D**ecimal)

Instruction type: Machine Instruction
Machine format: RX Instruction (Register and IndeXed Storage Instruction)

4E	R1	X2	B2	D2
0	7 8	11 12 15 16	19 20	31

Symbolic format:

	name	operation	operands
	[symbolic name]	CVD	R1,name2
or	[symbolic name]	CVD	R1,D2(X2,B2)

where R1 is a general register number. D2, X2 and B2 are the displacement, index register, and base register respectively used to calculate the second operand address.

. . . .

Rules:
- The second operand must be a doubleword. IBM S/360 requires that it reside on a doubleword integral boundary.
- The packed equivalent of the contents of R1 replaces the previous contents of the second operand.

Condition Code: The condition code remains unchanged.

Example:

	CVD	8,DBL2
DBL2	DS	D

Before execution of the CVD

	Bits (hex notation)	**Decimal**
Reg 8:	7F FF FF FF	2,147,483,647
DBL2:	irrelevant	

After execution of the CVD

	Bits (hex notation)	Decimal
Reg 8:	7F FF FF FF	2,147,483,647
DBL2:	00 00 02 14 74 83 64 7C	2,147,483,647

Note that overflow cannot occur as a result of the CVD instruction, for the doubleword (8-byte) second operand provides 15 decimal digit positions. This will always be enough to accommodate the decimal equivalent of a 31-bit number (contents of a register).

Note, too, that the CVD has a characteristic which is unusual in assembly language instructions; the result of the operation is placed in the *second operand* of the instruction. (It is not the only such instruction, however. We shall see others in chapter 8: the "store" instructions.)

Summary

This chapter has presented us with concepts which are very important and fundamental to the assembly language programmer. Positional representations of numbers were discussed, with detailed explanations of binary and hexadecimal representations, including arithmetic in these systems. Complement representation and subtraction by addition of complements were also demonstrated. The discussion of number systems included techniques for converting values from one such system into another.

Discussion of the role and treatment of binary numbers within the program was another important feature of this chapter. The need for conversion of numbers from one data format into another, the requirement for storing fixed point numbers on appropriate integral boundaries, and rules for placing binary constants and literals into main storage were each considered, along with appropriate instructions for conversion and constant definition.

Important Terms Discussed in Chapter 7

base (of a number system)
binary number system
byte-oriented operand feature

decimal instruction set
double-dabble

fixed point

hexadecimal number system

integral boundary

literals
literal pool

one's complement
overflow

payback
positional representation

radix (of a number system)

standard instruction set

ten's complement
two's complement

Questions

7-1. State two reasons for using the standard instruction set rather than the decimal set.

7-2. Name a method of representing numbers which is *not* a positional representation.

7-3. Perform the following binary additions.

    (a)   0 1 0 1 0 1 0 1 0 0   (b)   0 0 1 1 1 0 1 0 1
        + 0 0 0 1 1 1 0 1 1 1   + 0 0 0 1 1 0 1 0 1

    (c)   0 0 0 1 1 0 0 1 1   (d)   0 0 1 1 1 1 1 1
        + 0 0 1 1 0 0 1 1 0   + 0 0 1 1 1 1 1 1

7-4. Perform the following binary subtractions using the "borrowing" method.

    (a)   0 1 1 0 1 1 1 0   (b)   0 1 1 1 0 1 0 0
        − 0 0 1 1 0 1 0 1   − 0 0 0 0 1 0 0 1

    (c)   0 0 0 0 1 1 1 1   (d)   0 1 0 0 0 0 0 0
        − 0 0 0 0 1 0 0 1   − 0 0 0 1 1 1 1 1

7-5. Perform the following binary subtractions using the "payback" method.

    (a)   0 1 0 1 0 1 0 1   (b)   0 1 1 0 1 1 0 1
        − 0 0 1 0 1 0 1 0   − 0 0 0 1 1 1 1 1

    (c)   0 1 1 1 0 0 0 0   (d)   0 1 0 0 0 1 0 0
        − 0 0 0 0 1 1 1 1   − 0 0 0 0 1 0 0 1

7-6.   Perform the subtractions of problem 7-4 using the "payback" method.

7-7.   Give the 10's complement of the decimal numbers 764 and 123,456. Explain how they were obtained.

7-8.   Perform the following decimal subtractions using the complement method.

(a)   8 0 0
       − 4 5 6

(b)   7 4 0
       − 8 0 0

One of the subtractions above required an extra step. What was it?

7-9.   Find the two's complement of the following binary numbers.

(a)   0 1 0 1 0 1 1 1
(c)   0 1 1 1 1 1 1 1

(b)   1 1 1 1 0 0 1 1
(d)   1 0 0 0 0 0 0 1

7-10. Perform the following binary subtractions by "addition of the complements".

(a)   0 1 1 1 0 1 0 0
      − 0 0 1 1 0 0 1 1

(b)   1 0 0 1 1 0 1 1
      − 0 0 0 1 0 0 1 1

7-11. (a) Do either of the differences obtained in problem 7−10 require recomplementation? Why or why not?
       (b) Are the differences positive or negative? How do you know?

7-12. The problems below are to be treated as additions of signed binary numbers. In each case, tell whether the result is positive or negative.

(a)   0 1 1 1 0 1 1 1
        1 0 1 1 1 1 0 0

(b)   1 1 1 1 1 0 0 0
        0 1 0 1 0 1 1 1

7-13. Perform the following binary multiplication and long division.

(a)   (0 1 1 1 1) × (0 1 0 1)
(b)   (0 1 1 1 0 1 0) ÷ (0 1 1 1)

7-14. Interpret the following hexadecimal numbers (in decimal form).

(a) $(1A1)_{16}$
(c) $(ABD)_{16}$

(b) $(2022)_{16}$
(d) $(1234)_{16}$

7-15. Find the sums requested through hexadecimal addition.

(a)   1 2 4
       + A 9 C

(b)   A 0 B 0
       + 0 F F F

(c)   D 4 1
       + 1 4 D

(d)   1 2 3 A B 6
       + 0 A 4 5 7 1

7-16. Find the differences using the "borrowing" method for hexadecimal subtraction.

(a)   A24
       −045

(b)   CBA
       −ABC

7-17. Perform the following hexadecimal subtractions using the "payback" method.

(a)   BBB
       −9EE

(b)   245
       −154

7-18. Convert from binary form into hexadecimal form.

(a) 0 1 0 1 1 1 1 1

(b) 1 1 1 1 1 1 1 1

(c) 0 1 1 1 0 0 1 0

(d) 1 1 0 1 1 0 1 0 1 0 1 0 1 1 0 1

7-19. Convert from hexadecimal form into binary form.

(a) A B D

(b) 2 4 5 A F

(c) 1 2

(d) 0 1 F 6

7-20. Convert the decimal numbers below into binary form twice, using a different conversion technique each time.

(a) 285

(b) 33

7-21. Convert the following binary numbers into decimal form. Perform each conversion twice, using a different method each time.

(a) 0 1 0 1 0 1 0 0

(b) 0 1 1 1 0 1 1 1

7-22. Convert the decimal numbers below into hexadecimal form twice, using two different methods.

(a) 8400

(b) 96

7-23. Use three different methods to convert the following hexadecimal numbers into decimal form.

(a) A 0 5

(b) 5 8 9 D

7-24. What are the allowed lengths for fixed point numbers?

7-25. What is an integral boundary?

7-26. Is integral boundary alignment always required for fixed point numbers? Explain.

7-27. Indicate, using hexadecimal notation, the contents of main storage generated by each of the following constant definitions. In each case tell whether boundary alignment was performed.

(a)   DC   FL4'−4'
(b)   DC   H'13'
(c)   DC   H'−9,+70'
(d)   DC   HL1'5.86E1'

7-28. Given the following DC instructions,
    (a) Show (using hexadecimal notation) the assembled value of each constant.

(i)		DC	F'−3'
(ii)	TWO	DC	F'5'
(iii)		DC	H'−200'
(iv)	ZERO	DC	F'0'
(v)		DC	H'−1,−20,40'
(vi)		DC	FL4'0'
(vii)		DC	HL1'4.65E1'

    (b) Is there any difference between the assembled constants (iv) and (vi) above? Explain.

7-29. Write all instructions necessary to convert each of the following constants into binary format.

(a)	NUM1	DC	Z'46'
(b)	NUM2	DC	P'8'

7-30. Write all instructions necessary to convert a binary value in register 8, which will occupy 6 decimal digit positions, into zoned format.

7-31. Find any errors in the following instruction sequences.

    (a)

		CVD	6,LOC1
		UNPK	LOC2,LOC1
	LOC1	DS	PL4
	LOC2	DS	CL6

    (b)

		CVB	THERE,HERE
	HERE	DC	Z'5'

Chapter 8

Binary Integer Arithmetic

BINARY INTEGER ARITHMETIC

In this chapter we shall write an assembly language program which will require the computer to perform arithmetic with binary integers. We shall learn how to use several instructions for performing calculations (addition, subtraction, multiplication, and division) with binary numbers, as well as instructions which move binary data to and from registers.

8.1   AN INVENTORY REPORT PROBLEM

8.1.1   The Problem Described

Before we may request the computer to "solve" a problem, it is of course necessary that we understand the problem completely. Therefore we first present a detailed description of our program "input" — the raw data available to the program; the calculation or data manipulation that we wish the computer to perform; and the desired program output.

Consider a program whose purpose is to produce a simple inventory report. The input to our inventory report program consists of item records (records, each one of which contains information about a particular item which a company keeps in stock) on punched cards. Each record contains six fields relating to a particular item. A 4-digit item number (each item is assigned a unique identifying number) is recorded in columns 7 through 10; an old-on-hand amount (the number of such items in stock at the start of the inventory period) is recorded in columns 11 through 14; an issues amount (the amount by which the old-on-hand has been decreased during the inventory period) is recorded in columns 15 through 18; a receipt amount (the amount by which the old-on-hand has been increased during the inventory period) is recorded in columns 19 through 22; a unit price per item is recorded in columns 23 through 24; an item description is recorded in columns 26 through 45.

The program is to consider the input item records, and to produce the printed report described in figure 8.2.

As you can see, the report output is of three categories: header output, detail output, and total output. We first have a two-line "heading" which describes the output fields. One line is then skipped (blanks are printed) after which the "detail" output begins. Detail output consists of one output record (printed line) per item input record (punched card), with the item number, item description, old-on-hand, issues, and receipts as obtained from the input. Detail records will also have a new-on-hand amount (the number of items in stock after subtracting the issue amount from and adding the receipt amount to the old-on-hand); and the total price of such items which are in stock (obtained by multiplying the unit price per item by the new-on-hand). The "total" output consists of two lines, the first having the totals of the amounts in the new-on-hand and price fields, the second giving the average price per item (obtained by dividing the total price amount by the total new-on-hand amount).

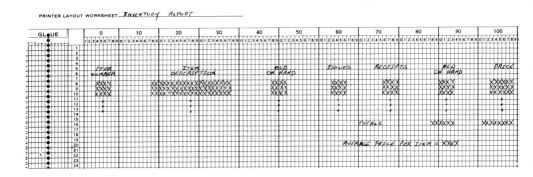

Figure 8.1
Input Layout for Inventory Report — 1

Figure 8.2
Output Layout for Inventory Report — 1

Note that for this problem, as for previous problems considered in this text, we have a uniform format for input records and output detail records. This uniform field organization is quite important, for it enables us to write programs in which the same instructions may be repeatedly used for different records of similar layout. Our instructions deal with *contents of fields* rather than with specific constant values. Therefore if we change field contents, we may use the same instructions to operate upon different numeric values over and over again.

8.1.2   Inventory Report Program Logic

We now plan and code the solution to the inventory problem described in section 8.1.1. As usual, our program logic is first described in flowchart form. The flowchart of figure 8.3 offers one possible method to use in writing our program.

The first step in our flowchart (symbol B1) instructs the computer to open the files (input card file and output printer file). You will recall (chapter 2, section 2.4) that a file must be OPENed before we may reference any records from that file. Steps C1, D1, and E1 of our program flowchart comprise the **header routine**. Steps F1 through J2 comprise the **detail routine**; steps A3 through E4 comprise the **total routine**.

The Header Routine

The second flowchart step (symbol C1) directs the computer to print the program heading lines, or "header output". The heading lines, lines 5 and 6 on our printer layout form, will serve as column headings in the final output report. Printing first page heading lines is generally performed before obtaining or manipulating the program data. The work of producing "heading" output is logically independent of the work of producing "detail" output (the main body of program output), for detail data is not necessary to implement the header routine. Flowchart symbol D1 then instructs the program to skip a line (note that line 7 on the printer layout form is blank). We next clear the output area (fill it with blanks) in preparation for the detail routine: the routine which produces the main program output. Clearing the output area may also have been accomplished by a DC instruction, as was explained in chapter 3, section 3.2.1.

The Detail Routine

Beginning with symbol F1, the flowchart describes the steps necessary for producing our detail lines. The computer first reads a card (symbol F1), for

Programmer: _____ Program No.: _____ Date: _____ Page: _____
Chart ID: _____ Chart Name: _____ Program Name: INVENTORY REPORT

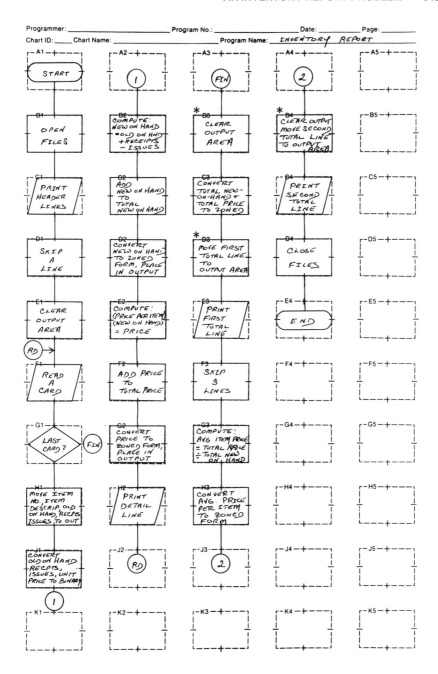

Figure 8.3
Flowchart for Inventory Report — 1

we must obviously have the appropriate data in main storage before it can be acted upon. A check is then performed to ensure that the card just read is not the "last card", that is, the "/*" card, which immediately follows our program data cards. (The test for the "/*" is actually performed by the macro definition for the assembly language macro which defines our card file: the "EOFADDR= " parameter of the DTFCD macro on DOS systems, and the "EODAD= " parameter of the DCB macro on OS systems.) If the card is indeed found to be the "/*" card, a branch takes place to the instruction called FIN. If the card is not the "/*" card, sequential execution continues with the processing of our input record, as will now be described.

The contents of the item number, item description, old-on-hand, issues, and receipts fields are moved from the input area into which they were read to the appropriate positions of the detail output area (symbol H1). The contents of the unit price field are not moved, for the printer layout description does not request them.

The next value required on our report output is the "new-on-hand" amount, obtained by subtracting the issues amount from old-on-hand and adding the receipt amount to the difference. Recall, however, that our numeric values were just read from data cards, and are stored in memory in zoned form. Arithmetic may not be performed by the computer on zoned numbers, therefore we convert (symbol J1) the old-on-hand, receipts, and issues fields into binary form in preparation for the computation of new-on-hand. At the same time we convert (symbol J1) the unit price field into binary form in preparation for a later computation. The flowchart continues with the actual computation of new-on-hand (symbol B2), then adds (symbol C2) the new-on-hand amount to a total-new-on-hand field in preparation for the total line at the end of the report. It then converts (symbol D2) the new-on-hand result from binary form (for computation with binary values naturally yields binary results) into zoned form and places it into the appropriate subfield of the detail output area.

The "price" is then computed (symbol E2) as the product of the item price and new-on-hand fields. The price value obtained is added (symbol F2) to a total-price field, in preparation for the total line. The price is then converted (symbol G2) into zoned form and placed into the appropriate part of the detail output area.

At this point, for the input record just read, we have item number, item description, old-on-hand, issues, receipts, new-on-hand, and price fields in the output area, as requested by the problem specifications. We are now ready to print a line (symbol H2). The record has been processed.

There may, however, be other input records which require similar processing! We therefore branch (symbol J2) back to RD (symbol F1), the instruction which reads a succeeding record and begins the process over again for the next input record. The process will be repeated over and over again for succeeding input records (the program has entered a loop) until eventually the "last card" ("/*" card) is detected (symbol G1). Program control is then transferred to the instruction at FIN (symbol A3).

The Total Routine

We first clear the output area (symbol B3) in preparation for a different output format. The total new-on-hand and total price fields are converted (symbol C3) to zoned form for output, and our first total line is printed (symbol E3). Recall that these totals were computed in our detail routine by continually adding old-on-hand and price values to total areas as the detail records were being processed (symbols C2 and F2). We then skip (symbol F3) three lines (note the three blank lines between the total lines on the printer layout form).

The second total line requires the average price per item. This value is now computed by dividing (symbol G3) the total price by the total new-on-hand amount. The quotient is then converted (symbol H3) into zoned form and the second total line is printed (symbol C4). The input and output files are then closed (symbol D4) and program execution ends (symbol E4).

It should be noted that one output area can serve for both detail and total output. That is, we can transfer the detail output fields to a certain main storage area and instruct the computer to print out the contents of that area. We may then transfer the total output information to that same main storage area and have the computer print its contents. In this way, we conserve the storage space required for defining separate areas for detail output and for each total line. In our flowchart, symbol B3 clears that common area after the detail lines have been printed, to prepare it to accept the first total line (symbol D3). Likewise, symbol B4 clears the output area to prepare it to accept the second total line.

In our coded version, we chose not to use this approach. Instead we described different output areas for detail lines, first total line, and second total line. Thus the starred flowchart symbols (B3, D3, and B4) are actually unnecessary for the program solution that we will present in section 8.1.3.

It would be very beneficial at this point for you to reread the program flowchart to be certain that you comprehend it fully, for a clear understanding of the program logic is necessary in order to write a correct program. If there is a point which is not absolutely clear, refer back to the discussion above to clarify the difficulty. You may then proceed with the actual program: the assembly language instructions which produce our inventory report.

8.1.3   The Inventory Report Program — Coded

We are now ready to examine the assembly language program to produce the inventory report described in section 8.1.1. The program listing is presented in figure 8.4.

8.1.4   The Inventory Report Program — Output

The output obtained after assembling and executing our inventory report program is presented in figure 8.5.

8.1.5   How the Instructions Work to Produce the Report

Let us first consider the file definitions and area definitions for the program of figure 8.4. Then we shall proceed with the discussion of the main body of the program which references those files and locations.

The DCB macro instructions in this OS version of our program (these would be DTF macros in a DOS version) assign the name ITMFILE to our input item card file, and the name RPTFILE to our output printer file. The data areas to be used by our program are described using combinations of DC and DS instructions.

The input area ITMREC is the 80-character area into which our item input records will be read. It contains fields INUM, IOLD, IISSUE, IRECPT, IUPRC, and IDESC to hold the respective item number, old-on-hand amount, issue amount, receipt amount, unit price per item, and description of the item.

The detail output area REPTREC is the 132-character area in which we arrange appropriate detail records for output. Fields ONUM, ODESC, OOLD, OISSUE, and ORECPT will contain respective item number, item description, old-on-hand, issue, and receipt values from the appropriate input item record. Fields ONEW and OPRC will contain the respective new-on-hand and price amounts which the program will compute. Note that the REPTREC fields are appropriately spaced to conform to the detail output line description on our printer layout form (figure 8.2).

```
LOC    OBJECT CODE          ADDR1 ADDR2   STMT  SOURCE STATEMENT

                                            1         PRINT NOGEN
CCCCCC                                      2         START 0
CCCCCC C5C0                         CCCC2   3    BGN  BALR  12,0
CCCCC2                                      4         USING *,12
                                            5    *
                                            6         OPEN  (ITMFILE,INPUT,RPTFILE,OUTPUT)
                                           14    **FOR DOS, PROGRAM FILES ARE OPENED BY
                                           15         OPEN  ITMFILE,RPTFILE
                                           16    *
CCCC12 1888                                17         SR    8,8     CLEAR REG 8 FOR TOTAL NEW-ON-HAND
CCCC14 1AAA                                18         SR    10,10   CLEAR REG 1C FOR TOTAL PRICE
                                           19    *
                                           20    * HEADER ROUTINE
CCCC16                                     21         PUT   RPTFILE,HEAD1
CCCC2C                                     26         PUT   RPTFILE,HEAD2
CCCC32                                     31         PUT   RPTFILE,BLANKS
CCCC4C D283 C287 C286   02289 02288       36         MVC   REPTREC,REPTREC-1
                                           37    *
                                           38    * DETAIL ROUTINE
CCCC46                                     39    RD   GET   ITMFILE,ITMREC
                                           43    * MOVE SOME INPUT DETAIL DATA TO OUTPUT
CCCC54 D703 C28A C23C   0228C 0223E       44         MVC   CNUM,INUM
CCCC5A D213 C298 C24F   0229A 02251       45         MVC   CDESC,IDESC
CCCC6C D703 C286 C24C   02286 02242       46         MVC   COLD,ICLD
CCCC66 D703 C2C5 C244   002C7 00246       47         MVC   OISSUE,IISSUE
CCCC6C D703 C2C2 C248   002C4 0024A       48         MVC   CRCPT,IRECPT
                                           49    * CONVERT DATA TO BINARY FORMAT FOR CALCULATION
CCCC72 F273 C5A6 C24C   0C5A8 0C242       50         PACK  DBL,ICLD
CCCC78 4F2C C5A6        0C5A8             51         CVB   2,CBL    OLD  ON-HAND INTO REG 2
CCCC7C F273 C5A6 C248   0C5A8 0024A       52         PACK  DBL,IRECPT
CCCC82 4F3C C5A6        0C5A8             53         CVB   3,DBL    RECEIPTS INTO REG 3
CCCC86 F273 C5A6 C244   0C5A8 00246       54         PACK  DBL,IISSUE
CCCC8C 4F40 C5A6        0C5A8             55         CVB   4,CBL    ISSUES INTO REG 4
CCCC9C F271 C5A6 C24C   0C5A8 0024E       56         PACK  DBL,IUPRC
CCCC96 4F7C C5A6        0C5A8             57         CVB   7,DBL    UNIT PRICE INTO REG 7
                                           58    * COMPUTE NEW-ON-HAND
CCCC9A 1A23                                59         AR    2,3
CCCC9C 1A24                                60         AR    2,4
CCCC9E 1A82                                61         AR    8,2      NEW-ON-HAND INTO REG 2
                                                                     TOTAL NEW-ON-HAND IN REG 8
                                           62    * NEW-ON-HAND INTO DETAIL OUTPUT (CONVERT INTO ZONED FORM)
CCCCAC 4E2C C5A6        0C5A8             63         CVD   2,DBL
CCCCA4 F337 C2ED C5A6   002EF 0C5A8       64         UNPK  CNEW,CBL
CCCCAA D300 C2E2 C2E3   002E4 002E5       65         MVZ   CNEW+3(1),CNEW+2    ELIMINATES SIGN FROM LAST BYTE
                                           66    * COMPUTE PRICE
CCCCBC 1C62                                67         MR    6,2      PRICE INTO REG 7
CCCCB2 1AA7                                68         AR    10,7     TOTAL PRICE IN REG 10
                                           69    * PRICE INTO DETAIL OUTPUT (CONVERT INTO ZONED FORM)
CCCCB4 4E7C C5A6        0C5A8             70         CVD   7,CBL
CCCCB8 F357 C2ED C5A6   002EF 0C5A8       71         UNPK  CPRC,CBL
CCCCBE D3CC C2F2 C2F1   002F4 002F3       72         MVZ   CPRC+5(1),OPRC+4    ELIMINATES SIGN FROM LAST BYTE
                                           73    * PRINT DETAIL LINE
CCCCC4                                     74         PUT   RPTFILE,REPTREC
                                           79    * GO BACK TO PROCESS NEXT DETAIL RECORD
CCCCC2 47F0 C044        00046             80         B     RD
                                           81    *
                                           82    * TOTAL ROUTINE
```

Figure 8.4

Inventory Report — 1 (Part 1)

```
LOC      OBJECT CODE        ADDR1  ADDR2   STMT  SOURCE STATEMENT

                                            83   *
CCCCC6   4E8C C5A6          004FC  C05A8    84   FIN   CVD   R4,DBL
CCCCCA   F357 C4E8 C4F2     CC4F5  C05A8    85         UNPK  TOTNEW,DBL        TOTAL NEW-ON-HAND TO TOTAL OUTPUT
CCCCD0   D3CC C4F3          CC4F5           86         MVZ   TOTNEW+5(1),TOTNEW*4
CCCCE6   4EA0 C5A6          C05A8           87         CVD   10,DBL
CCCCEA   F377 C4FB C5A6     004FD  C05A8    88         UNPK  TOTPRC,DBL        TOTAL PRICE TO TOTAL OUTPUT
CCCCFC   D300 C502 C501     C5C4   C0503    89         MVZ   TOTPRC+7(1),TOTPRC+6
CCCCFE                                      90         PUT   RPTFILE,BLANKS  SKIP A LINE
CCCC1C4                                     95         PUT   RPTFILE,TOT1    PRINT FIRST TOTAL LINE
CCCC12C                                    100         PUT   RPTFILE,BLANKS  SKIP
CCCC12E                                    105         PUT   RPTFILE,BLANKS  3
CCCC13C   9EAC 0C20         CC020          110         PUT   RPTFILE,BLANKS  LINES
CCCC14C   1DA8                             112         SRDA  10,32           PREPARE FOR BINARY DIVISION
CCCC142   4E8C C5A6         C05A8          115         DR    10,8            COMPUTE AVG PRICE PER ITEM, INTO REG 11
CCCC146   C337 C576 C5A6    00578  C05A8   116         CVD   11,DBL
CCCC14C   D3CC C579 C578    C57C   C057A   117         UNPK  AVG,DBL         AVG PRICE PER ITEM INTO TOTAL OUTPUT
CCCC152                                    118         MVZ   AVG+3(1),AVG+2
                                           119         PUT   RPTFILE,TOT2    PRINT SECOND TOTAL LINE
                                           120   *
CCCC16C                                    125         CLOSE (ITMFILE)
CCCC16A                                    126         CLOSE (RPTFILE)
                                           132   *FOR DOS, CLOSING FILES IS PERFORMED BY
                                           138         CLOSE ITMFILE,RPTFILE
                                           139   *
                                           140   *FOR DOS, THE END OF EXECUTION IS INSTRUCTED BY
CCC176   CA03                              141         SVC   3
                                           143         EOJ
                                           144   *
                                           145   * FILE DEFINITIONS
                                           146   *
                                           147   ITMFILE  DTFCD  DEVADDR=SYSRDR,IOAREA1=IN,BLKSIZE=80,RECFORM=FIXUN8,      C
CCC178                                                          WORKA=YES,EOFADCR=FIN
                                           201   RPTFILE  DTFPR  DEVADDR=SYSLST,IOAREA1=OUT,BLKSIZE=132,RECFORM=FIXUN8,    C
CCC1C8                                                          WORKA=YES
                                           255   *FOR DOS, FILE DEFINITIONS ARE PERFORMED BY THE DTF MACROS AND
                                           256   *
                                           257   ITMFILE  DTFCD  DEVADDR=SYSRDR,IOAREA1=IN,BLKSIZE=80,RECFORM=FIXUN8,
                                           258                   WORKA=YES,EOFADCR=FIN
                                           259   RPTFILE  DTFPR  DEVADDR=SYSLST,IOAREA1=OUT,BLKSIZE=132,RECFORM=FIXUN8,
                                           260                   WORKA=YES
CCC238                                     281   IN    DS   CL80     BUFFER FOR INPUT FILE
CCC238                                     262   OUT   DS   CL132    BUFFER FOR OUTPUT FILE
                                           263   *
                                           264   * DATA AREAS
                                           265   *
CCC23E                                     266   ITMREC  DS   OCL80        INPUT AREA
CCC242                                     267   INUM    DS   CL6
CCC246                                     769   ICLD    DS   CL4
CCC24A                                     270   IISSUE  DS   CL4
CCC24E                                     271   IRECPT  DS   CL4
CCC24E                                     272   IUPRC   DS   CL2
CCC250                                     274   IDESC   DS   CL20
CCC251                                     275
```

Figure 8.4
Inventory Report — 1 (Part 2)

```
LOC      OBJECT CODE            ADDR1 ADDR2  STMT   SOURCE STATEMENT

CCC265                                 276           DS    CL35
                                       277  *
                                       278  *            DETAIL OUTPUT AREA
CCC288  40                             279  REPTREC DC    C' '
CCC289                                 280  ONUM    DS    CL3
CCC28C                                 281          DS    CL4
CCC29C                                 282  ODESC   DS    CL10
CCC29A                                 283          DS    CL20
CCC2AE                                 284  COLD    DS    CL10
CCC28B                                 285          DS    CL4
CCC2C7                                 286  OISSUE  DS    CL11
CCC2C8                                 287          DS    CL4
CCC2D4                                 288  ORECPT  DS    CL9
CCC2D8                                 289          DS    CL4
CCC2E2                                 290  ONEW    DS    CL10
CCC2E6                                 291          DS    CL4
CCC2EF                                 292  OPRC    DS    CL9
CCC2F5                                 293          DS    CL24
                                       294  *
                                       295  *            FIRST TOTAL LINE
CCC3CD  404040404040404040             296  BLANKS  DC    CL132' '
                                       297  HEAD1   DC    CL132'  ITEM      ITEM    RECEIPTS    NEW        OLD'
CCC351  40404040C9E3C5D440             298  HEAD2   DC    CL132'  NUMBER    ISSUES   DESCRIPTION     ON HAND    PRICE   ON HAND'
CCC415  4040D5E4D4C2C5D9                            AND
                                       299  *
CCC459  4040404040404040               300  TCT1    DS    OCL132
CCC4CE  E3D6E3C1D3E2                    301          DC    CL6'TOTALS'
CCC4E4  4040404040404040               302          DC    CL12' '
CCC4FC  4040404040404040               303          DC    CL7' '
                                       304  TOTNEW  DS    CL6
CCC4F6  4040404040404040               305          DC    CL7' '
                                       306  TOTPRC  DS    CL8
CCC5C5  4040404040404040               307          DC    CL24' '
                                       308  *            SECOND TOTAL LINE
CCC51D  4040404040404040               309  TCT2    DS    OCL132
                                       310          DC    CL55' '
CCC55E  C1E5C5D9C1C7C540               311          DC    CL26'AVERAGE PRICE PER ITEM = '
                                       312  AVG     DS    CL4
CCC578  4040404040404040               313          DC    CL38' '
                                       314  *
CCC5A8                                 315  DBL     DS    0D
CCC5A8                                 316          DS    PL8
CCCCC0                                 317          END   BGN
```

Figure 8.4

Inventory Report — 1 (Part.3)

ITEM NUMBER	ITEM DESCRIPTION	OLD ON HAND	ISSUES	RECEIPTS	NEW ON HAND	PRICE
1CC4	RAINWEAR	0400	0058	CC60	0402	009648
1C1C	UMBRELLAS	0204	02CC	0110	0114	000912
1C17	MITTENS	0310	0250	01C4	0164	000328
1C2C	LADIES HANDBAGS	0108	0054	0C56	0110	003850
1C26	SKI MASKS	0255	0178	0055	0132	000792
1C3C	MENS CUTERWEAR	0202	0109	002C	0113	007797
2C15	GENERATORS	0099	0075	0010	0034	000442
2C2C	VOLTAGE REGULATORS	0095	0080	0046	0061	000915
2C79	BATTERIES	0085	0055	0030	006C	002580
3C49	SNOWMOBILES	0207	0168	01C0	0139	013344
4C11	FLOWER POTS	0155	0052	0064	0167	000668
4C13	FABRIC DYE	0083	0073	0060	0070	00C070
4C17	FLASHLIGHTS	0188	0160	0C20	0048	000144
4C2C	KEY RINGS	0035	0024	CC24	0C35	000070
4C2P	PICTURE FRAMES	0102	0010	C000	0092	000920
4C4C	PENS	0376	0282	C050	0144	000432
4C91	BALLOONS	0150	0101	0100	0149	000149
5CC4	LAMPS	0170	0140	0132	0162	001944
5CC7	PENCIL SHARPENERS	0094	0068	0010	0036	000468
5C16	FORMICA TABLES	0042	0024	C010	0028	000980
5C18	CAN OPENERS	0069	0046	C04C	0C63	000693

| | | TOTALS | | | 002323 | 00047146 |

AVERAGE PRICE PER ITEM ≈ 0020

Figure 8.5
Inventory Report — 1 Output

HEAD1 and HEAD2 describe (as constant definitions) the header lines required for the program header output. TOT1 and TOT2 describe the respective first and second total lines. The major parts of the lines are defined in constant form, and fields TOTNEW, TOTPRC, and AVG are reserved for the total new-on-hand, total price, and average price per item to be computed by the program. The field called DBL will be used in the program to hold numeric values which are temporarily in packed form (numbers must pass through packed form in order to effect proper conversion between binary and zoned forms).

Let us now focus our attention upon the main body of the program to see how our inventory· report was actually produced. Statement numbers referred to are those on the program listing.

The PRINT NOGEN, START, BALR, and USING instructions perform functions associated with "setting up" our program. The PRINT NOGEN instructs the assembler program to suppress the printing of macro definitions on the program listing. The START instruction directs the assembler to begin the assembly process, and to initialize the location counter to a value of 0. The instructions BALR 12,0 and USING *,12 initialize register 12 to a particular value (the address of the BALR instruction itself + 2) and inform the assembler that program addresses to be represented in base-displacement form are to use register 12 as the base register. If you do not recall the functions of the START, BALR, and USING instructions, refer back to chapter 2, section 2.4.

The instructions SR 8,8 and SR 10,10 clear registers 8 and 10, that is, each of registers 8 and 10 are filled with zeros (by subtracting its present contents from itself). This is in preparation for computing totals. Each time a new-on-hand or price amount is computed for a particular item record, the value will be added to the contents of register 8 or 10 respectively, so that once all the item records have been processed, the totals will be available in those registers. "Clearing" the registers is necessary before any addition takes place, to ensure that our values are not added to some unknown quantity already in the register.

The program now enters the "header routine", the set of instructions which produce heading output. The two PUT instructions print out the first and second heading lines (statements 21 and 26) and the instruction PUT RPTFILE,BLANKS causes the printer to space one line (one output line will be left blank). A MVC instruction then fills the detail output area with blanks in preparation for the next routine, in which detail lines will be arranged with blanks separating the data fields.

We continue our program with the "detail routine", the set of instructions which produces detail output. The first instruction of our detail routine is the GET statement (statement 39), for we cannot process a record until the input data has been read. Input fields which are to become part of the output detail record for this item are then moved to the appropriate positions of REPTREC (the detail output area). MVC instructions move contents of the item number, item description, old-on-hand, issues, and receipts fields.

Two additional output values are required for our report line: the new-on-hand and price quantities obtained through computation performed on our input values. In preparation for these computations, the program now converts the old-on-hand, receipts, issues, and unit price input amounts, first into packed form via PACK instructions and then from packed form into binary form via CVB (ConVert to Binary) instructions. For the first conversion, the instruction PACK DBL,IOLD considers the contents of IOLD, a zoned number, and converts it into packed form, placing the packed result into the first operand location, called DBL. (The PACK instruction is explained in detail in chapter 4, section 4.2.6). The instruction CVB 2,DBL considers the contents of its second operand, DBL (which now holds the packed number), converts it into binary form, and places it into its first operand register:

register 2. (The CVB instruction was explained in chapter 7, section 7.3.5.) You might note that DBL, the second operand of the CVB instruction, was defined on a doubleword integral boundary. The assembler requires that the CVB's second operand be so defined. Similar conversion procedures are performed for the receipts, issues, and unit price fields, placing their binary equivalents into registers 3,4, and 7 respectively.

We now compute new-on-hand by adding the receipts value (contents of register 3) to old-on-hand (contents of register 2) using the add instruction AR   2,3. The instruction SR   2,4 subtracts issues (contents of register 4) from the previous sum. New-on-hand is now contained in register 2. We add new-on-hand to register 8 for computation of a total new-on-hand value (the instruction AR   8,2). The new-on-hand is then converted into packed form (via the CVD instruction), then into zoned form, and is placed into the appropriate output subfield. The MVZ instruction eliminates the sign from the low-order byte of new-on-hand, so that the low-order digit will be properly printed (see chapter 5, section 5.2 for a discussion of this technique).

The price value (the price of all new-on-hand items for a particular record) is now computed as the product of the new-on-hand and the unit price (the price per item). The instruction MR   6,2 multiplies the contents of register 7, containing the unit price, by the contents of register 2, the new-on-hand. (Although the first operand is 6, the contents of register 7 will be accessed — see the discussion of the MR in section 8.2.3.) The product replaces the previous contents of register 7, the first operand. We next add the price to the contents of register 10 for the computation of a total price value (the instruction AR   10,7). Price is then converted, first into packed form via the CVD (ConVert to Decimal) instruction, which places the packed version into DBL, and then from packed form into zoned form and into the appropriate subfield   OPRC   of   the   detail   output   area,   via   the   instruction UNPK   OPRC,DBL. The MVZ instruction eliminates the sign from the low-order byte of OPRC for appropriate printing of the low-order digit.

Our detail line has now been arranged with field contents in appropriate output positions. The PUT instruction (statement 74) produces a detail output line. We then branch back to RD where we begin to process a new record. The program is in its loop, and will exit from the loop when, upon executing the GET statement, a "/*" (last card) is detected. Program control will then pass to the instruction called FIN (recall the OS   DCB parameter EODAD=FIN and the DOS   DTFCD parameter EOFADDR=FIN).

We next enter our "total routine", the set of instructions which produces the total lines. The total new-on-hand and total price fields are converted into packed format (via the CVD instructions). They are then converted into zoned format and placed into appropriate TOT1 subfields (via the UNPK instructions), and the signs are eliminated (via the MVZ instructions). The first total line is then printed, after which the three PUT   RPTFILE,BLANKS instructions cause the printer to space three lines in accordance with the output description. The instructions   SRDA   10,32 and DR   10,8 effect the division of the total price by the total new-on-hand to yield the average price per item. (See sections 8.2.4 and 8.2.5 for a discussion of these instructions.) The average is converted into packed form and then into zoned form and placed into the appropriate TOT2 subfield (via the CVD and UNPK instructions), and the sign is eliminated (via the MVZ instruction). The second total line is printed, the program files are closed, and control is returned to the supervisor program. Program execution has ended.

8.2   EXPLAINING   OUR   PROGRAM   INSTRUCTIONS: FIXED POINT ARITHMETIC

In this section, we shall present the assembly language instructions used for adding, subtracting, multiplying, and dividing binary fixed point numbers. We shall see that in these instructions, one operand is always a general register number, while the other is either a general register number or an address in main storage.

The contents of main storage used by these instructions are fixed point numbers, occupying a signed fullword or a signed halfword. The fullword and halfword operands will also have appropriate integral boundary requirements (addresses to be multiples of 4 or 2, respectively). In addition, the instructions which convert numbers to and from binary form have a doubleword integral boundary requirement.

Register contents used by the fixed point instructions will occupy the entire register (32 bits), however the divide instructions and some multiply instructions use a 64-bit operand occupying two adjacent registers.

8.2.1   Fixed-Point Addition Instructions: AR, A, AH

The fixed-point addition instructions add the contents of the second operand to the contents of the first operand, and the sum replaces the previous contents of the first operand.

Overflow occurs if the carry out of the sign position is not identical to the carry into the sign position. That is, if a "1" bit is carried into the sign position, a "1" must also be carried out of the sign position. If either carry takes place without the other, we say that overflow occurs. In the event of overflow, the condition code is set to 3 (and a program interruption may also take place). You may refer back to chapter 5, section 5.3, for a discussion of the condition code. Further explanation will be presented in chapter 13, section 13.3.1.

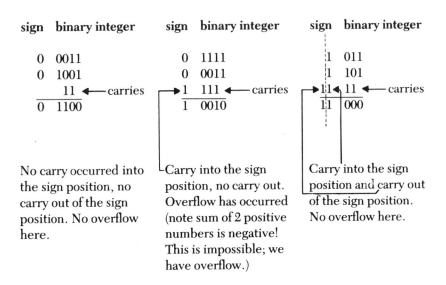

sign	binary integer		sign	binary integer		sign	binary integer
0	0011		0	1111		1	011
0	1001		0	0011		1	101
	11 ←—carries		1	111 ←—carries		11 11 ←—carries
0	1100		1	0010		11	000

No carry occurred into the sign position, no carry out of the sign position. No overflow here.

Carry into the sign position, no carry out. Overflow has occurred (note sum of 2 positive numbers is negative! This is impossible; we have overflow.)

Carry into the sign position and carry out of the sign position. No overflow here.

The fixed point addition instructions cause the following condition code settings:

0   if the sum = 0
1   if the sum < 0
2   if the sum > 0
3   if overflow occurs

A zero sum is represented as a positive binary number (sign bit = 0).

The AR Instruction

The AR Instruction (**A**dd **R**egisters)

Instruction type: Machine Instruction
Machine format: RR Instruction (Register to Register Instruction)

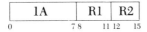

Symbolic format:

name	operation	operands
[symbolic name]	AR	R1,R2

where R1 and R2 are general register numbers (0 - 15)

. . . .

Rules:
- The contents of the first and second operands are interpreted as binary numbers.
- R1 and R2 may be the same register.

Example:

AR   2,3

Before execution of the AR			**After execution of the AR**		
	binary **(hex notation)**	**decimal**		**binary** **(hex notation)**	**decimal**
Reg 2:	00 00 00 40	64	Reg 2:	00 00 00 61	97
Reg 3:	00 00 00 21	33	Reg 3:	00 00 00 21	33

Example:

AR   5,5

	Before execution of the AR binary (hex notation)	decimal		After execution of the AR binary (hex notation)	decimal
Reg 5:	FF FF FF FB	-5	Reg 5:	FF FF FF F6	-10

Recall that negative binary numbers are represented in 2's complement notation with a sign bit of 1 (see chapter 7, section 7.2.1).

Example:

$$\text{AR} \qquad 6,7$$

	Before execution of the AR binary (hex notation)	decimal		After execution of the AR binary (hex notation)	decimal
Reg 6:	00 00 00 14	20	Reg 6:	00 00 00 00	0
Reg 7:	FF FF FF EC	-20	Reg 7:	FF FF FF EC	-20

Note here that the 0 result is represented as positive. Two's complement notation does not provide a negative zero.

The A Instruction

The A Instruction (**A**dd fullword)

Instruction type: Machine Instruction
Machine format: RX Instruction (Register and IndeXed Storage Instruction)

5A	R1	X2	B2	D2

0   7 8   11 12   15 16   19 20   31

Symbolic format:

	name	operation	operands
	[symbolic name]	A	R1,name2
or	[symbolic name]	A	R1,D2(X2,B2)

where R1 is a general register number (0–15). D2, X2, and B2 are the displacement, index register and base register respectively used to calculate the second operand address.

. . . .

Rules:
- The contents of the first and second operands are interpreted as binary numbers.
- The second operand must be a fixed point fullword: 32 bits long and located on a fullword integral boundary. That is, its address must be a multiple of 4 (in binary, this is an address whose low-order 2 bits are both 0's).

Example:

```
            A      4,NUMB
     NUMB   DC     F'6'
```

Before execution of the A	binary (hex notation)	decimal		After execution of the A	binary (hex notation)	decimal
Reg 4:	FF FF FF EF	−17	Reg 4:	FF FF FF F5	−11
NUMB:	00 00 00 06	6	NUMB:	00 00 00 06	6

Note that NUMB satisfies the fullword integral boundary requirement. A DC assembler instruction with operand type designation "F" stores a number in binary form with fullword length (32 bits) on a fullword integral boundary.

Example:

```
            A      8,TWO
     TWO    DC     F'2'
```

Before execution of the A	binary (hex notation)	decimal		After execution of the A	binary (hex notation)	decimal
Reg 8:	7F FF FF FF	2,147,483,647	Reg 8:	80 00 00 01	meaningless
TWO:	00 00 00 02	2	TWO:	00 00 00 02	2

The add instruction of this example results in an overflow condition. Note that before execution, register 8 already contained the largest possible positive binary number. Therefore adding 2 (or any positive value!) to it would naturally result in an overflow condition. The resulting sum is of course meaningless. What actually happened:

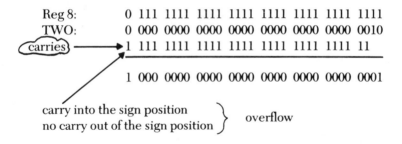

Reg 8:   0 111 1111 1111 1111 1111 1111 1111 1111
TWO: 0 000 0000 0000 0000 0000 0000 0000 0010
carries ──→ 1 111 1111 1111 1111 1111 1111 1111 11

             1 000 0000 0000 0000 0000 0000 0000 0001

carry into the sign position   ⎫
no carry out of the sign position   ⎬ overflow

The AH Instruction

The AH Instruction (**A**dd **H**alfword)

Instruction type: Machine Instruction
Machine format: RX Instruction (Register and IndeXed Storage Instruction)

4A	R1	X2	B2	D2
0	7 8	11 12 15 16	19 20	31

Symbolic format:

	name	operation	operands
	[symbolic name]	AH	R1,name2
or	[symbolic name]	AH	R1,D2(X2,B2)

where R1 is a general register number (0 —15). D2, X2 and B2 are the displacement, index register, and base register respectively used to calculate the second operand address.

. . . .

Rules:
- The contents of the first and second operands are interpreted as binary numbers.

- The second operand must be a fixed point halfword: 16 bits long and located on a halfword integral boundary. That is, its address must be a multiple of 2 (in binary this is an address whose low-order bit is 0).

For the AH instruction, the computer first expands the halfword second operand to a fullword before addition, by propagating the sign (a positive number is expanded with 16 leftmost 0's and a negative number is expanded with 16 leftmost 1's). Addition is then performed by adding the 32 bits of both operands.

Example:

```
              AH   7,HALF
HALF          DC   H'−23'
```

Before execution of the AH		**After execution of the AH**	
binary		**binary**	
(hex notation)	**decimal**	**(hex notation)**	**decimal**
Reg 7: 00 00 00 1E	30	Reg 7: 00 00 00 07	7
HALF: FF E9	−23	HALF: FF E9	−23

Note that HALF satisfies the halfword integral boundary requirement. A DC assembler instruction with operand type designation "H" stores a number in binary form with halfword length (16 bits) on a halfword integral boundary.

8.2.2   Fixed Point Subtraction Instructions: SR, S, SH

The fixed point subtraction instructions subtract the contents of the second operand from the contents of the first operand (unlike the case of addition, the *order* of the operands is important here!) The difference replaces the previous contents of the first operand.

The actual method used by the computer for subtraction follows: the computer first finds the one's complement of the number being subtracted (the second operand), and it then *adds* the one's complement *and* a low-order 1 to the contents of the first operand register. If you do not remember the binary complement representation or binary subtraction with complements, you may refer back to chapter 7, section 7.2.1.

Overflow occurs if the carry out of the sign position is not identical to the carry into the sign position, as is the case for the add instructions (above). It is also interesting to note here that subtracting a maximum negative number from a maximum negative number will yield a zero result with no overflow! This case is demonstrated below:

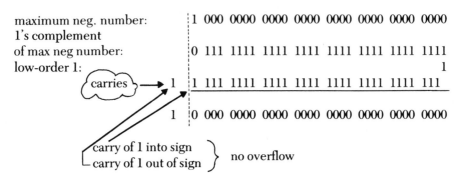

maximum neg. number: 1 000 0000 0000 0000 0000 0000 0000 0000
1's complement
of max neg number: 0 111 1111 1111 1111 1111 1111 1111 1111
low-order 1:   1

carries → 1   1 111 1111 1111 1111 1111 1111 1111 111

1   0 000 0000 0000 0000 0000 0000 0000 0000

carry of 1 into sign
carry of 1 out of sign   } no overflow

The fixed point subtraction instructions cause the following condition code settings:

>0   if the difference = 0
>1   if the difference < 0
>2   if the difference > 0
>3   if overflow occurs

A zero difference is represented as a positive binary number (sign=0).

The SR Instruction

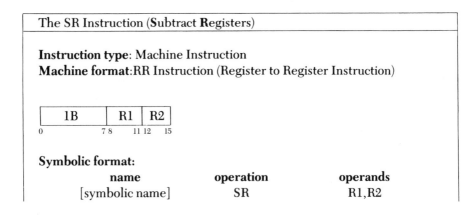

The SR Instruction (Subtract **R**egisters)

Instruction type: Machine Instruction
Machine format:RR Instruction (Register to Register Instruction)

1B	R1	R2
0 7 8 11 12 15		

Symbolic format:

name	operation	operands
[symbolic name]	SR	R1,R2

where R1 and R2 are general register numbers (0 — 15).

. . . .

Rules:
- The contents of the first and second operands are interpreted as binary numbers.
- The first and second operands may be identical. In this case, of course, the register is "cleared" — that is, it is filled with zeros.

Example:

$$\text{SR} \quad 6,4$$

Before execution of the SR			**After execution of the SR**		
	binary			**binary**	
	(hex notation)	**decimal**		**(hex notation)**	**decimal**
Reg 6:	00 00 00 28	40	Reg 6:	00 00 00 1E	30
Reg 4:	00 00 00 0A	10	Reg 4:	00 00 00 0A	10

Example:

$$\text{SR} \quad 9,9$$

Before execution of the SR			**After execution of the SR**		
	binary			**binary**	
	(hex notation)	**decimal**		**(hex notation)**	**decimal**
Reg 9	any number	any number	Reg 9:	00 00 00 00	0

Regardless of its previous contents, subtracting the contents of a register from itself yields a zero result.

The S Instruction

The S Instruction (Subtract fullword)

Instruction type: Machine Instruction
Machine format: RX Instruction (Register and IndeXed Storage Instruction)

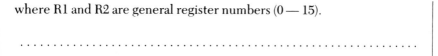

5B	R1	X2	B2	D2

0   7 8   11 12 15 16 19 20   31

Symbolic format:

	name	operation	operands
	[symbolic name]	S	R1,name2
or	[symbolic name]	S	R1,D2(X2,B2)

where R1 is a general register number (0-15). D2, X2 and B2 are the displacement, index register, and base register respectively used to calculate the second operand address.

. . . .

Rules:
- The contents of the first and second operands are interpreted as binary numbers.
- The second operand must be a fixed point fullword: 32 bits long and located on a fullword integral boundary. That is, its address must be a multiple of 4 (in binary, this is an address whose low-order 2 bits are both 0's).

Example:

$$S \quad 6,LOC1$$
$$LOC1 \quad DC \quad F'-1'$$

Before execution of the S			**After execution of the S**		
binary			binary		
(hex notation)		decimal	(hex notation)		decimal
Reg 6:	00 00 00 28	40	Reg 6:	00 00 00 29	41
LOC1:	FF FF FF FF	−1	LOC1:	FF FF FF FF	−1

Note that LOC satisfies the fullword integral boundary requirement, for it is defined by a DC instruction with the type designation "F".

Example:

$$S \quad 8,LOC2$$
$$LOC2 \quad DC \quad F'-1'$$

Before execution of the S			**After execution of the S**		
binary			binary		
(hex notation)		decimal	(hex notation)		decimal
Reg 8:	7F FF FF FF	2,147,483,647	Reg 8:	80 00 00 00	meaningless
LOC2:	FF FF FF FF	−1	LOC2:	FF FF FF FF	−1

The subtract instruction of this example results in an overflow condition. Before execution, register 8 contained the largest 32-bit number. Subtraction of a negative number from this is equivalent to addition of a positive number, resulting in overflow.

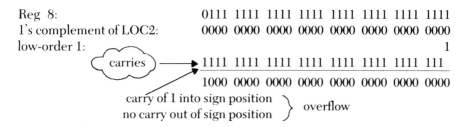

Reg 8:   0111 1111 1111 1111 1111 1111 1111 1111
1's complement of LOC2:   0000 0000 0000 0000 0000 0000 0000 0000
low-order 1:   1

carries ──→ 1111 1111 1111 1111 1111 1111 1111 111
            1000 0000 0000 0000 0000 0000 0000 0000

carry of 1 into sign position
no carry out of sign position } overflow

The SH Instruction

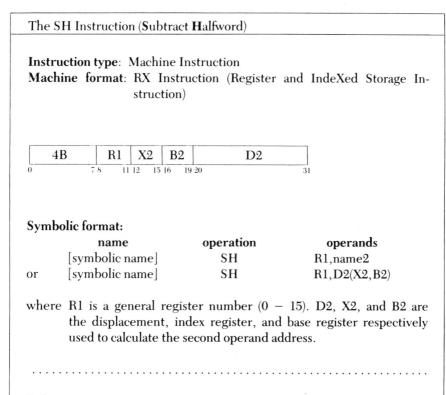

The SH Instruction (Subtract Halfword)

Instruction type: Machine Instruction
Machine format: RX Instruction (Register and IndeXed Storage Instruction)

4B	R1	X2	B2	D2
0 7 8	11 12	15 16	19 20	31

Symbolic format:

	name	operation	operands
	[symbolic name]	SH	R1,name2
or	[symbolic name]	SH	R1,D2(X2,B2)

where R1 is a general register number (0 − 15). D2, X2, and B2 are the displacement, index register, and base register respectively used to calculate the second operand address.

. . . .

Rules:
- The contents of the first and second operands are interpreted as binary numbers.

> • The second operand must be a fixed point halfword: 16 bits long
> and located on a halfword integral boundary. That is, its address
> must be a multiple of 2 (in binary, this is an address whose low-
> order bit is 0).

For the SH instruction, the computer first expands the halfword second
operand to a fullword before subtraction, by propagating the sign (a positive
number is expanded with 16 leftmost 0's, and a negative number is expanded with 16 leftmost 1's). Subtraction is then performed by adding the one's
complement of the 32-bit expanded second operand and a low-order 1 to the
first operand.

Example:

```
                        SH    5,THERE
            THERE       DC    H'5'
```

Before execution of the SH			**After execution of the SH**		
	binary			**binary**	
	(hex notation)	**decimal**		**(hex notation)**	**decimal**
Reg 5:	00 00 00 07	7	Reg 5:	00 00 00 02	2
THERE:	00 05	5	THERE:	00 05	5

Note that THERE satisfies the halfword integral boundary requirement, for
it is defined by a DC instruction with type designation "H".

8.2.3   Fixed-Point Multiplication Instructions: MR, M, MH

The fixed point multiplication instructions multiply the contents of the
second operand by the contents of the first operand register. For the MR
(Multiply Register) and M (Multiply) instructions, the product will occupy
an even-odd pair of registers; the even-numbered register of the pair is the
first operand of the instruction. For the MH (Multiply Halfword) instruction,
the product will replace the previous contents of the first operand register.

Overflow cannot occur when multiplying with the MR or M instructions.
Overflow is possible with the MH instruction, however the computer will
not indicate to us that it has in fact occurred.

The fixed point multiplication instructions leave the condition code setting
unchanged. A zero product is represented as a positive binary number (sign
bit = 0).

The MR Instruction

The MR Instruction (**Multiply Registers**)

Instruction type: Machine Instruction
Machine Format: RR Instruction (Register to Register Instruction)

1C	R1	R2

0   7 8   11 12   15

Symbolic format:

name	operation	operands
[symbolic name]	MR	R1,R2

where R1 is an even register number and R2 is a general register number (0 − 15).

. . . .

Rules: ˙
- The first operand R1 must be an even-numbered register. The odd-numbered register adjacent to R1, and following it, contains the multiplicand.
- The second operand R2 contains the multiplier.
- After execution, the even-odd register pair contains the product.

Example:

MR   4,6

| Before execution of the MR | | | After execution of the MR | | |

	binary (hex notation)	decimal		binary (hex notation)	decimal
Reg 4:	00 00 00 07	7	Reg 4:	00 00 00 00	72
Reg 5:	00 00 00 08	8	Reg 5:	00 00 00 48	
Reg 6:	00 00 00 09	9	Reg 6:	00 00 00 09	9

The instruction MR   4,6 multiplies the contents of register 5 by the contents of register 6 (the second operand). The first operand is an even-numbered register which actually addresses an *even-odd register pair*, the *odd* register of which contains the multiplicand. Thus the register numbered 4 addresses the even-odd pair consisting of registers 4 and 5, and register 5 contains the multiplicand. The second operand, register 6, contains the multiplier. In this example, (contents of register 5) × (contents of register 6) = $(8)_{10} \times (9)_{10} = (72)_{10}$. The product is a 64-bit signed binary integer occupying the even-odd register pair 4 − 5. The original contents of register 4 are destroyed.

Example:

MR   8,9

	Before execution of the MR			**After execution of the MR**		
	binary (hex notation)	**decimal**		**binary (hex notation)**	**decimal**
Reg 8:	00 00 00 0A	10	Reg 8:	00 00 00 00	
Reg 9:	FF FF FF FF	−1	Reg 9:	00 00 00 01	+1

The instruction MR   8,9 multiplies the contents of register 9 by itself. The multiplicand is in register 9 (the odd register of the even-odd pair 8−9, specified by the first operand) and the multiplier is in register 9 (the second operand). The product is thus: (contents of register 9) × (contents of register 9) = $(-1)_{10} \times (-1)_{10} = (+1)_{10}$. The original contents of register 8 are destroyed.

Example:

MR   7,9

This instruction is incorrect. The first operand R1 must be an even-numbered register.

The M Instruction

The M Instruction (**Multiply fullword**)
Instruction type: Machine Instruction

Machine format: RX Instruction (Register and IndeXed Storage Instruction)

5C		R1	X2	B2		D2	
0		7 8	11 12	15 16	19 20		31

Symbolic format:

	name	operation	operands
	[symbolic name]	M	R1,name2
or	[symbolic name]	M	R1,D2(X2,B2)

where R1 is an even register number. D2, X2, and B2 are the displacement, index register and base register respectively used to calculate the second operand address.

. . . .

Rules:
- The first operand R1 must be an even-numbered register. The odd-numbered register adjacent to R1, and following it, contains the multiplicand.
- The second operand must be a fixed point fullword: 32 bits long and located on a fullword integral boundary. That is, its address must be a multiple of 4 (in binary, this is an address whose low-order 2 bits are both 0's).
- The second operand location contains the multiplier.
- After execution, the even-odd register pair contains the product.

Example:

		M	2,M3
	M3	DC	F'−3'

Before execution of the M   **After execution of the M**

	binary (hex notation)	decimal		binary (hex notation)	decimal
Reg 2:	00 00 00 00	0	Reg 2:	FF FF FF FF	} −3
Reg 3:	00 00 00 01	+1	Reg 3:	FF FF FF FD	
M3:	FF FF FF FD	−3	M3:	FF FF FF FD	−3

The M instruction multiplies the contents of register 3 (the *odd* register of the even-odd register pair 2−3) by the contents of the fixed point fullword in location M3. In this example, (contents of register 3) × (contents of M3) = $(+1)_{10} \times (-3)_{10} = (-3)_{10}$, occupying register pair 2–3. Note the extension of the negative sign bit throughout register 2.

The MR and M Instructions: Why a Register Pair to Hold the Product?

Multiplication differs from addition and subtraction in one very important sense. Adding or subtracting two numbers will yield a sum or difference which is at most one digit longer than the longer of the two original numbers being added or subtracted. However, when multiplying two numbers, the length of the product may reach the sum of the lengths of the multiplicand and the multiplier. (The sum or difference of a 5-digit and a 6-digit number may reach 7 digits, but their product may reach 11 digits!) Results of multiplication are thus generally longer than results of addition and subtraction, and the assembly language multiply instruction must prepare for this possibility. The multiplicand and multiplier used by the MR and M instructions are each 32 bits long—actually 31 bits + the sign. Thus their product may occupy 62 bits + the sign, or 63 bits. (An exception is the product of 2 maximum negative numbers, which will occupy 63 bits + the sign.) Allowing a register pair (64 bits) for the product not only ensures enough room for the product, but also assures that overflow will not occur when using these instructions.

When multiplication takes place, the sign of a nonzero product is determined according to the rules of algebra (the product of 2 numbers of like sign is positive; the product of 2 numbers of unlike sign is negative). Then the computer "extends" the sign bit (repeats it) to the right until the first significant digit of the product is encountered. Thus the product will occupy the entire even-odd register pair.

In chapter 7, section 7.2.1, we discussed the actual procedure through which the computer performs binary multiplication (a pattern of addition, shifting, and possible complementation). It might be worthwhile for you to reread the discussion at this time. It will clarify exactly how the even-odd register pair is used—the step by step changes that its contents experience—during the multiplication process.

Programming Hint

It should be noted at this point that although the product will occupy a register pair, the significant part of the product along with a sign bit will usually fit into the low-order (odd) register. This will be the case as long as the product does not exceed $2^{31}-1$ or 2,147,483,647 if positive, -2^{31} or $-2,147,483,648$ if negative. (These are the binary numbers of largest absolute value which may fit into a register—see chapter 7, section 7.2.1.) The programmer will usually be able to judge, from knowledge of his data, whether the product is likely to exceed these amounts. (If the program calculates inventory new-on-hand amounts for store items, for example, one would have an idea whether the new-on-hand would be likely to reach the maximum register value!) Thus the programmer may usually ignore the contents of the even-numbered register, and consider only the significant part of the product plus the sign, in the odd-numbered register.

The MH Instruction

The MH Instruction (Multiply Halfword)

Instruction type: Machine Instruction
Machine format: RX Instruction (Register and IndeXed Storage Instruction)

4C	R1	X2	B2	D2
0	7 8	11 12	15 16 19 20	31

Symbolic format:

	name	operation	operands
	[symbolic name]	MH	R1,name2
or	[symbolic name]	MH	R1,D2(X2,B2)

where R1 is a general register number (0−15) and D2, X2, and B2 are the displacement, index register, and base register respectively used to calculate the second operand address.

. . . .

Rules:
- The first operand R1 contains the multiplicand.
- The second operand must be a fixed point halfword: 16 bits long and located on a halfword integral boundary. That is, its address must be a multiple of 2 (in binary, this is an address whose low-order bit is 0).
- The second operand location contains the multiplier.
- The product after multiplication replaces the multiplicand in R1.

For the MH instruction, the computer first expands the halfword second operand to a fullword before multiplication, by propagating the sign bit value 16 bit positions to the left. Multiplication is then performed by multiplying the 32 bits of both operands.

Example:

	MH	7,FIVE
FIVE	DC	H'5'

Before execution of the MH	**After execution of the MH**

	binary (hex notation)	decimal			binary (hex notation)	decimal
Reg 7:	00 00 00 06	6	Reg 7:		00 00 00 1E	30
FIVE:	00 05	5	FIVE:		00 05	5

Note that the MH may use any available register as its first operand (here an odd-numbered register was used). The result replaces the multiplicand in the first operand (register 7).

8.2.4 Fixed-Point Division Instructions: DR,D

Before execution, the fixed-point division instructions store their dividend in an *even-odd register pair* which is addressed in the instruction by the even register number (the high-order register of the register pair). The address of the register pair is the first operand R1 of the division instructions. The divisor will occupy a register (the second operand R2 of the DR—Divide Register—instruction) or a fullword location in main storage (the second operand of the D—Divide fullword—instruction).

The results of division are the quotient and the remainder. The quotient is in the odd-numbered register and the remainder is in the even-numbered register (R1) of the even-odd pair.

The sign of the quotient is determined by the rules of algebra. (If dividend and divisor are of like sign, the quotient will be positive. Otherwise, the quotient will be negative.) The sign of the remainder will be the same as that of the dividend. The only exception may be in the case of a zero quotient or remainder, which is always expressed as a positive binary number (sign bit = 0).

The fixed-point division instructions leave the condition code setting unchanged.

The DR Instruction

The DR Instruction (**D**ivide **R**egisters)

Instruction type: Machine Instruction
Machine format: RR Instruction (Register to Register Instruction)

1D	R1	R2

0   7 8   11 12   15

Symbolic format:

name	operation	operands
[symbolic name]	DR	R1,R2

where R1 is an even register number and R2 is a general register
number (0−15).

. . . .

Rules:
- The first operand R1 must be an even-numbered register.
- The even-odd register pair contains the dividend.
- The second operand R2 contains the divisor.
- After execution, R1 contains the remainder; the odd register of the
  even-odd pair contains the quotient.

Example:

$$DR \quad 4,6$$

Before execution of the DR   **After execution of the DR**

	binary (hex notation)	decimal			binary (hex notation)	decimal
Reg 4:	FF FF FF FF			Reg 4:	FF FF FF FE	−2
Reg 5:	FF FF FF E0	−32		Reg 5:	FF FF FF F6	−10
Reg 6:	00 00 00 03	+3		Reg 6:	00 00 00 03	+3

Note that the quotient replaces the low-order part of the dividend (register 5), while the remainder replaces the high-order part of the dividend (register 4). Note too that the sign of the quotient (-10) is determined by algebraic rules (the dividend and divisor were of unlike sign) while the remainder (-2) has the sign of the dividend.

The D Instruction

The D Instruction (**Divide fullword**)

Instruction type: Machine Instruction
Machine format: RX Instruction (Register and IndeXed Storage Instruction)

5D	R1	X2	B2	D2

0   7 8   11 12   15 16   19 20   31

Symbolic format:

	name	operation	operands
	[symbolic name]	D	R1,name2
or	[symbolic name]	D	R1,D2(X2,B2)

where R1 is an even register number. D2, X2 and B2 are the displacement, index register and base register respectively used to calculate the second operand address.

. . . .

Rules:
- The first operand R1 must be an even-numbered register. The even-odd pair contains the dividend.
- The second operand must be a fixed point fullword: 32 bits long, and located on a fullword integral boundary. That is, its address must be a multiple of 4 (in binary, this is an address whose low-order 2 bits are both 0's).
- The second operand contains the divisor.
- After execution, R1 contains the remainder. The odd register of the even-odd pair contains the quotient.

Example:

```
          D    8,TWO
TWO       DC   F'2'
```

Before execution of the D   **After execution of the D**

	binary (hex notation)	decimal
Reg 8:	00 00 00 00 ⎫	6
Reg 9:	00 00 00 06 ⎭	

	binary (hex notation)	decimal
Reg 8:	00 00 00 00	0
Reg 9:	00 00 00 03	3

Example:

```
          D    10,ONE
ONE       DC   F'1'
```

Before execution of the D   **After execution of the D**

	binary (hex notation)	decimal
Reg 10:	00 00 00 01 ⎫	8,589,934,591
Reg 11:	FF FF FF FF ⎭	

	binary (hex notation)	decimal
Reg 10:		dividend remains unchanged
Reg 11:		

In this example, the quotient would be of such magnitude that it could not be expressed as a 32-bit signed integer (it would have the same value as the dividend, whose significant portion occupies more than 32 bits). In such a case we say that a **fixed-point divide exception** is recognized. When this happens

- program interruption occurs
- division does not take place
- the dividend remains unchanged in the even-odd register pair

Note: A fixed point divide exception will likewise result when division is attempted with a divisor of 0.

8.2.5 Preparing for Fixed Point Division

Case I   Dividend is Positive

Given fixed-point fullword constants A and B, with A assumed to be positive, we may compute A/B as follows:

L	5,A	place A into reg 5
SR	4,4	fill reg 4 with zeros
D	4,B	compute A/B: quotient in reg 5, remainder in reg 4

The instruction L 5,A is a "load" instruction. It places the contents of the second operand fullword into the first operand register. (The "load" instructions will be explained in section 8.2.7.) In this case, we placed the dividend (A) into an odd-numbered register. We then filled the even-numbered register preceding it with zeros, to form the high-order part of the dividend, for a positive binary number may be expanded on the left with zeros. Division is then performed, with the even register in the first operand position. After execution, the quotient replaces the previous contents of the odd-numbered register of the even-odd pair.

Case II   Dividend is Negative

Given fixed-point fullword constants C and D, with C assumed to be negative, we may compute C/D as follows:

	L	7,C	place C into reg 7
	L	6,M1	fill reg 6 with ones
	D	6,D	compute C/D: quotient in reg 7, remainder in reg 6
M1	DC	F'−1'	

Here the quotient C is "loaded" into an odd-numbered register. The even-numbered register preceding it is filled with 1's (the binary number "−1" expressed in two's complement form consists of a string of 1's), for a negative binary number in two's complement form may be expanded on the left with 1's. Division is then performed as usual.

Case III   Sign of Dividend is Unknown

Assume now that we have fixed-point fullword constants E and F, of unknown sign. We wish to compute E/F. This problem differs from Case I and Case II above in that here we do not know whether to expand the dividend to the left with zeros (if it is positive) or with ones (if it is negative). The solution is, of course, to have the computer make this decision for us.

Perhaps the most obvious approach would be to "compare" the dividend value with zero. If the computer determines that the dividend value is less than zero (negative), we fill the even-numbered register with ones; otherwise (the dividend is positive or zero), we fill the even-numbered register with zeros. This approach, however, involves considerable programming effort, namely a "compare" instruction, a "decision-making" (branch) instruction, and instructions to handle both the positive and the negative case.

We shall demonstrate two alternate approaches to computing the quotient E/F of two fixed-point fullwords, each considerably more efficient than that which we have just described.

Approach 1:

L	5,E	place E into reg 5
M	4,=F'1'	multiply E by 1, with product in regs 4-5.
D	4,F	compute E/F: quotient in reg 5, remainder in reg 4.

Here we placed the fullword dividend into an odd-numbered register (register 5). Multiplying a number by 1, of course, does not change its magnitude. However, multiplying the dividend by 1 in this example yields the product in the even-odd register pair 4-5. The multiply instruction thus expands the dividend for us appropriately, with 0's if positive, and with 1's if negative. The division then follows, using the contents of the even-odd register pair 4-5 as the dividend.

Approach 2:

L	4,E	place E into reg 4
SRDA	4,32	shift E 32 bits to the right, into reg 5, with copies of the sign bit filling reg 4
D	4,F	

The first instruction in this segment places the contents of fullword E into register 4, an *even*-numbered register! The SRDA (Shift Right Double Algebraic) "shifts", or pushes, the data in the first operand register (register 4) to the *right* through what is essentially a *double* register addressed by the even-numbered register in the instruction (the even-odd register pair 4-5). The number of bit positions participating in the shift is described in the second operand (32 bits). The shift is **algebraic**, meaning that the bits filled in on the left of the register pair as a result of shifting are copies of the sign bit.

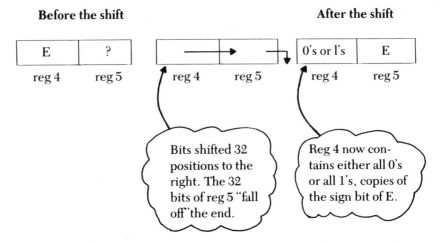

The net result of the instruction   SRDA   4,32   is to place E into register 5 with copies of its sign bit in register 4. We thus have an expanded version of E in the even-odd register pair 4-5. Division may then follow, using the contents of registers 4-5 as the dividend.

Note: The SRDA instruction belongs to a larger category of algebraic "shift" instructions which have many important programming uses. Some of these other uses will be discussed in chapter 9, section 9.5, along with a formal description of the instructions.

8.2.6   Some Program Examples

Now that we understand how the fixed-point addition, subtraction, multiplication, and division instructions work, it would be beneficial for us to examine some programs which use those instructions. The inventory report program of section 8.1 uses the RR arithmetic instructions AR, SR, MR, and DR.

In figures 8.6 and 8.7, we present two programs which make use of the fixed-point arithmetic instructions in RX form. We will also make use of some instructions which move data from main storage into registers (the "load" instructions) and from registers back into main storage (the "store" instructions). The load (LR, L, LH, LM) and store (ST, STH, STM) instructions will be described in section 8.2.7.

LOC	OBJECT CODE	ADDR1 ADDR2	STMT	SOURCE STATEMENT		17 NOV 78

```
                                    1 * PROGRAM 1
                                    2 *
                                    3 * THIS PRCGRAM CCMPUTES THE ARITHMETIC MEAN (AVERAGE) OF
                                    4 * 4 FIXED POINT CONSTANTS, 2 FULLWORDS AND 2 HALFWORDS
                                    5 * (NUM1 + NUM2 + NUM3 + NUM4)/4
                                    6 * MEAN VALUE IS LEFT IN A REGISTER
                                    7 *
CCCCCC                              8        START
CCCCCC 05C0                         9 BGN    BALR  12,0
              00002               10        USING *,12
CCCCC2 1B22                       11        SR    2,2            CLEAR REG 2 FOR SUM
CCCCC4 5A20 C022    C0024         12        A     2,NUM1         REG 2  NOW CONTAINS NUM1
CCCCC8 5A20 C026    C0028         13        A     2,NUM2         REG 2  NOW CONTAINS NUM1+NUM2
CCCCCC 4A20 C02A    C002C         14        AH    2,NUM3         REG 2  NOW CONTAINS NUM1+NUM2+NUM3
CCCC1C 4A20 C02C    C002E         15        AH    2,NUM4         REG 2  NOW CONTAINS NUM1+NUM2+NUM3+NUM4
CCCC14 8E20 0020    00020         16        SRDA  2,32           PREPARE FOR DIVISION
                                  17 *                          EXPANDED SUM IN REGS 2 AND 3
C0CC018 5D20 C02E   C0030         18        D     2,FCUR         QUOTIENT IN REG 3, REMAINDER IN REG 2
                                  19 * THE MEAN IS NCW IN REG 3
CCCC1C 5030 C032    C0034         20        ST    3,MEAN         PLACE MEAN VALUE INTO LOCATION MEAN
                                  21 *
CCCC2C 0A03                       22        SVC   3              ON DOS SYSTEMS THIS INSTRUCTION IS EOJ
                                  23 *
C0CC022 0000
CCCC24 C000C005                   24 NUM1   CC    F'5'
CCCC28 0C0CCC06                   25 NUM2   CC    F'6'
CCCC2C C007                       26 NUM3   DC    H'7'
CCCC2E 0008                       27 NUM4   CC    H'8'
CCCC3C C000C0C4                   28 FCUR   CC    F'4'          FULLWORD 4
CCCC34                            29 MEAN   DS    F
CCCCCC                            30        END   BGN
```

Figure 8.6
Computing the Arithmetic Mean

LOC	OBJECT CODE	ADDR1 ADDR2	STMT	SOURCE STATEMENT		17 NCV 78

```
                                    1 *
                                    2 * PROGRAM 2
                                    3 *
                                    4 * THIS PRCGRAM CCNSIDERS A CENTIGRADE TEMPERATURE C AND COMPUTES THE
                                    5 * EQUIVALENT FAHRENHEIT TEMPERATURE AS FOLLOWS
                                    6 * F = 9*C/5+32
                                    7 *
CCCC'                               8        START
CCCCCC C5C0                         9 HERE   BALR  12,0
              CC002               10        USING *,12
CCCCC2 5830 C016    C0018         11        L     3,C            LOAD C INTO ODD-ADDRESSED REGISTER
CCCCC6 5C20 C01A    C001C         12        M     2,F9           REGS 2 AND 3 NOW CONTAIN 9*C
CCCCCA 5D20 C01E    C0020         13        D     2,F5           REG 3 CONTAINS 9*C/5
                                  14 *                          REG 2 CONTAINS REMAINDER
CCCCCE 4A30 CC22    C0024         15        AH    3,H32          REG 3 CONTAINS 9*C/5 +32
                                  16 *
                                  17 * THE FAHRENHEIT TEMPERATURE IS NOW IN REG 3
                                  18 * NCTE THAT THE MULT INSTRUCTION, BY PLACING THE PRODUCT INTO AN
                                  19 * EVEN-ODD REGISTER PAIR, CONSTITUTED THE PREPARATION FOR DIVISION
                                  20 * WITH AN EXPANDED DIVIDEND FILLING THE REGISTER PAIR
                                  21 *
CCCC012 4030 C024   C0026         22        STH   3,FAHRHT       PLACE RESULT INTO LOCATION CALLED FAHRHT
CCCC16 0A03                       23        SVC   3              ON DOS SYSTEMS THIS INSTRUCTION IS EOJ
                                  24 *
CCCC18 C0000064                   25 C      CC    F'100'
CCCC1C 00000009                   26 F9     CC    F'9'          FULLWORD 9
CCCC2C 0000CC05                   27 F5     CC    F'5'          FULLWORD 5
CCCC24 0020                       28 H32    CC    H'32'         HALFWORD 32
CCCC26                            29 FAHRHT DS    H
CCCCCC                            30        END   HERE
```

Figure 8.7
Converting Centigrade into Fahrenheit

8.2.7 Data Movement: Register to Register, Main Storage to Register, Register to Main Storage

THE LOAD INSTRUCTIONS

The "load" instructions move data from register into register and from main storage into registers. We shall now discuss the Load Register, Load full-word, Load Halfword, and Load Multiple instructions. The Load Address instruction will be discussed in chapter 10, section 10.2.3.

The LR Instruction

The LR Instruction (Load **R**egister)

Instruction type: Machine Instruction
Machine format: RR Instruction (Register to Register Instruction)

18	R1	R2

0   7 8   11 12   15

Symbolic format:

name	operation	operands
[symbolic name]	LR	R1,R2

where R1 and R2 are general register numbers (0-15).

· ·

Rule:
- The second operand is the sending field; the first operand is the receiving field.

Condition Code: The condition code remains unchanged.

Example:

$$\text{LR} \quad 2,4$$

The contents of register 4 are placed into register 2. The contents of register 4 remain unchanged.

The L Instruction

The L Instruction (Load fullword)

Instruction type: Machine Instruction
Machine format: RX Instruction (Register and IndeXed Storage Instruction)

58	R1	X2	B2	D2

0   7 8   11 12   15 16   19 20   31

Symbolic format:

name	operation	operands
[symbolic name]	L	R1,name2
or [symbolic name]	L	R1,D2(X2,B2)

where R1 is a general register number. D2, X2, and B2 are the displacement, index register, and base register respectively used to calculate the second operand address.

. . . .

Rules:
- The second operand is the sending field; the first operand is the receiving field.
- The second operand is an aligned fixed-point fullword.

Condition Code: The condition code remains unchanged.

Example:

```
        L    3,WD
WD      DC   F'2'
```

The contents of WD (a fullword binary 2) are placed into register 3.

The LH Instruction

The LH Instruction (**L**oad **H**alfword)

Instruction type: Machine Instruction
Machine format: RX Instruction (Register and IndeXed Storage Instruction)

48	R1	X2	B2	D2

0　　　　　　7 8　　11 12　　15 16　　19 20　　　　　　　　　31

Symbolic format:

	name	operation	operands
	[symbolic name]	LH	R1,name2
or	[symbolic name]	LH	R1,D2(X2,B2)

where R1 is a general register number. D2, X2, and B2 are the displacement, index register, and base register respectively used to calculate the second operand address.

. . . .

Rules:
- The second operand is the sending field; the first operand is the receiving field.
- The second operand is an aligned fixed-point halfword.

Condition Code: The condition code remains unchanged.

The LH instruction first fetches the second operand halfword from main storage, then expands it to a fullword by propagating the sign bit through 16 high-order bits. The fullword equivalent of the second operand is then placed into the first operand register.

Example:

```
        LH   7,HALF
HALF    DC   H'8'
```

The contents of the aligned halfword HALF are placed into register 7.

The LM Instruction

The LM Instruction (Load Multiple)

Instruction type: Machine Instruction
Machine format: RS Instruction (Register and Storage Instruction)

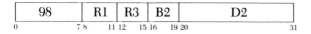

98	R1	R3	B2	D2

0   7 8   11 12   15 16   19 20   31

Symbolic format:

	name	operation	operands
	[symbolic name]	LM	R1,R3,name2
or	[symbolic name]	LM	R1,R3,D2(B2)

where R1 and R3 are general register numbers. D2 and B2 are the displacement and base register respectively used to calculate the second operand address.

. . . .

Rules:
- The second operand is the sending field. Registers R1 through R3 designate the receiving field.
- The second operand is an aligned fixed point fullword.

Condition Code: The condition code remains unchanged.

Example:

```
            LM   4,6,TABLE
    TABLE   DC   F'1'
            DC   F'2'
            DC   F'3'
```

The contents of main storage, beginning with TABLE, are placed into registers 4 through 6. That is, a fullword "1" will be placed into register 4, a fullword "2" into register 5, a fullword "3" into register 6. The LM instruction above performs the same job as three load (L) instructions:

$$
\begin{array}{ll}
\text{L} & \text{4,TABLE}
\end{array}
$$

$$
\begin{array}{ll}
\text{L} & \text{5,TABLE+4}
\end{array}
\left\{
\begin{array}{l}
\text{contents of storage 4} \\
\text{bytes (1 word) past} \\
\text{TABLE, into reg 5}
\end{array}
\right.
$$

$$
\begin{array}{ll}
\text{L} & \text{6,TABLE+8}
\end{array}
\left\{
\begin{array}{l}
\text{contents of storage 8} \\
\text{bytes (2 words) past} \\
\text{TABLE, into reg 6}
\end{array}
\right.
$$

Example:

```
        LM  8,8,HERE
HERE    DC  F'100'
```

The contents of HERE are placed into register 8. When R1 and R3 are equal, only one main storage word is placed into a single register.

Example:

```
         LM   14,1,THERE
THERE    DC   F'10'
         DC   F'20'
         DC   F'30'
         DC   F'40'
```

When the R1 register number is greater than the R3 register number, the registers "wrap around". That is, we consider that register 0 follows register 15. Thus the LM instruction of this example places a fullword "10" into register 14, a fullword "20" into register 15, a fullword "30" into register 0, a fullword "40" into register 1.

THE STORE INSTRUCTIONS

The "store" instructions move data from registers into main storage. We shall now discuss the Store fullword, Store Halfword, and Store Multiple instructions.

The ST Instruction

The ST Instruction (**ST**ore fullword)

Instruction type: Machine Instruction
Machine format: RX Instruction (Register and IndeXed Storage Instruction)

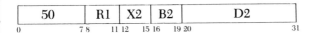

50	R1	X2	B2	D2

0   7 8   11 12   15 16   19 20   31

Symbolic format:

	name	operation	operands
	[symbolic name]	ST	R1,name2
or	[symbolic name]	ST	R1,D2(X2,B2)

where R1 is a general register number. D2, X2, and B2 are the displacement, index register, and base register respectively used to calculate the second operand address.

. . . .

Rules:
- The first operand is the sending field; the second operand is the receiving field.
- The second operand is an aligned fixed-point fullword.

Condition Code: The condition code remains unchanged.

Example:

```
                    ST   9,NUM1
          NUM1      DC   F'4'
```

The contents of register 9 are placed into the fullword location called NUM1. The previous contents of NUM1 (fullword binary 4) will be destroyed.

The STH Instruction

The STH Instruction (**ST**ore **H**alfword)

Instruction type: Machine Instruction
Machine format: RX Instruction (Register and IndeXed Storage Instruction)

40	R1	X2	B2	D2

0   7 8   11 12   15 16   19 20   31

Symbolic format:

name	operation	operands
[symbolic name]	STH	R1,name2
or [symbolic name]	STH	R1,D2(X2,B2)

where R1 is a general register number. D2, X2, and B2 are the displacement, index register, and base register respectively used to calculate the second operand address.

Rules:
- The first operand is the sending field; the second operand is the receiving field.
- The second operand is an aligned fixed-point halfword.

Condition Code: The condition code remains unchanged.

The Store Halfword instruction places the *low-order* 16 bits of the first operand register into the second operand halfword. The high-order 16 bits are not examined. This instruction will be used when the programmer knows the register contents to be of small enough magnitude to fit into a halfword location.

Example:

$$\text{STH 5,NUM2}$$
$$\text{NUM2   DC   H'10'}$$

The low-order 16 bits of register 5 are placed into NUM2, destroying the previous contents of NUM2 (halfword binary "10").

The STM Instruction

The STM Instruction (**ST**ore **M**ultiple)

Instruction type: Machine Instruction
Machine format: RS Instruction (Register and Storage Instruction)

90	R1	R3	B2	D2
0	7 8	11 12	15 16	19 20 31

Symbolic format:

	name	operation	operands
	[symbolic name]	STM	R1,R3,name2
or	[symbolic name]	STM	R1,R3,D2(B2)

where R1 and R3 are general register numbers. D2 and B2 are the displacement and base register respectively used to calculate the second operand address.

Rules:
- Registers R1 through R3 designate the sending field. The second operand is the receiving field.
- The second operand is an aligned fixed-point fullword.

Condition code: The condition code remains unchanged.

Example:

```
              STM  10,12,FLWD1
     FLWD1    DS   F
     FLWD2    DS   F
     FLWD3    DS   F
```

The contents of register 10 are placed into FLWD1, those of register 11 into FLWD2, and those of register 12 into FLWD3.

Example:

```
              STM  15,2,DATA
     DATA     DS   F
              DS   F
              DS   F
              DS   F
```

The general registers "wrap around", with register 0 following register 15. The STM above places the contents of register 15 into DATA, those of register 0 into memory beginning at DATA+4, those of register 1 into memory beginning at DATA+8, and those of register 2 into memory beginning at DATA+12.

Summary

Through the solution of a simple inventory problem, chapter 8 has presented a description of methods for performing addition, subtraction, multiplication and division with fixed-point values. Movement of data between registers and general memory was also considered.

Instructions described and illustrated in this chapter are: fixed-point addition instructions (AR, A, AH); fixed-point subtraction instructions (SR, S, SH); fixed-point multiplication instructions (MR, M, MH); fixed-point division instructions (DR, D); and instructions which move data between registers (LR), from main storage into registers (L, LH, LM), and from registers into main storage (ST, STH, STM).

Important Terms Discussed in Chapter 8

algebraic shift	fixed-point subtraction
even-odd register pair	load
fixed-point addition	store
fixed-point divide exception	
fixed-point division	wrap around
fixed-point multiplication	

Questions

8-1. Given two constants in zoned format, as follow:

$$
\begin{array}{lll}
A & DC & Z'3' \\
B & DC & Z'4'
\end{array}
$$

Write the instructions necessary to convert A and B into binary form, to compute their sum, to convert the sum into zoned form and to place the sum into a location call SUM.

8-2. Write the instructions to find double the difference between the contents of two halfword locations called HERE and THERE:

$$2 \times (HERE - THERE)$$

8-3. Given the contents of registers and main storage locations indicated below:

	Contents in decimal	Contents in binary (hex notation)			
Reg 2	1	00	00	00	01
Reg 3	−2	FF	FF	FF	FE
Reg 7	0	00	00	00	00
NUMB 1	−20	FF	FF	FF	EC
NUMB 2	256	00	00	01	00
NUMB 3	−1	FF	FF	FF	FF

Show the contents of the first operand location after execution of each instruction in the program segment below:

```
AR      2,3
D       2,NUMB3
M       6,NUMB1
S       7,NUMB3
M       2,NUMB3
DR      2,6
```

8-4. Assuming fullword main storage locations called CON1, CON2, and CON3, write the fixed point instructions to compute each of the following:

    (a)   CON1 × CON2/4

    (b)   6 × (CON3 + 10)

    (c)   (Reg 2) − (Reg 3) + (Reg 7)

8-5. Find the errors in each of the following program segments (there may be more than one error):

```
(a)                  AR      2,3          (b)                  SR      4,4
                     MR      3,7                               L       7,A
                     AH      7,CO                              M       6,ONE
        CONST        DC      F'2'                              D       6,4
                                                      A        DC      F'40'
                                                      ONE      DC      H'1'
```

```
(c)                  START               (d)                  START
        A            BALR    4,0             B                BALR    12,0
                     USING   *,4                              USING   *,12
                     SR      3,3                              SR      7,7
                     AR      13,6                             AH      7,ONE
                     AR      13,8                             MH      7,HUND
                     AR      4,2                              MH      7,HUND
                     A       13,ONE                           MH      7,HUND
                     SVC     3                                MH      7,HUND
        ONE          DC      F'1'                             MH      7,HUND
                     END     A                                SVC     3
                                             ONE              DC      H'1'
                                             HUND             DC      H'100'
                                                              END     B
```

8-6. Write instruction sequences to:
   (a) Divide the contents of register 4 (value unknown) by a fixed point constant:

$$\text{EIGHT} \quad \text{DC} \quad \text{F'8'}$$

   (b) Divide the contents of register 5 (value unknown) by the same constant. Place the quotient into a place called QUOT, and the remainder into a place called REM.

8-7. Given the contents of main storage locations as defined below:

THIS	DC	H'4'
PROBLEM	DC	F'7'
IS	DC	F'3'
VERY	DC	F'2'
EASY	DS	H

Show the contents of the receiving operand after execution of each instruction in the sequences below:

(a)
LH	5,THIS
L	6,IS
M	6,5
STH	7,EASY

(b)
LM	12,14,PROBLEM
AR	12,13
AR	12,14
STM	12,14,PROBLEM

(c)
L	8,IS
L	11,PROBLEM
SR	10,10
D	10,VERY
AR	11,8
STH	11,EASY
ST	10,IS

Program Exercises

8-1. Write an assembly language program to compute individual student exam averages, and the average class score on all the exams.

Input consists of student records on punched cards, with

field	card columns
STUDENT NAME	11-30
EXAM1	31-35
EXAM2	36-40
EXAM3	41-45

Output is a grade report with a header line, one detail line per student, and a total line, as follows:

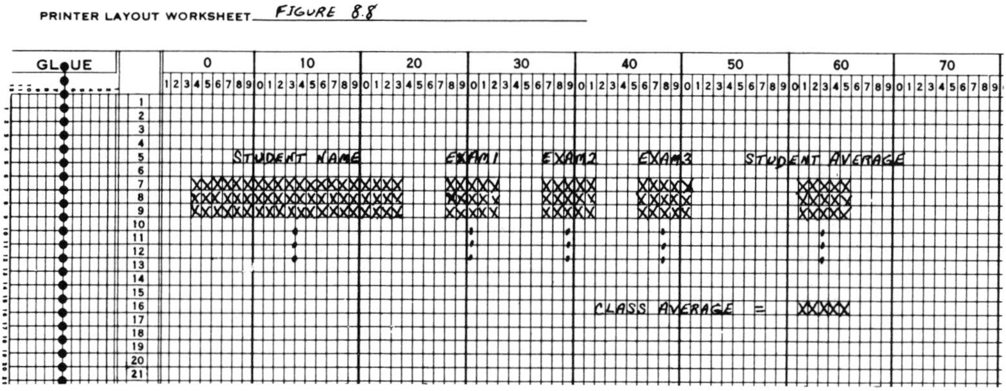

PRINTER LAYOUT WORKSHEET *FIGURE 8.8*

Figure 8.8

Note:

(1) Each average is to be computed as:

$$(EXAM1 + EXAM2 + EXAM3)/3$$

(2) The average class score is to be computed as:
total of all exam grades/total number of exams

(3) One line is to be skipped between the header line and the first detail line, and between the last detail line and the total line

(4) Computation is to be performed using fixed-point arithmetic.

8-2. Write an assembly language program to compute the area of triangles as $b \times h/2$ where b (the base of the triangle) and h (its height) are given.

The computation is to be performed using fixed-point arithmetic.

Input consists of punched card records with

field	card columns
b	1 - 3
h	4 - 6
ID NUMBER	7 - 10

Output consists of one header line, and one detail line per input record in the following form:

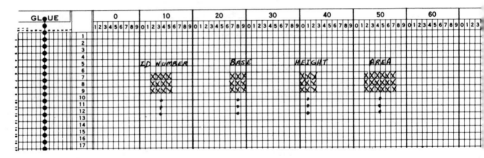

Figure 8.9

8-3. (a) Code the solution to exercise 4-7 (chapter 4) using fixed-point arithmetic.
     (b) Code the solution to exercise 4-8 (chapter 4) using fixed-point arithmetic.

Chapter 9

Binary Comparison, and Arithmetic with Non-Integer Values

BINARY COMPARISON, AND ARITHMETIC WITH NON-INTEGER VALUES

In chapter 8, we learned how to perform binary addition, subtraction, multiplication, and division, and we applied our knowledge of binary arithmetic to the solution of a simple inventory problem using integers. However, most true-to-life applications require working with non-integer values (monetary amounts will seldom involve dollars alone, but will rather be expressed as dollars and cents!). The discussion below will focus upon specific techniques for successful manipulation of such numbers. We shall also consider techniques for comparison of binary numbers, and for successive decision-making on the part of the computer.

9.1   INVENTORY REPORT PROBLEM—VERSION 2

In this section, we shall expand our inventory problem to include arithmetic operations with non-integer binary numbers and comparison of binary values.

Input will be in the form of item records on punched cards, as described on the input layout form of figure 9.1.

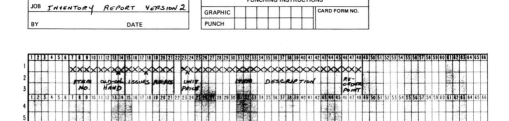

Figure 9.1
Input Layout for Inventory Report, Version 2

Note that **carats** (" ∧ ") are used to denote "implied decimal positions" within input fields. The decimal points are not punched on the cards, and hence will not be placed into the computer memory when the data is read. The presence of the decimal point is therefore *implied*, not actual, and it is the responsibility of the programmer to ensure that the numbers are treated in computation as though the decimal point were actually present. On the layout form of figure 9.1, the old-on-hand and issues fields each have 1 decimal position (for example, we may have 1.5 cases of beer and 1.8 pounds of nuts in stock). The price field has 2 decimal positions, and the receipts field remains a whole number.

The input to this expanded inventory problem also incorporates a new field: the reorder point, which represents the inventory amount below which the company will not permit the item stock (periodic new-on-hand) to fall.

In addition to the functions performed by the inventory program of chapter 8, this expanded version will require that the computer compare the new-on-hand to the reorder point. If the new-on-hand exceeds the reorder point, then new stock of this item need not be ordered; that is, the "reorder amount" will be 0. However if the new-on-hand does not exceed (is less than or equal to) the reorder point, then the program will compute:

reorder amount   = the integer amount by which the reorder point
                          exceeds new-on-hand + 200

                        = reorder point   −   integer part of new-on-hand
                          + 200

That is, enough items will be reordered to bring the amount of items in stock to 200 *above* the reorder point. This will allow for 200 items to be sold before reordering is again necessary.

The requested program output is described on the printer layout worksheet of figure 9.2. Notice that the output description indicates implied decimal positions. In a real-life situation, we would of course require actual decimal points to be printed within output fields. In chapter 10, we shall explain how to obtain actual decimal points as part of our output fields.

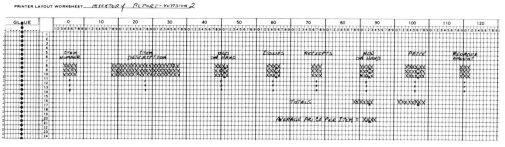

Figure 9.2
Output Layout for Inventory Report, Version 2

It is very tempting at this point to plunge immediately into planning and coding the solution to our revised problem. However a wiser and more systematic approach would be to first anticipate difficulties which may arise, and to consider various approaches to overcoming those difficulties. We shall consider each of the following programming concepts in turn, before embarking on the actual flowcharting and coding of our program:

- Adding and subtracting non-integer fixed-point fields
- Multiplying and dividing non-integer fixed-point fields
      Truncation and rounding
      Preparing for non-integer division
- The scale factor in binary arithmetic

9.2 TECHNIQUES FOR NON-INTEGER FIXED-POINT ARITHMETIC

9.2.1 Adding and Subtracting Non-Integer Fixed-Point Fields

If we were requested to compute the sum of the numbers 9.53, 6.4, and 7, we would arrange the numbers so that their decimal points are **aligned**:

$$
\begin{array}{r}
9.53 \\
6.4 \\
\underline{7.}
\end{array}
$$

In so doing, we assure that the digits being summed in any particular column have equivalent positional values.

The same procedure would be necessary when subtracting numbers. For example, $86.42 - 4$ would be arranged as

$$
\begin{array}{r}
86.42 \\
\underline{-4.}
\end{array}
$$

with decimal points in the minuend and subtrahend appropriately aligned.

If the need for alignment as a prelude to correct addition and subtraction is not perfectly clear to you at this point, refer to chapter 6, section 6.2.1 for a more extensive discussion of this matter.

Let us now see how this alignment is effected when adding and subtracting fixed-point numbers. Suppose that we wish to add fixed-point constants $9_\wedge 63$ and $4_\wedge 22$ (decimal positions are assumed by the programmer to be present; however the computer knows nothing of this). Arranging the numbers with appropriate alignment, we have

$$9_\wedge 63$$
$$\underline{4_\wedge 22}$$

which is exactly the way we would have arranged the values had they been integers! In other words, when we have an equal number of decimal positions in the numbers to be added (or subtracted), we need not instruct the computer to perform any additional steps for the sake of alignment. Either of the instruction sequences below will perform the desired addition:

	L	2,CON1	
	A	2,CON2	
	ST	2,SUM1	
	⋮		
CON1	DC	F'963'	$9_\wedge 63$
CON2	DC	F'422'	$4_\wedge 22$
SUM1	DS	F	

or

	LH	3,CON3	
	AH	3,CON4	
	ST	3,SUM2	
	⋮		
CON3	DC	H'963'	$9_\wedge 63$
CON4	DC	H'422'	$4_\wedge 22$
SUM2	DS	F	

Other solutions are possible. However any correct solution will require that one of the numbers to be summed be placed into a register before the second number is added to it, for the fixed-point addition instructions each have a register as the receiving field.

Let us now consider the subtraction: $17_\wedge 64 - 3_\wedge 1$. If these numbers were arranged without considering the decimal point, the solution would obviously be incorrect! However, unless precautions are taken, that is exactly what the computer will do, for the computer is unaware of any fractional values; it treats the fixed-point constants as integers! It is thus the programmer's responsibility to perform whatever steps are necessary to effect proper alignment. For this example, we wish to arrange the subtraction as follows:

$$17_\wedge64$$
$$\underline{-\ 3_\wedge1}$$

Notice that appending a low-order zero to the subtrahend "forces" proper alignment here. In general, it will be possible to align any numbers with differing decimal positions, by appending an appropriate number of low-order zeros to some of those numbers. The instruction sequence below will perform the desired subtraction:

```
           L      5,NUM2        ⎰ append low-order 0 to NUM2.
           M      4,F10         ⎱ NUM2 (extended) in register 5
           L      6,NUM1          NUM1 in register 6
           SR     6,5             NUM1 − NUM2 in register 6
           ST     6,DIFF          difference in DIFF
                  ⋮
F10        DC     F'10'
NUM1       DC     F'1764'         17∧64
NUM2       DC     F'31'           3∧1
DIFF       DS     F
```

We first placed the subtrahend (NUM2) — in this case the number to which a low-order zero must be appended — into an odd-numbered register (register 5). We then multiplied the subtrahend by 10. As we know, multiplication by 10 will have the effect of appending a low-order zero to the multiplicand (likewise, multiplication by 10^2 will append two low-order zeros, multiplication by 10^3 will append three low-order zeros, and so on), which is exactly what was required for correct alignment. The subtraction was then performed.

It is important to remember that the result of our subtraction has two decimal positions. That is, the number of decimal positions in a sum or difference is equivalent to the number of decimal positions in the actual numbers being added or subtracted. The method for inserting the actual decimal point into the result will be discussed in chapter 10.

Note that for this example, the multiplication might actually have been avoided, by defining NUM2 as F'310', and assuming the decimal position, as in $3_\wedge10$. However in many instances this may not be desirable; for example, we may be working with input values which will be used in other computations for which such additional zeros may be inappropriate.

Towards Deeper Understanding

You may have wondered why it was necessary to multiply here. Would it not have been possible to shift ("push") the subtrahend digits to the left in order to effect alignment? This technique is possible when dealing with packed numbers in which the decimal digits are identifiable (it is discussed in chapter 6, section 6.2.1 under "Shifting to the Left") however the numbers we are dealing with are binary! Shifting a binary number 1 bit position to the left will have the effect of multiplying the number by 2, not by 10, since every digit is being placed into a column worth twice the value of its original column! In fact it will not be possible to shift through binary columns to accomplish a multiplication by 10. Shifting 3 bit positions leftward is equivalent to multiplying by 8 (not enough), while shifting 4 bit positions leftward is equivalent to multiplying by 16 (too much). It will likewise be impossible to append *any* fixed number of low-order zeros to the decimal equivalent of a binary number (in other words, multiplication by a power of 10) by shifting binary fields.

Let us take a moment to test our understanding of alignment for addition and subtraction. For each pair of numbers below, indicate what adjustments, if any, are necessary in preparation for addition or subtraction. x represents a digit in the decimal equivalent of each number.

	A	**B**
(i)	xx$_\wedge$x	xxx
(ii)	xxx	$_\wedge$xxx
(iii)	x$_\wedge$xx	xx$_\wedge$xx
(iv)	$_\wedge$xxx	$_\wedge$xx

Are you ready? The adjustments necessary are:

(i)   append 1 low-order 0 to B (multiply by 10)
(ii)   append 3 low-order 0's to A (multiply by $10^3 = 1000$)
(iii)   none. A and B have the same number of decimal positions
(iv)   append 1 low-order 0 to B (multiply by 10)

9.2.2   Multiplying and Dividing Non-Integer Fixed-Point Fields

Let us now consider a typical problem requiring the multiplication and division of fixed-point fields. We wish to find the product of a 4-digit, 1-decimal position field (xxx$_\wedge$x) containing the number of items stocked (ITMAMT), and a 5-digit, 2-decimal position field (xxx$_\wedge$xx) containing the unit price per item (PRC).

Recall the general rules for interpreting the results of multiplication:

> maximum number of product digits = number of multiplicand digits + number of multiplier digits

> number of decimal positions in product = number of decimal positions in multiplicand + number of decimal positions in multiplier

Thus the product of ITMAMT and PRC will be at most 9 digits long (length of ITMAMT + length of PRC = 4 + 5 = 9) and will have three decimal positions (number of decimal positions in ITMAMT + number of decimal positions in PRC = 1 + 2 = 3). Schematically, we describe the multiplication as:

$$(xxx_\wedge x)(xxx_\wedge xx) = xxxxxx_\wedge xxx$$

Actually, the exact number of decimal digits in our product is not always of great importance in determining how much register space to leave for our binary product. The binary multiplication instructions only allow for a choice between fullword (the MH instruction) and doubleword (the MR and M instructions) products. The largest positive fullword binary number is equivalent to the decimal number 2,147,483,647 and the negative fullword binary number of largest absolute value is equivalent to decimal $-2,147,483,648$ (see chapter 7, section 7.2.1). Therefore as long as we are sure that our product will fall within the appropriate range, the MH instruction may be used; otherwise the MR or M instruction would be employed. The position of the decimal point in the product is *always* of great importance, however, for proper interpretation of our results.

The instructions below compute the product of sample ITMAMT and PRC fields:

```
        L       7,ITMAMT
        M       6,PRC          product = 656∧435
        ⋮

ITMAMT  DC      F'65'          6∧5
PRC     DC      F'10099'       100∧99
```

The product (the price of all the stocked items) is the value $656 \wedge 435$ in register 7. Quite obviously, a monetary amount with 3 decimal positions is inappropriate. The product must be restated as a 2-decimal position number, either by

• right truncation (the "dropping off" or elimination) of digits which exceed the desired length or accuracy. (Here, truncating the rightmost digit will yield the product $656_\wedge 43$) or by

- rounding the number to a particular accuracy, that is to the nearest tens, whole number, tenth, hundredth, or the like. (Here, rounding to the nearest hundredth will yield the product $656_\wedge 44$.)

We shall consider each of these alternatives as it applies to binary numbers.

- *Right Truncation*

  Eliminating the low-order digits of a number may be accomplished by dividing the number by an appropriate power of ten, and ignoring the remainder; the quotient will be the truncated result. The power of ten to serve as the divisor will be equivalent to the number of digits we wish truncated.

For example, the product of ITMAMT and PRC fields in the example above is a 3-decimal position number ($656_\wedge 435$). Truncating the rightmost digit may be accomplished by dividing the product by 10^1 and ignoring the remainder ($656435 \div 10 = 65643$); truncating the 2 rightmost digits may be accomplished by dividing the product by 10^2 ($656435 \div 100 = 6564$); and so on. Recall that the position of the decimal point is "imagined" by the programmer; from the computer's point of view, the numbers are integers. Therefore the division will be performed as though the dividend were an integer, and we simply assume the decimal point to be positioned between the same 2 digits as previously, with rightmost digit(s) appropriately truncated.

We expand the program segment above to truncate the rightmost product digit and place the result into a location called PROD.

```
              L      7,ITMAMT
              M      6,PRC          product = 656∧435
              D      6,=F'10'       quotient = 656∧43
              ST     7,PROD         place quotient into PROD
                 ⋮
ITMAMT        DC     F'65'          6∧5
PRC           DC     F'10099'       100∧99
PROD          DS     F
```

Notice that preparation for division was not necessary here. The multiplication left the product in an even-odd register pair as is required for binary division.

Towards Deeper Understanding

Did it occur to you that similar results may have been obtained by "shifting" the number rightward in the field, so that the unwanted digits "fall off" the end? This was possible when dealing with packed numbers in which the decimal digits were easily identifiable (see chapter 6, section 6.2.2). However in the case of binary numbers, shifting 1 bit-position rightward is equivalent to a division by 2, not by 10 (since every digit is being placed into a column with half the value of the original column); shifting 2 bit-positions rightward is equivalent to a division by 2^2; and so on. It will not be possible to shift through any number of binary columns to effect the equivalent of a division by a power of 10.

- *Rounding*

  In order to round a number to a certain accuracy, we cause the lowest-order digit that we wish to remain in the rounded result to be incremented by 1, if the digit to its right has the value 5 or greater. (The rounding process for packed numbers was discussed in chapter 6, section 6.2.2.) Rounding is accomplished by adding the value 5 (−5 if the number is negative) to the digit position immediately to the right of the lowest-order digit that we wish to keep. We then truncate any unwanted digits.

For example, in order to round $18_\wedge 465$ to the nearest hundredth, we add 5 to the digit immediately to the right of the digit 6 (the hundredths digit).

$$\begin{array}{r} 18_\wedge 465 \\ 5 \\ \hline 18_\wedge 47\cancel{0} \end{array}$$

Notice that the hundredths position was incremented by 1, as expected. Truncation of the low-order (thousandths) digit completes the rounding process.

Rounding $-19_\wedge 62789$ to the nearest tenth is accomplished as follows:

$$\begin{array}{r} -19_\wedge 62789 \\ - \qquad 5000 \\ \hline -19_\wedge 6\cancel{7}\cancel{7}\cancel{8}\cancel{9} \end{array}$$

An addition of −5000 was necessary here in order to ensure the addition of the digit value 5 to the position immediately to the right of the tenths column. Truncation of all digits to the right of the tenths column will complete the rounding process.

Let us modify the program segment which multiplies ITMAMT by PRC to find PROD. This time we shall round the product to the nearest whole number:

	L	7,ITMAMT	
	M	6,PRC	product = 656$_\wedge$435
	A	7,=F'500'	+ 500
			sum = 656$_\wedge$935 in register 7
	D	6,=F'1000'	quotient = 656$_\wedge$
	ST	7,PROD	place quotient into PROD
	⋮		
ITMAMT	DC	F'65'	6$_\wedge$5
PRC	DC	F'10099'	100$_\wedge$99
PROD	DS	F	

Adding 500 to the original product effects an addition of the digit value 5 to the column position immediately to the right of the one's column. Division by 10^3 (10^3 = 1000) and ignoring the remainder (in register 6) results in the truncation of the 3 low-order digits.

When performing division for purposes other than rounding, we follow the usual technique for determining the position of the decimal point in the quotient:

> If the divisor is integer, the decimal point in the quotient field will be in the same position as the decimal point in the dividend field.

> If the divisor is noninteger, we "move" the decimal point rightward in both the divisor and dividend fields for an equal number of positions, as many positions as are necessary to ensure that the divisor becomes integer.

In the latter case, (noninteger divisor), computer instructions will not be necessary to effect moving the decimal point within the divisor. Let us explain. The decimal point does not really exist; therefore we may assume the decimal point in the divisor to be moved to the right of its lowest-order digit. (We may actually assume the point to be anywhere we wish it to be; in this case, it is convenient to assume it to be to the right of the rightmost digit.) To maintain the integrity of the quotient, we will likewise assume the decimal point in the dividend to be moved the same number of positions as that of the divisor. This might, at times, require us to extend the dividend with low-order zeros, by multiplying the dividend by an appropriate power of 10.

Consider the following proposed divisions, where x represents a digit in the decimal equivalent of our number.

divisor	dividend		quotient
xxx	xxx∧x	No preparation necessary (divisor is integer)	xxx∧x
xx∧x	xx∧x x	No preparation necessary but points "assumed" to be moved	xxx∧x
x∧xx	xxx∧x0	Multiplication by 10 prepares dividend; necessary for point to be moved 2 positions rightward	xxxxx

In section 9.4, we shall see a programming example involving binary division with decimal points. Division will be performed in the computation of the "average price per item" for our expanded inventory report problem.

9.2.3   Using the Scale Factor in Binary Arithmetic

The examples of the previous section, featuring binary multiplication and division, used fixed-point data which was in integer form in main storage. The programmer *assumed* the presence of a point in the decimal equivalents of those fixed-point numbers. This is not, however, the only possible approach to dealing with binary fractional values.

Binary constants may be stored in fractional form in main storage. For example, the instruction DC FS3'2.25' will cause the binary equivalent of decimal 2.25 to be stored. The S in the operand portion means **scale factor**, and the integer value immediately following it indicates the number of bits to be used in storing the fractional portion of the constant. The storage of fullword 2.25 will be as follows:

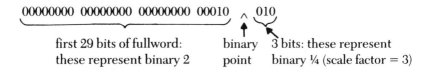

	first 29 bits of fullword:	binary	3 bits: these represent
	these represent binary 2	point	binary ¼ (scale factor = 3)

The binary point is assumed, but the low-order three bits of the bit configuration above is the appropriate representation of the fractional value .25.

Contrast this with the constant generated by DC   F'225':

00000000 00000000 00000000 11100001

For this latter constant, we assume the presence of a *decimal* point in the decimal equivalent of the number, (the value $_\wedge$25 cannot even be isolated in the binary equivalent of integer 2$_\wedge$25). However for the constant FS3'2.25', we assume the presence of a *binary* point.

The major difficulty in working with binary fractions is that most decimal fractions do not have exact binary equivalents. Therefore using binary fractions in our program will yield results which are usually not completely accurate. This fact was noted when we discussed binary representation in chapter 7, section 7.2.1.

We shall now rewrite the program segment of section 9.2.2 above which computes the product of ITMAMT (6$_\wedge$5) and PRC (100$_\wedge$99) fields, and rounds the product to the nearest integer. We store our binary constants in fractional form.

```
        L    7,ITMAMT  ⎧ product has 10 bits to the right of
        M    6,PRC     ⎨ the binary point:
                       ⎩ 00000000 00001010 010000 ∧01 10111101
        A    7,RND       sum has 10 bits to the right of the point
        SRA  7,10        shift off extra bits to obtain integer result

        ⋮

ITMAMT  DC   FS2'6.5'      00000000 00000000 00000000 000110∧10
PRC     DC   FS8'100.99'   00000000 00000000 01100100 ∧11111101
RND     DC   FS10'.5'      00000000 00000000 000000∧10 00000000
```

In the program segment above, the constant value 6.5 was precisely represented as 0110$_\wedge$10 (actually a scale factor of 1 would have been sufficient). However the fractional portion of decimal 100.99 is an infinitely repeating binary fraction which only approximates the value .99. Use of a larger scale factor would improve the accuracy of the representation, however a truly precise value could never be attained.

We begin the program segment by loading the contents of the ITMAMT field into register 7. Multiplying a 2-binary-position field (ITMAMT) by an 8-binary-position field (PRC) yields a product with 10 binary positions (the sum of the number of positions in the multiplier and multiplicand). Rounding is accomplished by first adding the binary fractional value .5 to the product, yielding a sum with 10 binary positions (the sum of 2 numbers, each having 10 binary positions, will itself have 10 binary positions). We then shift superfluous fractional bits out of the result register to obtain the desired integer result. The "shift" instruction used is the SRA or **Shift Right Algebraic**. The first operand of the SRA specifies the register whose contents are to be shifted (pushed) rightward, and the second operand specifies the number of bit positions to be shifted. In our program segment, the contents of register 7 are shifted 10 bit positions rightward, so that the 10 low-order bits (in this case, the fractional portion of the number) "fall off" the end and are lost. Emptied high-order bit positions are filled with copies of the sign bit (0's if the number is positive, 1's if the number is negative). A more extensive discussion of the SRA instruction will be given in section 9.5.

A most relevant question to consider at this point is whether it is better to perform binary arithmetic with fractional binary data, or with binary integer data using assumed decimal positions. The main advantage of working with binary fractions is that the technique enables us to replace a division with a shift instruction when truncating low-order numeric digits. Shifting is faster than multiplication or division, and in applications which involve much computation, the savings in time could be considerable.

Let us not, however, lose sight of the major drawback of working with binary fractions: results obtained will usually be approximate. Therefore when approximate results are not acceptable, fractional binary data should not be used.

9.3   COMPARING FIXED-POINT NUMBERS

Now that we have considered methods for performing arithmetic with non-integer binary numbers, we may focus our attention upon yet another fixed-point procedure which will be needed for computer solution of our expanded inventory report problem: that is, the comparison of binary numbers.

Comparing two numbers in assembly language is determining whether the value of one of them (the contents of the first operand) is equal to, less than, or greater than the value of the other (the contents of the second operand). If we call the first operand A and the second operand B, the "compare" instructions set the following values in the condition code: 0 if A=B; 1 if

A < B; 2 if A > B. The program must then test the condition code to determine its contents (which reflect the results of the comparison) and to branch (transfer program control) to an appropriate program routine, depending upon the particular condition code setting found. Comparison and branching have been discussed in chapter 5. If you feel that a review would be in order for you at this time, refer back to section 5.3 for a discussion of comparison, and to section 5.3.2 for a discussion of branching with the "extended mnemonic" instructions. Yet other ways of branching will be considered in chapter 11.

Now we shall focus upon the instructions which compare fixed-point numbers. There are three such instructions, each of which uses a register as its first operand. The choice of instruction for a particular case will be determined by the second operand: if it is a register, we use the CR instruction; if it is a main storage location, we use the C or CH instruction for fullword or halfword numbers respectively.

The CR, C, and CH instructions set the following values in the condition code:

    0   if contents of first operand = contents of second operand
    1   if contents of first operand < contents of second operand
    2   if contents of first operand > contents of second operand
    3   will not result from this instruction

The CR Instruction

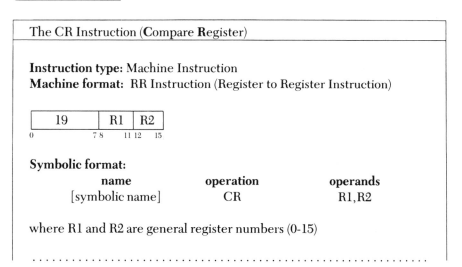

The CR Instruction (**C**ompare **R**egister)

Instruction type: Machine Instruction
Machine format: RR Instruction (Register to Register Instruction)

19	R1	R2

0   7 8   11 12   15

Symbolic format:

           name   operation   operands
     [symbolic name]   CR   R1,R2

where R1 and R2 are general register numbers (0-15)

Rules:
- The contents of both operands are treated as 32-bit signed integers.

Example:

    CR   4,5

If register 4 contains binary "-2" and register 5 contains binary "0", the value 1 will be set in the condition code. The contents of registers 4 and 5 remain unchanged.

Example:

    CR   6,6

This instruction will set the value 0 in the condition code. Any value is of course equal to itself. The contents of register 6 remain unchanged.

The C Instruction

The C Instruction (Compare fullword)

Instruction type: Machine Instruction
Machine format: RX Instruction (Register and IndeXed Storage Instruction)

59	R1	X2	B2	D2

0   7 8   11 12   15 16   19 20   31

Symbolic format:

	name	operation	operands
	[symbolic name]	C	R1,name2
or	[symbolic name]	C	R1,D2(X2,B2)

where R1 is a general register number. D2, X2, and B2 are the respective displacement, index register, and base register used to calculate the second operand address

. . . .

Rules:
- The contents of both operands are treated as 32-bit signed integers
- The second operand must be an aligned fixed-point fullword

Example:

	C	8,NEG
NEG	DC	F$'-9'$

If register 8 contains binary "+8", the C instruction will set the value 2 in the condition code. The contents of register 8 and of NEG remain unchanged.

The CH Instruction

The CH Instruction (**Compare Halfword**)

Instruction type: Machine Instruction
Machine format: RX Instruction (Register and IndeXed Storage Instruction)

49	R1	X2	B2	D2
0	7 8	11 12	15 16	19 20 31

Symbolic format:

name	operation	operands
[symbolic name]	CH	R1,name2
or [symbolic name]	CH	R1,D2(X2,B2)

where R1 is a general register number. D2,X2, and B2 are the respective displacement, index register, and base register used to calculate the second operand address.

. . . .

Rules:
- The contents of both operands are treated as 32-bit signed integers
- The second operand must be an aligned fixed-point halfword

Example:

```
             CH    12,FOUR
     FOUR    DC    H'4'
```

If register 12 contains binary "−2", the CH instruction will set the value 1 in the condition code. The contents of register 12 and of FOUR remain unchanged.

A Program Example

Let us consider a short program example which uses binary comparison. We wish to determine which of 3 fixed-point numbers (contents of fullword locations A, B, and C) is the largest, and to place that largest number into a fullword location called WINNER. The flowchart and corresponding assembly language program are presented in figures 9.3 and 9.4, respectively. Read them carefully.

Notice in the program that the contents of A, B, and C were loaded into registers before dealing with the main program logic. This enabled us to use the CR instruction (the register to register version) for all our program comparisons.

9.4 SOLVING THE INVENTORY REPORT PROBLEM WITH NON-INTEGER VALUES

We now present the flowchart and assembly language solution to the inventory report problem with non-integer values, described in section 9.1.

The basic program logic is of course similar to that of the inventory report problem of chapter 8. Modifications to our original flowchart (figure 8.3) which have been incorporated into the flowchart below are enclosed within dotted lines. Some of these additions designate alignment of fields in preparation for arithmetic with non-integers (symbols B2 and G4), others request the rounding of computational results (symbols G2 and J4). Symbols B3 through H3 describe steps which compare the new-on-hand amount to the reorder point, and find the appropriate reorder amount (which is zero if the new-on-hand exceeds the reorder point). Review the program flowchart of figure 9.5 carefully before proceeding to the assembly language solution.

Next read the assembly language solution of figure 9.6. You will notice that the boxed portions are additions and modifications to the program of chapter 8, and are labeled according to the flowchart symbols to which they correspond. It might be beneficial for you to read the program along with the discussion following it. Comments in the body of the program should also help to clarify the meaning of each step.

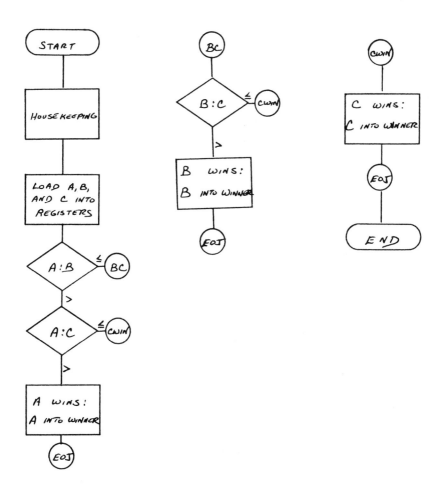

Figure 9.3
Flowchart: Comparing Three Fixed-Point Numbers

```
LOC     OBJECT CODE    ADDR1 ADDR2  STMT  SOURCE STATEMENT

CCCCCC                                1          PRINT NOGEN
CCCCCC  05C0                 C0002    2    BEGIN START 0
                                      3          BALR  12,0
                                      4          USING *,12
                                      5    *
CCCCC2  5820 C036           C0038     6          L     2,A         A INTO REGISTER 2
CCCCC6  5830 C03A           C003C     7          L     3,B         B INTO REGISTER 3
CCCCCA  5840 C03E           C0040     8          L     4,C         C INTO REGISTER 4
CCCCCE  1923                          9          CR    2,3         COMPARE A TO B
CCCC10  47D0 C020           C0022    10          BNH   BC          IF A>B, COMPARE B TO C
CCCC14  1924                         11          CR    2,4         OTHERWISE COMPARE A TO C
                                     12    *
CCCC16  47D0 C02E           C0030    13          BNH   CWIN        IF A>B, AND A>C, GO TO CWIN
CCCC1A  5020 C042           C0044    14    AWIN  ST    2,WINNER    OTHERWISE (A>B AND A>C), A IS LARGEST
CCCC1E  47F0 C032           C0034    15          B     EOJ         GO TO EOJ
                                     16    *
CCCC22  1934                         17    BC    CR    3,4         COMPARE B TO C
CCCC24  47D0 C02E           C0030    18          BNH   CWIN        IF A>B, AND B>C, GO TO CWIN
CCCC28  5030 C042           C0044    19    BWIN  ST    3,WINNER    OTHERWISE (A>B AND B>C), B IS LARGEST
CCCC2C  47F0 C032           C0034    20          B     EOJ         GO TO EOJ
                                     21    *
CCCC30  5040 C042           C0044    22    CWIN  ST    4,WINNER    C IS LARGEST
                                     23    *
CCCC34  0A03                         24    EOJ   SVC   3           STOP EXECUTION.  IN DOS, THIS INSTRUCTION
                                                                   IS EOJ
                                     25    *
                                     26    * AREA DEFINITIONS
                                     27    *
                                     28    *
CCCC36  C000                         29    A      DC   F'-2'
CCCC38  FFFFFFFE                     30    B      DC   F'0'
CCCC3C  00000000                     31    C      DC   F'+2'
CCCC44  00000002                     32    WINNER DS   F
CCCC4C                               33           END  BEGIN
CCCCC0
```

Figure 9.4
Comparing Three Fixed-Point Numbers

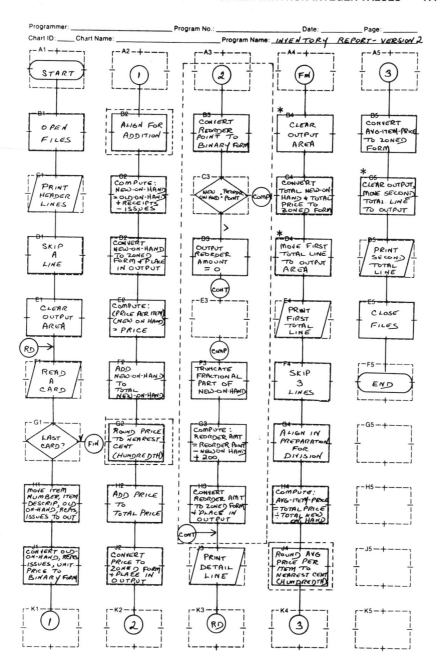

Figure 9.5
Flowchart for Inventory Report, Version 2

```
LOC    OBJECT CODE       ADDR1 ADDR2   STMT  SOURCE STATEMENT

                                        1         PRINT NOGEN
CCCCCC                                  2    BGN  START 0
CCCCC0 05C0                             3         BALR  12,0
                                        4         USING *,12
                                        5    *
CCCCC2                    C0002         6         OPEN  (ITMFILE,INPUT,RPTFILE,OUTPUT)
                                       14    *FOR DCS, PROGRAM FILES ARE OPENED BY
                                       15    *    OPEN ITMFILE,RPTFILE
                                       16    *
CCCC12 1B88                            17         SR    8,8         CLEAR REG 8 FOR TOTAL NEW-ON-HAND
CCCC14 1BAA                            18         SR    10,10       CLEAR REG 10 FOR TOTAL PRICE
                                       19    *
                                       20    * HEADER ROUTINE
CCCC16                                 21         PUT   RPTFILE,HEAC1
CCCC24                                 26         PUT   RPTFILE,HEAD2
CCCC32                                 31         PUT   RPTFILE,BLANKS
CCCC4C D283 C2DB C2DA   02DD 02DC      36         MVC   REPTREC,REPTREC-1
                                       37    * DETAIL ROUTINE
                                       38    * MOVE SOME INPUT DETAIL DATA TO OUTPUT
CCCC46                                 39    RD   GET   ITMFILE,ITMREC
CCCC54 D203 C2DE C290   02E0 0292      44         MVC   ONUM,INUM
CCCC5A D213 C2EC C2A3   02EE 02A5      45         MVC   CDESC,IDESC
CCCC60 D203 C294 C2A4   0296 02A6      46         MVC   CCLD,IOLD
CCCC66 D203 C319 C298   031B 029A      47         MVC   CISSUE,IISSUE
CCCC6C D202 C326 C29C   0329 029E      48         MVC   ORECPT,IRECPT
                                       49    * CONVERT DATA TO BINARY FORMAT FOR CALCULATION
CCCC72 F273 C5F6 C294   05F8 0292      50    RD   PACK  DBL,IOLD
CCCC78 4F20 C5F6        05F8           51         CVB   2,DBL       OLD ON-HAND INTO REG 2
CCCC7C F272 C5F6 C29C   05F8 029E      52         PACK  DBL,IRECPT
CCCC82 4F30 C5F6        05F8           53         CVB   3,DBL       RECEIPTS INTO REG 3
CCCC86 F273 C5F6 C298   05F8 029A      54         PACK  DBL,IISSUE
CCCC8C 4F40 C5F6        05F8           55         CVB   4,DBL       ISSUES INTO REG 4
CCCC8C F272 C5F6 C2A0   05F8 02A2      56         PACK  DBL,IUPRC
CCCC96 4F70 C5F6        05F8           57         CVB   7,DBL       UNIT PRICE INTO REG 7
                                       58    * ALIGN FOR ADDITION
CCCC9A 4C30 C612        C0614          59         MH    3,=H'10'    APPEND LOW-ORDER 0 TO RECEIPTS
                                       60    *                      NOW XXX BECOMES XXX∧0
                                       61    * COMPUTE NEW-ON-HAND
CCCC9E 1A23                            62         AR    2,3         OLD-ON-HAND + RECEIPTS = XXX∧X + XXX∧0
CCCCA0 1B24                            63         SR    2,4         NEW-ON-HAND = OLD-ON-HAND + RECEIPTS
                                       64    *                       - ISSUES = XXX∧X + XXX∧0 - XXX∧X
                                       65    *                      INTO REGISTER 2
CCCCA2 1A82                            66         AR    8,2         TOTAL NEW-ON-HAND IN REG 8
                                       67    * NEW-ON-HAND INTO DETAIL OUTPUT
CCCCA4 4E20 C5F6        05F8           68         CVD   2,DBL       (CONVERT INTO ZONED FORM)
CCCCA8 F337 C334 C5F6   00336 005F8    69         UNPK  ONEW,DBL
CCCCAE D300 C337 C336   00339 00338    70         MVZ   ONEW+3(1),ONEW+2   ELIMINATES SIGN FROM LAST BYTE
                                       71    * COMPUTE PRICE
CCCCB4 1C62                            72         MR    6,2         PRICE INTO REG 7
                                       73    *                      = (IXX∧XII∧XX) = XXXX∧XXX
CCCCB6 1AA7                            74         AR    10,7        TOTAL PRICE IN REG 10
                                       75    * ROUND PRICE TO NEAREST CENT (HUNDREDTHS)
CCCCB8 4A70 C614        C0616          76         AH    7,=H'5'     ROUND (INCREMENT HUNDREDTHS POSITION)
CCCCBC 5D60 C5FE        C0600          77         D     6,=F'10'    TRUNCATE LOW-ORDER (1000THS) DIGIT
                                       78    * PRICE INTO DETAIL OUTPUT (CONVERT INTO ZONED FORM)
```

B-2

G-2

Figure 9.6
Inventory Report, Version 2 (Part 1)

```
LOC     OBJECT CODE          ADDR1  ADDR2   STMT  SOURCE STATEMENT

CCCCCC  4E70 C5F6            C5F8           79         CVD   7,CBL
CCCCC4  F357 C341            C5F8   00343   80         UNPK  CPRC,DBL
CCCCCA  D300 C346 C348       C347           81         MVZ   CPRC+5(1),CPRC+4     ELIMINATES SIGN FROM LAST BYTE
                                            82    * CONVERT REORDER POINT INTO BINARY FORM
CCCCCC  F272 C5F6 C2B7       C2B9           83         PACK  DBL,IREORD
CCCCCC  4FB0 C5F6            C5F8           84         CVB   11,CBL
                                            85    *
CCCCCA  8E20 CC20            CC020          86         SRDA  2,32                 PLACE NEW-ON-HAND INTO ODD REG IN
                                            87    *                               PREPARATION FOR DIVISION
CCCCCE  5D20 C5FE            C0600          88         D     2,=F'10'             TRUNCATE-ORDER (FRACTIONAL) DIGIT
CCCCCE  1928                                89         CR    2,11                 COMPARE NEW-ON-HAND TO REORDER POINT
CCCCC2  4700 CCFO            C0F2           90         BNH   CMP                   IF NEW-ON-HAND NOT GREATER, GO TO CCMP
CCCCC8  D202 C351 C616       00353  C618    91         MVC   CREORD,=C'CCC'       OTHERWISE, REORDER AMT = 0
CCCCCE  47F0 C106            00108          92         B     CONT                 AND CONTINUE BELOW
                                            93    * NCW CCMPUTE RECRDER AMOUNT FOR NEW-ON-HAND NOT GREATER THAN RECRDER
                                            94    * PCINT
CCCCF2  1BB3                                95    CCMP  SR   11,3                 REORDER POINT - TRUNCATED NEW-ON-HAND
                                            96    *                               IN REG 11
CCCCF4  5AB0 C602            C604           97    CCMP  A    11,=F'200'           REORDER AMOUNT = (REORDER POINT
                                            98    *                               - TRUNCATED NEW-ON-HAND) + 200 IN REG 11
                                            99    * REORDER AMOUNT TO DETAIL OUTPUT (CONVERT TO ZONED FORM)
CCCCF8  4EB0 C5F6            C5F8          100          CVD   11,CBL
CCCCFE  F327 C351 C5F6       00353  C5F8   101          UNPK  CREORD,DBL
CCC1C2  D300 C353 C355       00355         102          MVZ   CREORD+2(1),OREORD
                                           103    * PRINT DETAIL LINE
CCC1C8                                     104    CCNT  PUT   RPTFILE,REPTREC
                                           109    * GO BACK TO PROCESS NEXT DETAIL RECORD
CCC116  47F0 CC44            00046         110          B     RD
                                           111    *
                                           112    * TCTAL RCUTINE
                                           113    *
CCC11A  4EB0 C5F6            C5F8          114    FIN   CVD   8,DBL
CCC11E  F542 C542 C5F6       00544         115          UNPK  TOTNEW,DBL          TOTAL NEW-ON-HAND TO TOTAL OUTPUT
CCC124  D300 C547 C546       00548         116          MVZ   TOTNEW+5(1),TOTNEW+4
CCC12A  4EA0 C5F6            C5F8          117          CVD   10,DBL
CCC12E  F377 C54F C5F6       00551         118          UNPK  TOTPRC,DBL          TOTAL PRICE TO TOTAL OUTPUT
CCC134  D300 C556 C555       00557         119          MVZ   TOTPRC+7(1),TOTPRC+6
CCC13A                                     120          PUT   RPTFILE,BLANKS      SKIP A LINE
CCC148                                     125          PUT   RPTFILE,TOT1        PRINT FIRST TOTAL LINE
CCC156                                     130          PUT   RPTFILE,BLANKS      SKIP
CCC164                                     135          PUT   RPTFILE,BLANKS            3
CCC172                                     140          PUT   RPTFILE,BLANKS            LINES
                                           145    * ALIGN IN PREPARATION FOR BINARY DIVISION TO 1000THS PLACE
                                           146    * AVG PRICE PER ITEM = TOTAL PRICE / TOTAL NEW-ON-HAND
                                           147    *                    = XXXXXX.XX / XXXXX.X
                                           148    *
                                           149    *
                                           150    *
CCC18C  BEAC CC20            CC020         151    SRDA  10,32                      PLACE TOTAL PRICE INTO REG 11 TO
                                           152    *                               PREPARE FOR ALIGNMENT
CCC184  5CAC C606            C608   00608  153          M     10,=F'100'           APPEND 2 LOW-ORDER O'S TO TOTAL PRICE
CCC188  1DA8                               154          DR    10,8                 COMPUTE AVG PRICE PER ITEM, INTO REG 11
                                           155    * ROUND AVG PRICE PER ITEM TO NEAREST CENT
CCC18A  5ABC C6CA            C60C   0060C  156          A     11,=F'5'             PREPARE FOR DIVISION (TRUNCATION)
CCC18E  5CAC C60E            C610   00610  157          M     10,=F'1'
```

Figure 9.6

Inventory Report, Version 2 (Part 2)

PAGE 4

17 NOV 78

```
LOC     OBJECT CODE       ADDR1 ADDR2  STMT  SOURCE STATEMENT

CCC192  5DA0 C5FE          00600  158   D    10,=F'10'
CCC196  4EB0 C5F6    C5F8          159   CVD  11,DBL
CCC19A  F337 C5CA C5F6 005CC 005F8  160  UNPK AVG,DBL
CCC1AC  D300 C5CD    005CF 005CE   161   MVZ  AVG+3(1),AVG+2   AVG PRICE PER ITEM INTO TOTAL OUTPUT
CCC1A6                            162   PUT  RPTFILE,TOT2     PRINT SECOND TOTAL LINE
                                  167  *
CCC1B4                            168   CLOSE (ITMFILE)
CCC1BE                            174   CLOSE (RPTFILE)
                                  180  *#FOR DOS, CLOSING FILES IS PERFORMED BY
                                  181  *       CLOSE ITMFILE,RPTFILE
                                  182  *
CCC1CA  0A03                      183         SVC  3
                                  184  *#FOR DOS, THE END OF EXECUTION IS INSTRUCTED BY
                                  185  *       EOJ
                                  186  *
                                  187  *  FILE DEFINITIONS
                                  188  *
CCC1CC                            189   ITMFILE DCB  DSORG=PS,MACRF=GM,DDNAME=SYSIPT,        C
                                              BLKSIZE=80,LRECL=80,EODAD=FIN
CCC22C                            243   RPTFILE DCB  DSORG=PS,MACRF=PM,DDNAME=SYSLST,        C
                                              BLKSIZE=132,LRECL=132

                                  297  *#FOR DOS, FILE DEFINITIONS ARE PERFORMED BY THE DTF MACROS AND
                                  298  *                    BUFFER DEFINITIONS
                                  299  *ITMFILE DTFCD DEVADDR=SYSRDR,IOAREA1=IN,BLKSIZE=80,RECFORM=FIXUNB,
                                  300  *             WORKA=YES,EOFADDR=FIN
                                  301  *RPTFILE DTFPR DEVADDR=SYSLST,IOAREA1=OUT,BLKSIZE=132,RECFORM=FIXUNB,
                                  302  *             WORKA=YES
CCC303                            303   IN   DS   CL80           BUFFER FOR INPUT FILE
CCC304                            304   OUT  DS   CL132          BUFFER FOR OUTPUT FILE
                                  305  *
                                  306  *
                                  307  *  DATA AREAS
                                  308  *
CCC28C                            309   ITMREC  DS   OCL80       INPUT AREA
CCC28C                            310   INUM    DS   CL6
CCC252                            311   INUM    DS   CL4         XXXX
CCC296                            312   ICLD    DS   CL4         XXX.X
CCC25A                            313   IISSUE  DS   CL3         XXX.X
CCC25E                            314   IRECPT  DS   CL3         XXX
CCC2A1                            315   IRECPT  DS   CL1
CCC2A2                            316   IUPRC   DS   CL3         X.XX
CCC2A5                            317   IDESC   DS   CL20
CCC2B9                            318   IRECRD  DS   CL3         XXX
CCC2BC                            319           DS   CL32
                                  320  *
CCC2DC  40                        321   REPTREC DC   C' '        DETAIL OUTPUT AREA
CCC02DD                           322   REPTREC DS   OCL132
CCC2DD                            323   ONUM    DS   CL3
CCC2E0                            324   ONUM    DS   CL4         XXXX
CCC2E4                            325   ODESC   DS   CL10
CCC3C2                            326   ODESC   DS   CL20
CCC3CC                            327   OOLD    DS   CL10
CCC310                            328   OOLD    DS   CL4         XXX.X
CCC31B                            329   OISSUE  DS   CL11
                                  330   OISSUE  DS   CL4         XXX.X
```

Figure 9.6

Inventory Report, Version 2 (Part 3)

```
LCC     OBJECT CODE        ADDR1  ADDR2   STMT   SOURCE STATEMENT

CCC31F                                    331    CRECPT   DS    CL9
CCC328                                    332             DS    CL3
CCC32B                                    333             DS    CL11
CCC33A                                    334    ONEW     DS    CL4          XXX
CCC343                                    335             DS    CL9
CCC349                                    336    OPRC     DS    CL6          XXX,A X
CCC353                                    337             DS    CL10         XXXX,A XX
CCC356                                    338    OREORC   DS    CL3          XXX
                                          339             DS    CL11

                                          340    *
CCC3E1  40404040404040C4C                 341    BLANKS   DC    CL132' '
CCC3E5  40404CC9E3C5D44C                  342    HEAD1    DC    CL132'              ITEM                ITEM              NEW           OLC
                                                                                 RECEIPTS                               PRIC
CCC465  4C40D5E4D4C2C5D9                  343    HEAD2    DC    CL132'            D        ISSUES      REORDER'     ON HC
                                                                                 CE        NUMBER     DESCRIPTION    ON HAND    C
                                                                                 AND                               AMOUNT'

                                          344    *
CCC4ED                                    345    TCT1     DS    OCL132            FIRST TOTAL LINE
CCC4ED  40404040404040404C               346             DC    CL69'  '
CCC532  E3D6E3C1D3E2                      347             DC    CL6'TCTALS'
CCC538  40404C404040404C                 348             DC    CL12' . '
CCC544                                    349    TCTNEW   DS    CL6          XXXXX,A X
CCC54A  40404C40404040                   350             DC    CL7' . '
CCC551                                    351    TOTPRC   DS    CL8          XXXXXX,A XX
CCC559  40404040404040404C               352             DC    CL24' . '

                                          353    *
CCC571                                    354    TOT2     DS    OCL132            SECOND TOTAL LINE
CCC571  40404040404040404C               355             DC    CL65' . '
CCC5B2  C1E5C5D9C1C7C540                  356             DC    CL26'AVERAGE PRICE PER ITEM = '
CCC5CC                                    357    AVG      DS    CL4          XX,A XX
CCC5CC  40404040404C4C40                 358             DC    CL38' . '

                                          359    *
CCC5F8                                    360    DBL      DS    OC
CCC5F8                                    361             DS    PL8
CCCCCC                                    362             END   BGN
CCC6CC  C00CCCCA                          363                   =F'10'
CCC6C4  C00CCCC8                          364                   =F'200'
CCC6C8  C0000064                          365                   =F'100'
CCC6CC  00000005                          366                   =F'5'
CCC61C  00000001                          367                   =F'1'
CCC614  C00A                              368                   =H'10'
CCC616  C005                              369                   =H'5'
CCC618  FCFCFCF0                          370                   =C'000'
```

Figure 9.6
Inventory Report, Version 2 (Part 4)

ITEM NUMBER	ITEM DESCRIPTION	OLD ON HAND	ISSUES	RECEIPTS	NEW ON HAND	PRICE	REORDER AMOUNT
11CC	HAMMER	2400	2000	12C	1600	100800	270
11C1	CHISEL	3200	1500	100	2700	256230	230
21C1	SCREWDRIVER	1250	1000	05C	0750	048750	245
6CC1	NAILS	1220	0605	075	1470	105840	173
6C1C	RAKE	5220	1210	060	5215	444318	199
7CCC	WRENCH	6230	2000	4CO	9020	802780	072
7C1C	FLOWER POT	2500	2000	2CO	2500	125000	190
7C2C	BOLTS	1700	0150	007	1720	104060	208
7C3C	TACKS	2700	0150	02C	2800	067200	205
7C4C	NUTS	3305	0200	030	3405	119175	160
8C1C	PINS	4000	2000	300	5000	025000	200
8C15	DYE	1250	0500	010	085C	010200	215
8C25	FERTILIZER	2250	1615	260	3235	084757	099
8C75	HOSE	0100	0040	003	0290	007038	341
9CCC	LIME	1000	0500	05C	1C00	024000	200

TOTALS   041355   23251480

AVERAGE PRICE PER ITEM = 5622

Figure 9.7
Inventory Report, Version 2 — Output

Examining the program of figure 9.6, we note few changes in the area definitions. The input area (ITMREC), detail output area (REPTREC), header lines (HEAD1 and HEAD2) and total areas (TOT1 and TOT2) are defined so that their field arrangements and descriptions correspond to program specifications (section 9.1). You might note that input fields IRECPT and IUPRC and detail output field ORECPT are different from the corresponding fields in chapter 8, to reflect the changed specifications. We also have a new input field (IREORD) which is to contain the item's reorder point, and a new output field (OREORD), to contain the computed reorder amount. Moreover, the fields IOLD, IISSUE, IIUPRC, OOLD, OISSUE, ONEW, and OPRC, as well as total fields, have implied decimal positions as indicated in the comment portions of the instructions which define them.

The procedure section of our program begins as usual, with establishing and initializing a base register (BALR and USING instructions) and OPENing program files. Registers 8 and 10 are filled with zeros in preparation for the accumulation of total amounts in these registers.

The header routine follows next, with the printing of two header lines (contents of HEAD1 and HEAD2) and a blank line (equivalent to "skipping" a line). The detail output area is filled with blanks in preparation for further processing.

The detail routine begins by moving certain input fields to the detail output area. The input fields moved (item number, item description, old-on-hand, issues, and receipts) are those which are to be reproduced unchanged as part of the detail output record for that item. The old-on-hand, receipts, issues, and unit price input fields are then converted to binary form in preparation for computation.

The computation of new-on-hand includes adding receipts to old-on-hand and subtracting issues from that sum. Old-on-hand has one implied decimal position ($xxx_\wedge x$) while receipts is integer (xxx). Therefore the fields must be aligned by appending a low-order zero to receipts, effected by multiplying the receipts field by 10. We then compute new-on-hand as: old-on-hand + receipts − issues ($xxx_\wedge x$ + $xxx_\wedge 0$ − $xxx_\wedge x$). Every new-on-hand amount is added to register 8, in which we keep a running total of new-on-hand values. New-on-hand is then converted to zoned form and placed in the appropriate part of the detail output area.

We next compute "price" as the product of the just-calculated new-on-hand ($xxx_\wedge x$) and the unit price obtained from input ($x_\wedge xx$). The product is of the form $xxxx_\wedge xxx$, with 3 decimal positions. The product is added to register

10 where the total of all price fields is accumulated. Rounding this number to the nearest 100th is accomplished by adding 5 and dividing the resulting sum by 10 (see section 9.2.2). Price is then converted into zoned form and placed in the detail output area.

Now the program must determine whether the computed new-on-hand amount is smaller in value than the reorder point, for the item under consideration. In other words, we wish to know whether the item amount in stock is low enough to necessitate replenishing that stock. If the amount is not low enough (new-on-hand > reorder point), the "reorder amount" will be 0 (reordering is unnecessary). Otherwise (new-on-hand ≤ reorder point) we must compute the amount required to be reordered (reorder amount) for that item.

The computation of the reorder amount is accomplished by first truncating the fractional portion of new-on-hand (new-on-hand has one decimal position, so that division by 10 will effect this truncation — see section 9.2.2). We then subtract the integer portion of new-on-hand from the reorder point (to find the amount by which the new-on-hand falls short of the reorder point) and add 200 to the difference. (This computation follows the program specifications of section 9.1 above.) The computed reorder amount is converted into zoned form and placed into the detail output area.

The detail output area contains the item number, item description, old-on-hand, issues, receipts, new-on-hand, price, and reorder amount for the current item, as designated by the program output specifications. A detail line is printed, and the processing of the current record has ended. Program control is then transferred to the instruction called RD, which reads a new record, and the entire detail routine is repeated for the next record. The program has entered a loop.

Exit from the loop takes place when the "last card" (the " /* " card) is read. At that time, program control is passed to the instruction called FIN, as instructed by the macro which defined the input file (DCB for OS systems, DTFCD for DOS systems). The program has entered the routine which produces total output.

After converting the total new-on-hand and total price fields into zoned form and positioning them appropriately in TOT1, a line is skipped, and the first total line is printed. Three more lines are then skipped, as designated on the output layout form.

Computing the average price per item for the second total line requires some preparation. The divisor (total new-on-hand) has one decimal position, while the dividend (total price) has two decimal positions. We wish a quotient with three decimal positions, to be rounded back to two. Since the decimal points are assumed, we may mentally "move" both divisor and dividend decimal points one position rightward, as we would in performing the division on paper:

$$
\begin{array}{r}
\text{xx} \wedge \text{x} \\
\text{xxxxx} \wedge \text{x} \overline{\smash{\big)}\,\text{xxxxxx} \wedge \text{x} \; \text{x}}
\end{array}
$$

However this will yield a quotient with only one decimal position! It is therefore necessary for us to append 2 zeros to the dividend before dividing:

$$
\begin{array}{r}
\text{xx} \wedge \text{xxx} \\
\text{xxxxx} \overline{\smash{\big)}\,\text{xxxxxx} \wedge \text{x00}}
\end{array}
$$

This will yield a 3-decimal-position quotient which we afterwards round back to two decimal positions (by adding 5 to the quotient, and then dividing by 10 to eliminate the rightmost digit). The resultant average price per item is converted into zoned form, placed into the appropriate part of TOT2, and the second total line is printed. The program files are then closed, and execution is terminated.

9.5   ALGEBRAIC SHIFT INSTRUCTIONS

The program segment of section 9.2.3 and the program of section 9.4 made use of shift instructions (the SRA and SRDA instructions) to "push" register bits rightward. Assembly language uses four algebraic shift instructions to move bits sideways through the general registers: the SRA and SRDA instructions shift the data rightward, and the SLA and SLDA instructions shift the data leftward. The algebraic shift instructions have many possible uses in programs which manipulate binary data in registers. It is therefore appropriate for us to describe them and to consider their uses at this time.

We notice that the algebraic shifts are all machine instructions in RS format. However the third operand R3 is never used.

ALGEBRAIC RIGHT SHIFTS

As noted above, two algebraic instructions shift data rightward within registers. The SRA (**S**hift **R**ight **A**lgebraic) shifts data within a single register, and the SRDA (**S**hift **R**ight **D**ouble **A**lgebraic) shifts data within 2 registers (an even-odd pair, the first of which is even-numbered), treating them as a single 64-bit register.

The first operand of the SRA or SRDA instruction indicates the respective single register, or even-odd register pair, to be shifted. The second operand contains the shift amount: the number of bits to be shifted out of the register or register pair. We shall first outline the basic construction and rules of the SRA and SRDA instructions. Then we shall consider some examples of their use.

The SRA Instruction

The SRA Instruction (**S**hift **R**ight **A**lgebraic)

Instruction type: Machine Instruction
Machine format: RS Instruction (Register and Storage Instruction)

8A	R1	////	B2	D2

0   7 8   11 12   15 16   19 20   31

Symbolic format:

	name	operation	operands
	[symbolic name]	SRA	R1,constant
or	[symbolic name]	SRA	R1,D2(B2)

where R1 is a general register number. D2 and B2 are the displacement and base register specifying an address, the *low-order 6 bits* of which indicate the number of bit positions to be shifted.

. . . .

Rule:
- Using the second operand form above, a 0 in the B2 field means that the computation of the shift amount, involving the contents of a register, is not to take place.

The SRDA Instruction

The SRDA Instruction (Shift **R**ight **D**ouble **A**lgebraic)

Instruction type: Machine Instruction
Machine format: RS Instruction (Register and Storage Instruction)

| 8E | R1 | ⧹⧹ | B2 | D2 |

0   7 8   11 12   15 16   19 20   31

Symbolic format:

	name	operation	operands
	[symbolic name]	SRDA	R1,constant
or	[symbolic name]	SRDA	R1,D2(B2)

where R1 is an *even* register number. D2 and B2 are the displacement
        and base register specifying an address the *low-order 6 bits* of
        which indicate the number of bit positions to be shifted.

· ·

Rules:
- The first operand must be an even-numbered register.
- Using the second operand form above, a 0 in the B2 field means
  that the computation of the shift amount, involving the contents of
  a register, is not to take place.

The SRA and SRDA instructions result in the following condition code settings:

>   0   if result $=$ 0
>   1   if result $<$ 0
>   2   if result $>$ 0
>   3   will not result from these instructions

The SRA and SRDA instructions have 32-bit and 64-bit first operands, respectively. For each instruction, the sign of the first operand remains unchanged. All *other* bits of the first operand are moved rightward as many bit
positions as are specified in the second operand. Low-order bits are shifted
off the right end of the respective register or register pair, and are lost. (The

instructions do not inspect those bits to determine what values are being lost.) High-order bit positions which are vacated are filled with copies of the sign bit: 0's if the original number was positive, 1's if the original number was negative. Thus we see that the shift instructions maintain the sign of the original numbers.

Assume the following original register contents:

Register 8:   00101111010111111111000001011010
Register 9:   11111111111111110000000010101010

The examples below give the changed register contents after the execution of the indicated instructions. We assume the above contents of registers 8 and 9 before execution of each instruction below.

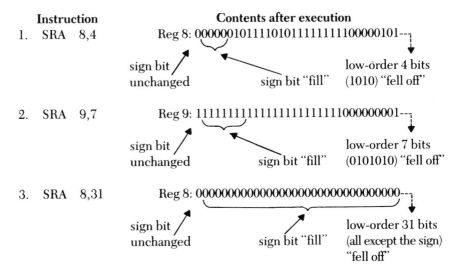

Instruction	Contents after execution
1. SRA 8,4	Reg 8: 00000010111101011111111100000101
2. SRA 9,7	Reg 9: 11111111111111111111111111000000001
3. SRA 8,31	Reg 8: 00000000000000000000000000000000

When all the bits of a positive number are shifted rightward (shift amounts 31 − 63), the register will contain all 0's.

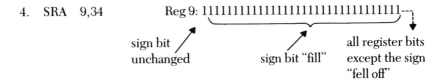

| 4. SRA 9,34 | Reg 9: 11111111111111111111111111111111 |

When all the bits of a negative number are shifted rightward (shift amounts 31 − 63), the register will contain all 1's.

5.   SRDA   8,8   Reg 8: 00000000010111101011111111110000

sign bit
unchanged

sign bit
"fill"

Reg 9: 01011010111111111111111100000000--

low-order 8 bits "fell off"

Notice that the first operand specifies the register *pair* 8-9. The sign of the doubleword is the sign of the even-numbered (high-order) register, and the leftmost bit of the odd-numbered register is shifted in the same manner as any other numeric bit.

Shifting rightward algebraically is equivalent to dividing by a power of 2 (the particular power of 2 is determined by the number of bit-positions being shifted) and rounding *downward*.

For example, the number +9, or 000...01001 binary, shifted 1 bit-position rightward, yields 4: 00...0100. Note that $9 \div 2^1 = 4$, with a remainder of 1 which is ignored.

Likewise, the number −14 or 111...10010 binary, shifted 2 bit-positions rightward, yields −4: 11...100. Note that $-14 \div 2^2 = -14 \div 4 = -3$ with a remainder. Rounding downward gives us the value −4. (Remember that for negative numbers, numbers with a larger absolute value are smaller in actual value. If a person owes 4 dollars, he has *less* money than if he owes 3 dollars.)

Of course, if the division by a power of 2 does not yield a remainder, the result of the right shift will be the exact quotient value. For example, the number +8 or 000...01000 binary, shifted 2 positions rightward, yields +2: 00...010. Note that $8 \div 2^2 = 8 \div 4 = 2$.

The SRA and SRDA instructions may be used in assembly language programs whenever division by a power of 2 is required. In fact, the shift instructions require less execution time than do the fixed-point divide instructions, hence they are preferred.

ALGEBRAIC LEFT SHIFTS

The algebraic instructions which shift data leftward within registers are the SLA (**Shift Left Algebraic**), which shifts data within a single register, and the SLDA (**Shift Left Double Algebraic**), which shifts data within an even-odd register pair, treating it as a single 64-bit register.

The first operand of the SLA or SLDA instruction indicates the respective single register or even-odd register pair to be shifted. The second operand contains the shift amount.

The SLA Instruction

The SLA Instruction (**Shift Left Algebraic**)

Instruction type: Machine Instruction
Machine format: RS Instruction (Register and Storage Instruction)

8B	R1	////	B2	D2

0   7 8   11 12   15 16   19 20   31

Symbolic format:

	name	operation	operands
	[symbolic name]	SLA	R1,constant
or	[symbolic name]	SLA	R1,D2(B2)

where R1 is a general register number. D2 and B2 are the displacement and base register specifying an address, the *low-order 6 bits* of which indicate the number of bit positions to be shifted.

. . . .

Rules:
- Using the second operand form above, a 0 in the B2 field means that the computation of the shift amount, involving the contents of a register, is not to take place.

The SLDA Instruction

The SLDA Instruction (**S**hift **L**eft **D**ouble **A**lgebraic)

Instruction type: Machine Instruction
Machine format: RS Instruction (Register and Storage Instruction)

```
|    8F    |   R1  |////|  B2  |      D2      |
0          7 8    11 12  15 16  19 20          31
```

Symbolic format:

	name	operation	operands
	[symbolic name]	SLDA	R1,constant
or	[symbolic name]	SLDA	R1,D2(B2)

where R1 is an *even* register number. D2 and B2 are the displacement and base register specifying an address, the *low-order 6 bits* of which indicate the number of bit positions to be shifted.

. . . .

Rules:
- The first operand must be an even-numbered register.
- Using the second operand form above, a 0 in the B2 field means that the computation of the shift amount, involving the contents of a register, is not to take place.

The SLA and SLDA instructions result in the following condition code settings:

- 0   if result = 0
- 1   if result < 0
- 2   if result > 0
- 3   if overflow results

The SLA and SLDA instructions have 32-bit and 64-bit first operands, respectively. For each instruction, the sign of the first operand remains unchanged during execution, and all the other bits are shifted leftward the number of bit positions specified by the second operand. High order bits (excluding the sign, which remains) are shifted off and "lost", and low-order register positions which are vacated are filled with zeros. If a bit unlike the sign is shifted out of position 1 (the second high-order position), we say that **overflow** (an error condition) occurs. This ensures that the shift operation will not change the sign of the original register contents.

Assume the following original register contents:

Register 10:   111111111111001000101010111110000
Register 11:   00000000010000001100001111110011

The examples below give the changed register contents after the execution of the indicated instructions. We assume the above contents of registers 10 and 11 before execution of each instruction below.

Instruction	**Contents after execution**

1.   SLA   10,6   Reg 10: 1 ⌐1111100100010101011110000000000

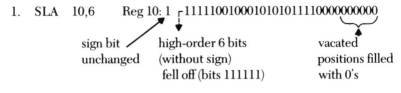

      sign bit   high-order 6 bits   vacated
      unchanged   (without sign)   positions filled
                   fell off (bits 111111)   with 0's

2.   SLA   11,8   Reg 11: 0 ⌐100000011000011111100110000000

      sign bit   high-order 8 bits   vacated
      unchanged   fell off   positions
                   (bits 00000000)   filled with 0's

3.   SLA   11,9   This instruction will result in overflow. Example 2 above shifted the register contents 8 bit positions leftward. The 9th numeric bit is a "1" bit, which differs from the sign bit (the sign bit is 0). This is overflow.

4.   SLA   10,31   Reg 10: 1 ⌐0000000000000000000000000000000

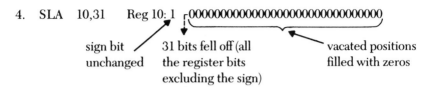

      sign bit   31 bits fell off (all   vacated positions
      unchanged   the register bits   filled with zeros
                   excluding the sign)

When all the bits of a negative number are shifted leftward (shift amounts $31-63$), the register will contain the value -2^{31}. For negative numbers, shifting all the register bits leftward will result in overflow (unless the original register contents were -1). However program interruption will occur only when the fixed-point overflow mask bit is one (this will be explained in chapter 13).

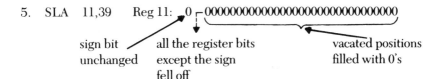

5.   SLA   11,39   Reg 11: 0 0000000000000000000000000000000000

sign bit   all the register bits   vacated positions
unchanged   except the sign   filled with 0's
                 fell off

For positive numbers, shifting all the register bits leftward (shift amounts 31— 63) will result in overflow (unless the original register contents were zero). However program interruption will occur only when the fixed-point overflow mask bit is one (see chapter 13).

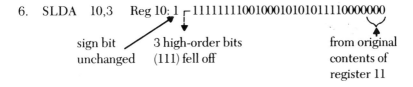

6.   SLDA   10,3   Reg 10: 1 1111111100100010101011110000000

sign bit   3 high-order bits   from original
unchanged   (111) fell off   contents of
                                             register 11

Reg   11:   0000001000000110000111111110000000

vacated positions
filled with zeros

Notice here that the first operand, register 10, specifies the even-odd register pair 10-11. The shift instuction treats the pair as a single 64-bit register. The sign is the leftmost bit of register 10, and the leftmost bit of register 11 is treated in the same manner as any other numeric bit.

Shifting leftward algebraically is equivalent to multiplication by a power of 2. The number of bit positions being shifted is the power of 2 by which the value is multiplied. For example, the number +21, or binary 00...010101, shifted 1 bit-position leftward, yields 42: 0 0...0101010. Likewise, the

0   zero fill

number −21, or binary 1...101011,shifted 2 bit-positions leftward, yields −84:

1 1...10101100 ($-21 \times 2^2 = -21 \times 4 = -84$).

11   zero fill

The SLA and SLDA instructions may be used in place of fixed-point multiplication instructions when multiplication by a power of 2 is required. Moreover, they are faster than the fixed-point multiplication instructions, and their use is therefore preferred.

Summary

In this chapter, we presented techniques for performing computation with non-integer fixed-point data.

The instructions for comparing fixed-point numbers (CR, C, CH) were also described. The left and right algebraic shift instructions were discussed and illustrated.

Uses for our newly-presented instructions and techniques were demonstrated through the solution of an expanded version of the inventory report problem of chapter 8.

Important Terms Discussed in Chapter 9

align	rounding
carat	scale factor
fixed-point comparison	truncation

Questions

9-1. Given two fixed-point constants, A and B, with implied decimal positions as indicated,

```
A       DC      F'256'      2ʌ56
B       DC      H'684'      68ʌ4
```

(a) Write the instructions necessary to compute A + B and to place the result into a fullword location called SUM.

(b) Write the instructions necessary to compute A × B and to place the product into a fullword location called PROD.

(c) Write the instructions to round PROD (from (b) above) to the nearest tenth.

(d) Write the instructions to compute B ÷ A. Find the quotient to the tenths position, and then round to the nearest whole number.

9-2. Consider numbers of the forms described below, with x representing a digit in the decimal equivalent of the number. Tell what adjustments are necessary to round the numbers to the appropriate accuracies.

(a) $x_\wedge xxxx$ to the nearest 1000th
(b) $x_\wedge xx$ to the nearest whole number
(c) $xxx_\wedge xx$ to the nearest 10th
(d) $xxx_\wedge xxxx$ to the nearest whole number
(e) $xxx_\wedge xxxx$ to the nearest 100th

9-3. Consider divisors and dividends of the forms described below. Indicate the preparation, if any, necessary to compute A ÷ B to the tenths position.

	Divisor (B)	**Dividend (A)**
(a)	$xx_\wedge x$	$xxx_\wedge x$
(b)	$x_\wedge xx$	$x_\wedge xxx$
(c)	$x_\wedge xxx$	$x_\wedge xx$
(d)	$xx_\wedge$	$xxx_\wedge$
(e)	$x_\wedge xxxxx$	$x_\wedge x$

9-4. State one advantage to using binary fractions over binary integer values with "imagined" decimal positions. State one disadvantage.

9-5. Given the following binary constants

```
NUM1    DC    FS4'5.2'    00000000000000000000000000101.0011
NUM2    DC    FS3'4.25'   00000000000000000000000000100.010
```

Write the instructions necessary to find the product of NUM1 and NUM2, and to round that product to the nearest whole number.

9-6. Assume that register 2 contains the value +17, and register 3 contains −8. Tell what condition code settings will result after execution of each of the following instructions.

```
(a)    CR     2,3
(b)    C      3,=F'0'
(c)    CH     3,=H'−8'
(d)    AR     2,3
       CR     3,2
(e)    CR     2,2
```

9-7. Given a fullword location called J containing an unknown binary number, write a program segment to add 1 to J if J is positive; add 2 to J if J is negative; do nothing with J (stop execution) if J is zero.

Program Exercises

9-1. Consider three fixed-point fullword locations called X,Y, and Z containing unknown binary quantities.

X	DS	F
Y	DS	F
Z	DS	F

Write an assembly language program to place these numbers into ascending sequence in main storage. That is, we wish the smallest of the three numbers to be in X, the next larger number in Y, and the largest in Z.

9-2. Consider program input on cards as described below:

Field	Card Columns	
Item Description	1 − 20	
Item Cost	21 − 25	xxx$_\wedge$xx
Labor Charge	26 − 29	xx$_\wedge$xx
Freight Charge	30 − 32	xxx$_\wedge$
Tax Rate	33 − 34	$_\wedge$xx

The program will accept one input record per item, and will compute the final cost as follows:

Final Cost = Item Cost + Labor Charge + Freight Charge
+ (Tax Rate) (Item Cost)

The Final Cost is to be rounded to the nearest cent (hundredth).

Program output will consist of 2 heading lines, and one detail line per input record, as described below:

ITEM	ITEM	FINAL
(13 − 16)	(31 − 34)	(41 − 45)
DESCRIPTION	COST	COST
(10 − 20)	(31 − 34)	(42 − 45)
x$_x$xxxxxxxxxxxxxxxxxx	xxx$_\wedge$xx	xxxx$_\wedge$xx
xxxxxxxxxxxxxxxxxxxx	xxx$_\wedge$xx	xxxx$_\wedge$xx
xxxxxxxxxxxxxxxxxxxx	xxx$_\wedge$xx	xxxx$_\wedge$xx
⋮	⋮	⋮
(6 — 25)	(31 — 35)	(41 — 46)

Editing and More Advanced Branching and Looping

Unit 4

Chapter 10

Toward More Readable Printed Output: Editing and Forms Control

TOWARD MORE READABLE PRINTED OUTPUT

This chapter will be concerned with improving the appearance of program output. We will introduce several new instructions, each of which will serve in some way to make our output more readable.

For numeric fields, (sections 10.1 — 10.2) we have the "edit" instructions
- The ED (**ED**it) instruction
- The EDMK (**ED**it and Mar**K**) instruction

For forms control (section 10.3) we have
- The CNTRL (**C**o**NTR**o**L**) macro instruction
- The PRTOV (**PR**in**T O**Verflow) macro instruction

10.1   THE ED (EDit) INSTRUCTION

The ED ("edit") instruction is a very powerful "special purpose" instruction whose function is to improve the appearance and readability of printed numeric output. In particular, it may be used to
- suppress leading zeros — that is, to replace insignificant zeros with other characters, usually blanks
- insert special characters, such as commas and decimal points, between the digits of numeric fields
- cause certain insignificant zeros to be printed while others are suppressed (for example, we might want a field with 0005 to be printed ƀƀ.05)
- produce a negative indication to the right of a negative field
- perform any or all of the above for more than one field, with one instruction

The EDit is a storage to storage (SS) instruction with one length factor, designated by the first operand. Before execution of the ED instruction, the second operand — the source field — contains a *packed number* which is to be prepared for output. The first operand field contains a special collection of characters which we call a **pattern**. The particular makeup of the pattern — its characters, and the order in which they are arranged — will determine how the ED instruction treats the packed number in the second operand. After execution of the ED instruction, the "edited" result (that is, the number prepared for output with digits converted to zoned form, commas and decimal points inserted, and the like) will replace the pattern in the first operand. The second operand is not affected by instruction execution.

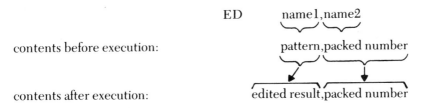

contents before execution:

contents after execution:

The pattern designates how the numeric field is to be treated. The study of the ED instruction is thus largely the study of pattern construction.

The ED pattern may use a combination of characters from among four types:

name of character	hexadecimal code	binary code
digit selector	20	0010 0000
significance starter	21	0010 0001
field separator	22	0010 0010
message character	any other characters	

In the following sections, we will explain the functions of each of the pattern characters above. We will then combine them into patterns to treat numeric data in different ways.

10.1.1 Suppressing Leading Zeros

Let us consider a 3-byte field called FLDA containing a packed integer value. We wish to define a pattern which will prepare the number for output with all leading (insignificant) zeros replaced by blanks.

We first note that a 3-byte packed number may be described in the following general form:

$$dd \quad dd \quad ds$$

where "d" is a 4-bit numeric code (0000-1001) and
     "s" is a 4-bit sign code (1100 for + and 1101 for −, using EBCDIC
        form)

The Pattern

The pattern will be defined as a constant in hexadecimal form. The first character of any pattern is the **fill character** — the character with which the programmer intends to replace insignificant zeros. If we wish leading zeros suppressed by blanks, the fill character will be a hexadecimal 40 (0100 0000 in binary), the EBCDIC representation for the character "blank" (see Appendix A, side ⑩).

For the remainder of the pattern, we correspond a special control character called a **digit selector** (hexadecimal 20) to each packed digit of the numeric field — in this case, we have 5 digits, hence 5 digit selectors.

Note: We use hexadecimal notation for control characters, for there do not exist printed characters with those particular computer configurations. Thus, although X′C1′ is the character A (C′A′) and X′40′ is the character blank (C′ ′), X′20′, X′21′, and X′22′ (the edit control characters) do not have representations as printed characters.

The pattern to edit FLDA may thus be defined:

PATTERN   DC   X′402020202020′

and the instruction to edit FLDA with this pattern is

ED   PATTERN,FLDA

During instruction execution, the computer scans both operands from left to right. The pattern is examined first; the fill character is noted and is left untouched in the leftmost pattern position.

The scanning of the pattern then continues rightward. When a digit selector is found, the computer looks to the second operand for a packed digit. What happens next will depend upon the state of the **significance indicator** — a switch whose respective on and off states designate whether or not significance (a non-zero source digit or a significance starter in the pattern) has been encountered in the scanning of a particular field. (An exception to this rule is presented in section 10.1.4.) The significance indicator is off at the start of an edit operation.

If a digit selector is encountered while the significance indicator is off (that is, significance has not yet been established in this field), then the corresponding source digit is examined for significance. A zero (code 0000) in the source field will cause the digit selector to be replaced in the first operand with a fill character. Any other valid numeric code (0001 through 1001) in the source field will cause the digit selector to be replaced in the first operand with a zoned version of the digit: F1 for 1, F2 for 2, and so on.

If a digit selector is encountered while the significance indicator is on, the digit selector will be replaced in the pattern by the appropriate zoned digit, even if the digit is zero.

Let us consider the instruction sequence to edit FLDA with sample field contents.

Example 1:

	MVC	OUTA,PATTERNA
	ED	OUTA,FLDA

$\vdots$

FLDA	DC	PL3'200'
PATTERNA	DC	X'402020202020'
OUTA	DS	CL6

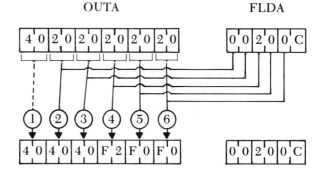

Before execution of the ED:

After execution of the ED:

Circled numbers represent the order of occurrence.

In the above example, leading zeros are replaced by the fill character, while significant zeros are converted to zoned form. The significance indicator was turned on at step 4. Note that the sign has been ignored.

Note too that had FLDA contained all significant digits (for example, all 2's: 22 22 2C) the fill character would still remain in the first character position of the edited result. The fill character is noted during the editing process but is itself left untouched. Moreover, the first pattern character is *by de-finition* the fill character; hence every pattern will have one. Each pattern will thus contain at least one character more than there are digits in the packed field (the fill character, plus one digit selector character per packed digit).

Example 2:

```
            MVC     OUTB,PATTERNB
            ED      OUTB,FLDB

               ⋮

FLDB        DC      PL2'0'
PATTERNB    DC      X'40202020'
OUTB        DS      CL4
```

Circled numbers represent the order of occurrence.

In this example, significance was not established in the field; hence the editing operation filled the result field with blanks.

The fill character, while often a blank, may actually be any character the programmer may wish. In fact, for monetary amounts, particularly on computer-generated checks, it is fairly common to see an asterisk (hexadecimal 5C) used as a fill character. This is known as **asterisk protection**, for it serves to make fraudulent tampering with checks more difficult.

The example below shows the results of editing sample data with two different fill characters.

Example I:

before editing	after editing	
	pattern: 402020202020	pattern: 5C2020202020
1) 98765	98765	*98765
2) 08765	8765	**8765
3) 00765	765	***765
4) 00065	65	****65
5) 00005	5	*****5
6) 00000		******

Note that the asterisk remains in the first character position, as it is left un-touched by the edit instruction. This is true with the blank as fill character as well, however the blank is not visible in the edited form.

10.1.2   Punctuating Numeric Fields

Punctuating numeric fields is accomplished by the insertion of **message characters** into the pattern. Any pattern character other than the fill character and the control characters X′20′, X′21′, and X′22′ are message characters. (The X′21′ and X′22′ will be discussed later in this chapter.)

When a message character is encountered while scanning the pattern, the resultant operation will depend upon the state of the significance indicator. If the indicator is on (that is, significance has been established in the field) the message character will be untouched in the result. If the indicator is off (that is, significance has not been established) the message character will be replaced by the fill character.

Let us examine the instruction sequence to edit a 7-digit numeric field as-sumed to have 2 decimal positions. A comma will be inserted after the second digit when it is significant. Note that a comma is represented by X′6B′, and a decimal point by X′4B′(see Appendix A, side ⑩).

Example 3:

```
                MVC    OUTC,PATC
                ED     OUTC,FLDC

                  ⋮

   FLDC         DC     P′9876543′
   PATC         DC     X′4020206B2020204B2020′
   OUTC         DS     CL10
```

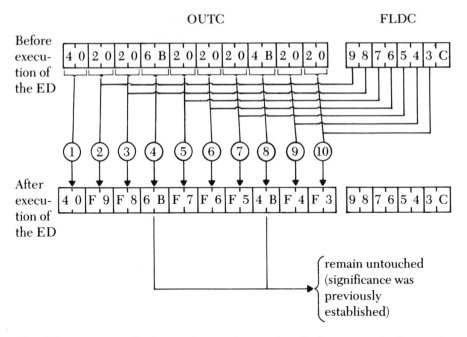

The following example demonstrates the results of editing sample data with a comma and a decimal point as message characters.

Example II:
pattern: 5C20206B2020204B2020

	before editing	after editing
1)	9876543	* 98,765.43
2)	0876543	** 8,765.43
3)	0076543	**** 765.43
4)	0006543	***** 65.43
5)	0000543	****** 5.43
6)	0000043	********43
7)	0000003	*********3
8)	0000000	**********

We note that the last entry of the above example, containing 7 zeros, has 10 asterisks in its edited form! This is so because the fill character itself remained, and each of the 2 message characters was replaced by the fill character, as were each of the seven zeros, for significance was never established in that field.

Note also that in the 6th and 7th entries of the above example, the edited results have no decimal point, although we assumed the field to be a 2-decimal-position field. The edited results apparently desired are *******.43 and *******.03 respectively. In other words, we wish to establish significance in the field (cause the significance indicator to be turned on) so that certain message characters and/or zeros will be printed *before an actual significant digit is encountered* during the scanning of the field. To overcome this difficulty, we need a special control character called the **significance starter**.

10.1.3 The Significance Starter: Establishing Early Significance

The significance starter (hexadecimal 21) is a control character with two functions. Firstly, it functions exactly as does a digit selector in that it corresponds to a packed digit in the left-to-right scan. Secondly, if the significance indicator has not yet been turned on when the significance starter is encountered, the significance starter will cause the significance indicator to be turned on, so that all *succeeding* characters (including message characters and zero digits) will be treated exactly as though an actual significant digit had been encountered.

Note that if the significance starter corresponds to an insignificant packed zero, that zero will *not* be treated as significant in the editing process. Any characters which follow that zero, however, will be so treated.

The example below illustrates editing with zero suppression, comma and decimal point as message characters, and use of the significance starter to ensure results with decimal positions.

Example III:
   pattern: 4020206B2020214B2020

	before editing	**after editing**
1)	9876543	98,765.43
2)	0876543	8,765.43
3)	0076543	765.43
4)	0006543	65.43
5)	0000543	5.43
6)	0000043	.43
7)	0000003	.03
8)	0000000	.00

Entries 6,7,and 8 above demonstrate how the significance starter will establish significance before an actual non-zero digit has been encountered. For entries 1 through 5, however, significance was established earlier in the left-to-right scan.

You may note from the examples that the total number of digit selectors and significance starters in the pattern should be exactly equal to the number of *digits* in the field being edited. It is good programming practice to check this whenever you code editing routines.

Another interesting point to be noted here is the effect of the significance starter on an all-zero field: the zero digits which occur after the significance starter will be printed. Contrast this with the last entry in Example II, in which the fill character replaced every packed digit.

There may, however, be times when it is desirable to fill a zero field completely with blanks or with asterisks, while maintaining the position of the significance starter for other possible field contents.

We may accomplish both ends by testing the condition code to see if the field which was edited contained all zeros. The execution of the ED instruction causes the condition code to be set as follows:

$$
\begin{array}{ll}
0 & \text{if all source digits} = 0 \\
1 & \text{if source field} < 0 \text{ (negative)} \\
2 & \text{if source field} > 0 \text{ (positive)}
\end{array}
$$

Thus, after editing the field using the significance starter, we may test the condition code to see whether it is set to zero (a zero result). If it is not, the program will proceed normally. If the setting indicates a zero result, we instruct the computer to fill the field with fill characters before proceeding with normal program execution.

Example 4:

```
              MVC     RESULT,PATRN
              ED      RESULT,NUMBER
              BC      6,PROCEED              cond code not 0
              MVC     RESULT+1(9),RESULT
    PROCEED   .
              .
              .
    NUMBER    DC      P'9876543'
    PATRN     DC      X'4020206B2020214B2020'
    RESULT    DS      CL10
```

The instruction BC 6,PROCEED will transfer program control to the instruction called PROCEED if the condition code is not 0. (The BC instruction will be explained in chapter 11.) Note that the second MVC instruction is executed *only* if the condition code = 0. It causes a blank (the first character of RESULT after the ED instruction has been executed) to be propagated throughout the RESULT field (see the discussion of the MVC in section 2.4). If the condition code is not 0 after execution of the ED instruction, a branch is performed to the instruction called PROCEED, and the second MVC instruction is ignored.

10.1.4   Signed Fields: A Negative Suffix

Our discussion of editing has thus far been concerned with the digit portion of numeric fields. Let us now focus on sign indication.

As we know, the sign of a packed number is located in the low-order portion of the low-order (rightmost) byte of the field. Each time a packed digit is fetched from the high-order portion of a byte, the low-order portion of that byte is examined to determine whether it contains a sign code. If a sign code is not found, the editing process continues until a digit is fetched from the high-order portion of the *next* byte, at which time the search is again made for the sign. Eventually, of course, a sign will be detected. If a negative sign is found, editing will proceed normally, the significance indicator remaining on if it had previously been on, or remaining off had significance not been established. If a positive sign is found, the digit in the high-order portion of the byte is edited normally, and the *significance indicator is turned off*. Thus, when a sign is detected, the significance indicator serves as a sign indicator: off for positive or zero, on for negative.

If we extend our pattern with message characters after the last digit selector, those characters will be printed for negative amounts and will not be printed for non-negative amounts. Typical sign indications would include a minus sign (60 in hexadecimal) or the symbol CR (meaning "credit", often used in business reports: C3 D9 in hexadecimal). However, any message character(s) desired are permissible.

Example IV illustrates editing with comma and decimal point, significance starter, and sign indication. Use of two different fill characters is demonstrated.

Example IV:

before editing		after editing
	pattern: 4020206B2020214B20204060	pattern: 5C20206B2020214B20204060
9876543+	98,765.43	*98,765.43**
0876543+	8,765.43	**8,765.43**
0076543+	765.43	****765.43**
0006543+	65.43	*****65.43**
0000543+	5.43	******5.43**
0000043+	.43	*******.43**
0000003+	.03	*******.03**
0000000+	.00	*******.00**
9876543−	98,765.43 −	*98,765.43 −
0000003−	.03 −	*******.03 −
0000000.−	.00 −	*******.00 −

You will notice from the table that asterisks are printed to the right of positive quantities in the rightmost column. This occurs because the characters "4060" in the pattern are message characters which are replaced by the fill character when the significance indicator is off, as is the case when a positive sign is encountered. The same thing occurred for the pattern with a blank fill character, however blanks are not evident on printed output. In actual practice, the case of asterisks being printed rightmost in the output field is not likely to occur very often. Asterisk protection is used most often for computer-generated checks. Such patterns will generally not provide for negative indication, for there is no point to printing checks for negative amounts!

At this point it should be clear to the reader that the ED instruction provides only for automatic negative indication to the *right* of a field! If we wish to print a minus sign to the left of a field, we may test the condition code after normal editing has been accomplished, and place a minus sign to the left of the edited result if a condition code setting of 1 (meaning "negative") is found. We may likewise place a plus sign to the left of positive results, however this is usually unnecessary, since unsigned numbers are generally assumed to be positive.

Consider the following instruction sequence:

			contents after execution					
			WORK−1		WORK			
	MVC	WORK,PAT	?	40	21	4B	20	20
	ED	WORK,NUMB	?	40	40	4B	F0	F4
	BC	11,CONTINUE						
	MVI	WORK−1,C′−′	60	40	40	4B	F0	F4
CONTINUE	:							
	:							
NUMB	DC	PL2′−4′	contains 00 4D					
PAT	DC	X′40214B2020′						
	DS	CL1						
WORK	DS	CL5						

The branch instruction BC   11,CONTINUE (see chapter 11) will transfer program control to the instruction called "CONTINUE" if the condition code is *not* set to 1 (the instructions BNM CONTINUE or BNL CONTINUE would accomplish the same; see chapter 11). In our example, a negative number was edited, hence the condition code was set to 1, and the branch did not take place. Instead, execution proceeded with the MVI instruction which placed a minus sign to the left of the edited result. When printed, the result would appear thus:

   −ƀƀ.04 where ƀ symbolizes a blank.

10.1.5   Editing Several Fields with One Instruction

It is possible to describe one pattern to edit several fields, so that they may all be edited with one ED instruction. This requires the use of yet another control character called a **field separator**, hexadecimal 22, to separate those parts of the extended pattern which correspond to different fields. It is itself replaced by the fill character, and it turns off the significance indicator. Several points must be noted, however, if you wish to use this technique:

- The leftmost character of the extended pattern is treated as the fill character for the entire pattern. Thus each field must use the same fill character.
- The condition code setting after instruction execution reflects only the sign of the *last* field edited.
- Fields to be so edited must be adjacent in storage.

Suppose that we wish to edit 3 packed fields which are 2, 3, and 2 bytes long, respectively. The fields are to appear in the following respective forms:

XXX.X; X,XXX.X−; XXXCR with a blank fill character, and with at least one blank separating each of the fields. The example below gives sample data to illustrate possible results:

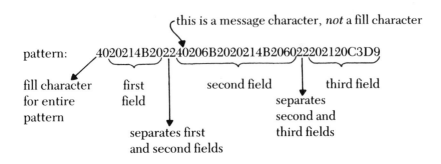

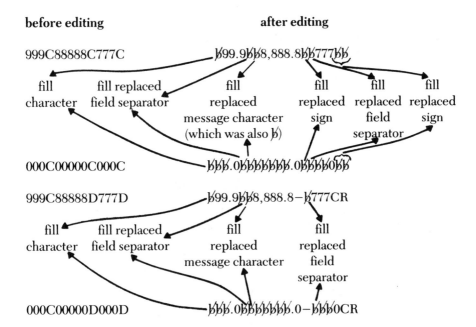

Note here that the fields were adjacent in storage.

Note too that the blank (X'40') following the first field separator is a message character used to provide extra space between the edited results, and is not a fill character. Actually, any message character might have been used here with the same final result, for the significance indicator is off at this point in the left-to-right scan (the field separator turns it off). You will recall that when the significance indicator is off, message characters are replaced by the fill character.

Some Additional Edit Reminders

Before we summarize the workings of the ED instruction, it would be well to emphasize several points which are rather common causes of error for beginning programmers.

We have already noted that the total number of digit selectors plus the total number of significance starters in a pattern should be exactly equal to the number of digits in the packed field being edited. Let us further state that this number will always be odd, for by its very nature a packed field will always contain an odd number of digits (2 per byte + 1 in the low-order byte). Remember always that we do not edit numbers—we edit *fields*! Thus, even though you might be sure (from knowledge of your data) that the number to be edited is a 2-digit number, it will have at least one high-order zero when in packed form (24 would be 024C) and the pattern must be written for a 3-digit number, the leftmost digit of which will be zero-suppressed in the edited result. If the pattern is written for a 2-digit number, the high-order zero will be fetched along with the digit to its right (recall that editing proceeds from left to right) and the low-order digit will be truncated in the edited result.

You have probably noticed, from examining the examples presented in this chapter, that we generally move the pattern to another location—either a work area or an output area—before editing. That is, the first operand of the ED instruction contains a copy of the pattern rather than the original pattern. A typical example would be:

```
              MVC     WORK,PATRN
              ED      WORK,NUMBER

                :

NUMBER        DS      PL2
PATRN         DC      X'40214B202060'
WORK          DS      CL6
```

In order to understand why we wish to edit onto a *copy* of the pattern rather than onto the original, we must envision the program segment as it would appear within the main program. The typical business program will perform the same operations many times, each time on different data. This is accomplished in the program by looping: using the same instructions over and over again. If we were to edit a number onto an original pattern (as opposed to a copy of such) as follows,

```
            ED      PATRN,NUMBER
             .
             .
NUMBER      DS      PL2
PATRN       DC      X'40214B202060'
```

the packed number in NUMBER would be properly edited—the first time! The edited result, however, replaces the previous contents of the first operand location—in this case destroying the original pattern in the process! Later on during program execution, when the instructions loop back to re-use this program segment, the pattern will have been destroyed and will no longer be available.

It is therefore good programming practice to move the pattern to a work area or directly to the output area before editing. In this way we ensure that the original pattern will be preserved for further use, either elsewhere in the program for another field of similar layout, or at the same point of the program. Then looping will bring us back to the point at which we each time copy the pattern, and only the copy is destroyed during the editing process.

One final note of caution: when moving the pattern to a work area or an output area, be sure that the receiving field is equal to the pattern in length! Too short a receiving field will cause part of the pattern to be lost. Too long a field will cause more to be moved than you would actually want. One exception would be a case in which you might want to use the leftmost portion of a longer pattern to edit a shorter field. For example, suppose we wished to edit a 2-byte (3-digit) packed field containing a whole number without using a significance starter, and happened to have the pattern:

```
PAT         DC      X'402020206B2020214B2060'
```

We might code the following:

			contents of WORK after execution			
	MVC	WORK,PAT	40	20	20	20
	ED	WORK,NUM	40	40	F4	F4

NUM	DC	PL2'044'
PAT	DC	X'402020206B2020214B2060'
WORK	DS	CL4

Recall (section 2.4) that the number of bytes moved by the MVC instruction is determined by the first operand length. Thus only the leftmost 4 bytes of PAT are moved and used here for editing.

Note that using the leftmost portion of a longer pattern precludes using that feature of the ED instruction which automatically signs negative fields. However, we may still test the condition code for a setting of "1" (a negative indication) and then move the sign or signs into place with additional instructions (see section 10.1.4).

10.1.6   The ED Instruction Summarized

The ED Instruction (**ED**it)

Instruction type: Machine Instruction
Machine format: SS Instruction (Storage to Storage Instruction)

DE	L	B1	D1	B2	D2
0	7 8	15 16 19 20	31 32	35 36	47

Symbolic format:

	name	operation	operands
	[symbolic name]	ED	name1,name2
or	[symbolic name]	ED	D1(L,B1),D2(B2)

where D1 and B1 are the displacement and base register respectively used to calculate the first operand address, and D2 and B2 are the displacement and base register respectively used to calculate the second operand address. L is the operand length.

. . . .

Rules:
- The second operand must contain a packed number.
- The first operand must contain an edit pattern. Characters include the digit selector (X'20'), significance starter (X'21'), field separator (X'22') and message character(s) (any other characters).
- Overlapping operands give unpredictable results.

Condition Code:

0	if last source field = 0
1	if last source field < 0
2	if last source field > 0
3	cannot result from this instruction

Table 1 (opposite page) summarizes the editing functions. The leftmost 4 columns indicate conditions which may exist before execution of the ED instruction. The rightmost 2 columns indicate the type of character placed in the result, and the new state of the significance indicator, which result from executing the ED instruction under that particular combination of conditions.

10.2   THE EDIT AND MARK INSTRUCTION

The Edit and Mark (EDMK) instruction functions exactly as does the Edit instruction, except that it performs one additional step, which makes it possible for the programmer to provide floating symbols to the left of the printed field.

10.2.1   Fixed vs Floating Symbols

A floating symbol is one which appears immediately to the left of the first significant digit of the field, rather than at a fixed point of the field.

The most commonly used floating symbols are the dollar sign and the arithmetic signs: plus and minus.

CONDITIONS				RESULTS	
pattern character	signi- ficance indi- cator	source digit	low- order half of source byte	result character	new setting of signi- ficance indicator
digit selector	off	0	(i)	fill character	off
"	off	1-9	not plus	source digit	on
"	off	1-9	plus	source digit	off
"	on	0-9	not plus	source digit	on
"	on	0-9	plus	source digit	off
significance starter	off	0	not plus	fill character	on
"	off	0	plus	fill character	off
"	off	1-9	not plus	source digit	on
"	off	1-9	plus	source digit	off
"	on	0-9	not plus	source digit	on
"	on	0-9	plus	source digit	off
message character	off	(ii)	(ii)	fill character	off
"	on	(ii)	(ii)	message character	on
field separator	(i)	(ii)	(ii)	fill character	off

(i) does not affect result
(ii) source digit not examined

TABLE 1

The chart below illustrates 2 ways of printing some sample data, using fixed and floating dollar signs.

fixed $	floating $
$ 19,876.54	$19,876.54
$ 9,876.54	$9,876.54
$ 876.54	$876.54
$ 76.54	$76.54
$ 6.54	$6.54

Coding for a Fixed Dollar Sign

A few moments' thought will surely determine how to produce a fixed dollar sign in our printed output: after normal editing is completed, simply move the dollar sign into place! In fact, the dollar sign may be moved right over the fill character, which remains leftmost in the edited result and is generally superfluous after editing has been performed.

Consider the following instruction sequence to edit a 3-byte currency field with a fixed dollar sign:

		contents of WORK after execution

MVC	WORK,PAT	40 20 20 21 4B 20 20 C3 D9
ED	WORK,NUMB	40 40 F4 F3 4B F2 F1 40 40
MVI	WORK,C'$'	5B 40 F4 F3 4B F2 F1 40 40

$$\vdots$$

NUMB	DC	PL3'4321'	contains 04 32 1C
PAT	DC	X'402020214B2020C3D9'	
WORK	DS	CL9	

Note that the symbol "$" is represented in computer memory as a hexadecimal 5B.

If the contents of WORK were printed after execution of the above sequence of instructions, the results would appear as: $b̸43.21b̸b̸ where b̸ is the character blank. A similar procedure was followed in section 10.1.4 to obtain a minus sign to the left of negative fields.

Fixed symbols, therefore, present no problem. The difficulty with floating symbols arises because we wish them printed to the left of the *first significant character*! Not only is the location of a first significant character unknown at the time the program is being written (instructions are written to work with *variable fields*, not with constants), but the location of the first significant digit will very likely be different each time editing is done, even on the same field, since field contents change!

The following section will demonstrate how the EDMK instruction may be used to produce floating symbols.

10.2.2 Using the EDMK Instruction

The EDMK instruction is identical to the ED instruction in every way, but performs one additional function. It places the *address* of the first significant digit of the edited result into register 1, *if* detecting that digit caused the significance indicator to be turned on. This address is precisely what we need, for floating symbols are to be placed into the address preceding that of the first significant digit.

There is one problem, however. If the significance indicator is turned on by a significance starter in the pattern rather than by a significant digit, the EDMK instruction will not place anything into register 1. This fact should not be too distressing, however, once we realize that we may write the code for this case on our own, for we already know the address of the significance starter!

We will therefore first load the *address* (*not* the contents) of the location following the significance starter into register 1. Then we execute the EDMK instruction. If significance is established by the significance starter, then the character immediately following it becomes the "first significant character" for this field, and its address is in register 1, for we placed it there! If significance is established earlier by detecting an actual significant digit before the significance starter is reached, the EDMK instruction will place the address of that digit into register 1, destroying that which we had previously placed there! In either case, after execution of the EDMK instruction, we will have the address of the first significant character of the field in register 1.

Suppose that we have a 3-byte currency field to be edited with 2 decimal positions, a CR symbol for negative amounts, and a floating dollar sign.

Example:

contents of WORK after execution

MVC	WORK,PATRN	40 20 20 21 4B 20 20 40 C3 D9	
		WORK+4	
LA	1,WORK+4		
EDMK	WORK,AMT	40 40 40 F2 4B F1 F1 40 40 40	
		WORK+3	
BCTR	1,0		
MVI	0(1),C'$'	40 40 5B F2 4B F1 F1 40 40 40	
		WORK+2	

$\vdots$

AMT	DC	PL3'211'	contains 00 21 1C
PATRN	DC	X'402020214B202040C3D9'	
WORK	DS	CL10	

In this example, the pattern is defined as usual, and moved to an area called WORK, where the editing is to take place. Examining the pattern in WORK, we note that if significance is later established in our packed field by the significance starter, the decimal point (X'4B') will be the "first significant character" of the field. We thus use the LA (Load Address) instruction to place the *address* of the decimal point into register 1. (The deciimal point, X'4B', is the 5th character of the field, hence WORK+4.) The LA instruction will be explained in greater detail in the next section.

The EDMK instruction is executed next. In addition to editing the number in AMT as would the ED instruction, the EDMK notes that significance was established in this particular field *not* by the significance starter, but by the detection of the significant digit "2". The EDMK instruction thus places the address of the location in which the edited "2" is found (the 4th byte of WORK, hence WORK+3) into register 1, destroying the address which had been previously stored in register 1 by the LA instruction. WORK+3 thus replaces WORK+4 in register 1.

The purpose of identifying the first significant character is to find the location into which the dollar sign is to be placed. We wish to move the dollar sign into the position *preceding* the first significant character, not over it! We now have the address of the first significant character in register 1. Reducing the value of that address by 1 will give us the location number into which we will place the dollar sign, in this case, the address of WORK+2. The BCTR (**B**ranch on **C**oun**T** **R**egister) instruction with a second operand of 0 reduces the contents of the first operand register (in this example, register 1) by 1 and does not branch. It is the simplest and most efficient way of reducing the contents of a register by 1. (Alternate methods would involve one of the binary subtract instructions S or SH, for we assume contents of registers to be in binary form.) The BCTR instruction is explained more extensively in chapter 11.

The final instruction in our program segment moves the dollar sign into place. We know that the address of the location into which we wish to place the dollar sign is in register 1. However, without knowing the exact value of the data (and we certainly do *not* know its value at the time these instructions are written), we do not know what that location is! We know only that its address is in register 1.

We may overcome this apparent difficulty by using a "base-displacement" method for describing the first operand of the MVI instruction. The general form is D(B)   (D means "displacement", B means "base register") which may be interpreted as: the address which may be found by considering the content of register B (where B is some register number) and adding to it the number D (where D is a non-negative decimal number).

The instruction MVI   0(1),C'$' of our program segment thus moves the character "$" into that location which is found by adding zero (the displacement) to the contents of register 1 (the base register). Adding zero to any quantity leaves its value unchanged, so we are moving the "$" into the location given by the contents of register 1. (The displacement of 0 obviously did not contribute to the result here, but was necessary to conform to the required notation for base-displacement addressing.)

The field of our program segment, when printed, will appear thus:
    ⌀⌀$2.11⌀⌀⌀   where ⌀ is the character blank.

The example below gives sample data and edited results when using the instruction sequence explained above to produce a decimal point, CR sign indication for negative fields, and floating dollar sign.

Example V:
        pattern: 402020214B202040C3D9

before editing	after editing
54321+	$543.21
04321+	$43.21
00321+	$3.21
00021+	$.21
00001+	$.01
00000+	$.00
54321−	$543.21 CR
00000−	$.00 CR

It would be a very valuable exercise at this point to review these values along with the instruction sequence above to ensure that you understand how each edited result was obtained.

One further note before we summarize the EDMK instruction: when several fields are edited with one EDMK instruction (through use of field separators), the address of the first significant character which established significance for each field is in turn stored in register 1. However, after execution has been completed, *only* the first significant character of the last field edited remains in register 1. Therefore it would be possible to insert a floating currency symbol *only* in the last field of that group.

10.2.3 The EDMK Instruction Summarized

The EDMK Instruction (**ED**it and Mar**K**)

Instruction type: Machine Instruction
Machine format: SS Instruction (Storage to Storage Instruction)

DF	L	B1	D1	B2	D2

0   7 8   15 16   19 20   31 32   35 36   47

Symbolic format:

	name	operation	operands
	[symbolic name]	EDMK	name1,name2
or	[symbolic name]	EDMK	D1(L,B1),D2(B2)

where D1 and B1 are the displacement and base register respectively
        used to calculate the first operand address, and D2 and B2 are
        the displacement and base register respectively used to calculate
        the second operand address. L is the operand length.

. . . .

Rules:
- The second operand must contain a packed number.
- The first operand must contain an edit pattern. Characters include the digit selector (X'20'), significance starter (X'21'), field separator (X'22') and message character(s) (any other characters).
- Overlapping operands give unpredictable results.

Condition Code:

  0   if last source field $= 0$

  1   if last source field < 0

  2   if last source field > 0

  3   cannot result from this instruction

Table 1 (section 10.1.6), which summarizes the editing functions, applies to the EDMK instruction as well. In addition, the EDMK places the address of each first significant result character (provided the significance indicator was off before it was examined) into register 1.

The LA Instruction

The LA Instruction (**L**oad **A**ddress)

Instruction type: Machine Instruction

Machine format: RX Instruction (**R**egister and Inde**X**ed Storage Instruction)

41	R1	X2	B2	D2

0   7 8   11 12   15 16   19 20   31

Symbolic format:

	name	operation	operands
	[symbolic name]	LA	R1,name2
or	[symbolic name]	LA	R1,D2(X2,B2)

where R1 is a general register number. D2, X2, and B2 are the displacement, index register, and base register respectively used to calculate the second operand address.

Condition Code: The condition code remains unchanged.

The LA instruction places the *address* (not the contents) of the second operand location into the low-order 24 bits of the first operand register (bits 8 — 31). The high-order 8 bits are set to 0 (bits 0 — 7). Any address may be represented in base-displacement form in 24 bits.

Example:

LA   2,PLACE

⋮

PLACE   DC   CL2'AB'

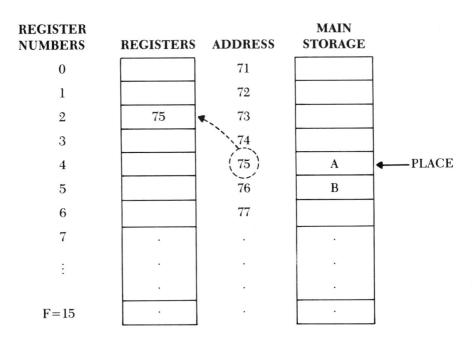

Note that the *address* assigned to PLACE (the second operand) is stored in register 2 (the first operand). The *contents* of the second operand location are not inspected by the LA instruction.

10.3   FORMS CONTROL AND STACKER SELECTION

In addition to producing computer output which is correct and legible, we would like to see our printed results properly spaced on the output forms, with appropriate top and bottom margins and other intermediate spacing as desired. Have you taken this for granted? Well, it is the programmer's responsibility to provide the proper spacing and skipping instructions. In this section we will discuss 2 macro instructions which control the movement of continuous form printer units. For forms control,

The CNTRL (**CoNTRoL**) macro instruction will be used to:
- ensure that our output begins at the top of a new page
- control spacing as desired: single, double, or triple spacing; skipping over a portion of a page for special formatting.

The PRTOV (**PRinT OV**erflow) macro instruction will:
- test for page overflow at some predesignated position, then branch to an appropriate routine.

We will also discuss carriage control techniques for spooled systems.

10.3.1 Carriage Control

The continuous form printer devices commonly used with IBM/360 and 370 computers have carriage mechanisms which operate under control of a **carriage control tape**. The carriage mechanisms are able to accommodate forms of many different lengths. Appropriate tapes are prepared for forms of different lengths and are punched to conform to the spacing desired by the installation for that form.

Figure 10.1 illustrates the alignment of the carriage control tape with a printer form. The tape should be positioned so that the top line is even with the top of the form. Note how the tape is marked into vertical columns (numbered 1 through 12) which we call **channels** and into horizontal rows which correspond to printed rows on the continuous form. Holes may be punched in the carriage control tape in any or all channels. They will be punched in rows which correspond to positions of the form to which we wish the paper skipped in our program. For example, if we were printing on line 5 and the next line were to be printed 10 lines below that, we would instruct the computer to skip, say, to channel 3, which was punched corresponding to line 15 on the printed form. The actual skipping will be controlled by computer instruction. In general, a punch in channel 1 will be made in the position at which we wish our first line to be printed. A punch will be made in either channel 9 or 12 to designate the last line to be printed (overflow). After the channels have been punched, the tape line corresponding to the bottom edge of the form is cut and the bottom edge of the tape is glued to the top portion marked GLUE.

The holes in the center of the tape are prepunched and are unrelated to the channel punches. They serve merely to place the tape on a pin-feed mechanism which causes the tape to advance along with the movement of the actual printer carriage.

As we shall see, the instructions which provide for skipping will refer to channel numbers to designate form positions to which advancement is to take

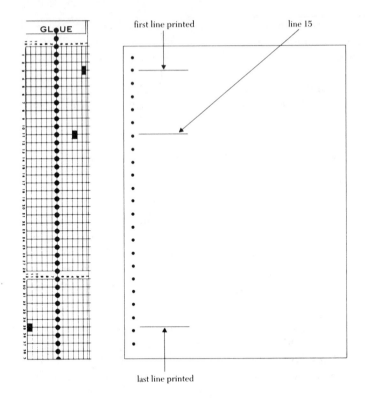

Figure 10.1
Carriage Control Tape and Continuous Form Paper

place. The carriage control tape must be properly prepared and mounted if our instructions are to perform properly.

10.3.2 The CNTRL Macro Instruction

Each PUT instruction designating a printer file provides automatic carriage movement of 1 space for each line. The CNTRL macro may be used to provide extra spacing. In addition, it may be used to **select** (choose) the stacker of read-punch units into which we wish punched card output to fall or from which we wish to read.

The CNTRL Instruction (**CoNTRoL**)

Instruction type: Macro Instruction
Symbolic format:

name	operation	operands
[symbolic name]	CNTRL	filename,code,n,m

. . . .

Rules:
- On DOS systems, the DTF macro defining the file whose output is to be controlled by the CNTRL instruction must include the parameter CONTROL=YES.
- On OS systems, the DCB macro defining the file whose output is to be controlled by the CONTRL instruction must include the parameter MACRF=PMC.
- The first 2 parameters (filename,code) are required; the last 2 are optional
- The parameters must appear in the above order. If the third parameter is omitted, a second comma after the second parameter should be used to indicate the omission.
- The first parameter (filename) must be the same symbolic name assigned to the file by the DTF or DCB macro.
- The second parameter (code) specifies the type of operation we wish performed.
- The third parameter (n) is used when we wish either
    - stacker selection, or
    - immediate carriage control (the carriage moves as soon as the CNTRL instruction is encountered)
- The fourth parameter (m) is used when we wish delayed carriage control (the computer will wait until after the next write command, and only then will carriage movement take place).

The following chart summarizes the possible parameter entries for the CNTRL macro.

UNIT	MNEMONIC CODE	n	m	COMMAND
2540 Card Reader	PS	1 2 3		select pocket 1, 2, or 3
2520, 1442 Card Read-Punch	SS	1 2		select stacker 1 or 2
	E			Eject to stacker 1 (1442 only)
1403, 1404, 1443 1445 Printers	SP	1 2 3	1 2 3	carriage space 1, 2, or 3 lines
	SK	1-12 (i)	1-12 (j)	skip to channel (i) immediate and/or channel (j) delayed

Spacing and Skipping

Example 1:

```
PUT     OUTFILE,OUTAREA
CNTRL   OUTFILE,SP,2
```

Here the PUT macro causes the printer to automatically space 1 line. Then the CNTRL macro causes an immediate double space. The net effect of the two instructions is therefore 3 spaces between lines.

Example 2:

```
CNTRL   OUTFILE,SP,,2
PUT     OUTFILE,OUTAREA
```

In this example, the CNTRL macro designates *delayed* spacing of 2 lines; that is, the spacing will take place after execution of the next PUT instruction. In this situation, the automatic single spacing will not take place. Thus the net effect of these two instructions is only 2 spaces between lines.

Example 3:

```
PUT     OUTFILE,OUTAREA
CNTRL  OUTFILE,SK,1
```

The CNTRL macro above will cause an immediate skip to channel 1 (the top of the next page).

Example 4:

```
CNTRL  OUTFILE,SK,,1
PUT     OUTFILE, OUTAREA
```

This CNTRL macro will cause a skip to channel 1 after execution of the PUT instruction.

In general, any combination of space and skip commands issued consecutively will result in proper execution of them all, with the following exceptions:
  1. If there are more than 1 consecutive immediate skip instructions for the same printer file, only the first will be executed. The others will be ignored.
  2. If there are more than 1 consecutive delayed skip and/or space instructions for the same printer file, only the last will be executed.

Stacker Selection

"Stacker selection" is directing a card to a particular pocket or stacker of a card input/output device. We shall consider the 2540 Card Read-Punch unit as an example.

The 2540 Card Read-Punch has 5 stackers into which cards may fall.

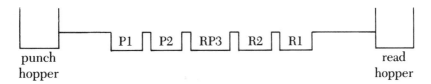

When cards are read they normally fall into stacker R1 on the reader side, and cards being punched normally fall into stacker P1 on the punch side. However the CNTRL macro may override these conventions to allow cards being read to fall into pocket R1, R2, or RP3 and punched cards to fall into pocket P1, P2 or RP3, depending upon whether the third parameter of the CNTRL is specified as 1,2, or 3, respectively.

Example 5:

```
GET     INFILE,INAREA
CNTRL  INFILE,PS,3
```

The CNTRL macro above will select the card being read into pocket RP3.

When selecting stackers from the read side:
- The CNTRL macro must *follow* the GET (may not precede it)
- Once the CNTRL macro is used with one GET for a file, it must be used with every GET for that file (although different pockets may be used).

Example 6:

```
CNTRL  OUTFILE,PS,2
PUT     OUTFILE,OUTAREA
```

The CNTRL instruction will select the card being punched into stacker P2.

When selecting stackers from the punch side:
- The CNTRL macro must *precede* the PUT for that record
- The CNTRL *need not*, however, precede every PUT for the file.

10.3.3   The PRTOV Macro Instruction

The PRTOV macro is the programmer's means of recognizing the end of a page (the last line upon which we wish to print: usually channel 12), so that he may skip to channel 1 of the next page and continue from there with new headings or detail output.

The PRTOV Instruction (**PR**in**T OV**erflow)

Instruction type: Macro Instruction
Symbolic format:

name	operation	operands
[symbolic name]	PRTOV	filename,n,routine-name

. . . .

Rules:
- On DOS systems, the DTF macro defining the file whose output is to be cnotrolled by the PRTOV instruction must include the parameter PRINTOV=YES.
- The first 2 parameters are required; the third is optional.
- The parameters must appear in the above order.

- The first parameter (filename) must be the same symbolic name assigned to the file by the DTF or DCB macro.
- The second parameter (n) specifies the channel punch with which the programmer intends to signal an overflow (end of page) condition. This is usually channel 12, but channel 9 may also be used.
- The third parameter (routine-name) is the name of a routine (a group of instructions) to which we wish program control to transfer upon sensing an overflow condition. (The return address — that of the instruction following the PRTOV — will be saved in general register 14.)
- If the third parameter is omitted and an overflow condition is sensed, an automatic skip is effected to channel 1 (the top of the next page), and execution continues sequentially.
- In the absence of an overflow condition, program execution continues sequentially, without any skipping.
- The routine to which we branch by means of the PRTOV instruction may not contain another PRTOV instruction.

Example 7:

```
PUT     OUTFILE,OUTAREA
PRTOV   OUTFILE,12
```

The PRTOV macro above tests for an overflow condition. (Actually, sensing channel 12 in this case will cause an overflow indicator to be turned on, and the instruction tests the overflow indicator.) If an overflow condition does not exist, nothing occurs and the next sequential instruction is executed. If the overflow indicator is on, an automatic skip will be effected to the top of the next page, and then program execution continues sequentially.

Example 8:

```
                    PUT     OUTFILE,OUTAREA
                    PRTOV   OUTFILE,12,ROUTINE
         NEXT       :

         ROUTINE ST    14,HOLD   save address of NEXT
                    :
subroutine          L     14,HOLD   put address of NEXT back into
                                    register 14

                    BR    14        branch back to NEXT
                    :
```

In this example, the PRTOV instruction tests for an overflow condition. If the overflow indicator is off, sequential execution continues. If the overflow indicator is on, a skip to channel 1 is *not* effected. Instead the address of the instruction following the PRTOV ("NEXT" in this example) will be automatically placed into register 14 and an automatic branch will be effected to the "subroutine", a group of instructions the first of which is named ROUTINE (indicated by the third parameter).

At ROUTINE, the address of NEXT (now in register 14) is stored in a main storage location (called HOLD in our program), and the succeeding instructions will be executed sequentially. At the end of the routine, the address of NEXT is placed back into register 14 from HOLD (by the instruction L 14,HOLD), and the BR 14 instruction tells the computer to "branch to the location whose address is to be found in register 14"; in other words, branch back to NEXT. The BR instruction will be explained further in chapter 12.

The reason that it was necessary to save the contents of register 14 during execution of the routine is that certain other macro instructions make use of that register. By saving its contents, we protect the address of NEXT from being inadvertently destroyed.

A more extensive discussion of branching to program routines will be found in chapter 11.

10.3.4   Carriage Control on Spooled Systems

Many S/360 and S/370 systems use a technique called **spooling** for the reading and writing of data sets. Spooling is used to improve throughput by minimizing the time necessary for input and output with such slow-speed I/O devices as the card reader and printer. Spooling is always supported by special software.

For card input on a spooled system, cards are read **off-line** (they may alternately be read during **slack** periods, that is, when the computer is in **wait state** — see chapter 13) directly onto a faster device such as disk or tape. Then the card image data is read by the computer directly from the high-speed device. As can be seen, this technique circumvents (or at worst, minimizes) the deleterious effect of the slower input device on I/O time.

Likewise, printed output on a spooled system is spooled to a high-speed device such as disk or tape. The output data is printed later, either off-line or during the computer's slack periods.

The CNTRL and PRTOV macros discussed above cannot be used to control vertical spacing on systems with spooled output. Instead, we control vertical spacing of printed output records by appending a special **carriage control character** (also called a **spacing control character**) to the beginning of each such record. The choice of control character used will determine the type of spacing effected.

The most common control characters and their respective effects upon spacing are noted below:

carriage control character	effect upon spacing
b̸ (blank)	normal single space
0	double space to the next line
−	triple space to the next line
+	suppress spacing before printing the next line
1	skip to top of next page before printing the next line

Note that the carriage control character is an *extra* character on the output record and must be the *first* character of the record. That is, an output record which would ordinarily be defined to be 132 characters long would now be defined to consist of 133 characters, the first of which is the carriage control character.

Note too that the sole purpose of the carriage control character is to give carriage control commands to the printer. It is itself *not printed* on the output line.

10.4   THE COMRG AND TIME MACRO INSTRUCTIONS

The COMRG Macro

The COMRG ("Communications Region") macro instruction is used on DOS systems to obtain the *address* of a special area of the DOS supervisor called the **Communications Region**. The Communications Region contains, among other things, the current date which the computer operator communicates to the system on a daily basis as part of a standard procedure. Once the address of the Communications Region is obtained, the programmer may obtain information from that region for his own use.

The COMRG Instruction (**COM**munications **ReG**ion)

Instruction type: Macro Instruction
Symbolic format:

name	operation	operand	
[symbolic name]	COMRG		$\left\{\begin{array}{l}\text{operand(s)}\\ \text{not}\\ \text{allowed}\end{array}\right.$

Example:

```
        COMRG
        MVC     DATE,0(1)
        ⋮
DATE        DS      CL8
```

The COMRG instruction places the address of the Communications Region into register 1. Register 1 is always used. We do not, however, know what that address is; we know only that it is in register 1. The instruction MVC DATE,0(1) therefore uses the base-displacement mode of addressing, where D(B) implies an address computed by adding the contents of a register (B) to a displacement (D). We may interpret the MVC instruction as follows: move the contents of the address obtained by adding the contents of register 1 to 0 (that is, the contents of the address in register 1, which is the contents of the communications region) into the place called DATE. The MVC instruction thus places the current date into a location called DATE where it may be used as, say, part of a heading line.

The TIME Macro

The TIME macro instruction is used on OS systems to obtain the date and time of day.

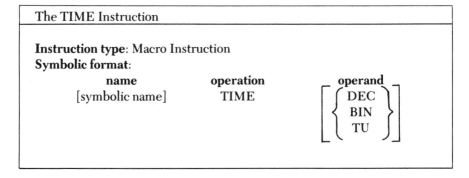

The TIME Instruction

Instruction type: Macro Instruction
Symbolic format:

name	operation	operand
[symbolic name]	TIME	$\left[\left\{\begin{array}{l}\text{DEC}\\ \text{BIN}\\ \text{TU}\end{array}\right\}\right]$

Upon execution of the TIME macro, the date is placed into register 1 as packed decimal digits of the form 00yydddc. "yy" are the last two digits of the year, "ddd" is the day of the year, and "c" is the sign, which will be hexadecimal F. For example, if the date returned is of the form 0079032F, the date is February 1, 1979; that is, the 32nd day of 1979. The date would be unpacked for printing. For example, we might code

```
              TIME                    place date into register 1
              ST      1,PLACE         store date in packed form
              UNPK    DBL,PLACE       unpack date for printing
                ⋮

PLACE         DS      F
DBL           DS      D
```

The time of day is placed into register 0 in the form specified in the operand portion of the TIME instruction:

- DEC yields packed decimal digits of the form HHMMSSth where HH is hours, MM is minutes, SS is seconds, t is .1 second, and h is .01 second. The packed digits can be unpacked by changing the "h" value to a zoned sign and using the UNPK instruction.
- BIN yields a binary number indicating the time in units of .01 second.
- TU yields a binary number indicating the time in **timer units** (a timer unit is 26.04166 microseconds).

If the operand portion is omitted altogether, the time of day will be given in the form of packed digits, as though an operand of DEC had been coded.

10.5   A REPORT PROGRAM WITH EDITING AND FORMS CONTROL

In this section, we present a simple program which makes use of the techniques introduced in this chapter. Read the program carefully to be sure that you understand the reasons behind each step. If there is a point which is not perfectly clear, refer back to the appropriate section to review the relevant technique.

Program input will be in the form of item records on punched cards. One card will be supplied per item. Each card will contain 3 fields, as described on figure 10.2. An item number will be recorded in columns 41 through 47; the unit price of the item will be recorded in columns 10 through 13; the number of such items sold will be recorded in columns 22 through 24.

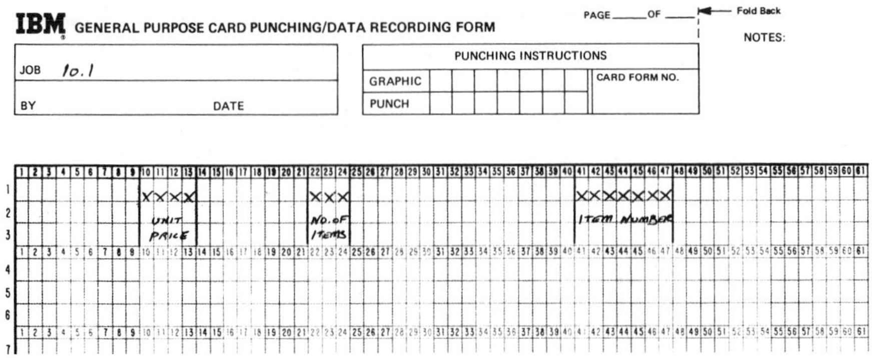

Figure 10.2
Input Layout for Report Program with Editing and Forms Control

The purpose of the program will be to produce a printed report, as described on the printer layout worksheet of figure 10.3.

Note that the first header line contains the page number. The program should provide for the possibility of printed output extending to more than one page, with each page appropriately numbered and containing its own header lines. Output fields should be edited as indicated, with floating dollar signs in the unit-price field.

Figure 10.4 is a flowchart describing the program logic. The program listing and output are shown in figure 10.5.

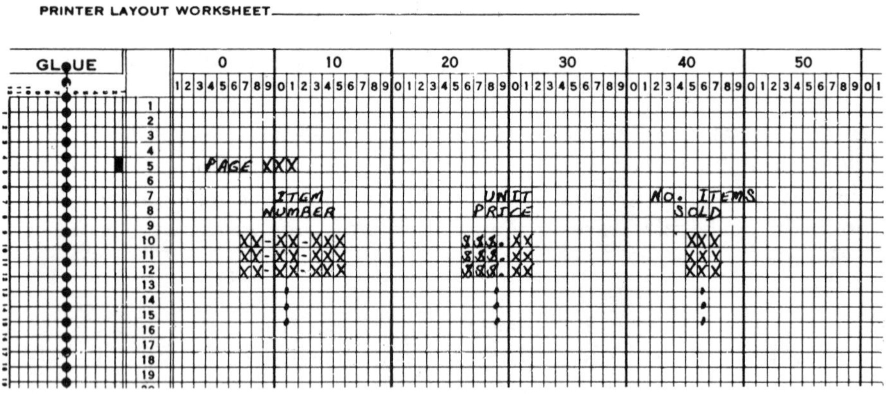

Figure 10.3
Output Layout for Report Program with Editing and Forms Control

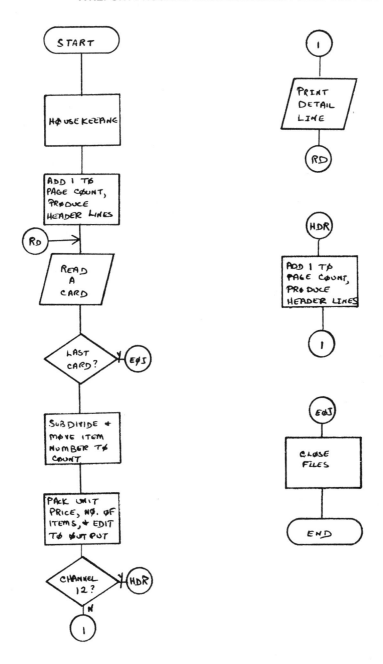

Figure 10.4
Flowchart for Report Program with Editing and Forms Control

```
LOC   OBJECT CODE    ADDR1 ADDR2  STMT   SOURCE STATEMENT                                          17 NOV 78

                                    1          PRINT NOGEN
CCCCC0                              2          START
                                    3  * SET UP BASE REGISTER
CCCCCC 0560                         4  BEGIN   BALR  6,0
                           CC002    5          USING *,6
                                    6  *
                                    7  * PROCEDURES
                                    8  *
                                    9  * THIS PROGRAM WILL ACCEPT ONE CARD PER ITEM, WITH ITEM NUMBER, UNIT
                                   10  * PRICE, AND NUMBER OF SUCH ITEMS SOLD.
                                   11  * OUTPUT WILL INCLUDE HEADER LINES ON EACH PAGE, WITH APPROPRIATE PAGE
                                   12  * NUMBER AND DATE. DETAIL OUTPUT WILL CONSIST OF EDITED VERSIONS OF THE
                                   13  * INPUT FIELDS
                                   14  *
                                   15  * HOUSEKEEPING
CCCCC2                             16          OPEN  (INPT,INPUT,OUTPT,OUTPUT)
                                   24  * FOR DOS PROGRAMS, FILES ARE OPENED BY
                                   25  *      OPEN  INPT,OUTPT
                                   26  * FIRST PAGE HEADINGS
CCC012                             27          CNTRL OUTPT,SK,1
CCC022 D234 62B3 62B2 002B5 C02B4  33          MVC   OUTAREA,OUTAREA-1           CLEAR OUTPUT AREA
CCC028 D203 62EF 6389 C02F1 C038B  34          MVC   PAGENO,PATPAGE
CCC02E DE03 62EF 6387 002F1 C0389  35          ED    PAGENO,PAGE
CCC034                             36          PUT   OUTPT,HEADER1
CCC042                             41          CNTRL OUTPT,SP,1
CCC05C                             46          PUT   OUTPT,HEADER2
CCC05E                             51          PUT   OUTPT,HEADER3
CCC06C                             56          CNTRL OUTPT,SP,1
                                   61  *
                                   62  * DETAIL ROUTINE
                                   63  *
CCC07A                             64  READ    GET   INPT,INAREA
CCC088 D201 62B9 628A 002BB C028C  69          MVC   OITM1,ITM1                  SUBDIVIDE
CCC08E D201 62BC 628C C02BE C028E  70          MVC   OITM2,ITM2                  ITEM
CCC094 D202 62BF 628E 002C1 C0290  71          MVC   OITM3,ITM3                  NUMBER
                                   72  *
CCC09A F223 638D 626B 0038F C026D  73          PACK  PPRICE,PRICE
CCC0A0 D206 62CB 639C C02CD C0392  74          MVC   OPRICE,PATI
CCC0A6 4110 62CF             002D1 75          LA    1,OPRICE+4
CCC0AA DF06 62CB 638D 002CD C039F  76          EDMK  OPRICE,PPRICE              EDMK UNIT PRICE
CCC0BC C610                        77          BCTR  1,0
CCC0B2 925B 1C00            00000  78          MVI   0(1),C'$'
                                   79  *
CCC0B6 F212 6397 6277 00399 C0279  80          PACK  PNUM,NUM
CCC0BC D203 62DE 6399 C02EC C039B  81          MVC   ONUM,PAT2
CCC0C2 DE03 62DE 6397 002E0 00399  82          ED    ONUM,PNUM                  EDIT NO. ITEMS SOLD
                                   83  *
CCC0C8                             84          PRTOV OUTPT,12,HEADRT             TEST FOR PAGE OVERFLOW
CCC1C8                            102          PUT   OUTPT,OUTAREA
CCC116 47F0 6078            C007A  107          B     READ
                                  108  *
                                  109  * HEADER SUBROUTINE
CCC11A 50E0 639E            C03A0 110  HEADRT  ST    14,SAVE
CCC11E                            111          CNTRL OUTPT,SK,1
C0012E FA10 6387 63A6 00389 C03A8 117          AP    PAGE,=P'1'
```

Figure 10.5 (Part 1)
Report Program Using ED, EDMK, CNTRL, PRTOV

LOC	OBJECT CODE	ADDR1	ADDR2	STMT	SOURCE STATEMENT	

```
COC134 D2O3 62EF 6389 CO2F1 CO38B   118         MVC   PAGENC,PATPAGE
CCC13A DE03 62EF 6387 CC2F1 CO389   119         ED    PAGENC,PAGE
CCC14C                              120         PUT   CUTPT,HEADER1
CCC14E                              125         CNTRL CUTPT,SP,1
CCC15C                              130         PUT   CUTPT,HEADER2
CCC16A                              135         PUT   CUTPT,HEADER3
CCC178                              140         CNTRL CUTPT,SP,1
CCC186 58E0 639E          003A0     145         L     14,SAVE          RESTORE RETURN ADRS TO REG 14
CCC18A C7FE                         146         BR    14               RETURN
                                    147 *
CCC18C                              148 FINISH  CLOSE (INPT)
CCC196                              154         CLOSF (CUTPT)
                                    160 * FOR DOS PROGRAMS, FILES ARE CLOSED BY
                                    161 *         CLOSE INPT,CUTPT
CCC1A2 CA03                         162         SVC   3
                                    163 * FOR DOS, PROGRAM EXECUTION IS HALTED BY
                                    164 *         EOJ
                                    165 *
                                    166 * FILE DEFINITIONS
                                    167 *
                                    168 INPT    CCB   CSCRG=PS,MACRF=GM,DDNAME=SYSIPT,BLKSIZE=80,LRECL=80,   C
CCC1A4                                            ECDAD=FINISH,RECFM=F
                                    222 OUTPT   CCB   DSORG=PS,MACRF=PMC,DDNAME=SYSLST,BLKSIZE=53,LRECL=53,   C
CCC2E4                                            RECFM=F
                                    276 * FOR DOS PROGRAMS, FILE DEFINITIONS ARE PERFORMED BY THE DTF MACROS
                                    277 * AND BUFFER DEFINITIONS
                                    278 *INPT   DTFCD DEVADCR=SYSRDR,IOAREA1=INA,EOFADDR=FINISH,WORKA=YES
                                    279 *CUTPT  DTFPR DEVADCR=SYSLST,IOAREA1=OUTA,BLKSIZE=132,CONTROL=YES,
                                    280 *                 WORKA=YES
                                    281 *INA    DS    CL80             BUFFER FOR INPUT FILE
                                    282 *OUTA   DS    CL132            BUFFER FOR OUTPUT FILE
                                    283 *
                                    284 * AREA DEFINITICNS
                                    285 *
CCC264                              286 INAREA  CS    0CL80
CCC264                              287         CS    CL9
CCC26D                              288 PRICE   CS    CL4
CCC271                              289         CS    CL8
CCC279                              290 NUM     CS    CL3
CCC27C                              291         CS    CL16
CCC28C                              292 ITMNC   DS    0CL7
CCC28C                              293 ITM1    CS    CL2
CCC28E                              294 ITM2    DS    CL2
CCC29C                              295 ITM3    CS    CL3
CCC293                              296         DS    CL33
                                    297 *
CCC2B4 40                           298         CC    C' '
CCC2B5                              299 CUTAREA DS    0CL53
CCC2B5                              300         CS    CL6
CCC2BB                              301 OITMNC  CS    0CL9
CCC2BB                              302 OITM1   CS    CL2
CCC2BD                              303         CS    CL1
CCC2BE                              304 OITM2   CS    CL2
CCC2CO                              305         CS    CL1
CCC2C1                              306 OITM3   CS    CL3
```

Figure 10.5 (Part 2)
Report Program Using ED, EDMK, CNTRL, PRTOV

LOC   OBJECT CODE   ADDR1 ADDR2   STMT   SOURCE STATEMENT

```
CCC2C4                                    307            DS    CL9
CCC2CD                                    308 CPRICE     DS    CL7
CCC2D4                                    309            DS    CL12
CCC2E0 ONUM                               310 ONUM       DS    CL4
CCC2E4                                    311            DS    CL6
                                          312 *
CCC2EA                                    313 HEADER1    DS    0CL53
CCC2EA 404040                             314            DC    CL3' '
CCC2ED D7C1C7C5                           315            DC    CL4'PAGE'
CCC2F1                                    316 PAGENO     DS    CL4
CCC2F5 404040404040404040                 317            DC    CL42' '
                                          318 *
CCC31F 404040404040404040                 319 HEADER2    DC    CL53'      ITEM              UNIT           NO. ITEMS'
                                          320 *
CCC354 404040404040404D5                  321 HEADER3    DC    CL53'      NUMBER           PRICE            SOLD'
                                          322 *
CCC389 C01C                               323 PAGE       DC    PL2'1'                         RUNNING COUNT OF PAGE NUMBERS
CCC38B 40202020                           324 PATPAGE    DC    X'40202020'
                                          325 *
CCC38F                                    326 PPRICE     DS    PL3
CCC392 402020214B2020                     327 PAT1       DC    X'402020214B2020'
CCC399                                    328 PNUM       DS    PL2
CCC39B 40202120                           329 PAT2       DC    X'40202120'
                                          330 *
CCC3AC                                    331 SAVE       DS    F
                                          332 *
CCCCC0                                    333            END   BEGIN
CCC3A8 1C                                 334                   =P'1'
```

Figure 10.5 (Part 3)
Report Program Using ED, EDMK, CNTRL, PRTOV

PAGE   1

ITEM NUMBER	UNIT PRICE	NC. ITEMS SCLD
C1 01 CC2	$56.55	250
C1 01 CC2	$32.40	283
C1 01 CO2	$73.21	328
C1 01 CO3	$1.23	210
C1 01 CC5	$65.42	529
C1 01 CC5	$82.01	432
C1 01 CC8	$32.25	324
C1 01 OC8	$32.15	222
C1 01 CC8	$23.45	421
C1 01 CC8	$65.33	460
C1 01 012	$99.55	200
C1 03 CC4	$68.54	258
C1 03 CC6	$3.32	583
C1 03 CC6	$78.90	276
C1 03 CC6	$42.03	500
C1 03 012	$14.59	452
C1 05 CC7	$8C.12	299
C1 05 CC7	$60.10	486
C1 1C CC2	$86.CO	384
C3 02 003	$79.00	236
C3 02 CC3	$54.20	599
C3 04 012	$67.80	421
C4 01 CC5	$4.50	521
C4 01 CC6	$47.90	200
C6 01 CC2	$61.CC	100
C6 03 CC4	$82.50	RO
C6 03 CC6	$5C.20	240
C6 04 CC7	$72.45	163
C6 C4 CC8	$89.56	333
C6 05 CC1	$60.00	182
C6 C5 CC3	$35.00	401
C6 05 CC4	$.05	511
C7 01 CC1	$.35	225
C7 01 CC3	$1.40	400
C7 01 CC5	$22.5C	60
C7 02 CC7	$68.25	44
C7 03 CC2	$12.58	150
C7 03 CC4	$26.89	85
C7 03 CC6	$14.99	32
C8 02 CC2	$38.70	15
C8 02 CC3	$14.56	277
C8 02 CC4	$30.00	310
C8 02 CC6	$40.50	282
C8 04 CC4	$65.85	414
C8 04 CC2	$50.75	193
C8 04 CC7	$39.99	600
C8 04 CC8	$69.80	9
C9 04 CC3	$70.25	295
C9 04 004	$.50	350
C9 04 CC5	$2.50	65
C9 04 CC8	$85.55	42

Figure 10.5 (Part 4)
Report Program Using ED, EDMK, CNTRL, PRTOV

PACE   2

ITEM NUMBER	UNIT PRICE	NC. ITEMS SCLD
10 01 CO1	$22.42	230
1C 01 CC2	$4C.6U	166
10 02 CC2	$2C.5C	222
10 05 003	$88.CC	100
1C 06 CC2	$99.99	50
1C 06 CO8	$56.35	10
1C 06 C1C	$65.95	4
11 01 CC5	$79.CO	260
13 02 CC4	$44.CO	180

Figure 10.5 (Part 5)
Report Program Using ED, EDMK, CNTRL, PRTOV

Summary

In this chapter, we examined a number of techniques for improving the appearance of printed program output.

The Edit instruction was presented, and its use demonstrated, for suppressing leading zeros, punctuating numeric fields, and appending a negative indication to the right of negative numeric output. The use of one Edit instruction to operate upon several numeric fields was demonstrated, although certain restrictions did apply.

The Edit and Mark instruction was also discussed for editing fields and for producing floating symbols on numeric output.

Several other new instructions were introduced: the CNTRL, PRTOV, COMRG, and TIME macro instructions. Carriage control for spooled systems was likewise considered.

The use of the ED, EDMK, CNTRL, and PRTOV instructions was demonstrated through a coded program example in section 10.5.

Important Terms Discussed in Chapter 10

asterisk protection	floating symbol
carriage control	message character
carriage control character	
carriage control tape channel	overflow indicator
communications region	pattern
digit selector	significance indicator
	significance starter
edit	spacing control character
	stacker selection
field separator	
fill character	timer unit
fixed symbol	

Questions

For questions 1 through 4, write appropriate DC instructions to establish patterns for editing packed numeric fields as described.

10-1. A 3-byte field is to be edited with blanks suppressing leading zeros, 2 decimal positions, and the character "−" (minus) to the right of the field in the event of negative output: xxx∧xx−

10-2. A 4-byte field designating a monetary amount is to be edited with asterisk protection, comma between the second and third digits, 2 decimal positions, and "CR" to the right of negative fields. Zero suppression should occur up to the decimal point: xx,xxx∧xxCR

10-3. A 2-byte field containing a whole number is to be edited. Leading zeros are to be suppressed by blanks, and field contents of all zeros should be printed with exactly one (low-order) zero. No provision should be made for printing a sign.

10-4. A 4-byte field containing a whole number is to be edited with appropriate commas, and the characters "NEG" to the right of negative output. An all-zero field should be fully suppressed by blanks: x,xxx,xxxNEG

10-5. Assume that a 3-byte packed field called NUM1 is to be edited with the instructions

	MVC	FLD,PAT	
	ED	FLD,NUM1	
NUM1	DC	PL3'123'	00 12 3C
PAT	DC	X'4020214B20202060'	
FLD	DS	CL8	

Illustrate the contents of the fields' NUM1, PAT and FLD *after* execution of the ED instruction.

10-6. A 4-byte packed field called NUM2 is edited as follows:

	MVC	AREA,PATRN	
	ED	AREA,NUM2	
NUM2	DC	PL4'−27'	00 00 02 7D
PATRN	DC	X'5C20206B2020214B2020C3D9'	
AREA	DS	CL12	

What will be in AREA after execution of the ED instruction? Illustrate using hexadecimal notation.

10-7. Why must the edit pattern be written in hexadecimal? Why not use character type definitions (for example, C'   ' instead of X'40')?

10-8. Why were such control characters as X'20', X'21', ad X'22' chosen for editing, instead of such EBCDIC characters as, for example, C'X', C'Y', and C'Z'?

10-9. Will the significance indicator *always* be turned on when the first nonzero source digit is encountered? Explain.

10-10. Write the assembly language instructions to store the packed number 012345678D in the computer, and to edit the number so that it will look like $ḃḃ123,456.78CR on output. Note that the output has a fixed dollar sign.

10-11. Write the assembly language instructions to edit the contents of a 3-byte field called FLD with 2 decimal positions, "−" (minus sign) to the right of the number if it is negative, and a floating dollar sign. Some sample data would be

field contents	desired output
23467D	$234.67−
00005C	$.05

10-12. Illustrate the appearance of the results of editing a field containing 00002C with each of the following patterns:

(i)   X'40202020202060'
(ii)   X'40202021202060'
(iii) X'5C2020214B2020C3D9'

10-13. Write an instruction which you would place at the beginning of an assembly language program to ensure that the output will begin at the top of a new page. Assume that the printer file is called PRFLE.

10-14. Describe the type of printer spacing that will result from each of the following instruction sequences. PRNTFL is the name of a printer file, and OUTAREA is the name of the output area.

```
(i)   CNTRL      PRNTFL,SP,,1
      PUT        PRNTFL,OUTAREA

(ii)  PUT        PRNTFL,OUTAREA
      CNTRL      PRNTFL,SP,3
```

10-15. Write an instruction to test for a page overflow condition and to branch to an instruction called HERE when channel 12 is detected. The printer file is called PRFILE.

10-16. Given the instruction
         COMRG
Write a statement to place the current date into a field called DATE. How should DATE be defined?

10-17. What entries must be designated in the printer file definition in order that we may use the CNTRL and PRTOV macros for DOS programs? for OS programs?

Program Exercises

10-1. In chapter 6, section 6.3, we presented a payroll program which performed computation with numbers having assumed decimal positions. However the program output did not contain decimal points.

Expand the program of section 6.3 so that the output will appear as designated in figure 10.6. The notation $$$.XX denotes a field with floating $ and significance established for all characters, including both the decimal point and all characters to the right of the decimal point.

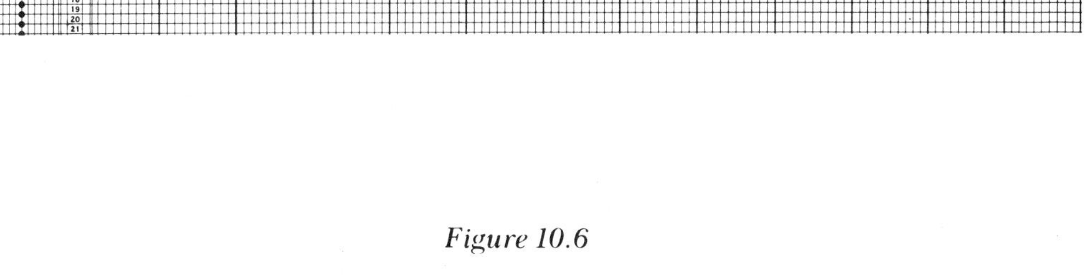

Figure 10.6

10-2. Write an assembly language program which has input as follows:

Field	Card Columns	
ACTNO (account number)	1-3	xxx
PRINC (principal amount)	5-9	xxx $\wedge$ xx
INT (interest)	10-11	$\wedge$ xx

For example, a PRINC field of 099$_\wedge$86 and an INT field of $_\wedge$08 would designate an interest rate of 8% on the amount $99.86.

The program is to compute

$$\begin{aligned}
\text{NEWAMT} &= (\text{PRINC})(\text{INT}) + \text{PRINC} \\
&= (\text{xxx}_\wedge\text{xx})(_\wedge\text{xx}) + \text{xxx}_\wedge\text{xx} \\
&= \text{xxx}_\wedge\text{xxxx} + \text{xxx}_\wedge\text{xx} \\
&= \text{xxxx}_\wedge\text{xxxx}
\end{aligned}$$

Round NEWAMT to the nearest penny.

Output is to be two header lines and one detail line per input record as follows:

ACCOUNT	PRINCIPAL	INTEREST	NEW
(5-11)	(16-24)	(32-39)	(48-50)
NUMBER			AMOUNT
(5-10)			(47-52)
XXX	$$$.XX	.XX	$$$$.XX
XXX	$$$.XX	.XX	$$$$.XX
XXX	$$$.XX	.XX	$$$$.XX
:	:	:	:
(6-8)	(17-22)	(36-38)	(46-52)

Chapter 11

More on Branching and Looping

MORE ON BRANCHING AND LOOPING

In this chapter we shall discuss various coding techniques which require the computer to "decide" the course of action to be followed during program execution. These techniques will involve looping and the use of specialized conditional branch instructions.

We have already seen examples of comparison and branching in assembly language (chapters 5 and 9); however, the programs of this chapter will more clearly demonstrate the power that conditional branching affords the programmer. Indeed, it is this very capacity for decision-making and transfer of control (along with a vast storage capacity) that so greatly distinguishes the computer from many other calculating devices.

11.1   A SOCIAL SECURITY PROBLEM

In this section, we discuss techniques for solving a problem which we call a "social security problem", whose solution requires the introduction of new instructions for branching. In particular, we shall explain the BC and BCR instructions, and a special group of instructions called the "extended mnemonics".

11.1.1   The Problem Described

We shall first consider a problem which is part of most real-life payroll programs: the computation of social security tax. As you know, the social security payroll tax is computed as a fixed percentage of an individual's gross earnings up to a maximum salary level. The tax is not paid on that part of one's salary which exceeds the designated maximum level.

In the example below, we take the percentage to be 7.0%, with a maximum base salary of $20,000. Earnings which exceed $20,000 are not subject to the tax. An individual earning $21,000 will not pay social security tax (also called FICA: Federal Insurance Contributions Act) on $1,000: the amount by which his salary exceeds $20,000.

A typical approach to computing FICA on a weekly basis is described in the flowchart of figure 11.1. We assume that several values are known: the amount of FICA already paid in the current year (OLDFICA), the cumulative year-to-date earnings up until the current week (OLDYTD), and the current weekly earnings (EARN). The program is to compute TAX: the amount of FICA which is due for the current week.

Note that the maximum amount that any individual need pay is $1,400.00 per year: 7.0% of $20,000. Thus there may be cases in which the weekly TAX is zero, (that is, when OLDFICA = $1,400.00) or in which TAX need be paid on only part of the current week's salary (if EARN brings the year-to-date salary over the $20,000 mark).

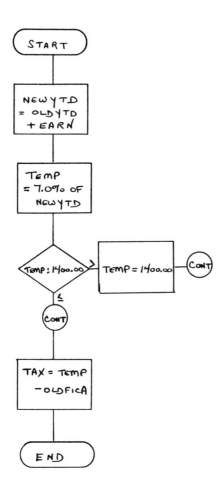

Figure 11.1
Flowchart for Social Security Problem

We begin with the computation of the new year-to-date salary (NEWYTD): the sum of the old year-to-date salary and the current weekly earnings. TEMP is then calculated as 7.0% of NEWYTD. This is the amount of cumulative year-to-date FICA *if* FICA is indeed required on the *total* current weekly earnings. Now we must test to see whether that is indeed the case.

The contents of TEMP are compared to $1,400: the maximum yearly FICA. If TEMP is less than or equal to $1,400, it follows that EARN must have brought the new year-to-date salary to an amount which is less than or equal to $20,000 respectively. In either case, FICA is required for the current week. We already know the cumulative yearly FICA amounts including this week (TEMP) and excluding this week (OLDFICA). The current weekly amount is thus the difference between these values: TAX = TEMP − OLDFICA.

Now assume that in the comparison, TEMP (7.0% of the NEWYTD) was found to *exceed* $1,400 in value. This implies one of two conditions: either the $20,000 mark was passed before the current week even began (OLDYTD exceeded $20,000) or the mark was passed with the addition of EARN to OLDYTD. (For example, if OLDYTD = $19,750 and EARN = $300, then NEWYTD = $20,050, TEMP would exceed $1,400 and FICA would need to be paid on $250 of EARN, with the remaining $50 not subject to the tax.) The conditions are treated alike in the problem flowchart: the previous value of TEMP is replaced by $1,400, and OLDFICA is then subtracted from this amount to yield the current week's FICA. Note here that had OLDYTD exceeded $20,000, then OLDFICA = $1,400 so that TAX would be 0 (TAX = TEMP − OLDFICA = $1,400 − $1,400 = 0). This is certainly valid, for the social security base had already been passed. On the other hand, had the addition of EARN brought the year-to-date salary over the $20,000 mark, then TAX would have been the difference between $1,400 and OLDFICA (TAX = TEMP − OLDFICA = $1,400 − OLDFICA).

The above method for computing the amounts of social security payments is certainly not the only possible approach to this problem. It is, however, the shortest in flowchart form (and hence in program form) and it leads to more accurate results than other typical approaches (see section 11.1.4).

The comparison of TEMP to 1,400 and the resulting decision to branch or not to branch is of crucial importance to the solution of this problem. We may code the problem using the instructions for comparison and branching introduced in chapters 5 or 9. However, we should like at this point to consider a more generalized approach to branching than the extended mnemonics (section 5.3.2), and to have a more detailed discussion of what actually happens when a program branch takes place.

11.1.2   The Condition Code and Instruction Address Register

The condition code is a 2-bit field which resides in a special part of the CPU. It is part of a very important 64-bit register called the PSW: Program Status Word. The PSW is fully discussed in chapter 13. As we already know, two bits may contain binary values 00, 01, 10, or 11: 0, 1, 2, or 3 respectively. The condition code may be set by various instructions, including compare instructions, logical instructions, and many arithmetic instructions. The particular condition code value set by an instruction will reflect the instruction's outcome. For example, compare instructions will set values 0, 1, or 2, depending upon whether the first operand is respectively equal to, smaller than, or greater than the second operand in value. The settings of 0, 1, 2, or 3 by arithmetic instructions denote respective zero, negative, postive or overflow results.

The conditional branch instruction (described in the next section) tests the condition code and, depending upon its setting, determines whether program control will continue sequentially or will be diverted. Note that:

- Once the condition code is set, it remains unchanged until reset by another instruction. Thus the "testing" need not occur immediately after the condition code is set, as long as the relevant operation is not separated from the branch instruction by another instruction which sets the condition code.
- A branch may be initiated based upon the result of *any* instruction which sets the condition code, not only the results of compare instructions.
- It is not possible to "suppress" the setting of the condition code.

The instruction address register is another PSW field which is important to the branching process. It contains the main storage address of the next instruction to be executed at each point during the program cycle.

Recall that when programs are run, the object program (the program in its ready-to-run machine language form) is loaded into main storage before execution begins. At the same time, the address of the first instruction is placed into the instruction address register. The computer then knows which instruction is to be retrieved, namely, the instruction whose address is in the instruction address register. The contents of the instruction address register are then incremented by 2, 4, or 6, depending upon the number of bytes in the current instruction (see chapter 1 for instruction formats). The computer will again retrieve the instruction whose address is now in the register. This continuous process leads to sequential instruction execution.

A branch instruction places the address of the instruction to which control will be transferred into the instruction address register. This causes any further instruction execution to begin at that address.

Now that the true nature of the branch is understood we are ready to examine two branch instructions : the BC (Branch on Condition) and BCR (Branch on Condition to Register) instructions. There are a number of other branch instructions, some of which will be discussed later in this chapter.

11.1.3   The BC and BCR Instructions

The Branch on Condition and Branch on Condition to Register instructions are alike except for the way in which their second operand is interpreted. Each of them will be described in turn.

The BC Instruction (**B**ranch on **C**ondition)

Instruction type: Machine Instruction
Machine format: RX Instruction (Register and IndeXed Storage
                          Instruction)

47	M1	X2	B2	D2
0	7 8	11 12	15 16 19 20	31

Symbolic format:

	name	operation	operands
	[symbolic name]	BC	mask,name2
or	[symbolic name]	BC	M1,D2(X2,B2)

where M1 is a 4-bit mask. D2,X2, and B2 are the displacement, index register, and base register respectively used to calculate the second operand address.

. . . .

Rules:
   • The first operand may contain one of the values 0-15.
   • The second operand is the address in main storage which will replace the current value in the instruction address register, *if* the condition code setting complies with the specification of M1.

Condition Code: The condition code remains unchanged.

The first operand of the BC instruction is a 4-bit code called a **mask**. It specifies a condition or a choice of conditions, one of which must be met in order that the branch to the second operand location be effected. The four bits of the mask correspond to the four possible condition code settings as follows:

mask bit position value :   8   4   2   1
condition code :   0   1   2   3

The branch is "successful" (that is, transfer of control takes place) when the condition code setting has a corresponding mask bit of 1.

For example, the instruction BC   8, HERE will cause a branch to the instruction called HERE when the condition code value is 0. Note that a mask bit position of 8 corresponds to a condition code setting of 0. (In this case, the mask in binary form is 1000.) Likewise, BC   1,THERE will cause a branch to the instruction called THERE when the condition code value is 3. (In this case, the mask in binary form is 0001.)

The instruction BC   10,THERE will cause a branch to THERE when the condition code is set *either* to 0 *or* to 2. (The mask in binary is 1010: decimal 10, or binary bits 8 and 2, correspond to condition code settings 0 and 2.)

The BCR Instruction (Branch on Condition to Register)

Instruction type: Machine Instruction
Machine format: RR Instruction (Register to Register Instruction)

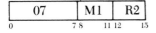

name	operation	operands
[symbolic name]	BCR	M1,R2

Symbolic format:

where M1 is a 4-bit mask. R2 is a register whose contents denote the second operand address.

. . . .

Rules:
- The first operand may contain one of the values 0 —15.
- The second operand is a register whose *contents* (actually the low-order

> 24 bits of the contents) will replace the current value of the instruction address register, *if* the condition code setting complies with the specification of M1.
> - A second operand of 0 means "no branch", regardless of the condition.

Condition Code: The condition code remains unchanged.

This instruction is identical to the BC instruction, with the exception that the second operand designates a register whose *contents* give the location to which the branch will take place.

For example, if register 5 contains 0000964A, the instruction BCR 12,5 will cause a branch to the instruction stored at 0000964A if the condition code is set to either 0 or 1.

Likewise the instruction BC 8,LOC accomplishes the same as the instructions
```
        LA      4,LOC
        BCR     8,4
```

Note that the LA instruction places the *address* of LOC into register 4. The BCR will cause a branch to the location whose address is in register 4 (in this case LOC), if the condition code is set to 0.

Also note the following:
- A first operand of 15 (binary 1111, all bits are ones) is an unconditional branch. (After all, one of the conditions must be met, since all possible conditions are specified!)
- A first operand of 0 (binary 0000) means no branch or no-operation. A no-operation instruction does have uses, although they might not be obvious at this time.

Table 11.1 summarizes the mask values and the respective condition code settings which they test.

mask(in bits)	mask(in decimal)	condition code
0000	0	none
0001	1	3
0010	2	2
0011	3	2,3
0100	4	1
0101	5	1,3
0110	6	1,2
0111	7	1,2,3

1000	8	0
1001	9	0,3
1010	10	0,2
1011	11	0,2,3
1100	12	0,1
1101	13	0,1,3
1110	14	0,1,2
1111	15	all (0,1,2,3)

Table 11.1
Mask Values and Corresponding Condition Code Settings

Table 11.2 summarizes the condition code settings for System/370 binary, decimal, logical, and input/output instructions. A complete list including settings for all System/370 machine instructions may also be found in Appendix A, side ⑤ .

11.1.4   The Social Security Problem — Coded

We now present the assembly language code for the social security problem using decimal (packed) values. The flowchart is reproduced in figure 11.2 with numbered flowchart symbols corresponding to numbered boxed sections on the program listing (figure 11.3).

In this program, the assumed OLDYTD amount $19,900 plus the EARN (current weekly earnings) amount brings the NEWYTD over the social security base to $20,100. Thus 7.0% of $20,100 exceeds the maximum yearly FICA amount ($1,400). The instruction BC   12,CONT will cause a branch to CONT if condition 12 is met: that is, if TEMP is found to be equal to or less than $1,400 (condition code settings of 0 or 1 respectively: mask 1100 binary or 12 decimal). In this case, the contents of TEMP exceeded $1,400, therefore the branch did not occur. Instead the program continued with the value of MAXTAX ($1,400) replacing the previous contents of TEMP in storage. FICA (called TAX in the program) was then computed as the difference between the value in TEMP (the maximum possible FICA) and OLDFICA (the cumulative year-to-date FICA).

Towards Deeper Understanding
You may have wondered why, in planning the solution to the social security problem, a method was chosen in which tax was computed for a particular week by subtracting the old year-to-date social security from 7.0% of the new year-to-

Condition-Code Settings

	CODE STATE						CODE STATE		
	0	1	2	3			0	1	2	3
Fixed-Point Arithmetic						*Status Switching*				
Add H/F	zero	< zero	> zero	overflow		Test and Set	zero	one	--	--
Add Logical	zero, no carry	not zero, no carry	zero, carry	not zero, carry		*Input/Output Operations*				
Compare H/F	equal	low	high	--		Halt I/O	interruption pending	CSW stored	burst op stopped	not operational
Load and Test	zero	< zero	> zero	carry						
Load Complement	zero	< zero	> zero	overflow		Start I/O	successful	CSW stored	busy	not operational
Load Negative	zero	< zero	--	--						
Load Positive	zero	--	> zero	overflow		Test Channel	available	interruption pending	burst mode	not operational
Shift Left Double	zero	< zero	> zero	overflow						
Shift Left Single	zero	< zero	> zero	overflow		Test I/O	available	CSW stored	busy	not operational
Shift Right Double	zero	< zero	> zero	--						
Shift Right Single	zero	< zero	> zero	--		NOTES				
Subtract H/F	zero	< zero	> zero	overflow		available	Unit and channel available			
Subtract Logical	--	not zero, no carry	zero, carry	not zero, carry		burst op stopped	Burst operation stopped			
Decimal Arithmetic						busy	Unit or channel busy			
Add Decimal	zero	< zero	> zero	overflow		carry	A carryout of the sign position occurs			
Compare Decimal	equal	low	high	--		complete	Last result byte nonzero			
Subtract Decimal	zero	< zero	> zero	overflow		CSW stored	Chanel status word stored			
Zero and Add	zero	< zero	> zero	overflow		equal	Operands compare equal			
Floating-Point Arithmetic						F	Fullword			
Add Normalized S/L	zero	< zero	> zero	--		> zero	Result is greater than zero			
Add Unnormalized S/L	zero	< zero	> zero	--		H	Halfword			
Compare S/L	equal	low	high	--		halted	Data transmission stopped. Unit in halt-reset mode			
Load and Test S/L	zero	< zero	> zero	--						
Load Complement S/L	zero	< zero	> zero	--		high	First operand compares high			
Load Negative S/L	zero	< zero	--	--		incomplete	Nonzero result byte; not last			
Load Positive S/L	zero	--	> zero	--		L	Long precision			
Subtract Normalized S/L	zero	< zero	> zero	--		< zero	Result is less than zero			
Subtract Unnormalized S/L	zero	< zero	> zero	--		low	First operand compares low			
						mixed	Selected bits are both zero and one			
Logical Operations						not operational	Unit or channel not operational			
And	zero	not zero	--	--		not zero	Result is not all zero			
Compare Logical	equal	low	high	--		one	Selected bits are one			
Edit	zero	< zero	> zero	--		overflow	Result overflows			
Edit and Mark	zero	< zero	> zero	--		S	Short precision			
Exclusive Or	zero	not zero	--	--		zero	Result or selected bits are zero			
Or	zero	not zero	--	--						
Test Under Mask	zero	mixed	--	one						
Translate and Test	zero	incomplete	complete	--						

Table 11.2

Condition Code Settings for Binary, Decimal, Logical and I/O Operations.

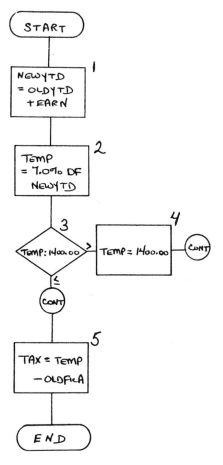

Figure 11.2
Flowchart for Social Security Problem

date earnings. A much more direct approach would at first glance involve simply computing 7.0% of all or part of each week's salary (EARN) until the social security base is reached (that is, until NEWYTD > 20,000)!

In order to understand why the latter approach is not used, let us consider an example. An individual earns a weekly salary of $482.50. Computing 7.0% of 482.50 yields 33.775, or $33.78 weekly social security payment, rounding to the nearest cent. After working for 41 weeks at this rate, the individual has earned $19,782.50 and paid FICA at $33.78 per week — a total of $1384.98 for the 41 weeks. For the 42nd week, the person has only to pay tax on the $217.50 of his salary which will bring the taxed amount up to the social security base. 7.0% of

```
LOC     OBJECT CODE     ADDR1 ADDR2   STMT  SOURCE STATEMENT

                                        1  *
                                        2     PRINT NOGEN
CCCCCC                                   3  FICA  START 0
CCCCCC  0580                             4  A     BALR  11,0
                                0002     5        USING *,11
                                        6  *
000002  F853 B04D B042  0004F 00044     7        ZAP   NEWYTD,OLDYTD        1
000008  FA32 B04D B04A  0004F 0004C     8        AP    NEWYTD,EARN
                                        9  *
00000E  F853 B051 B04D  00053 0004F    10        ZAP   TEMP,NEWYTD     TEMP- 00 00 20 10 00 0C
000014  FC51 B051 B05A  00053 0005C    11        MP    TEMP,P7         TEMP- 00 14 07 00 00 0C      2
00001A  FA51 B051 B05C  00053 0005E    12        AP    TEMP,P500       TEMP- 00 14 07 00 50 0C
000020  F153 B051 B051  00053 00053    13        MVO   TEMP,TEMP(4)    TEMP- 00 00 01 40 70 0C      3
                                       14  *
000026  F953 B051 B05E  00053 00060    15        CP    TEMP,MAXTAX     TEMP- SAME AS ABOVE
                                       16  *
00002C  47C0 B034        00036         17        BC    12,CONT         TEMP- SAME AS ABOVE
                                       18  *
000030  F853 B051 B05E  00053 00060    19        ZAP   TEMP,MAXTAX     TEMP- 00 00 01 40 00 0C      4
                                       20  *                          SINCE 1407.00 > 1400.00
000036  F823 B057 B053  00059 00055    21  CONT  ZAP   TAX,TEMP+2(4)   TAX- 01 40 00 0C
00003C  FB23 B057 B046  00059 00048    22        SP    TAX,OLDFICA     TAX- 00 00 70 0C             5
                                       23  *
000042  0A03                           24        SVC   3              FOR DOS, THIS INSTRUCTION IS EOJ
                                       25  *
000044  1990000C                       26  OLDYTD  DC  P'19900.00'
000048  0139300C                       27  OLDFICA DC  P'1393.00'
00004C  20000C                         28  EARN    DC  P'200.00'
00004F                                 29  NEWYTD  DS  PL4
000053                                 30  TEMP    DS  PL6
000059                                 31  TAX     DS  PL3
00005C  070C                           32  P7      DC  P'.070'
00005E  500C                           33  P500    DC  P'500'
000060  0140000C                       34  MAXTAX  DC  P'1400.00'
000000                                 35          END A
```

Figure 11.3
Social Security Problem Listing

$217.50 is 15.225, or \$15.23 to the nearest cent. Thus the individual has paid \$1384.98 FICA for the first 41 weeks, plus \$15.23 FICA for the 42nd week, bringing his total payment to \$1400.21, which is more than the \$1,400.00 maximum amount! The difficulty with this method is that the tax on weekly earnings is rounded up each week by a fraction of a cent. Over a period of many weeks, the loss of accuracy accumulates.

The method used in this chapter balances the effect of rounding each week. The person pays \$33.78 tax the first week. For the second week, 7.0% of the NEWYTD (\$965) yields 67.55 in TEMP. Since TEMP $<$ 1400.00, the second week's payment will be TAX = TEMP − OLDFICA = 67.55 − 33.78 = 33.77, one cent less than that of the first week. For the third week, 7.0% of the NEWYTD (1447.50) yields 101.33 in TEMP. Since TEMP $<$ 1400.00, the third week's payment will be TAX = TEMP − OLDFICA = 101.33 − 67.55 = 33.78. The payment for the fourth week will be \$33.77, for the fifth week \$33.78, and so on. The cumulative effect of rounding by this method will never be more than a fraction of a cent off.

11.1.5   The Extended Mnemonic Instructions

The "extended mnemonic instructions" are branch instructions, each of which will test for specific condition code setting(s) as a condition for branching. The extended mnemonics have been discussed earlier (chapter 5, section 5.3.2).

We may now understand that the extended mnemonics are not instructions in themselves, but are merely convenient "extensions" of the BC and BCR instructions. They eliminate the necessity for using the mask codes. The operation portion of an extended mnemonic in its machine language form embodies the *same operation code* as the BC or BCR instruction (depending upon whether the extended mnemonic instruction is in RX or RR form, respectively), and incorporates the M1 (mask) portion as well. Only one operand is required, corresponding to the second operand of the conditional branch instruction.

For example, BH   INST1 (Branch on High) becomes the same machine language instruction as BC   2,INST1. BNE   INST2 (Branch Not Equal) becomes the same machine language instruction as BC   7,INST2; and BNER   4 (Branch Not Equal to Register) becomes the same machine language instruction as BCR   7,4.

Table 11.3 presents the complete list of extended mnemonics along with the equivalent conditional branch instructions.

Meaning	Extended Code		Conditional Branch	
	RX	**RR**	**RX**	**RR**
Unconditional Branch	B loc2	BR R2	BC 15,loc2	BCR 15,R2
No Operation	NOP loc2	NOPR R2	BC 0,loc2	BCR 0,R2

For use after comparison: A compared to B

Meaning	Extended Code		Conditional Branch	
Branch on A High	BH loc2	BHR R2	BC 2,loc2	BCR 2,R2
Branch on A Low	BL loc2	BLR R2	BC 4,loc2	BCR 4,R2
Branch on A Equal B	BE loc2	BER R2	BC 8,loc2	BCR 8,R2
Branch on A Not High	BNH loc2	BNHR R2	BC 13,loc2	BCR 13,R2
Branch on A Not Low	BNL loc2	BNLR R2	BC 11,loc2	BCR 11,R2
Branch on A Not Equal B	BNE loc2	BNER R2	BC 7,loc2	BCR 7,R2

For use after arithmetic instructions:

Meaning	Extended Code		Conditional Branch	
Branch on Plus	BP loc2	BPR R2	BC 2,loc2	BCR 2,R2
Branch on Minus	BM loc2	BMR R2	BC 4,loc2	BCR 4,R2
Branch on Zero	BZ loc2	BZR R2	BC 8,loc2	BCR 8,R2
Branch on Not Plus	BNP loc2	BNPR R2	BC 13,loc2	BCR 13,R2
Branch on Not Minus	BNM loc2	BNMR R2	BC 11,loc2	BCR 11,R2
Branch on Not Zero	BNZ loc2	BNZR R2	BC 7,loc2	BCR 7,R2
Branch on Overflow	BO loc2	BOR R2	BC 1,loc2	BCR 1,R2

Table 11.3
Extended Mnemonics and Equivalent Conditional Branch Instructions

Note that table 11.3 contains many identical instructions. For example, the BH and BP operation codes do the same thing (they each test for the same condition code setting and are each equivalent to a BC operation with a mask of 2), as do the BL and BM instructions. We are merely provided with operation mnemonics which are easy and convenient to use.

Note too, that we do not have extended mnemonics to test for every possible condition. The instruction BC   12,HERE, for example, cannot be rewritten as an extended mnemonic.

11.2   A TABLE HANDLING PROBLEM

An important category of programming problems involves the use of data in the form of "tables". The solution of these problems requires the use of special techniques, including looping, and the use of base registers, index registers, or specialized branch instructions. These concepts will be illustrated below.

11.2.1   What Are Tables?

A **table** is a grouping of logically related data items which are stored in some systematic way, usually in adjacent storage locations. As you might well imagine, tables are used extensively for many business (as well as mathematical) computer applications in which large groups of data items are to be processed.

An example might be a list, each entry of which contains the name, address, and telephone number of an employee in a particular firm. The list would be stored sequentially in main storage and referenced by program routines which need the information. The term **list** refers to a one-dimensional table. The items in the table are **table entries**.

Tables may be multi-dimensional as well. Consider the case of an insurance company which determines benefit premiums based upon two criteria: the applicant's age and health category. Assume that an individual may be placed into one of health categories 1, 2, 3, or 4, depending upon his physical condition at the time of application. Then a table such as the one in figure 11.4 may be used to determine the applicant's premiums per year for a given life insurance policy.

age / health	1	2	3	4
18-25	100.75	124.50	142.00	178.75
25-33	123.25	136.00	152.25	189.00
34-42	134.75	150.00	185.75	210.00
43-49	162.00	194.50	224.00	264.50

Figure 11.4
A Two-Dimensional Table

The table in figure 11.4 is 2-dimensional. If we wished to store this table in the computer's main storage, the entries might be placed into contiguous locations as follows:
100.75 / 124.50 / 142.00/ 178.75 // 123.25 / 136.00 / 152.25 / 189.00 //
134.75 / 150.00 / 185.75 / 210.00 // 162.00 / 194.50 / 224.00 / 264.50//

Examining the values above, you will see that the double slashes separate the age entries. However each age entry itself contains a 4-item list of premium values for health categories within the particular age grouping. (The appearance is actually that of a table within a table.)

This logic may be extended to tables of more than 2 dimensions. However in this chapter we will be concerned with one-dimensional tables only.

11.2.2   The Problem Described

Let us consider the following problem: a business organization has a list of amounts invested in its ventures by private individuals over the past several years. One manager, convinced that small investors are contributing a large percentage of the total investment, wishes to prove this by computing the sum of all investment amounts not greater than $200.

Assuming for the sake of brevity that there are 10 investment amounts to be considered (in practice, of course, there would be many more), the values might be stored in consecutive storage locations, that is, in the form of a list:

```
LIST    DC    F'50'
        DC    F'105'
        DC    F'530'
        DC    F'200'
        DC    F'250'
        DC    F'100'
        DC    F'70'
        DC    F'1000'
        DC    F'60'
        DC    F'975'
```

It would certainly be possible to examine each item in the list to determine whether or not it is greater than $200, by issuing ten different "compare" instructions, one for each item. However, this would not be a very efficient method. The most obvious solution is to code a **loop** to handle the comparison. In fact, one major advantage of storing data in table form is that the systematic organization of the data lends itself naturally to the type of programming in which a set of instructions may be repeated over and over again, each time on a different table entry.

One possible flowchart for the problem above is given in figure 11.5.

You will notice, upon examining the flowchart, that the portion within the dotted lines describes the steps required to "solve" the problem: that is, to test the value of individual data items and to compute the sum. The other steps were required

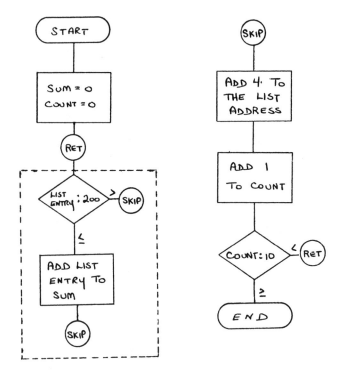

Figure 11.5
Summing Selected Items in a List

to control the loop itself: to set it up and to determine when we have done enough (whenever COUNT reaches a value of 10).

Previous chapters have dealt with looping. However at this point it will be beneficial for us to examine the nature of the loop more closely.

11.2.3   Loop Structure

A program loop consists of four components, or steps. The steps may be programmed separately, or several may be included in one instruction. However they are always clearly identifiable and must all be present for proper functioning of the loop. They are:
- initialization
- body of the loop

- adjustment
- test for exit

We shall consider each of these steps in turn.

Initialization

This step is the preparation for the loop and should precede the loop itself. Typically, counters are set (initialized to zero or some other value) and any preparation necessary for the proper functioning of the loop is performed. In figure 11.5, setting the SUM and COUNT areas to 0 constitutes the initialization.

Body of the Loop

This step is the heart of the loop. In figure 11.5, the portion within the dotted lines constitutes the body of the loop. These instructions are repeated for each entry in the table, and constitute the processing for which purpose the loop was constructed.

Adjustment

The adjustment often involves the incrementing or decrementing of a counter—a storage location whose purpose is to "count" the number of times the loop has been performed—so that an exit may be made at the proper time. The adjustment may involve other actions, however. It might be necessary to "adjust" contents of other storage locations in preparation for the repetitive processing of the body of the loop. In figure 11.5, for example, the step "ADD 4 TO THE LIST ADDRESS" is an adjustment which ensures that when the body of the loop is next executed, the instructions will act upon a field which is 4 bytes *after* the previously handled field in storage. This enables us to use the *same* instructions to act each time upon succeeding data fields. The step "ADD 1 TO COUNT" is also part of the adjustment, since we are incrementing the counter which will be used for exiting from the loop.

Test for Exit

Quite obviously, we are required to meet some specified criteria in order to exit from the loop at the proper time. In some of our earlier programs, for example, we explained the parameter EODAD = name of the DCB data set definition for OS programs (for DOS, EOFADDR = name of the DTFCD file definition) as instructing the computer to test for a "/*" card each time a record was read from the card file. When the "/*" card was found, an automatic branch was to be taken to some specified instruction. (In our programs, this was often an instruction called FINISH). This was actually the test and exit from a loop which read and processed succeeding card records. In figure 11.5, the comparison of the contents of COUNT to 10 constitutes the test for exit, which is satisfied when

COUNT reaches 10. The test for exit can assume various forms. The condition to be tested for in any particular case will naturally vary with the problem.

We reproduce the flowchart of figure 11.5 (in figure 11.6), along with a schematic diagram of its loop structure.

The four loop components outlined above need not always occur in the order presented. The initialization should always precede the loop itself. However, the adjustment and/or test for exit may precede the body of the loop, especially in situations in which it is not unlikely that the loop will be bypassed altogether (in other words, the exit criteria may be initially satisfied). However all four steps must be present in order for the loop to function properly within the program.

Now that we have a clear understanding of loop structure, we are tempted to plunge immediately into coding the solution to the problem presented in section 11.2.2. However the logic required to code from figure 11.5 may be further clarified by considering base registers and index registers to help us reference table entries. Thus we will defer coding the solution to our problem until after we have discussed these concepts.

11.2.4   Using Base Registers and Index Registers for Table Reference

Base Registers and Address Modification

Assembly language instructions may explicitly reference a main storage location by describing its address as the sum of a constant (the displacement) and the contents of a register (a base register). We have already seen this technique used in the section on the EDMK instruction (chapter 10, section 10.2.2). Briefly, if we wish to add the number in main storage location 100 to the number in register 5, we may use the following:

```
          LA      4,100
          A       5,0(4)
```

The LA instruction says "load the address of the location numbered 100 into register 4". (This is, of course, redundant. The address of location 100 is 100!) The LA instruction has placed the number 100 into register 4. The same thing might have been accomplished by the statements

```
          L       4,HUND
HUND      DC      F'100'
```

but the LA instruction enabled us to avoid a constant definition.

The notation 0(4) in the instruction A   5,0(4) may be interpreted as follows: Consider the address found by adding the contents of register 4, the base register (register 4 contains 100, since we just put it there), to the number 0, the

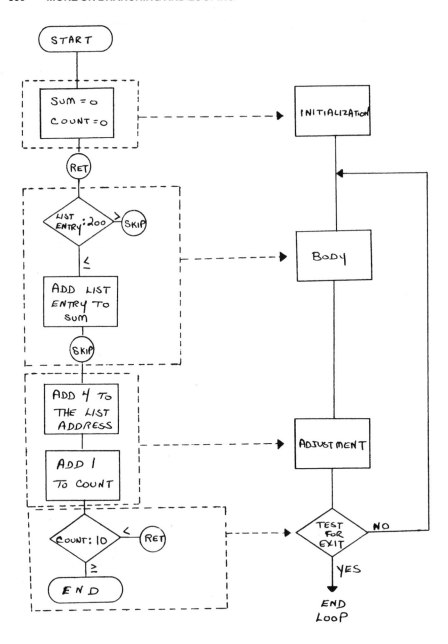

Figure 11.6
Flowchart with Illustration of Loop Structure

displacement; 100 plus 0 equals 100. Therefore the instruction A 5,0(4) causes the contents of location 100 to be added to the contents of register 5.

The general form of address is D(B) where D is the displacement and B is the base register. Note that
- The number of our "base" (the register number) must be enclosed in parentheses
- The displacement must precede the parentheses
- A displacement must be used, even if its value is zero
- The displacement must have a non-negative integer value.

The advantage of using base-displacement addressing in our programs is that it enables us to modify the effective address being referenced by changing either the contents of the base register or the displacement.

In the flowchart of figure 11.6, for example, LIST (the beginning address of our table) might be referenced in base-displacement form. Then the address of each item in the list may be incremented by adding 4 to the appropriate base register. Of course we would also have to initialize the base register before entering the loop. For example, suppose we choose register 4 as our base and register 3 to hold our sum. Then we have the flowchart of figure 11.7.

Note on figure 11.7 that the test for exit from the loop could just as well be made by testing register 4 as by testing the counter. Register 4 is initialized in value to the address of LIST and is incremented by 4 each time the loop is processed. Thus register 4 references LIST, LIST+4, LIST+4·2, LIST+4·3, ..., LIST+4·9 in its 10 times around the loop. When register 4 contains the address of LIST+4·10, the loop has been processed 10 times. (We say LIST+4·10 and not LIST+4·9, for the incrementing of register 4 takes place after the body of the loop, and before the test for exit.) It is thus possible to eliminate COUNT entirely! The resulting flowchart (figure 11.8) is one instruction shorter than that of figure 11.7, but is admittedly a bit more difficult to follow.

Figure 11.8 shows the revised version of our program flowchart, along with the assembly language instructions necessary for its implementation. Corresponding flowchart and program segments have been numbered accordingly.

Note the instruction C 4,=A(LIST+40) in the program segment numbered 4. It compares the contents of register 4 to the *address* of LIST+40, to test for an exit from the loop at the proper time. A literal has been used here,

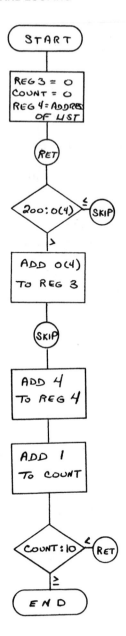

Figure 11.7
Looping, Using Base Register for Address Modification

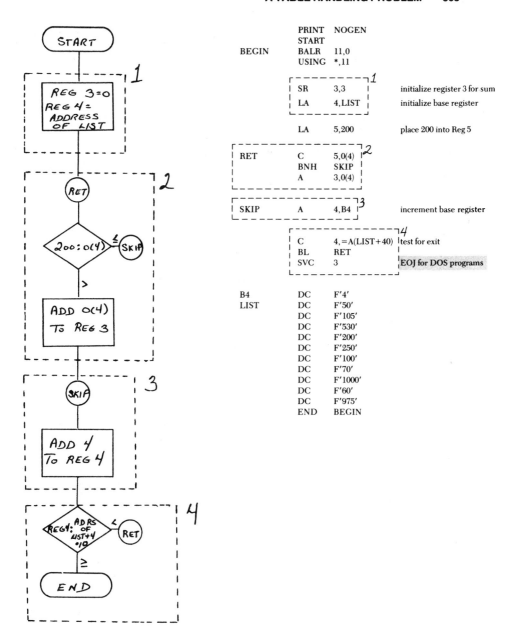

Figure 11.8
Program Using Register 4 as a Base Register for Address Modification

with the designation A(loc) meaning "the address of" loc. See chapter 3, section 3.3, for a more complete discussion of literals, and chapter 12, section 12.2.1, for a discussion of "address constants".

Index Registers and Address Modification

Assembly language provides yet another method for generating effective addresses, which may be used with *instructions in RX format only*. Besides considering a main storage address as the sum of a displacement and the contents of a base register, it may be computed as the sum of a displacement, the contents of a base register, and the contents of an **index register**.

RX Instructions (**R**egister and Inde**X**ed Storage)

You will recall (see chapter 1, section 1.4.2) that the general form of an RX instruction is

name	operation	operands
[symbolic name]	mnemonic operation code	R1,name2

or	[symbolic name]	mnemonic operation code	R1,D2(X2,B2)

where the first operand R1 is a register number, and D2,X2, and B2 are the *displacement, index register*, and *base register* respectively *used to calculate the second operand address*.

The translation of an RX instruction with second operand D2(X2,B2) into machine language is as follows:

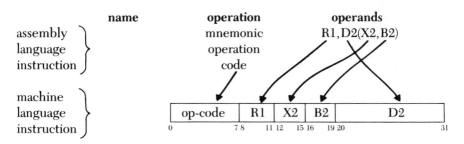

Note, for example, the translation of the RX instruction into machine language, described in figure 11.9.

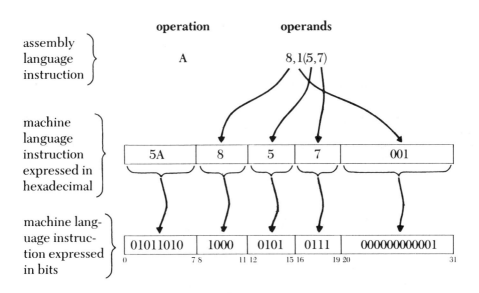

Figure 11.9
Translation of an RX Instruction into Machine Language

In this section, we will be mainly concerned with the expression of the second operand of an RX instruction in the form D2(X2,B2) where D2 is the displacement, X2 is the index register, and B2 is the base register.

Example 1:

LA	5,4	places 4 into register 5
LA	7,6	places 6 into register 7
A	8,1(5,7)	

The add instruction will add the contents of location number 11 (contents of register 5 + contents of register 7 + 1) to the contents of register 8.

The technique demonstrated in example 1 is not always feasible. In cases for which it is either not practical or not convenient to use two register contents (X2 and B2) for the computation of an address, we may use an index register X2 along with an *implied* (as opposed to an explicitly designated) base register in order to compute an effective address.

Example 2:

LA	4,0	places 0 into register 4
A	3,LIST(4)	

When the assembler computes the effective address of the second operand of the add instruction, it will add the contents of register 4 to the address of LIST. LIST + 0 = LIST (register 4 contains 0, since the LA instruction placed it there), so that the net effect of the instruction A   3,LIST(4) will be to add the contents of LIST to the contents of register 3. (Note, however, that by changing the contents of register 4, we may change the effective address of the second operand.)

The add instruction of example 2 is an RX instruction. Let us see how the assembler will translate this instruction into machine language so that it will fit the required format for RX instructions:

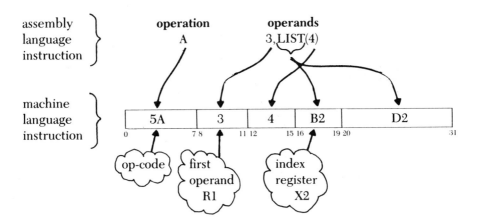

The operation code and first operand are translated as usual. The second operand has register number 4 in parentheses; register 4 is the *index register* X2 for this instruction. However the second operand must also have base register and displacement values (B2 and D2) in order for the instruction to be translated in accordance with the machine language specifications for RX instructions! The instruction does not specify values B2 and D2, therefore the assembler will have to "find" them.

The assembler knows that the second operand address is computed by adding:

address of LIST + contents of register 4

The assembler will use the program base register number B2 as defined by the USING instruction, and the appropriate displacement value D2 such that the contents of B2 + D2 will be equal in value to the address of LIST. The programmer need not be concerned with what those values B2 and D2 actually are! The assembler will choose correct values so that the second operand address will be computed by adding:

$$\underbrace{\text{contents of B2} + \text{D2}}_{\text{address of LIST}} + \text{contents of register 4}$$

We say that the second operand of the add instruction used an **implied base register**, for the base register, although specified by the programmer in the USING instruction, was not explicitly designated by the programmer in this instruction. The appropriate program base register number and displacement value will be incorporated into the machine language version of the instruction by the assembler.

The flowchart and assembly language instructions of figure 11.10 demonstrate an alternative to the coding of figure 11.8. The program uses register 6 as an index register and successively increments the contents of register 6 by 4 to process data items which are located at 4-byte (fullword) intervals in core. Note that the test to end the looping process is the comparison of register 6 to 40. Register 6 is initialized to 0 and is incremented by 4 after the processing of each table entry. Thus, when 10 entries have been processed, register 6 will contain 40.

In summary, we see that base registers and index registers for address modification are very powerful tools for programming with data items which are stored in consecutive storage locations. The techniques demonstrated in this section are equally useful for handling items which are stored in any systematic way, for appropriate routines can then be developed to obtain addresses by modifying register contents or displacements. Modification of displacements has not been presented in this section, for the technique is not as elegant nor as widely used as those that we have considered.

11.2.5   The Table Problem with Branch on Index Instructions

In this section we will demonstrate how the Branch on Index instructions may be used to simplify the looping process. As we have seen, incrementing a counter or an address and testing that location for exit is almost standard in the looping process. Indeed, in figure 11.10, three instructions were devoted to adjustment and testing:

A	6,B4	incrementing the index register (adjustment)
C	6,B40	test for exit
BL	RET	return if exit criteria not satisfied

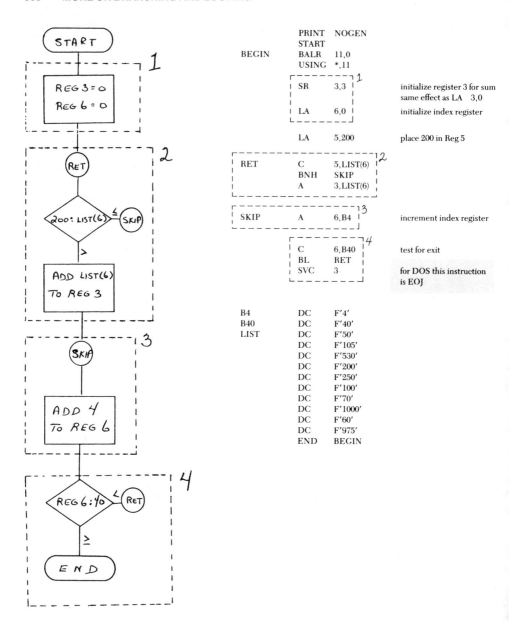

Figure 11.10
Program Using Register 6 as an Index Register for Address Modification

The Branch on Index instructions combine these steps into one instruction. We shall first describe the instructions. Then we shall use them to code alternate (simpler) versions of the program of figure 11.10.

The BXH and BXLE Instructions

The BXH Instruction (**B**ranch on Inde**X** **H**igh)

Instruction type: Machine Instruction
Machine format: RS Instruction (Register and Storage Instruction)

86	R1	R3	B2	D2

0   7 8   11 12   15 16   19 20   31

Symbolic format:

	name	operation	operands
	[symbolic name]	BXH	R1,R3,name2
or	[symbolic name]	BXH	R1,R3,D2(B2)

where R1 and R3 are register numbers. D2 and B2 are the displacement and base register respectively used to calculate the rightmost operand address.

. . . .

Rules:
- The register specified by R1 will be an index register.
- The register specified by R3 will contain an increment.
- If R3 is even, the next higher register will contain the limit.
- If R3 is odd, it contains both the increment and the limit.
- The rightmost operand contains the address to which control will be transferred when
    contents of R1 + contents of R3 > limit
- The increment may be of any magnitude.

Condition Code: The condition code remains unchanged.

The Branch on Index High instruction performs three of the steps generally necessary for loop processing. It combines addition, comparison, and a conditional branch. The first operand register (R1) is treated as the index register and must be initialized elsewhere in the program. The middle operand register (R3) contains the amount by which R1 will be incremented (or decremented) each time the BXH is executed. The limit (that is, the value to which the instruction compares R1) is found in an *odd* register only. If R3 is odd, it serves as both increment and limit. If R3 is even, the next higher-numbered register (which is naturally odd) serves as the limit. The BXH instruction adds the contents of R3 to the contents of R1, replacing the previous contents of R1 with the sum. It then compares R1 to the limit. If R1 is greater than the limit in value (that is, if R1 is "high"), then a branch is effected to the instruction at name2. If R1 is less than or equal to the limit, sequential execution continues.

Example:

```
              LA      9,0
              LA      10,10
              LA      11,10
              BXH     9,10,LOOP
CONTINUE      .
              :
              :
```

The contents of register 9 (zero) + contents of register 10 (ten) are not greater than the contents of register 11 (ten). Hence the branch will not take place. Sequential execution continues.

Example:

```
              LA      9,8
              L       11,M2
              BXH     9,11,LOOP
CONTINUE
              :
              :

M2            DC      F'−2'
```

The contents of register 9 (eight) + contents of register 11 (minus two) are greater than the contents of register 11 (minus two). Hence program control will be transferred to the instruction called LOOP.

The BXLE Instruction (**B**ranch on Inde**X** **L**ow or **E**qual)

Instruction type: Machine Instruction
Machine format: RS Instruction (Register and Storage Instruction)

87	R1	R3	B2	D2

0   7 8   11 12   15 16   19 20   31

Symbolic format:

name	operation	operand
[symbolic name]	BXLE	R1,R3,name2
or [symbolic name]	BXLE	R1,R3,D2(B2)

where R1 and R3 are register numbers. D2 and B2 are the displacement and base register respectively used to calculate the rightmost operand address.

. . . .

Rules:

- The register specified by R1 will be an index register.
- The register specified by R3 will contain an increment.
- If R3 is even, the next higher register will contain the limit.
- If R3 is odd, it contains both the increment and the limit.
- The rightmost operand contains the address to which control will be transferred when
      contents of R1 + contents of R3 ≤ limit
- The increment may be of any magnitude.

Condition code: The condition code remains unchanged.

The BXLE instruction is identical to the BXH, except that the branch will take place when the sum of the index (R1) and the increment (R3) is less than or equal to the limit. If the sum is greater than the limit, sequential execution continues.

Example:

```
              LA      7,4
              LA      8,2
              LA      9,50
              BXLE    7,8,BRANCH
      CONT    .
              .
              .
```

The contents of register 7 (four) + contents of register 8 (two) are less than the contents of register 9 (fifty). Therefore program control will transfer to the instruction at BRANCH.

Example:

```
                    LA      5,20
                    LA      11,20
                    BXLE    5,11,BRANCH
        CONT        .
                    .
```

The contents of register 5 (twenty) + contents of register 11 (twenty) are greater than the contents of register 11 (twenty). Sequential execution will continue.

We are now ready to code the program of figure 11.10, using the BXLE instruction. The listing of this version of the program is given in figure 11.11.

Note that some extra instructions are required before the loop, in order to initialize the index, increment and limit registers. However, keep in mind that the initialization occurs only once, and is well worth the savings of instructions within the loop itself, for such instructions would be executed many times.

We first clear register 3 to zero, for that register is to hold the sum. We then load the three registers to be used by the BXLE instruction for index, increment, and limit purposes, with their desired contents. The body of the loop remains the same as in the version of figure 11.10. The operation of the instruction BXLE   6,8,RET may be described as follows, for each pass through the loop:

Number of Pass	Register 6 Before Incrementing		Register 8		Register 6 After Incrementing		Limit	Branch Back to RET?
1	0	+	4	=	4	<	36	yes
2	4	+	4	=	8	<	36	yes
3	8	+	4	=	12	<	36	yes
4	12	+	4	=	16	<	36	yes
5	16	+	4	=	20	<	36	yes
6	20	+	4	=	24	<	36	yes
7	24	+	4	=	28	<	36	yes
8	28	+	4	=	32	<	36	yes
9	32	+	4	=	36	=	36	yes
10	36	+	4	=	40	>	36	no

Note that the limit value used in this version was 36 (the previous version used a value of 40), for the test here was for "less than or equal to" while the previous version tested for "less than" only (the instruction BL   RET, see figure 11.10).

```
LOC     OBJECT CODE   ADDR1 ADDR2  STMT  SOURCE STATEMENT

CCCCCC                              1          PRINT NOGEN
CCCCCC                              2          START
CCCCCC  C5B0                 CCC02  3  BEGIN   PALR  11,0
                                    4          USING *,11
CCCCC4  1B33                        5          SR    3,3        CLEAR REG 3 FOR SUM
CCCCC8  4160 CCC0           C0000   6          LA    6,0        INITIALIZE INDEX REGISTER
CCCCCC  4180 CC04           C0004   7          LA    8,4        INCREMENT = 4
CCCCCC  4190 CC24           C0024   8          LA    9,36       LIMIT = 36
CCCCC1C 415C CCC8           C00C8   9          LA    5,200      PLACE 2C0 INTO REG 5
CCCCC14 5956 B026           C0028  10  RET     C     5,LIST(6)
CCCCC18 47DC B01E           C0020  11          BNH   SKIP
CCCCC1C 5A36 B026           C0028  12          A     3,LIST(6)
CCCCC2C 8768 BC12           C0014  13  SKIP    BXLE  6,8,RET    ADDS 4 TO REGISTER 6, COMPARES SUM
                                   14  *                        TO 36, BRANCHES BACK IF (REG 6)≤36
                                   15  *                        FOR DOS THIS INSTRUCTION IS EOJ
CCCCC24 CA03                       16          SVC   3

CCCCC28 CCCC                CCC0   17  LIST    DC    F'50'
CCCCC2B CCCCCC32                   18          DC    F'105'
CCCCC2C CCCCC69                    19          DC    F'530'
CCCCC3C CCCCC212                   20          DC    F'200'
CCCCC34 CCCCCCC8                   21          DC    F'250'
CCCCC38 CCCCCCFA                   22          DC    F'100'
CCCCC3C CCCCC64                    23          DC    F'70'
CCCCC4C CCCCC46                    24          DC    F'1000'
CCCCC44 CCCCC3E0                   25          DC    F'65'
CCCCC48 CCCCC041                   26          DC    F'975'
CCCCC4C CCCCC3CF                   27          END   BEGIN
```

Figure 11.11
Program Using Register 6 as an Index Register,
and BXLE Instruction to Control the Loop

For the sake of completeness, we present the final version of our program in figure 11.12, using the BXH instruction. Note that the nature of the test by this instruction makes a negative increment more natural, and we may thus code the problem working backwards through LIST.

11.2.6 Loop Control with the BCT and BCTR Instructions

The Branch on Count instructions (BCT and BCTR) provide the adjustment and testing functions for exit from a loop, as well as the decision that an exit from the loop should or should not be implemented. You will see that they are a bit more restrictive than the BXLE and BXH instructions in that they do not allow the programmer to choose increment and limit values (those values are predetermined). However in situations to which these instructions are applicable, they are concise and simple to use.

We shall first describe the instructions, and then provide examples of their use. Note that their functions are essentially equivalent. The BCT and BCTR are of the RX and RR types, respectively.

The BCT Instruction (**B**ranch on Coun**T**)

Instruction type: Machine Instruction
Machine format: RX Instruction (Register and IndeXed Storage Instruction)

46	R1	X2	B2	D2
0	7 8	11 12	15 16 19 20	31

Symbolic format:

	name	operation	operands
	[symbolic name]	BCT	R1,name2
or	[symbolic name]	BCT	R1,D2(X2,B2)

where R1 is a register number. D2,X2, and B2 are the displacement, index register, and base register respectively used to calculate the second operand address.

. . . .
Rules:
- The register specified by R1 should contain the counter (the number to be decremented and compared to zero).

```
LOC      OBJECT CODE   ADDR1  ADDR2   STMT   SOURCE STATEMENT

000000                                  1    *
                                        2          PRINT NOGEN
                                        3          START
000000   05B0                           4   BEGIN  BALR  11,0
                                        5          USING *,11
000002   1B33                           6          SR    3,3          CLEAR REGISTER 3 FOR SUM
000004   4160 0024            00024     7          LA    6,36         INITIALIZE INDEX REG TO 36
000008   4880 B024            00026     8          LH    8,MFCUR      INCREMENT = -4
00000C   4190 0000            0000C     9          LA    9,0          LIMIT = 0
000010   4150 00C8            000C8    10          LA    5,200        PLACE 200 INTO REGISTER 5
000014   5956 B026            00028    11   RET    C     5,LIST(6)
000018   47D0 B01E            0001E    12          BNH   SKIP
00001C   5A36 B026            00028    13          A     3,LIST(6)
000020   8668 B012            00014    14   SKIP   BXH   6,8,RET      DECREASES REGISTER 6 BY 4, COMPARES
                                                                     RESULT TO ZERO, BRANCHES BACK IF
                                                                     (REG 6)>0
                                        15   *
                                        16   *
000024   0A03                           17          SVC   3           FOR DOS THIS INSTRUCTION IS EOJ
                                        18   *
000026   FFFC                           19   MFCUR  DC    H'-4'
000028   00000032                       20   LIST   DC    F'50'
00002C   00000069                       21          DC    F'105'
000030   00000212                       22          DC    F'530'
000034   000000C8                       23          DC    F'200'
000038   000000FA                       24          DC    F'250'
00003C   00000064                       25          DC    F'100'
000040   00000046                       26          DC    F'70'
000044   000003E8                       27          DC    F'1000'
000048   00000041                       28          DC    F'65'
00004C   000003CF                       29          DC    F'975'
                                        30          END   BEGIN
```

Figure 11.12

Program Using Register 6 as an Index Register, and BXH Instruction to Control the Loop

> • The second operand specifies the address to which control will be transferred when contents of R1 ≠ 0.

Condition code: The condition code remains unchanged.

The first operand register in the BCT holds the counter that will determine when an exit will occur from the loop. When the BCT is executed, the contents of R1 are automatically reduced by a value of 1. The new contents are then compared to zero. If the contents of R1 are not equal to zero (R1 ≠ 0) then control will pass to the instruction specified by the second operand address (usually back to the beginning of the loop). If the contents of R1 are equal to zero (R1 = 0) then execution will continue sequentially (no branch—usually the exit from the loop).

Example:

```
              SR      5,5
              LA      4,10
LOOP          A       5,NUMB
              BCT     4,LOOP
FINISH        .
              .
```

In this example, register 5 was first cleared to 0, and the number 10 was loaded into register 4. The contents of NUMB were then added into register 5 ten times. The summary below describes what happened during each pass through the loop.

Number of Pass	Register 4 Before Decrementing	Register 4 After Decrementing		Branch Back to LOOP?
1	10	9	(> 0)	yes
2	9	8	(> 0)	yes
3	8	7	(> 0)	yes
4	7	6	(> 0)	yes
5	6	5	(> 0)	yes
6	5	4	(> 0)	yes
7	4	3	(> 0)	yes
8	3	2	(> 0)	yes
9	2	1	(> 0)	yes
10	1	0	(= 0)	no (exit from loop)

The BCTR Instruction (**B**ranch on **C**oun**T** **R**egister)

Instruction type: Machine Instruction
Machine format: RR Instruction (Register to Register Instruction)

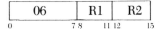

06	R1	R2
0	7 8 11 12	15

Symbolic format:

name	operation	operands
[symbolic name]	BCTR	R1, R2

where R1 and R2 are register numbers.

. . . .

Rules:
- The register specified by R1 should contain the counter.
- The register specified by R2 should contain the address of the location to which control will be transferred when contents of R1 ≠ 0.
- If R2 = 0, no branch will take place.

Condition Code: The condition code remains unchanged.

The BCTR instruction is identical to the BCT, except that the branch location is specified indirectly, as the location *whose address is in the second operand register*.

Example:

	LA	3, LOOP	load address of
			LOOP into Reg 3
	SR	5,5	
	LA	4,10	
LOOP	A	5, NUMB	
	BCTR	4,3	
FINISH	:		
	:		

These instructions perform the same function as those of the example above (for the BCT). The difference here is that the branch to LOOP is described as a branch to the instruction whose address is in register 3. (The address of LOOP is in register 3, since we placed it there!)

Programming Hints

1. The BCTR instruction may be used with a second operand of 0 as a "quick and easy" way of subtracting 1 from the contents of a register, in situations in which branching is not desirable at all! The instruction BCTR 3,0 will reduce the contents of register 3 by 1. The zero in the second operand means "no branch", for register 0 cannot be used for purposes of addressing (this is true for all instructions which use this type of indirect branching, including the BR and BALR instructions discussed in chapter 12). Moreover, this method of subtracting 1 from the contents of a register is quite efficient, for it avoids the need to define a constant value of 1 (with either a DC instruction or with a literal) and the instruction itself, being of the RR type, occupies only 2 bytes of storage! In fact, you might recall that we used this very feature of the BCTR to decrease the contents of register 1 by 1 when inserting floating characters to the left of edited fields (section 10.2.2).

2. One note of caution should be added at this point. In programming situations in which the first operand register is not loaded immediately prior to the looping process, it is a good practice to test the contents of R1 for a zero value before entering the loop. Consider, for example, the following case:

                LOOP   AR   3,4
                                BCT   5,LOOP
                                :
                                :

    If by some chance register 5 contained a zero prior to entering the loop, the BCT would first reduce the contents of register 5 to -1, and *then* test for equality with zero, which it will not find; therefore a branch will be effected back to LOOP. After the second execution of the loop, register 5 will be reduced to -2, then to -3, and so on, until the maximum negative binary number is reached. The Branch on Count instructions ignore the overflow occurring when the maximum negative binary number is transformed into the maximum positive binary number by the next reduction. The decrementing will continue until finally the value in R1 reaches zero! (If you do not remember binary representation with complements, refer back to chapter 7.) This is obviously a situation that we wish to avoid, and a simple test to ensure an acceptable initial count value is in order.

The program of figure 11.13 demonstrates how the BCT instruction may be used to control looping in the table problem considered earlier in this chapter. Note

```
LCC   OBJECT CODE   ADDR1 ADDR2   STMT   SOURCE STATEMENT

                                    1   *
                                    2         PRINT NOGEN
                                    3         START
CCCCCC                              4   BEGIN BALR  11,0
CCCCCC  C5B0                        5         USING *,11
CCCCC2  1B33                        6         SR    3,3        CLEAR REG 3 FOR SUM
CCCCC4  4190 CC0A          CCC0A    7         LA    9,10       INITIALIZE COUNT TO 10
CCCCC8  4150 CCC8          CCC08    8         LA    5,200      PLACE 2CC INTO REG 5
CCCCCC  4160 CC00          CCC00    9         LA    6,LIST(6)  INITIALIZE INDEX REGISTER
CCCC1C  5956 BC2A                  10   RET   C     5,LIST(6)
CCCC14  4700 BC1A                  11         BNH   SKIP
CCCC18  5A36 B02A                  12         A     3,LIST(6)
CCCC1C  5A60 BC26                  13   SKIP  A     6,B4       INCREMENT INDEX REGISTER
CCCC2C  4690 BC0E                  14         BCT   9,RET      REDUCES CONTENTS OF REG 9 BY 1, COMPARES
                                                                RESULT TO C, BRANCHES BACK IF (REG 9) =0
                                   15   *
                                   16   *
CCCC24  CAC3                       17         SVC   3          FOR DOS, THIS INSTRUCTION IS EOJ

CCCC26  CC00                       18   B4    DC    F'4'
CCCC28  CCCCC004                   19   LIST  DC    F'50'
CCCC2C  CCCCC32                    20         DC    F'105'
CCCC3C  CCCCC069                   21         DC    F'530'
CCCC34  CCCCC212                   22         DC    F'200'
CCCC38  CCCCCCC8                   23         DC    F'250'
CCCC3C  CCCCCFA                    24         DC    F'100'
CCCC4C  CCCC0064                   25         DC    F'700'
CCCC44  CCCCC046                   26         DC    F'1000'
CCCC48  CCCCC3E8                   27         DC    F'65'
CCCC4C  CCCCC41                    28         DC    F'95'
CCCC5C  CCCCC3CF                   29         END   BEGIN
CCCCCC  0000C3CF
```

Figure 11.13

Program Using the BCT Instruction to Control the Loop

that the count register has been initialized to 10, for the loop is to be processed 10 times (once for each table entry). Note too that the index is separate from the count, hence it must be incremented separately (this was not the case in the other versions of this program; see figures 11.10, 11.11, and 11.12).

Summary

In this chapter, various techniques for branching and loop control have been discussed, along with the functions of the condition code and the instruction address register fields. The use of base registers and index registers for address modification has also been presented, along with a demonstration of table reference using those techniques.

The solution to a problem involving the computation of FICA up to an assumed social security base has been flowcharted and coded. Programs have been presented that reference a one-dimensional table in storage through varied looping techniques.

Several new instructions have been introduced: the BC (branch on condition), the BCR (branch on condition to register), the BXH (branch on index high), the BXLE (branch on index low or equal), the BCT (branch on count), and the BCTR (branch on count register). In addition, the complete list of extended mnemonics has been presented.

Important Terms Discussed in Chapter 11

address modification	implied base register
adjustment (of loop)	index register
	initialization (of loop)
base register	
body (of loop)	list
branch	loop
condition code	table
extended mnemonic	

Questions

11-1. Assume that the contents of registers 2, 3, and 4 are as follow:
Register 2: 0000012A
Register 3: 00001044
Register 4: 001000FE

Indicate whether the branch to THERE will take place for each of the following program segments:

a) AR   2,3   d) LR   8,3
    BC   2,THERE   CR   2,8
                               BC   10,THERE

b) CR   4,2   e) CR   3,4
    SR   2,3   BC   15,THERE
    BC   5,THERE

c) SR   4,4
    BC   7,THERE

11-2. Write two different instructions each of which will clear register 5 to zero without the use of constants or literals.

11-3. Write the conditional branch instructions which are equivalent in function to the extended mnemonics below:
    a)   BE   LOW
    b)   BNL   PLACE
    c)   BO   PLACE
    d)   BNMR   11
    e)   NOPR   5
    f)   BH   B

11-4. Write a program segment to compute the sum of 5 consecutive halfwords in memory, beginning at location X. Use the BCT instruction to control the loop.

11-5. Assume that we have a 20-element list in storage beginning at a location called TABLE. Each list entry is a fullword long. Write a flowchart and assembly language instructions to store the list entries in reverse order beginning at a location called TABLE2. (Hint: You might use the BXLE or BXH instruction here.)

11-6. Consider three fullwords in storage called X, Y, and Z whose contents are unknown. Write a flowchart and assembly language code to sort these data elements into descending order in main storage. (Hint: You might want to place the values into registers before sorting.)

11-7. Write a program to search a list of twenty halfword values for all items smaller than 100, and to replace those items with the number 100. Use the BXLE instruction to control the loop.

11-8. Assume that we have twenty 2-byte elements in consecutive order beginning in main storage location LOC. Write a flowchart and assembly language instructions to find the largest number in this list, and to place that number into a location called LARGE. If there is more than one of the largest value, choose any one.

11-9. Consider a 15-word list beginning at location LISTX. Write the instructions to compute the mean value (average).

11-10. Now consider the list of question 9. But assume that we do not know how many entries the list contains. We do know, however, that the last element of the list will contain a zero. Write a program to compute the mean value (average). (Note that the program must determine how many values are actually present.)

11-11. State exactly what preparation must be made before using the BXLE, BXH, or BCT instructions. Which (if any) of these instructions is most useful? Least useful? Why?

11-12. What is the advantage of using base registers and index registers in table reference?

Unit

5

Operating System Concepts

Chapter 12

Subroutines and Subroutine Linkage

12.1   THE NEED FOR SUBROUTINES

12.1.1   A Programming Dilemma: Providing Output Headings Page by Page

Previous program examples in this text have provided program output with heading lines. However, with the exception of the program of section 10.5, we have contented ourselves with headers on the first page of output only.

We shall now consider a program which produces headers at the top of the first page, and at the top of each succeeding page upon detection of an "end of page" condition.

Program input will be in the form of student records on punched cards, as shown in figure 12.1. Each record will consist of 3 fields: a student identification number recorded in columns 1-9; a student name in columns 11-30; a student telephone number in columns 31-42.

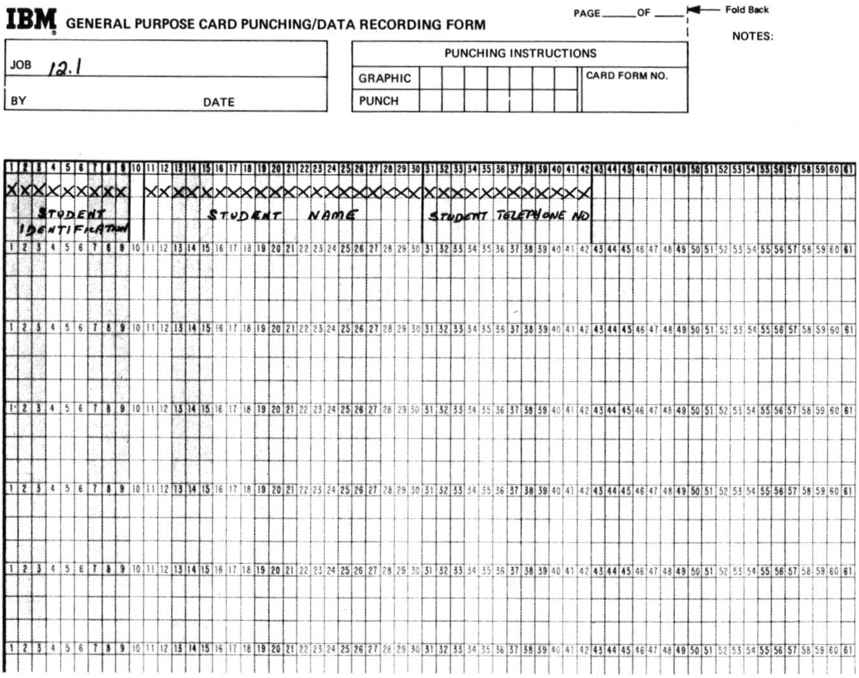

Figure 12.1
Input Layout for Header Program

The purpose of our program will be to instruct the computer to consider the input data and to produce output in the form of a report, with heading lines at the top of each output page, and one line skipped between heading and detail lines. The program will be instructed to proceed to a succeeding page after processing 50 lines on the current page. The output format desired is illustrated in figure 12.2.

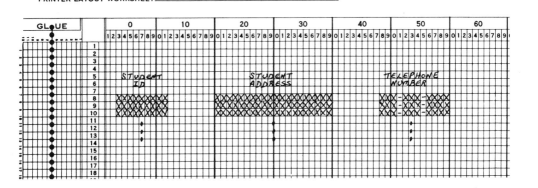

Figure 12.2
Output Layout for Header Program

We will flowchart the problem solution in this section. However, the actual coding will be deferred to section 12.2.2. The program flowchart is presented in figure 12.3.

Note the two identical flowchart segments in figure 12.3 enclosed within dotted lines. The first segment produces headings on a first output page, while the second produces headings on succeeding pages of output.

From a practical point of view, the repetition of identical flowchart segments (and hence instruction repetition in the resulting program!) would seem to be unnecessary at best, wasteful of computer storage and programmer effort.

A more efficient technique would involve writing the program segment only once, branching to it whenever it is needed, and returning to the point of departure after the program segment has been executed. Figure 12.4 is a revised version of the flowchart of figure 12.3. It utilizes the branching technique just described.

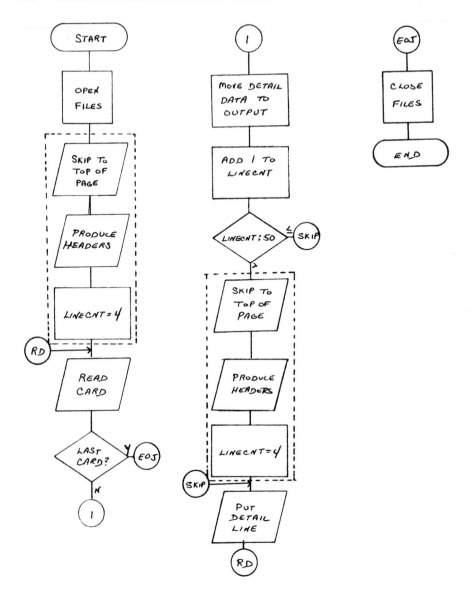

Figure 12.3
Flowchart for Header Program

Note the new flowchart symbol introduced in figure 12.4:

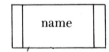

This symbol denotes a predefined set of operations—a **subroutine**—which is

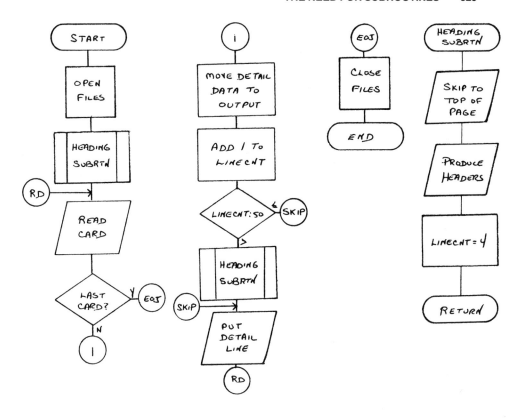

Figure 12.4
Revised Flowchart for Header Program

assumed to be described independently and identified by name (the name within the symbol).

Note too that the actual subroutine description begins with a terminal sign identifying the subroutine by name. Likewise the termination of the "HEADING SUBRTN" described in figure 12.4 is identified by the word RETURN enclosed in a terminal sign. This denotes that execution does not halt upon completion of the subroutine. Instead, control is returned to the point of the main program which immediately follows the branch to the subroutine.

12.1.2 What Are Subroutines?

Some Basic Definitions

In a general sense, a **subroutine** is a group of instructions which perform a particular function. An **open subroutine** is repeated within a program whenever its services are required. A **closed subroutine** is found only once in main storage, and is branched to or called by other routines which use it. An open subroutine is illustrated within the dotted lines in figure 12.3; a closed subroutine called HEADING SUBRTN is illustrated in figure 12.4.

In our discussion of subroutines, we shall also use the following terms:
Calling routine: A program which invokes a subroutine.
Called routine: A subroutine which is invoked by a calling routine.

Subroutines may be classified as internal or external. An **internal subroutine** is assembled along with the calling program. An **external subroutine** is assembled separately. When larger programs are subdivided to be written and debugged separately, the units are external subroutines which will be joined or "linked" together prior to execution of the completed project. When written, each of these independent programming units is known as a **control section** (or CSECT). The control sections are linked together by a special operating system program called the **linkage editor**. The workings of the linkage editor will be briefly considered in section 12.4.

Why Subroutines?

The use of subroutines in today's programming is not merely advantageous—it is often indispensable! When a subroutine at one storage location is branched to from many points within a program instead of being inserted whenever its services are required, valuable storage space is saved.

Moreover, once written, the subroutine may be separately assembled (or compiled), debugged, and tested, and then incorporated into other programs requiring its services, thus avoiding substantial duplication of programming effort.

In the case of larger commercial applications, a problem might actually be segmented into a number of separate subroutines, each to be written, assembled, and debugged separately. The main program might then consist essentially of successive branches to the appropriate subroutines. The entire project is in this way greatly simplified.

In a yet larger sense, the typical user program may be considered a subroutine of the operating system which controls computer operations. The user program is "called" by the supervisor program, and "returns" control to the supervisor after its execution.

A key idea in these days of "structured programming" is the development of a program in "modular" fashion; that is, as a set of independent linked subroutines.

The following section will demonstrate the use of internal subroutines in the program application described above (section 12.1.1): producing program headers. External subroutines will be considered in section 12.3.

12.2   INTERNAL SUBROUTINES

12.2.1   Entry To and Return From Internal Subroutines: The BAL, BALR, and BR Instructions

Entry to the internal heading subroutine would appear at first glance to be a simple matter indeed, involving an unconditional branch when the need becomes apparent (after opening files, or when LINECNT exceeds 50 in value in the flowchart of figure 12.4). The difficulty, however, involves returning to the proper point of the main program after subroutine execution! Even in the simple example of section 12.1.1, we have two possible return points. After each subroutine execution, we wish to return to the program instruction which immediately follows the unconditional branch to the subroutine. Thus we must use an unconditional branch instruction which, prior to branching, saves the address of the next sequential instruction of the calling program, so that the return may later be effected to that address. Assembly language provides two such instructions: The BAL and BALR instructions.

The BAL Instruction (**B**ranch **A**nd **L**ink)

Instruction type: Machine Instruction

Machine format: RX Instruction (Register and IndeXed Storage Instruction)

45	R1	X2	B2	D2
0	7 8 11 12	15 16	19 20	31

Symbolic format:

	name	operation	operands
	[symbolic name]	BAL	R1,name2
or	[symbolic name]	BAL	R1,D2(X2,B2)

where R1 is a general register number (0-15). D2,X2, and B2 are the respective displacement, index register, and base register used to calculate the second operand address

---

Condition Code: The condition code remains unchanged.

The BAL instruction takes the address of the instruction which *follows* it in main storage (the BAL instruction itself occupies 4 bytes, hence the address in question is that of the BAL instruction + 4) and places it into the register designated as the first operand of the instruction.

After this is done, the program branches to the instruction stored at name2.

Example:

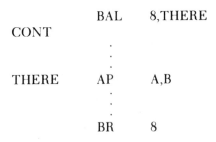

If, prior to execution, the machine language version of the BAL instruction were stored beginning in location 100 of main storage (an RX instruction occupies 4 bytes, hence the BAL will occupy locations 100-103), then the instruction would place the value 104, the address of CONT, into register 8. An unconditional branch is then effected to THERE (in figure 12.5, the instruction at main storage location 200). The subroutine has now been "called". The "return" to the instruction following the BAL is effected by the BR 8 instruction, the last instruction of our subroutine. The BR instruction is an extended mnemonic (see chapter 11). It causes an unconditional branch to that instruction whose address is contained in the operand register. In the example above, register 8 contains the address of CONT (the BAL instruction placed it there) hence BR 8 will cause a return to CONT, the instruction immediately following the BAL.

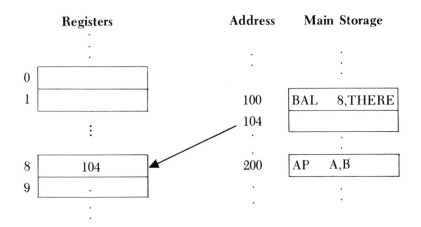

Figure 12.5
Storage of Succeeding Address by BAL Instruction

The BALR instruction has been described in section 2.4. For convenience, we repeat the description below:

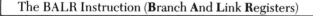

The BALR Instruction (**B**ranch **A**nd **L**ink **R**egisters)

Instruction type: Machine Instruction

Machine format: RR Instruction (Register to Register Instruction)

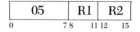

| 05 | R1 | R2 |

0   7 8   11 12   15

Symbolic format:

name	operation	operands
[symbolic name]	BALR	R1,R2

where R1 and R2 are general register numbers (0-15).

Condition Code: The condition code remains unchanged.

The BALR instruction places the address of the instruction which follows it in main storage (the BALR, an RR instruction, occupies 2 bytes, hence the address in question is that of the BALR instruction + 2) into the register designated as its first operand.

The instruction then effects a branch to that instruction whose *address* is found in the second operand register. There is one exception: A second operand of 0 means that no branch is to take place.

Example 1:

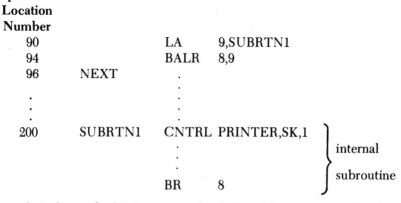

Location Number			
90		LA	9,SUBRTN1
94		BALR	8,9
96	NEXT	.	
.		.	
.		.	
.		.	
200	SUBRTN1	CNTRL	PRINTER,SK,1
		.	
		.	
		.	
		BR	8

internal subroutine

In example 1 above, the LA instruction loads the *address* associated with the name SUBRTN1 (that is, the address of the CNTRL instruction—in this case the value 200) into register 9. The BALR instruction then places the address of the instruction *following* it (that is, the address of NEXT, here the value 96) into register 8. It then effects a branch to the instruction whose address is found in register 9. Register 9 contains the address of SUBRTN1 (the LA instruction placed it there!), hence a branch to SUBRTN1 takes place. The subroutine has now been "called".

The "return" to the main routine is effected by the BR 8 instruction, the last instruction of our subroutine. In the example above, register 8 contains the address of NEXT (the BALR instruction placed it there). Hence BR 8 will cause a return to NEXT, the instruction immediately following the BALR.

The example below demonstrates another way of placing a subroutine address into a register so that the BALR may be used to effect the linkage. Here we use a special type of constant called an **address constant** or **adcon**. This constant has the form

name	operation	operand
[symbolic name]	DC	A(name)

It stores the *address* of the location whose name is in parentheses into a binary fullword location in main storage. The fullword location in which the address is stored may be referred to by the symbolic name assigned by the programmer in the name portion of the adcon. Thus the statement AD DC A(B) stores the address of a location called "B" in another storage location called "AD".

Example 2:

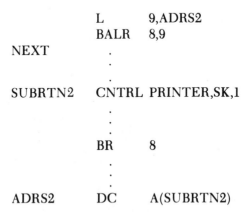

```
                          L       9,ADRS2
                          BALR    8,9
              NEXT          .
                            .
                            .
              SUBRTN2     CNTRL   PRINTER,SK,1
                            .
                            .
                            .
                          BR      8
                            .
                            .
                            .
              ADRS2       DC      A(SUBRTN2)
```

In example 2 above, the L instruction loads the contents of ADRS2—that is, the address of SUBRTN2—into register 9. The BALR instruction then places the address of NEXT into register 8, and effects a branch to the instruction whose address is stored in register 9—that is, a branch to SUBRTN2. The return to the main routine is effected by the BR 8 instruction, as in example 1 above.

12.2.2 Our Heading Program Coded: An Example Using Subroutines

Now that we understand how internal subroutine linkage is accomplished by the BAL, BALR, and BR instructions, we are ready to present, in figure 12.6, the coded solution to the flowchart of section 12.1.1.

Note that we accomplished the initial branch to SUBRTN at the beginning of the program with the instruction BAL 8,SUBRTN, while the branch in

```
  LOC   OBJECT CODE     ADDR1 ADDR2  STMT    SOURCE STATEMENT
                                        1 * THIS PROGRAM ACCEPTS STUDENT RECORDS EACH WITH STUDENT-ID, STUDENT
                                        2 * NAME, AND STUDENT TELEPHONE NUMBER.
                                        3 * EACH OUTPUT PAGE WILL CONTAIN 2 HEADING LINES, 1 SKIPPED LINE, AND
                                        4 * APPROPRIATELY SPACED DETAIL LINES.
                                        5 *
                                        6             PRINT NOGEN
CCCCCC                                   7             START 0
CCCCCC 05C0                              8 BEGIN       BALR  12,0
                            00002        9             USING *,12
CCCCC2                                  10             OPEN  (INFILE,INPUT,OUTFILE,OUTPUT)
                                        18 * FOR DOS SYSTEMS, FILES ARE OPENED BY
                                        19 *       OPEN  INFILE,OUTFILE
                                        20 *
                                        21 * BRANCH TO HEADING SUBROUTINE
                                        22 *
CCCC12 4580 C05C             C005E      23             BAL   8,SUBRTN
                                        24 *
CCCC16                                  25 RD          GET   INFILE,INAREA
CCCC24 D208 C2D0 C27E 02D02 C0280       30             MVC   ONUMBER,INUMBER
CCCC2A D213 C2E1 C288 002E3 002EA       31             MVC   CNAME,INAME
CCCC3C D20B C2FD C29C 002FF 0029E       32             MVC   CPHONE,IPHONE
CCCC36 FA10 C352 C354 00354 C0356       33             AP    LINECNT,ONE        INCREMENT LINE COUNTER
CCCC3C F911 C352 C355 00354 C0357       34             CP    LINECNT,FIFTY      COMPARE LINE COUNTER TO 50-OVERFLOW
CCCC42 4700 C04A             0004C       35             BNH   NOSUB              IF NO OVERFLOW, BRANCH PAST HEADING
                                        36 *                                       SUBROUTINE
CCCC46 4190 CC5C             CC05E      37             LA    9,SUBRTN           OTHERWISE LOAD SUBROUTINE ADDRESS
CCCC4A C589                             38             BALR  8,9                AND BRANCH TO HEADING SUBROUTINE
                                        39 *
CCCC4C                                  40 NCSUB       PUT   OUTFILE,OUTAREA    PRINT A LINE
CCCC5A 47F0 C014             C0016      45             B     RD
                                        46 *
                                        47 * HEADING SUBROUTINE
                                        48 *
CCCC5E                                  49 SUBRTN      CNTRL OUTFILE,SK,1       SKIP TO CHANNEL 1
CCCC6E                                  55             PUT   OUTFILE,HEADER1    WRITE FIRST HEADER
CCCC7C                                  60             PUT   OUTFILE,HEADER2    WRITE SECOND HEADER
CCCC8A                                  65             CNTRL OUTFILE,SP,1       SKIP A LINE
CCCC58 D201 C352 C357 00354 C0359       70             MVC   LINECNT,FOUR       RESET LINE COUNTER TO 4, SINCE AFTER
                                        71 *                                      HEADING WE'RE READY FOR 4TH PRINTED
                                        72 *                                      LINE
CCCC9E 07F8                             73             BR    8                  RETURN TO MAIN ROUTINE
                                        74 *
CCCCAC                                  75 EOJ         CLOSE (INFILE)
CCCCAA                                  81             CLOSE (OUTFILE)
                                        87 * FOR DOS SYSTEMS, FILES ARE CLOSED BY
                                        88 *       CLOSE INFILE,OUTFILE
CCCCB6 0A03                             89             SVC   3
                                        90 * FOR DOS SYSTEMS, EXECUTION IS HALTED BY
                                        91 *       EOJ
                                        92 *
                                        93 * DEFINE FILES, CONSTANTS, MAIN STORAGE LOCATIONS
                                        94 *
                                        95 INFILE      DCB   DSORG=PS,MACRF=GM,DDNAME=SYSIPT,BLKSIZE=80,LRECL=80,    C
CCCCB8                                        EODAD=EOJ
CCC118                                 149 OUTFILE     DCB   DSORG=PS,MACRF=PMC,DDNAME=SYSLST,BLKSIZE=132,LRECL=132
```

Figure 12.6 (Part 1)
Program with Internal Subroutine Linkage

the event of overflow was accomplished by loading the address of SUBRTN into register 9 (LA 9,SUBRTN) and then branching to the address contained in register 9. Actually the choice of branching techniques was arbitrary; either technique could have been used in either case. We may likewise have used an adcon:

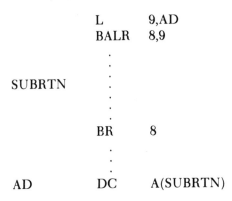

```
 LOC   OBJECT CODE     ADDR1 ADDR2  STMT    SOURCE STATEMENT

                                    203 * FOR DOS PROGRAMS, FILE DEFINITIONS ARE PERFORMED BY THE DTF MACROS
                                    204 * AND BUFFER DEFINITIONS
                                    205 *INFILE  DTFCD DEVADDR=SYSRDR,IOAREA1=INA,EOFADDR=FINISH,WORKA=YES
                                    206 *OUTFILE DTFPR DEVADDR=SYSLST,IOAREA1=OUTA,BLKSIZE=132,CONTROL=YES,
                                    207 *               WORKA=YES
                                    208 *INA     DS    CL80                BUFFER FOR INPUT FILE
                                    209 *OUTA    DS    CL132               BUFFER FOR OUTPUT FILE
CCC178                              210 HEADER1 CS    OCL132
CCC178 4C4040                       211         CC    CL3' '
CCC178 E2E3E4C4C5D5E3               212         CC    CL7'STUDENT'
CCC1E2 404040404C4C4C4C4C           213         DC    CL15' '
CCC1S1 E2E3E4C4C5D5E3               214         CC    CL7'STUDENT'
CCC158 4C4C4C404C4C4C4C             215         CC    CL16' '
CCC1A8 E3C5D3C5D7C8D6D5             216         CC    CL9'TELEPHCNE'
CCC1E1 404040404040404040           217         CC    CL75' '
CCC1FC                              218 HEADER2 CS    OCL132              SECOND HEADER
CCC1FC 4C404C404C                   219         DC    CL5' '
CCC2C1 C9C4                         220         CC    CL2'IC'
CCC2C3 404040404C4C404040           221         CC    CL19' '
CCC216 D5C1D4C5                     222         CC    CL4'NAME'
CCC21A 4C4C4C404C4C4C4C             223         CC    CL19' '
CCC22C D5E4D4C2C5D9                 224         CC    CL6'NUMBER'
CCC233 40404C404C4C4C4040           225         CC    CL77' '
                                    226 *
CCC28C                              227 INAREA  CS    OCL80               INPUT AREA
CCC28C                              228 INUMBER CS    CL9
CCC28S                              229         DS    CL1
CCC2EA                              230 INAME   CS    CL20
CCC29E                              231 IPHCNE  CS    CL12
CCC2AA                              232         DS    CL38
                                    233 *
CCC2CC                              234 OUTAREA CS    OCL132              OUTPUT AREA
CCC2CC 4040                         235         CC    CL2' '
CCC2C2                              236 CNUMBER DS    CL9
CCC2CB 404040404C4C4C4C4C           237         CC    CL8' '
CCC2E3                              238 ONAME   CS    CL20
CCC2F7 404040404C4C4040             239         CC    CL8' '
CCC2FF                              240 CPHCNE  CS    CL12
CCC3CB 4C4C404C4C4C4C4C4C           241         CC    CL73' '
                                    242 *
CCC354 C00C                         243 LINECNT DC    PL2'0'              LINECNT INITIALIZED TO ZERO
CCC356 1C                           244 CNE     CC    P'1'
CCC357 C50C                         245 FIFTY   CC    P'50'
C0C359 C04C                         246 FOUR    CC    PL2'4'
CCCCCC                              247         END   BEGIN
```

Figure 12.6 (Part 2)
Program with Internal Subroutine Linkage

STUDENT ID	STUDENT NAME	TELEPHONE NUMBER
32C214200	ALEBA ROY	577-235-0214
856324578	ANDREWS ANNETTE	212-042-3215
4112CC320	ANTMAN FRED	212-200-3254
857321045	BENEDICT ELIZABETH	577-242-5136
5746325R7	BROWN LORI	212-021-2478
1C2C30526	BURNS ANDREW	212-023-0247
652321474	COSENTINO SUSAN	411-245-2366
35P658574	CRANE ANNA	212-024-2865
856320212	DALEY ROBERT	422-252-6387
32C542175	DAVIS FRED	577-235-0298
32C145852	DOE JOHN	212-878-8787
632985476	EATON JOHN	577-250-3000
32C325412	ECKSTEIN LINDA	212-025-2857
5E7E54321	EMANUELE RITA	577-980-3214
653C87542	FRANCES RITA	577-235-0231
C12C35647	FRANK ALICE	577-023-8567
565856325	FREEMAN DAVID	712-024-2121
5R7650341	FRENCH SUZANNE	577-224-5784
352145624	GODFATHER THE	577-416-5774
563254124	HAMILTON GEORGE	212-024-5200
142574852	HARRY JAMES	212-123-4567
650245121	HERE IAM	577-025-6868
C21320520	HIRSCH DANIEL	577-023-0202
585687421	HOPE JOYCE	212-452-0209
5P6530248	JENKINS SAM	212-854-6857
754852541	KILPATRICK JOSEPH	577-252-3541
854210235	KILROY	577-612-6161
C2C12458S	LAMBERTI BILL	577-254-2365
C2314257R	LAMBERTI ELIO	212-032-0279
353241578	LANDER ROY	577-421-5454
244155745	LAZZARIO TONY	577-252-3421
632142502	LEWIS MARCIA	212-021-5421
541254125	LEWIS REGINALD	212-352-0200
744583216	LORD BRIAN	212-233-3254
565E74235	LUPO MARIA	577-245-2424
457245132	MARANO BETH	212-021-5468
52C321420	MARCANO MILLICENT	212-421-2457
653C23021	MARTIN TONY	577-57R-5635
653214578	MCINTOSH ROBERT	212-024-5687
2C1245235	NAPOLEON VITO	577-578-5757
541C20320	PASCALE DIANNE	577-542-6320
654252350	REID CHERYL	212-025-6369
421C23541	ROCHESTER BURTON	212-425-5454
R41C23542	ROMANO ALICIA	212-023-5324
6542C3203	RUBIN MICHELLE	577-085-6547
652351245	RYDER EASY	577-57R-9898

Figure 12.6 (Part 3)
Program with Internal Subroutine Linkage

STUDENT ID	STUDENT NAME	TELEPHONE NUMBER
9R7654321	SALZBERG ANDREW	577-235-0247
147258369	SETTEMBRE ERNESTO	577-254-8569
652487124	SIEGEL NANCY	212-032-0214
63C585647	SILVERMAN DEBORAH	212-525-0214
C21424525	SROUR GIL	577-025-6589
C2C2C2023	TORRES MIGUEL	212-025-3653
321024754	TRUMAN JACOB	577-578-5666
124120325	WISE GABRIEL	577-421-2523
856425174	YORK MICHAEL	632-212-4252

Figure 12.6 (Part 4)
Program with Internal Subroutine Linkage

12.3   EXTERNAL SUBROUTINES

12.3.1   The Need for Linkage Conventions

Register Conventions

The program of section 12.2.2 above demonstrated a typical subroutine linkage. There was no difficulty in providing communication between the main routine and the subroutine. For example, the "calling" instructions

BAL 8,SUBRTN and BALR 8,9 required another instruction to return control to the calling routine. This "return" instruction was BR 8. The need for this method of return was obvious as long as the operation of the BAL and BALR was understood.

External subroutines, however, are often written by different programmers! In such cases it becomes very important to establish standard register assignments—uses set by convention for particular registers—in order to ensure proper communication between routines. For example, Programmer A may write the instruction BALR 14,15 in his calling routine. Programmer B, writing the called routine and unaware of register conventions, may code BR 8 as his return instruction. This obviously will not establish proper subroutine linkage. There are two ways of avoiding such difficulties. One is constant close contact between writers of calling and called routines, a situation which is impractical. The alternative is the adherance to standard conventions for register use. These standards allow both calling and called routines assurance that uses to which the linkage registers are put by one will be the same uses to which they are put by the other.

Saving Register Contents

Systems/360 and 370 have 16 general registers which are used by every program routine, including the supervisor program. It is quite possible that the contents of some registers used by a calling routine will be destroyed by instructions in a called subroutine. Attempting to avoid this situation by assigning certain registers to each routine is not always practical or feasible, since Systems/360 and 370 have only 16 general registers available, and many of these are set aside for special uses (such as program base registers and linkage registers). Each routine should thus have access to as many registers as possible without fear of losing important data. Thus, it is the established practice that when a subroutine receives control, it saves the contents of the 16 general registers for the calling program. Immediately before returning control to the main program, the original register contents are restored. Thus both calling and called routines have complete use of the registers, the only restrictions being special uses designated for registers 0,1,13,14 and 15. Saving and restoring register contents will be more fully discussed in section 12.3.4.

12.3.2   Entry To and Return From External Subroutines

Entry to the Subroutine

Suppose that we wish, in our main program, to effect a branch to a subroutine called RTNA which was compiled separately from our program. The instruction BAL 14,RTNA would not work, for RTNA is not defined in the main program. In fact the assembler would consider this statement to be erroneous. Likewise the instruction sequences

```
LA      15,RTNA
BALR    14,15
```

and

$$
\begin{array}{ll}
\text{L} & \text{15,ADDRTNA} \\
\text{BALR} & \text{14,15}
\end{array}
$$

.
.
.

ADDRTNA   DC   A(RTNA)

both reference RTNA, an undefined name.

The EXTRN and ENTRY Statements

We must have a way of telling the assembler that although RTNA cannot be assigned an address at present (during the assembly phase), the correct address of RTNA will be placed into ADDRTNA by the linkage editor program—a special operating system program—after both the calling and called routines have been assembled.

The linkage editor considers separate **object modules**—the results of separate assembly and/or compilation—and **links** them together to form one program. The general method by the which the linkage editor accomplishes this linkage is described in section 12.4. For now, however, let us understand what the programmer must do in order for the linkage editor to accomplish its task.

The EXTRN Statement

The programmer must notify the assembler that certain symbols will be referenced within this routine, yet are defined externally. These **external symbols** are identified by the assembler instruction

operation	operands
EXTRN	name1,name2,...

In addition to notifying the assembler of the external nature of certain names, the EXTRN statement informs the linkage editor that an appropriate address for the name must be communicated to the calling program. This is accomplished as follows: The assembler places the symbol used in the operand portion of the EXTRN statement, and its starting address (the address of the adcon in which the symbol is used), into a special control dictionary called the **ESD** (external symbol dictionary), as an *external* symbol. The ESD is created by the assembler at the same time that it creates the object module during the assembly process.

The ENTRY Statement

The linkage editor may link many different object modules. Suppose that the linkage editor is to join routines 1,2 and 3. RTNA is described as an external symbol by routine 1. Furthermore suppose that both routines 2 and 3 use the symbol RTNA; that is, different addresses are associated with RTNA in each of routines 2 and 3. Which of these RTNA addresses is the proper address to be incorporated into routine 1? The linkage editor obviously would not know unless the programmer specifies this information. The assembler statement

operation	operands
ENTRY	name1,name2...

notifies the assembler program that the operand symbols are to be placed in the ESD as *entry* symbols, along with their addresses in the object module. If the address of RTNA in routine 2 were to be incorporated into routine 1, then routine 2 would have the statement ENTRY RTNA and routine 3 would have no such statement.

An **external symbol** is one that is used in an object module but is defined elsewhere (in another object module). An **entry symbol** is defined in the object module and used elsewhere (in *another* object module, although it may be used in the defining module as well).

The symbol RTNA, for example, would be found twice in ESDs, once as an EXTRN (external) symbol, once as an ENTRY symbol.

Thus the EXTRN and ENTRY statements cause their respective operands to be placed in the ESD. As long as the linkage editor is provided with an ENTRY symbol to match each EXTRN symbol, all symbolic linkage will be properly handled for the programmer.

Note, however, that:
● For the EXTRN instruction to be used, the program must provide an address constant (adcon) for each operand symbol.
● For the ENTRY instruction to be used, each operand symbol must be defined (assigned an address) within the routine.

Example 1:

```
      ° CALLING PROGRAM
                EXTRN RTNA
      PROG1         .
                    .
                    .
                    .
                L       15,ADDRTNA
                BALR    14,15
                    .
                    .
      ADDRTNA   DC      A(RTNA)      adcon provided for
          °                          EXTRN symbol RTNA
                END     PROG1
```

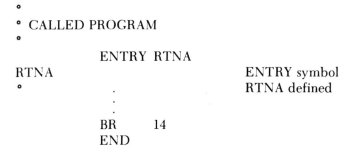

```
*
* CALLED PROGRAM
*
              ENTRY  RTNA
RTNA                                    ENTRY symbol
*          .                            RTNA defined
           .
           .
           BR      14
           END
```

Example 2:

**Assembler-
assigned
location
numbers**

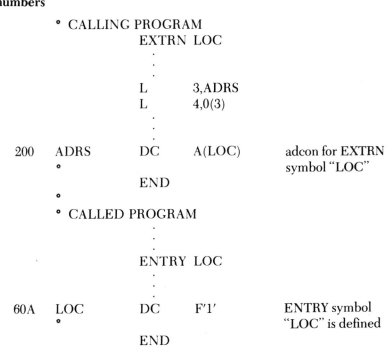

```
    * CALLING PROGRAM
                  EXTRN  LOC
                  .
                  .
              L        3,ADRS
              L        4,0(3)
                  .
                  .
200   ADRS        DC       A(LOC)        adcon for EXTRN
      *                                  symbol "LOC"
                  END
      *
    * CALLED PROGRAM
                  .
                  .
              ENTRY  LOC
                  .
                  .
60A   LOC         DC       F'1'          ENTRY symbol
      *                                  "LOC" is defined
                  END
```

The ESD for the calling program of example 2 would have (among others)
the entry

symbol	type	location
LOC	EXTRN	200

The ESD for the called program of example 2 would have (among others) the entry

symbol	type	location
LOC	ENTRY	60A

The linkage editor, in resolving the two object modules, will place the number 60A (the address of LOC) into location 200 of the calling program, where that address is referenced.

The instruction L   3,ADRS   of the calling program places the contents of ADRS (the address of LOC which was placed in ADRS by the linkage editor) into register 3. The instruction L   4,0(3)   then considers the contents of the address in register 3 (the contents of LOC, that is, the fullword number "1") and places it into register 4.

Thus we see that the use of appropriate EXTRN and ENTRY statements may enable us to reference not only names of other routines to enable proper transfer of control between routines (example 1, above) but also to reference contents of locations defined in other routines (example 2, above).

The V-Type Address Constant
An alternate method for effecting a branch to an external subroutine is to use a **V-type address constant** to define the address of the subroutine entry point. The constant has the form

name	operation	operand
symbolic name	DC	V(name)

It places the address of the location whose name is in parentheses into a binary fullword location in main storage. That fullword location may be referred to by the symbolic name assigned by the programmer in the name portion of the V-type address constant. The V-type adcon differs from the A-type adcon in that the operand address of a V-type adcon is automatically assumed by the assembler to be external (that is, defined elsewhere—not within the same program or control section). An EXTRN to inform the assembler that the address is external and is therefore unnecessary.

Example 3:

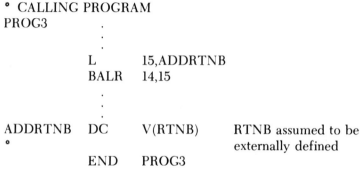

```
      ° CALLING PROGRAM
      PROG3         .
                    .
                    .
                    L       15,ADDRTNB
                    BALR    14,15
                    .
                    .
      ADDRTNB  DC       V(RTNB)        RTNB assumed to be
           °                           externally defined
               END      PROG3
```

```
  ○
  ○  CALLED PROGRAM
  ○
  RTNB            .
                  .
                  .
         BR    14
         END
```

Two other acceptable variations for entry to external subroutines involve the use of literals:

```
         EXTRN  RTNC
           .
           .
           .
         L       15,=A(RTNC)   EXTRN statement
                                required
         BALR    14,15
           .
           .
           .
```

or

```
         L       15,=V(RTND)   EXTRN statement
                                not required
         BALR    14,15
           .
           .
```

It should be noted that whenever the BALR instruction was used to effect a branch to an external subroutine, register 15 was used to hold the address of the subroutine. The standard linkage conventions dictate that register 15 always be used for this purpose.

Return From The Subroutine

As you may note from examples 1 and 3 above, the point of return to the main routine from an external subroutine is placed by the BALR instruction into register 14. The standard linkage conventions dictate that register 14 always be used for this purpose. The actual return is accomplished by the BR instruction. Return from an external subroutine is thus identical in technique to return from an internal subroutine.

12.3.3   Passage of Data Between Calling and Called Routines

It is often necessary for transfer of data to take place between calling and called routines. For example, if a subroutine is to compute the square root of a number, then the value of the number whose square root is to be determined must be communicated to the subroutine, and the resultant square root value must, after subroutine execution, be transmitted to the main program.

Likewise if a subroutine is to compute the mean (arithmetic average) of several values, the original values must first be passed to the subroutine, and the mean will be passed back to the calling routine after subroutine execution. We are thus concerned with techniques for passing parameter values between calling and called routines. A **parameter** is a variable that assumes a constant value throughout any one subroutine use. However its value may change when the subroutine is used again by the same main routine or by other main routines.

The standard linkage conventions determine that when parameter values are to be passed between calling and called routines, register 1 will hold the address of the **parameter list**. The parameter list is a list which may contain

- the parameter values *themselves*, in which case we say that we **call by value**, or
- the *addresses* of the parameters, in which case we say that we **call by name**.

The preferred method, the "call by name", is demonstrated in the example below.

Example 1:

```
        *CALLING ROUTINE
        CALL          .
                      .
                      .
#1              LA    1,PARAMLST   address of parameter
                                   list into R1
#2              L     15,ADDSUB    entry point to
                                   subroutine into R15
                BALR  14,15
                      .
                      .
        ADDSUB  DC    V(SUBRTN)
        *
        PARAMLST DC   A(PARAM1)    parameter list
                 DC   A(PARAM2)
                 DC   A(ANSWER)
        *
        PARAM1  DS    F            parameter values
        PARAM2  DS    F
        ANSWER  DS    F
                      .
                      .
                END   CALL
```

```
        ○
        ○  CALLED ROUTINE
        ○           ENTRY  SUBRTN
                      .
                      .
 #3   SUBRTN   L      2,0(1)
```
contents of address in register 1 (*address* of PARAM1) into R2

```
 #4            L      3,4(1)
```
contents of address in register 1 + 4 (address of PARAM2) into R3

```
 #5            L      7,0(2)
```
PARAM1 into R7

```
 #6            L      8,0(3)
```
PARAM2 into R8

$\left.\begin{array}{c} . \\ . \\ . \end{array}\right\}$ processing steps

```
 #7            L      9,8(1)
```
place address of 3rd entry in parameter list (address of ANSWER) into R9

```
 #8            ST     10,0(9)
```
store processing results (R10 optional choice) in location given by contents of R9, i.e., in ANSWER

```
               BR     14
```
return to calling routine

Figure 12.7 considers sample (arbitrary) addresses for PARAMLST, PARAM1, PARAM2, ANSWER, and SUBRTN, as defined in example 1. It demonstrates how these address values are manipulated and referenced within the program. The number on each connecting line refers to the particular program instruction which causes the data to be transferred.

The calling routine of example 1 above lists the *addresses* of 3 parameters—PARAM1, PARAM2, and ANSWER—in its parameter list PARAMLST. It is assumed that PARAM1 and PARAM2 contain values to be transmitted to the subroutine, while ANSWER is to receive a result value from the subroutine. The "call by name" is effected by the instruction LA 1,PARAMLST, which places the address of the parameter list (the *address* of the list which contains the *addresses* of the parameters—read that again!) into register 1. The next two instructions L   15,ADDSUB
                                   BALR 14,15
effect the branch to SUBRTN.

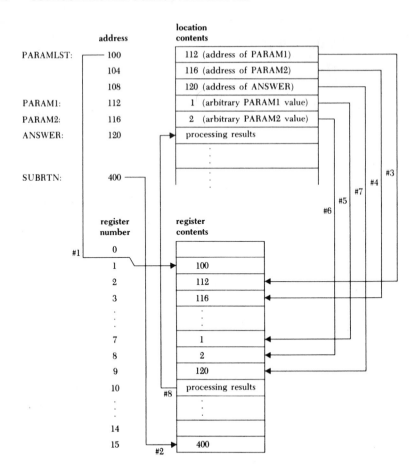

Figure 12.7

Once in SUBRTN, the instruction L 2,0(1) loads the contents of register 1—the *address* of PARAM1—into register 2, while the instruction L 3,4(1) loads the contents of the location which is 4 bytes past that given by the contents of register 1—that is the address of PARAM2, (since address constants are four bytes long!)—into register 3. We now have the addresses of PARAM1 and PARAM2 in registers 2 and 3 respectively. (You might note here that both addresses could have been loaded with a single "load multiple" instruction: LM 2,3,0(1); see section 8.2.7 for a discussion of the LM.)

The subroutine, however, requires the actual values of PARAM1 and PARAM2, not their addresses. The instruction L 7,0(2) therefore loads the "contents of the address contained in register 2," that is, the value PARAM1 (obviously the contents of the address of PARAM1 is the value PARAM1) into register 7. Likewise, the instruction L   8,0(3) loads the value PARAM2 into register 8. The passage of two data values from the calling routine to the subroutine has now been effected, and the subroutine may proceed with whatever processing of these values may be required.

Let's assume that some result value in register 10 is obtained by the subroutine, and is to be passed back to the calling routine and stored in the location ANSWER of the calling routine. The instruction L   9,8(1) loads the contents of the location obtained by adding 8 to the contents of register 1 (that is the address of ANSWER, which is in core 8 bytes past the address of PARAMLST) into register 9. Then, ST   10,0(9) stores the contents of register 10 (assumed to be subroutine results) into the location whose address is found in register 9—that is, into ANSWER.

Other Methods

The method described above for establishing a block of parameter addresses and loading the address of that block into register 1 is the standard method, and can be used regardless of the number of parameters required. Alternative methods may be considered. However they are limited in their applicability.

If only one or two parameters exist, the parameter values themselves may be placed into register 1 or registers 0 and 1. Registers 0 and 1 are the only registers used for passing values between routines, according to the standard linkage conventions. This is a straightforward method; however it can be used for passing one or two fullword values only.

A second alternative is to place the addresses of the parameters into registers 0 and 1 (rather than the address of the addresses). Here too, however, we limit ourselves to two parameter values. Moreover, in the interpretation of base-displacement addresses, the value 0 in a base register or index register field is interpreted to mean that the register is not to be used in the computation of the address. Hence placing an address into register 0 limits our ability to reference that address (in order to obtain its contents) by the methods employed in the example above. The statement L   3,4(0), for example, loads the contents of *location number 4* and does not consider the contents of register 0 at all!

We see, therefore, that the standard linkage convention for establishing a parameter address list and "pointing" to it through the contents of register 1 is indeed the most versatile of available techniques.

12.3.4   Saving and Restoring Register Contents

Saving Register Contents

When control is passed from a routine A to a routine B, the very first job of the subroutine is to save the contents of the 16 general registers as received from routine A. This affords routine B freedom in using the registers for its own purposes. The standard convention is for routine A to establish a special 18-word "save area". Routine B then stores the contents of registers 14,15,0,1,2,...,12, into words 4 through 18 of routine A's save area. However, how can routine B reference an area defined in routine A? In order to make this possible, the main program must pass the address of its save area to routine B by placing it in register 13. Routine A might load the address of SAVEA (its save area)—of course any name could be used— into register 13 as follows:

```
                LA      13,SAVEA
                  .
                  .
                  .
SAVEA           DS      18F
```

Then, upon receiving control, routine B will execute the instruction

```
                STM     14,12,12(13)
```

This instruction causes the storing of the contents of registers 14 through 12 (recall that the registers have the "wrap-around" feature, with register 0 immediately following register 15—thus 14 through 12 means 14,15,0,1,...,12) into that location given by the "contents of register 13 + 12". That is, the register storage will begin 12 bytes or 3 words past the beginning address of SAVEA— in the 4th word of SAVEA. The first 3 words of SAVEA are reserved for other uses.

Word 2 of Save Area

Note that all of routine A's register contents have been stored except for register 13, which contains the address of its save area SAVEA. Register 13 thus holds the "key" to the other register contents, and its contents must be safely stored in an area defined by routine B. If routine B is a "lowest-level" subroutine, that is it will not call any other subroutine and will not call on any supervisor services, then the contents of register 13 may be stored in any full-word location. However, if routine B is a "higher-level" subroutine (by far the more common case), then it will establish its *own* 18-word save area. It is then the convention that routine B will store the contents of register 13, as received from routine A, in the second word of its (routine B's) save area. Likewise if routine B calls a subroutine C, then routine C will store the contents of registers 14,15,0,...,12 back in words 4 through 18 of routine B's save area, and the contents of register 13 as received from routine B will be placed in the second word of routine C's save area, and so on.

Let us recap the steps for saving register contents in instruction form, assuming RTNA to be the calling program and RTNB to be the called routine.

```
✸
RTNA          .
              .
              .
              LA      13,SAVEA      address of SAVEA in R13
              .
              .
              .
SAVEA         DS      18F
✸             .
              .
              .
RTNB          STM     14,12,12(13)  contents of A's R14-R12 in
                                    words 4-18 of SAVEA

              BALR    12,0
              USING   ✸,12
              ST      13,SAVEB+4    contents of A's R13 (ad-
                                    dress of SAVEA) into word
                                    2 of SAVEB
              .
              .
              .
SAVEB         DS      18F
```

Note that the exact order of the first 4 instructions of RTNB is very important. RTNB is to be assembled separately from RTNA. Therefore it uses the BALR and USING instructions to initialize a base register (the BALR initializes its first operand register) and to establish addressability.

Note that the USING instruction notifies the assembler program that its second operand is to be an implied base register—that is the second operand register is to be assumed to contain the value indicated in the first operand of the USING instruction, and addresses in base-displacement form are to be calculated by the assembler based upon that assumption., If you do not remember the functions of the BALR and the USING instructions in establishing addressability, refer back to chapter 2, section 2.4.

When we initialize a base register, its previous contents are lost! Therefore it is important that we *store* the previous contents of that register which is to be used by RTNB as the base, *before* we initialize it. We may simply have stored the contents of register 12 (any register other than 13 might have been chosen) before establishing addressability, as follows:

```
              ST      12,68(13)
              BALR    12,0
              USING   ✸,12
```

However it is just as easy to store all 15 registers (they do have to be stored eventually) with one instruction:

```
              STM     14,12,12(13)
```

But what of the storage of the contents of register 13? Could this have been accomplished before establishing addressability? No. Remember that the contents of register 13 are to be stored in the save area of the called routine. Thus the addressability of routine B's save area must be established *before* the instruction ST   13,SAVEB+4 can be assembled or executed.

Word 3 of Save Area

We have just described storing the address of the *calling* routine's save area (SAVEA) into word 2 of the *called* routine's save area (SAVEB).

Yet another action which is designated by the standard linkage conventions, but which is not mandatory, is storing the address of the called routine's save area (SAVEB) into word 3 of the calling routine's save area (SAVEA). This may be accomplished by expanding the code for saving register contents as follows:

```
RTNA            .
                .
                .
                LA      13,SAVEA
                .
                .
SAVEA           DS      18F
                .
                .
RTNB            STM     14,12,12(13)
                BALR    12,0
                USING   *,12
                ST      13,SAVEB+4      save address of SAVEA
                                        in word 2 of SAVEB
```

LA	15,SAVEB	address of SAVEB into register 15
ST	15,8(13)	address of SAVEB into that location which is 8 bytes past the beginning of SAVEA, i.e. into word 3 of SAVEA (register 13 contains the address of SAVEA)
LR	13,15	now put the address of SAVEB into register 13 (in preparation for another subroutine call by RTNB)

The purpose of the boxed instructions is to store the address of SAVEB into word 3 of SAVEA. The LA instruction places the address of SAVEB into register 15 (an intermediate location—actually any register, other than the base register, or register 13 whose present contents will be used by the next instruction, may have been used). The instruction ST   15,8(13) then stores the address of SAVEB (which we just placed into register 15) into the third word of SAVEA. Note that register 13 contains the address of SAVEA (it was placed there by RTNA) so that 8(13) represents a displacement of 8 bytes from the address of SAVEA—that is, the third word of SAVEA!

The instruction LR   13,15 loads the address of SAVEB into register 13. Recall that the standard linkage conventions designate that the address of a routine's save area be stored by the routine in register 13. RTNA accomplished this with the instruction   LA   13,SAVEA and RTNB accomplished this with the instruction LR   13,15.

Figure 12.8 illustrates the makeup of the 3 save areas. Word 1 of the save areas is not used in the type of linkage pattern that we are discussing in this chapter.

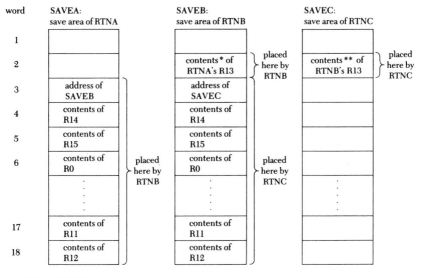

* address of SAVEA
**address of SAVEB

Figure 12.8

Restoring Register Contents

After the subroutine has accomplished its work, it must return control to the main program. The code to do this is called the **exit code**. The subroutine first places whatever results need be transmitted back to the main program either into locations given in the parameter list (see section 12.3.3) or into register 0. It must then restore the register contents which were saved during subroutine execution. This is accomplished by two instructions which undo the effects of those used to save the register contents. The instruction L   13,SAVEB+4 places the contents of the second word of the save area (where contents of register 13 were stored) back into register 13. Then the instruction LM   14,12,12(13) replaces the original contents of registers 14,15,0,...,12.

If, however, the subroutine placed a result value into register 0 to be transmitted back to the main routine, then restoring the contents of register 0 will destroy that result! In such a case we must use two Load Multiple instructions:

LM	14,15,12(13)	to restore the contents of registers 14 and 15, and
LM	1,12,24(13)	to restore the contents of registers 1-12.

12.3.5   Summary: Responsibilities of Calling and Called Routines

We shall now summarize the responsibilities that the calling routine and the called routine must fulfill in order for proper linkage to be accomplished. The standard linkage conventions are, of course, adhered to, as has been the case throughout this chapter.

Responsibilities of Calling Routine

1a   Define an 18-word save area and place its address in register 13.
2a   If parameters are to be passed between routines (whether into or out of):
Define areas to hold those parameters
Define a parameter list with addresses of those parameters
Load the address of the parameter list into register 1.
3a   Place the address of the called routine into register 15.
4a   Load the address of the return point to the calling routine into register 14.
5a   Branch to the address in register 15.

Responsibilities of Called Routine

1b   Store contents of registers 14 through 12 (from calling routine) in words 4 through 18 of the calling routine save area.

2b   Establish addressability (USING instruction)

3b° Define an 18-word save area.
     Store contents of register 13 (from calling routine) in second word of the subroutine save area.

4b°° Place address of subroutine save area into the third word of the calling routine save area.

5b° Place address of subroutine save area into register 13.
     Processing $\Big\}$ includes steps 2a through 5a above if branch to another subroutine is to occur

6b   Restore address of calling routine save area from second word of subroutine save area, to register 13.

7b   Restore previous contents of registers 14 through 12 from words 4 through 18 of the calling routine save area.

8b   Return to calling routine by branch to the address in register 14.

° denotes steps necessary for branch by this subroutine to another subroutine.
°° denotes nonmandatory steps.

In instruction form, assuming RTNA to be a higher-level routine which in turn calls RTNB, we have:

```
            ENTRY  RTNA
            EXTRN  RTNB
            START
RTNA        STM    14,12,12(13)    step 1b
            BALR   12,0
            USING  *,12            step 2b
            ST     13,SAVEA+4      step 3b
            LA     13,SAVEA        step 1a need be done only
               .                          once by calling rou-
               .                          tine, even if many
               .                          other subroutine calls
               .                          are later made by
               .                          this routine.
            L      15, ADRTNB      step 3a
            BALR   14,15           steps 4a, 5a
               .
               .
            L      13,SAVEA+4      step 6b
            LM     14,12,12(13)    step 7b
            BR     14              step 8b
SAVEA       DS     18F
ADRTNB      DC     A(RTNB)
            END    RTNA
```

```
                ENTRY RTNB
RTNB            STM     14,12,12(13)      step 1b
                BALR    12,0
                USING   *,12              step 2b
                ST      13,SAVEB+4        step 3b
                LA      13,SAVEB          step 1a     ⎫ unnecessary if
                L       15,=V(RTNC)       step 3a     ⎪ RTNB is a lowest
                  .                                   ⎪ level subroutine
                  .                                   ⎬ —(will not call
                  .                                   ⎪ other subroutines
                BALR    14,15             steps 4a,5a ⎪ or use supervisor
                  .                                   ⎭ services)
                  .
                  .
                L       13,SAVEB+4        step 6b
                LM      14,12,12(13)      step 7b
                BR      14                step 8b
SAVEB           DS      18F
                END     RTNB
```

Note that the steps noted to the right of the instructions for RTNA include those necessary for both calling and called routines, for RTNA is, in effect, fulfilling both functions. For RTNB, however, steps 1a through 5a may be eliminated in the event that it is a lowest level subroutine.

Note too that the save area of a calling routine is important in that it holds the routine's register contents while control is in the hands of a subroutine. After control has been restored to the calling routine, however, (with original register contents restored), the register save area contents are no longer needed. Therefore subsequent subroutine calls from the routine may utilize the *same* save area to *again* store the register contents immediately prior to another subroutine branch. It follows that loading the address of the save area into register 13 (step 1a in RTNA above) need be done only once near the beginning of a calling routine, and need not be repeated for other subroutine calls from that routine. The other steps involved in the calling process must, however, be repeated in order to assure proper linkage.

We now summarize the special functions of registers 0,1,13,14, and 15 as used in standard subroutine linkage. Note that these registers are used as indicated not only by programmers, but by the operating system macros as well.

Register Number	Register Function	Contents
0	Parameter Register	Single word output of a subroutine
1	Parameter Register	Input or output subroutine parameters
	or Parameter Address List Register	or Address of a main storage area which contains *either* the address of the parameters—(the parameters may be either input to, or output from, the subroutine) or parameter values
13	Save Area Register	Address of register save area (in calling routine) to be used by the subroutine
14	Return Register	Address of calling routine instruction to which control is to return after subroutine execution.
15	Entry Point Register	Address of point of entry to the subroutine

Towards Deeper Understanding

1. The BALR and USING instructions in the main routine initialize the base register and establish addressability for that routine. That is, the instruction USING °,12 informs the assembler that program addresses are to be expressed in the form of a displacement of a certain amount from the value "°" (meaning "present contents of location counter"; see chapter 2, section 2.4). Likewise, in the instruction sequence

```
        BALR   12,0
        USING  B,12
   B           .
               .
               .
```

the USING instruction informs the assembler that addresses are to be expressed in terms of their displacement from B. The maximum displacement value, however, is $4095 = 2^{12} - 1$. Therefore any location values which are more than 4095 bytes past B in main storage would not be addressable.

This difficulty can be avoided by using a more advanced version of the USING instruction, with several base registers indicated:

```
        BALR   8,0
        USING  B,8,9,10,11
B       LM     9,11,ADRS
          .
          .
          .
ADRS    DC     A(B+4096,B+8192,B+12288)
```

The instruction USING B,8,9,10,11 tells the assembler that base register values through B+12288 may be used. However the BALR instruction only loads register 8! Therefore we must load registers 9,10, and 11 ourselves with the appropriate initial values. Care must be taken, however, that the address constant ADRS extend not further than 4095 bytes past B, otherwise it will itself be non-addressable, and the loading could not then take place.

2. With regard to establishing addressability for a subroutine, the example above uses the statements

```
RTNB    STM    14,12,12(13)
        BALR   12,0
        USING  *,12
```

The BALR instruction initializes register 12 and the USING instruction informs the assembler that register 12 is to be used as a base register. Actually, however, the calling routine (RTNA) has already initialized register 15 with the address of RTNB! We may take advantage of this fact by requesting the assembler to calculate base-displacement address values using the present contents of register 15 (placed there by RTNA in the statement L 15,ADRTNB) as a base, without having to initialize any register with a new value.

We may thus code

```
        ENTRY  RTNB
        USING  *,15
RTNB    STM    14,12,12(13)
```

Note that in this case the USING instruction may precede the STM instruction, for it is not tied to the BALR instruction or to any instruction which will alter the contents of the register.

12.3.6   The SAVE, RETURN and CALL Macros

Assembly language provides us with 3 macro instructions which somewhat simplify linkage to and from subroutines.

The SAVE Macro

Instruction type: Macro Instruction
Symbolic format:

name	operation	operands
[symbolic name]	SAVE	(r1,r2)

where r1 and r2 are register numbers

The macro expansion of the SAVE instruction is a STore Multiple (STM). instruction which stores the contents of registers r1 through r2 in the proper words of the register save area in accordance with the standard linkage conventions. That is, the contents of registers beginning with register 14 are placed into consecutive storage locations beginning with the fourth word of the save area: 12(13).

Example:

                        SAVE   (14,12)
    has the macro expansion   STM   14,12,12(13)

Example:

                        SAVE   (4,6)
    has the macro expansion   STM   4,6,36(13)

The RETURN Macro

Instruction type: Macro Instruction
Symbolic format:

name	operation	operands
[symbolic name]	RETURN	(r1,r2)

where r1 and r2 are register numbers

The macro expansion of the RETURN instruction is:
   (i) A Load Multiple (LM) instruction which restores the original contents of registers r1 through r2 from the register save area, and
  (ii) The instruction BR   r1 which returns control to the calling routine

Example:

```
    RETURN   (14,12)
has the macro expansion   LM      14,12,12(13)
                          BR      14
```

Example:

```
                STM     14,12,12(13)
                BALR    12,0
                USING   *,12
                   .
                   .
                   .
                LM      14,12,12(13)
                BR      14
```

may be replaced by

```
                SAVE    (14,12)
                BALR    12,0
                USING   *,12
                   .
                   .
                   .
                RETURN  (14,12)
```

The SAVE and RETURN macros also include some optional parameters which we shall not consider in this text.

The CALL macro may be used to provide a parameter list and to establish subroutine entry point and return point addresses. Whether using this instruction or the methods considered earlier, the entry point must be identified by an ENTRY instruction in the called control section if the entry name is not the same as the control section name.

The CALL macro is of the form:

operation	operands
CALL	name1(name2,name3,...)VL

When the macro is expanded
- A V-type address constant is created for name1, and the address is loaded into register 15. Thus name1 is the subroutine entry point.
- A-type address constants are created for the parameters coded within parentheses, and the address of the first parameter (name2) is put into register 1. Thus the macro expansion creates a parameter list and places the address of the list into register 1. The programmer simply designates (within parentheses) which parameters are to be passed.

- VL designates that the high-order bit of the last A-type address constant be set to 1.

Upon execution of the CALL macro, the address of the instruction following the CALL is loaded into register 14. Control is then passed to the instruction at name1, using a branch and link instruction.

Other forms of the CALL instruction are available for use. However we shall not present them in this text. For further discussion of the SAVE, RETURN, and CALL macros, refer to the IBM publication *IBM System/360 Operating System Supervisor Services and Macro Instructions* (GC28-6646).

12.3.7 A Program Example

In this section we illustrate a routine which calls a subroutine to find the sum of two binary values. The main routine too, however, is considered a subroutine of the operating system. It therefore stores the operating system registers in a save area, with the assumption that register 13 already contains the address of that save area. Before ending, the main routine restores the operating system registers and returns control to the operating system. The routine utilizes the SAVE, RETURN, and CALL macro instructions.

Read the program of figure 12.9 very carefully along with the comments to the right of the instructions. If there is any step which is not perfectly clear, refer back to the appropriate section of this chapter for clarification.

12.4 THE LINKAGE EDITOR AND SUBROUTINE LINKAGE

This section deals with an important topic, but much discussion is required for it to be fully understood. The following discussion is only a brief overview. For a more detailed explanation of the linkage editor, one may refer to the appropriate IBM publication.

The smallest unit of a program which may be separately stored or relocated is known as a **control section**. A programmer distinguishes a control section by beginning it with either the START assembler instruction or with another assembler instruction called the CSECT (Control **SECT**ion). It is possible to write a single program consisting of several control sections each of which may be assembled, debugged, and tested separately. Thus separate subroutines may be defined as individual control sections by use of CSECT instructions.

After an assembly language program is written, it is acted upon by the assembler whose main output is an object program in machine language called an **object module**. During the assembly process, the assembler also

```
    LOC   OBJECT CODE      ADDR1 ADDR2  STMT    SOURCE STATEMENT

                                          1            PRINT NOGEN
CCC0C0                                     2 RINA      CSECT
CCCC00                                     3            SAVE  (14,12)
0C00C4 0580                                6            BALR  11,0
                                00006       7            USING *,11
                                            8 *
000006 50D0 B07E              00084         9            ST    13,SAVE1+4
0C000A 41D0 B07A              00080        10            LA    13,SAVE1
CCCCCE                                     11            OPEN  (PRINTER,OUTPUT)
CC001A                                     17            CALL  SUBR,(NUM1,NUM2,NAS1)
C0003A 5880 B06E              00074        31            L     8,NAS1          LOAD CONTENTS OF NAS1 INTO R8
00003E 4E80 B0C2                           32            CVD   8,DBL
CCC042 F377 B0D5 B0C2 000DB  000C8         33            UNPK  OUT+10(8),DBL
CC0048                                     34            PUT   PRINTER,OUT-1
CC0056                                     39            CLOSE (PRINTER)
                                           45 *
000062 58D0 B07E              00084        46            L     13,SAVE1+4
CC0066                                     47            RETURN (14,12)
                                           50 *            AREA DEFINITIONS
CC006C 00000008                            51 NUM1      DC    F'8'
0C0070 00000009                            52 NUM2      DC    F'9'
C00074 00000000                            53 NAS1      DC    F'0'
CC0078 C0000000                            54 NAS2      DC    F'0'
00007C 00000000                            55 NAS3      DC    F'0'
                                           56 *
CCC08C 0000000000000000                    57 SAVE1     DC    18F'0'
CC00C8                                     58 DBL       DS    D
000CD0 40                                  59            DC    C' '
0CC0C1 4040404040404040                    60 OUT       DC    CL50' '
000103                                     61 PRINTER   DCB   DSORG=PS,MACRF=PM,DDNAME=SYSLST,RECFM=FB,
000168                                                        LRECL=50,BLKSIZE=50
000168                                    115 SUBR      CSECT
C0016C 05A0                               116            SAVE  (14,12)
                                          119            BALR  10,0
                                0016E     120            USING *,10
                                          121 *
00C16E 50D0 A02A              00198       122            ST    13,SAVE2+4
000172 41D0 A026              00194       123            LA    13,SAVE2
000176 9835 1000              00000       124            LM    3,5,0(1)       LOAD PARAMETER ADDRESS
00017A 1B88                               125            SR    8,8            CLEAR GPR8
                                          126 *            COMPUTATIONS
C0017C 5A80 3000              00000       127            A     8,0(0,3)       ADD NUM1 TO GPR8
000180 5A80 4000              00000       128            A     8,0(0,4)       ADD NUM2 TO GPR8
000184 5080 5000              00000       129            ST    8,0(0,5)       STORE RESULT INTO NAS1
                                          130 *
000188 58D0 A02A              00198       131            L     13,SAVE2+4
00018C                                    132            RETURN (14,12)
000192 0000
00C194 0000000000000000                   135 SAVE2     DC    18F'0'
CCC0C0                                    136            END   RINA
```

Figure 12.9
Program with External Subroutine Linkage

constructs a table of the symbols used in the program, along with each symbol's length, its value or location, and the statements in which it is referred to in the program. The location of a symbol is actually a *relative* location. The START instruction assigns a tentative start location—it initializes a "location counter". The locations calculated by the assembler then express the displacement of those storage locations from the initial location counter value.

Assembler program output thus includes the:
  object module
  program listing
  diagnostics listing
  cross reference listing

external symbol dictionary (ESD)
relocation dictionary (RLD)

The Linkage Editor

Once assembled, the object module must be acted upon by the **linkage editor**, a service program, before it can be executed. If several object modules (control sections) are to be processed as one program, the linkage editor will process each one in turn, and combine them to create a single **load module**, which is executable. In fact, the routines to be linked may have been originally written in any higher level programming language, for the linkage editor combines **object modules**—the results of assembly or compilation.

Other assembler output besides the object code itself is used as input to the linkage editor. This includes the external symbol dictionary (ESD) and relocation dictionary (RLD). These dictionaries supply the information necessary for the linkage editor to resolve differences between the various object modules.

The ESD contains any references in a problem program which may be needed for establishing links with other programs. It contains *at least* the program name as defined in a START or a CSECT statement, its length, and its starting address (address initialized in the assembler's location counter). It will also contain the name, length, and starting address of any V-type address constants, EXTRN symbols, and ENTRY symbols.

The RLD describes each address constant found during assembly, including:
 (i) the control section in which the adcon is used
(ii) the control section in which the adcon is defined
(iii) the type of adcon it is (V-type, A-type)
(iv) its length
 (v) its assembled address

The linkage editor considers the ESD and RLD data found in the object modules of the CSECTS which are to be joined. It builds composite dictionaries of this data, and resolves all linkages between the control sections.

Recall now that the location numbers assigned by the assembler program establish only relative locations of instructions and data within the control section. Relocation of the program can therefore be accomplished without difficulty, by simply reassigning the location at which program storage begins. The linkage editor relocates each control section, by adding a relocation factor to the value of the assembler's location counter at the beginning of each assembly. The address values of adcons are also changed during link-editing to reflect the relocated values of the symbols which are represented.

The entire **load module** is then assigned to a contiguous area of main storage. It is now executable. Under DOS systems, it is also nonrelocatable.

Summary

In this chapter, we have discussed the subroutine concept, and demonstrated a number of programming techniques for coding subroutine logic.

We have been concerned with closed subroutines. The programmer first establishes a means of branching to the subroutine and of returning to the point of the program at which he left. Methods are devised for communication between the sections of code—for passage of data to the subroutine and passage of results back to the main program. Yet another consideration was ensuring that a "called routine" does not destroy the contents of the general registers placed there by the "calling routine", for the 16 general registers may be used by all program routines, including the supervisor program.

Standard procedures have been established for accomplishing successful subroutine communication. We call these the standard linkage conventions. This chapter presented two full program examples demonstrating both internal and external subroutine logic through adherance to the standard linkage conventions.

Important Terms Discussed in Chapter 12

adcon
address constant
addressability

call
call by name
call by value
called routine
calling routine
closed subroutine
control section

entry symbol
external subroutine
external symbol
exit code

internal subroutine

linkage editor
load module

main routine

object module
open subroutine

parameter
parameter list

return

save area
subroutine

Questions

12-1. What is the difference between an **open subroutine** and a **closed subroutine**?

12-2. Distinguish between the terms **calling routine** and **called routine**. Is it possible for a routine to fall within both categories?

12-3. What distinguishes an **internal subroutine** from an **external subroutine**?

12-4. Which of the following instructions accomplish the same thing? Assume that the program has the following constants defined:

A	DC	F'1'
AD	DC	A(A)

    (a) L   2,AD
    (b) L   2,A
    (c) LA   2,AD
    (d) LA   2,A

12-5. For each of the instruction sequences below, indicate what value in placed into register 14.

    (a)
```
            START   0
            BALR    14,2
```

    (b)
```
            START   16
            BAL     14,THERE
                .
                .
                .
THERE           .
                .
```

12-6. What is the difference in function between the BALR instructions in the following instruction sequence?

```
            START   0
            BALR    2,0
            USING   *,2
            LA      4,INST
            BALR    5,4
                .
                .
INST            .
                .
                .
```

12-7. What registers are used for the standard linkage conventions? What is the use of each?

12-8. Under what condition(s) do we use EXTRN and ENTRY statements?

12-9. Distinguish between a "call by name" and a "call by value".

12-10. List two advantages to storing the address of the parameter address list in register 1, as opposed to simply placing the parameter values themselves into registers 0 and 1.

12-11. What values will be placed into an 18-word save area by a subroutine?

12-12. Can a subroutine store the contents of a main routine's registers in a save area which it itself provides? Explain.

12-13. Is it possible for a main routine to store all of its own register contents before branching to a subroutine and then to restore them after the return? Explain.

12-14. A main routine A is to call subroutine B twice and subroutine C three times. How many save areas are necessary? Explain.

12-15. If by some chance a subroutine did not change the contents of the registers, would it be necessary to restore their contents before the return? Explain. What if the subroutine uses only one register, say register 7?

12-16. Assume that we expect our program to occupy up to 8192 bytes of core. We then begin by writing

```
            BALR    6,0
            USING   C,6,7
              .
              .
              .
      C       .
              .
```

Write instruction(s) necessary to initialize register 7. (The BALR initializes register 6.)

12-17. Consider the instruction sequence below at the beginning of a subroutine:

```
            STM     14,12,12(13)
            BALR    12,0
            USING   *,12
            ST      13,SAVEB+4
```

(a) May we have placed the ST instruction before the BALR-USING pair? Why or why not?
(b) May we have placed the BALR-USING pair before the STM instruction? Why or why not?

12-18. What are the macro expansions for the following two instructions?

(a)   SAVE   (5,10)
(b)   RETURN (15,12)

12-19. Distinguish between an **object module** and a **load module**.

12-20. What is an ESD? An RLD? Why are they necessary?

Program Exercises

12-1. Write a lowest level subroutine to compute the square of a fullword binary value. That is, given a value x, the subroutine is to compute x^2.

Then write a higher level routine (itself a subroutine of the operating system) to read in two values I and J, convert them into binary form, and to find $I^2 - J^2$ using the lowest level subroutine which you have just written.

12-2. Write a subroutine to accept a 4-byte packed number with 3 implied decimal positions (form: dd dd$_\wedge$dd ds where d is a packed digit and s is the sign) and to round it to the nearest hundredth.

Then write a higher level subroutine to compute the product of two packed constants:

| A | DC | P'23.40' |
| B | DC | P'5.68' |

and to round the product to the nearest hundredth, using the subroutine which you have just written.

Chapter 13

Some Operating System Features: Virtual Storage the Program Status Word the Interrupt System

13.1   WHAT IS AN OPERATING SYSTEM?

An **operating system** is a collection of programs whose purpose is to effectively manage the resources of a computer system. These resources include

- Hardware resources: main storage, secondary storage, registers, and input/output devices.
- Data resources: generalized programs and data which may be kept in the computer for use by other programs and programmers. These generalized programs and data are called program "libraries".
- Human resources: programmers, operators, and users. The functions of an operating system are to improve the ways in which these system resources are utilized, and to make their utilization more efficient.

Naturally, there will be conflicting ideas among people concerned with developing and using operating systems as to exactly what constitutes efficient utilization of a system. Moreover, many agreed-upon objectives will often be in conflict. For example, two important objectives of most operating systems are to increase **throughput** (the amount of actual processing done by the computer in a fixed time span) and to increase **availability** (a programmer should have access to the computer as often as possible, and with a minimum amount of waiting time). By necessity, *in*creasing throughput (the computer is busier) will have the effect of *de*creasing availability, and vice versa. Other operating system objectives may include minimizing **turnaround time** (the amount of time which elapses from the time a job is submitted to the time it is completed); minimizing **response time** (on "time-shared" systems in which many individuals request to use the same computer at the same time, response time is the amount of time which elapses between the request to access the computer, and the computer's response); providing for computer security (assuring that non-authorized individuals do not have access to programs or data); providing for system reliability (for example, "backup" may be provided in the event that part of a system should fail). There may be many other operating system objectives; they will vary depending upon the size, use, and general nature of the particular system. Moreover, the objectives, whatever they may be, should be pursued with a realistic respect for the cost that achieving such objectives may entail.

The purpose of this chapter is not to discuss how operating systems are written (entire books have been written on the subject!). However, the reader should be aware of the fact that operating systems do differ, and that our discussion of operating systems for the IBM System/360 and System/370 may not necessarily be applicable in all respects to other operating systems. As computers themselves vary and as system objectives and requirements vary, so will operating systems.

13.2   VIRTUAL STORAGE SYSTEMS

Briefly, virtual storage techniques are methods for managing computer resources so that the size of programs need not be restricted by the size of main storage. Programs may be written as though the computer had much more main storage than is actually available. A basic premise behind the idea of virtual storage is that it is not necessary for an entire program to be present in real storage at once, for after all the CPU can only execute one instruction at a time!

In a virtual storage system, the entire program is stored on an auxiliary storage device and is divided into smaller parts called segments or pages, some of which will be in real storage as well. Each time an address is referenced by the program, a special operating system module determines whether the appropriate program page is in real storage. If it is, the virtual address is translated into a real address and instruction execution proceeds. If it is not, the page is transferred into real storage before address translation and instruction execution take place. In a virtual storage system, program addresses (called virtual addresses) are relative to the beginning of the segment and/or page in which the appropriate instruction or data is located.

Before we can fully appreciate how a virtual storage system works, it will be necessary for us to introduce and to discuss several very important programming concepts, including the concepts of storage allocation, relocation, segmentation, and paging. These topics will be considered in sections 13.2.1 and 13.2.2. Section 13.2.3 will present a precise description of what virtual storage is, and subsequent sections will explain how program execution takes place in virtual storage systems, coding for virtual storage, and benefits of virtual storage.

Storage Allocation

An important capability for which the operating system may provide is that of **multiprogramming.** Multiprogramming allows two or more programs to reside in storage simultaneously, and to be executed concurrently. In general, main storage is divided into sections each of which can be occupied by a different program. Although simultaneous execution of more than one program by one CPU is impossible, the operating system may provide for execution of part of another program whenever a given program is idle, as when, say, an I/O operation is being processed. When the new program pauses, the operating system can transfer control back to the original program or to yet another program. In this way, the CPU's idle time is minimized.

It is obvious that we must not allow a program in one portion of storage to change the data or instructions of programs in other portions of storage. We must prevent one program from addressing locations which are beyond the limits of its own allocated storage area. Storage allocation is thus an important activity of the operating system.

We shall now discuss some methods by which the operating system allocates storage area.

13.2.1   Relocation

When a source program is written, whether in Assembly Language or in any other non-machine language, the programmer assigns symbolic names to instructions, to data descriptions, and to input/output descriptions (such as files and records). We say that the source program exists in **symbolic name space,** and the programmer uses these symbolic names in the description and processing of his program logic.

Once the source program is written, it is submitted to a compiler or assembler for translation into machine language. During this procedure, sequential addresses replace the symbolic names. These addresses begin at some fixed location and continue sequentially from there. The resulting range of relative addresses is called the program **address space**. The linkage editor may then combine the address spaces of several programs to form a larger address space (see chapter 12, section 12.4).

The address space must be converted into **real storage** locations in order for the instructions which are stored in those locations, or which reference those addresses, to be used. (Throughout the book we have referred to "main storage" or "main memory"; in this chapter we shall use the term "real storage", to distinguish it from "virtual storage", which we shall discuss in more detail in section 13.2.3.)

The conversion of addresses in a program's address space into actual location numbers in real storage is called **relocation.** There are two basic types of relocation, distinguished by the *time* at which the relocation occurs.
  * **Static Relocation:** The program is assigned to ("bound" to) definite real storage locations at **load time;** that is, at the time that the program is loaded into main storage for execution.
  * **Dynamic Relocation:** The program is not bound to definite real storage locations. A program may be moved and main storage reallocated *during program execution.*

Let us first consider a system which uses neither of these relocation types, so that we may appreciate the difference. For System/360 under the DOS operating system, the address space (result of compilation) begins with 0 (a zero "origin") and is relocatable. The linkage editor converts the address space into real storage locations with a different origin. The result of the link-editing is thus tied to definite sequential storage locations and will be loaded into those same locations for every execution (unless, of course, it is link-edited again). It is possible to have several programs in storage, executing at the same time (multiprogramming). However, careful planning is necessary so that disjoint real storage areas be assigned to the programs to be loaded. Otherwise programs assigned to the same or overlapping locations must wait for the completion of programs currently in real storage.

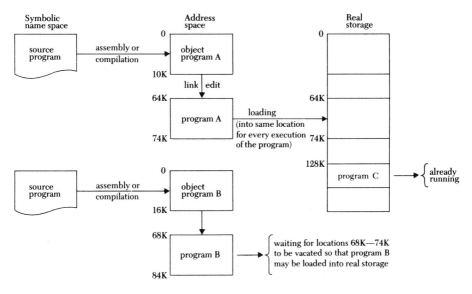

Figure 13.1
Simple Program Loading

As you can see from figure 13.1, two steps are accomplished by the linkage editor. Firstly, addresses are relocated; that is, actual storage locations are assigned. Secondly, the resultant program is physically loaded into main storage.

A major disadvantage of this type of storage allocation ("simple program loading") is that a program ready to be loaded into main storage may have to wait for the storage area assigned to it to be vacated, for another program may be occupying some of that same storage area. This is true in spite of the fact that other contiguous main storage areas of sufficient size may be available at this time.

Note from figure 13.2 that although there is sufficient unused storage available (72K – 120K), programs B and C must wait until the execution of program A is completed (since programs B and C have been assigned to real storage loca-

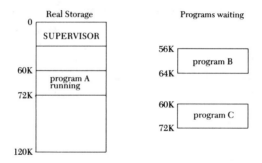

Figure 13.2
Programs Waiting for Assigned Real Storage Areas

tions some of which are currently being used by program A). This difficulty can be eliminated by the use of static relocation.

STATIC RELOCATION

A system which uses static relocation waits to relocate (to assign real storage locations) until program load time, just before execution begins. This has great advantage over simple program loading in that real storage addresses may be more efficiently allocated to provide for multiprogramming. Note from figure 13.3 that under static relocation, relocation is accomplished as the program is being loaded. Thus the program can be assigned to storage locations which are immediately available. However the program is bound to definite locations throughout execution; relocation is still not possible during execution. Static relocation for management of real storage is performed by the OS operating system on System/360 computers.

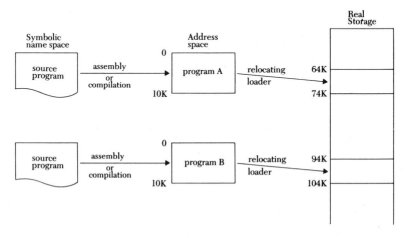

Figure 13.3
Static Relocation

DYNAMIC RELOCATION

A system with the capability for dynamic relocation assigns real storage locations *during execution;* storage may also be *re*allocated during execution.

Before we consider how dynamic relocation works, let us understand why it is desirable. We have already stated that for systems which use static relocation, each program occupies contiguous real storage locations. When several programs have been thus loaded, there are often unused areas left between them. Each of these areas individually may not be large enough to hold another program, although the total amount of unused storage may be substantial. We call this condition **fragmentation** of real storage. Fragmentation will occur on all systems using static relocation.

Dynamic relocation attempts to avoid fragmentation to as great an extent as possible. The program is divided into parts called **segments** (sometimes the segments may be further subdivided into smaller parts called **pages**). The segments into which the program is divided can then fit into the parts of real storage which are unused, so that much of the real storage thought to be lost due to fragmentation can now be used.

Moreover, the address space of a program which uses dynamic relocation never becomes bound to real storage locations. The addresses of each segment begin with 0, and addresses within the segment are expressed relative to the origin of the segment (as being "displaced" by a certain amount from the beginning of the segment). These **relative addresses** are translated during program execution by a special hardware feature called the **DAT Feature** or **Dynamic Address Translation Feature.**

In the next section, we shall discuss the address structure as well as the DAT feature for dynamic relocation systems.

13.2.2   Techniques for Dynamic Relocation: Segmentation and Paging

A SEGMENTATION SYSTEM

In a segmentation system, the operating system will segment (subdivide) the program, with each program segment assigned a unique number and with **relative addresses** expressed as **displacements** from the origin of the segment.

```
        segment
        number      displacement
      ┌──────────┬────────────────────────┐
      │          │                        │
      └──────────┴────────────────────────┘
```

Figure 13.4
Two-Part Address Structure
in a Segmentation System

Segment addresses will consist of two parts: the segment number, and the displacement, as in figure 13.4. This two part address structure is imperative.

Suppose, for example, that we wish to reference location 100 of segment 3 of the program schematically segmented below:

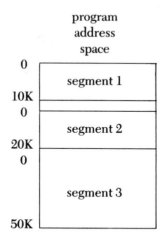

Saying "location 100" would evoke the response "*which* location 100"? Each segment has a location numbered 100! Thus we need the two-part address structure: [3 | 100] will indicate that we wish to reference location 100 of segment 3.

A 24-bit relative address (System/370 has a 24-bit address structure) might be structured as follows:

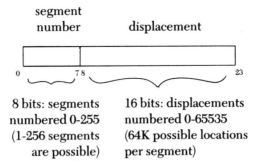

(Other subdivisions of the 24-bit address, allowing different amounts of segments and different sized segments, are also possible.)

The relative addressing shown above seems all well and good, however the

CPU references real storage locations using **absolute** addresses only! Obviously, if our segmented program is to be executed, the relative addresses must be translated into absolute addresses. This is done as follows: A special register in real storage called the **segment table origin register** (STOR) "points" to the real storage origin address of a table (called a **segment table**) which **maps** the segments of the program currently being executed. Every segmented program in real storage has its own segment table. The individual entries in the segment table give the origin, in real storage, of the program segments. When a program is interrupted and another begins execution, the origin address of the second program's segment table will replace that of the first in the STOR.

Given the STOR and segment table of figure 13.5, we see that the relative address is translated as follows:

(i)   The STOR points to the origin of the appropriate segment table.

(ii)   The segment number in the relative address points to the appropriate entry in the segment table found by step (i). The real storage location corresponding to that segment number is the origin address of the segment in real storage.

(iii)   The origin address found by step (ii) is added to the displacement, giving the absolute address.

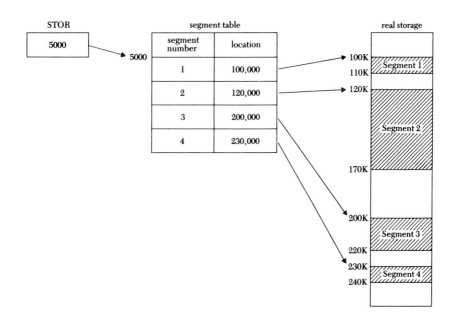

Figure 13.5
Finding the Origin of Program Segments
in Real Storage

Example:

relative address | 3 | 1000

Referring to figure 13.5

(i)   Find segment table at 5000

(ii)   Segment number 3 in the relative address points to the 3rd entry in the table, location 200,000.

(iii) Add: 200,000 + displacement
       = 200,000 + 1,000
       = 201,000
       = absolute address

Note:

- The type of address translation shown above is performed *continuously* during program execution, each time an address is referenced.
- The address translation is performed automatically by the Dynamic Address Translation Feature (DAT), a *hardware* feature.
- Program segments may be relocated even during execution. The DAT will change the segment table entry appropriately.

It is now fairly easy to understand and appreciate the importance of segmentation in storage allocation. Suppose that two programs, A and B, occupy real storage locations as in figure 13.6, and program C is to be loaded into storage at this time. Unless we use segmentation, program C will have to wait until either program A or B is completed, in spite of the fact that the total unused storage area is sufficient to hold program C (100K to 120K and 200K to 260K comprise more than the 64K required for program C).

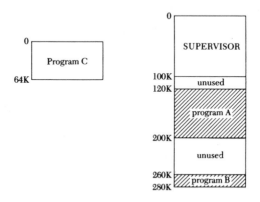

Figure 13.6
Program Ready for Segmentation and Loading

However, using segmentation, program C can be loaded as described in figure 13.7.

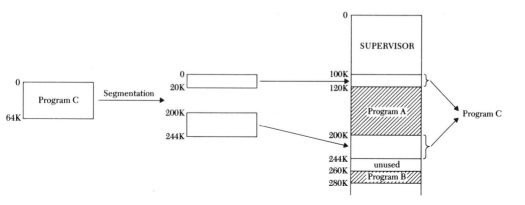

Figure 13.7
Program Segmentation and Loading
into Available Real Storage

A SEGMENTATION AND PAGING SYSTEM

Thus far, we have seen that segmenting programs has the effect of reducing fragmentation of real storage. However, fragmentation will still exist, for the program segments will not necessarily fill the real storage fragments entirely. The segments may therefore be subdivided into yet smaller parts called **pages.** Pages are always fixed in size; we shall assume a page size of 4K in our discussion. The program pages will be placed into areas of real storage which are 4K in size. We shall call such real storage areas **page frames.**

Another level has thus been added to the address space: the structure is that of program segments, pages within segments, and locations within pages.

The address structure has also taken on a new dimension, as illustrated in figure 13.8.

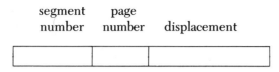

Figure 13.8
Three-Part Address Structure
in a Segmentation and Paging System

The "segment number" identifies the particular program segment in which the location is to be found; the "page number" identifies the page within the segment; and the "displacement" is the distance from the beginning of the page.

A typical 24-bit address structure might be:

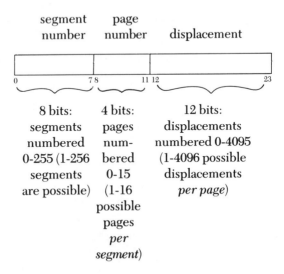

Now let us see how a three-part relative address of this type may be translated into an absolute address. You will recall that a segmentation system required one segment table to map the address space of a program. A segmentation and paging system requires a single segment table and more than one **page table.** In fact a page table will be used for *each program segment.*

Given the STOR, segment table and page tables of figure 13.9, a three-part relative address is translated as follows:

(i)   The STOR points to the origin of the appropriate program segment table.

(ii)   The segment number in the relative address points to the appropriate entry in the segment table found by step (i). The entry in the segment table points to the origin of that segment's page table.

(iii) The page number in the relative address then points to the appropriate entry in the page table found by step (ii). The entry in the page table identifies a real storage location which is the origin address of the page frame in real storage.

(iv)   The origin address found by step (iii) is added to the displacement, giving the absolute address.

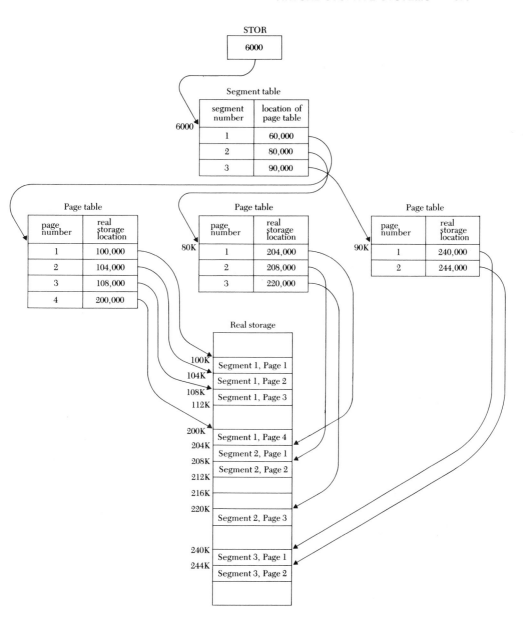

Figure 13.9
Referencing Program Pages
Within Segments in Real Storage

Example:

relative address

2	2	2000

Referring to figure 13.9

(i)   Find segment table at 6000.

(ii)   Segment number 2 in the relative address points to the second entry in the segment table. This gives the location of the page table for segment 2 as 80,000.

(iii) Page number 2 in the relative address points to the second entry in the page table which begins at 80,000. Real storage location number 208,000 is now identified as the origin of the page in real storage where our address is found.

(iv)   Add: 208,000 + displacement
            = 208,000 + 2000
            = 210,000
            = absolute address

As for segmentation systems, the address translation described above for segmentation and paging systems is performed continuously and automatically during execution by the Dynamic Address Translation Feature (DAT). Programs may also be relocated during execution.

How are Page Frames Assigned?

Thus far, our discussion of segmentation and paging has centered about dynamic address translation using segment tables and page tables. We have discussed how the contents of real storage locations may be referenced, but have assumed all along that the program pages were already stored in appropriate page frames of real storage. Let us now consider the question of how the operating system manages real storage. That is, how are page frames assigned by the operating system to program pages? This job is accomplished by use of another table called the **page frame table,** illustrated in figure 13.10.

page frame number	program ID	segment and page number	status
1			1
2			1
3			1
4			1
5			0
6			0
7			0
.			.
.			.
.			.

Figure 13.10
Page Frame Table
(with sample contents)

The page frame table is used by the operating system to record how various page frames of real storage are allocated to user programs. Real storage is divided into page frames of fixed size, say 4K. Each entry of the page frame table describes one page frame in main storage, and has four parts:

- The **page frame number** identifies the particular page frame described in the entry.
- The **program ID** identifies, by name, the program whose page is in the page frame being described.
- The **segment and page number** identifies the page which is contained in the page frame.
- The **status** tells whether or not the page frame is available. Status = 0 means the page frame is available; status = 1 means it is not.

As programs are loaded into real storage, page frames with a status of 0 are allocated to program pages, and the appropriate status entries are set to 1. When the program ends, its status entries are reset to 0. The page frame table continuously maps the use of real storage.

What about execution time?

If the address translation described above (including referencing the STOR, the segment table and page tables) were to be performed for each address referenced in a program, the effect would be a slowing of execution time. In order to counter this, the systems include special hardware devices called **associative array registers;** System/370 provides eight such devices. The associative array registers identify the eight *most recently referenced* pages from the executing program. These pages are each identified by segment and page number and the page frame location in which it is found (see figure 13.11).

Segment and page number		Reference bit	Page frame location
1	2	0	36,000
2	1	1	44,000
2	2	1	48,000
.	.	.	.
.	.	.	.
.	.	.	.
8	7	1	64,000

Figure 13.11
Associative Array Registers
(with sample contents)

When a relative address is referenced in a program, the segment and page number from the address are compared to the segment and page numbers in all eight associative array registers simultaneously. This occurs at the same time that translation begins via the segment and page tables. If the segment and page numbers match a register entry, the corresponding page frame location in the register is joined to the relative address displacement to give the real storage address, and the reference bit of the register is turned on (set to 1). You can see that it is possible for all the reference bits to eventually become 1. When this happens, the hardware will turn them all off (reset all to 0).

If the relative address does not match any of the associative array register entries, translation will continue through completion via the segment and page tables. Note that the address thus found (through the tables) would now be the most recently referenced page. The system must therefore place its segment and page numbers and its page frame location into one of the associative array registers. The register chosen will be one which has not been recently referenced (reference bit = 0). Thus the associative array registers continually identify the eight most recently referenced pages in a program being executed. In actual practice, most address translation occurs through the associative array registers, so that time is not very much increased as a result of referencing segment and page tables. The assumption used to justify the continued identification of the most recently referenced program pages by the associative array registers is that the pages which were most recently used are more likely to be needed again soon. Thus, reference to those pages least recently used will be replaced by reference to those pages most recently used.

13.2.3   Virtual Storage (VS): Its Meaning and Its Structure

In the previous section, we discussed how a program's address space may be structured into segments and pages, and how real storage is structured into page frames which are the same size as pages. The maximum size of an address space is determined by the address structure of the computer system. Thus an 8-bit allocation for the segment number determines that 1 to 256 segments may be used per program; a 4-bit allocation for the page number determines that 1 to 16 pages may be referenced per segment. System/370 has a 24-bit address structure. Therefore its address space has at most 16,777,216 addressable locations or 16 megabytes. The size of the address space is much larger than the size of real storage! We say that the system has a **virtual storage** which may occupy *up to* 16 megabytes (it may occupy less). Virtual storage is, in effect, a large address space. It is usually substantially larger than the size of the computer's real storage. (Real storage typically consists of 1 or 2 megabytes, although physically it *could* be larger).

At this point, you are probably wondering: just *where is* virtual storage? Virtual storage cannot be seen, for it is, as we have stated above, an address space. However programs and data which reside in virtual storage must be in some physical location too; in particular, they are in the auxiliary storage which we call **external page storage.** This external storage (physically, this is usually on disk or drum) is divided into page-size compartments called **slots**; each slot will hold one page.

It is important to understand, however, that virtual storage and auxiliary storage are *not* equivalent. Virtual storage is an **address space.** The programs and data which are in virtual storage exist *physically* in auxiliary storage. There may be other parts of virtual storage which are not currently being used; they comprise what we call **potential address space** and *do not physically exist*, not in auxiliary storage and not anywhere else.

Virtual storage is allocated to programs in whole segments. The parts of segments left unused, and whole segments which are not allocated, comprise the potential address space. The potential address space (unused virtual storage) is shaded in figure 13.12.

On IBM systems, virtual storage uses the segment-page structure, as does real storage for dynamic relocation systems. However, virtual storage uses fixed length segments (64K each); every segment contains 16 pages, each of which is 4K in size.

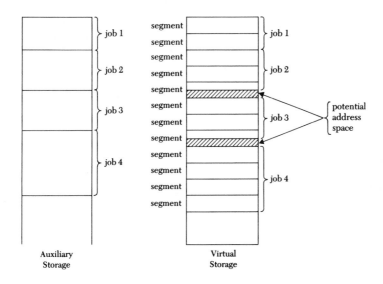

Figure 13.12
Virtual Storage: An Address Space

We call addresses that reference virtual storage **virtual addresses** (see figure 13.13). Virtual addresses are relative addresses; physical locations will not be associated with those addresses until execution time. (Those virtual addresses which, at a particular time, are part of the potential address space, will of course not be associated with any physical location.)

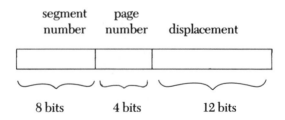

Figure 13.13
Virtual Address Structure

In order for a computer instruction to be executed or for data to be referenced by an executing program, the respective instruction and/or data must be in the computer's real storage. In a virtual storage system, the virtual address is first examined and the operating system determines if the page in which the data is found is in real storage. If it is in real storage, there is no problem: the virtual address is translated into a real address and execution proceeds. If the page is not in real storage, its slot in external page storage must be identified, and the data must then be transferred into real storage. In the next section, we shall discuss how page locations are identified and how the operating system determines whether or not a page is in real storage, so that the determination may be made to move or not to move a copy of a page from its slot in external storage to the appropriate page frame in real storage.

13.2.4   Program Execution in a Virtual Storage System

Let us assume that a program has been loaded into virtual storage and is executing. We will now consider the question of how virtual addresses are interpreted so that the appropriate instructions or data may be retrieved for use during execution. The procedure described in our discussion is illustrated in figure 13.14.

As in the segmentation and paging system described in section 13.2.2, the STOR (segment table origin register) points to the origin of the appropriate segment table. When a virtual address requires translation, the segment number will identify the entry in the segment table which in turn points to the origin of the appropriate page table. In our previous discussion of segmentation and paging systems, the page table gave the origin of a page frame. This origin address was joined to the relative address displacement to give the real storage address. In a virtual storage system, however, we have an additional

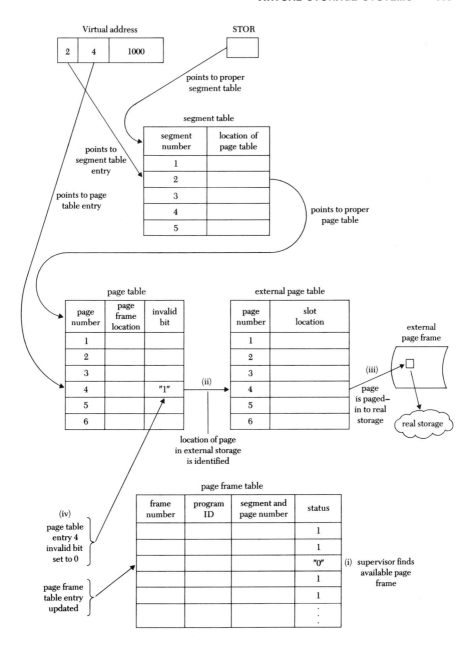

Figure 13.14
Interpreting and Referencing a Virtual Address

consideration: not every page is actually present in a real storage location at the time of reference! The page table must therefore indicate not only the page frame locations for those pages which are in real storage. It must also tell the system when a page is *not* in real storage. This is accomplished by an additional bit in each entry of the page table, called an **invalid bit.** When the invalid bit is set to 0, the page is in real storage; when set to 1, the page is not in real storage.

Suppose that the invalid bit is found to be set to 0. Then the page frame location is joined to the virtual address displacement to give a real storage address, and program execution proceeds as planned. If the invalid bit is set to 1, however, the page does not reside in real storage: we say that we have a **page fault.** Control is now passed to the supervisor (an interrupt occurs) and the page must now be brought into real storage from external storage. This is called a **page-in** operation. We outline its steps below (see figure 13.14):

(i)   The supervisor will search the page frame table to find an available page frame (one whose corresponding status bit = 0: see section 13.2.2). Once an appropriate page frame has been found, (the case in which none is available will be considered shortly), then

(ii)   We must find the location of the page in external storage. This is done by going to the appropriate page entry in a table called the **external page table.** This table corresponds each page number with an appropriate **slot location**—that is, with the location of the page in external storage.

(iii)   We then find the appropriate slot in the external page storage, and the page is "paged-in": that is, it is transmitted from external storage to the page frame identified by (i).

(iv)   The page table is updated to show the new real storage location of the page, with invalid bit set to 0. The page frame table is updated to show the program ID, and the segment and page numbers stored in the identified frame.

The virtual address is now translated into a real storage address, and execution resumes.

The paging-in procedure described above is all well and good, provided the supervisor finds an available page frame in real storage (step (i)). Suppose, however, that an available page frame is not found: that is, all status bits of the page frame table are set to 1. Then the page which is needed must replace one which is currently in main storage. This procedure is called **swapping.** In order to choose the page to be replaced, the system will use the **LRU** (Least Recently Used) rule: that is, the pages which have not been referenced recently will be the first pages to be replaced. (The assumption is that a page which was recently used is more likely to be needed again soon, requiring the system to bring it back into real storage within a short time span. This assumption was also the basis for use of the associative array registers, described in section 13.2.2.) Another bit in the page frame table (see figure 13.15), called the **reference bit,** is used by the system to determine whether a particular page was recently used. The reference bit is automatically turned on (set to 1) whenever the data stored in the appropriate page frame is referenced. (When all the reference bits eventually become 1, they are reset to 0, similar to the procedure followed by the associative array registers.) The supervisor thus scans the reference bits to determine which page is to be replaced (one whose reference bit is set to 0).

page frame table

frame number	program ID	segment and page number	status	reference bit	change bit
			1	1	1
			1	0	0
			1	1	0
			1	0	1
			1	1	1

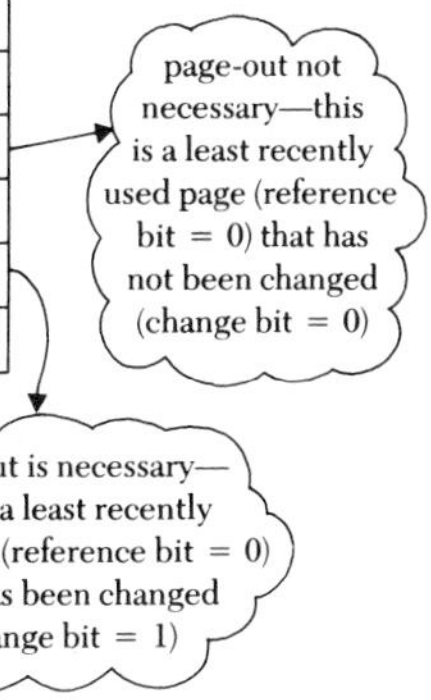

page-out not necessary—this is a least recently used page (reference bit = 0) that has not been changed (change bit = 0)

page-out is necessary—this is a least recently used page (reference bit = 0) that has been changed (change bit = 1)

Figure 13.15
Page Frame Table Showing
Reference Bits and Change Bits

Once the page is identified, the invalid bit of the page table entry associated with that particular page is set to 1 (meaning that the page can no longer be assumed to be in real storage). The supervisor has now selected the page frame to be replaced. It is not yet ready, however, to replace the previous contents of that page frame with the data required by our program.

One additional question must still be answered: Have the contents of the page which is to be replaced been changed since that page was paged-in? The answer to this question is given by yet another bit of the page frame table (see figure 13.15), called the **change bit.**

- If the change bit is set to 0 (the contents of the page were not changed), then there is a copy of the page in external page storage, and therefore no need to "hold onto" the information on that page. The system may proceed to page-in the page needed by the program, update the page table and page frame tables appropriately, translate the virtual address to a real storage address, and proceed to program execution.

- If the change bit is set to 1 (the contents of the page were changed since having been paged-in), the page must be **paged-out:** that is, a copy of the page must be transmitted from real storage to external storage, for there is currently no copy of the *changed* data in external storage. Any later program reference to that page would thus not reflect the latest (correct) page contents. The system may select any slot in external page storage for the page-out operation, and will then update the external page table to reflect the new slot location of that particular page. Once the page-out has been completed, the needed program page may be paged-in to the now available page frame, and the page and page frame tables are updated appropriately. The virtual address is translated into a real storage address, and program execution proceeds.

We refer to the page-in and page-out procedure as **paging.** This activity is also called **demand paging,** for pages are brought into real storage only when requested ("demanded") by the program. Note too that the paging operations are input/output operations. As with all I/O operations in a multiprogramming environment, other programs are activated and executed by the CPU while the data transmission is taking place.

13.2.5   Single Virtual Storage vs Multiple Virtual Storages

Virtual storage systems may have either a single virtual storage or multiple virtual storages. We outline certain characteristic features of each below. A good understanding of the workings of each, as well as their respective advantages and limitations, will require much further study. This summary is meant only to acquaint the reader with the basic differences between the two types of VS implementations.

SINGLE VIRTUAL STORAGE

- (i)   Its maximum size is determined by the address structure of the particular computer, although a virtual storage smaller than the maximum may be used. (Our 24 bit address structure allows a maximum VS of 16 megabytes.)
- (ii)   The virtual storage is the *system's* (as opposed to a program's) *address space*. The virtual storage is then allocated to user programs with one segment allocated to each such program. It therefore follows that
- (iii) One segment table will be sufficient to map the *entire* virtual storage. As usual, each segment will have an associated page table.

MULTIPLE VIRTUAL STORAGES

In a virtual storage system with multiple virtual storages, each user has his own virtual storage.

(i)   The maximum size of virtual storage is still determined by the address structure of the particular computer. Obviously, a user's storage may not exceed the maximum.

(ii)   Virtual storage is the *user's address space* (as opposed to the system's address space for a single virtual storage system).

(iii)   *Each virtual storage* is mapped by a segment table. As usual, each segment will have an associated page table.

13.2.6   Coding for Virtual Storage

The practices which the programmer should follow when coding for virtual storage do differ from techniques used when coding for static relocation systems. In general, the programmer is less concerned with the total amount of storage required by the program, and is more concerned with a reduction of page faults — and thus of paging — during program execution. Some general guidelines to keep in mind are summarized below:

- The program should provide for **locality of reference.** That is, instructions and/or data which are to be used with each other should be stored near each other, and those which are to be used less often should be kept separate.

    In particular, most processing should be sequential. However, such routines as error routines (which will not be executed often, if at all), should be stored separately, perhaps as separate subroutines.

    Other short subroutines which are to be used only a few times, should be included in the main body of code whenever they would otherwise have been "called". While this would increase the amount of virtual storage, it will serve to reduce page faults and real storage requirements.

    When subroutines are necessary, they should be as near as possible to the routines which will call them.

- The program should require a **minimum use of real storage.** This will be accomplished by writing modular code, and then arranging those modules which will be used frequently as near to each other as possible. These routines will stay in real storage for longer periods of time (because of their frequent use); if they are arranged close to each other, a minimum of real storage will be required.

- Programs should strive for **validity of reference.** That is, we wish to avoid long searches for data and any data retrieval which is unnecessary (this will also minimize paging). In this regard, we try to minimize indirect addressing (the instruction MVC PLACE,0(2) requires the computer to examine register 2 before retrieving the information to be moved from the appropriate real storage location). We also try to minimize certain data structures which require a great deal of searching.

13.2.7 Advantages of Virtual Storage

Virtual storage systems provide many benefits to their users, some of which have been hinted at in the discussions above. In particular

- Fragmentation of real storage is minimized.
- Applications may be processed which require much more storage space than is available in the computer's real storage. A program written for a virtual storage system has, in effect, a much larger storage space available to it.
- A virtual storage system may be able to process more jobs, since programs might not require their entire set of instructions and data for each execution.
- In multiple virtual storage systems, system protection is greatly improved. Each user has his own address space, and is prevented from infringing upon the address space assigned to other users.
- The operating system is *itself* structured in real storage. That is, many portions of the system itself are paged, and do not require real storage space unless their use is requested. The system is thus less limited in the number of resident operating system functions which may be required. This is so since these operating system modules will only require real storage when they are used, unlike static relocation systems in which full-time real storage residence is required.

The interested reader is referred to the following IBM publications for more information on virtual storage:

Introduction to Virtual Storage in System/370 . . . . GR20-4260
Introduction to DOS/VS GC33-5370
OS/VS1 Planning and Use Guide GC24-5090
OS/MFT, OS/MVT, and OS/VS1 CRSE Concepts and Facilities . . GC30-2012
OS/VS Supervisor Services and Macro Instructions GC27-6979
      (more information on VS software)
IBM System/370 System Summary GA22-7001
      (summary of VS components)
IBM Data Processing Glossary GC20-1699
      (gives VS terminology)

13.3   SOME KEY FEATURES OF SYSTEM DESIGN

The way in which computer hardware is designed will greatly affect the design of all software, including the operating system. In fact, we have already stated (in section 13.1) that one purpose of operating systems is the management of the hardware resources of the computer. In this section, we shall examine some important features of IBM System/360 and System/370 computers with which both machine hardware and the operating system are intimately involved.

13.3.1   The Program Status Word in BC Mode

The **Program Status Word** (or PSW) is a 64-bit register (a doubleword long!) which resides in a special part of the CPU. The PSW consists of various fields, each of which has a unique role. The fields in the first word of the PSW function to control the overall operation of the computer system. The fields in the second word of the PSW contain information to control what happens to a program during execution.

The PSW for IBM 360 systems is organized in what is called **Basic Control Mode** or BC Mode. IBM 370 systems have two PSW modes, the Basic Control Mode or BC Mode (which is essentially identical to that of the PSW for 360 systems) and the **Extended Control Mode** or EC Mode, which is used when the special system feature called virtual storage is implemented. We shall first discuss the Program Status Word in BC Mode, which is illustrated in figure 13.16.

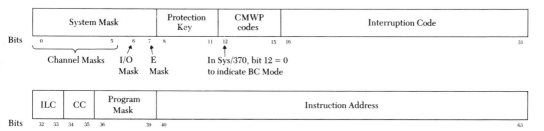

Figure 13.16
Program Status Word for Sys/360;
and for Sys/370 in BC Mode

The Condition Code (CC)

One field of the PSW with which we have already been acquainted is the condition code (bits 34–35). Recall that the condition code is set by compare instructions to indicate the results of comparisons, and by various other instructions (such as decimal and binary add and subtract instructions, binary shift instructions, and others) to indicate the signs of result fields or the occurrence of arithmetic overflow. Column ⑤ of the IBM System/370 Reference Summary (see Appendix A) summarizes the condition code settings which result from the execution of assembly language instructions.

The Instruction Length Code (ILC) and the Instruction Address

The execution of computer instructions actually involves two steps: the instruction cycle during which the instruction is fetched from main storage and is decoded; and the execution cycle, during which the instruction is actually executed (the computer "does" what the instruction "tells" it to do). Have you wondered how the computer knows, in considering the series of 0's and 1's which comprise the object code, when one instruction ends and the next begins; or how the computer knows, after execution of an instruction, where to "find" the next instruction to be executed? The answers to these questions are intimately tied to the workings of the Instruction Length Code (bits 32–33) and the Instruction Address (bits 40–63) fields of the PSW.

You will recall (chapter 1, section 1.4.2) that addresses in System/360 and 370 are expressed in base-displacement form: a general purpose register is chosen by the programmer to act as a base register for the program, and is loaded with a number which serves as the start address for the program. Addresses are then expressed as being displaced by a certain amount from the contents of the base register:

absolute address = contents of base register + displacement

Displacements are limited to 4095 bytes (hexadecimal FFF). If a program requires more than that, a new base register must be supplied for each additional 4096 bytes to be used by the program. The new base register will be loaded with a number which exceeds the contents of the previous base register by 4096, thus establishing a new reference point which begins immediately after the old reference point left off.

Note that the use of base-displacement addressing allows us to reference absolute addresses of considerable magnitude using only 16 bits. The base register is expressed in 4 bits (the general registers are numbered 0-15, or 0000–1111 using bits) while the displacement is expressed in 12 bits (the upper limit for the displacement is FFF, or 1111 1111 1111 using bits, which is equivalent to 4095 decimal).

When execution of a program segment begins, the object code for the first instruction is fetched by the CPU and the address of the instruction is placed into the instruction address field of the PSW. The CPU then examines the first 2 bits of the operation code. If the first 2 bits are 00, the instruction is of a format which is 2 bytes or 1 halfword long. If the first 2 bits are 10 or 01, the instruction is of a format which is 4 bytes or 2 halfwords long. If the first 2 bits are 11, the instruction is of a format which is 6 bytes or 3 halfwords long.

The Instruction Length Code of the PSW (bits 32–33) is then set to 1 (01 binary), 2 (10 binary), or 3 (11 binary) to designate the respective number of halfwords in the instruction being executed. The instruction address field is incremented appropriately (by the number of bytes of the current instruction) to "point" to the address of the *next* instruction to be executed. For the next instruction cycle the CPU will fetch the instruction at the (newly incremented) address in the instruction address field.

Let us assume, as an example, that the program segment below is to be executed. Register 10 (hexadecimal A) is the base register and is assumed to contain 1B0000 at the start of the segment. Displacements too are indicated in hexadecimal form.

Instruction Address			Instruction			
			Object Code			
Hexadecimal	Base-Displacement		(hexadecimal)	Source	Code	
1B0002	A	002	1B22	LOOP	SR	2,2
1B0004	A	004	5A20A100		A	2,1
1B0008	A	008	47F0A002		B	LOOP

Object Code (in bits)
0001 1011 0010 0010
0101 1010 0010 0000 1010 0001 0000 0000
0100 0111 1111 0000 1010 0000 0000 0010

When the first instruction cycle begins, the object code for the first instruction, (1B22 hexadecimal or 0001 1011 0010 0010 in bits) is fetched by the CPU, and the address 1B0002 is placed into the instruction address register. The object code is examined and is found to begin with the bits 00; this is a signal for the instruction length code field to be set to $(01)_2$ and for the instruction address field to be incremented by 2 (the current instruction is 1 halfword or 2 bytes long) to the binary value (hex notation 1B0004) which in base-displacement form, is expressed as A004. The instruction 1B22 is then decoded by the CPU and executed.

The computer then examines the instruction address field, finds the value 1B0004 and the instruction at 1B0004 (object code 5A20A100) is fetched by the CPU. This object code is examined and is found to begin with 01, hence the instruction length code is set to $(10)_2$ and the instruction address is incremented by 4 (the current instruction is 2 halfwords or 4 bytes long) to the binary value (hex notation 1B0008) which in base-displacement form is expressed as A008. The instruction 5A20A100 is then decoded by the CPU and executed.

The computer now examines the instruction address field, finds the value 1B0008 and the instruction at 1B0008 (object code 47F0A002) is fetched by the CPU. This object code is examined and is found to begin with 01, hence the instruction length code is set to $(10)_2$ and the instruction address is incremented by 4 to the value 1B000C. The instruction 47F0A002 is decoded and executed. However, the instruction 47F0A002 is a *branch* instruction, and its execution places the address specified in its second operand, A002 (hexadecimal 1B0002), into the instruction address field! Thus, during the next instruction cycle, the CPU will fetch the instruction at 1B0002. A "branch" has been effected, overriding the usual sequential execution of program instructions.

Of special note here is that updating PSW fields (including setting the instruction length code and incrementing the instruction address) is a *hardware* function. That is, it is *not* controlled by computer instruction and is therefore accomplished at very high speed.

The Protection Key

Bits 8–11 of the PSW comprise the protection key. Storage is allocated to programs in units of 2048 bytes (we say in units of 2K) on System/360 and 370 computers. A special 4-bit "storage key" (a 4-bit code) is assigned to each 2048-byte block as it is assigned, with the same key being assigned to each such block of a program. Thus a program occupying 20K would occupy ten 2K blocks each having the identical storage key. Accessing such a program would not be possible unless the protection key in the PSW at the time of access matches the key of the block to be accessed. In other words, the protection key (bits 8–11) of the PSW is compared to the storage key. If the keys match, or if the protection code is 0 (the key used by the supervisor), the program may be accessed; otherwise, an "interruption" occurs. (This is called a "protection exception". Interrupts will be discussed in section 13.3.3.) The purpose of such protection is to ensure that a program in core does not interfere with other programs which may be in core at the same time. Different protection keys are assigned to different programs.

On some models, storage is not protected; on others protection is supplied only for instructions which change the contents of main storage ("store" operands). On yet other models protection is supplied for instructions which both store information in main storage and access ("fetch") information from main storage.

PSW Bit 12

On the System/360, bit 12 of the PSW indicates whether a code called ASCII-8 (bit 12=1) or whether EBCDIC code (bit 12=0) will be used to represent values. We have assumed EBCDIC representation throughout this text.

On the System/370, bit 12 of the PSW has a different meaning. It serves to indicate whether the PSW is in BC mode (bit 12=0) or in EC mode (bit 12=1). Our discussion thus far pertains to BC mode.

PSW Bits 14–15: WP Codes

The W position (bit 14) of the PSW indicates whether the CPU is in **wait state** (bit 14=1) or in **running state** (bit 14=0).

When the computer is in running state, instructions are being processed. However in wait state, instructions are not being executed; instead the computer is "awaiting" the completion of some action (for example, the completion of an input or output operation) before resuming its processing. Interruption may occur in either wait state or running state. ("Wait state" should be distinguished from "stop state" which is entered and left only through operator intervention and in which even program interruption may not occur. When not in "stop state", the CPU is said to be in "operating state".)

The P position (bit 15) of the PSW indicates whether the CPU is in **problem state** (executing a problem program; bit 15=1) or in **supervisor state** (bit 15=0). Certain "privileged" instructions, including some which change the PSW itself, may only be executed when the computer is in supervisor state. That is, when bit 15=1, none of these privileged instructions can be used. Bit 15 therefore serves to protect against unwarranted use of those instructions.

The remaining PSW fields include bits 0–7 (the system mask), bit 13 (the M or "Machine check" mask), bits 16–31 (the interruption code) and bits 36–39 (the program mask). These bits are all associated with interrupts, and with the exception of the interruption code, are all **mask bits**, meaning that they may be set to 0 or 1 to control whether program interrupts will occur (mask bit = 1) or will not occur (mask bit = 0) under specified conditions. In the interest of better understanding, our discussion of the remaining PSW fields for BC Mode will be incorporated into our discussion of the interrupt system in section 13.3.3.

13.3.2   The Program Status Word in EC Mode

A second form of the Program Status Word for IBM 370 systems is the Extended Control Mode or EC Mode. Some of the fields of the PSW in EC Mode are similar in function and in position to those of the PSW in BC Mode. Others are similar in function but have been moved, either to different bit positions in the PSW or to special **control registers** which are provided by System/370 (see figure 13.18). Some new PSW fields have been established, while others are left unused (although they will undoubtedly be used in the future, as system capabilities expand). The PSW in EC Mode is illustrated in figure 13.17.

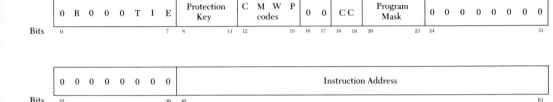

Figure 13.17
Program Status Word in EC Mode

We first note that the instruction address (bits 40–63), the protection key (bits 8–11), and the CMWP codes (bits 12–15) are identical in both function and location to those PSW fields in BC Mode. Recall that for System/370, bit 12 designates the PSW Mode: for EC Mode, bit 12 will always be 1.

The condition code has been moved (from bits 34–35 in BC Mode to bits 18–19 in EC Mode), as has the program mask (from bits 36–39 in BC Mode to bits 20–23 in EC Mode); however these fields remain unchanged in function.

Bit 1 (labeled "R" in figure 13.17) is the **program event recording** mask. That is, it controls whether (bit 1 = 1) or not (bit 1 = 0) program recording will take place. Program event recording is a System/370 feature which is a useful aid to debugging. It provides a "trace" or record of certain program activities or "events". Control registers 9, 10, and 11 (figure 13.18) are associated with program event recording. Bits 0,1,2, and 3 of control register 9 may be used to mask the respective recording of a successful branch, of fetching an instruction from a designated main storage area, of altering the contents of a main storage area, or of altering the contents of designated general registers. Bits 16–31 of control register 9 designates which *general* registers will be examined for change of contents. Control registers 10 and 11 contain the respective starting and ending addresses of the main storage area which is to be examined for change of content.

Bit 5 (labeled "T" in figure 13.17) specifies whether or not **translation mode** (that is, dynamic address translation) will be used. When bit 5 = 1, dynamic address translation will be used; when bit 5 = 0, it will not. Note from figure

13.18 that control register 1 gives the segment table length and segment table address in bit positions 0–7 and 8–25 respectively. Control register 1 thus contains the Segment Table Origin Register discussed in section 13.2.2. Note too

CONTROL REGISTERS

CR	Bits	Name of field	Associated with	Init.
0	0	Block-multiplex'g control	Block-multiplex'g	0
	1	SSM suppression control	SSM instruction	0
	2	TOD clock sync control	Multiprocessing	0
	8-9	Page size control	⎫	0
	10	Unassigned (must be zero)	⎬ Dynamic addr. transl.	0
	11-12	Segment size control	⎭	0
	16	Malfunction alert mask	⎫	0
	17	Emergency signal mask	⎬ Multiprocessing	0
	18	External call mask		0
	19	TOD clock sync check mask	⎭	0
	20	Clock comparator mask	Clock comparator	0
	21	CPU timer mask	CPU timer	0
	24	Interval timer mask	Interval timer	1
	25	Interrupt key mask	Interrupt key	1
	26	External signal mask	External signal	1
1	0-7	Segment table length	⎫ Dynamic addr. transl.	0
	8-25	Segment table address	⎭	0
2	0-31	Channel masks	Channels	1
8	16-31	Monitor masks	Monitoring	0
9	0	Successful branching event mask	⎫	0
	1	Instruction fetching event mask		0
	2	Storage alteration event mask	⎬ Program-event record'g	0
	3	GR alteration event mask		0
	16-31	PER general register masks	⎭	0
10	8-31	PER starting address	Program-event record'g	0
11	8-31	PER ending address	Program-event record'g	0
14	0	Check-stop control	⎫ Machine-check handling	1
	1	Synch. MCEL control	⎭	1
	2	I/O extended logout control	I/O extended logout	0
	4	Recovery report mask	⎫	0
	5	Degradation report mask		0
	6	Ext. damage report mask	⎬ Machine-check handling	1
	7	Warning mask		0
	8	Asynch. MCEL control		0
	9	Asynch. fixed log control	⎭	0
15	8-28	MCEL address	Machine-check handling	512

Figure 13.18
Control Registers

that bits 8–12 of control register 0 give the page and segment sizes to be used in dynamic address translation.

Bit 6 (labeled "I" in figure 13.17) is the input/output mask. If bit 6 = 0, all I/O interrupts are blocked. Otherwise, control register 2 (see figure 13.18), which contains mask bits for individual channels will mask channel interrupts individually (their function was performed by bits 0–6 in the PSW in BC Mode). Interrupts will be considered in detail in section 13.3.3.

Bit 7 (labeled "E" in figure 13.17) is the external mask. If bit 7 = 0, all external interrupts are blocked. Otherwise, various external mask bits in control register 0 will mask external interrupts individually depending upon the cause of the interrupt.

The remaining PSW bit positions (bits 0, 2, 3, 4, 16–17, 24–31, and 32–39) are unused in EC Mode, as of this writing.

You will find the names and functions of fields in the 15 control registers summarized on side ⑬ of the System/370 Reference Summary (Appendix A). This chart is reproduced for your convenience in figure 13.18.

13.3.3 The Interrupt System

An **interrupt** is a transfer of computer control to a module of the operating system which will "handle" the cause of the interruption. Our discussion of the interrupt system will attempt to answer the following basic questions:

- What conditions cause interrupts to occur?
- What is the mechanism through which an interrupt is accomplished?
- What happens when interrupts from different sources occur at the same time?
- What determines whether an interrupt will or will not occur?

What Conditions Cause Interrupts to Occur?

Interrupts are categorized according to the conditions which cause them to occur. There are six classes of interrupts, each of which shall be explained in turn.

1. Restart (only on System/370)
2. External
3. Supervisor call
4. Program
5. Machine check
6. Input/output

RESTART INTERRUPTS

A restart interrupt occurs only on the System/370 by pushing the "restart" key on the operator's console.

EXTERNAL INTERRUPTS

An external interrupt occurs when a signal is transmitted to the CPU from either

- a clock or timer (for example, a program may exceed the time limit which has been set for it)
- the interrupt key on the operator's console
- an external device connected to the CPU (for example, another computer on-line to this one may transmit the interrupt signal)

The interrupt effects a transfer of control to an operating system module called the **external interrupt handler**.

SUPERVISOR CALL INTERRUPTS

A supervosor call interrupt is effected by the execution of an SVC (**S**uper**V**isor **C**all) instruction. (The SVC instruction has been discussed in chapter 2, section 2.4.) The interrupt effects a transfer of control to an operating system module called the **SVC interrupt handler**. The SVC instruction may or may not be written by the programmer; it might be part of a macro definition, the programmer having written the original macro instruction.

PROGRAM INTERRUPTS

A program interrupt occurs as a result of some condition arising from a problem program. A number of different error conditions can cause program interruption, as every programmer discovers, with either resignation or dismay! The interrupt effects a transfer of control to the operating system module called the **program interrupt handler**, and places a special "interruption code" in the PSW field designated for that purpose (bits 16–31). We list the program interruption codes in figure 13.19, along with the respective conditions which cause those interruptions. However, we defer detailed discussions of most of those interrupt conditions to the chapter on debugging (chapter 14, section 14.4.2).

MACHINE CHECK INTERRUPTS

A machine check interrupt occurs as a result of some machine or hardware failure. The interrupt effects a transfer of control to the operating system module called the **machine check interrupt handler**.

INPUT/OUTPUT INTERRUPTS

Input/output interrupts occur during the processing of input or output operations (that is, when data is about to be read into or to be written out of main

Program Interruption Codes

0001	Operation exception
0002	Privileged operation exception
0003	Execute exception
0004	Protection exception
0005	Addressing exception
0006	Specification exception
0007	Data exception
0008	Fixed-point overflow exception
0009	Fixed-point divide exception
000A	Decimal overflow exception
000B	Decimal divide exception
000C	Exponent overflow exception
000D	Exponent underflow exception
000E	Significance exception
000F	Floating-point divide exception
0010	Segment translation exception
0011	Page translation exception
0012	Translation specification exception
0013	Special operation exception
0040	Monitor event
0080	Program event (code may be combined with another code)

Figure 13.19
Program Interruption Codes

storage). When an input or output operation is to take place, special devices called **channels** relieve the CPU from the need to process certain of the I/O functions. When the channel completes its I/O functions, it signals the CPU, causing the condition which we call an input/output interrupt. A transfer of control is effected to the operating system module called the **I/O interrupt handler**.

The Mechanism Through Which an Interrupt is Accomplished

The successful occurrence of an interrupt is accomplished through the interaction of hardware functions and operating system routines. Both the hardware and the software elements assume the allocation of certain areas of main storage for specific uses. These main storage areas occupy the low end of memory, beginning with location zero.

In order to visualize what happens when an interrupt occurs, let us consider a problem program currently being executed. We assume that the program protection key is 1010, and that the instruction address field of the PSW contains a value equivalent to B100 hexadecimal; that is, B100 is the address of the *next* instruction to be executed. (Recall from section 13.3.1 that the instruction address is incremented to the address of the next instruction *before* execution of the current instruction.) When the interrupt signal is transmitted to the CPU, the following action takes place (see figure 13.20).

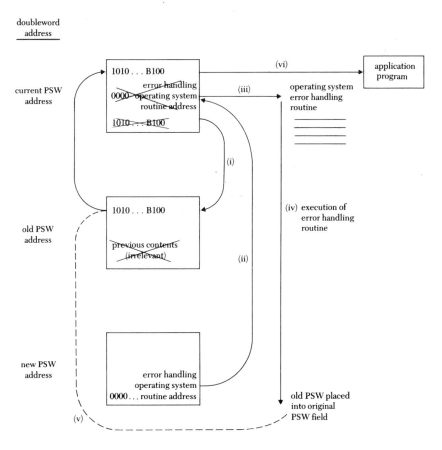

Figure 13.20
The Interrupt Mechanism

(i)   The contents of the current PSW (called the "initial program loading PSW"), containing the protection key 1010 and the instruction address B100, will be placed into a *different* doubleword called the "old PSW" field.

(ii)   The contents of yet a third doubleword, the "new PSW" field, are then placed into the (original) initial program loading PSW field. This new PSW contains the protection key 0000 (the protection key for the operating system). The instruction address field will contain the address of the operating system module which handles interrupts belonging to the same class as the interrupt which has just occurred.

(iii)   The CPU then follows its usual procedure (see section 13.3.1) for determining which instruction is to be executed next: it examines the instruction address field of the current PSW, which at this point will contain the address of the appropriate operating system interrupt handler (step (ii) put it there!). Hence a branch is effected to that operating system routine.

(iv)   The interrupt handler performs whatever functions are appropriate for handling the interruption. These functions are variable. They will depend upon the class of interrupt and the particular cause of the interrupt, and may differ from one operating system to another. For example, the action of the SVC interrupt handler will depend upon the numeric code in the operand of the SVC instruction (see chapter 2, section 2.4). The program interrupt handler may terminate the job and print out a diagnostic (error) message; it may, in addition to the above, print out a "dump" of certain main storage locations; it may do neither of the above, depending on the cause of the interrupt and the setting of PSW bits 36–39 (this will be explained shortly). The machine check interrupt handler will generate diagnostic information with regard to the cause of machine failure; however under OS systems the routine attempts either to correct the problem or to circumvent it so that processing will continue, while under DOS systems the CPU is placed into wait state (processing will not continue).

(v)   The last instruction of the interrupt handler places the old (original) PSW back into the initial program loading PSW location. (If control is not to be returned to the application program, another PSW may be placed into the initial program loading PSW.)

(vi)   Reloading the original PSW causes control to be returned to the next sequential instruction of the application program.

The current PSW (that is, the PSW governing the computer's operations at any particular time) occupies a fixed location in main storage. However, the old PSW and new PSW addresses differ for each interrupt class. Each new PSW contains (in its instruction address field) the address of the operating system interrupt routine appropriate for that class. The addresses of the old and new PSW fields are given in figure 13.21. Note that all addresses whose contents are used are doublewords (multiples of 8).

Thus if the CPU determined that an I/O interrupt were to occur,

- The contents of the initial program loading PSW would be placed into hex location 38 (the I/O old PSW).

- The contents of the new PSW at hex location 78 would be placed into the current PSW field.
- After examining the new PSW in the current PSW field, a branch would be effected to the I/O error handling routine of the operating system.
- The I/O error handling routine would be executed.
- The last step of the error handling routine would cause the contents of the doubleword at hex location 38 to be returned to the current PSW field.
- The CPU would then examine the instruction address of the current PSW and effect a branch back to the application program (to the instruction following that which caused the I/O interrupt).

| Address | | | |
Decimal	Hexadecimal	Length	Purpose
24	000018	doubleword	external old PSW
32	000020	doubleword	supervisor call old PSW
40	000028	doubleword	program old PSW
48	000030	doubleword	machine check old PSW
56	000038	doubleword	input/output old PSW
64	000040	doubleword	channel status word
72	000048	word	channel address word
76	00004C	word	unused
80	000050	word	timer
84	000054	word	unused
88	000058	doubleword	external new PSW
96	000060	doubleword	supervisor call new PSW
104	000068	doubleword	program new PSW
112	000070	doubleword	machine check new PSW
120	000078	doubleword	input/output new PSW
128	000080	varies	diagnostic scan-out area (used after machine check)

Figure 13.21
Permanent Storage Assignments
for Old and New PSW Fields

The Simultaneous Occurrence of Different Interrupt Conditions

When different interrupt conditions occur simultaneously, they are taken in the following order of priority:

1. Machine check
2. Supervisor call
3. Program

4. External
5. Input/output
6. Restart (Sys/370 only)

However the actual execution of the appropriate operating system error handling routines occurs in the reverse order. Let us explain.

Suppose that supervisor call, external, and input/output interrupts all occurred at the same time. They are taken in priority order as follows: the current PSW is placed into the SVC old PSW location (hex 000020), and the SVC new PSW is placed into the current PSW location; then the current PSW (now the same as the contents of the SVC new PSW) is placed into the external old PSW location (hex 000018), and the external new PSW is placed into the current PSW location; then the current PSW (now the same as the contents of the external new PSW) is placed into the input/output old PSW location (hex 000038), and the input/output new PSW is placed into the current PSW location.

It is time for the interrupt routines to be processed. The current PSW now "points" to the input/output interrupt handler, so that routine is executed first; the contents of the input/output old PSW (containing the external new PSW) are returned to the current PSW. The current PSW now "points" to the external interrupt handler, so that routine is executed next; the contents of the external old PSW (containing the SVC new PSW) are returned to the current PSW. The current PSW now "points" to the SVC interrupt handler, so that routine is executed next; the contents of the SVC old PSW (the original application program PSW) are returned to the current PSW. The current PSW now "points" to the application program, to which control is now returned.

Note from the above example that the execution of the interrupt handling routines occurs in the reverse order from that in which the interrupts were taken.

Controlling the Occurrence or Non-Occurrence of Particular Interrupts

Certain PSW bits function as mask bits: they may be set to 1 or 0, to indicate whether a particular interrupt is to occur (corresponding mask bit = 1) or is not to occur (corresponding mask bit = 0).

The **system mask** (PSW bits 0–7) indicates whether interrupts associated with input and output channels (PSW bits 0–6) or external signals (PSW bit 7) are to be taken. External signals may arise from the timer, the interrupt key on the console, or other external devices. The individual bits and their corresponding sources of interrupt are noted in figure 13.22.

Channels are special-purpose hardware devices through which transfer of information is effected between the I/O devices and the computer. The CPU communicates with the appropriate channel when an actual I/O operation is to take place (when an I/O interrupt *has been taken*) and the channel reports back to the CPU when its job (buffering, counting the number of bytes read or written, and incrementing core addresses) has been completed. When a channel mask bit is 0, the corresponding channel may not interrupt the CPU; the interrupt will remain pending until the bit is reset to 1.

System Mask Bit	Source of Interrupt
0	channel 0
1	channel 1
2	channel 2
3	channel 3
4	channel 4
5	channel 5
6	mask for channel 6 *and up*
7	external mask

Figure 13.22
System Mask Bits

Likewise, when the external mask bit is 0 the external signal may not interrupt the CPU. It too will remain pending until bit 7 is reset to 1.

The machine check mask bit (bit 13) does not allow a machine check interrupt, when set to 0. When bit 13 is set to 1, the machine check is allowed.

The **program mask** (bits 36–39) controls the occurrence or non-occurrence of the four program exceptions listed in figure 13.23, as follows:

Program Mask Bit	Program Exception
36	fixed-point overflow
37	decimal overflow
38	exponent underflow
39	significance

Figure 13.23
The Program Mask

Fixed-point overflow and decimal overflow were discussed along with the description of binary and decimal arithmetic instructions (chapters 8 and 4 respectively), and will be reviewed in chapter 14. The exponent underflow and significance exceptions occur with floating point operations, which are beyond the scope of this book.

Let us understand why masking is provided for input/output, external, and machine check interrupts. Suppose that a machine check interrupt occurred, causing the current PSW, say that of the application program, to be stored in the machine check old PSW (hex location 000030). The machine check new PSW is then placed into the current PSW location; it "points" to the machine check interrupt handler and *contains a 1-bit in position 13*, prohibiting any further machine check interrupts from occurring until after the interrupt has been processed and the machine check old PSW contents restored. To understand why this masking is necessary, consider the consequences were another machine check interrupt to be taken prior to the restoration of the old PSW contents: the contents of the current PSW at the time of the second interrupt (moved in during the first interrupt from the machine check new PSW) would replace the contents of the machine check old PSW, destroying them. The original application program PSW would thus be lost! Masking PSW bit 13 to prevent additional machine check interrupts while the first is being processed is therefore an important safeguard.

Masking is needed for input/output and external interruptions, to prevent the same type of occurrence. However, masking is not provided for program or SVC interrupts. We say that masking for program or SVC interrupts is not necessary, on the assumption that execution of the program interrupt handler will not cause another program interrupt (the routine should be error-free!) and that the SVC interrupt handler is written so that it will not initiate another SVC interrupt.

13.4 THE IBM 3033 PROCESSOR

Throughout the text, we have discussed computer capabilities and characteristics as they apply to the IBM System/360 and System/370 series. It is worthwhile, at this point, to note the recent addition of a new member of the IBM System/370 "family": the IBM 3033 Processor.

Of great importance to us as applications programmers is the fact that only very minimal software differences exist between the 3033 Processor and the System/370 Model 168. In fact the 3033 offers greater processing power and an instruction execution rate which is 1.6 to 1.8 times the rate of the System/370 Model 168 with identical programs, when running under the operating system module known as OS/VS2 Release 3.

While maintaining compatibility with System/370 computers, the 3033 does provide expanded capabilities: In particular,
- Programming support provided includes such operating systems versions as MVS, SVS, and VM/370. This will serve to facilitate the maintenance and modification of already existing programs on this system.
- Processor storage is sold in increments of two megabytes with four, six, or eight megabytes available per processor.

- Two console display terminals are provided as a standard feature, and each is individually addressable. Both displays may be concurrently used by operators, or one may be used for system production while another is used for running channel or console microdiagnostics.
- Faster cycle time is provided than with the System/370 (58 nanoseconds, as opposed to 80 nanoseconds with the Sys/370 Model 168)
- Main storage is complemented with increased buffer storage size (64K).
- Other features are available on an optional basis, including the expansion of the standard twelve I/O channels to sixteen; channel to channel adapters; channel interfaces for attaching high-speed devices

The IBM 3033 with DASD (Direct Access Storage Device), printer, and console is illustrated in figure 13.24. Since software compatibility with the System/370 series is maintained, our study of assembly language for the 370 under OS control will be applicable to the writing of assembly language programs for the IBM 3033 Processor as well.

Courtesy of IBM Corporation

Figure 13.24
IBM 3033 Processor with
DASD, Printer, and Console

Summary

This chapter introduced us to some very important operating systems concepts.

Virtual Storage systems were introduced, along with a discussion of relocation, including simple program loading, static relocation, and dynamic relocation. Techniques for dynamic relocation considered in this chapter include segmentation systems, and segmentation and paging systems. In addition, we distinguished single from multiple virtual storage systems, discussed various advantages of virtual storage systems, and advised as to appropriate techniques and approaches to be used when coding for virtual storage.

We discussed the Program Status Word (PSW) in both BC and EC Modes and the respective functions of the various PSW fields.

The interrupt system was described, including classes of interrupts, interrupt priority, and interrupt masking.

The IBM 3033 Processor, a recent addition to the System/370 family, was introduced.

Important Terms Discussed in Chapter 13

address space

associative array registers

availability

BC mode

change bit

condition code

control registers

DAT feature

demand paging

displacement

dynamic address translation feature

dynamic relocation

EC mode

external interrupt

external mask

external page frame

external page storage

external page table

fragmentation

input/output interrupt

input/output mask

instruction address

instruction length code

interrupt

interruption code

invalid bit

least recently used rule (LRU)

load time

locality of reference

machine check interrupt

mask bit

multiple virtual storages

multiprogramming

operating system

page

page fault

page frame

page frame table

page-in

page-out

page table

potential address space

problem state

program event recording

program interrupt

program mask

program status word (PSW)

protection key

real storage

reference bit
relative address
relocation
response time
restart interrupt
running state

segment
segment table
segment table origin register (STOR)
segmentation
simple program loading
single virtual storage
slot
static relocation
status bit

supervisor call interrupt
supervisor state
swapping
symbolic name space
system mask

throughput
translation mode
turnaround time

validity of reference
virtual address
virtual storage (VS)

wait state

Questions

13-1. What is an operating system?

13-2. State six possible objectives of an operating system. Will these objectives apply to all operating systems?

13-3. What is multiprogramming?

13-4. Distinguish between a program in symbolic name space and one in address space.

13-5. (a) What is program relocation?
(b) Name the two basic types of relocation, and distinguish between them.

13-6. State a major disadvantage of simple program loading.

13-7. (a) Name a computer system which uses simple program loading.
(b) Name a computer system which uses static relocation.

13-8. What is the major advantage of static relocation systems over those that use simple program loading? What major difficulty with regard to allocation of main storage still remains with static relocation systems? What type of relocation system attempts to resolve this difficulty, and how?

13-9. Is static relocation performed by system software or hardware? What about dynamic relocation?

13-10. Distinguish between an absolute address and a relative address. Which type of address does the CPU use to reference real storage locations?

13-11. Summarize the steps necessary to translate a relative address in a segmentation system.

13-12. How is fragmentation avoided in a segmentation system?

13-13. Summarize the steps necessary to translate a relative address in a segmentation and paging system.

13-14. When does the address translation for segmentation systems and for segmentation and paging systems take place? Is this translation directed by the programmer? Explain.

13-15. Distinguish between a page and a page frame.

13-16. What is the function of a page frame table?

13-17. What determines the segment size and page size in a segment-page formatted address space?

13-18. What are the three components of the virtual address structure in a VS system which uses segmentation and paging?

13-19. What is the function of the associative array registers?

13-20. What rule does the system use in deciding which associative array register to replace?

13-21. Translate the following relative addresses, using the associative array registers of figure 13.11.

	segment number	page number	displacement
(a)	2	2	0500
(b)	1	4	0648
(c)	1	2	1024

13-22. How does the system determine which associative array register to choose in order to store the segment number, page number, and page frame location of a newly translated address?

13-23. What is the maximum virtual storage size of a computer whose address register is 24 bits long?

13–24. Translate the following relative addresses, using the segment and page tables of figure 13–9.

	segment number	page number	displacement
(a)	1	3	1600

(b)	3	2	0050

(c)	2	1	0004

13–25. In what physical location are programs and data which reside in virtual storage?

13–26. Distinguish between address space and potential address space.

13–27. What are the respective segment and page sizes for virtual storage on IBM systems?

13–28. What is demand paging?

13–29. What is a page fault? How and when does a virtual storage system sense a page fault?

13–30. The occurrence of a page fault signals the need for what type of operation?

13–31. How does the virtual storage system locate the page to be paged-in?

13–32. What is a slot location?

13–33. Suppose that paging-in is called for, but there is no page frame available whose corresponding status bit=0. What will happen?

13–34. The best page replacement rule is considered to be the LRU rule. What does this mean? Which bit of the page frame table helps the implementation of this rule?

13–35. How does the virtual storage system know whether the contents of a page which is to be replaced have been changed since that page was paged-in? Why is this important to know?

13–36. State whether each of the following features characterizes systems with a single virtual storage, systems with a multiple virtual storage, or both types of systems.
   (a) The maximum size of virtual storage is determined by the computer's address structure.
   (b) The virtual storage is the system's address space.
   (c) The virtual storage is the user's address space.

13-37. We have said that when loading programs for virtual storage systems, we should load all frequently used subroutines near each other in virtual storage. Why?

13-38. List three general guidelines to keep in mind when coding for virtual storage systems.

13-39. State five advantages of virtual storage systems.

13-40. Tell what the letters in the following terms stand for:
(a) DAT
(b) STOR

13-41. What do the letters PSW stand for? Distinguish between the overall functions of the fields in the first and second words of the PSW.

13-42. What are the only possible condition code settings? From what do these settings, or changes in these settings, result?

13-43. We know that the instruction address field of the PSW is incremented automatically before execution of an instruction, to the address of the next sequential instruction. How, then, is a departure from sequential execution effected?

13-44. One PSW bit has a different function on 360 systems than it does on 370 systems. Identify this bit by number, and distinguish between its different functions.

13-45. (a) Distinguish between wait state and running state.
(b) Distinguish between problem state and supervisor state.
(c) Distinguish between stop state and operating state.

13-46. Bit 5 of the PSW in EC mode specifies whether or not translation mode will be used. What does this mean? Which control registers have associated functions?

13-47. What are the respective functions of bits 6 and 7 of the PSW in EC mode?

13-48. (a) What is an interrupt?
(b) List the six classes of interrupts.
(c) Which class of interrupt is likely to be of most concern to the applications programmer? Explain.

13-49. Briefly summarize the six steps which we described as comprising the interrupt mechanism.

13-50. The occurrence of interrupts belonging to which class(es) may be controlled through masking? For which interrupt classes is masking not provided?

13-51. Suppose that a machine check and a program interrupt occur simultaneously. Which will be taken first? Which interrupt handler will be executed first? Explain.

13-52. What is the setting of bit 15 in the new PSW fields, that is, during the execution of interrupt handling routines?

Chapter 14

Debugging

DEBUGGING

An error in a computer program is called a **bug,** and the process of correcting those errors is called **debugging.** Debugging is virtually always a necessary part of the total process of writing programs and bringing them to correct completion. Programmers are human and are thus unable to write the "perfect" program without a certain allowance for errors to occur. In fact, in determining time schedules for the completion of programming projects, a responsible manager will always allot a sufficient amount of time for such debugging procedures.

14.1   THE BEST DEBUGGING MEDICINE IS PREVENTIVE

Debugging may actually be said to begin when the programming problem is first defined. Certainly, a problem which is not properly analyzed or defined will have to be reanalyzed at some later stage, necessitating not only the reanalysis, but also the reworking of the entire programming effort which was based upon that defective analysis.

There may likewise be faults in the design of program logic. Such faults will almost certainly require a very great debugging effort, for they too will require that the coding process be at least partially repeated.

Assuming that the problem was properly analyzed and its logic correctly designed for an efficient solution, coding errors may arise. We shall be concerned in this chapter with coding errors resulting from:

(i)   Violations of the rules associated with writing statements in the language, or

(ii)   Incorrect translation of the logical steps (as described in, say, a problem flowchart) into programming-language instructions.

Our first debugging responsibility is thus to take great care in our initial writing. It is very important to:

- Be neat and organized in our work.
- Keep all documents (such as layout forms, flowcharts) for reference.
- Comment the program liberally. Good comments may be especially invaluable at later stages of debugging, for they describe one's train of thought and one's reasons for using certain procedures or instructions. Moreover, a good program may be used for quite some time and may require modification or expansion at some later date. Certainly, comments will prove to be quite useful in deciphering the logical detail of a pro-

gram, months, or even years, after its initial writing, possibly by an individual other than the one who wrote the program originally!

Once the problem has been analyzed, the logic designed, and the code written, the stage of *actual* debugging has been reached. The programmer will begin by **desk-checking** his program both before and after it is keypunched. Section 14.2 will describe a systematic approach to desk-checking.

14.2 DESK-CHECKING

Desk-checking is the process of checking the coding forms (before keypunching) and punched cards (after keypunching) to catch any clerical or logical errors which the programmer may notice. If desk-checking is done carefully, the programmer will almost always spot at least some trivial coding errors or keypunching errors and will thus eliminate an assembly or possibly a program run with data. In brief, when checking the coded program, you should pay special attention to the following points:

- Check to see that all instruction names begin in column 1; that there is at least one blank between instruction names and operations, and between operations and operands; that blanks are not embedded within either names, operations, or operand fields.
- Double-check your DCB (for OS systems) or DTF (for DOS systems) macros to be sure that the proper operands are present and are spelled correctly, with required commas separating those operands.
- Double-check the descriptions of all input and output records. Be sure that they conform to the problem specifications and that they contain the required total number of characters.
- Check to see that names are not defined more than once, and that all names used in the operand portions of instructions are, in fact, defined. (This will require that you create a list of all names used in operands as you scan the program. Then check this list against the name portions of DC and DS instructions.)

It is also wise to check the logical flow of your program.

- Compare your program code to the program flowchart, to be sure that the program "flow" corresponds (that routines are placed in the proper order; that when the program branches to a program statement, the operand portion of the branch instruction references the proper statement, whether directly or indirectly).
- Follow the "flow" of your program for each possible condition that may arise. (For example, in a payroll problem, see where the instructions will

lead if the individual worked overtime or did not work overtime; if the individual passed the social security base or did not.) This way you will be assured that program routines which handle different conditions are arrived at appropriately.

- Check that all loops are initialized properly, and that the condition which determines the exit from the loop is, in fact, the appropriate condition. (For example, if the loop is "counting" the number of lines to be printed on the page, and we would like 50 lines to be printed, should the counter be tested for "equal to" 50? "less than" 50? This will depend upon how the counter is initialized and whether or not the test for exit from the loop precedes the incrementation of the counter.)
- Check to see that all counters and accumulators (for example, areas in which totals are being accumulated) are initialized appropriately.

After the program has been keypunched, the punched cards should be checked against the coding sheets. It may be possible for you to get an **80–80 listing** of your keypunched deck (an exact copy of your deck, with each of the 80 columns represented as an appropriate printed character on the listing). In such a case, the listing may be checked against the coding sheets.

Once the desk-checking has been concluded, the source deck is ready to be submitted for assembly and/or execution.

14.3   DIAGNOSTICS

We are already familiar with the fact that when programs are assembled, different types of printed output are produced along with the object module. This printed output includes the:
- External symbol dictionary (ESD)
- Assembly listing
- Using map
- Cross-reference listing
- Relocation dictionary (RLD)
- Diagnostic listing
- Load map

For purposes of debugging in this section, we will make use of the assembly listing, the cross-reference listing, and the diagnostic listing, each of which appears on its own page as part of the program output.

Figure 14.1 (parts 1–4) shows the assembly listing, cross-reference listing, and

```
LOC    OBJECT CODE      ADDR1 ADDR2   STMT  SOURCE STATEMENT

                                        1  *
                                        2         PRINT NOGEN
                                        3         START
                                        4  *
CCCCCC                                  5  BEGIN  BALR  11,0
CCCCC  C5D0                             6         USING *,11
                                        7  *
CCCCC2                    CCCC2         8         OPEN  (INFILE,INPUT,OUTFILE,OUTPUT)
                                       16  *+FOR ECS,OPEN  INFILE,OUTFILE
                                       17  *
                                       18  *
CCCC12                                 19  +      PUT   OUTFILE,HEADER1
CCCC2C                                 24  +      PUT   OUTFILE,HEADER2
CCCC2E                                 29  +      PUT   OUTFILE,BLANKS
CCCC32  CCC0 CCC0         CCCC0        31  +      LA    0,BLANKS      LOAD PARAMETER REG 0
        *** ERROR ***
CCCC3C  CCC0 CCC0                      34  +      PUT   OUTFILE,HEADER3
CCCC4A                                 39  +      PUT   OUTFILE,BLANKS
CCCC4E  CCC0 CCC0         CCCC0        41  +      LA    0,BLANKS      LOAD PARAMETER REG 0
        *** ERROR ***
                                       44  *
CCCC5B  D213 B34F 616A    C0351 C016C  45  REPEAT GET   INFILE,INAREA
CCCC5E  D20E B367 B17E    C0369 C017E  46  *
CCCC64  D201 B37E B1RD    C03BC C01BF  47         MVC   CNAME,INAME
CCCC6A  D202 B385 B19F    C03B7 C0191  48         MVC   CTITLE,ITITLE
CCCC7C  D202 B38F B192    C0391 C0194  49         MVC   DCIV,ICIV
CCCC76  B393 B195         C0197        50         MVC   CDEPT,IDEPT
CCCC7C  CCC0 CCC0 CCCC    CCCC0        51         MVC   DAREA,IAREA
                                       52         MVC   CNUM,INUM
                                       53         MVC   DEXT,IEXT(3)
                                       54  *
CCCCP2                                 55         PUT   OUTFILE,OUTLINE
                                       60  *
CCCCSC  CCC0 CCC0         CCCC0        61         B     REPEAT.
        *** ERROR ***
                                       62  *
CCCCS4                                 63  EOJ
CCCCSE                                 69         CLOSE (INFILE)
                                                  CLOSE (OUTFILE)
                                       75  *+FOR ECS,CLOSING PROGRAM FILES IS DONE BY
                                       76         CLOSE INFILE,OUTFILE
                                       77  *
CCCCAA  0A03                           78         SVC   3
        *** ERROR ***                  79  +FOR ECS,THE SVC 3 IS REPLACED BY
                                       80  *      EOJ
                                       81  *
                                       82  * FILE DEFINITIONS
                                       83  *
COCCAC                                 84  INFILE  DCB  DSORG=PS,MACRF=GM,DDNAME=SYSIPT,   C
                                                        BLKSIZE=80,LRECL=80,EODD=EOJ       C
CCC1CC                                138  OUTFILE DCB  DSORG=PS,MACRF=PM,DDNAME=SYSLST,   C
                                                        BLKSIZE=132,LRECL=132
                                       192  *
```

Figure 14.1 (Part 1)
An Assembly Listing with Diagnostics

```
LCC  OBJECT CODE      ADDR1 ADDR2   STMT   SOURCE STATEMENT                                              PAGE   3

                                                                                                         17 NOV 78

                                    193 *FOR DOS, THE CCB'S ARE REPLACED BY
                                    194 *INFILE  CTFCD DEVADDR=SYSRDR,IOAREA1=IN,BLKSIZE=80,
                                    195 *              RECFORM=FIXUNB,WORKA=YES,EOFADDR=EOJ
                                    196 *CUTFILE CTFPR DEVADDR=SYSLST,IOAREA1=OUT,BLKSIZE=132,
                                    197 *              RECFORM=FIXUNB,WORKA=YES
                                    198 *IN      DS    CL80     IN IS NAME OF INPUT BUFFER AREA FOR DOS
                                    199 *CUT     DS    CL132    OUT IS NAME OF OUTPUT BUFFER AREA FOR DOS
                                    200 *
                                    201 *  AREA DEFINITIONS
                                    202 *
                                    203 *  INPUT AREA
CCC1C                               204 INAREA  DS    OCL80
CCC1C                               205 INAME   DS    CL20
CCC3C                               206 ITITLE  DS    CL15
CCC4F                               207 IDIV    DS    CL2
CCC51                               208 IDEPT   DS    CL3
CCC54                               209 IPHONE  DS    OCL13
CCC54                               210 IAREA   DS    CL3
CCC57                               211 INUM    DS    CL7
CCC5E                               212 IEXT    DS    CL3
CCC61                               213 *
                                    214 *  HEADER LINES
                                    215 *
CCC1BC  4C404C4C4C4C4C404C          217 HEADER1 DC    CL137'          MICKEY MOUSE
CCC24C  4C404C404C4C4C4C4C          218 HEADER2 DC    CL132'      ETRAP INC.'
CCC2C4  4C4C404C4C4C404C4C          219 HEADER3 DC    CL132'      DIRECTORY'
                                    220 *
                                    221 *  CUTPUT LINE
                                    222 *
CCC348  4C404C404C4C404C4040        223 CUTLINE DS    OCL132
CCC34B                              224 CNAME   DS    CL20*
CCC351  40404C40                    225               DS    CL5*
CCC365  40404C40                    226               DS    CL4*
CCC369                              227 CTITLE  DS    CL15
CCC378  4C404C4C4C4C404C4C          228               DS    CL8*
CCC38C  40404040                    229 CDIV    DS    CL2
CCC3P2                              230               DS    CL5*
CCC387  4C404C404C4C4040            231 CDEPT   DS    CL3
CCC3EA                              232               DS    CL7*
CCC354  40                          233 CAREA   DS    CL3
CCC351                              234               DS    CL1*
CCC355                              235 CNUM    DS    CL7
CCC35C  40404040                    236               DS    CL4*
CCC3AC                              237 CEXT    DS    CL3
CCC3A3  4C404C4C4C4C404C4C          238               DC    CL41*'
CCCCCC                              239               END   BEGIN
```

Figure 14.1 (Part 2)
An Assembly Listing with Diagnostics

CROSS-REFERENCE

SYMBOL	LEN	VALUE	DEFN	REFERENCES			
BEGIN	2	000C00	5	239	41		
BLANKS		****UNDEFINED****		31			
CCJ	4	00CC94	65	106			
HEADER1	132	00C1BC	217	21			
HEADER2	132	00C240	218	26			
HEADER3	132	00C2C4	219	36			
IAREA	3	00C194	21C	51			
IDEPT	3	00C191	20B	50			
IDIV	2	00C19F	207	49			
IEXT	3	00C19E	212	53			
INAME	2C	00C16C	205	47			
INAREA	8C	00C0AC	204				
INFILE	4	00C0AC	8P	12	67		
INUM	7	00C197	211	52			
IPHONE	13	00C194	206	48			
ITITLE	15	000180	233	51			
OAREA	3	00C387	231	50			
ODIV	3	000380	229	49			
OEXT	3	00C3A0	237	53			
ONAME	2C	00C351	235	47			
ONUM	7	00C395	227	52			
OTITLE	15	000369	142	14	20	25	30
OUTFILE	4	00C10C	223	35	40	56	73
OUTLINE	132	00C348	273	57			
REPEAT		****UNDEFINED****		61			

Figure 14.1 (Part 3)
Cross Reference Listing for
Assembly Language Program with Diagnostics

DIAGNOSTICS

```
STMT   ERROR CODE   MESSAGE

  31   ASMG024      NEAR OPERAND COLUMN    3--UNDEFINED SYMBOL
  41   ASMG024      NEAR OPERAND COLUMN    3--UNDEFINED SYMBOL
  45   ASMG088      UNDEFINED OPERATION CODE
  53   ASMG008      NEAR OPERAND COLUMN   12--INVALID DISPLACEMENT
  61   ASMG024      NEAR OPERAND COLUMN    1--UNDEFINED SYMBOL
  79   ASMG088      UNDEFINED OPERATION CODE


   6 STATEMENTS FLAGGED IN THIS ASSEMBLY
  12 WAS HIGHEST SEVERITY CODE


 2860 SYSLIB SOURCE RECORDS,    97 SYSIN SOURCE RECORDS,
   25 SYSLIN OUTPUT RECORDS,   173 SYSPRINT OUTPUT RECORDS
```

Figure 14.1 (Part 4)
Diagnostic Listing for
Assembly Language Program with Diagnostics

diagnostic listing for a version of the telephone directory problem of chapter 3, into which some errors have been deliberately introduced. We shall explain the meanings of the information in the various columns of each of the three types of output listings presented. We will then use the information in those listings to find and to correct the errors in the program.

Let us first consider the assembly listing (figure 14.1, part 1). The rightmost column of the listing is labeled SOURCE STATEMENT. It lists the assembly language instructions to be translated by the assembler program. The first source statement of our program, the PRINT NOGEN instruction, is an assembler instruction which "tells" the assembler not to print the expansions of any macro instructions which may be part of the program, so that only the instructions actually written by the programmer and submitted to the assembler will be noted on the listing. However, for cases in which error conditions affect the proper translation of the macro, those parts of the macro definition affected by the error will indeed become part of the listing. They will be identified by the symbol " + " to their left, immediately to the right of the statement number (under the column labeled STMT, standing for "statement") which identifies such instructions. In figure 14.1, part 1, statements 31 and 41 were not written by the programmer; they are the parts of the macro definitions for statements 29 and 39 respectively which were affected by error condition(s) in those macros.

We have already stated that the column headed by the word STMT contains **ST**ate**M**en**T** numbers which were generated by the assembler to identify the program statements. It is certainly more convenient, in discussing the program, to speak of "statement 24" rather than to speak of "the second PUT statement of the program"! You may have noticed that statement numbers appear to be "skipped" after each macro instruction. For example, statement number 8 (the OPEN instruction) is followed by statement number 16; actually, statements 9–15 do exist, however they comprise the macro definition, which does not appear on the listing.

The leftmost column of the listing is headed by the letters LOC, standing for "**LOC**ation counter". The location counter is the means by which the assembler keeps track of the relative locations and lengths of instructions, constants, and reserved areas. The location counter is initialized by the START instruction, and is incremented as instructions are translated and as storage areas are assigned. Note from figure 14.1, part 1, that statement 47 is stored at location 58; the MVC instruction occupies 6 bytes, hence the next statement, statement number 48, has location counter value 5E (58+6=5E). The location counter was not incremented after statement number 3, the START instruction, for it is an assembler instruction, hence has no object code, and is therefore neither translated nor stored.

The column headed OBJECT CODE has the machine language translation of the corresponding program source statements. For instructions which are not translated, the OBJECT CODE column remains blank. When an error condition prevents the translation of an instruction, the printed object code will consist of all zeros and the line immediately beneath that which contains the instruction will have the note °°° ERROR °°° in the OBJECT CODE column (see, for example, statements 31, 41, 53, and 61 in figure 14.1, part 1). For DC instructions, the OBJECT CODE column will usually have the first eight bytes of the generated constant (to override this, we use the PRINT instruction; see chapter 2, section 2.4). For DS instructions, the OBJECT CODE column will be left blank, since those instructions do not cause constants to be stored.

The columns headed ADDR1 and ADDR2 contain the location counter values for the respective first and second operands of the corresponding instructions. Note that these location counter values are *not* expressions of addresses as displacements. Operand addresses are, however, expressed in base-displacement form by the OBJECT CODE. For cases in which either one or both of the operands do not exist or are register numbers, the appropriate ADDR1 and/or ADDR2 columns remain blank.

We now direct our attention to the cross-reference listing in figure 14.1, part 3. The leftmost cloumn, headed SYMBOL, lists all symbolic names referenced by the program, in alphabetical order. The LEN column gives the **LEN**gth associated with the corresponding symbol; lengths are expressed in bytes. Thus the symbol BEGIN has a length of 2, for it is the name of the BALR instruction which in machine language form occupies 2 bytes. Likewise, the symbol IEXT has a length of 3, for it is the name of a storage area defined as IEXT DS CL3, having Character Length 3. The VALUE column gives the location counter value associated with the symbol (the value of the location counter at the point of the program at which the symbol is defined). The DEFN column gives the number of the statement at which the symbol is defined. The REFERENCES column gives the statement numbers of all statements that reference the symbol; that is, all statements that use the symbol in their operand portions. Note in figure 14.1, part 3, that the symbol BLANKS is said to be °°°°UNDEFINED°°°° although it is "referenced" by the statements numbered 31 and 41. This is obviously a program error (all symbols referenced by program instruction(s) must be defined!) and will require correction.

Diagnostics are syntax errors which are discovered by the assembler (or by the appropriate compiler, for programs written in other languages). The word syntax refers to the sentence structure rules within a language, including the order of parts of instructions (name, operation code, operands), the order of operands, and the like. When syntax errors do not appear in the program, the diagnostic listing will not appear; instead the message NO STATEMENTS FLAGGED IN THIS ASSEMBLY will be printed following the cross-reference listing. For programs in which diagnostics do exist, a diagnostic listing is produced (see figure 14.1, part 4). On the diagnostic listing, each error is identified by the number of the statement in which it occurs (the STMT column). A message briefly explains the cause of the error from the assembler's point of view, and an ERROR CODE refers to an expanded explanation of the cause of the error as given in an IBM manual titled *IBM System/360 Operating System Error Messages and Codes,* Form GC28–6631 (for OS systems) or *DOS and TOS Assembler Language,* Form GC24–3414 (for DOS systems). In most cases, the message provided as part of the diagnostic listing is sufficient, and reference to the manual will not be necessary.

A word of caution is in order here. The error messages given will not necessarily give the cause of the error as seen by the programmer; they will give the cause of the error from the point of view of the *assembler program*. If the cause of the error is not immediately apparent to the programmer (very often it will be), the programmer will have to simulate the "thinking" of the assembler. He must determine what condition(s) would cause the assembler to consider that an error, of the type described in the message, actually occurred. We will now demonstrate how to approach the messages from this point of view by examining the diagnostic messages of figure 14.1, part 4, and using them to correct the syntax errors in our program.

The first diagnostic error listed for our program is at statement number 31. We are told that the error is NEAR OPERAND COLUMN 3 and that the error is that of an UNDEFINED SYMBOL. Looking in the program at statement 31, we note the "+" symbol immediately to the right of the statement number. This tells us that statement number 31 is part of the macro expansion of the macro which preceded it: statement 29. We may thus examine statement 31 near operand column 3 to determine the cause of the error, however any correction will be made with regard to statement 29, which is the instruction that the programmer wrote! Examining statement 31, we note that the only symbol in the operand portion is the symbol "BLANKS", which is, in fact, undefined, just as the message noted! Thus statement 29 turns out to be correct in itself, however it referenced an undefined symbol! The intent of the statement was to print a blank line, so that the remedy will be to add the constant definition BLANKS DC CL132 ´ ´ to the program and to leave statement 29 as is.

The second diagnostic error listed is at statement number 41. This error is also NEAR OPERAND COLUMN 3 — — UNDEFINED SYMBOL. Looking at statement 41 in the program, we see a situation identical to that of statement 31 above: the statement references the symbol "BLANKS" which is undefined. Thus adding the constant definition of BLANKS will serve to eliminate the cause of this diagnostic as well.

The next diagnostic error is listed at statement 45, as an UNDEFINED OPERATION CODE. Looking at the instruction, however, we see the operation code GET, which is perfectly valid! Here we have a prime example of how the error from the *assembler's* point of view may be very different from the error from the *programmer's* point of view! If you examine statement 45 carefully, you will probably notice the cause of the error without the aid of any message: the name of the instruction, REPEAT, was keypunched in column 2 of the card instead of column 1, as is proper. Now let us see how the assembler arrived at its printed message. The name portions of instructions must begin in column 1; therefore when the assembler found column 1 blank, it assumed that this instruction had no name (names, after all, are not required in assembly language instructions!). Assuming that there is no name, the next part of the instruction encountered must (from the assembler's point of view) be the operation code! Thus the assembler interpreted the symbol REPEAT to be the operation code. When viewed as such, we do indeed have an UNDEFINED OPERATION CODE, although from the programmer's point of view the error was in the keypunching of the name. We see, therefore, that the error messages cannot always be taken literally; one must often use a bit of ingenuity to decipher them.

The next diagnostic error listed is at statement 53: NEAR OPERAND COLUMN 12 — — INVALID DISPLACEMENT. For this statement, the error message does diagnose the problem properly from the programmer's point of view. The second operand of the MVC instruction has a length factor of 3 (this is the DISPLACEMENT referred to by the message). You may recall that the number of characters affected by the MVC instruction is determined by the *first* operand, so that a stated length in the second operand is interpreted to be invalid. The remedy, of course, is to simply remove the length factor, leaving the instruction to read MVC   OEXT,IEXT.

Statement 61 is the next to be noted on the diagnostic listing, with the message NEAR OPERAND COLUMN 1 — — UNDEFINED SYMBOL. Examining the statement in the program, B REPEAT, all seems to be in order! However recall that the symbol REPEAT, the name of the instruction to which statement 61 intends to branch, was not recognized by the assembler as a name (statement 45). When we correct the problem in statement 45, the diagnostic in statement 61 will be likewise corrected.

Our last diagnostic refers to statement 79: UNDEFINED OPERATION CODE. Do you recognize the difficulty with this statement? There is certainly nothing wrong with any operation code, for this statement was not intended to be an instruction at all. It was obviously intended to be a comment, but the asterisk in column 1 was omitted. The assembler, finding nothing in column 1, assumed that this statement was not a comment, therefore it must be an in- struction without a name portion. The first symbol encountered, the symbol FOR, would therefore (from the assembler's point of view) be an operation code and, as such, is invalid. The remedy, of course, is simply to keypunch the appropriate asterisk in column 1 of the card.

Before we leave the subject of diagnostics, let us take special note of several points:
- The diagnostic messages must not always be taken literally.
- The number of diagnostic messages does not necessarily reflect the num- ber of actual program errors. For example, an error in defining a symbol or neglecting to define a symbol will generate a message every time that symbol is referenced.
- The cross-reference listing may be of great aid in correcting diagnostics. For example, suppose that the program was not consistent in its spelling of a particular name: say both the terms INAREA and IAREA were used in the program to describe the input area. The remedy would be to define the area one way, say as INAREA, and then to assure that every reference to the area referred to INAREA. The cross-reference listing, under the REFERENCES column, will identify every program reference to both INAREA and to IAREA, making the appropriate changes both simpler to perform and more accurate.

Figure 14.2 shows our program and its cross-reference listing after correction of the errors described above. Note the absence of a diagnostic listing once the errors have been corrected. Instead we find the message NO STATEMENTS FLAGGED IN THIS ASSEMBLY.

14.4   TESTING THE PROGRAM

Suppose that all the diagnostic errors in a program have been eliminated. We still are not sure that the program will produce the desired output. The next phase in the debugging process is **testing** the program, first with sample data and then with real data, simulating every possible type of condition that the program may encounter. We then check the results of these **test runs** for ac- curacy. Only when such accuracy has been determined for every conceivable type of data condition which may arise, is the program finally considered to be debugged.

```
LOC     OBJECT CODE              ADDR1 ADDR2   STMT   SOURCE STATEMENT

                                               1    *
                                               2          PRINT NCGEN
                                               3          START
                                               4    *
CCCCCC  C5R0                     CC002          5    BEGIN   PALR  11,0
                                               6          USING *,11
CCCCC2                                          7    *
                                               8          CPEN  (INFILE,INPUT,OUTFILE,OUTPUT)
                                              16    *
CCCCC2                                         17  *FCR CCS,CPEN  INFILE,OUTFILE
                                              18    *
CCCC12  D213 B3E3 B17A  CO3E5 CO17C           19          PUT   OUTFILE,HEACER1
CCCC2C  D20F B3FB B18E  CC3FD CO190           24          PUT   OUTFILE,HEADER2
CCCC72  D201 B412 B19D  CO414 CO19F           79          PUT   OUTFILE,BLANKS
CCCC7E  D202 B419 B19F  CC41B CO1A1           34          PUT   OUTFILE,HEADER3
CCCC7E  D202 B423 B1A2  CC425 CO1A4           39          PUT   OUTFILE,BLANKS
CCCC4A  L706 B427 B1A5  CC429 CO1A7           44    *
CCCCEA  D2C2 B432 B1AC  CC434 CO1AE           45    REPEAT  GET   INFILE,INAREA
                                              50    *
CCCCEE  D213 B3E3 B17A  CO3E5 CO17C           51          MVC   CNAME,INAME
CCCCEC  D20E B3FB B18E  CC3FD CO190           52          MVC   CTITLE,ITITLE
CCCC72  B412 B19D B19D  CO414 CO19F           53          MVC   CCIV,IDIV
CCCC7E  D202 B419 B19F  CC41B CO1A1           54          MVC   CCEPT,IDEPT
CCCC7E  B423 B1A2       CC425 CO1A4           55          MVC   OAREA,IAREA
CCCC4  L706 B427 B1A5   CC429 CO1A7           56          MVC   CNUM,INUM
CCCCEA  D2C2 B432 B1AC  CC434 CO1AE           57          MVC   CEXT,IEXT
                                              58    *
CCCCSC                                        59          PUT   OUTFILE,OUTLINE
                                              64    *
CCCCSE  47FC BC56        CC05B                65          B     REPEAT
                                              66    *
CCCCA2                                        67    ECJ     CLOSE (INFILE)
CCCCAE                                        73          CLOSF (CUTFILE)
                                              79  *FCR CCS,CLOSING PROGRAM FILES IS DONE BY
                                              80    *    CLOSF INFILE,OUTFILE
CCCCRA  CA03                                  81    *
                                              82          SVC   3
                                              83  *FCR CCS,THE SVC 3 IS REPLACED BY
                                              84    *    ECJ
                                              85    *
                                              86    *  FILE DEFINITICNS
                                              87    *
CCCCHC                                        98  INFILE   DCB   DSORG=PS,MACRF=GM,CDNAME=SYSIPT,      C
                                             197  *FCR CCS, THE DCB'S ARE REPLACED BY
                                             198  *INFILE  CTFCD  DEVADDR=SYSRDR,IOAREA1=IN,BLKSIZE=80,
                                             199          RECFORM=FIXUNB,WORKA=YES,EOFADDR=EOJ
CCC11C                                       142  CUTFILE  CCB   DSCRG=PS,MACRF=PM,CDNAME=SYSLST,      C
                                             200  *CUTFILE CTFPR  DEVADDR=SYSLST,IOAREA1=OUT,BLKSIZE=132,
                                             201          RECFORM=FIXUNB,WORKA=YES
CCC132                                                   BLKSIZE=132,LRECL=132
                                             202  *IN      DS    CL80    IN IS NAME OF INPUT BUFFER AREA FOR DOS
                                             203  *OUT     DS    CL132   OUT IS NAME OF OUTPUT BUFFER AREA FOR DOS
                                             204    *
```

Figure 14.2 (Part 1)
An Assembly Listing Without Diagnostics

```
LOC      OBJECT CODE          ADDR1  ADDR2    STMT  SOURCE STATEMENT

                                             205  * AREA DEFINITIONS
                                             206  *
                                             207  * INPUT AREA
CCC17C                                       208  INAREA   DS    0CL80
CCC17C                                       209  INAME    DS    CL70
CCC1CC                                       210  ITITLE   DS    CL15
CCC1DF                                       211  IDIV     DS    CL2
CCC1A1                                       212  IDEPT    DS    CL3
CCC1A4                                       213  IPHONE   DS    0CL13
CCC1A4                                       214  IAREA    DS    CL3
CCC1A7                                       215  INUM     DS    CL3
CCC1AD                                       216  IEXT     DS    CL3
CCC1D1                                       217  IEXT     DS    CL27
                                             218  *
                                             219  * HEADER LINES
                                             220  *
CCC1CC   4C4C4C404C4C4C4040                  221  HEADER1  DC    CL132'        MICKEY MOUSE
                                                                             ETRAP INC.'
CCC25C   4C4C4C4C4C4C4C4C4C                  222  HEADER2  DC    CL132'        TELEPHONE C
                                                                             DIRECTORY'
CCC2C4   4C4C4C4040404C4C4C                  273  HFADER3  DC    CL132'        TITLE     C
CCC358   4C4C40404040404040                                                    DIVISION
                                             724  BLANKS   DC    CL132'   NAME                DEPT          EXT'
                                                                                   TELEPHONE NO.
                                             725  *
                                             726  * OUTPUT LINE
                                             727  *
CCC3EC                                       728  OUTLINE  DS    0CL132
CCC3EC   4C4C40404C4C4C4C4C                  229  ONAME    DS    CL9*
CCC3F9   404040404C                          230  ONAME    DS    CL20
CCC3FL                                       231  CTITLE   DS    CL4*
CCC4CC   4C4C40404040404C4C                  232  CTITLE   DS    CL15
CCC414                                       233  ODIV     DS    CL8*
CCC416   404C404C4C                          234  ODIV     DS    CL2
CCC41B                                       235  CDEPT    DS    CL5*
CCC41E   4C4C40404040404C4C                  236  CDEPT    DS    CL3
CCC425                                       237  OAREA    DS    CL7*
CCC428   40                                  238  OAREA    DS    CL3
CCC429                                       239  CNUM     DS    CL1*
CCC43C   4C4C4C4C                            240  CNUM     DS    CL7
CCC434                                       241  CEXT     DS    CL4*
CCC437   404040404C4C4C4C4040                242  CEXT     DS    CL3
CCCCCC                                       243           DC    CL41' '
                                             244           END   BEGIN
```

Figure 14.2 (Part 2)
An Assembly Listing Without Diagnostics

CROSS-REFERENCE

SYMBOL	LEN	VALUE	DEFN	REFERENCES		
BEGIN	2	000000	5	244	41	
BLANKS	132	000358	274	31		
CCJ	4	0000C4	69	110		
HEADER1	132	0001CC	221	21		
HEADER2	132	000250	222	26		
HEADER3	132	0002D0	223	36		
IAREA	3	0001A4	214	55		
ICFPT	3	0001A1	212	54		
IDIV	2	00019F	211	53		
IEXT	3	0001AE	216	57		
INAME	2C	0001AE	209	51		
INAREA	8C	00017C	208	47		
INFILE	4	0000CC	92	12	46	71
INLM	7	0001A7	215	56		
IPHONE	13	0001A4	213			
TITLE	15	000190	21C	52		
OAREA	3	000425	238	55		
OCFPT	2	000414	234	53		
OEXT	3	000434	242	57		
ONAME	2C	0003F5	230	56		
ONLM	7	000429	24C	52		
OTITLE	15	0003FD	232	14	20	25
OUTFILE	4	00C11C	146	35	40	60	30 77
CLTLINE	132	0003DC	228	61		
REPEAT	4	0CCC58	46	65		

Figure 14.2 (Part 3)
Cross Reference Listing for
Assembly Language Program Without Diagnostics

PAGE   6

17 NOV 78

RELOCATION DICTIONARY

POS.ID	REL.ID	FLAGS	ADDRESS	POS.ID	REL.ID	FLAGS	ADDRESS	POS.ID	REL.ID	FLAGS	ADDRESS
01	01	08	C00009	01	01	08	C0000C	01	01	08	C000A9
01	01	08	C000B5	01	01	08	C000DD				

NO STATEMENTS FLAGGED IN THIS ASSEMBLY

2869 SYSLIB SOURCE RECORDS,   98 SYSIN SOURCE RECORDS
27 SYSLIN OUTPUT RECORDS,   157 SYSPRINT OUTPUT RECORDS

Figure 14.2 (Part 4)
Relocation Dictionary for
Assembly Language Program Without Diagnostics

14.4.1   Test Data

Test data must usually be prepared, at least to some extent, by the programmer. The first step in the procedure would be to list every condition which must be tested by the program. For example, in a payroll program which computes employees' salaries and deducts both payroll tax and social security tax, the test data should include:

- An employee who did not work overtime, one who did work overtime, one who did not work at all. (We do not want a check made out for $0.00! On the other hand, perhaps the employee has "sick days" accumulated and should be paid anyway!)
- An employee with 0 dependents, with 4 dependents (an average case), with 12 dependents (an unusual case).
- An employee whose cumulative earnings so far have not passed the social security tax base, one whose cumulative earnings have just reached the social security tax base, one whose cumulative earnings have passed the social security tax base.

Other conditions may also affect the payroll computation. Should deductions be made for union dues? for pension contributions? towards extra medical benefits? The test data should take each condition, and, in fact, each combination of conditions into account.

Once each possible program condition has been listed and test data has been designed to fit each possibility, the program should be tested in stages, using the following general guidelines:

- Test for more general program conditions first (involving the main logic of the program) and then proceed to the more minor conditions and unusual cases.
- Graduate the testing very slowly, adding only a few new conditions for each test run. This way when an error does occur, you will have limited its possible causes.
- Be sure to test minimum and maximum as well as intermediate data values.
- It is a good idea to introduce some deliberately erroneous data to be sure that the program handles it appropriately. (If the data says that an individual worked an impossible number of hours this week, say 200 hours, will the program produce a check based on that amount? Will the program terminate? Will the program produce an "error" message of its own stating that it received erroneous data? The latter procedure is the most preferred of the three. It is not a good idea to have the program terminate, for one error of this type would not be reason enough to cancel the entire program. Processing should continue, and the cause of the error can be looked into later.)

After the program has been tested using test data, it should be run using "real" data. For example, input data will be used containing information describing actual employee salaries and options, using a relatively large volume of data.

The last stage in the testing of the program would involve what is called a **system run** or **system test.** This means that we test the workings of the program in conjunction with other systems programs with which it may have some interconnection. For example, the output of some other program may be the input to our program, or our program's output may constitute the input to yet another program. The programs should be tested to see that they work smoothly *together* and without error, before they are first attempted in a real-life situation (such as the production of actual payroll checks, or the ordering of actual inventory products), in which an error could have very unpleasant, if not serious, consequences.

Before leaving our discussion of test data, we should like to relay a very relevant incident which the authors know to have actually occurred not long ago. An individual incurred a bill from a certain manufacturing firm, which was paid in full not long after it was received. However, shortly after the bill was paid, another bill was received in the mail for $0.00! Endless telephone calls and conversations with the people at the manufacturing concern did not stop the barrage of mail that followed, threatening fines, penalties, and court action if the amount owed were not paid. The matter was finally resolved when the beleaguered individual hit upon an idea: a check for zero dollars and zero cents was written and sent in as "payment". The barrage of threatening mail was halted, and the matter stood resolved. The cause of the above mishap is really rather obvious. The program which handled incoming payments was not properly tested to deal with conditions in which the bill was paid in full with no further credit extended to the buyer. Had such testing been properly done, much aggravation (and, we would venture to guess, loss of customers!) would have been avoided. It is certainly not farfetched to assume that this incident was repeated a number of times for different customers, and must eventually have been resolved by proper adjustment of the culprit program.

14.4.2   Program Interruptions: The Program-Check Message

When a computer program violates one of the rules of the system under which it is running, we say that an **exception** occurs. An exception causes what is known as a **program interrupt**: program execution is halted, and control of the computer is transferred to the supervisor program. The cause of the interrupt will be printed in a message to the programmer called a **program-check message**, and very often a **dump** will be produced. That is, the contents of certain parts of storage and of registers, as well as other relevant information, will be printed.

The interrupt procedure has been described in chapter 13, section 13.3.3, along with a discussion of the various classes of interrupts and their respective causes. In this chapter we will be concerned with only one interrupt class: the **program interrupt**, or **program-check interrupt**.

When a program interrupt occurs, the interruption code field of the PSW (the PSW is a special doubleword containing key information regarding the status of the system; see chapter 13, sections 13.3.1 and 13.3.2) contains a special code which identifies the cause of the error. There are fifteen types of program exceptions which may be so identified.

Interruption Code 001 (decimal 1): Operation Exception
The operation code of the instruction to be executed is illegal. That is, it is not recognized by the system as a valid operation code. In such a case, instruction execution is suppressed (execution will not be attempted).

Interruption Code 002 (decimal 2): Privileged Operation Exception
The operation code of the instruction to be executed is that of a privileged instruction, that is, of an instruction which may be executed only when the computer is in supervisor state. If the computer is in problem state when such an instruction is encountered, the operation is suppressed.

Interruption Code 003 (decimal 3): Execute Exception
Illegal use of the EX (**EX**ecute) instruction causes this type of interrupt. (We have not studied the EX instruction.)

Interruption Code 004 (decimal 4): Protection Exception
Every block of a user program in main storage is protected by a 4-bit storage key which is matched with the protection key of the PSW (bits 8–11 of the PSW at the time the program block is executing). The storage keys are assigned by the operating system. The supervisor itself has a protection key of 0000_2. When the storage key of the area being accessed does not match the protection key, a protection exception occurs (see chapter 13, section 13.3.1 for further discussion of the protection key). For virtual storage systems, protection exceptions will result only for attempts to improperly access real (not virtual) addresses.

Interruption Code 005 (decimal 5): Addressing Exception
An addressing exception occurs when the effective address of an instruction operand (an instruction address or a data address) is outside the limits of avail-

able computer storage. (For example, there may be 64K available, and an instruction tries to access location number 70,000.) For virtual storage systems, addressing exceptions will occur only when an attempt is made to access locations outside the limits of available real storage (not of virtual storage).

Interruption Code 006 (decimal 6): Specification Exception

A specification exception occurs when an instruction operand designates an improper main storage address or register number. For example, register operands of certain instructions are required to be even-numbered (we have seen this requirement for the first operands of the MR, M, DR, and D instructions). Instructions in RX or RS format require that certain operands be aligned on halfword, fullword, or doubleword integral boundaries (this does not apply when the byte oriented operand feature is installed). Branch instructions must specify a branch to an even-numbered address; an attempt to branch to an odd-numbered address will result in a specification exception.

Interruption Code 007 (decimal 7): Data Exception

If the operand codes of instructions are not as required by the instruction, a data exception occurs. For example, the decimal arithmetic instructions AP, SP, MP, and DP require that both operands contain valid packed numbers, with valid digit codes and sign codes. Many other assembly language instructions have similar requirements.

Interruption Code 008 (decimal 8): Fixed-Point Overflow Exception

A fixed-point overflow exception occurs when the results of certain binary integer add, subtract, or load instructions (the instructions AR, A, AH, SR, S, SH, LCR, LPR; we have not studied the LCR and LPR instructions) are too large to fit into 32 bits. In addition, fixed-point overflow resulting from any of these instructions will cause the condition code to be set to 3.

A fixed-point overflow exception may or may not cause a program interrupt, depending upon the setting of the fixed-point overflow mask bit of the PSW (bit 36 of the PSW in BC mode, or bit 20 of the PSW in EC mode). If the fixed-point overflow mask bit is set to 1, a fixed-point overflow exception will cause an interrupt; if the mask bit is set to 0, a fixed-point overflow exception will not cause an interrupt. The user program itself may set the program mask bit on and off by use of the SPM (**S**et **P**rogram **M**ask) instruction, one of the few non-privileged instructions which alter the PSW itself.

Interruption Code 009 (decimal 9): Fixed-Point Divide Exception

A fixed-point divide exception may occur as a result of two possible conditions. The quotient resulting from a binary division (DR or D instruction) may be too large to be expressed in 32 bits and will therefore not fit into the even-numbered register of the first operand (this condition will also occur if an attempt is made to divide by zero). The second possible cause of a fixed-point divide exception is an attempt to convert a number into binary form via the CVB instruction, and the binary number is too large to fit into the first operand register.

If a fixed-point divide exception occurs as a result of a DR or D instruction, division will be suppressed (will not occur); however, if the cause of the exception is a CVB instruction, the instruction is executed, and the high-order portion of the result which does not fit into the register is ignored. Program interruption will always occur.

Interruption Code 00A (decimal 10): Decimal Overflow Exception

A decimal overflow exception occurs when the result of a decimal addition or subtraction (the AP, SP, and ZAP instructions) is too large to fit into the first operand location. In addition, decimal overflow by any of these instructions will cause the condition code to be set to 3.

A decimal overflow exception may or may not cause a program interrupt, depending upon the setting of the decimal overflow mask bit of the PSW (bit 37 of the PSW in BC mode, or bit 21 of the PSW in EC mode). If the decimal overflow mask bit is set to 1, a decimal overflow exception will cause an interrupt; if the mask bit is set to 0, a decimal overflow exception will not cause an interrupt. The user may set the program mask bit on and off by use of the SPM instruction.

Interruption Code 00B (decimal 11): Decimal Divide Exception

A decimal divide exception occurs when the quotient resulting from the execution of a decimal divide (DP) instruction is too large to fit into the first operand. Overflow cannot occur. When a decimal divide exception is recognized, the operation is suppressed.

Interruption codes 00C through 00F (decimal 12 through 15) describe program exceptions which occur as a result of attempts to improperly use floating-point instructions. The floating-point instructions are not discussed in this text; however, for the sake of completeness, we list the causes of the four floating-point program exceptions below.

Interruption Code 00C (decimal 12): Exponent Overflow Exception

The result of a floating-point operation is greater than or equal to 16^{64}.

Interruption Code 00D (decimal 13): Exponent Underflow Exception

The result of a floating-point operation is less than 16^{-64}.

Interruption Code 00E (decimal 14): Significance Exception

When the fraction resulting from a floating-point operation is zero, and the significance mask bit of the PSW is one, a significance exception occurs and a program interruption takes place.

Interruption Code 00F (decimal 15): Floating-Point Divide Exception

This occurs when a floating-point division by zero is attempted.

The fifteen interruption codes listed and described above serve to identify the *causes* of errors occurring during program execution. They do not, however, identify which program instruction is causing the problem. For this, we must direct our attention to the total output produced when an interrupt occurs, including the program dump.

14.4.3   Program Dumps

A **dump** is the reproduced contents of certain parts of main storage and of registers, possibly including certain other information which may serve to help the programmer identify the cause(s) of program errors.

There are three basic categories of dumps produced by the operating system:

- **Dynamic** dumps, requested by the programmer through use of the SNAP macro instruction (for OS systems) or the PDUMP macro instruction (for DOS systems).
- **Abend** dumps, obtained through use of the DUMP operand in the OS macro ABEND.
- **Core-image** dumps, supplied automatically by the system, should a *system* routine fail.

We shall briefly consider each of these categories of dumps in turn. However for a complete discussion as well as illustrations of various dump formats and guidance in using the dumps, refer to the IBM manual, *Programmer's Guide to Debugging* (Form GC28-6670).

Dynamic Dumps

Dynamic dumps are produced at the point of program execution at which they are requested, regardless of whether or not an error occurred at that point in the program. After the dump is produced, program execution continues with the next sequential program instruction. Therefore dynamic dumps can be used many times throughout the course of program execution to trace changes in register and main storage contents. After the program has been debugged and is working properly, the PDUMP or SNAP instructions will no longer be needed, and may then be removed.

The PDUMP macro instruction (for DOS systems only) is of the form

name	operation	operands
[symbolic name]	PDUMP	name1,name2
or [symbolic name]	PDUMP	(R1),(R2)

In the first form of the instruction, the operands are the beginning and ending addresses of the storage area to be dumped by the instruction. The contents of main storage will be printed up until, but not including, the contents of the second operand area.

In the second form of the instruction, the operands are register numbers enclosed within parentheses. The parentheses may be interpreted to mean "the contents of", so that the contents of the registers noted within parentheses are, in fact, the beginning and ending addresses of those storage areas which are to be dumped.

For example, given AREA1 and AREA2 defined as follows:

```
AREA 1      DS      CL50
AREA 2      DS      CL20
```

we may write

```
PDUMP    AREA1,AREA2
```

to dump the contents of AREA1 only. (The instruction requests a dump *up until, but not including* the contents of AREA2.)

The same dump may be indirectly specified as follows:

```
LA      2,AREA1
LA      4,AREA2
PDUMP   (2),(4)
```

If we wish to display the contents of *both* AREA1 and AREA2, we may write

```
PDUMP    AREA1,AREA2+20
```

```
or   LA      2,AREA1
     LA      4,AREA2+20
     PDUMP   (2),(4)
```

The choice of registers in the above examples is, of course, arbitrary.

The SNAP macro instruction (for OS systems only) is of the form

name	**operation**	**operands**
[symbolic name]	SNAP	ID=decimal number,
		STORAGE=(beginning location,
		ending location),PDATA=(REGS),
		DCB=dcbname

The ID operand is a decimal number used to identify the dump, for if SNAP macros are issued at several points within the program, it might otherwise be difficult to identify the point during program execution at which the dump was issued.

The STORAGE operand indicates the beginning and ending addresses of those storage areas which are to be dumped. The contents of main storage up until, but not including, the second operand location will be dumped.

The PDATA operand is used to specify information to be displayed by the macro in addition to the main storage areas specified. PDATA=(REGS) means that we want to have the contents of the registers displayed.

The DCB operand indicates the name of a special data control block, which describes a special data set. The data control block must be defined as follows:

dcbname	DCB	DSORG=PS,RECFM=VBA,
		MACRF=(W),BLKSIZE=nnn,
		LRECL=125,DDNAME=ddname

where nnn is 882 (for MFT systems) or either 882 or 1632 (for MVT systems). The ddname must be specified on a DD job control language statement, and must be some name other than SYSABEND or SYSUDUMP. This data control block is discussed in greater detail in the IBM manual *Data Management Services* (Form GC26–3746).

Figure 14.3, part 1, shows the corrected version of the program shown in figures 14.1 and 14.2 above, with the SNAP macro included (statement 60). Note the SNAP operand DCB=DCBAD, and the definition of the data control block named DCBAD in statement 213. Notice too that the data set was OPENed by statement 8 (if the program is to be processed by the loader, a CLOSE macro should also be issued for the SNAP data control block). The DDNAME chosen was SOKDUMP, an arbitrary choice.

Notice, on the program listing, that the SNAP macro was placed before the

PUT instruction (statement 76) within the program loop. This means that a dump will be produced each time the loop is executed, that is, once for each data card read. Had the SNAP been placed after the branch instruction, it would have been outside the program loop and executed only once during the entire program execution.

Figure 14.3 parts 2–8 shows the results of the SNAP macro for the seven times that it was executed by our program. Let us examine this output and learn how it is to be interpreted. Our discussion will refer to circled letters hand-drawn on the output to identify the various parts of the SNAP output.

We first notice that the dump includes: (A), the name of the job taken from the job card; (B), the name of the job step during which the dump was produced; (C), the time of day at which the dump was produced (the time is given in hours, minutes, and seconds, based upon a 24-hour clock); (D), the date that the dump was produced (78321 means the **321**st day of **1978** starting from 1/1/78). The dump also provides, in (E), the **ID**entification number as determined by the SNAP macro itself. Note in statement 60 that our instruction used the operand ID=1. Had the operand used been ID=10, (E) would have appeared as ID = 010.

Our SNAP macro included the operand PDATA=(REGS). This means that we wish the contents of registers displayed as they appear when the SNAP is being executed. We see those contents displayed under the printed note REGS AT ENTRY TO SNAP. Part (F) gives the contents of the **FL**oa**T**ing point **R**egisters numbered 0, 2, 4, and 6, hence the note FLTR 0–6. The floating-point registers are each a doubleword long, and are displayed in hexadecimal notation (16 hexadecimal characters are used to represent a doubleword, for each hexadecimal character represents 4 bits). Actually, the floating point registers are not used by this particular program and their contents therefore do not interest us here.

The contents of the 16 general registers are displayed on the next two printed lines (part (G)) with registers 0 through 7 (REGS 0–7) on the first line and registers 8 through 15 (REGS 8–15) on the second. These register contents are also displayed using hexadecimal notation. The register contents are displayed in order, proceeding from left to right. Thus general register 0 contains 00045FF8, general register 1 contains A0206898, . . . , general register 4 contains 002048C4, and so on. Our program instructions do not use the general registers, with the exception of register 11, the base register, which is loaded by statement 5: the instruction BALR 11,0. Actually, the BALR instruction places the contents of the instruction length code (2 bits), condition code (2 bits), and program mask (4 bits) fields of the PSW into bits 0–7 of the first operand register (register 11). The address of the next instruction to be executed is placed into bits 8–31 of the first operand register. Our program was loaded into memory beginning at location 206800; the first executable instruction was the BALR, which occupies 2 bytes (bytes 206800 and 206801), the next executable instruction is at 206802, which we see on the dump in bit positions 8–31 of register 11 (underlined on figure 14.3, part 2).

Part (H) on our program dump lists main storage addresses at intervals of 8 fullwords. Part (I) shows the contents of main storage requested to be displayed by the SNAP macro, beginning with INAREA and continuing up until, but not including, HEADER3 (STORAGE=INAREA,HEADER3). The contents of main storage are displayed using hexadecimal notation (2 hexadecimal digits per byte), beginning with the byte whose number is listed under the heading STORAGE (part (H)), and continuing for 8 fullwords, across the line. The first line is an exception, for the contents of storage were requested beginning only at INAREA, which begins at location 2069F8 (see the value 1F8 at the definition of INAREA, statement 276, under the LOC column). Likewise, the last byte displayed is the byte immediately preceding HEADER3.

Part (J) shows the EBCDIC characters corresponding to the hexadecimal notation of part (I), where such correspondence exists. Where no such correspondence exists, we would see series of periods in part (J). Notice that beginning with location 2069F8, the hexadecimal notation C3C1D4D7 represents the EBCDIC characters C,A,M, and P, and beginning with location 2069FC, hexadecimal C2C5D3D3 represents the respective EBCDIC characters B, E, L, and L. The line which describes eight fullword locations beginning at 206AA0 contains a string of the hexadecimal character 40; this is translated in part (J) as a line of "blanks".

Considering the overall picture of the contents of main storage from part (J), we notice in figure 14.3 part 2, that the input data includes the name CAMPBELL ANNE, title ASST MANAGER, division and department numbers 01 and 001 respectively, telephone number 214 244 5324, extension 444. Figure 14.3 part 3 shows the dump which results from the *second* execution of the SNAP macro. That dump occurred after a second data card was read into main storage, destroying the data read in from the first card! Here we see the input data in storage as including the name FARR HAROLD, title MANAGER, division and department numbers 12 and 345 respectively, telephone number 670 234 5557, extension 772. The contents of the floating point and general registers, as well as the contents of other parts of memory which were displayed, remain identical to those of figure 14.3 part 2, since the program execution occurring between the printing of each of these dumps did not affect those areas.

LCC	OBJECT CODE	ADDR1	ADDR2	STMT	SOURCE STATEMENT
				1 *	PRINT NCGEN
				2	START
				3	
				4 *	
CCCCCC	O5BO			5 BEGIN	BALR 11,0
CCCCCC			CCOO2	6	USING *,11
				7 *	
CCCCC2				8	CPEN (INFILE,INPUT,OUTFILE,OUTPLT,DCBAD,OUTPUT)
				18 *	
				19 **	
				20 **	
CCCC16				21	PUT OUTFILE,HEACER1
CCCC24				26	PUT OUTFILE,HEADER2
CCCC32				31	PUT CUTFILE,BLANKS
CCCC4C				36	PUT CUTFILE,HEADER3
CCCC4E				41	PUT CUTFILE,BLANKS
				46 *	
CCCC5C				47 REPEAT	GET INFILE,INAREA
				52 *	
CCCC6A	D213 B45F B1F6	CC461	CO1F8	53	MVC CNAME,INAME
CCCC7C	D20E B477 B20A	CC479	C020C	54	MVC CTITLE,ITITLF
CCCC76	D201 B48E B219	CC490	C021B	55	MVC OCIV,ICIV
CCCC7C	C202 B495 B21B	CC497	C021D	56	MVC CCEPT,IDEPT
CCCCE2	C202 B49F B21E	CC4A1	C0220	57	MVC CAREA,IAREA
CCCCE8	C206 B4A3 B221	CC4A5	C0223	58	MVC CNUP,INUM
CCCC54	C202 B4AE B228	CC4AC	C022A	59	MVC CEXT,TEXT
				60	SNAP ECP=DCBAD,IC=1,STORAGE=(INAREA,HEADER3),PDATA=(IREGS)
				75 *	
CCCCP6				76	PUT CUTFILE,OUTLINE
				81 *	
CCCCC4	47F0 BC5A		CC05C	82	B REPEAT
				83 *	
CCCCC8				84 ECJ	CLCSE (INFILE)
CCCCD2				90	CLOSE (CUTFILE)
				96 **	
				97 **	
				98 *	
CCCCCE	CA03			99	SVC 3
				100 **	
				101 **	
				102 *	FILE CEFINITICNS
				103 **	
				104 *	
CCCCEC				105 INFILE	CCB CSCRG=PS,MACRF=GM,DDNAME=SYSIPT, C
					BLKSIZE=80,LRECL=80,EODAD=EOJ
CCC14C				159 OUTFILE	CCB CSORG=PS,MACRF=M,DDNAME=SYSLST, C
					BLKSIZE=132,LRECL=132
CCC1AC				213 DCBAD	CCB CSORG=PS,RECFM=VBA,MACRF=(W),BLKSIZE=1632,LRECL=125, C
					CDNAME=SOKDUMP
				264 *	
				265 *	
				266 *	
				267 *	
				268 *	
				269 *	

Figure 14.3 (Part 1a)

A Program Using the Snap Macro

```
LOC     OBJECT CODE       ADDR1 ADDR2   STMT   SOURCE STATEMENT

                                        270    *
                                        271    *
                                        272    *
                                        273    *      AREA DEFINITIONS
                                        274    *
                                        275    *      INPUT AREA
CCC1F8                                  276    INAREA   DS   0CL80
CCC1F8                                  277    INAME    DS   CL20
CCC3CC                                  278    ITITLE   DS   CL15
CCC21B                                  279    IDIV     DS   CL2
CCC21D                                  280    IDEPT    DS   CL3
CCC22C                                  281    IPHONE   DS   0CL13
CCC22C                                  282    IAREA    DS   CL3
CCC223                                  283    INUM     DS   CL7
CCC22A                                  284    IEXT     DS   CL3
CCC22D                                  285             DS   CL27
                                        286    *
                                        287    *      HEADER LINES
                                        288    *
CCC248  404040404C404C404C4C            289    HEADER1  DC   CL132'                MICKEY MOUSE'
CCC2CC  4C4C40404C404C4C4C40            290    HEADER2  DC   CL132'ETRAP INC.'
CCC35C  404040404C4C404C4C4C            291    HEADER3  DC   CL132'DIRECTORY'
CCC3E4  404040404C4C404C4C4C                           NAME        DIVISION  DEPT   TELEPHONE NO.      EXT'
                                                                                                  TELEPHONE C
                                                                                   TITLE        C
                                        292    BLANKS   DC   CL132' '
                                        293    *
                                        294    *      OUTPUT LINE
                                        295    *
CCC458                                  296    OUTLINE  DS   0CL132
CCC458  404040404C404C4C4C40            297             DS   CL9'  '
CCC461  40404040                        298    ONAME    DS   CL20
CCC475                                  299             DS   CL4'  '
CCC479  4C4C4C4C4C4C4C4C40              300    OTITLE   DS   CL15
CCC48C                                  301             DS   CL8'  '
CCC452  4C4040404C                      302    CDIV     DS   CL2
CCC457                                  303             DS   CL5'  '
CCC49A  4C4C4C4C4C4C4C40                304    ODEPT    DS   CL3
CCC4A1  4C                              305             DS   CL7'  '
CCC4A4  4C                              306    CAREA    DS   CL3
CCC4A5  40404040                        307             DS   CL1'  '
CCC4AC                                  308    ONUM     DS   CL7
CCC4BC                                  309             DS   CL4'  '
CCC4E3  404040404C4C404C4C4C            310    OEXT     DS   CL3
CCCCCC                                  311             DC   CL41' '
                                        312             END  BEGIN
```

Figure 14.3 (Part 1b)
A Program Using the Snap Macro

```
Ⓐ JOB RYTHREE1    Ⓑ STEP ASM      Ⓒ TIME 104748   Ⓓ DATE 78321   Ⓔ ID = CC1                                    PAGE 0001

REGS AT ENTRY TO SNAP
Ⓕ FLTR 0-6    01C0045800083C001   010001400030008            00046AF00CFFC000   0000000000000C000
Ⓖ REGS 0-7    CC045FF8   A0206898   00203900   00206800        02048C4   CCC01388   CC1FD884   00204921
  REGS 8-15   802C3D9A   CC1FF15C   00206800   60206802        00206CCC   02046F0    4020686A   C00086C8

STORAGE
Ⓗ
206FEC                                                          C3C1D4D7 C2C5D3D3   *........8...8....CAMPBELL*
2C6ACC   40C1D5D5 C5404040 4C404040 C1E2E2E3   40404CF0 F1FCF0F1   * ANNE     ASST MANAGER   01001*
206A20   F2F1F4F2 F4F4F5F3 F2F40404 40404040   40404040 40404040   *21424532444*
2C6A4C   4C4C4C40 40404040 4C404040 40404040   C9C3D2C5 E4E2C5E3   *
2C6A6C   40404040 40404040 40404040 40404040   E840D4D6 D9C1D740   *MICKEY MOUSETRAP*
206A8C   C9D5C34B 40404040 40404040 40404040   4C404040 4C404040   *INC.*
206AAO   40404040 40404040 4C404040 40404040   4C404040 4C404040   *

LINE 206ACO SAME AS ABCVE
206AEC   40404040 4C404040 40404040 40404040   E3C5D3C5 D7C8D6D5 C540C4C9   *RECTORY      TELEPHONE DI*
2C6BCC   D9C5C3E3 D6D9E840 4C404040 4C404040   40404040 40404040 4C404C40   *
206B20   40404040 40404040 40404040 40404040                              *
206B40   40404040 40404040 40404040

ENC OF DUMP
```

location 2069F8, the beginning of INAREA

location 2069FC

location 206B53 the byte preceding HEADER.3

Ⓘ   Ⓙ

Figure 14.3 (Part 2)
Results of the Snap Macro

```
JOB RYTHREE1         STEP ASM             TIME 104748   DATE 78321    ID = CC1                         PAGE 0C01

REGS AT ENTRY TO SNAP

     FLTR 0-6      01CCC458CC83C001       0100014000030008             00046AF00CFFC000        00C0C000000CC000

     REGS 0-7      00045FF8   A0206898    00203900   00206800          002048C4   CCCC1388    C01FD884   00204921
     REGS 8-15     8C2C3D9A   CC1FF15C    C0206800   60206802          00206CCC   C02046F0    4020686A   C00086C8

STORAGE

2C69EC                                                                     C6C1D9D9 40C8C1D9   *............8...8...'....FARR HAR*
2C6ACC    D6D3C440 4C404040 40404040 D4C1D5C1    C7C5D94C 40404040 4C4C40F1 F2F3F4F5   *OLD          MANAGER          12345*
206A2C    F6F7F0F2 F3F4F5F5 F5F7F7F7 F2404040    40404040 40404040 40404040 4C404C40   *6702345557772                     *
206A4C    40404040 40404C40 40404040 40404040    40404040 404C4040 40404040 40404C40   *                                  *
2C6A6C    4C40404C 4C40404C 40404040 404040D4    C9C3D2C5 E840C4D6 E4E2C5E3 D9C1D740   *                  MICKEY MOUSETRAP *
206A8C    C9D5C34B 4C404040 40404040 40404040    40404040 404C4040 4C4C4040 4C4C4040   *INC.                              *
206AA0    40404040 40404040 4C404040 40404040    40404040 40404040 40404040 40404040   *                                  *
      LINE 206AC0 SAME AS ABCVE
206AE0    40404040 40404040 4C404040 40404040    40404040 E3C5C3C5 C7C8D6D5 C540C4C9   *                      TELEPHONE DI*
2C6BCC    D9C5C3E3 D6D9E840 40404040 40404040    40404040 40404040 40404040 40404C40   *RECTORY                           *
206B2C    40404040 40404040 4C404040 40404040    40404040 4040404C 40404040 40404040   *                                  *
206B40    40404040 404C4040 4C404040 40404040    40404040                              *                                  *

ENC OF DUMP
```

Figure 14.3 (Part 3)
Results of the Snap Macro

```
JOB RYTHREE1          STEP ASM          TIME 104748   DATE 78321    ID = CC1                                          PAGE 0001

REGS AT ENTRY TO SNAP

   FLTR 0-6     010CC04580083C001   010001400030008                   CC04AFCCFFCCC0      000C0000000C0000

   REGS 0-7     CC045FF8  AC2C6A98  C1E2E2E3   C9D5D5C9  C1C7C509   00C203900  00206800   002048C4  CCC01388   001FD884   CC204921
   REGS 8-15    802C3D9A  001FF15C            8Q2C3D9A  00206800   6D206802              00206CDC  002046F0   4020686A   CC0086C8

STORAGE

2C69EC                                                        CTC5D6D9 C7C540E6    *..........8...8........GEORGE W*
20 6ACC   C9D5D5C9 C5404040 4C404040 C1E2E2E3   40C4C1D5 C1C7C5D9 40404040 4C4C4C4C  *INNIE      ASST MANAGER  02100*
2C6A2C   F4F5F6F7 F8F9FCF1 F2F3FCF2 F1404040   40404040 40404040 4C4C4040 4C404040  *456789012 3221                *
2C6A4C   40404040 40404040 40404040 40404004   40404040 40404040 40404040 40404040  *                              *
2C6A6C   4C4C4C4C 4C4C4C4C 4C4C4C4C 4C404040   C9C3D7C5 E840C4D6 E4E2C5E3 D9C1D740  *INC.            MICKEY MOUSETRAP*
2C6A8C   C9D5C34B 4C4C4C4C 4C404040 40404040   40404040 40404040 40404040 40404040  *INC.                          *
2C6AAC   40404040 SAME AS ABCVE

2C6AEC   40404040 40404040 4C404040 40404040   40404040 E3C5D3C5 C7C8D6D5 C540C4C9  *            TELEPHONE DI*
2C6BCC   09C5C3E3 D6D9E840 4C4C4C4C 40404040   40404040 4C404040 4C404040 4C404040  *RECTORY                       *
2C6B2C   4C4C4C4C 4C4C4C4C 4C4C4040 40404040   40404040 40404040 40404040 40404040  *                              *
2C6B4C   40404040 4C404040 4C404040 40404040   40404040

ENC CF DUMP
```

Figure 14.3 (Part 4)
Results of the Snap Macro

```
JOB RYTHREE1        STEP ASM        TIME 104748    DATE 78321    ID = 001                                    PAGE 0001

REGS AT ENTRY TC SNAP

   FLTR 0-6    010C045B0083C001  0100014000030008                  C0046AFC0CFFCCC0    0CCCCC00CCCCC000

   REGS C-7    CCC45FF8  AC2C6898  C2E4E8C5    00203900  00206800    00204BC4  CCC01388    001FD884  CC204921
   REGS 8-15   8C2C3D9A  C01FF15C  40404040    00206800  60206802    00206CDC  C02C46F0    4C2C686A  CC0086C8

STORAGE

2C49EC                                                    D1C5C1D5 E24CC2D3   *.........8...8...*....JEANS BL*
2C6ACC  E4C54040 40404040 C2E4E8C5  C9404040 40404040 40404040 40404040 F3F0F3F2  *UE      BUYER            03032*
2C6A2C  F4F5F6F7 F8F9F0F1 F2F3F5F4  40404040 40404040 40404040 40404040 40404040  *4567890123544                *
2C6A4C  4C4C4C40 40404040 40404040  40404040 40404040 40404040 40404040 40404040  *                             *
2C6A6C  40404040 40404040 40404040  40404040 C9C3D2C5 E84DC4C6 E4E2C5E3 D9C1D740  *          MICKEY MOUSETRAP   *
2C6A8C  C9D5C34B 40404040 40404040  40404040 40404040 40404040 40404040 40404040  *INC.                         *
2C6AAC  40404040 40404040 40404040  40404040 40404040 40404040 40404040 40404040  *                             *
   LINE 2C6ACC SAME AS ABOVE
2C6AE0  4C404040 4C404040 40404040  40404040 40404040 E3C5D3C5 D7C8D6D5 C540C4C9  *              TELEPHONE DI*
2C6BCC  D9C5C3E3 D6D9E840 40404040  40404040 40404040 40404040 40404040 40404040  *RECTORY                      *
2C6B2C  40404040 40404040 40404040  40404040 40404040 40404040 40404040 40404040  *                             *
2C6B4C  40404040 40404040 4C404040  40404040 40404040                             *                             *

ENC OF DUMP
```

Figure 14.3 (Part 5)
Results of the Snap Macro

```
JOB RYTHREE1        STEP ASM        TIME 104748   DATE 78321   ID = CO1                    PAGE OCO1

RECS AT ENTRY TO SNAP

    FLTR 0-6    C1CCC4580C83CCC1    01000140CC030008    0004AF00CFFC000    0000000000CCC000

    REGS 0-7    CC045FF8  A0206898  00203900  00206800  00204BC4  CC001388  001FD884  C0204921
    REGS 8-15   A02C3D9A  C01FF15C  60206800  60206802  C0206CDC  C02046F0  4020686A  00008608

STORAGE

2069EC  C3C1D3E5 C9D54040 40404040 E7C1D3C5 C1D6C8D5 E2D6D540  *........8...8...*....JOHNSON *
206ACC  F4F5F6F7 F8F9FCF1 F2F3F5F2 F1404040 40404040 F4F0F2F2  *CALVIN    SALESMAN      04022*
206A2C  40404040 40404040 40404040 40404040 40404040 4C404C40  *4567890123521*
206A4C  40404040 40404040 40404040 40404040 E4E2C5E3 D9C1D740  *          MICKEY MOUSETRAP*
206A8C  C9D5C34B 40404040 40404040 40404040 40404040 40404040  *INC.*
206AAC  40404040 40404040 40404040 40404040 40404040 40404040  *                    *
        LINE 206AC0 SAME AS ABOVE
206AEC  40404040 40404040 4C404040 40404040 E3C5D3C5 D7C8D6D5 C5404040  *         TELEPHONE DI*
206BCC  D9C5C3E3 D6D9E840 40404040 40404040 4C404040 40404040          *RECTORY*
206B2C  40404040 40404040 40404040 40404040 40404040                   *                    *
206B4C  40404040 40404040 40404040

END OF DUMP
```

Figure 14.3 (Part 6)
Results of the Snap Macro

```
JOB RYTHREE1          STEP ASM          TIME 104748    DATE 78321    ID = CO1                          PAGE CCO1

REGS AT ENTRY TO SNAP

    FLTR 0-6    C1CC0458C083CCO1    010001400030008       00046AF00CFFOC00    00CCCCOCCOCCCCO0

    REGS 0-7    CC045FF8  A0206898    00203900  00206800   002048C4  CCC01388   001FD884  C0204921
    REGS 8-15   8C2C3D9A  001FF15C    00206800  60206802   00206CDC  C02046F0   4C20686A  C0008 6C8

STORAGE

206EC
206ACC   C4C14040 40404040 D709C9D4    C5400AC9 D5C9E2E3   C4C5C9D9 40C7D6D3   *.........8...'...MEIR GCL*
206A2C   F7F8F8F2 F1F3F4F5 FCF2F0F2    40404040 40404040   C5D940F0 F5F0F4F4   *DA 78821345 02024  PRIME MINISTER 05044*
206A40   40404040 40404040 4C404040    40404040 40404040   40404040 4C4C4C40   *                  *
206AE0   40404040 40404040 40404040    C9C302C5 0840D406   E4E2C5E3 D9C1D740   *       INC.     MICKEY MOUSETRAP *
206AEC   C9D5C34B 4C4C4C40 40404040    40404040 40404040   40404040 4CC40440   *INC.             *
206AAC   40404040 40404040 40404040    40404040 40404040   40404040 4CC40440   *                 *

LINE 206AC0 SAME AS ABOVE

206AEC   40404040 40404040 40404040    40404040 E3C5D3C5   D7C8D6D5 C540C4C9   *          TELEPHONE DI*
206BCO   D9C5C3E3 D6D9E840 40404040    40404040 40404040   40404040 40404040   *RECTORY          *
206B20   40404040 40404040 40404040    40404040 40404040   40404040 4CC40440   *                 *
206B4C   40404040 40404040 4C4C4040    40404040                                *          *

END OF DUMP
```

Figure 14.3 (Part 7)
Results of the Snap Macro

```
JOB RYTHREE1          STEP ASM          TIME 104748   DATE 78321    ID = C01                                        PAGE 0001

REGS AT ENTRY TO SNAP

   FLTR 0-6       0100045800083C001      0100014000030008          0004AF00CFFC0C0      0000000000000000

   REGS 0-7      C00045FF8   A0206898   00203900   00206800      02048C4   CCC01388   001FD884   00204921
   REGS 8-15     8C2C3C9A    001FF15C   00206800   60206802      0206CDC   002046F0   4020686A   C00086C8

STORAGE

2065EC                                                     E2D4C9E3  C840D1D6   *..........8...8....*....SMITH JO*
2C6ACC   C8D54C40  40404040  40404040  04C1D5C1   C7C5D940  40404040  40C40F1   FCFCF3F4   *HN            MANAGER    10034*
206A2C   F4F5F6F7  F8F9F0F1  F2F3F6F5  F5404040   40404040  40404040  40404040  40404040   *456789012365                 *
206A4C   4C404040  40404040  4C404040  40404040   40404040  40404040  40404040  40404040   *                             *
2C6A6C   4C4C4040  40404040  40404040  404040C4   C9C3D2C5  E840D4D6  E4E2C5E3  D9C1D74C   *             MICKEY MOUSETRAP *
2C6A8C   C9D5C348  40404040  40404040  40404040   40404040  40404040  40404040  40404040   *INC.                         *
2C6AAC   40404040  40404040  40404040  40404040   40404040  40404040  40404040  40404040   *                             *
         LINE 206AC0  SAME AS ABOVE
2C6AEC   40404040  40404C4C  40404040  40404040   40404040  E3C5D3C5  D7C8D6D5  C540C4C9   *            TELEPHONE DI*
2C8BCC   D9C5C3E3  D6D9E840  40404040  40404040   40404040  40404040  40404040  40404040   *RECTORY                      *
2C6B2C   40404040  40404040  4C404040  40404040   40404040  40404040  40404040  40404040   *                             *
2C6B4C   40404040  40404040  4C404040  40404040   40404040                                 *                       *

END OF DUMP
```

Figure 14.3 (Part 8)
Results of the Snap Macro

Abend Dumps

An abend dump is requested by use of the ABEND macro instruction. This instruction is of the form

name	**operation**	**operands**
[symbolic name]	ABEND	completion code,DUMP

where the completion code is some decimal integer smaller than or equal to 4095. The completion code will be printed as part of the dump and serves to identify the dump.

The programmer must also provide a job control statement: a DD statement with a ddname of SYSABEND. This statement would be of the form

    //SYSABEND DD SYSOUT=A

if the program is being executed without a catalogued procedure, or

    //GO.SYSABEND DD SYSOUT=A

if the program is run in the GO step of a catalogued procedure. If in doubt as to which statement you should use, inquire from the appropriate computer center personnel.

Actually, the dump provided using the DD statement with ddname SYSABEND provides many pages of output, much of which is not intelligible except to systems programmers. It is not necessary to understand this output except in the very unusual cases of *very* obscure errors which may have somehow affected or have been affected by areas of main storage other than the user program itself.

The abend dump with ddname SYSABEND does, of course, provide a dump of main storage locations. The operating system space is printed first, and the user's (program's) space is printed last. The form of this part of the dump is similar to what we have seen in examining the dump provided by the SNAP macro: the contents of storage are printed in hexadecimal form. When they exist, EBCDIC character representations corresponding to hexadecimal notations are printed. When main storage bytes do not correspond to EBCDIC characters, periods are printed instead. Figure 14.4 shows an abend dump with ddname SYSABEND. We have presented, for demonstration purposes, only the first three pages of what was in fact a 25-page dump.

The programmer may feel that the dump produced by use of the ddname SYSABEND is more than is needed or desired. In such case, a DD statement with the ddname SYSUDUMP may be provided. This will cause a dump only of the problem program areas and system control areas associated with the program.

```
JOB RYELEVN1          STEP ASM           TIME 181522    DATE 78171                                          PAGE 0001

COMPLETION CODE       USER = 0001

PSW AT ENTRY TO ABEND FFE50000 60197852

TCB 030DE8   RHP   000167D8   PIE    00000000   DEB  0036D03C   TIO 00035F0   CMP   80000001   TRN  00000000
             MSS   02043708   PK-FLG EU850400   FLG  0002F10    LLS 0C03A510  JLB   00000000   JPQ  00037828
             FSA   011AD760   TCB    00000000   TME  00000000   JST 00C330E8  NTC   00000000   OTC  00042760
             LTC   00000000   IQE    00000000   ECB  000374EC   TSF 2C000000  D-PQE 00054FA0   SQS  00041168
             NSTAE 00000000   TCT    8003A1F8   USER 00000000   DAR 00000000  RESV  00000000   JSCB 87036DBC
             RESV  C0019867   IOB    00000000

ACTIVE RBS

PRB 0395C8   RESV  00000000   APSW   00000000   WC-SZ-STAB 00040082   FL-CDE 000437B8   PSW FFE50006 4018DD10
             Q/TTR C0000000   WT-LNK 00037DE8

PRB 04268B   RESV  00000000   APSW   00000000   WC-SZ-STAB 00040002   FL-CDE C003AE88   PSW FFE50006 4019002A
             Q/TTR C0000000   WT-LNK 000395CA

PRB 036490   RESV  00000000   APSW   00000000   WC-SZ-STAB 00040007   FL-CDE 00037828   PSW FFE50000 60197852
             Q/TTR C0000000   WT-LNK U0042688

SVRB 0165C8  TAR-LN 0053023H  APSW  F9F0F1C3   WC-SZ-STAB 0016D002   TQN 00000000   PSW 00040033 5001F1F2
             C/TTR  CC00D719   WT-LNK 00038490
             RG 0-7 F4000070   P00C0001   00194900   00197955   00195AA8   0001388    0018E884   0019840C
             RG 8-15 80194D9A  00190150   00197800   60197R02   00197974   00195F0    60194E12   00197800
             EXTSA  00002986   8F1AD240   00000000   00000000   FFD30000   0016664    0016664C   E28EE2C9
                    CCC1E0F1   C9C5C1E8   C4F90000   00000000   00000000   00000000   00000000   00000000
                    CC000000   00000000

SVRB 0167D8  TAR-LN 0018C5C8  APSW  F1F0F5C1   WC-SZ-STAB 0016D002   TQN 00000000   PSW FF04000C 503D8FAA
             Q/TTR  C000A51?   WT-LNK 0016SCR
             RG 0-7 45EC09L0E  00016628   8001F0F7   00020050   00033DE8   00016SC8   03033DE8   00016SC8
             RG 8-15 00033DE6  4001F03A   00033DE9   C00396E9   0001664C   00016664   40010140   00000000
             EXTSA  E2E9F2C9   C5C1F0F1   C02047?D   18F247F0   C0181801   C0000000   41I0C022   0A2207FE
                    C0CC2F3   C1C5D940   40404040   404007FF   00000000   00000000   00000000   00000000
                    C0000000   00000000   00000000   00000000

LOAD LIST

NE 0003D6A8  RSP-CDE 02059AD0   NE 0003B878  RSP-CDE 0105A2F8   NE 0003BD60  RSP-CDE 0105A228
NE C0043AA8  RSP-CDE 0105A1F8   NE 00041CD0  RSP-CDE 01033D30   NE 00042208  RSP-CDE 0105A428
NE C004261A  RSP-CDE 0105A398   NE 00042630  RSP-CDE 04059C00   NE 000429A0  RSP-CDE 060542F8
NE C0042E5C  RSP-CDE 04059BD0   NE C0042B78  RSP-CDE 0405A288   NE 00042C70  RSP-CDE 0405A228
NE C0043CF8  RSP-CDE 0405A1F8   NE 00043D40  RSP-CDE 0405A328   NE 00043ED0  RSP-CDE 0105A288
NE C0044058  MSP-CDE 05059H60   NE 00048CC0  RSP-CDE 0205A1B8   NE 00000000  RSP-CDE 0205A358

CDE
```

Figure 14.4 (Part 1)
An Abend Dump

XL

047388	ATR1 0B	NCDE 000000	ROC-RB 00039C8	NM ASMG	USE 01	EPA 18DD00	ATR2 20	XL/MJ 0489A8
C34E88	ATR1 0B	NCDE 033D30	ROC-RB 00042688	NM ASMGRTA	USE 01	EPA 190000	ATR2 20	XL/MJ 041A28
037828	ATR1 0H	NCDE 034E88	ROC-RB 0003R490	NM ASMGFPP	USE 01	EPA 190A18	ATR2 20	XL/MJ 042678
C59AD0	ATR1 B0	NCDE 059B00	ROC-RB 00000000	NM IGC0A05A	USE 01	EPA 3D8810	ATR2 28	XL/MJ 059AC0
05A2F8	ATR1 B0	NCDE 05A328	ROC-RB 00000000	NM IGG019CC	USE 02	EPA 3F44F8	ATR2 20	XL/MJ 05A2E8
05A228	ATR1 R0	NCDE 05A258	ROC-RB 00000000	NM IGG019BA	USE 01	EPA 3F40E8	ATR2 20	XL/MJ 05A218
05A1F8	ATR1 R0	NCDE 05A228	ROC-RB 00000000	NM IGG019BB	USE 02	EPA 3F3E88	ATR2 20	XL/MJ 05A1E8
C33D30	ATR1 03	NCDE 043788	ROC-RB 00000000	NM ASMGIS01	USE 01	EPA 196E88	ATR2 20	XL/MJ 048858
05A42R	ATR1 B0	NCDE C5445R	ROC-RB 00000000	NM IGG019AA	USE 02	EPA 3F58E0	ATR2 20	XL/MJ 05A418
05A398	ATR1 B0	NCDE 05A3C8	ROC-RB 00000000	NM IGG019AQ	USE 01	EPA 3F4E88	ATR2 20	XL/MJ 05A388
C59C00	ATR1 R0	NCDE 059C30	ROC-RB 00000000	NM IGG019BC	USE 01	EPA 3D9970	ATR2 20	XL/MJ 059BF0
059BC0	ATR1 B1	NCDE 059C00	ROC-RB 00000000	NM IGG019CO	USE 01	EPA 3D9878	ATR2 20	XL/MJ 059BC0
05A2R8	ATR1 30	NCDE 05A2F8	ROC-RB 00000000	NM IGG019CH	USE 02	EPA 3F5058	ATR2 20	XL/MJ 05A2A8
05A298	ATR1 BC	NCDE 05A358	ROC-RB 00000000	NM IGG019CI	USE 01	EPA 3F4AD8	ATR2 20	XL/MJ 05A318
C59B60	ATR1 H1	NCDE C5A2B8	ROC-RB 00000000	NM IGG019FN	USE 01	EPA 3F4878	ATR2 20	XL/MJ 05A278
05A1B8	ATR1 H0	NCDE 05A1F8	ROC-RB 00000000	NM IGG019AI	USE 02	EPA 3F4068	ATR2 20	XL/MJ 059B50
05A35R	ATR1 B0	NCDE 05A398	RJC-R3 00000000	NM IGG019AR	USE 02	EPA 3F4D78	ATR2 20	XL/MJ 05A1A8
								XL/MJ 05A348

| | | | LN | | ADR | | LN | | ADR |

6489A8	SZ CCC0010	NO 00000001	80002300	0018DD00
041A2R	SZ 0CC0010	NO 00000001	80000800	00190000
04267R	SZ 0CC001C	NO 00000001	80005ER	00190A18
C59ACO	SZ 0CC0010	NO 00000001	8000037F0	003D8810
05A2ER	SZ CCC0010	NO 00000001	8000030P	003F44F8
05A218	SZ CCC0010	NO 00000001	800001C0	003F40E8
05A1E8	SZ CCC0010	NO 00000001	80000178	003F3E88
048858	SZ 0CC0010	NO C0000001	80000948	0196E88
05A418	SZ CCC001C	NO 00000001	800000A0	003F58E0
05A388	SZ CCCC010	NU 00000001	80000178	003F4E88
059BF0	SZ CCC0010	NO 00000001	8000014R	003D9970
059BC0	SZ CCCC010	NO 00000001	800000F8	003D9878
05A2A8	SZ 0CC0010	NO 00000001	80000080	003F5058
05A318	SZ CCCC010	NO 00000001	800002A0	003F4AD8
C5A27R	SZ CCC0010	NC 00000001	80000260	003F4878
C59B50	SZ CCC0010	NC C0000001	R0C0007R	003F4800
05A1A8	SZ CCC0010	NO 00000001	80000080	003F4068
05A348	SZ CCC0010	NO 00000010	80000110	003F4D78

DEB

C36DCO	00007248	00007248	00007248	00000000	00000000	U04028E0	0000724R	CCC07248
036D20	10036DBC	CR0C0C00	8FC00000	01000000	10000000	EF1AD240	UFC00000	03033DE8
036D40	0001C001	00000000	00000000	0000007D	C2C2C2C1	C3C30000	02036D18	8300472C
C36D8C	0CC0C000	00000000	00000000	00000000	00000000	00000000	00000000	CCCCCCC0

DEB

| 036DBC | | | | 003F5058 | 003F4800 |

ASPO CBO IS RYEL .... *
* ....Y*
* ..H................*
* ....*BBACC.......*
* ....6....*

Figure 14.4 (Part 2)
An Abend Dump

```
                                                                                                    PAGE 0003
036DA0  00007248 003D9878 00007248 00000000   0000010F 00003BE2 11000000 08033DE8   *.......................S.......Y*
036DC0  100397D4 C8000000 17000000 01000000   10000000 EF18E6D4 04036D98 18003260   *...MH...............WM.. ....-*
036DE0  0000003D 0004C046 0006004B 00010001   00000000 00000000 00000000 C2C2C2C1   *............................BBBA*
036FC0  C6D5C3C8 C3F0C3C3 C3C4C2C3 00000000   00000000 00000000 00000000 00000000   *FNCHCOCCCDBC....................*

DEB

C397AC                                        003F5058 003F4800 00007248 003D9878   *.................&..............*
C397CC  00007248 00000000 0000010E 00003BE2   11000000 08033DE8 10039864 C8C00000   *...............S.......Y....H...*
C397EC  17000000 01000000 10000000 EF18E668   040397B0 18003260 00000034 0001003D   *.............W........-........*
0398C0  0003004B 00010001 00000000 00000000   00000000 C2C2C2C1 C6D5C3C8 C3F0C3C3   *...................BBBAFNCHCOCC*
C39820  C3C4C2C3 00000000 00000000 00000000   00000000 00000000                     *CDBC.......................H....*

DEB

039840  003F5058 003F4800 00007248 003D9878   00007248 00000000 0000010C 00003BE2   *..&...........................S*
C39860  11000000 08033DE8 100398F4 C8000000   17000000 01000000 10000000 EF18E5FC   *.......Y...4H.................V.*
C3988C  04039840 18003260 0000002A 00060034   0000004B 00010001 00000000 00000000   *... ...-........................*
C398AC  00000000 C2C2C2C1 C6D5C3C8 C3F0C3C3   C3C4C2C3 00000000 00000000 00000000   *....BBBAFNCHCOCCCDBC............*
C398C0  00000000 D9E8C5D3                                                           *....RYEL.. ......................*

DEB

0398C0                                        00007248 00007248 00007248 00007248   *....RYEL.. ......................*
0398EC  00007248 00000000 00000000 00409BE0   0F000000 03033DE8 10036F34 C8000000   *............. .........Y.. .H...*
C399C0  1F000000 01000000 10000000 EF18E818   020398D0 B300458C 00010001 00000000   *.............Y..................*
C3992C  00000000 00000079 C1D9C1C9 C3C30000   00000000 00000000 00000000 00000000   *........ARAICC..................*
C3994C  00000000 00000000                                                           *................&...............*

DEB

036F00                                        00007248 00007248 00007248 00007248   *...Y...Q...&....................*
036F20  00007248 00000000 00000000 00419FE0   0F000000 03033DE8 1003A17C 68000000   *.....................Y...'.....*
036F40  10004000 01000000 10000000 EF18E884   02036F10 B30046F8 00010001 00000000   *.. ..........Y... ....8.........*
C36F60  00000000 00000050 C1D8C1C1 C3C30000   00000000 00000000 00000000 00000000   *.......&AQAACC..................*
036F80  00000000 00000000                                                           *................................*

DEB

C3A140                                                          003F5058 003F4800   *     ..............&.......&.....*
C3A160  00007248 003D9878 00007248 C0000001   92000518 00003BE0 13000000 07033DE8   *...............................Y*
03A180  0203B77C 49000000 10000000 03000000   10000000 EF18E740 0403A158 58003C2C   *...'..................X ........*
03A1A0  000001C1 001201C1 00120001 50003C2C   000001A6 000001B0 001200D1 50003C2C   *...A...A....&...............J&...*
C3A1C0  000001B1 000001B2 00120026 0102C2C2   C2C1C6D5 C3C8C3F0 C3C3C2C3 00000000   *.............BBBAFNCHCOCCBC....*
C3A1E0  00000000 00000000 00000000 C0001196                                         *.................O...........-*

DEB

03B740                                                          00007248 003F4800   *..P&...........................*
```

Figure 14.4 (Part 3)
An Abend Dump

After a dump is produced using the ABEND macro, control is not returned to the user program. The dump is provided only in the case of abnormal termination of a job.

INDICATIVE DUMPS

An **indicative dump** is provided when the programmer has requested an abnormal termination dump but has not provided a DD statement with either the name SYSABEND or SYSUDUMP. The indicative dump contains information about the program and the cause of program interruption.

When a program exception causes the interruption, the indicative dump will show a **completion code**, a 3-digit code the first two digits of which will be 0C and the third of which will be the interruption code number (1 means operation exception, 2 means privileged operation exception, and so on; see section 14.4.2). One or two sets of general register contents are given, as well as the contents of the floating point registers. The contents of main storage immediately preceding and including the instruction that is executed when the interrupt occurs is also displayed, in hexadecimal form (in total, 12 bytes of storage will be displayed). An additional section of the indicative dump, called the ACTIVE RB LIST, provides other information about the status of the program. Indicative dumps are provided by operating systems with MFT and are not provided by operating systems with MVT.

Core Image Dumps

If a *system* routine (not a *program* routine) fails, the operating system automatically provides a dump of main storage, containing diagnostic information. This is called a **core image dump**. This dump is not printed automatically, but a special program called the IMDPRDMP Service Aid program may be invoked to obtain such a printout. A discussion of the IMDPRDMP program and of the formats of the core image dump may be found in the IBM publication *Service Aids* (Form GC28–6719).

The discussion of program dumps above was meant to acquaint the reader with the types of dumps available to the programmer. It also communicated a general sense for which dumps should be invoked and under what conditions they may be found most useful. In the next section, we shall demonstrate how to use a dump to find the cause of a simple program error. However, true proficiency in the use of dumps and a good understanding of which dump features and elements will be useful under particular program conditions will be gained only after considerable debugging experience. As with programming itself, experience will prove to be the best teacher.

Should the programmer have specific questions with regard to the interpretation or use of the program dumps described in this section, the following IBM publications may prove useful (they should be available for reference in any computer center which uses an IBM 360 or 370 computer using the OS operating system).

IBM System/360 Operating System Messages and Codes GC28–6631
IBM System/360 Operating System Programmers Guide
           to Debugging GC28–6670
OS/VS1 Debugging Guide GC24–5093
OS/VS2 Debugging Guide GC28–0632

14.4.4 Analyzing a Dump: A Debugging Example

Let us now consider a simple debugging example. We shall trace the cause of a program interrupt by analyzing a dump of main storage areas occupied by the program at the time of error.

Figure 14.5 is identical to program 7.1 of chapter 7, with an error introduced. The program is to consider the contents of fields called OLD, RECPT, and ISSUE; to compute OLD+RECPT−ISSUE; and to place the result of such computation into a main storage area called NEW. Computation is to be performed using binary values, and the result is to be converted into zoned form for placement into NEW.

The program of figure 14.5 was executed on an IBM S/370 computer under OS control. Execution was terminated by the occurrence of a program interrupt; the system provided the printed output of figures 14.6 and 14.7 to aid us in our debugging efforts.

Upon examining the program dump of figure 14.7, we note that the first few lines provide us with information specific to the particular instruction and error condition which caused the interrupt to occur.

With regard to the instruction which caused the interrupt, we are told that the ADDRESS OF NEXT INSTRUCTION is 2CF020, and that the INSTRUCTION LENGTH is 4 BYTES.

We know, from examining the **load map** of figure 14.6, that our program object module was loaded into main storage beginning at location 2CF000 (note the value 2CF000 under the column heading LOCATION on the load map) and occupied 48 bytes of storage (note the value 000048 under the column heading LENGTH on the load map). Thus, if the ADDRESS OF NEXT INSTRUCTION is 2CF020, the address is *20 main storage bytes past the beginning of our stored object program*. All numeric values referred to are expressed in hexadecimal; thus 20 bytes hexadecimal means 32 bytes decimal.

PAGE 2

30 NOV 78

```
LOC    OBJECT CODE       ADDR1 ADDR2   STMT      SOURCE STATEMENT

000000 05F0                               1          START
000000 05F0              00002            2  A       BALR  11,0
                                          3          USING *,11
                                          4  *
000002 F273 B03E B02E    00040 00030      5          PACK  DBL,OLD      CONVERT OLD INTO PACKED FORM, AND
                                          6  *                         PLACE INTO DBL
000008 4F40 B03E         00040            7          CVB   4,DBL        BINARY OLD INTO REG 4
00000C F271 B03E B032    00040 00034      8          PACK  DBL,RECPT    CONVERT OLD INTO PACKED FORM, AND
                                          9  *                         PLACE INTO DBL
000012 4F50 B03E         00040           10          CVB   5,DBL        BINARY RECPT INTO REG 5
000016 F271 B03E B034    00040 00036     11          PACK  DBL,ISSUE    CONVERT ISSUE INTO PACKED FORM, AND
                                         12  *                         PLACE INTO DBL
00001C 4F60 B03E         00040           13          CVB   6,DBL        BINARY ISSUE INTO REG 6
000020 1A45                              14          AR    4,5          ADD   OLD + RECPT INTO REG 4
000022 1B46                              15          SR    4,6          SUBTRACT  (OLD + RECPT)-ISSUE INTO REG 4
000024 4E40 B03E         00040           16          CVD   4,DBL        CONVERT BINARY RESULT INTO PACKED FORM,
                                         17  *                         PLACE INTO DBL
000028 F327 B036 B03E    00038 00040     18          UNPK  NEW,DBL      CONVERT PACKED RESULT INTO ZONED FORM, AND
                                         19  *                         PLACE INTO NEW
00002E 0A03                              20          SVC   3            STOP EXECUTION
                                         21  *                         IN DOS, THIS INSTRUCTION IS EOJ
                                         22  *
000030 F1F0F0F0C0                        23  OLD     DC    Z'1000'
000034 F5C0                              24  RECPT   DC    Z'50'
000036 072C                              25  ISSUE   DC    P'72'
000038                                   26  NEW     DS    CL3
00003D                                   27  DBL     DS    D
000040                                   28          END   A
```

Figure 14.5

A Program Example Resulting in an Interruption

LOAD MAP   30 NOV 78

CSECT NAME LOCATION LENGTH
/NONAME/   2CF000   000048

Figure 14.6
A Load Map

ASMG3C4I   EXECUTION ERROR.

ADDRESS OF NEXT INSTRUCTION   2CF020
INSTRUCTION LENGTH   4 BYTES
INTERRUPTION CODE   0007   INVALID DATA
CONDITION CODE   2

REGISTERS AT TIME OF ERROR

R	HEX	DECIMAL	R	HEX	DECIMAL	R	HEX	DECIMAL	R	HEX	DECIMAL
0	F3C00070	-0218103696	1	002C5AA4	0002906788	2	002CC100	0002932992	3	002CF000	0002945024
4	CC0003E8	0000001000	5	00000032	0000000050	6	002C6084	0002908292	7	002CFC00	0002948096
8	802CC55A	-2144549478	9	002C795C	0002914652	A	002CF000	0002945024	8	602CF002	1613557762
C	002CF048	0002945096	D	002CCEF0	0002936560	E	602CC612	1613547026	F	002CF000	0002945024

FPR0	+01.000030 00030001	FPR2	+01.000036 00010001	FPR4	-61.B937C9 3F78334F	FPR6	+00.000000 00000000
	+.CCCC0000000000000 E+00		+.000000000000000 E+00		-.393914939744453323 E+40		+.000000000000000 E+00

STORAGE AT TIME OF ERROR

```
2CFCCC  058F273 B03EB02E 4F40B03E F271B03E   B0324F50 B03EF271 B03EB034 4F60B03E   *.2.......2.....6..2.....-.*
2CF020  1A451B46 4E40B03E F327B036 B03E0A03   F1F0FC0 F5CO072C 01000036 0001000A   *..+..3......100.5.........*
2CF040  00000000 000007C2 01000038 00020008   79B4C000 00000017 01000030 0003000C   *.......8.................*
```

END OF TASK

Figure 14.7
A Program Dump Caused by Execution Error

Referring to our program listing, we note that the assembler's location counter has assigned program address values (under the column heading LOC) beginning with the value 000000. Thus the address identified as being 20 bytes past the beginning of our object program is the address numbered 000020 on our listing; the instruction at 000020 is statement number 14: an AR instruction. However, this address is, according to the message on our dump, the address of the *NEXT INSTRUCTION!* In other words, had the interruption *not* occurred, the next instruction to be executed *would have been* the instruction at location 000020. It therefore follows that the instruction which caused the interruption is the one which *precedes* that of location 000020. Referring back to the listing of figure 14.5, we see that the instruction preceding that which begins at 000020 is the instruction beginning at 00001C: statement 13. We conclude that statement 13, a CVB instruction, was the cause of the program interrupt.

Redirecting our attention to the program dump, we again note the message that the INSTRUCTION LENGTH, that is the length of the instruction which caused the interrupt, is 4 BYTES. We have already determined the CVB instruction of statement 13 to have caused the interrupt, and examination of the instruction object code (4F60B03E) verifies the 4-byte length.

Examination of the culprit statement, CVB   6,DBL, does not reveal the cause of the error. The instruction conforms to the standard RX format with a register number as the first operand and an aligned doubleword as the second operand. We therefore turn again to the program dump for direction.

The next message on the dump informs us of the cause of the error: the INTERRUPTION CODE is 0007, and the message INVALID DATA indicates that we should examine the contents of the instruction operands to determine the validity of the data being acted upon.

We know from our studies that the CVB instruction considers a packed number in its second operand field; converts it into binary form; and replaces the previous contents of the first operand register with the binary result. The previous contents of the first operand register cannot possibly be considered to constitute invalid data, since they are neither examined nor acted upon by the instruction, but are simply replaced by the results of the conversion. The fault must therefore lie with the contents of the second operand field, DBL, which should consist of a valid packed number for conversion. We see from statement 27 that the name DBL has been assigned by the assembler to location counter value 000040, that is to the location which begins 40 bytes past the beginning of the program.

Returning to figure 14.7, the section labeled STORAGE AT TIME OF

ERROR displays the contents of main storage beginning at location 2CF000, the beginning location of the object program. DBL begins 40 bytes past the beginning of the program, at location 2CF040, and is eight bytes long. The eight bytes of storage beginning at location 2CF040 on the dump are shown to contain 00000000 000007C2; this is not a valid packed number! The cause of the interrupt is now evident.

How did an improper value find its way into DBL? Examination of the other program statements shows that ISSUE was defined to contain a packed number (statement 25), which was then acted upon by a PACK instruction (statement 11) yielding the incorrect value! The PACK instruction was itself acting incorrectly by attempting to pack an already packed number. However the PACK instruction does not check its operand contents for validity, therefore the error was not caught until the CVB instruction, which *does* check its second operand for validity, found the value to be incorrect.

We may remedy the program difficulty by defining ISSUE as a zoned number using the statement

          ISSUE   DC   Z'72'

ISSUE will then be appropriately packed and converted to binary.

Alternately, we may choose to define ISSUE as a packed number, but to place it on a doubleword integral boundary and extend its length to eight bytes:

                   DS   0D
          ISSUE   DC   PL8'72'

The PACK instruction of statement 11 would then be eliminated; the CVB would be sufficient for proper conversion to binary form.

Summary

In this chapter, a systematic approach to debugging computer programs was presented.

The premise was advanced that programs should be as carefully planned and as error-free as possible in their initial version. A systematic approach to desk-checking, to correction of program diagnostics (syntax errors), and to test runs using carefully prepared test data was then demonstrated. The chapter also introduced the use of several types of program dumps which are available to the programmer, as aids in his debugging efforts.

Important Terms Discussed in Chapter 14

abend dump
addressing exception

bug

completion code
core-image dump
cross-reference listing

data exception
debugging
decimal divide exception
decimal overflow exception
desk-checking
diagnostic
diagnostic listing
dump
dynamic dump

eighty-eighty (80–80) listing
exception
execute exception
exponent overflow exception

exponent underflow exception

fixed-point divide exception
fixed-point overflow exception
floating-point divide exception

indicative dump

operation exception

privileged operation exception
program-check interrupt
program-check message
program interrupt
protection exception

significance exception
specification exception
system run
system test

test data
test run

Questions

14-1. Distinguish between coding errors and logical errors. Errors in which of these categories will be more difficult to correct?

14-2. What is the first phase of checking a program for coding errors?

14-3. What is an 80–80 listing? What is its use in program debugging?

14-4. List seven different types of assembler output aside from the object module.

14-5. How are operand addresses expressed on the assembler listing as part of an instruction's OBJECT CODE? Are operand addresses represented in another form elsewhere on the listing? Explain.

14-6. Can one always know the cause of an error from reading a diagnostic message? Why or why not?

14-7. When testing a program, why is it important to include minimum and maximum values in the construction of test data?

14-8.   What is meant by the term system run?

14-9.   What is an exception?

14-10. Explain what is meant by an interruption code. How many such codes are there?

14-11. Name the three categories of program dumps.

14-12. Explain the meaning of each operand in the instruction below:
```
SNAP   DCB=DCBAD,ID=1,STORAGE=(AREA1,AREA2),
       PDATA=(REGS)
```

14-13. Name the macros used to obtain partial dumps under both DOS and OS systems.

14-14. What type of dump is produced should a system routine (as opposed to a program routine) fail? Is this dump provided automatically? Explain.

Appendices

Appendix
A

IBM System/370
Reference Summary

System/370 Reference Summary

GX20-1850-2

Third Edition (March 1974)

This edition supersedes GX20-1850-1. It includes new machine instructions and control register functions associated with multi-processing, and the new instructions CS, CDS, CLRIO, IPK, and SPKA. To the extent that space allows, additional non-TP devices most often attached to System/370s have been added to the I/O command code tables.

The card is intended primarily for use by S/370 assembler language programmers. It contains basic machine information on Models 115 through 168 summarized from the *System/370 Principles of Operation* (GA22-7000), frequently used information from *OS/VS and DOS/VS Assembler Language* (GC33-4010), command codes for various I/O devices, and a multi-code translation table. The card will be updated from time to time. However, the above manuals and others cited on the card are the authoritative reference sources and will be first to reflect changes.

The names of instructions essentially new with S/370 are shown in italics. Some machine instructions are optional or not available for some models. For those that are available on a particular model, the user is referred to the appropriate functional characteristics manual. For a particular installation, one must ascertain which optional hardware features and programming system(s) have been installed. The floating-point and extended floating-point instructions, as well as the instructions listed below, are not standard on every model. Monitoring (the MC instruction) is not available on the Model 165.

Conditional swapping	CDS, CS
CPU timer and clock comparator	SCKC, SPT, STCKC, STPT
Direct control	RDD, WRD
Dynamic address translation	LRA, PTLB, RRB, STNSM, STOSM
Input/output	CLRIO, SIOF
Multiprocessing	SIGP, SPX, STAP, STPX
PSW key handling	IPK, SPKA

Comments about this publication may be sent to the address below. All comments and suggestions become the property of IBM.

IBM Corporation, Technical Publications/Systems, Dept. 824, 1133 Westchester Avenue, White Plains, N. Y. 10604

MACHINE INSTRUCTIONS ②

NAME	MNEMONIC	OP CODE	FOR MAT	OPERANDS
Add (c)	AR	1A	RR	R1,R2
Add (c)	A	5A	RX	R1,D2(X2,B2)
Add Decimal (c)	AP	FA	SS	D1(L1,B1),D2(L2,B2)
Add Halfword (c)	AH	4A	RX	R1,D2(X2,B2)
Add Logical (c)	ALR	1E	RR	R1,R2
Add Logical (c)	AL	5E	RX	R1,D2(X2,B2)
AND (c)	NR	14	RR	R1,R2
AND (c)	N	54	RX	R1,D2(X2,B2)
AND (c)	NI	94	SI	D1(B1),I2
AND (c)	NC	D4	SS	D1(L,B1),D2(B2)
Branch and Link	BALR	05	RR	R1,R2
Branch and Link	BAL	45	RX	R1,D2(X2,B2)
Branch on Condition	BCR	07	RR	M1,R2
Branch on Condition	BC	47	RX	M1,D2(X2,B2)
Branch on Count	BCTR	06	RR	R1,R2
Branch on Count	BCT	46	RX	R1,D2(X2,B2)
Branch on Index High	BXH	86	RS	R1,R3,D2(B2)
Branch on Index Low or Equal	BXLE	87	RS	R1,R3,D2(B2)
Clear I/O (c,p)	CLRIO	9D01	S	D2(B2)
Compare (c)	CR	19	RR	R1,R2
Compare (c)	C	59	RX	R1,D2(X2,B2)
Compare and Swap (c)	CS	BA	RS	R1,R3,D2(B2)
Compare Decimal (c)	CP	F9	SS	D1(L1,B1),D2(L2,B2)
Compare Double and Swap (c)	CDS	BB	RS	R1,R3,D2(B2)
Compare Halfword (c)	CH	49	RX	R1,D2(X2,B2)
Compare Logical (c)	CLR	15	RR	R1,R2
Compare Logical (c)	CL	55	RX	R1,D2(X2,B2)
Compare Logical (c)	CLC	D5	SS	D1(L,B1),D2(B2)
Compare Logical (c)	CLI	95	SI	D1(B1),I2
Compare Logical Characters under Mask (c)	CLM	BD	RS	R1,M3,D2(B2)
Compare Logical Long (c)	CLCL	0F	RR	R1,R2
Convert to Binary	CVB	4F	RX	R1,D2(X2,B2)
Convert to Decimal	CVD	4E	RX	R1,D2(X2,B2)
Diagnose (p)		83		Model-dependent
Divide	DR	1D	RR	R1,R2
Divide	D	5D	RX	R1,D2(X2,B2)
Divide Decimal	DP	FD	SS	D1(L1,B1),D2(L2,B2)
Edit (c)	ED	DE	SS	D1(L,B1),D2(B2)
Edit and Mark (c)	EDMK	DF	SS	D1(L,B1),D2(B2)
Exclusive OR (c)	XR	17	RR	R1,R2
Exclusive OR (c)	X	57	RX	R1,D2(X2,B2)
Exclusive OR (c)	XI	97	SI	D1(B1),I2
Exclusive OR (c)	XC	D7	SS	D1(L,B1),D2(B2)
Execute	EX	44	RX	R1,D2(X2,B2)
Halt I/O (c,p)	HIO	9E00	S	D2(B2)
Halt Device (c,p)	HDV	9E01	S	D2(B2)
Insert Character	IC	43	RX	R1,D2(X2,B2)
Insert Characters under Mask (c)	ICM	BF	RS	R1,M3,D2(B2)
Insert PSW Key (p)	IPK	B20B	S	
Insert Storage Key (p)	ISK	09	RR	R1,R2
Load	LR	18	RR	R1,R2
Load	L	58	RX	R1,D2(X2,B2)
Load Address	LA	41	RX	R1,D2(X2,B2)
Load and Test (c)	LTR	12	RR	R1,R2
Load Complement (c)	LCR	13	RR	R1,R2
Load Control (p)	LCTL	B7	RS	R1,R3,D2(B2)
Load Halfword	LH	48	RX	R1,D2(X2,B2)
Load Multiple	LM	98	RS	R1,R3,D2(B2)
Load Negative (c)	LNR	11	RR	R1,R2
Load Positive (c)	LPR	10	RR	R1,R2
Load PSW (n,p)	LPSW	82	S	D2(B2)
Load Real Address (c,p)	LRA	B1	RX	R1,D2(X2,B2)
Monitor Call	MC	AF	SI	D1(B1),I2
Move	MVI	92	SI	D1(B1),I2
Move	MVC	D2	SS	D1(L,B1),D2(B2)
Move Long (c)	MVCL	0E	RR	R1,R2
Move Numerics	MVN	D1	SS	D1(L,B1),D2(B2)
Move with Offset	MVO	F1	SS	D1(L1,B1),D2(L2,B2)
Move Zones	MVZ	D3	SS	D1(L,B1),D2(B2)
Multiply	MR	1C	RR	R1,R2
Multiply	M	5C	RX	R1,D2(X2,B2)
Multiply Decimal	MP	FC	SS	D1(L1,B1),D2(L2,B2)
Multiply Halfword	MH	4C	RX	R1,D2(X2,B2)
OR (c)	OR	16	RR	R1,R2

MACHINE INSTRUCTIONS (Contd) ③

NAME	MNEMONIC	OP CODE	FORMAT	OPERANDS
OR (c)	O	56	RX	R1,D2(X2,B2)
OR (c)	OI	96	SI	D1(B1),I2
OR (c)	OC	D6	SS	D1(L,B1),D2(B2)
Pack	PACK	F2	SS	D1(L1,B1),D2(L2,B2)
Purge TLB (p)	PTLB	B20D	S	
Read Direct (p)	RDD	85	SI	D1(B1),I2
Reset Reference Bit (c,p)	RRB	B213	S	D2(B2)
Set Clock (c,p)	SCK	B204	S	D2(B2)
Set Clock Comparator (p)	SCKC	B206	S	D2(B2)
Set CPU Timer (p)	SPT	B208	S	D2(B2)
Set Prefix (p)	SPX	B210	S	D2(B2)
Set Program Mask (n)	SPM	04	RR	R1
Set PSW Key from Address (p)	SPKA	B20A	S	D2(B2)
Set Storage Key (p)	SSK	08	RR	R1,R2
Set System Mask (p)	SSM	80	S	D2(B2)
Shift and Round Decimal (c)	SRP	F0	SS	D1(L1,B1),D2(B2),I3
Shift Left Double (c)	SLDA	8F	RS	R1,D2(B2)
Shift Left Double Logical	SLDL	8D	RS	R1,D2(B2)
Shift Left Single (c)	SLA	8B	RS	R1,D2(B2)
Shift Left Single Logical	SLL	89	RS	R1,D2(B2)
Shift Right Double (c)	SRDA	8E	RS	R1,D2(B2)
Shift Right Double Logical	SRDL	8C	RS	R1,D2(B2)
Shift Right Single (c)	SRA	8A	RS	R1,D2(B2)
Shift Right Single Logical	SRL	88	RS	R1,D2(B2)
Signal Processor (c,p)	SIGP	AE	RS	R1,R3,D2(B2)
Start I/O (c,p)	SIO	9C00	S	D2(B2)
Start I/O Fast Release (c,p)	SIOF	9C01	S	D2(B2)
Store	ST	50	RX	R1,D2(X2,B2)
Store Channel ID (c,p)	STIDC	B203	S	D2(B2)
Store Character	STC	42	RX	R1,D2(X2,B2)
Store Characters under Mask	STCM	BE	RS	R1,M3,D2(B2)
Store Clock (c)	STCK	B205	S	D2(B2)
Store Clock Comparator (p)	STCKC	B207	S	D2(B2)
Store Control (p)	STCTL	B6	RS	R1,R3,D2(B2)
Store CPU Address (p)	STAP	B212	S	D2(B2)
Store CPU ID (p)	STIDP	B202	S	D2(B2)
Store CPU Timer (p)	STPT	B209	S	D2(B2)
Store Halfword	STH	40	RX	R1,D2(X2,B2)
Store Multiple	STM	90	RS	R1,R3,D2(B2)
Store Prefix (p)	STPX	B211	S	D2(B2)
Store Then AND System Mask (p)	STNSM	AC	SI	D1(B1),I2
Store Then OR System Mask (p)	STOSM	AD	SI	D1(B1),I2
Subtract (c)	SR	1B	RR	R1,R2
Subtract (c)	S	5B	RX	R1,D2(X2,B2)
Subtract Decimal (c)	SP	FB	SS	D1(L1,B1),D2(L2,B2)
Subtract Halfword (c)	SH	4B	RX	R1,D2(X2,B2)
Subtract Logical (c)	SLR	1F	RR	R1,R2
Subtract Logical (c)	SL	5F	RX	R1,D2(X2,B2)
Supervisor Call	SVC	0A	RR	I
Test and Set (c)	TS	93	S	D2(B2)
Test Channel (c,p)	TCH	9F00	S	D2(B2)
Test I/O (c,p)	TIO	9D00	S	D2(B2)
Test under Mask (c)	TM	91	SI	D1(B1),I2
Translate	TR	DC	SS	D1(L,B1),D2(B2)
Translate and Test (c)	TRT	DD	SS	D1(L,B1),D2(B2)
Unpack	UNPK	F3	SS	D1(L1,B1),D2(L2,B2)
Write Direct (p)	WRD	84	SI	D1(B1),I2
Zero and Add Decimal (c)	ZAP	F8	SS	D1(L1,B1),D2(L2,B2)

Floating-Point Instructions

NAME	MNEMONIC	OP CODE	FORMAT	OPERANDS
Add Normalized, Extended (c,x)	AXR	36	RR	R1,R2
Add Normalized, Long (c)	ADR	2A	RR	R1,R2
Add Normalized, Long (c)	AD	6A	RX	R1,D2(X2,B2)
Add Normalized, Short (c)	AER	3A	RR	R1,R2
Add Normalized, Short (c)	AE	7A	RX	R1,D2(X2,B2)
Add Unnormalized, Long (c)	AWR	2E	RR	R1,R2
Add Unnormalized, Long (c)	AW	6E	RX	R1,D2(X2,B2)
Add Unnormalized, Short (c)	AUR	3E	RR	R1,R2
Add Unnormalized, Short (c)	AU	7E	RX	R1,D2(X2,B2)

c. Condition code is set.
n. New condition code is loaded.
p. Privileged instruction.
x. Extended precision floating-point.

Floating-Point Instructions (Contd) ④

NAME	MNEMONIC	OP CODE	FORMAT	OPERANDS
Compare, Long (c)	CDR	29	RR	R1,R2
Compare, Long (c)	CD	69	RX	R1,D2(X2,B2)
Compare, Short (c)	CER	39	RR	R1,R2
Compare, Short (c)	CE	79	RX	R1,D2(X2,B2)
Divide, Long	DDR	2D	RR	R1,R2
Divide, Long	DD	6D	RX	R1,D2(X2,B2)
Divide, Short	DER	3D	RR	R1,R2
Divide, Short	DE	7D	RX	R1,D2(X2,B2)
Halve, Long	HDR	24	RR	R1,R2
Halve, Short	HER	34	RR	R1,R2
Load and Test, Long (c)	LTDR	22	RR	R1,R2
Load and Test, Short (c)	LTER	32	RR	R1,R2
Load Complement, Long (c)	LCDR	23	RR	R1,R2
Load Complement, Short (c)	LCER	33	RR	R1,R2
Load, Long	LDR	28	RR	R1,R2
Load, Long	LD	68	RX	R1,D2(X2,B2)
Load Negative, Long (c)	LNDR	21	RR	R1,R2
Load Negative, Short (c)	LNER	31	RR	R1,R2
Load Positive, Long (c)	LPDR	20	RR	R1,R2
Load Positive, Short (c)	LPER	30	RR	R1,R2
Load Rounded, Extended to Long (x)	LRDR	25	RR	R1,R2
Load Rounded, Long to Short (x)	LRER	35	RR	R1,R2
Load, Short	LER	38	RR	R1,R2
Load, Short	LE	78	RX	R1,D2(X2,B2)
Multiply, Extended (x)	MXR	26	RR	R1,R2
Multiply, Long	MDR	2C	RR	R1,R2
Multiply, Long	MD	6C	RX	R1,D2(X2,B2)
Multiply, Long/Extended (x)	MXDR	27	RR	R1,R2
Multiply, Long/Extended (x)	MXD	67	RX	R1,D2(X2,B2)
Multiply, Short	MER	3C	RR	R1,R2
Multiply, Short	ME	7C	RX	R1,D2(X2,B2)
Store, Long	STD	60	RX	R1,D2(X2,B2)
Store, Short	STE	70	RX	R1,D2(X2,B2)
Subtract Normalized, Extended (c,x)	SXR	37	RR	R1,R2
Subtract Normalized, Long (c)	SDR	2B	RR	R1,R2
Subtract Normalized, Long (c)	SD	6B	RX	R1,D2(X2,B2)
Subtract Normalized, Short (c)	SER	3B	RR	R1,R2
Subtract Normalized, Short (c)	SE	7B	RX	R1,D2(X2,B2)
Subtract Unnormalized, Long (c)	SWR	2F	RR	R1,R2
Subtract Unnormalized, Long (c)	SW	6F	RX	R1,D2(X2,B2)
Subtract Unnormalized, Short (c)	SUR	3F	RR	R1,R2
Subtract Unnormalized, Short (c)	SU	7F	RX	R1,D2(X2,B2)

EXTENDED MNEMONIC INSTRUCTIONS†

Use	Extended Code* (RX or RR)	Meaning	Machine Instr.* (RX or RR)
General	B or *BR*	Unconditional Branch	BC or BCR 15,
	NOP or NOPR	No Operation	BC or BCR 0,
After Compare Instructions (A:B)	BH or *BHR*	Branch on A High	BC or BCR 2,
	BL or *BLR*	Branch on A Low	BC or BCR 4,
	BE or *BER*	Branch on A Equal B	BC or BCR 8,
	BNH or *BNHR*	Branch on A Not High	BC or BCR 13,
	BNL or *BNLR*	Branch on A Not Low	BC or BCR 11,
	BNE or *BNER*	Branch on A Not Equal B	BC or BCR 7,
After Arithmetic Instructions	BO or *BOR*	Branch on Overflow	BC or BCR 1,
	BP or *BPR*	Branch on Plus	BC or BCR 2,
	BM or *BMR*	Branch on Minus	BC or BCR 4,
	BNP or *BNPR*	Branch on Not Plus	BC or BCR 13,
	BNM or *BNMR*	Branch on Not Minus	BC or BCR 11,
	BNZ or *BNZR*	Branch on Not Zero	BC or BCR 7,
	BZ or *BZR*	Branch on Zero	BC or BCR 8,
After Test under Mask Instruction	BO or *BOR*	Branch if Ones	BC or BCR 1,
	BM or *BMR*	Branch if Mixed	BC or BCR 4,
	BZ or *BZR*	Branch if Zeros	BC or BCR 8,
	BNO or *BNOR*	Branch if Not Ones	BC or BCR 14,

*Second operand not shown; in all cases it is D2(X2,B2) for RX format or R2 for RR format.
†For OS/VS and DOS/VS; source: GC33-4010.

EDIT AND EDMK PATTERN CHARACTERS (in hex)

20—digit selector	40—blank	5C—asterisk
21—start of significance	4B—period	6B—comma
22—field separator	5B—dollar sign	C3D9—CR

CONDITION CODES ⑤

Condition Code Setting	0	1	2	3
Mask Bit Value	8	4	2	1

General Instructions

Add, Add Halfword	zero	<zero	>zero	overflow
Add Logical	zero,	not zero,	zero,	not zero,
	no carry	no carry	carry	carry
AND	zero	not zero	—	—
Compare, Compare Halfword	equal	1st op low	1st op high	—
Compare and Swap/Double	equal	not equal	—	—
Compare Logical	equal	1st op low	1st op high	—
Exclusive OR	zero	not zero	—	—
Insert Characters under Mask	all zero	1st bit one	1st bit zero	—
Load and Test	zero	<zero	>zero	—
Load Complement	zero	<zero	>zero	overflow
Load Negative	zero	<zero	—	—
Load Positive	zero	—	>zero	overflow
Move Long	count equal	count low	count high	overlap
OR	zero	not zero	—	—
Shift Left Double/Single	zero	<zero	>zero	overflow
Shift Right Double/Single	zero	<zero	>zero	—
Store Clock	set	not set	error	not oper
Subtract, Subtract Halfword	zero	<zero	>zero	overflow
Subtract Logical	—	not zero,	zero,	not zero,
		no carry	carry	carry
Test and Set	zero	one	—	—
Test under Mask	zero	mixed	—	ones
Translate and Test	zero	incomplete	complete	—

Decimal Instructions

Add Decimal	zero	<zero	>zero	overflow
Compare Decimal	equal	1st op low	1st op high	—
Edit, Edit and Mark	zero	<zero	>zero	—
Shift and Round Decimal	zero	<zero	>zero	overflow
Subtract Decimal	zero	<zero	>zero	overflow
Zero and Add	zero	<zero	>zero	overflow

Floating-Point Instructions

Add Normalized	zero	<zero	>zero	—
Add Unnormalized	zero	<zero	>zero	—
Compare	equal	1st op low	1st op high	—
Load and Test	zero	<zero	>zero	—
Load Complement	zero	<zero	>zero	—
Load Negative	zero	<zero	—	—
Load Positive	zero	—	>zero	—
Subtract Normalized	zero	<zero	>zero	—
Subtract Unnormalized	zero	<zero	>zero	—

Input/Output Instructions

Clear I/O	no oper in progress	CSW stored	chan busy	not oper
Halt Device	interruption pending	CSW stored	channel working	not oper
Halt I/O	interruption pending	CSW stored	burst op stopped	not oper
Start I/O, SIOF	successful	CSW stored	busy	not oper
Store Channel ID	ID stored	CSW stored	busy	not oper
Test Channel	available	interruption pending	burst mode	not oper
Test I/O	available	CSW stored	busy	not oper

System Control Instructions

Load Real Address	translation available	ST entry invalid	PT entry invalid	length violation
Reset Reference Bit	R=0, C=0	R=0, C=1	R=1, C=0	R=1, C=1
Set Clock	set	secure	—	not oper
Signal Processor	accepted	stat stored	busy	not oper

CNOP ALIGNMENT

DOUBLEWORD							
WORD				WORD			
HALFWORD		HALFWORD		HALFWORD		HALFWORD	
BYTE	BYTE	BYTE	BYTE	BYTE	BYTE	BYTE	BYTE

0,4	2,4	0,4	2,4
0,8	2,8	4,8	6,8

ASSEMBLER INSTRUCTIONS† ⑥

Function	Mnemonic	Meaning
Data definition	DC	Define constant
	DS	Define storage
	CCW	Define channel command word
Program sectioning and linking	START	Start assembly
	CSECT	Identify control section
	DSECT	Identify dummy section
	DXD*	Define external dummy section
	CXD*	Cumulative length of external dummy section
	COM	Identify blank common control section
	ENTRY	Identify entry-point symbol
	EXTRN	Identify external symbol
	WXTRN	Identify weak external symbol
Base register assignment	USING	Use base address register
	DROP	Drop base address register
Control of listings	TITLE	Identify assembly output
	EJECT	Start new page
	SPACE	Space listing
	PRINT	Print optional data
Program Control	ICTL	Input control
	ISEQ	Input sequence checking
	PUNCH	Punch a card
	REPRO	Reproduce following card
	ORG	Set location counter
	EQU	Equate symbol
	OPSYN*	Equate operation code
	PUSH	Save current PRINT or USING status
	POP	Restore PRINT or USING status
	LTORG	Begin literal pool
	CNOP	Conditional no operation
	COPY	Copy predefined source coding
	END	End assembly
Macro definition	MACRO	Macro definition header
	MNOTE	Request for error message
	MEXIT	Macro definition exit
	MEND	Macro definition trailer
Conditional assembly	ACTR	Conditional assembly loop counter
	AGO	Unconditional branch
	AIF	Conditional branch
	ANOP	Assembly no operation
	GBLA	Define global SETA symbol
	GBLB	Define global SETB symbol
	GBLC	Define global SETC symbol
	LCLA	Define local SETA symbol
	LCLB	Define local SETB symbol
	LCLC	Define local SETC symbol
	SETA	Set arithmetic variable symbol
	SETB	Set binary variable symbol
	SETC	Set character variable symbol

SUMMARY OF CONSTANTS†

TYPE	IMPLIED LENGTH, BYTES	ALIGNMENT	FORMAT	TRUNCA-TION/PADDING
C	—	byte	characters	right
X	—	byte	hexadecimal digits	left
B	—	byte	binary digits	left
F	4	word	fixed-point binary	left
H	2	halfword	fixed-point binary	left
E	4	word	short floating-point	right
D	8	doubleword	long floating-point	right
L	16	doubleword	extended floating-point	right
P	—	byte	packed decimal	left
Z	—	byte	zoned decimal	left
A	4	word	value of address	left
Y	2	halfword	value of address	left
S	2	halfword	address in base-displacement form	—
V	4	word	externally defined address value	left
Q*	4	word	symbol naming a DXD or DSECT	left

†For OS/VS and DOS/VS; source: GC33-4010.
*OS/VS only.

I/O COMMAND CODES ⑦

Standard Command Code Assignments (CCW bits 0-7)

xxxx 0000	Invalid	tttt tt01	Write
tttt 0100	Sense	tttt tt10	Read
xxxx 1000	Transfer in Channel	tttt tt11	Control
tttt 1100	Read Backward	0000 0011	Control No Operation

x—Bit ignored. †Modifier bit for specific type of I/O device

CONSOLE PRINTERS

Write, No Carrier Return	01	Sense	04
Write, Auto Carrier Return	09	Audible Alarm	0B
Read Inquiry	0A		

3504, 3505 CARD READERS/3525 CARD PUNCH

Source: GA21-9124

Command	Binary	Hex
Sense	0000 0100	04
Feed, Select Stacker	SS10 F011	
Read Only*	11D0 F010	
Diagnostic Read	1101 0010	D2
Read, Feed, Select Stacker*	SSD0 F010	
Write RCE Format*	0001 0001	11
<u>3504, 3505 only</u>		
Write OMR Format†	0011 0001	31
<u>3525 only</u>		
Write, Feed, Select Stacker	SSD0 0001	
Print Line*	LLLL L101	

Bit Meanings

<u>SS</u>	<u>Stacker</u>
00	1
01/10	2
<u>F</u>	<u>Format Mode</u>
0	Unformatted
1	Formatted
<u>D</u>	<u>Data Mode</u>
0	1–EBCDIC
1	2–Card image
<u>L</u>	<u>Line Position</u>
	5-bit binary value

*Special feature on 3525. †Special feature.

PRINTERS: 3211/3811 (GA24-3543), 3203/IPA, 1403*/2821 (GA24-3312)

	After Write	*Immed*
Space 1 Line	09	0B
Space 2 Lines	11	13
Space 3 Lines	19	1B
Skip to Channel 0†	–	83
Skip to Channel 1	89	8B
Skip to Channel 2	91	93
Skip to Channel 3	99	9B
Skip to Channel 4	A1	A3
Skip to Channel 5	A9	AB
Skip to Channel 6	B1	B3
Skip to Channel 7	B9	BB
Skip to Channel 8	C1	C3
Skip to Channel 9	C9	CB
Skip to Channel 10	D1	D3
Skip to Channel 11	D9	DB
Skip to Channel 12	E1	E3

Write without spacing	01
Sense	04
Load UCSB without folding	FB
Fold†	43
Unfold†	23
Load UCSB and Fold (exc. 3211)	F3
UCS Gate Load (1403 only)	EB
Load FCB†	63
Block Data Check	73
Allow Data Check	7B
Read PLB†	02
Read UCSB†	0A
Read FCB†	12
Diag. Check Read (exc. 3203)	06
Diagnostic Write†	05
Raise Cover†	6B
Diagnostic Gate†	07
Diagnostic Read (1403 only)	02

*UCS special feature; IPA diagnostics are model-dependent. †3211 only.

3420/3803, 3410/3411 MAGNETIC TAPE

(**Indicates 3420 only)

See GA32-0020, -0021, -0022 for special features and functions of specific models.

Write	01
Read Forward	02
Read Backward	0C
Sense	04
Sense Reserve**	F4
Sense Release**	D4
Request Track-in-Error	1B
Loop Write-to-Read**	8B
Set Diagnose**	4B
Rewind	07
Rewind Unload	0F
Erase Gap	17
Write Tape Mark	1F
Backspace Block	27
Backspace File	2F
Forward Space Block	37
Forward Space File	3F
Data Security Erase **	97
Diagnostic Mode Set **	0B

Mode Set 1 (7-track)

Density	Parity	DC	Trans	Cmd
200	odd	on	off	13
		off	off	33
			on	3B
	even	off	off	23
			on	2B
556	odd	on	off	53
		off	off	73
			on	7B
	even	off	off	63
			on	6B
800	odd	on	off	93
		off	off	B3
			on	BB
	even	off	off	A3
			on	AB

Mode Set 2 (9-track), 800 bpi	CB
Mode Set 2 (9-track), 1600 bpi	C3
Mode Set 2 (9-track), 6250 bpi**	D3

I/O COMMAND CODES (Contd) ⑧

DIRECT ACCESS STORAGE DEVICES:

3330-3340 SERIES (GA26-1592, -1617, -1619, -1620);
2305/2835 (GA26-1589); **2314, 2319** (GA26-3599, -1606)

	Command	MT Off	MT On*	Count
Control	Orient (c)	2B		Nonzero
	Recalibrate	13		Nonzero
	Seek	07		6
	Seek Cylinder	0B		6
	Seek Head	1B		6
	Space Count	0F		3 (a); nonzero (d)
	Set File Mask	1F		1
	Set Sector (a,f)	23		1
	Restore (executes as a no-op)	17		Nonzero
	Vary Sensing (c)	27		1
	Diagnostic Load (a)	53		1
	Diagnostic Write (a)	73		512
Search	Home Address Equal	39	B9	4
	Identifier Equal	31	B1	5
	Identifier High	51	D1	5
	Identifier Equal or High	71	F1	5
	Key Equal	29	A9	KL
	Key High	49	C9	KL
	Key Equal or High	69	E9	KL
	Key and Data Equal (d)	2D	AD	Number of bytes (including mask bytes) in search argument
	Key and Data High (d)	4D	CD	
	Key and Data Eq. or Hi (d)	6D	ED	
Continue Scan	Search Equal (d)	25	A5	
	Search High (d)	45	C5	
	Search High or Equal (d)	65	E5	
	Set Compare (d)	35	B5	
	Set Compare (d)	75	F5	
	No Compare (d)	55	D5	
Read	Home Address	1A	9A	5
	Count	12	92	8
	Record 0	16	96	Number of bytes to be transferred
	Data	06	86	
	Key and Data	0E	8E	
	Count, Key and Data	1E	9E	
	IPL	02		
	Sector (a,f)	22		1
Sense	Sense I/O	04		24 (a); 6 (d)
	Read, Reset Buffered Log (b)	A4		24
	Read Buffered Log (c)	24		128
	Device Release (e)	94		24 (a); 6 (d)
	Device Reserve (e)	B4		24 (a); 6 (d)
	Read Diagnostic Status 1 (a)	44		16 or 512
Write	Home Address	19		5 (exc. 7 on 3340)
	Record 0	15		8+KL+DL of R0
	Erase	11		8+KL+DL
	Count, Key and Data	1D		8+KL+DL
	Special Count, Key and Data	01		8+KL+DL
	Data	05		DL
	Key and Data	0D		KL+DL

* Code same as MT Off except as listed.
a. Except 2314, 2319.
b. 3330-3340 Series only; manual reset on 3340.
c. 2305/2835 only.
d. 2314, 2319 only.
e. String switch or 2-channel switch feature required; standard on 2314 with 2844.
f. Special feature required on 3340.

IBM

International Business Machines Corporation
Data Processing Division
1133 Westchester Avenue, White Plains, New York 10604
(U.S.A. only)

IBM World Trade Corporation
821 United Nations Plaza, New York, New York 10017
(International)

Printed in U.S.A. GX20-1850-2

CODE TRANSLATION TABLE ⑨

Dec.	Hex	Instruction (RR)	BCDIC	EBCDIC(1)	ASCII	7-Track Tape BCDIC(2)	EBCDIC Card Code	Binary
0	00			NUL	NUL		12-0-1-8-9	0000 0000
1	01			SOH	SOH		12-1-9	0000 0001
2	02			STX	STX		12-2-9	0000 0010
3	03			ETX	ETX		12-3-9	0000 0011
4	04	SPM		PF	EOT		12-4-9	0000 0100
5	05	BALR		HT	ENQ		12-5-9	0000 0101
6	06	BCTR		LC	ACK		12-6-9	0000 0110
7	07	BCR		DEL	BEL		12-7-9	0000 0111
8	08	SSK			BS		12-8-9	0000 1000
9	09	ISK			HT		12-1-8-9	0000 1001
10	0A	SVC		SMM	LF		12-2-8-9	0000 1010
11	0B			VT	VT		12-3-8-9	0000 1011
12	0C			FF	FF		12-4-8-9	0000 1100
13	0D			CR	CR		12-5-8-9	0000 1101
14	0E	MVCL		SO	SO		12-6-8-9	0000 1110
15	0F	CLCL		SI	SI		12-7-8-9	0000 1111
16	10	LPR		DLE	DLE		12-11-1-8-9	0001 0000
17	11	LNR		DC1	DC1		11-1-9	0001 0001
18	12	LTR		DC2	DC2		11-2-9	0001 0010
19	13	LCR		TM	DC3		11-3-9	0001 0011
20	14	NR		RES	DC4		11-4-9	0001 0100
21	15	CLR		NL	NAK		11-5-9	0001 0101
22	16	OR		BS	SYN		11-6-9	0001 0110
23	17	XR		IL	ETB		11-7-9	0001 0111
24	18	LR		CAN	CAN		11-8-9	0001 1000
25	19	CR		EM	EM		11-1-8-9	0001 1001
26	1A	AR		CC	SUB		11-2-8-9	0001 1010
27	1B	SR		CU1	ESC		11-3-8-9	0001 1011
28	1C	MR		IFS	FS		11-4-8-9	0001 1100
29	1D	DR		IGS	GS		11-5-8-9	0001 1101
30	1E	ALR		IRS	RS		11-6-8-9	0001 1110
31	1F	SLR		IUS	US		11-7-8-9	0001 1111
32	20	LPDR		DS	SP		11-0-1-8-9	0010 0000
33	21	LNDR		SOS	!		0-1-9	0010 0001
34	22	LTDR		FS	"		0-2-9	0010 0010
35	23	LCDR			#		0-3-9	0010 0011
36	24	HDR		BYP	$		0-4-9	0010 0100
37	25	LRDR		LF	%		0-5-9	0010 0101
38	26	MXR		ETB	&		0-6-9	0010 0110
39	27	MXDR		ESC	'		0-7-9	0010 0111
40	28	LDR			(		0-8-9	0010 1000
41	29	CDR			)		0-1-8-9	0010 1001
42	2A	ADR		SM	*		0-2-8-9	0010 1010
43	2B	SDR		CU2	+		0-3-8-9	0010 1011
44	2C	MDR			,		0-4-8-9	0010 1100
45	2D	DDR		ENQ	-		0-5-8-9	0010 1101
46	2E	AWR		ACK	.		0-6-8-9	0010 1110
47	2F	SWR		BEL	/		0-7-8-9	0010 1111
48	30	LPER			0		12-11-0-1-8-9	0011 0000
49	31	LNER			1		1-9	0011 0001
50	32	LTER		SYN	2		2-9	0011 0010
51	33	LCER			3		3-9	0011 0011
52	34	HER		PN	4		4-9	0011 0100
53	35	LRER		RS	5		5-9	0011 0101
54	36	AXR		UC	6		6-9	0011 0110
55	37	SXR		EOT	7		7-9	0011 0111
56	38	LER			8		8-9	0011 1000
57	39	CER			9		1-8-9	0011 1001
58	3A	AER			:		2-8-9	0011 1010
59	3B	SER		CU3	;		3-8-9	0011 1011
60	3C	MER		DC4	<		4-8-9	0011 1100
61	3D	DER		NAK	=		5-8-9	0011 1101
62	3E	AUR			>		6-8-9	0011 1110
63	3F	SUR		SUB	?		7-8-9	0011 1111

CODE TRANSLATION TABLE (Contd) ⑩

Dec.	Hex	Instruction (RX)	BCDIC	EBCDIC(1)	ASCII	7-Track Tape BCDIC(2)	EBCDIC Card Code	Binary
64	40	STH	Sp	Sp	@	(3)	no punches	0100 0000
65	41	LA			A		12-0-1-9	0100 0001
66	42	STC			B		12-0-2-9	0100 0010
67	43	IC			C		12-0-3-9	0100 0011
68	44	EX			D		12-0-4-9	0100 0100
69	45	BAL			E		12-0-5-9	0100 0101
70	46	BCT			F		12-0-6-9	0100 0110
71	47	BC			G		12-0-7-9	0100 0111
72	48	LH			H		12-0-8-9	0100 1000
73	49	CH			I		12-1-8	0100 1001
74	4A	AH		¢ ¢	J		12-2-8	0100 1010
75	4B	SH	.	. .	K	B A 8 21	12-3-8	0100 1011
76	4C	MH	⌑)	< <	L	B A 84	12-4-8	0100 1100
77	4D		[	((	M	B A 84 1	12-5-8	0100 1101
78	4E	CVD	<	+ +	N	B A 842	12-6-8	0100 1110
79	4F	CVB	‡	| |	O	B A 8421	12-7-8	0100 1111
80	50	ST	& +	& &	P	B A	12	0101 0000
81	51				Q		12-11-1-9	0101 0001
82	52				R		12-11-2-9	0101 0010
83	53				S		12-11-3-9	0101 0011
84	54	N			T		12-11-4-9	0101 0100
85	55	CL			U		12-11-5-9	0101 0101
86	56	O			V		12-11-6-9	0101 0110
87	57	X			W		12-11-7-9	0101 0111
88	58	L			X		12-11-8-9	0101 1000
89	59	C			Y		11-1-8	0101 1001
90	5A	A		! !	Z		11-2-8	0101 1010
91	5B	S	$	$ $	[	B 8 21	11-3-8	0101 1011
92	5C	M	*	* *	\	B 84	11-4-8	0101 1100
93	5D		]	))	]	B 84 1	11-5-8	0101 1101
94	5E	AL	;	; ;	^	B 842	11-6-8	0101 1110
95	5F		Δ	¬ ¬	_	B 8421	11-7-8	0101 1111
96	60	STD	-	- -	`	B	11	0110 0000
97	61		/	/ /	a	A 1	0-1	0110 0001
98	62				b		11-0-2-9	0110 0010
99	63				c		11-0-3-9	0110 0011
100	64				d		11-0-4-9	0110 0100
101	65				e		11-0-5-9	0110 0101
102	66				f		11-0-6-9	0110 0110
103	67	MXD			g		11-0-7-9	0110 0111
104	68	LD			h		11-0-8-9	0110 1000
105	69	CD			i		0-1-8	0110 1001
106	6A	AD			j		12-11	0110 1010
107	6B	SD	,	, ,	k	A 8 21	0-3-8-1	0110 1011
108	6C	MD	%(	% %	l	A 84	0-4-8	0110 1100
109	6D	DD	¥	_ _	m	A 84 1	0-5-8	0110 1101
110	6E		\	> >	n	A 842	0-6-8	0110 1110
111	6F	SW	⇥	? ?	o	A 8421	0-7-8	0110 1111
112	70	STE			p		12-11-0	0111 0000
113	71				q		12-11-0-1-9	0111 0001
114	72				r		12-11-0-2-9	0111 0010
115	73				s		12-11-0-3-9	0111 0011
116	74				t		12-11-0-4-9	0111 0100
117	75				u		12-11-0-5-9	0111 0101
118	76				v		12-11-0-6-9	0111 0110
119	77				w		12-11-0-7-9	0111 0111
120	78	LE			x		12-11-0-8-9	0111 1000
121	79	CE		`	y		1-8	0111 1001
122	7A	AE	ǂ	: :	z	A	2-8	0111 1010
123	7B	SE	#	# #	{	8 21	3-8	0111 1011
124	7C	ME	@'	@ @	|	84	4-8	0111 1100
125	7D	DE	:	' '	}	84 1	5-8	0111 1101
126	7E	AU	>	= =	~	842	6-8	0111 1110
127	7F	SU	√	" "	DEL	8421	7-8	0111 1111

1. Two columns of EBCDIC graphics are shown. The first gives standard bit pattern assignments. The second shows the T-11 and TN text printing chains (120 graphics).
2. Add C (check bit) for odd or even parity as needed, except as noted.
3. For even parity use CA.

TWO-CHARACTER BSC DATA LINK CONTROLS

Function	EBCDIC	ASCII
ACK-0	DLE,X'70'	DLE,0
ACK-1	DLE,X'61'	DLE,1
WACK	DLE,X'6B'	DLE, ;
RVI	DLE,X'7C'	DLE,<

CODE TRANSLATION TABLE (Contd)   ⑪

Dec.	Hex	Instruction and Format	BCDIC	EBCDIC(1)	ASCII	7-Track Tape BCDIC(2)	EBCDIC Card Code	Binary
128	80	SSM -S					12-0-1-8	1000 0000
129	81			a	a		12-0-1	1000 0001
130	82	LPSW -S		b	b		12-0-2	1000 0010
131	83	Diagnose		c	c		12-0-3	1000 0011
132	84	WRD -SI		d	d		12-0-4	1000 0100
133	85	RDD		e	e		12-0-5	1000 0101
134	86	BXH		f	f		12-0-6	1000 0110
135	87	BXLE		g	g		12-0-7	1000 0111
136	88	SRL		h	h		12-0-8	1000 1000
137	89	SLL		i	i		12-0-9	1000 1001
138	8A	SRA					12-0-2-8	1000 1010
139	8B	SLA -RS		{			12-0-3-8	1000 1011
140	8C	SRDL		≤			12-0-4-8	1000 1100
141	8D	SLDL		(			12-0-5-8	1000 1101
142	8E	SRDA		+			12-0-6-8	1000 1110
143	8F	SLDA		+			12-0-7-8	1000 1111
144	90	STM					12-11-1-8	1001 0000
145	91	TM -SI		j	j		12-11-1	1001 0001
146	92	MVI		k	k		12-11-2	1001 0010
147	93	TS -S		l	l		12-11-3	1001 0011
148	94	NI		m	m		12-11-4	1001 0100
149	95	CLI		n	n		12-11-5	1001 0101
150	96	OI -SI		o	o		12-11-6	1001 0110
151	97	XI		p	p		12-11-7	1001 0111
152	98	LM -RS		q	q		12-11-8	1001 1000
153	99			r	r		12-11-9	1001 1001
154	9A						12-11-2-8	1001 1010
155	9B			}			12-11-3-8	1001 1011
156	9C	SIO, SIOF		⊡			12-11-4-8	1001 1100
157	9D	TIO, CLRIO }S		)			12-11-5-8	1001 1101
158	9E	HIO, HDV		±			12-11-6-8	1001 1110
159	9F	TCH		■			12-11-7-8	1001 1111
160	A0			¬			11-0-1-8	1010 0000
161	A1		~	a			11-0-1	1010 0001
162	A2		s	s			11-0-2	1010 0010
163	A3		t	t			11-0-3	1010 0011
164	A4		u	u			11-0-4	1010 0100
165	A5		v	v			11-0-5	1010 0101
166	A6		w	w			11-0-6	1010 0110
167	A7		x	x			11-0-7	1010 0111
168	A8		y	y			11-0-8	1010 1000
169	A9		z	z			11-0-9	1010 1001
170	AA						11-0-2-8	1010 1010
171	AB			⌐			11-0-3-8	1010 1011
172	AC	STNSM }SI		⌐			11-0-4-8	1010 1100
173	AD	STOSM		[			11-0-5-8	1010 1101
174	AE	SIGP -RS		≥			11-0-6-8	1010 1110
175	AF	MC -SI		●			11-0-7-8	1010 1111
176	B0			°			12-11-0-1-8	1011 0000
177	B1	LRA -RX		1			12-11-0-1	1011 0001
178	B2	See below		2			12-11-0-2	1011 0010
179	B3			3			12-11-0-3	1011 0011
180	B4			4			12-11-0-4	1011 0100
181	B5			5			12-11-0-5	1011 0101
182	B6	STCTL }RS		6			12-11-0-6	1011 0110
183	B7	LCTL		7			12-11-0-7	1011 0111
184	B8			8			12-11-0-8	1011 1000
185	B9			9			12-11-0-9	1011 1001
186	BA	CS					12-11-0-2-8	1011 1010
187	BB	CDS }RS		⌐			12-11-0-3-8	1011 1011
188	BC			┐			12-11-0-4-8	1011 1100
189	BD	CLM		]			12-11-0-5-8	1011 1101
190	BE	STCM }RS		≠			12-11-0-6-8	1011 1110
191	BF	ICM		—			12-11-0-7-8	1011 1111

Op code (S format):

B202 - STIDP	B207 - STCKC	B20D - PTLB
B203 - STIDC	B208 - SPT	B210 - SPX
B204 - SCK	B209 - STPT	B211 - STPX
B205 - STCK	B20A - SPKA	B212 - STAP
B206 - SCKC	B20B - IPK	B213 - RRB

CODE TRANSLATION TABLE (Contd)   ⑫

Dec.	Hex	Instruction (SS)	BCDIC	EBCDIC(1)	ASCII	7-Track Tape BCDIC(2)	EBCDIC Card Code	Binary
192	C0		?	{		B A 8 2	12-0	1100 0000
193	C1		A	A	A	B A 1	12-1	1100 0001
194	C2		B	B	B	B A 2	12-2	1100 0010
195	C3		C	C	C	B A 2 1	12-3	1100 0011
196	C4		D	D	D	B A 4	12-4	1100 0100
197	C5		E	E	E	B A 4 1	12-5	1100 0101
198	C6		F	F	F	B A 4 2	12-6	1100 0110
199	C7		G	G	G	B A 4 2 1	12-7	1100 0111
200	C8		H	H	H	B A 8	12-8	1100 1000
201	C9		I	I	I	B A 8 1	12-9	1100 1001
202	CA						12-0-2-8-9	1100 1010
203	CB						12-0-3-8-9	1100 1011
204	CC			∫			12-0-4-8-9	1100 1100
205	CD						12-0-5-8-9	1100 1101
206	CE			⑂			12-0-6-8-9	1100 1110
207	CF						12-0-7-8-9	1100 1111
208	D0			}		B 8 2	11-0	1101 0000
209	D1	MVN	J	J	J	B 1	11-1	1101 0001
210	D2	MVC	K	K	K	B 2	11-2	1101 0010
211	D3	MVZ	L	L	L	B 2 1	11-3	1101 0011
212	D4	NC	M	M	M	B 4	11-4	1101 0100
213	D5	CLC	N	N	N	B 4 1	11-5	1101 0101
214	D6	OC	O	O	O	B 4 2	11-6	1101 0110
215	D7	XC	P	P	P	B 4 2 1	11-7	1101 0111
216	D8		Q	Q	Q	B 8	11-8	1101 1000
217	D9		R	R	R	B 8 1	11-9	1101 1001
218	DA						12-11-2-8-9	1101 1010
219	DB						12-11-3-8-9	1101 1011
220	DC	TR					12-11-4-8-9	1101 1100
221	DD	TRT					12-11-5-8-9	1101 1101
222	DE	ED					12-11-6-8-9	1101 1110
223	DF	EDMK					12-11-7-8-9	1101 1111
224	E0		‡	\		A 8 2	0-2-8	1110 0000
225	E1						11-0-1-9	1110 0001
226	E2		S	S	S	A 2	0-2	1110 0010
227	E3		T	T	T	A 2 1	0-3	1110 0011
228	E4		U	U	U	A 4	0-4	1110 0100
229	E5		V	V	V	A 4 1	0-5	1110 0101
230	E6		W	W	W	A 4 2	0-6	1110 0110
231	E7		X	X	X	A 4 2 1	0-7	1110 0111
232	E8		Y	Y	Y	A 8	0-8	1110 1000
233	E9		Z	Z	Z	A 8 1	0-9	1110 1001
234	EA						11-0-2-8-9	1110 1010
235	EB						11-0-3-8-9	1110 1011
236	EC			⌐			11-0-4-8-9	1110 1100
237	ED						11-0-5-8-9	1110 1101
238	EE						11-0-6-8-9	1110 1110
239	EF						11-0-7-8-9	1110 1111
240	F0	SRP	0	0	0	8 2	0	1111 0000
241	F1	MVO	1	1	1	1	1	1111 0001
242	F2	PACK	2	2	2	2	2	1111 0010
243	F3	UNPK	3	3	3	2 1	3	1111 0011
244	F4		4	4	4	4	4	1111 0100
245	F5		5	5	5	4 1	5	1111 0101
246	F6		6	6	6	4 2	6	1111 0110
247	F7		7	7	7	4 2 1	7	1111 0111
248	F8	ZAP	8	8	8	8	8	1111 1000
249	F9	CP	9	9	9	8 1	9	1111 1001
250	FA	AP		I			12-11-0-2-8-9	1111 1010
251	FB	SP					12-11-0-3-8-9	1111 1011
252	FC	MP					12-11-0-4-8-9	1111 1100
253	FD	DP					12-11-0-5-8-9	1111 1101
254	FE						12-11-0-6-8-9	1111 1110
255	FF			EO			12-11-0-7-8-9	1111 1111

ANSI-DEFINED PRINTER CONTROL CHARACTERS
(A in RECFM field of DCB)

Code	Action before printing record
blank	Space 1 line
0	Space 2 lines
-	Space 3 lines
+	Suppress space
1	Skip to line 1 on new page

MACHINE INSTRUCTION FORMATS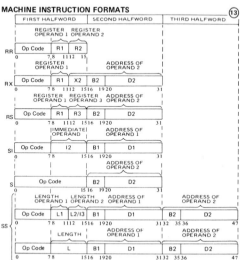

CONTROL REGISTERS

CR	Bits	Name of field	Associated with	Init.
0	0	Block-multiplex'g control	Block-multiplex'g	0
	1	SSM suppression control	SSM instruction	0
	2	TOD clock sync control	Multiprocessing	0
	8-9	Page size control		0
	10	Unassigned (must be zero)	Dynamic addr. transl.	0
	11-12	Segment size control		0
	16	Malfunction alert mask		0
	17	Emergency signal mask		0
	18	External call mask	Multiprocessing	0
	19	TOD clock sync check mask		0
	20	Clock comparator mask	Clock comparator	0
	21	CPU timer mask	CPU timer	0
	24	Interval timer mask	Interval timer	1
	25	Interrupt key mask	Interrupt key	1
	26	External signal mask	External signal	1
1	0-7	Segment table length	Dynamic addr. transl.	0
	8-25	Segment table address		0
2	0-31	Channel masks	Channels	1
8	16-31	Monitor masks	Monitoring	0
9	0	Successful branching event mask		0
	1	Instruction fetching event mask		0
	2	Storage alteration event mask	Program-event record'g	0
	3	GR alteration event mask		0
	16-31	PER general register masks		0
10	8-31	PER starting address	Program-event record'g	0
11	8-31	PER ending address	Program-event record'g	0
14	0	Check-stop control	Machine-check handling	1
	1	Synch. MCEL control		1
	2	I/O extended logout control	I/O extended logout	0
	4	Recovery report mask		0
	5	Degradation report mask		0
	6	Ext. damage report mask	Machine-check handling	1
	7	Warning mask		0
	8	Asynch. MCEL control		0
	9	Asynch. fixed log control		0
15	8-28	MCEL address	Machine-check handling	512

PROGRAM STATUS WORD (BC Mode)

0-5 Channel 0 to 5 masks
6 Mask for channel 6 and up
7 (E) External mask
12 (C=0) Basic control mode
13 (M) Machine-check mask
14 (W=1) Wait state
15 (P=1) Problem state

32-33 (ILC) Instruction length code
34-35 (CC) Condition code
36 Fixed-point overflow mask
37 Decimal overflow mask
38 Exponent underflow mask
39 Significance mask

PROGRAM STATUS WORD (EC Mode)

1 (R) Program event recording mask
5 (T=1) Translation mode
6 (I) Input/output mask
7 (E) External mask
12 (C=1) Extended control mode
13 (M) Machine-check mask
14 (W=1) Wait state

15 (P=1) Problem state
18-19 (CC) Condition code
20 Fixed-point overflow mask
21 Decimal overflow mask
22 Exponent underflow mask
23 Significance mask

CHANNEL COMMAND WORD

CD—bit 32 (80) causes use of address portion of next CCW.
CC—bit 33 (40) causes use of command code and data address of next CCW.
SLI—bit 34 (20) causes suppression of possible incorrect length indication.
Skip—bit 35 (10) suppresses transfer of information to main storage.
PCI—bit 36 (08) causes a channel program controlled interruption.
IDA—bit 37 (04) causes bits 8-31 of CCW to specify location of first IDAW.

CHANNEL STATUS WORD (hex 40)

5 Logout pending
6-7 Deferred condition code
32 (80) Attention
33 (40) Status modifier
34 (20) Control unit end
35 (10) Busy
36 (08) Channel end
37 (04) Device end
38 (02) Unit check
39 (01) Unit exception

40 (80) Program-controlled interruption
41 (40) Incorrect length
42 (20) Program check
43 (10) Protection check
44 (08) Channel data check
45 (04) Channel control check
46 (02) Interface control check
47 (01) Chaining check
48-63 Residual byte count for the
last CCW used

PROGRAM INTERRUPTION CODES

0001	Operation exception	000C	Exponent overflow excp
0002	Privileged operation excp	000D	Exponent underflow excp
0003	Execute exception	000E	Significance exception
0004	Protection exception	000F	Floating-point divide excp
0005	Addressing exception	0010	Segment translation excp
0006	Specification exception	0011	Page translation exception
0007	Data exception	0012	Translation specification excp
0008	Fixed-point overflow excp	0013	Special operation exception
0009	Fixed-point divide excp	0040	Monitor event
000A	Decimal overflow exception	0080	Program event (code may be
000B	Decimal divide exception		combined with another code)

⫽ED STORAGE LOCATIONS ⑮

ea, ec.	Hex addr	EC only	Function
⫽ 7	0		Initial program loading PSW, restart new PSW
⫽ 15	8		Initial program loading CCW1, restart old PSW
⫽ 23	10		Initial program loading CCW2
⫽ 31	18		External old PSW
⫽ 39	20		Supervisor Call old PSW
⫽ 47	28		Program old PSW
⫽ 55	30		Machine-check old PSW
⫽ 63	38		Input/output old PSW
⫽ 71	40		Channel status word (see diagram)
⫽ 75	48		Channel address word [0-3 key, 4-7 zeros, 8-31 CCW address]
⫽ 83	50		Interval timer
⫽ 95	58		External new PSW
⫽-103	60		Supervisor Call new PSW
⫽-111	68		Program new PSW
⫽-119	70		Machine-check new PSW
⫽-127	78		Input/output new PSW
⫽-133	84		CPU address assoc'd with external interruption, or unchanged
⫽-133	84	X	CPU address assoc'd with external interruption, or zeros
⫽-135	86	X	External interruption code
⫽-139	88	X	SVC interruption [0-12 zeros, 13-14 ILC, 15:0, 16-31 code]
⫽-143	8C	X	Program interrupt. [0-12 zeros, 13-14 ILC, 15:0, 16-31 code]
⫽-147	90	X	Translation exception address [0-7 zeros, 8-31 address]
⫽-149	94		Monitor class [0-7 zeros, 8-15 class number]
⫽-151	96	X	PER interruption code [0-3 code, 4-15 zeros]
⫽-155	98	X	PER address [0-7 zeros, 8-31 address]
⫽-159	9C		Monitor code [0-7 zeros, 8-31 monitor code]
⫽-171	A8		Channel ID [0-3 type, 4-15 model, 16-31 max. IOEL length]
⫽-175	AC		I/O extended logout address [0-7 unused, 8-31 address]
⫽-179	B0		Limited channel logout (see diagram)
⫽-187	B9	X	I/O address [0-7 zeros, 8-23 address]
⫽-223	D8		CPU timer save area
⫽-231	E0		Clock comparator save area
⫽-239	E8		Machine-check interruption code (see diagram)
⫽-251	F8		Failing processor storage address [0-7 zeros, 8-31 address]
⫽-255	FC		Region code*
⫽-351	100		Fixed logout area*
⫽-383	160		Floating-point ⫽egister save area
⫽-447	180		General register save area
⫽-511	1C0		Control register save area
⫽ †	200		CPU extended logout area (size varies)

⫽ vary among models; see system library manuals for specific model.
⫽cation may be changed by programming (bits 8-28 of CR 15 specify address).

⫽MITED CHANNEL LOGOUT (hex B0)

⫽CU id	Detect		Source	000	Field validity flags	TT	00	A	Seq.
0	3	4	7 8	12 13	15 16	23 24	26	28 29	31

⫽CPU	12 Control unit
⫽Channel	16 Interface address
Main storage control	17-18 Reserved (00)
Main storage	19 Sequence code
⫽CPU	20 Unit status
⫽Channel	21 Cmd. addr. and key
Main storage control	22 Channel address
Main storage	23 Device address

24-25 Type of termination	
00 Interface disconnect	
01 Stop, stack or normal	
10 Selective reset	
11 System reset	
28(A) I/O error alert	
29-31 Sequence code	

⫽CHINE-CHECK INTERRUPTION CODE (hex E8)

MC conditions	000	00	Time	Stg. error	0	Validity indicators
	8	9	13 14	16	18 19 20	31

⫽00	0000	0000	00	Val.	MCEL length
	39 40	45 46	48	55 56	63

⫽ystem damage	14 Backed-up
⫽nstr. proc'g damage	15 Delayed
⫽ystem recovery	16 Uncorrected
⫽imer damage	17 Corrected
⫽iming facil. damage	18 Key uncorrected
⫽xternal damage	20 PSW bits 12-15
⫽lot assigned (0)	21 PSW masks and key
⫽egradation	22 Prog. mask and CC
⫽arning	23 Instruction address

24 Failing stg. address	
25 Region code	
27 Floating-pt registers	
28 General registers	
29 Control registers	
30 CPU ext'd logout	
31 Storage logical	
46 CPU timer	
47 Clock comparator	

DYNAMIC ADDRESS TRANSLATION ⑯

VIRTUAL (LOGICAL) ADDRESS FORMAT

Segment Size	Page Size		Segment Index	Page Index	Byte Index
64K	4K	Bits	8 - 15	16 - 19	20 - 31
64K	2K	0 - 7	8 - 15	16 - 20	21 - 31
1M	4K	are	8 - 11	12 - 19	20 - 31
1M	2K	ignored	8 - 11	12 - 20	21 - 31

SEGMENT TABLE ENTRY

PT length	0000*	Page table address	00*	I
0	3 4	7 8	28 29	31

*Normally zeros; ignored on some models.   31 (I) Segment-invalid bit.

PAGE TABLE ENTRY (4K)

Page address		00	
0	11 12 13		15

12 (I) Page-invalid bit.

PAGE TABLE ENTRY (2K)

Page address		I	
0	12 13 14		15

13 (I) Page-invalid bit.

HEXADECIMAL AND DECIMAL CONVERSION

From hex: locate each hex digit in its corresponding column position and note the decimal equivalents. Add these to obtain the decimal value.

From decimal: (1) locate the largest decimal value in the table that will fit into the decimal number to be converted, and (2) note its hex equivalent and hex column position. (3) Find the decimal remainder. Repeat the process on this and subsequent remainders.

Note: Decimal, hexadecimal, (and binary) equivalents of all numbers from 0 to 255 are listed on panels 9 – 12.

HEXADECIMAL COLUMNS

	6		5		4		3		2		1
HEX	= DEC	HEX	= DEC	HEX	= DEC	HEX	= DEC	HEX	= DEC	HEX	= DEC
0	0	0	0	0	0	0	0	0	0	0	0
1	1,048,576	1	65,536	1	4,096	1	256	1	16	1	1
2	2,097,152	2	131,072	2	8,192	2	512	2	32	2	2
3	3,145,728	3	196,608	3	12,288	3	768	3	48	3	3
4	4,194,304	4	262,144	4	16,384	4	1,024	4	64	4	4
5	5,242,880	5	327,680	5	20,480	5	1,280	5	80	5	5
6	6,291,456	6	393,216	6	24,576	6	1,536	6	96	6	6
7	7,340,032	7	458,752	7	28,672	7	1,792	7	112	7	7
8	8,388,608	8	524,288	8	32,768	8	2,048	8	128	8	8
9	9,437,184	9	589,824	9	36,864	9	2,304	9	144	9	9
A	10,485,760	A	655,360	A	40,960	A	2,560	A	160	A	10
B	11,534,336	B	720,896	B	45,056	B	2,816	B	176	B	11
C	12,582,912	C	786,432	C	49,152	C	3,072	C	192	C	12
D	13,631,488	D	851,968	D	53,248	D	3,328	D	208	D	13
E	14,680,064	E	917,504	E	57,344	E	3,584	E	224	E	14
F	15,728,640	F	983,040	F	61,440	F	3,840	F	240	F	15
	0 1 2 3		4 5 6 7		0 1 2 3		4 5 6 7		0 1 2 3		4 5 6 7
	BYTE				BYTE				BYTE		

POWERS OF 2

2^n	n
256	8
512	9
1 024	10
4 096	12
8 192	13
16 384	14
32 768	15
65 536	16
131 072	17
262 144	18
524 288	19
1 048 576	20
2 097 152	21
4 194 304	22
8 388 608	23
16 777 216	24

POWERS OF 16

	16^n	n
$2^0 = 16^0$	1	0
$2^4 = 16^1$	16	1
$2^8 = 16^2$	256	2
$2^{12} = 16^3$	4 096	3
$2^{16} = 16^4$	65 536	4
$2^{20} = 16^5$	1 048 576	5
$2^{24} = 16^6$	16 777 216	6
$2^{28} = 16^7$	268 435 456	7
$2^{32} = 16^8$	4 294 967 296	8
$2^{36} = 16^9$	68 719 476 736	9
$2^{40} = 16^{10}$	1 099 511 627 776	10
$2^{44} = 16^{11}$	17 592 186 044 416	11
$2^{48} = 16^{12}$	281 474 976 710 656	12
$2^{52} = 16^{13}$	4 503 599 627 370 496	13
$2^{56} = 16^{14}$	72 057 594 037 927 936	14
$2^{60} = 16^{15}$	1 152 921 504 606 846 976	15

Appendix
B

Input/Output
Macros

OS/370   Input/Output Macros

name	operation	operands

[symbolic name]   OPEN $\left(\text{dcbname}, \left[\left(\begin{Bmatrix} \text{INPUT} \\ \text{OUTPUT} \\ \text{INOUT} \\ \text{OUTIN} \\ \text{RDBACK} \\ \text{UPDAT} \end{Bmatrix} \begin{bmatrix} \text{DISP} \\ \text{,REREAD} \\ \text{LEAVE} \end{bmatrix} \right) \right] \right.$

$\left. \begin{bmatrix} , \text{dcbname}, \left[\left(\begin{Bmatrix} \text{INPUT} \\ \text{OUTPUT} \\ \text{INOUT} \\ \text{OUTIN} \\ \text{RDBACK} \\ \text{UPDAT} \end{Bmatrix} \begin{bmatrix} \text{DISP} \\ \text{,REREAD} \\ \text{LEAVE} \end{bmatrix} \right) \right] \end{bmatrix} \dots \right)$

[symbolic name]   CLOSE $\left(\text{dcbname}, \begin{bmatrix} \text{DISP} \\ \text{REREAD} \\ \text{LEAVE} \end{bmatrix} \right.$

$\left. \begin{bmatrix} , \text{dcbname}, \begin{bmatrix} \text{DISP} \\ \text{REREAD} \\ \text{LEAVE} \end{bmatrix} \end{bmatrix} \dots \right)$

[symbolic name]   GET $\begin{Bmatrix} (1) \\ \text{dcbname} \end{Bmatrix} \begin{bmatrix} , \begin{Bmatrix} (0) \\ \text{workaddress} \end{Bmatrix} \end{bmatrix}$

[symbolic name]   PUT $\begin{Bmatrix} (1) \\ \text{dcbname} \end{Bmatrix} \begin{bmatrix} , \begin{Bmatrix} (0) \\ \text{workaddress} \end{Bmatrix} \end{bmatrix}$

dcbname   DCB $\text{DSORG} = \begin{Bmatrix} \text{PS} \\ \text{PSU} \end{Bmatrix}$

$, \text{MACRF} = \begin{Bmatrix} (\text{GM or GL or GT or} \\ \quad \text{GMC or GLC or GTC}) \\ (\text{PM or PL or PT or} \\ \quad \text{PMC or PLC or PTC}) \end{Bmatrix}$

name	operation	operands

,DDNAME=name of data set, given on DD
     statement

$$[,RECFM=\begin{cases} U[T][A \text{ or } M] \\ V[B \text{ or } T][A \text{ or } M] \\ F[B \text{ or } S \text{ or } T \text{ or } BS \text{ or } BT \text{ or } ST \\ \quad \text{or } BST][A \text{ or } M] \end{cases}$$

$$[,DEVD=\begin{cases} DA \\ TA[,DEN=0 \text{ or } 1 \text{ or } 2][,TRTCH \\ \quad =C \text{ or } E \text{ or } T \text{ or } ET] \\ PT[,CODE=1 \text{ or } F \text{ or } B \text{ or } C \text{ or} \\ \quad A \text{ or } T \text{ or } N] \\ PR[,PRTSP=0 \text{ or } 1 \text{ or } 2 \text{ or } 3] \\ PC \text{ or } RD[,MODE=C \text{ or } E] \\ \quad [,STACK=1 \text{ or } 2] \end{cases}$$

[,EODAD=address of end-of-data set routine for
     input data sets]

[,BLKSIZE=1 to 32, 760 bytes maximum per block]

[,LRECL=1 to 32, 760 bytes in F-format
     record; specify maximum bytes in
     V-format record]

[,BFTEK=S or E]

[,BUFNO=1 — 255 buffers]

[,BFALN=F or D]

[,BUFL=1 to 32, 760 bytes per buffer]

[,BUFCB=address of buffer pool]

[,EXLST=address of exit list]

[,EROPT=ACC or SKP or ABE]

[,SYNAD=address of user's routine for I/O
     errors which are uncorrectable]

[,OPTCD=W or C or WC]

DOS/370   Input/Output Macros (for card and printer I/O)

name	operation	operands
[symbolic name]	OPEN	$\left\{\begin{array}{c}\text{filename1}\\(r1)\end{array}\right\}\left[\begin{array}{cc}, & \left\{\begin{array}{c}\text{filename2}\\(r2)\end{array}\right\}\,...\begin{array}{c}\text{filename16}\\\text{maximum}\end{array}\end{array}\right]$
[symbolic name]	CLOSE	$\left\{\begin{array}{c}\text{filename1}\\(r1)\end{array}\right\}\left[\begin{array}{cc}, & \left\{\begin{array}{c}\text{filename2}\\(r2)\end{array}\right\}\,...\begin{array}{c}\text{filename16}\\\text{maximum}\end{array}\end{array}\right]$
[symbolic name]	GET	$\left\{\begin{array}{c}\text{filename}\\(1)\end{array}\right\}\left[, \left\{\begin{array}{c}\text{workname}\\(0)\end{array}\right\}\right]$
[symbolic name]	PUT	$\left\{\begin{array}{c}\text{filename}\\(1)\end{array}\right\}\left[, \left\{\begin{array}{c}\text{workname}\\(0)\end{array}\right\}\right]$
[symbolic name]	CNTRL	$\left\{\begin{array}{c}\text{filename}\\(1)\end{array}\right\}$,code[,n][,m]
[symbolic name]	PRTOV	$\left\{\begin{array}{c}\text{filename}\\(1)\end{array}\right\}, \left\{\begin{array}{c}9\\12\end{array}\right\}\left[, \left\{\begin{array}{c}\text{routine name}\\(0)\end{array}\right\}\right]$

name	operation	operands	remarks
filename	DTFCD		Required for card files. Symbolic filename must be assigned.
		DEVADDR=SYSnnn	Required. Specifies symbolic unit associated with the file.
		DEVICE= $\left\{\begin{array}{c}2540\\1442\\2520\\2501\end{array}\right\}$	Required for I/O device other than 2540.
		IOAREA1=name	Required. Associates a symbolic address with the file.
		IOAREA2=name	Associates a second symbolic address with a combined file.
		IOREG=(r)	Required if two I/O areas are used. Specify r (register 2-12).

name	operation	operands	remarks
		EOFADDR=name	Required for input or combined file, to specify name of end-of-file routine.
		TYPEFLE= $\begin{cases} \text{INPUT} \\ \text{OUTPUT} \\ \text{CMBND} \end{cases}$	Required for files other than input files, to specify whether file is input, output, or combined.
		WORKA=YES	Include if records are processed in work areas.
		RECFORM= $\begin{cases} \text{FIXUNB} \\ \text{UNDEF} \\ \text{VARUNB} \end{cases}$	Required if file is other than FIXUNB, to specify record format.
		BLKSIZE=n	Required for all files to designate length of I/O area(s).
		RECSIZE=(r)	Required for undefined records. Let r = register containing the length of the output record.
		CONTROL=YES	Required if a CNTRL macro is issued to the file.
		SSELECT=n	Required for stacker selection to a pocket other than NR or NP. n is the stacker select character.
filename	DTFPR		Required for printer files. Symbolic filename must be assigned.
		DEVADDR=SYSnnn	Required. Specifies a symbolic unit associated with the file.
		DEVICE= $\begin{cases} 1403 \\ 1404 \\ 1443 \\ 1445 \end{cases}$	Required for I/O device other than 1403.
		IOAREA1=name	Required. Associates a symbolic address (output area) with the file.
		IOAREA2=name	Required if two I/O areas are specified, to name the second output area.

name	operation	operands	remarks
		IOREG=(r)	Required if two output areas are used. Specify r (register 2-12).
		WORKA=YES	Include if records are processed in work areas.
		RECFORM= $\begin{cases} \text{FIXUNB} \\ \text{UNDEF} \\ \text{VARUNB} \end{cases}$	Required if file is other than FIXUNB, to specify record format.
		BLKSIZE=n	Required if n≠121, where n designates the length of the output area. If the record is not of fixed length, n will designate the length of the longest record.
		RECSIZE=(r)	Required for undefined records. Let r=register containing the length of the output record.
		CONTROL=YES	Required if a CNTRL macro is issued to the file.
		PRINTOV=YES	Required if a PRTOV macro is issued to the file.

Appendix
C

Job Control
Statements

OS Job Control Statements

The JOB Statement

//Name	Operation	Operand	P/K	Comments
//jobname	JOB	([account number] [,additional accounting information,...])	P	Can be made mandatory
		[programmer's name]	P	Can be made mandatory
		[CLASS=jobclass]	K	Assign A–O.
		[COND=((code,operator),...)]	K	Maximum of 8 tests
		[MSGCLASS=output class]	K	Assign A–Z, 0–9.
		$\text{MSGLEVEL}=\left(\begin{bmatrix}0\\1\\2\end{bmatrix}\begin{bmatrix},0\\,1\end{bmatrix}\right)$	K	
		[NOTIFY=user identification]	K	Notify user of job completion. For MVT with TSO.
		[PRTY=priority]	K	Assign 0–13.

$\left[RD=\left\{ \begin{matrix} R \\ RNC \\ NC \\ NR \end{matrix} \right\} \right]$	K	Restart definition
$\left[REGION=\left\{ \begin{matrix} valueK \\ value0K \end{matrix} \right\} \left[,value1K \right] \right]$	K	For MVT
$\left[RESTART=\left\{ \begin{matrix} * \\ stepname \\ stepname.procstepname \end{matrix} \right\} \left[,checkid \right] \right]$	K	For deferred restart
$\left[ROLL=\left\{ \begin{matrix} YES \\ NO \end{matrix} \right\} \left\{ \begin{matrix} ,YES \\ ,NO \end{matrix} \right\} \right]$	K	Rollout/rollin. For MVT.
$\left[TIME=\left\{ \begin{matrix} (minutes,seconds) \\ 1440 \end{matrix} \right\} \right]$	K	Assigns job CPU time limit.
$\left[TYPRUN=HOLD \right]$	K	Holding a job in job queue.

Legend:

P   Positional parameter.
K   Keyword parameter.
{ }   Choose one.
[ ]   Optional; if more than one line is enclosed, choose one or none.

OS Job Control Statements

The EXEC Statement

//Name	Operation	Operand	P/K	Comments
//[stepname]	EXEC	PGM={program name / *.stepname.ddname / *.stepname.procstepname.ddname} [PROC=]procedure name	P	Identifies program or cataloged procedure
		[ACCT=(accounting information,...) / ACCT.procstepname=(accounting information,...)]	K	Accounting information for step
		COND=({(code,operator) / (code,operator,stepname) / (code,operator,stepname.procstepname)},...[,][EVEN/ONLY])	K	Maximum of 8 tests, or 7 tests if EVEN or ONLY is coded
		COND.procstepname=({(code,operator) / (code,operator,stepname) / (code,operator,stepname.procstepname)},...[,][EVEN/ONLY])		
		[DPRTY=(value1,value2) / DPRTY.procstepname=(value1,value2)]	K	Assign values of 0-15. For MVT.
		[PARM=value / PARM.procstepname=value]	K	Parentheses or apostrophes enclosing value may be required

	K	
$RD=\begin{Bmatrix}R\\RNC\\NC\\NR\end{Bmatrix}$ $RD.procstepname=\begin{Bmatrix}R\\RNC\\NC\\NR\end{Bmatrix}$	K	Restart definition
$REGION=(\begin{Bmatrix}valueK\\value_0K\end{Bmatrix}[,value_1K])$ $REGION.procstepname=(\begin{Bmatrix}valueK\\value_0K\end{Bmatrix}[,value_1K])$	K	For MVT
$ROLL=(\begin{Bmatrix}YES\\NO\end{Bmatrix}\begin{Bmatrix},YES\\,NO\end{Bmatrix})$ $ROLL.procstepname=(\begin{Bmatrix}YES\\NO\end{Bmatrix}\begin{Bmatrix},YES\\,NO\end{Bmatrix})$	K	Rollout/rollin. For MVT.
$TIME=\begin{Bmatrix}(minutes,seconds)\\1440\end{Bmatrix}$ $TIME.procstepname=\begin{Bmatrix}(minutes,seconds)\\1440\end{Bmatrix}$	K	Assigns step CPU time limit.

Legend :

P   Positional parameter.
K   Keyword parameter.
{   Choose one.
[] Optional; if more than one line is enclosed, choose one or none.

OS Job Control Statements

		The DD Statement
//Name	Operation	Operand

//Name	Operation	Operand
// ⎡ ddname procstepname. ddname ⎤	DD	⎡ * DATA ⎤ [DUMMY] [DYNAM] [AFF=ddname] ⎡ DCB=(list of attributes) DCB=({ dsname / *.ddname / *.stepname.ddname / *.stepname.procstepname.ddname } [,list of attributes]) ⎤ [DDNAME=ddname] DISP=(⎡ NEW / OLD / SHR / MOD ⎤ ⎡ ,DELETE / ,KEEP / ,PASS / ,CATLG / ,UNCATLG / , ⎤ ⎡ ,DELETE / ,KEEP / ,CATLG / ,UNCATLG ⎤) { DSNAME / DSN } = { dsname / dsname(member name) / dsname(generation number) / dsname(area name) / &&dsname / &&dsname(member name) / &&dsname(area name) / *.ddname / *.stepname.ddname / *.stepname.procstepname.ddname } ⎡ FCB=(image-id [,ALIGN / ,VERIFY]) ⎤ LABEL=([data set seq #] ⎡ ,SL / ,SUL / ,AL / ,AUL / ,NSL / ,NL / ,BLP / , ⎤ ⎡ ,PASSWORD / ,NOPWREAD / , ⎤ [,IN / ,OUT] [,] ⎡ EXPDT=yyddd / RETPD=nnnn ⎤) [OUTLIM=number] [QNAME=process name]

P/K	Comments
P	To define a data set in the input stream.
P	To bypass I/O operations on a data set (BSAM and QSAM)
P	To request dynamic allocation. For MVT with TSO.
K	One way to request channel separation.
K	To complete the data control block. See Glossary of DCB Subparameters.
K	To postpone the definition of a data set.
K	To assign a status, disposition, and conditional disposition to the data set
K	To assign a name to a new data set or to identify an existing data set. An unqualified name is 1-8 characters, beginning with an alphabetic or national character.
K	To specify forms control information. The FCB parameter is ignored if the data set is not written to a 3211 printer.
K	To supply label information
K	To limit the number of logical records you want included in the output data set.
K	Specifies the name of a TPROCESS macro which defines a destination queue for messages received by means of TCAM.

The DD Statement (con't)

//Name	Operation	Operand
// [ddname procstepname. ddname]	DD	(see below)

$$\left[\begin{cases} ^1 \text{SPACE}=(\begin{cases} \text{TRK} \\ \text{CYL} \\ \text{blocklength} \end{cases}, (\text{primary} [,\text{secondary}] [,\text{directory}\atop ,\text{index}])) [,\text{RLSE}] [{,\text{CONTIG}\atop ,\text{MXIG}\atop ,\text{ALX}}] \\ ^2 \text{SPACE}=(\text{ABSTR},(\text{primary quantity},\text{address} [,\text{directory}\atop ,\text{index}])) \end{cases}\right]$$

$$\left[\text{SPLIT}=\begin{cases} (n,\text{CYL},(\text{primary quantity} [,\text{secondary quantity}])) \\ n \\ (\text{percent},\text{blocklength},(\text{primary quantity} [,\text{secondary quantity}])) \\ \text{percent} \end{cases}\right]$$

$$\left[\text{SUBALLOC}=(\begin{cases} \text{TRK} \\ \text{CYL} \\ \text{blocklength} \end{cases}, (\text{primary} [,\text{secondary}] [,\text{directory}]))\right]$$

$$\left[\text{SYSOUT}=(\text{classname} [,\text{program name}] [,\text{form number}]), [\text{OUTLIM}=\text{number}]\right]$$

$$[\text{TERM}=\text{TS}]$$

$$\left[\text{UCS}=(\text{character set code} [,\text{FOLD}] [,\text{VERIFY}])\right]$$

$$\left[\begin{cases} \text{UNIT}=(\begin{bmatrix} \text{unit address} \\ \text{device type} \\ \text{group name} \end{bmatrix} [,\text{unit count}\atop ,\text{P}] [,\text{DEFER}] [,\text{SEP}=(\text{ddname},\dots)]) \\ \text{UNIT}=\text{AFF}=\text{ddname} \end{cases}\right]$$

$$\left[\begin{cases} \text{VOLUME} \\ \text{VOL} \end{cases}=([\text{PRIVATE}] [,\text{RETAIN}] [,\text{volume seq} \#] [,\text{volume count}] [,]\right]$$

Legend:

P   Positional parameter.

K   Keyword parameter.

{ }   Choose one.

[ ]   Enclosing subparameter, indicates that subparameter is optional; if more than one line is enclosed, choose one or none.

[ ]   Enclosing entire parameter, indicates that parameter may be optional, depending on what type of data set you are defining

	P/K	Comments
$\left[,\text{ROUND}\right])$	K	[1] To assign space on a direct access volume for a new data set [2] To assign specific tracks on a direct access volume for a new data set
	K	To assign space on a direct access volume for a new data set. Data sets share cylinders.
$\left\{\begin{array}{l},\text{ddname}\\,\text{stepname.ddname}\\,\text{stepname.procstepname.ddname}\end{array}\right\})\Big]$	K	To request part of the space on a direct access volume assigned earlier in the job
	K	To route a data set through the output stream. For classname, assign A–Z or 0–9.
	K	To indicate to the system that the input or output data being defined is coming from or going to a time sharing terminal.
	K	To request a special character set for a 1403 printer
	K	To provide the system with unit information
$\left[\begin{array}{l}\text{SER=(serial number,...)}\\\text{REF=dsname}\\\text{REF=*.ddname}\\\text{REF=*.stepname.ddname}\\\text{REF=*.stepname.procstepname.ddname}\end{array}\right]\Big])$	K	To provide the system with volume information

DOS Job Control Statements

The summary below includes selected statements and commands:
- Job Control Statements (JCS) to be preceded by //b̸ in positions 1, 2, and 3 respectively
- Job Control Commands (JCC)
- Single Program Initiation Commands (SPI)

Name	Operation	Operand	Remarks
//	JOB accepted by JCS	jobname [accounting information]	jobname : one to eight alphameric characters accounting information : one to 16 characters
[//]	EXEC accepted by JCS, SPI	| progname |	progname : one to eight alphameric characters. Used only if the program is in the core image library
[//]	ASSGN accepted by JCS JCC SPI	SYSxxx, address $\left[\left\{\begin{matrix},X'ss'\\,ALT\end{matrix}\right\}\right]$ [TEMP]	SYSxxx: can be SYSRDR SYSIPT SYSIN – Invalid for SPI SYSPCH SYSLST SYSOUT SYSLOG SYSLNK } Invalid for SPI SYSREC SYSRLB SYSSLB SYSCLB – Only valid for JCC SYS000 – SYSmax address: can be X'cuu', UA, or IGN X'cuu': c = 0–6 uu = 00–FE (0–254) in hex UA: unassign IGN: unassign and ignore (Invalid for SYSCLB, SYSRDR, SYSIPT, and SYSIN) X'ss': used for magnetic tape only. (table below) ALT: specifies alternate unit (Invalid for SYSCLB) TEMP: only valid for JCC. Assignment for logical unit is destroyed by next JOB statement.

ss	Bytes per Inch	Parity	Translate Feature	Convert Feature
10	200	odd	off	on
20	200	even	off	off
28	200	even	on	off
30	200	odd	off	off
38	200	odd	on	off
50	556	odd	off	on
60	556	even	off	off
68	556	even	on	off
70	556	odd	off	off
78	556	odd	on	off
90	800	odd	off	on
A0	800	even	off	off
A8	800	even	on	off
B0	800	odd	off	off
B8	800	odd	on	off
C0	800	single density 9 track tape		
C0	1600	single density 9 track tape		
C0	1600	dual density 9 track tape		
C8	800	dual density 9 track tape		

Name	Operation	Operand	Remarks
//	OPTION accepted by: JCS	option 1 [, option 2, . . .]	option: can be any of the following:
			LOG Log control statements on SYSLST
			NOLOG Suppress LOG option
			DUMP Dump registers and main storage on SYSLST in the case of abnormal program end
			NODUMP Suppress DUMP option
			LINK Write output of language translator on SYSLNK for linkage editing
			NOLINK Suppress LINK option
			DECK Output object module on SYSPCH
			NODECK Suppress DECK option
			LIST Output listing of source module on SYSLST
			NOLIST Suppress LIST option
			LISTX Output listing of object module on SYSLST
			NOLISTX Suppress LISTX option
			SYM Punch sumbol deck on SYSPCH
			NOSYM Suppress SYM option
			XREF Output symbolic cross-reference list on SYSLST
			NOXREF Suppress XREF option
			ERRS Output listing of all errors in source program on SYSLST
			NOERRS Suppress ERRS option
			CATAL Catalog program or phase in core image library after completion of Linkage Editor run
			STDLABEL Causes all DASD or tape labels to be written on the standard label track
			USRLABEL Causes all DASD or tape labels to be written on the user label track
			PARSTD Causes all DASD or tape labels to be written on the partition standard label track
			48C 48-character set
			60C 60-character set
			SYSPARM='string' specifies a value for assembler system variable symbol and SYSPARM
[//]	PAUSE accepted by: JCS JCC SPI	[comments]	Causes pause immediately after processing this statement. PAUSE statement is always printed on 1052 (SYSLOG). If no 1052 is available, the statement is ignored.
/*	ignored accepted by: JCS	ignored	columns 1 and 2 are the only columns checked.
/&	ignored accepted by: JCS	[comments]	columns 1 and 2 are the only columns checked. Comments are printed on SYSLOG and SYSLST at EOJ.
*	accepted by: JCS	comments	column 2 must be blank.

Appendix D

Answers to Odd-numbered Questions

CHAPTER 1

1-1.   The computer is very different indeed from an adding machine. It is an electronic device capable of performing many operations at high speeds by following a set of instructions called a program. Thus a job which will take a human using a desk calculator a number of years may be completed by a computer in several seconds.

1-3.   The six components are: storage unit, ALU, control unit, input unit(s), output unit(s), and auxiliary storage unit(s).

1-5.   It is an electronic unit, typically a metallic element, which may be magnetized. It is called a core.

1-7.

Phrase		Phrase as it appears in storage					
TOV	in binary	1110	0011	1101	0110	1110	0101
	in hex	E	3	D	6	E	5
HIY	in binary	1100	1000	1100	1001	1110	1000
	in hex	C	8	C	9	E	8
76	in binary	1111	0111	1111	0110		
	in hex	F	7	F	6		

1-9.   The control unit.

1-11.   Eighty symbols may be punched on one Hollerith card.

1-13.   The card reader.

1-15.   Card reader — input device
Printer — output device

1-17.   Field — an organized collection of related characters. On a punched card, it may be represented as a group of consecutive columns which logically belong together.
Record — an organized collection of related fields
File — an organized collection of related records.

1-19.   A/R file (accounts receivable), A/P file (accounts payable), N/A file (name and address), and the like

1-21.   A register is an organized collection of electronic circuits capable of retaining a number. It is generally a 32-bit independent storage unit.

1-23. In the IBM 360 and 370 computers there are three types of registers: floating point registers; general purpose registers; control registers.

1-25. No, only numeric or logical information may be placed in a register. This information will be stored in straight binary format.

1-27. Perhaps the problem might not have arisen had the programmer avoided using register zero. It is quite possible that during the first few executions of the program, the computer was not in need of register zero for its operations. However register zero is among those the computer may use whenever it has the need.

1-29.

Base register	Displacement	Effective address
5	62A	2 9 9 B
8	24F	8 A 3
9	F75	F F F
11	54F	4 0 0 0

1-31. No. One base register will not suffice, since the displacement can be at most 4095, which is less than the 5000 storage positions he needs.

1-33. The op-code (operation code) and one or more operands.

1-35.

RR
RX
RS
SI
SS   Version 1
SS   Version 2
S   (for instructions concerned with advanced functions)

1-37. 16 bits are required (4 bits for the base register and 12 bits for the displacement). If indexing is utilized, a total of 20 bits will be required (4 bits for the index register + 16 bits as above).

1-39. A main storage address is specified in assembler language by use of a symbolic name.

1-41. The assembler program will translate assembler language programs into machine language.

CHAPTER 2

2-1. (a) assembler instructions
      (b) machine instructions
      (c) macro instructions

2-3. Assembler language (or assembly language) instructions are instructions written in mnemonic (or symbolic) code. Assembler instructions are a category of assembly language instructions.

2-5. Machine instructions are translated into machine language.

2-7. They are usually found in the macro library.

2-9. Yes. In fact, it may be reused indefinitely, since the assembler merely copies those instructions and does not destroy them.

2-11. Yes. In fact, they must, if present, adhere to the following order:
      (1) name
      (2) operation
      (3) operand(s)
      (4) comments

2-13. The maximum length of a name is 8 characters.

2-15. To identify and/or describe the data to be acted upon by the instruction.

2-17. The name portion must begin in column 1. The operation portion must be preceded by at least one blank. The operand and comment portions, if present, must be separated from the operation portion and from each other by at least one blank.

2-19. START   4096.

2-21. The assembler keeps track of locations as instructions are translated, by incrementing the location counter by the amount 2, 4, or 6 depending upon the length in bytes of the instruction stored.

2-23. For DOS systems, the operands IOAREA1=symbolic name in DTF instructions defining input or output files identify by name those areas to be used for input or output respectively. However, use of the additional (optional) operand WORKA=YES in such DTF instructions will cause buffering to take place, with the areas specified as IOAREA1 being used as buffer (intermediate) areas only. Work areas are designated in the operand portions of GET and PUT statements.

For OS systems, buffering is provided automatically. The actual input and output areas are not specified by the programmer. However, the work areas are designated in the operand portions of GET and PUT statements.

2-25. The instruction will cause the location number of the executable instruction which follows the BALR to be placed into register 5.

2-27. For OS systems, data sets are activated by
    OPEN   (FBIFILE,INPUT,CIAFILE,OUTPUT)
    Data sets are deactivated by
    CLOSE   (FBIFILE,CIAFILE)

For DOS systems, files are activated by
    OPEN   FBIFILE,CIAFILE
    Files are deactivated by
    CLOSE   FBIFILE,CIAFILE

2-29. BOTTLE is the receiving field. WATER is the sending field.

2-31. (a)

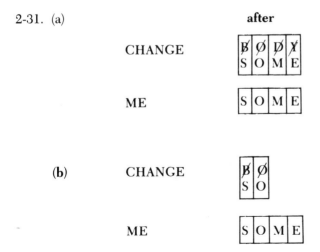

2-33. The term "extended mnemonic" refers to an abbreviated version of a machine instruction, which is supplied by the manufacturer for the programmer's convenience.

2-35. They notify the computer to terminate program execution.

2-37. 1. Operation should be spelled START.
2. The address identified as the EOFADDR, that is, the address called STOP, is not defined anywhere in the program.
3. The last operand of the DTFPR should say CONTROL=YES.
7. The first operand of the OPEN is incorrectly spelled; it should read "HELLO."
10. One may only branch to a location which contains an instruction; the location "HI" does not. (In this program, it would probably make more sense to branch to RETURN, so that additional records may be read.)
11. The operation "CLOSE" should precede the operands "HELLO, GOODBYE."
13. The END instruction should be the last instruction in an assembly language program. It should appear after the DS statements in this program.

CHAPTER 3

3-1. 1. Understanding the problem—describing input and output, and flow-charting the program logic.
2. Coding the solution.
3. Recording on an input medium.
4. Assembly, link-editing, execution.
5. Testing and debugging.

3-3. A flowchart describes the sequence of logical steps necessary to solve a problem through use of the computer. There may be many correct flowcharts for any particular problem. The number of steps and the amount of detail presented may vary from programmer to programmer. Moreover, the choice of wording used within flowchart symbols may vary.

3-5. (a) packed: 07 5C   zoned: F7 C5
      (b) packed: 04 2D   zoned: F4 D2
      (c) packed: 80 0D   zoned: F8 F0 D0
      (d) packed: 0C   zoned: C0

3-7. (a)   DC   C'AQU'
                       DC   X'C1D8E4'
                       DC   B'110000011101100011100100'

      (b)   DC   C'138'
                       DC   X'F1F3F8'
                       DC   X'111100011111001111111000'

      (c)   DC   Z'-492'
                       DC   C'49K'
                       DC   X'F4F9D2'

      (d)   DC   Z'+8'
                       DC   C'H'
                       DC   X'C8'

3-9. EBCDIC, hexadecimal and binary constants may not exceed 256 bytes. Packed and zoned constants may not exceed 16 bytes.

3-11. The duplication factor in the operand portion of a DC instruction allows repetition of a constant a number of times in consecutive storage locations.

3-13. A literal may be used in the operand portion of an instruction, replacing the use of a name in that operand. The name, if used, would have to be defined by a DC (or DS) instruction. Thus the use of a literal enables the programmer to avoid a separate area and/or constant definition.

3-15. The literal pool is a special place, usually at the end of the program, used to store assembled data specified by literals in the program.

3-17. Both the DC and DS instructions
        • define and reserve storage area
        • specify the size of the area being reserved
        • associate a name with the area (optional)
      In addition, *only* the *DC instruction* places constant data into the area.

3-19.
OUT	DS	0CL132
	DC	CL3' '
A1	DS	CL3
	DC	CL6' '
B1	DS	CL2
	DC	CL6' '
C1	DS	CL4
	DC	CL6' '
D1	DS	CL1
	DC	CL101' '

Note that the fields should be assigned names which differ from those of the input fields. Duplicate names are not permitted in assembly language programs. The DC instructions above may be replaced by DS instructions; the output area would then be "cleared" during program execution.

CHAPTER 4

4-1.
ONE:	5C
TWO:	00 00 00 00 2C

4-3.
HERE:	00 02 00 0C

4-5. (a)
	AP	NUM3,NUM2
	SP	NUM3,NUM1
	ZAP	LOC,NUM3
	⋮	
LOC	DS	PL2

(b)
	ZAP	LONG,NUM2
	MP	LONG,NUM2
	UNPK	AREA,LONG
	⋮	
LONG	DS	PL2
AREA	DS	CL3

(c)

	ZAP	PLACE,NUM3
	DP	PLACE,NUM1
	⋮	
PLACE	DS	0PL4
QUOT	DS	PL2
REM	DS	PL2

(d)

	UNPK	ZNUM1,NUM1
	UNPK	ZNUM2,NUM2
	UNPK	ZNUM3,NUM3
	⋮	
ZNUM1	DS	CL3
ZNUM2	DS	CL2
ZNUM3	DS	CL3

4-7.

	AP	SUM,NUM1
	AP	SUM,NUM2
	AP	SUM,NUM3
	AP	SUM,NUM4
	AP	SUM,NUM5
	AP	SUM,NUM6
	ZAP	DIVID,SUM
	DP	DIVID,SIX
	UNPK	RESULT,DIVID(2)
SUM	DC	PL2'0'
SIX	DC	P'6'
DIVID	DS	PL3
RESULT	DS	CL2
NUM1	DC	P'10'
NUM2	DC	P'11'
NUM3	DC	P'12'
NUM4	DC	P'13'
NUM5	DC	P'14'
NUM6	DC	P'15'

4-9. 1. B will contain 10 0F
2. A will contain 24 2C
3. A will contain 23 9C
4. B will contain 00 3C
5. B will contain 00 9C
6. E will contain 00 00 9C
7. E will contain 00 9C 0C

4-11. Such instructions are present in virtually all assembly language programs, therefore they are not considered part of the logic particular to the program being described. Their indication on the program flowchart would therefore be superfluous.

4-13. The instructions are all of SS (Storage to Storage) format.

4-15. (a) correct
   (b) incorrect. The second operand is not a packed number.
   (c) correct.
   (d) incorrect. The second operand does not have an implied length ("PLACE2+1" was not defined and has no associated length, although "PLACE2" has). Therefore an explicit length must be supplied.
   (e) incorrect. PLACE2 is not long enough to hold both the quotient and the remainder. The contents of PLACE2 should have first been ZAPed into a longer location.
   (f) incorrect. Division by zero is not allowed. A divide exception will occur.
   (g) correct.
   (h) correct.
   (i) incorrect. PLACE1 will not be large enough to hold the product. 02000C requires 3 bytes, and PLACE1 is only 2 bytes long.
   (j) correct. The difference will be negative. However, this is perfectly acceptable.

4-17. For the AP, SP, and ZAP instructions, the maximum length of either operand is 16 bytes. For the MP instruction, the first operand field may not exceed 16 bytes, but the second operand field may not exceed 8 bytes in length. For the DP instruction, the maximum dividend and divisor lengths are 16 bytes and 8 bytes, respectively. The maximum quotient size is 15 bytes.

4-19. To prepare for arithmetic operations, the number must be more than simply "placed" into a longer field. It must be right justified in the longer field and extended on the left with high-order zeros. That is, the number itself must be extended in size appropriately, to "fit" the longer field; the ZAP instruction does precisely that. The MVC, on the other hand, left justifies the value being moved, and pads it on the right with blanks; the result is a value which, for arithmetic purposes, would not even be considered to be numeric. A combination of MVC instructions would be necessary, one to move zeros into appropriate high-order positions, and a second using a relative addressing technique to right justify the number in the receiving field.

CHAPTER 5

5-1. (a) GOOD⌿DAY
      (b) 1984
      (c) 198D
      (d) CATCH⌿22

5-3. (a) The sign (either + or −) is keypunched in the low-order column, *right over* the low-order digit of the number.
      (b) Negative data must be input in signed form. Positive data need not, since an unsigned input value is, in any case, assumed by the computer to be positive.

5-5. (a) D8 D9 E7 Ⓒ8
      (b) Ⓒ8 Ⓒ9 D7 E8
      (c) Ⓒ8 E9 Ⓒ7 Ⓒ8
      (d) D8 D9 E7 F8
      Circled bytes were not changed through execution of the MVZ.

5-7.
```
            UNPK    NUM,PNUM
            MVZ     NUM+2(1),NUM+1
            CP      PNUM,=P'0'
            BNL     SKIP
            MVI     NUM−1,C'−'
   SKIP      ⋮
```

5-9. (a) **B**ranch (unconditional); any cc setting
      (b) **No OP**eration (no branch); no cc setting
      (c) **B**ranch on **A L**ow; cc=1
      (d) **B**ranch on **A N**ot **E**qual to B; cc≠0
      (e) **B**ranch on **P**lus; cc=2
      (f) **B**ranch on **N**ot **M**inus; cc≠1
      (g) **B**ranch on **Z**ero; cc=0

5-11. Statements 95, 101, 105, 124, and 127 eliminated the signs from the low-order bytes of the affected fields, so that the low-order printed characters will be printed as digits. The fields were not tested for sign, since it is assumed that an individual's gross pay, tax, and net pay will never (logically) be negative amounts!

5-13. (a) cc = 1
      (b) cc = 0
      (c) cc = 1
      (d) cc = 1
      (e) cc = 1

5-15. No. The collating sequences for packed and zoned numbers are not based upon ascending or descending binary values, unless the comparison is performed upon: two packed numbers, both of which are unsigned; two zoned numbers, both of which are unsigned; or two zoned numbers, both of which are positive.

CHAPTER 6

6-1. An implied decimal point is one which is present only in the programmer's mind; it is not actually stored, not on the input, output or storage media. A real decimal point is actually stored on the appropriate media.

6-3. (a)

	ZAP	LONGER, FIELD
	MP	LONGER, =P'100'
LONGER	DS	PL4

(b)

	MVC	RES1(3), FIELD
	MVC	RES1+3(1), =X'00'
	MVN	RES1+3(1), RES1+2
	MVN	RES1+2(1), =X'00'
	:	
RES1	DS	PL4

(c)

	MVC	RES2(3), FIELD
	MVI	RES2+3, X'0F'
	NC	RES2+3(1), RES2+2
	NI	RES2+2, X'F0'
	:	
RES2	DS	PL4

6-5. (a) xxxx∧xx ; 4 bytes
      (b) xxxxxx∧xxxxx ; 6 bytes
      (c) xxxx∧xxxx ; 5 bytes
      (d) xxxxx ; 3 bytes

6-7. (a) add 50 (−50 for a negative field value)
      (b) add 5 (−5 for a negative field value)
      (c) add 500 (−500 for a negative field value)
      (d) add 500 (−500 for a negative field value)
      (e) add 50 (−50 for a negative field value)
      (f) add 50000 (−50000 for a negative field value)
      (g) add 5 (−5 for a negative field value)
      (h) add 500 (−500 for a negative field value)

6-9. (a)   ZAP   LNG1,X
                       MP   LNG1,=P'10'
                       AP   LNG1,Y
                       AP   LNG1,=P'5'
                       MVO   LNG1,LNG1(5)
                        ⋮
            LNG1   DS   PL6

      (b)   ZAP   LNG2,X
                       MP   LNG2,Y
                       AP   LNG2,=P'500'
                       MVO   LNG2,LNG2(4)
                        ⋮
            LNG2   DS   PL6

      (c)   ZAP   LNG3,X
                       MP   LNG3,Y
                       MP   LNG3,Z
                       AP   LNG3,=P'500000'
                       MVN   LNG3+3(1),LNG3+6
                       ZAP   LNG3,LNG3(4)
                        ⋮
            LNG3   DS   PL7

(d)
```
              ZAP       TEMP,Z
              MP        TEMP,=P'100'
              SP        Y,TEMP
              MVO       Y,Y(2)
              MVO       Y,Y(2)
                        ⋮
    TEMP      DS        PL3
```

6-11.
```
              ZAP       RESULT,TOTAL
              MP        RESULT,=P'1000'
              DP        RESULT,NUMB
              AP        QUOT,=P'5'
              MVN       RESULT+8(1),QUOT+5
              MVO       RESULT,QUOT
                        ⋮
    RESULT    DS        0PL9
    QUOT      DS        PL6
    REM       DS        PL3
```

6-13. Statement 105 scaled the gross pay field in preparation for division by 4, for the computation of tax. The program specification designated that the tax was to be computed to the nearest cent (hundredth). Thus, it was necessary for the computation to be carried to the thousandths position, to then be rounded back to the nearest hundredth. Statement 105 therefore extended the gross pay with a low-order (rightmost) zero, that is, to the thousandths position.

6-15. (a)
```
              LH        6,M1
              SRP       CONS1,0(6),5
                        ⋮
    M1        DC        H'-1'
    CONS1     DC        P'682.444'
```

(b)
```
              LH        10,M2
              SRP       CONS2,0(10),10
                        ⋮
    M2        DC        H'-2'
    CONS2     DC        P'-76.89'
```

(c)	LH	8,M1
	SRP	CONS3,0(8),5
	⋮	
M1	DC	H'−1'
CONS3	DC	P'98.69'

(d)	LH	9,M2
	SRP	CONS4,0(9),10
	⋮	
M2	DC	H'−2'
CONS4	DC	P'66.666'

CHAPTER 7

7-1. (a) Binary arithmetic is faster than decimal arithmetic.
      (b) Storage of binary numbers is often more compact.

7-3.

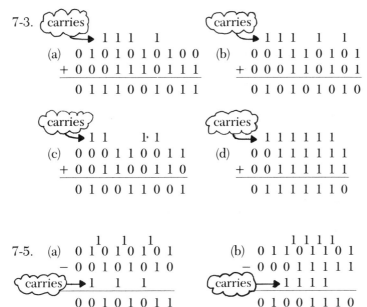

7-5. (a)

```
          1   1   1
    0 1 0 1 0 1 0 1
  − 0 0 1 0 1 0 1 0
 carries ▶ 1   1   1
  ─────────────────
    0 0 1 0 1 0 1 1
```

(b)

```
              1 1 1
    0 1 1 0 1 1 0 1
  − 0 0 0 1 1 1 1 1
 carries ▶ 1 1 1 1
  ─────────────────
    0 1 0 0 1 1 1 0
```

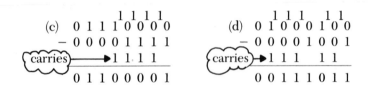

$$
\begin{array}{ll}
\text{(c)} & \overset{1\ 1\ 1\ 1}{0\ 1\ 1\ 1\ 0\ 0\ 0\ 0} \\
& -\ 0\ 0\ 0\ 0\ 1\ 1\ 1\ 1 \\
\hline
\end{array}
$$

7-7. (a) Ten's complement $= 10^n - N = 10^3 - 764 = 236$
      (b) Ten's complement $= 10^n - N = 10^6 - 123{,}456 = 876{,}544$

7-9. (a) $0\ 1\ 0\ 1\ 0\ 1\ 1\ 1$ $----$ $\begin{array}{l} 1\ 0\ 1\ 0\ 1\ 0\ 0\ 0 \\ \hphantom{1\ 0\ 1\ 0\ 1\ 0\ 0\ } 1 \end{array}$

two's complement $\longrightarrow$ $1\ 0\ 1\ 0\ 1\ 0\ 0\ 1$

(b) $1\ 1\ 1\ 1\ 0\ 0\ 1\ 1$ $----$ $\begin{array}{l} 0\ 0\ 0\ 0\ 1\ 1\ 0\ 0 \\ \hphantom{0\ 0\ 0\ 0\ 1\ 1\ 0\ } 1 \end{array}$

two's complement $\longrightarrow$ $0\ 0\ 0\ 0\ 1\ 1\ 0\ 1$

(c) $0\ 1\ 1\ 1\ 1\ 1\ 1\ 1$ $----$ $\begin{array}{l} 1\ 0\ 0\ 0\ 0\ 0\ 0\ 0 \\ \hphantom{1\ 0\ 0\ 0\ 0\ 0\ 0\ } 1 \end{array}$

two's complement $\longrightarrow$ $1\ 0\ 0\ 0\ 0\ 0\ 0\ 1$

(d) $1\ 0\ 0\ 0\ 0\ 0\ 0\ 1$ $----$ $\begin{array}{l} 0\ 1\ 1\ 1\ 1\ 1\ 1\ 0 \\ \hphantom{0\ 1\ 1\ 1\ 1\ 1\ 1\ } 1 \end{array}$

two's complement $\longrightarrow$ $0\ 1\ 1\ 1\ 1\ 1\ 1\ 1$

7-11. (a) Binary results in the computer never require complementation. Unlike the decimal representation which we are accustomed to using, negative binary numbers are always expressed in complement form and remain in that form in the computer memo┐
      (b) Difference (a) is positive: Sign (leftmost) bit is 0.
          Difference (b) is negative: Sign (leftmost) bit is 1.

7-13. (a)
$$
\begin{array}{r}
0\ 1\ 1\ 1\ 1 \\
\times\ \ 0\ 1\ 0\ 1 \\
\hline
0\ 1\ 1\ 1\ 1 \\
0\ 1\ 1\ 1\ 1 \\
\hline
1\ 0\ 0\ 1\ 0\ 1\ 1
\end{array}
$$

(b)
$$
\begin{array}{r}
1\ 0\ 0\ 0 \\
0\ 1\ 1\ 1\ \overline{)\ 0\ 1\ 1\ 1\ 0\ 1\ 0} \\
0\ 1\ 1\ 1 \\
\hline
0\ 0\ 1\ 0
\end{array}
$$

7-15.
$$
\begin{array}{ll}
\text{(a)} & \begin{array}{r} 1\ 2\ 4 \\ +\ \text{A}\ 9\ \text{C} \\ \hline \text{B}\ \text{C}\ 0 \end{array} \qquad
\text{(b)} & \begin{array}{r} \text{A}\ 0\ \text{B}\ 0 \\ +\ 0\ \text{F}\ \text{F}\ \text{F} \\ \hline \text{B}\ 0\ \text{A}\ \text{F} \end{array}
\end{array}
$$

(c)   D 4 1   (d)   1 2 3 A B 6
     + 1 4 D   + 0 A 4 5 7 1
     ───────   ─────────────
      E 8 E   1 C 8 0 2 7

carries ──────────▶ 1 1

7-17. (a)   B ^{1} B ^{1} B   (b)   2 ^{1} 4 5
          − 9   E   E   − 1   5 4
            1   1   1
          ─────────   ─────────
          1   C   D   0 F 1

7-19. (a) A B D   =   (1 0 1 0 1 0 1 1 1 1 0 1)$_2$
         / | \
       1010 1011 1101

(b) 2   4   5   A   F = (0 0 1 0 0 1 0 0 0 1 0 1 1 0 1 0 1 1 1 1)$_2$
   / | \   \   \
  0010 0100 0101 1010 1111

(c) 1   2   =   (0 0 0 1 0 0 1 0)$_2$
    /   \
   0001 0010

(d) 0 1 F 6   =   (0 0 0 1 1 1 1 1 0 1 1 0)$_2$
    / / \ \
  0000 0001 1111 0110   Some extraneous zeros omitted here.

7-21.

(a) **Method 1**:
    01010100 = 0 + 1 × 2^6 + 0 + 1 × 2^4 + 0 + 1 × 2^2 + 0 + 0
             =   64   +   16   +   4
             = 84

    Method 2: (double-dabble)
    0   1   0   1   0   1   0   0
    0   2   4   10   20   42   84 + 0   =   84

(b) **Method 1**:
    01110111 = 0 + 1×2^6 + 1×2^5 + 1×2^4 + 0 + 1×2^2 + 1×2^1 + 1×2^0
                    64   +   32   +   16   +   4   +   2   +   1
             = 119

Method 2: (double-dabble)

0	1	1	1	0	1	1	1		
0	2	6	14	28	58	118 +	1	=	119

7-23. (a)**Method 1**:

$$A05 = 10 \times 16^2 + 0 + 5 \times 16^0$$
$$= 2560 + 5$$
$$= (2565)_{10}$$

Method 2: Positional values of hexadecimal digits from chart.

A in column 3:   2560
5 in column 1:   5
                    —————————
                    $(2565)_{10}$

Method 3:

         10
       $\times 16$
      —————
      160 + 0 = 160
             $\times 16$
            —————
            2560 + 5 = $(2565)_{10}$

(b) **Method 1**:

$$589D = 5 \times 16^3 + 8 \times 16^2 + 9 \times 16^1 + 13 \times 16^0$$
$$= 20480 + 2048 + 144 + 13$$
$$= (22685)_{10}$$

Method 2: Positional values of hexadecimal digits from chart.

5 in column 4:   20480
8 in column 3:   2048
9 in column 2:   144
D in column 1:   13
                    —————————
                    $(22685)_{10}$

Method 3:

          5
       $\times 16$
      —————
        80 + 8 = 88
              $\times 16$
             —————
             1408 + 9 = 1417
                        $\times 16$
                       —————
                       22672 + 13 = $(22685)_{10}$

7-25. A number is on an integral boundary if its address is a multiple of its length in bytes.

7-27. (a) FF FF FF FC   no alignment
      (b) 00 0D   halfword alignment
      (c) FF F7 00 4 6   halfword alignment
      (d) 3 A   no alignment
      integer part of $5.86 \times 10^1 = 58.6$, is $(58)_{10}$

7-29. (a)

	PACK	DBL,NUM1
	CVB	2,DBL
	⋮	
NUM1	DC	Z'46'
DBL	DS	D

(b)

	CVB	3,NUM2
	⋮	
	DS	0D
NUM2	DC	P'8'

7-31. (a) 1. LOC1 should be aligned on a doubleword boundary.
      2. LOC2 should be seven bytes long in order to ensure sufficient room for the zoned results.

(b) 1. The second operand of the CVB instruction must contain a packed number (contents in this example are zoned).
    2. The first operand of the CVB must be a general register number.

CHAPTER 8

8-1.

	PACK	D,A
	CVB	2,D
	PACK	D,B
	CVB	3,D
	AR	2,3
	CVD	2,D
	UNPK	SUM,D
	⋮	
D	DS	D
SUM	DS	CL2

8-3.   Reg 2 will contain -1
       Reg 2 will contain 0 (the remainder); Reg 3 will contain $+2$ (the quotient)
       Regs 6-7 will contain 0
       Reg 7 will contain $+1$ $(0-(-1))$
       Regs 2-3 will contain -2 $(+2(-1))$
       Regs 2-3 remain unchanged : divide exception

8-5.   (a) The MR instruction may not have an odd-addressed first operand.
           The AH instruction must have a halfword second operand; more-
           over, the second operand must be defined.

       (b) The M instruction must have a fullword second operand. Division
           by zero (register 4 contains 0) is not allowed.

       (c) The program changes the contents of the base register (AR   4,2).
           This is not allowed. Also, register 13 may not be used (it is re-
           served, by convention, for other uses).

       (d) Overflow will result from the repeated multiplications.

8-7.   (a)   Reg 5 will contain $+4$
             Reg 6 will contain $+3$
             Reg 6 will contain high-order 0's, reg 7 will contain $+12$
             EASY will contain $+12$

       (b)   Reg 12 will contain $+7$, reg 13 will contain $+3$, reg 14 will contain $+2$
             Reg 12 will contain $+10$
             Reg 12 will contain $+12$
             PROBLEM will contain $+12$, IS will contain $+3$, VERY will con-
             tain $+2$

       (c)   Reg 8 will contain $+3$
             Reg 11 will contain $+7$
             Reg 10 will contain 0
             Reg 10 will contain $+1$, reg 11 will contain $+3$
             Reg 11 will contain $+6$
             EASY will contain $+6$
             IS will contain $+1$

CHAPTER 9

9-1. (a)   LH   3,B   68∧4 in reg 3
                   M   2,=F'10'   68∧40 in reg 3
                   A   3,A   A+B(2∧56+68∧40) in reg 3
                   ST   3,SUM   A+B in SUM
          SUM   DS   F

      (b)   L   3,A   A in reg 3
                   MH   3,B   A×B in reg 3
                   ST   3,PROD   A×B in PROD
          PROD   DS   F

                or

                   LH   3,B   B in reg 3
                   M   2,A   A×B in regs 2-3
                   ST   3,PROD   A×B in PROD
          PROD   DS   F

      (c)   L   5,PROD   xxx∧xxx in reg 5
                   A   5,=F'50'   +   50
                                        ──────────────
                                        xxx∧xxx
                   SR   4,4   zeros in reg 4 (PROD is positive)
                   D   4,=F'100'   truncate low-order 2 digits:
                                        xxx∧x in reg 5
                   ST   5,ROUND   rounded result in ROUND
          ROUND   DS   F

      (d)   L   7,B   68∧4 (dividend) in reg 7
                   M   6,=F'100'   extend B (dividend) with 2 low-
                                        order zeros   2.56 ⟌68.400
                   D   6,A   compute B÷A to tenths position
                   A   7,=F'5'   add 5 to quotient
                   D   6,=F'10'   truncate low-order (tenths) digit
                   ST   7,QUOT   place rounded result into QUOT
          QUOT   DS   F

9-3. (a) Multiply A by 10 (append one low-order 0 to A)
      (b) No preparation necessary
      (c) Multiply A by 100 (append two low-order 0's to A)
      (d) Multiply A by 10 (append one low-order 0 to A)
      (e) Multiply A by 100000 (append five low-order 0's to A)

9-5.

```
            L       9,NUM1
            M       8,NUM2       product has 7 bits to the right of
                                 the binary point.
            A       9,ROUND
            SRA     9,7          shift off extra bits to obtain integer
            ⋮                    result

ROUND       DC      FS7'.5'
```

9-7.

```
            START
BGN         BALR    11,0
            USING   *,11
            L       2,J
            C       2,=F'0'
            BH      POS          if J > 0 go to POS
            BL      NEG          if J < 0 go to NEG
            B       EOJ          if J = 0 go to EOJ
POS         A       2,=F'1'
            B       EOJ
NEG         A       2,=F'2'
EOJ         SVC     3
J           DS      F
            END     BGN
```

CHAPTER 10

10-1.

```
            DC      X'402020214B202060'
```

10-3.

```
            DC      X'40202120'
```

10-5. NUM1 will contain   00 12 3C   unchanged
      PAT will contain   40 20 21 4B 20 20 20 60   unchanged
      FLD will contain   40 F0 F0 4B F1 F2 F3 40   edited results

10-7. The edit pattern must contain control characters (such as X'20', X'21', X'22') as well as other characters. The control characters cannot be represented with character type definitions (there are no EBCDIC characters with those exact bit configurations), hence the pattern must be described using hexadecimal notation.

10-9. No. Although this is usually the case, an exception is the case in which significance is established in the last byte of a positive source field. In this case the significance indicator will remain off. See section 10.1.4. (Another possible exception is the case in which the significance indicator is *already* on when the nonzero digit is encountered. For example, a significance starter in the pattern may have turned it on.)

10-11.

```
                      MVC     AREA,PAT
                      LA      1,AREA+4
                      EDMK    AREA,FLD
                      BCTR    1,0
                      MVI     0(1),C'$'
                        ⋮
          FLD         DS      PL3
          PAT         DC      X'402020214B202060'
          AREA        DS      CL8
```

10-13.   CNTRL   PRFLE,SK,1

10-15.   PRTOV   PRFILE,12,HERE

10-17. For DOS, the DTFPR instruction must contain the parameter
              CONTROL=YES for use of the CNTRL
              PRINTOV=YES for use of the PRTOV
       For OS, the printer file DCB instruction must contain the parameter
              MACRF=PMC, "C" meaning "CNTRL".

CHAPTER 11

11-1. (a) yes   test for cc = 2
                sum is positive
      (b) yes   test for cc = 1 or 3
                difference is negative
      (c) no   test for cc = 1, 2, or 3
                difference is zero
      (d) no   test for cc = 0 or 2
                reg 2 < reg 8
      (e) yes   unconditional branch

11-3. (a)   BC   8,LOW
      (b)   BC   11,PLACE
      (c)   BC   1,PLACE
      (d)   BCR   11,11
      (e)   BCR   0,5
      (f)   BC   2,B

11-5.   LA   2,TABLE+76
                   LA   4,TABLE2
                   LA   5,4
                   LA   6,TABLE2+76
      MOVE   L   10,0(2)
                   ST   10,0(4)
                   S   2,B4
                   BXLE   4,5,MOVE
                   ⋮
      TABLE   DS   F ⎫
                   ⋮   ⎬ 20 times
                   DS   F ⎭
      TABLE2   DS   F ⎫
                   ⋮   ⎬ 20 times
                   DS   F ⎭
      B4   DC   F'4'

11-7.   LA   6,0
                   LA   8,2
                   LA   9,38
                   LA   2,100
      LOOP   C   2,LOC(6)   100:list item
                   BNH   INCR   branch if 100 ≯ list item
                   ST   2,LOC(6)
      INCR   BXLE   6,8,LOOP
                   ⋮
      LOC   DS   H ⎫
                   ⋮   ⎬ 20 times
                   DS   H ⎭
      B100   DC   H'100'
                   ⋮

11-9.		SR	10,10
		LA	2,LISTX+56
		L	4,=F'−4'
		LA	5,LISTX−4
AD		A	10,0(2)
		BXH	2,4,AD
DIV		SRDA	10,32
		D	10,=F'15'
		ST	11,AVG

$$\vdots$$

LISTX	DS	F

15 times

	DS	F
AVG	DS	F

11-11. For the BXLE and BXH instructions, one must initialize an index register, an increment register, and a limit register (the limit register is the same as the increment register if the increment register is odd; it is the next higher numbered register if the increment register is even). For the BCT, a count register (R1) must be initialized. The BXLE and BXH are more useful than the BCT, for the programmer may choose his own increment and limit. Thus it may be possible to use other program elements (such as contents of index registers) as the criteria for exiting from the loop.

CHAPTER 12

12-1. An *open subroutine* is repeated within a program whenever it is required. A *closed subroutine* is coded once and branched to whenever needed.

12-3. An *internal subroutine* is assembled together with the calling program, while an *external subroutine* is assembled separately.

12-5. (a) The value 2. The START initializes the location counter to 0 and, being an assembler instruction, requires no core storage. The BALR is an RR machine instruction, hence occupies 2 bytes of storage: locations 0 and 1. The location number following the BALR, "2", is placed by the BALR into its first operand, register 14.

(b) The value 20. The analysis for part (a) applies to (b) as well, except that the START initializes the location counter to 16 and the BAL is an RX instruction occupying 4 bytes.

12-7. Registers 0,1,13,14,15
Register 0: Single word subroutine output
      1: A parameter value, or the address of a list containing either parameter values or parameter addresses
     13: Address of save area in calling routine
     14: Return address
     15: Branch address

12-9. "Call by value": the parameter list contains the parameters themselves. "Call by name": the parameter list contains the addresses of parameters.

12-11. Contents of registers 14 through 12 are placed into words 4 through 18 of the save area. Word 2 contains the address of the *calling* routine's save area (the routine which *called* the program in which the save area is found). Word 3 contains the address of the save area in a subroutine which *is called by* the program in which the save area is found. Word 1 is used by the operating system.

12-13. Yes. It would be possible, but not preferable. The storage of register contents is a necessary part of subroutine linkage. It is not in any way related to the logic of the main program, but *is* necessary for the subroutine, so that the subroutine is the proper vehicle for effecting that storage.

12-15. No. The purpose of saving and restoring register contents is to assure that both routines have full use of the registers. If the subroutine makes no use of the registers, it is not necessary either to save them or to restore them. If the subroutine uses only register 7, then only register 7 need be saved and restored. However, very little execution time is lost by adhering to the conventions and saving and restoring all the register contents, and this is still the recommended course of action.

12-17. (a) No. Addressability must be established for SAVEB *before* it can be referenced by an instruction. The BALR-USING pair establishes this addressability.

(b) No. The BALR, by initializing register 12 with a new value, destroys its previous contents. If we do not store the original contents of register 12 first, those contents will be lost.

12-19. An object module is the output of the assembler program. It is relocatable (uses relative addresses) and non-executable. A load module is the output of the linkage editor program. It is executable, and under DOS systems it is non-relocatable (it is assigned to definite storage locations).

CHAPTER 13

13-1. An operating system is a collection of programs whose purpose is to manage and to improve the efficiency of the resources of a computer system.

13-3. Multiprogramming is an operating system capability which allows two or more programs to reside in storage simultaneously and to be executed concurrently.

13-5. (a) Relocation is the process of converting addresses in a program's address space into actual real storage location numbers.
   (b) The two types of relocation are:
   Static Relocation: the program is bound to definite real storage locations at load time.
   Dynamic Relocation: the program is not bound to definite real storage locations.

13-7. (a) System/360 under DOS control
   (b) System/360 under OS control

13-9. Static relocation is a type of software relocation. Dynamic relocation is a type of hardware relocation.

13-11. (i) The origin of the appropriate segment table is pointed to by the STOR (Segment Table Origin Register).
   (ii) The segment number in the relative address points to the appropriate entry in the segment table, which gives the location number in real storage at which the appropriate segment begins.
   (iii) The origin address of step (ii) is added to the displacement given in the relative address. This sum is the absolute address.

13-13. (i)   The origin of the appropriate segment table is pointed to by the STOR (Segment Table Origin Register).
   (ii) The segment number in the relative address points to the appropriate segment table entry. This entry points to the origin of the page table for that segment.
   (iii) The page number in the relative address points to the appropriate page table entry, which gives the location number in real storage at which the appropriate page begins.
   (iv) The origin address of step (iii) is added to the displacement given in the relative address. This sum is the absolute address.

13-15. A page is a subdivision of a computer program. A page frame is a subdivision of real storage.

13-17. The relative address structure determines the segment size and page size.

13-19. The associative array registers hold the most recently referenced program segment and page numbers, along with their corresponding page frame locations.

   For each relative address referenced by the program, the system compares the address to the addresses in the associative array registers. If the appropriate segment and page number is found in one of the registers, address translation is completed with the registers. Otherwise, translation will occur with the segment and page tables.

   The main function of the associative array registers is thus to improve execution speed by providing for faster relative address translation (the comparisons of relative addresses to all the associative array registers occur simultaneously).

13-21. (a) 48,500
   (b) Cannot be translated using the registers of figure 13.11. We need segment and page tables.
   (c) 37,024.

13-23. 16 megabytes, or 16,777,216 bytes.

13-25. They are in auxiliary storage, or external page storage.

13-27. On IBM systems, fixed length segments are 64K, and each segment contains 16 fixed length pages, each of which is 4K in size.

13-29. A page fault is said to exist when the particular page being referenced by the virtual address does not reside in real storage. This is sensed during address translation, when the corresponding page table entry's invalid bit is set to 1.

13-31. The page to be paged-in is somewhere in external storage. Therefore the system finds the appropriate entry in the external page table, which corresponds the desired page with the appropriate slot location.

13-33. The needed page must then replace one currently in main storage. This is called swapping.

13-35. Each entry of the page frame table has a bit called a change bit. If the contents of a page have not been changed, the change bit is set to 0; if they have been changed, the change bit is set to 1.

This is important to know, for if the contents of the page have been changed, there is no copy of the changed data in external storage! Therefore a paging-out operation will be necessary, so that later program reference to the page will reflect the most up-to-date page contents.

13-37. Routines which are frequently used will tend to stay in real storage. If such routines are loaded near to each other, the result will be a reduced number of page faults, a major objective when coding for VS systems.

13-39. 1. Real storage fragmentation is minimized.
2. Programs may be written that require more storage space than is available in real storage.
3. More jobs may be processed, since the entire instruction set of each particular job might not need to reside in real storage for each execution.
4. Improved system protection is characteristic of multiple virtual storage systems, since individual users are prevented from infringing upon the address space of other users.
5. Full time operating system residence is not required, since the operating system is itself structured in real storage.

13-41. PSW stands for Program Status Word. The fields of the first PSW word control the overall operation of the computer system. The fields of the second PSW word contain information which controls what will happen to an individual program during execution.

13-43. The execution of branch instructions causes the placement of the branch address into the instruction address field. Such placement destroys the address of the next sequential instruction which was previously there due to automatic address incrementation.

13-45. (a) Wait state: Instructions are not being executed; the completion of some action (for example, an I/O operation) is being awaited.
Running state: Instructions are being executed.

    (b) Problem state: Privileged instructions, including some which change PSW fields, may not be executed.
Supervisor state: Execution of privileged instructions is permitted.

    (c) Stop state: Instruction execution of any kind may not take place, due to operator intervention. Not even program interruption may occur.
Operating state: When the computer is not in stop state, it is said to be in operating state.

13-47. Bit 6 is the I/O mask, indicating whether all I/O interrupts are to be blocked (bit 6=0) or whether channel interrupts will be individually masked through mask bits in control register 2 (bit 6=1).

Bit 7 is the external mask, indicating whether all external interrupts are to be blocked (bit 7=0) or whether external interrupts will be individually masked through mask bits in control register 0 (bit 7=1).

13-49. (i) The contents of the current PSW are placed into the field designated as the old PSW field for the appropriate interrupt class.
    (ii) The contents of the new PSW field for the interrupt class (including the address of the appropriate interrupt handler) are placed into the current PSW field.
    (iii) A branch is effected to the appropriate operating system interrupt handler.
    (iv) The interrupt handler is executed, performing whatever steps are needed to handle the interruption.
    (v) The original PSW, now in the old PSW field, is placed back into the initial program loading PSW location by the last step of the interrupt handler.
    (vi) Control is returned to the next sequential instruction of the application program.

13-51. The designated order of priority dictates that the machine check interrupt be taken first, before the program interrupt. However execution of the program interrupt handler will occur before execution of the machine check interrupt handler. The following describes the procedure. The current PSW is first placed into the machine check old PSW location, and the machine check new PSW is placed into the current PSW location (the machine check interrupt is taken first). Then the contents of the current PSW (now the same as the machine check new PSW) are placed into the program old PSW location, and the program new PSW is placed into the current PSW location.

The current PSW now points to the program interrupt handler, so it is executed first; the contents of the program old PSW (containing the machine check new PSW) are returned to the current PSW. The current PSW now points to the machine check interrupt handler, so it is executed next; the contents of the machine check old PSW (the original application program PSW) are returned to the current PSW. Control is then returned to the application program.

CHAPTER 14

14-1. Coding errors are program errors resulting either from violations of language rules, or from incorrect translation of design steps into computer instructions. Logical errors, on the other hand, result from faults or weaknesses in the design of program logic.

Logical errors will be more difficult to correct, for they require not only the reworking or reanalyzing of program logic, but also the repetition of all coding which was based upon that faulty analysis.

14-3. An 80-80 listing is an exact printed copy of a keypunched deck. It is useful for desk-checking, for the listing may then be checked against the coding sheets, instead of the punched cards being checked against the coding sheets.

14-5. Operand addresses are expressed as part of the OBJECT CODE in base-displacement form. However the columns headed ADDR1 and ADDR2 on the listing contain location counter values for main storage operands, expressed in straight hexadecimal (*not* in displacement) form.

14-7. Test data should include minimum and maximum data values in order to ensure that program fields are defined so that the entire range of allowed values will be appropriately accommodated and dealt with by the program.

14-9. An exception is the condition which occurs when a computer program violates a rule of the system under which it is running.

14-11. (i)   Dynamic dumps
(ii) Abend dumps
(iii) Core-image dumps

14-13. For DOS systems, we use the PDUMP macro; for OS systems, we use the SNAP macro.

Glossary

A

abend dump — A type of dump provided only in the case of abnormal termination of a job. It is obtained through the use of the DUMP operand in the OS macro ABEND. After this dump is produced, control is not returned to the user program.

absolute addressing — Refers to a technique for referencing locations in main storage by specifying the actual location numbers assigned to particular locations by the manufacturer.

adcon — See *address constant*

address — A number assigned by the manufacturer to a particular main storage location.

address constant — Also known as an adcon. A constant which stores the address of the location whose name appears in parentheses in its operand portion: DC   A (name)

address modification — Changing or modifying the effective address referenced by an instruction. This may be accomplished by such techniques as altering the contents of a base register or index register, or by altering a displacement value.

address space — The range of relative addresses that are bounded by the program(s) and are available to the programmer.

addressing exception — An exception which occurs when the effective address of an instruction operand (an instruction address or a data address) is outside the limits of available computer storage.

adjustment (of loop) — The collection of steps performed in preparation for exiting from a loop at the proper time. It may involve the incrementing and/or the decrementing of a counter, or changing the contents of storage locations in preparation for the repetitive processing of the body of the loop.

algebraic shift — A type of shift in which the bits filled in to the left of the field or register(s) as a result of shifting are copies of the sign bit.

align — To line up, or bring into adjustment, the components of a field.

ALU — See *arithmetic and logical unit*

arithmetic and logical unit (ALU) — That part of the CPU in which arithmetic and logical operations are performed. It consists of electronic circuits whose function is to perform operations such as addition, complementation, shifting and comparison.

assembler — See *assembler program*

assembler instruction — An instruction written by the programmer to provide the translator (assembler) with directions for proper translation of an assembler source module into a machine language object module.

assembler language — A machine oriented language in which the op-code and operands are replaced by symbolic names.

assembler program — A computer program which translates symbolic input code into machine instructions.

assembly phase — See *assembly time*

assembly time — The time during which the assembler translates a source program into object code.

associative array registers — In virtual storage systems, these registers are special purpose devices, much faster than real storage, that are used to compensate for the relatively slow speed of table translation.

asterisk protection — Refers to the use of the asterisk (hexadecimal 5C) as a fill character when dealing with monetary amounts, particularly on computer-generated checks. It serves to make fraudulent tampering with checks more difficult.

auxiliary storage — Memory units which hold information but are separate from the actual computer. Typical examples are magnetic tape and disk.

availability — The percentage of time in a certain time span that a piece of equipment is working correctly.

B

base (of a number system) — See *radix*

base register — A general purpose register which has been designated as the base register; it contains a base, or starting address, to be used in translating addresses from base-displacement form, or index-base-displacement form, into absolute form.

basic control mode (BC Mode) — A mode in which the features of the System/360 are operational, or in which features of the System/370 without virtual storage may be operational. Also refers to the specific organization of the PSW for System/360, or for System/370 without virtual storage.

BC mode — See *basic control mode*

binary constant — A group of bits (0's and 1's) specified in the operand portion of a DC instruction.

binary number system — A positional representation system with a radix of two.

bit — A binary digit (0 or 1)

body (of loop) — The heart of the loop. The set of instructions which are repeated each time control passes through the loop, and which constitute the processing for which purpose the loop was constructed.

branch — A transfer of control from one instruction to another instruction which does not sequentially follow the first.

bug — An error in a program. It can be a syntax error or an error in the logic of the program.

byte — A unit of 8 bits.

byte-oriented operand feature — A feature which allows operands of binary instructions to begin at any address, not necessarily at the appropriate halfword, fullword, or doubleword boundary.

C

call — The process of transferring control to a called routine from a calling routine.

call by name — Passing the addresses of the parameters to a subroutine.

call by value — Passing the actual parameter values to a subroutine.

called routine — A subroutine which is invoked by a calling routine.

calling routine — A program routine which invokes a subroutine.

carat — A symbol ("∧") used to denote an implied decimal point.

card layout form — A special form used to pictorially represent the fields of a punched card.

card reader — An input unit which senses the presence or absence of holes in each column of a punched card, converts holes punched in cards into electrical impulses, and then transmits the data to the main memory of the computer.

carriage control — Refers to the control of the movements of the printer carriage.

carriage control character — A character appended to the beginning of each printer record to control vertical spacing of printed output.

carriage control tape — A tape with control codes which control the vertical and horizontal positioning of the printer carriage and of the paper feed unit.

central processing unit (CPU) — The unit of a computing system which contains the primary storage, the arithmetic and logical unit and the control unit. It is here that the actual manipulation of data takes place.

change bit — For virtual storage systems, a bit in the page frame table which is turned on whenever data is stored into the page residing in the bits associated real storage page frame.

closed subroutine — A subroutine which is found only once in main storage, and is branched to or called by other routines which use it.

coding — The process of writing computer instructions.

coding form — A form developed by computer manufacturers to facilitate the keypunching of instructions in the correct columns of punched cards.

comment — A short explanatory remark which the programmer may insert in order to explain the workings of his program.

communications region — A special area of the DOS supervisor which contains, among other things, the current date which the computer operator communicates to the system on a daily basis as part of a standard procedure.

comparison — The determination of the relationship between the contents of two locations. This is done by compare instructions which determine whether the value of one location's contents is equal to, less than, or greater than the value of a second location's contents. A comparison is usually followed by a decision.

compilation — The process by which a compiler translates a program written in a nonmachine language into machine language.

compiler — A computer program that translates programs written in a source language (usually a higher level language such as FORTRAN or COBOL) into machine language.

completion code — A 3-digit code, the first two digits of which will be 0C and the third of which will be the interruption code number. This code is provided by the indicative dump when a program exception causes an interruption.

computer — An electronic computational device having the following characteristics:
a) internal storage
b) stored program (instructions)
c) capability to modify a set of instructions during execution of a program.

computer language — A language with which one can communicate with the computer.

computer system — This refers to the aggregate of the CPU together with one or more input and output units.

condition code — A field in the PSW whose contents reflect the results of comparisons, or of arithmetic or logical operations.

conditional branch — An instruction which causes the computer either to branch (transfer control to another instruction) or not to branch (continue sequential execution) depending upon the setting of the condition code at the time of execution.

connector symbol — A symbol used in a flowchart to indicate entry to or exit from another part of the program flowchart.

constant — A symbol or a group of consecutive symbols stored in computer memory by the assembler program for use during program execution.

control registers — A set of registers provided by System/370, comprising information fields. These fields relate to or control various aspects of the overall operation of the computer system,or of events which may occur during program execution.

control section — Refers to those independent programming units which are written, stored, relocated and debugged separately, and are then joined or "linked" together prior to execution of the complete program. It is abbreviated CSECT.

control unit — The part of a digital computer or processor which acts as a "general manager", controlling the various operations of the computer. It controls the input and output of the computer and the communication between the various components of the computer. It interprets program instructions, initiates I/O devices, commences execution of a computer program and ensures that everything is done at the proper time and in the right sequence.

core-image dump — A dump of main storage containing diagnostic information. This dump is supplied automatically by the system, should a *system* routine (not a *program* routine) fail.

core memory — A type of storage which is composed of tiny rings called *cores* which are arranged in rows and strung on wires.

CPU — See *central processing unit.*

cross-reference listing — A listing produced by the assembler from information encountered in the source module. It lists, in alphabetical order, each symbolic name referenced by the program; the length associated with the corresponding symbol; the value of the location counter at the point of the program at which the symbol is defined; the number of the statement at which the symbol is defined; and the statement numbers of all statements that reference the symbol.

D

DAT feature — See *dynamic address translation feature.*

data — Facts or figures about something, from which conclusions can be drawn.

data exception — An exception in which the operand codes of instructions are not as required by the instruction.

debugging — The process of finding and correcting errors in a program.

decimal arithmetic — In assembly language terminology, refers to arithmetic with numeric values in packed format.

decimal divide exception — An exception which occurs when the quotient resulting from the execution of a decimal divide instruction is too large to fit into the first operand. Overflow cannot occur. When a decimal divide exception is recognized, the operation is suppressed.

decimal instruction set — Refers to the set of machine language instructions for the IBM 360/370 which deal with values in packed or decimal form.

decimal overflow exception — An exception which occurs when the result of a decimal addition or subtraction is too large to fit into the first operand location.

decision symbol — A symbol used in a flowchart to indicate alternate paths which may be chosen by the computer during processing. The choice of path will depend upon the presence or absence of some condition.

demand paging — In virtual storage systems, the activity of paging in and paging out, as required to execute programs and to dynamically share real storage among users.

desk-checking — The process of checking the coding forms (before keypunching) and punched cards (after keypunching) to catch any clerical or logical errors which the programmer may notice.

detail line — A type of output line containing information which varies from record to record.

diagnostic — A syntax error which is discovered by the assembler (or by the appropriate compiler, for programs written in other languages).

diagnostic listing — A listing of syntax errors discovered by the assembler (or by the appropriate compiler, for programs written in other languages). This listing is produced following the listing of the source module.

digit selector — A special control character (hexadecimal 20) in an edit pattern. Each such character corresponds to a packed digit of the numeric field to be edited.

disk — A circular metal plate with magnetic material on both sides, capable of storing information magnetically.

displacement — Represents the number of storage locations which the effective address is displaced (removed) from the base address in relative addressing.

documentation — Information about a program which includes layout forms, flowcharts, listings, explanations, and directives to users.

double dabble — A technique for converting binary numbers into decimal form, consisting of repeated multiplications by 2 and additions. The high-order bit value is doubled, the result added to the next rightmost bit; the sum is then doubled, added to the next rightmost bit, and so on, until the last bit value has been added.

doubleword — A unit of 8 bytes (2 words).

dump — The printing of the contents of certain parts of storage and of registers, as well as other relevant information which may serve to help the programmer identify the cause(s) of program error.

duplication factor — A value in the operand portion of a DC instruction that indicates the number of times a constant immediately following this value is to be repeated in consecutive storage locations.

dynamic address translation feature (DAT) — A special CPU hardware facility which translates relative addresses each time an instruction or data element is referenced during program execution in a virtual storage system.

dynamic dump — A type of dump produced at the point of program execution at which it is requested, regardless of whether or not an error occurred at that point in the program. It is requested by the programmer through use of the SNAP macro instruction (for OS systems) or the PDUMP macro instruction (for DOS systems). After the dump is produced, program execution continues with the next sequential program instruction.

dynamic relocation — A type of relocation in which the program is not bound to definite real storage locations. A program may be moved and main storage reallocated *during program execution.*

E

EBCDIC — See *extended binary coded decimal interchange code.*

EC mode — See *extended control mode.*

edit — The process of improving the appearance and readability of printed numeric output.

effective address — Refers to the actual address calculated by a computer when an instruction specifies relative addressing.

eighty-eighty (80–80) listing — An exact printed copy of a source deck, with each of the 80 columns of a punched card represented as an appropriate printed character on the listing.

end-of-file condition — A condition reached when the card reader attempts to read a record and there are no more to be found.

entry symbol — A symbol which is defined in an object module and used elsewhere (in another object module, although it may be used in the defining module as well).

even-odd register pair — Two consecutive registers, the first an even numbered register and the second an odd numbered register.

exception — A condition which occurs when a computer program violates one of the rules of the system under which it is running.

execute — To perform a task or carry out an instruction.

execute exception — An exception caused by illegal use of the EX (*EXecute*) instruction.

execution phase — See *execution time*.

execution time — The amount of time it takes a computer to perform the operations specified by program instructions.

exit code — The code used to return control to the main program after a subroutine has accomplished its function.

explicit length — A length (of a constant or storage area) which is explicitly specified by the programmer, either by definition, or as part of an instruction operand.

exponent overflow exception — An exception which occurs when the result of a floating-point operation is greater than or equal to 16^{64}.

exponent underflow exception — An exception which occurs when the result of a floating-point operation is less than 16^{-64}.

extended binary coded decimal interchange code (EBCDIC) — An 8–bit code, used for character representation. It can represent as many as 256 distinct characters and is used by many modern computer systems.

extended control mode (EC mode) — A mode in which all System/370 features may be operational, including virtual storage capabilities. Also refers to the specific organization of the PSW for System/370 with virtual storage.

extended mnemonics — A special group of assembly language instructions supplied by the computer manufacturer for the convenience of the programmer. They are alternate forms of some machine instructions, but are simpler in their symbolic form since their symbolic op-code incorporates both the operation and the first operand information of the original.

external interrupt — An interrupt which occurs when a signal is transmitted to the CPU from either a clock or timer; the interrupt key on the operator's console; or an external device connected to the CPU.

external mask — A PSW bit whose respective on or off states designate whether or not an external signal may interrupt the CPU.

external page storage — In virtual storage systems, that part of auxiliary storage that is used to store pages.

external page table — In virtual storage systems, a table which corresponds each page number with an appropriate slot location; that is, with the location of the page in external storage.

external subroutine — A subroutine which is not assembled together with the calling program, but is assembled separately.

external symbol — A symbol which is referenced within an object module, but is defined elsewhere (in another object module).

F

field — A collection of characters which belong together as a logical unit.

field separator — An edit control character (hexadecimal 22) used to separate those parts of an extended edit pattern which correspond to different fields. It is itself replaced by the fill character, and it turns off the significance indicator.

file — An organized collection of related records.

fill character — The character with which the programmer intends to replace insignificant zeros in a field to be edited. It is the first character of any edit pattern.

fixed-point constant — A binary number placed by the assembler into main storage, and aligned on a proper integral boundary.

fixed-point divide exception — An exception which may occur as a result of two possible conditions. The first possible cause is the quotient of a fixed point division being of such magnitude that it cannot be expressed as a 32-bit signed integer. The second possible cause is an attempt to convert a number into binary form via a CVB instruction, and the binary number being too large to fit into the first operand register.

fixed-point overflow exception — An exception which occurs when the results of certain binary integer add, subtract, or load instructions are too large to fit into 32 bits.

fixed symbol — A symbol which appears at a specific (fixed) point of a field.

floating point divide exception — An exception which occurs when a floating point division by zero is attempted.

floating point registers — Refers to the four special registers, each 64 bits long, which are used to hold numbers in floating point format. They are used primarily for scientific applications.

floating symbol — A symbol which appears immediately to the left of the first significant character of a field, rather than at a fixed point of a field.

flowchart — A pictorial description of the structure and general sequence of operations involved in the logical solution of a programming problem.

flowchart template — A tool, in which many shapes are outlined, developed to aid the programmer in drawing flowcharts.

fragmentation — The condition which results when several programs have been loaded, and there are areas between them. Each of these areas individually may not be large enough to hold another program; however, the total amount of unused storage may be substantial.

free form coding — Coding guidelines which do not designate specific columns for each portion of an instruction. For assembly language, free form coding guidelines designate the name portion (if present) to begin in column 1; the operation portion to be preceded by at least one blank; the operand and comment portions, if present, to be separated from the operation and from each other by at least one blank; coding not to extend beyond column 71.

fullword (word) — A unit of 4 bytes (2 halfwords)

G

general purpose register (GPR) — Refers to the sixteen 32–bit registers which may be used by the programmer or operating system for various tasks. The information in these registers is stored in straight binary format.

GPR — See *general purpose register.*

H

halfword — A unit of 2 bytes.

heading line — A type of output line which is composed of constant information determined by the user and implemented by the programmer.

hexadecimal constant — A group of one or more hexadecimal digits (0 through F) indicated in the operand portion of a DC instruction.

hexadecimal number system — A positional representation with base or radix 16.

high-order bit — The leftmost bit of a number or of a configuration of bits.

Hollerith card — The standard punched card named after Herman Hollerith, its inventor, used for representing alphanumeric data. Each column holds one character, which is represented by 1, 2 or 3 holes punched into designated row positions of the column.

housekeeping — Operations or routines in a program or computer system which pertain to functions that are necessary in order to maintain control and which must be performed for proper processing to be accomplished. For example, housekeeping may involve establishing program base registers, setting up certain constants or variables to be used in processing, initialization, file identification, and the like.

I

I/O (input/output) — 1. Media, techniques, and devices use to communicate with the computer.
2. Information and data involved in this communication.

immediate (instructions or operands) — Refers to the inclusion of operand data in the instruction stream itself.

implied base register — A base register not explicitly designated by the programmer in a given instruction. It is, however, defined by the USING instruction as a program base register and is therefore part of the expression of the address in base-displacement form.

implied length — A length (of a constant or storage location) which is not specified by the programmer. The number of storage positions is instead determined by the assembler according to predetermined rules.

index register — In the index-base-displacement method of relative addressing, the programmer chooses two GPR's: one is the base register and the other is the index register. The contents of the index register are used for calculation of the effective address.

indicative dump — A dump provided when the programmer has requested an abnormal termination dump, but has not provided a DD statement with either the name SYSABEND or SYSUDUMP. The indicative dump contains information about the program and the cause of program interruption.

initialization (of loop) — Refers to any preparation necessary for the proper functioning of a loop, such as the setting of counters to zero (or to some other value).

input — Data which is transferred or is to be transferred from a storage medium outside the computer into the computer's main storage.

input area — Main storage locations into which a computer places input data.

input/output interrupt — An interrupt which occurs during the processing of input or output operations, when a channel signals the CPU that its I/O functions have been completed.

input/output mask — A group of PSW bits each of whose respective on or off settings indicates whether or not interrupts associated with the corresponding input or output channel are to be taken.

input/output symbol — A symbol used in flowcharts to describe input and output operations.

instruction address field — A PSW field into which instruction addresses are placed, for appropriate incrementation prior to instruction execution. After incrementation, the instruction address points to the address of the next instruction to be executed.

instruction format — The allocation of parts of instructions, differentiating between various instruction components such as names, operations, and operands.

instruction length code — A field in the PSW which is set to 1, 2, or 3, to reflect the respective number of halfwords in an instruction. This occurs after the instruction address is fetched by the CPU and placed into the PSW instruction address field, prior to instruction execution.

integral boundary — A field is said to be on an integral boundary if its address (its starting or leftmost location) is a multiple of its length in bytes.

internal subroutine — A subroutine which is assembled along with the calling program.

interrupt — A transfer of computer control to an operating system module which will "handle" the cause of the interruption (that is, of this break in the normal sequence of instruction execution).

interruption code — A specific numeric code placed into the appropriate PSW field to designate the occurrence of a program error condition.

invalid bit — In System/370 virtual storage systems, a bit in the page table whose setting reflects whether or not the associated page is in real storage.

J

JCL — See *job control language*.

job control language (JCL) — A language which instructs the operating system what to do; each operating system has its own job control language. (For example, JCL statements for IBM's Disk Operating System guide the program through the assembly, link-edit, and execution phases.) JCL instructions are not part of assembly language; their exact form will vary from one computer installation to another, and may even vary in the same installation from time to time.

L

least recently used rule (LRU) — In virtual storage systems, a rule used to select pages for replacement. It designates that the least recently used pages (those that have not been referenced in a long time) should be the first to be replaced. The LRU rule thus attempts to keep the most recently referenced pages in real storage.

left justify — To align on the leftmost side of a field.

length factor — That part of the operand portion of a DC or DS instruction which assigns a length in bytes to the constant or storage area being defined.

linkage editor — A special-purpose program supplied by the computer manufacturer. It transforms the object module into the load module, which is then read into or maintained in main storage for execution.

list — Refers to a one-dimensional table.

literal — A specification of data to be used in a program. It is written in the same way as is the operand of a DC instruction but is preceded by an equal sign (=).

literal pool — An area of main storage into which the values of the data specified by literals are assembled.

load — To place data into a register, either from main storage or from another register.

load module — A revised form of an object module which is suitable for loading into main storage for execution. This revised form is the transformation of the object module by the linkage editor.

load time — The time at which the program is loaded into main storage for execution.

loading — The process of placing data or information from auxiliary or external storage into the internal storage of a computer.

locality of reference — The phenomenon which occurs when the reference pattern of a program, during execution, dwells within a relatively small number of pages for relatively long periods of time.

location counter — A counter used by the assembler to keep track of which locations in memory to use for the storage of each instruction.

logical comparison — A type of comparison in which operand contents being compared are treated as unsigned binary values.

logical product — The result of the operation performed by the logical operator AND. The AND function has the value 1 if both operands have the value 1; otherwise, it has the value 0.

loop — A sequence of instructions that is executed repeatedly until a specified criterion is satisfied.

low-order bit — The rightmost bit of a number or of a configuration of bits.

LRU — See *least recently used rule.*

M

machine check interrupt — An interrupt which occurs as a result of some machine or hardware failure.

machine instruction — An instruction written by the programmer in assembly language and subsequently translated by the assembler into a machine language instruction.

machine language — The language which a particular computer was designed to understand without translation.

macro instruction — An assembler language statement to be replaced by the assembler with more than one machine language instruction. It is written by the programmer to represent a set sequence of instructions which may be repeated several times in the same program or in different programs.

macro library — A collection of sets of instruction sequences, stored in memory, which are retrieved by macro instructions.

magnetic tape — A storage medium upon which bits are recorded magnetically as a means of retaining data.

main storage — See *real storage.*

mainline — The main body of program logic.

mask — A pattern of characters or bits used to test or alter another field.

mask bit — A bit configuration in which bits are set to 0 or 1 to control the occurrence or nonoccurrence of certain operations, or for the purpose of testing or altering another field.

message character — Refers to any pattern character other than the fill character and the control characters X'20', X'21' and X'22'.

modifier — That part of the operand portion of a DC or DS instruction which describes the length in bytes to be assigned by the assembler to the appropriate constant or storage area.

multiple constants — Several constants defined with a single DC instruction.

multiple virtual storages — A virtual storage system in which each user has his own virtual storage: that is, the virtual storage is the user's address space. (For segmentation, *each* virtual storage is mapped by a segment table.)

multiprogramming — An important capability for which the operating system may provide, which allows two or more programs to reside in storage simultaneously, and to be executed concurrently.

N

numeric punch — On a Hollerith punched card, a punch in one of the rows numbered 0–9.

O

object deck — The set of punched cards containing an object program.

object listing — The copy of an object program printed out by the computer.

object module — The set of machine language instructions created by the assembler when it translates program source statements.

object program — The block of machine language code created by an assembler or by a compiler as a result of translating a source module.

object statement — A machine language statement which is part of the object program created by an assembler or by a compiler.

one's complement — The representation obtained from a given binary number by changing all 0–bits to 1's and all 1–bits to 0's.

op-code — See *operation code*.

open subroutine — A subroutine which is repeated within a program whenever its services are required.

operand — That portion of an instruction which identifies and/or describes the data to be acted upon by the instruction.

operating system — A collection of programs whose purpose is to effectively manage the resources of a computer system.

operation code — The most important part of an instruction, it tells the computer what type of operation is to be done, and implies the type of data to be acted upon by the instruction.

operation exception — An exception in which the operation code of the instruction to be executed is illegal. That is, it is not recognized by the system as a valid operation code. In such a case, instruction execution is suppressed.

output — Information transferred to auxiliary or external storage from a computer's main storage.

output area — A set of storage locations which the programmer designates for output purposes.

overflow — The generation of operational results whose storage requirements exceed the capacity of the register(s) and/or storage location(s) designated for holding those results.

P

packed number — A signed number stored in memory in a special form suitable for use in decimal arithmetic operations. In a packed constant, digits are "packed" two per byte with the exception of the low-order byte. The rightmost half of the low-order byte contains the sign (hexadecimal C for positive, and hexadecimal D for negative).

pad — To fill out a fixed block of information with dummy characters, items, or records. "Padding" may occur in the leftmost or rightmost portion of a block, as designated.

padding character — The character or character type used to pad a given area.

page — 1. In a segmentation and paging system, a subdivision of a segment. Segments may thus be divided into one or more units called pages which are fixed in size.

2. A subdivision of a program (without segmentation).

page fault — In virtual storage systems, the condition which results when a program references instruction(s) and/or data in some page which does not reside in real storage.

page frame — In virtual storage systems, an area of real storage which can contain a page.

page frame table — In virtual storage systems, a table which is used by the operating system to record how page frames of real storage are allocated to user programs. Each entry of this table describes one page frame in main storage.

page-in — In virtual storage systems, the transfer of a copy of a page from a slot in external page storage into a page frame in real storage.

page-out — In virtual storage systems, the transfer of a copy of a page from its page frame in real storage to a slot in external page storage. The appropriate external page table entry is also updated to designate the new slot location.

page table — In virtual storage systems, a table each of whose entries identifies a real storage location which is the origin address of a page frame in real storage.

parameter — A variable that assumes a constant value throughout any one subroutine use. However, its value may change when the subroutine is used again by the same main routine or by other main routines.

parameter list — A list which may contain either the parameter values to be passed from a main routine to a subroutine or the addresses of the parameters.

pattern — A special collection of characters (defined as a hexadecimal constant) in the first operand field of an ED instruction. The pattern determines how the packed number in the second operand is to be treated by the ED instruction.

pocket selection — See *stacker selection*.

positional representation — A representation of numbers in which digits may assume different values depending upon the position, or column, of the number that they occupy.

potential address space — Comprises those areas (segments and/or pages) of virtual storage which are not currently allocated.

printer — One of the most popular output devices, providing information in readable form. The medium generally used is continuous form paper.

printer layout form — A special form used to assist the programmer in planning the arrangement of printed output.

privileged operation exception — An exception occurring when the CPU is in problem state, and the operation code of the instruction to be executed is that of a privileged instruction (that is, of an instruction which may be executed only when the computer is in supervisor state). If the computer is in problem state when such an instruction is encountered, the operation is suppressed.

problem state — The CPU state in which problem programs are executed, but execution of privileged instructions is prohibited.

process symbol — A symbol used in a flowchart to indicate any processing operation other than: the beginning or termination of a program or subroutine; input/output operations; decisions.

program — 1. A set of instructions arranged in proper sequence which tells the computer how to solve a particular problem.
2. A plan or procedure for solving a problem.
3. The coded instructions and data for the solution of a problem.

program-check interrupt — See *program interrupt.*

program-check message — A printed message to the programmer indicating the cause of a program interrupt.

program event recording — A System/370 feature which provides a trace, or record, of certain program activities or events.

program interrupt — An interrupt which occurs as a result of some condition arising from a problem program (such as certain error conditions).

program mask — A PSW field containing a 4–bit mask, whose bit settings control the occurrence or nonoccurrence of the following four program exceptions: fixed-point overflow; decimal overflow; exponent underflow; significance.

program relocation — See *relocation.*

program status word (PSW) — A 64–bit register consisting of fields each of which functions in some unique way to control the overall operation of the computer system, or to control what happens to a program during execution.

programmer — One who writes computer programs. May refer to one who codes, or to one who analyzes a problem, breaks it down into discrete steps and expresses those steps in a computer language.

programming — The activity of writing computer programs. May refer to coding, or to analyzing a problem, breaking it down into discrete steps, and expressing those steps in a computer language.

protection exception — An exception occurring when the storage key of the area being accessed does not match the protection key.

protection key — A PSW field containing a 4–bit code. This code must match the storage key of a memory block in order for access of the block to be permitted.

PSW — See *program status word.*

punched card — A card of definite size and shape, suitable for punching data or information for input and/or output purposes. Specific configurations of punches in a column represent particular characters.

R

radix (of a number system) — An integer that defines a system of representing numbers by positional notation. That is, an integer, powers of which will determine column values in a given number system.

real storage — Storage from which the CPU can directly obtain data and instructions, and to which results of processing can be directly returned.

receiving area — An area designated for incoming data and/or instructions.

record — An organized collection of related fields.

reference bit — In virtual storage systems, a bit in the associative array registers which is set to 1 or 0 to indicate whether or not the associated program pages were recently referenced.

register — A discrete storage unit of fixed length which is conceptually similar to, but is physically separate from, main storage.

relative address — An address which is expressed as a displacement from (relative to) an origin.

relative addressing — Refers to a technique for referencing locations in main storage using some fixed address (a base address) as a reference point.

relocation — 1. Refers to the conversion of addresses in a program's address space into actual location numbers in real storage.
2. Compensating for a change in the origin of a program, a CSECT, or a page by modifying appropriate address constants.

response time — On "time-sharing" systems in which many individuals request to use the same computer at the same time, response time is the amount of time which elapses between the request to access the computer, and the computer's response.

restart interrupt — An interrupt which occurs on the System/370 by pushing the "restart" key on the operator's console.

retrieval — The accessing or collection of information from a storage unit.

return — The process of transferring control back to the calling routine from a called routine.

right justify — To align on the rightmost side of a field.

rounding — The process of determining the value of a quantity to a certain accuracy, according to some rule.

running state — The CPU state in which instructions are being processed.

S

save area — An 18-word area used to store the contents of the registers of a calling routine A when control is passed from the calling routine A to the called routine B.

scale factor — A multiplier used by the programmer to modify the location of a decimal point in a field, as, for example, in preparation for some arithmetic procedure.

secondary storage — See *auxiliary storage.*

segment — In virtual storage systems, a subdivision of a program's address space.

segment table — In virtual storage systems, a table in real storage each entry of which identifies the origin of a segment in real storage.

segment table origin register (STOR) — In virtual storage systems, a register in real storage which "points" to the real storage origin address of a segment table. The segment table pointed to maps the segments of the program currently being executed.

segmentation — The process of dividing a program's address space so that only part of the program need be in storage at any particular time during program execution. That is, only those program segments currently required for execution need be in main storage.

sending field — The instruction operand field whose contents are to be processed by the instruction.

shifting — The movement of field digits in a particular direction: to the left, or to the right.

significance exception — An exception which occurs when the fraction resulting from a floating-point operation is zero, and the significance mask bit of the PSW is one. When a significance exception occurs, a program interruption takes place.

significance indicator — A system switch, not under programmer control, whose respective on and off states designate whether or not significance (a nonzero source digit or a significance starter in the edit pattern) has been encountered in the scanning of a particular field.

significance starter — An edit control character with two functions. Firstly, it functions exactly as does a digit selector in that it corresponds to a packed digit in the left-to-right scan. Secondly, if the significance indicator has not yet been turned on when the significance starter is encountered, the significance starter will cause the significance indicator to be turned on, so that all succeeding characters will be treated exactly as though an actual significant digit had been encountered.

simple program loading — A type of storage allocation in which addresses are relocated (that is, actual storage locations are assigned) *before load time*. The resultant program is then loaded into the assigned main storage locations.

single virtual storage — A virtual storage system in which the virtual storage is the system's address space (as opposed to a program's address space). (For segmentation, the entire VS may be mapped by a single segment table.)

slot — For virtual storage systems, a slot is a record area in external page storage; it is the same size as a page.

source deck — A set of punched cards containing a source program.

source listing — A source program, when printed out by the computer.

source program — A program written in a source language; that is, in a language that requires translation. The program will thus constitute the input to a language translator (to an assembler or a compiler).

source statement — A statement written by a programmer in a source language; that is, in a language which requires translation before execution.

spacing control character — See *carriage control character*.

specification exception — An exception which occurs when an instruction operand contains an improper main storage address or register number.

spooling — A technique supported by special software for the reading and writing of data sets. Card input is read off-line or during slack periods onto a high-speed device; card image data is then read into memory from that device. Printed output is likewise spooled to a high-speed device, and printed off-line or during slack periods. Throughput is improved by minimizing the time necessary for input and output with such slow-speed I/O devices as the card reader and printer.

stacker selection — Directing a card to a particular pocket or stacker of a card input and/or output device.

standard instruction set — Refers to the set of IBM 360/370 machine language instructions which deal with values in fixed point form.

static relocation — A type of relocation in which the program is assigned to definite real storage locations *at the time that the program is loaded* into main storage for execution.

status bit — A bit which constitutes one of the four parts of each entry in the page frame table; it tells whether or not a particular page frame is available. If the status bit is zero, the page frame is available; if the status bit is one, the page frame is not available.

stop state — The CPU state in which instruction execution of any kind may not take place, due to operator intervention. Not even program interruption may occur.

STOR — See *segment table origin register.*

storage unit — Any device onto which information can be copied and held until needed, at which time it can be retrieved.

store — To copy data from a register into main storage.

subroutine — A group of instructions which perform a particular function.

supervisor call interrupt — An interrupt which is effected by the execution of an SVC (supervisor call) instruction.

supervisor state — The CPU state in which the execution of privileged instructions (such as certain instructions which manipulate the PSW itself, or certain input and output manipulations) is permitted.

swapping — In virtual storage systems, the procedure through which a needed page replaces one which is currently in real storage.

symbolic name space — The combination of symbolic instructions and symbolic names created by the programmer to implement a computer application.

system mask — A PSW field whose bit settings indicate whether or not interrupts associated with input and output channels, or with external signals, are to be taken.

system run — See *system test*.

system test — A test of the workings of the program in conjunction with other systems programs with which it may have some interconnection.

T

table — A grouping of logically related data items which are stored in some systematic way, usually in adjacent storage locations.

ten's complement — The ten's complement of a given n-digit number is that number obtained by subtracting the given number from 10^n. That is, $10^n - N$, where N is the given n-digit number.

terminal symbol — A symbol used in a flowchart to depict the beginning or the end of a program or of a subroutine.

test data — Refers to data used to test the correctness of a program. A program is run using test data, to simulate every possible type of condition that the program may encounter.

test run — Refers to that part of the debugging process which consists of running the program using manufactured data to simulate every possible type of condition that the program may encounter. The results of these program runs are then checked against the known correct results for the particular problem.

throughput — The amount of actual processing done by the computer in a fixed time span.

timer unit — 26.04166 microseconds.

translation mode — Refers to the use of dynamic address translation by the computer system.

truncation — The process of dropping part of a field (the rightmost part for right truncation; the leftmost part for left truncation).

turnaround time — The amount of time which elapses from the time a job is submitted to the time it is completed.

two's complement — 1. A representation which has 0's in those binary columns whose values total one less than the absolute value of the number whose complement is being represented.
2. The two's complement of a given n-bit number is that number obtained by subtracting the given number from 2^n. That is, 2^n-N where N is the given n-digit number.

V

validity of reference — The phenomenon under which unnecessary or extraneous retrieval of data from real storage is avoided.

virtual address — A relative address which refers to a location in virtual storage. Virtual addresses are translated into real storage addresses when they are to be used.

virtual storage (VS) — Addressable storage that simulates real storage, and from which instructions and data are transferred into real storage. Virtual storage is an *address space* that may be much larger than real storage. The maximum size of this address space is determined by the system's address structure.

VS — See *virtual storage*.

W

wait state — The CPU state in which instructions are not processed, but interrupts are allowed. The CPU is awaiting the completion of some action (such as an I/O operation) before processing is resumed.

word — See *fullword*.

wrap around — A way of numbering in a cyclic manner so that the last numbered location or register is followed by the first.

Z

zone portion — The high-order 4 bits of a byte.

zone punch — A punch in row 0,11, or 12 of a Hollerith punched card.

zoned number — A signed number in which each digit occupies one byte, and consists of two parts: the zone portion and the digit portion. Each digit, with the exception of the low-order digit, has hexadecimal F in the zone portion, and a 4–bit representation of the decimal value of the digit in the digit portion. The low-order byte contains the sign (hexadecimal C for positive, hexadecimal D for negative) in its zone portion.

Index